The Great War in Russian Memory

INDIANA-MICHIGAN SERIES IN RUSSIAN
AND EAST EUROPEAN STUDIES

Alexander Rabinowitch and
William G. Rosenberg,
general editors

THE
Great War in Russian Memory

Karen Petrone

Indiana University Press

BLOOMINGTON AND INDIANAPOLIS

This book is a publication of

Indiana University Press
601 North Morton Street
Bloomington, Indiana 47404-3797 USA

www.iupress.indiana.edu

Telephone orders   800-842-6796
Fax orders   812-855-7931
Orders by e-mail   iuporder@indiana.edu

♾ The paper used in this publication meets the minimum requirements of the American National Standard for Information Sciences—Permanence of Paper for Printed Library Materials, ANSI Z39.48-1992.

Manufactured in the United States of America

Library of Congress Cataloging-in-Publication Data

Petrone, Karen.
    The Great War in Russian memory / Karen Petrone.
        p. cm. — (Indiana-Michigan series in Russian and East European studies)
    Includes bibliographical references and index.
    ISBN 978-0-253-35617-8 (cloth : alk. paper) 1. World War, 1914–1918—Social aspects—Soviet Union. 2. World War, 1914–1918—Influence. 3. Collective memory—Soviet Union—History. 4. War memorials—Soviet Union—History. 5. War and society—Soviet Union—History. 6. Political culture—Soviet Union—History. 7. Patriotism—Soviet Union—History. 8. Soviet Union—Social conditions—1917–1945. 9. Soviet Union—Politics and government—1917–1936. 10. Soviet Union—Politics and government—1936–1953. I. Title.
    D524.7.S65P48 2011
    940.3′47—dc22

                                                                                                        2011007765

1 2 3 4 5   16 15 14 13 12 11

For Ken, Mara, and Anya

Only in the ancient book, not effaced by anything, and somewhere in the depths of each of our souls, not completely trampled, lives the prohibition "Thou shalt not kill."

—IL'IA ERENBURG, *The Face of War*

Contents

Acknowledgments   *xi*

1   *Introduction · The Great War in Russian Memory*   1

2   *Spirituality, the Supernatural, and the Memory of World War I*   31

3   *The Paradoxes of Gender in Soviet War Memory*   75

4   *Violence, Morality, and the Conscience of the Warrior*   127

5   *World War I and the Definition of Russianness*   165

6   *Arrested History*   199

7   *Disappearance and Reappearance*   246

8   *Legacies of the Great War*   282

Notes   *301*

Bibliography   *339*

Index   *359*

ACKNOWLEDGMENTS

In September of 2001 I was home on sabbatical, working on a new project that I thought was about Soviet-era soldiers' memoirs from both world wars, when I heard a news report on the radio that a plane had hit one of the towers of the World Trade Center. As a native New Yorker, I turned on the television in time to witness the second plane hit the second tower. There is no doubt that the events of that day and their ongoing aftermath have influenced the way in which I approach war, religion, heroism, patriotism, mobilization, and the morality of violence in this book. This is most certainly a "post-9/11" work.

There were a few twists and turns on the path to this book, but one of the most significant turning points was when one of my best friends from high school, Doug Mao, recruited me to take part in the Modernist Studies Association Annual Conference in 2002, of which he was the Program Chair. Because Modernist Studies is primarily a literature conference, I decided to present a paper on Soviet World War I literature—and the focus of my project suddenly shifted to encompass all World War I cultural production, and only World War I cultural production. For a few years the going was rough; although I was finding interesting material, prominent scholars in the field warned me that World War I memory and World War I literature were not Soviet categories, journals rejected my articles, and I wavered.

Then in 2006, under the auspices of the Social Theory Program at the University of Kentucky, I co-taught a graduate seminar on emotion with colleagues Wallis Miller, Jeff Peters, and Richard Smith. During that semester, Jay Winter came to speak at the University of Kentucky. His encouraging and supportive response to my research helped me to see that this was indeed a project well worth pursuing.

At this critical juncture, the National Council for Eurasian and East European Research granted me a National Research Fellowship. I am deeply grateful to Bob Huber and all the NCEEER staff for their support. I also very much appreciate the time that Barbara Clements, Robert Edelman, and Katerina Clark spent writing what must have seemed like an endless number of recommendations for grants and fellowships. The University of Kentucky College of Arts and Sciences and Office of the Vice President for Research have generously supported this research through conference travel money, a Research Committee Grant, and a Summer Faculty Research Fellowship. Steven Hoch, former Dean of the College of Arts and Sciences, was particularly steadfast in his support of this project. In conjunction with the NCEEER award, he arranged for me to have three consecutive semesters of leave time, without which this book could not have been written. I am truly grateful for Steve's faith in my work, and for the support of the current Dean Mark Kornbluh.

And then there are my esteemed collaborators on other projects, who enriched this project by allowing it to cross-pollinate with new thoughts, ideas, and fields. Interactions with these colleagues profoundly enriched this book. Many thanks to my dear friend and mentor Valerie Kivelson, with whom I was privileged to explore Muscovite cultural history. It has also been a great pleasure to work with Jie-Hyun Lim on issues of gender and mass dictatorship. I wish to thank Jie-Hyun for his stimulating work on comparative mass dictatorship and for introducing me to a transnational community of scholars stretching from Hanyang University in Seoul, South Korea, throughout Europe and the United States. Special thanks must go to my most long-standing collaborator and dear friend, Choi Chatterjee. We have been through a lot together during the writing of this book—including a month living together in a one-room apartment in Moscow, organizing conferences, working on two collaborative articles and grant proposals, and much else in between. This book would not be what it is without Choi.

The University of Kentucky has been a warm, friendly, and stimulating intellectual home for the sixteen years that I have been here. My colleagues in the Department of Russian and Eastern Studies have unfailingly supported me over the years. Jeanmarie Rouhier-Willoughby read several chapter drafts and gave me wonderful feedback on folk belief. I have benefited from many discussions about this work with Cynthia Ruder and Igor Sopronenko, who have also helped with translations. Jerry Janecek shared his unpublished work with me, and he and Susan Janecek have also warmly extended their hospitality over the last several years at "the dacha." Anna Voskresensky generously assisted with some very troublesome translations. To all of you, bol'shoe spasibo!

I am also indebted to *all* of my colleagues in the Department of History at the University of Kentucky. Although I cannot thank every one of you by name, I want you all to know how much I enjoy being a part of our particular community of scholars on the seventeenth floor! Many times throughout this process I have been stressed out and running against a deadline, and our staff members Tina Hagee, Carol O'Reilly, Kari Burchfield, and Rachelle Green have been there to help when I needed them. I thank you all for your kindness and your dedication to your work.

I have many mentors in the History Department and would like especially to thank Daniel Rowland for his thoughtful comments on this book manuscript, and for inspiring me to think about the contributions that I can make to my local community as I make my contributions to scholarship. I very much value his friendship and his example. In the last several years, Francie Chassen-Lopez has been extraordinarily supportive both as department chair and as a friend, for which I thank her. It is a pleasure to work closely with my colleagues in Modern European History. I thank Phil Harling and Alayna Wilburn for our stimulating and creative partnership in producing our online course on war and society, and for their patience during the last stages of this book's production. Phil, along with Jim Albisetti, Ellen Furlough, and Jeremy Popkin, have created a nurturing intellectual atmosphere in which ideas about World War I memory could be tested and discussed.

I also appreciate the supportive friendships among scholars in other fields and would like especially to thank former chair Dan Smith, David Hamilton, Mark Summers, Dan Gargola, and Kathi Kern for their support. For the last thirteen years, I have benefited from daily debriefing at the office next door, occupied by Gretchen Starr-LeBeau. Our informal lunches, scholarly and professional consultations, and general blowing off of steam mean a great deal to me, and I thank her for her kindness, friendship, and unstinting support throughout the years.

The University of Kentucky is especially strong in the quality of its librarians. I want to thank Gordon Hogg and Carrie Lewis for their hard work on the Scott Soviet Military Research Collection. I would also like to thank Frank Davis, Judy Fugate, and Shawn Livingston for being an enormous help over the years. I am happy to take this opportunity to thank the highly professional and efficient archivists and librarians at the Hoover Institution and the Bakhmeteff Archive, and also in Moscow at the Russian State Library, INION, GIM OPI, GARF, RGALI, RGASPI, RGVA, and RGVIA. I would particularly like to thank Mariia Katagoshchina at GIM OPI for sharing her scholarly work with me.

One of the great pleasures of my job at Kentucky has been the possibility to work with wonderful students. Over the years, interactions with many students have contributed to the conceptualization of this work. I would like to thank my graduate students Keziban Acar, Keri Manning, Aaron Weinacht, and Jami Bartek for the intellectual stimulation that their projects have provided. I thank Phil Stosberg, Jeremiah Nelson, and especially John Davis for providing excellent, good-natured, and timely research help as well as intellectual stimulation.

This book has greatly benefited from careful and expert readers who have helped me craft this project. I would like to thank Joshua Sanborn and Peter Gatrell for their immensely knowledgeable and constructive comments on the manuscript. Many thanks also to Janet Rabinowitch and Candace McNulty for their editorial comments and to Dan Pyle and Marvin Keenan for their work on the manuscript.

This work has been enriched by the comments of participants at various conferences and workshops. Many thanks to Robert Thurston, Scott Kenworthy, Stephen Norris, and the participants at the Midwest Russian History Workshop at Miami University of Ohio in March 2003; Michael David-Fox, Peter Holquist, and the participants in the Harvard-Maryland Workshop on Transnational Histories at the University of Maryland in May 2003; Diane Koenker, John Randolph, Mark Steinberg, and the participants at the Midwest Russian History Workshop at the University of Illinois in February 2007 for their especially thoughtful comments on the religion chapter; and Mark Cornwall and all the participants of the 2007 "Sacrifice and Regeneration" conference in Southampton, England, for opening up my eyes to the complexity of the legacy of the Great War in Eastern Europe.

Many other scholars in the field have made substantial contributions to this work. Melissa Stockdale has been extremely supportive personally and professionally as a scholar of World War I, as has Lisa Kirschenbaum as a scholar of memory. As a cultural historian straying into military history, I have benefited greatly from the advice and counsel of Bruce Menning, Dave Stone, and Roger Reese. I am also greatly indebted to each one of the scholars named below for the important contributions that they have made to my work. I appreciate their scholarly expertise, collegiality, and friendship over the years. Warm thanks go to David Brandenberger, Maria Bucur, Jane Burbank, Mollie Cavender, Rebecca Friedman, Sheila Fitzpatrick, Cathy Frierson, Cora Granata, Dan Healey, Betsy Hemenway, Hubertus Jahn, Pearl James, Claudia Koonz, Cheryl Koos, Alf Lüdtke, Julia Mannherz, Laura Phillips, Sarah Phillips, Peter Pozefsky, David Ransel, Bill Rosenberg, Irina Tarakanova, Nina Tumarkin, Erika Wolf, and Denise Youngblood.

I would also like to thank my entire extended family in New York, California, and Florida, especially Mary Efron, Diana Hartman, and Carmen

Maggiore, for their outpouring of love and support over the decades. Your visit to Lexington in August 2009 meant so much to all of us! It is also hard to imagine how I could have made it through the long process of writing this book without the friendship of Dana Rabin and Craig Koslofsky, Debra Hensley and Melissa Watt (whose talents as a photographer are also much appreciated), Deborah Field and Mark Schneyer, Emilie Greco, Evelyn Schwarz, François and Angie Leroy, Michele and Ziggy Rivkin-Fish, Nancy Schoenberg and Mark Swanson, Wendy Rowland, and Wes Willoughby. To Beate Popkin, Sally Zwicker, and Jane Kottmyer, many thanks for nurturing my children, animals, and garden while I was writing this book!

It is hard to put into words my appreciation for Ken Slepyan, who fits into practically every category above. No one has looked at more drafts of this manuscript than Ken has, or has been more encouraging, and the book is much better for his wise counsel and expert knowledge on military and social history. I also have appreciated Ken's good humor, creative thinking, and his dedication to good pedagogy as we have collaborated on the writing of a Soviet history textbook. But Ken's support of this project does not stop at the professional. His deceptively quiet yet wicked sense of humor has helped me through many difficult moments. None of the travel to research this book or to attend scholarly conferences could have been done without Ken "holding down the fort" and caring for our two daughters, the cat, the dog, and the late guinea pig. He has been an exemplary partner in scholarship and in life, and I dedicate this book to him, and to our two children, Mara and Anya. When I began this project, Mara was five and Anya only two years old. Over the nine years that it took to write this book, they have developed vibrant and charming personalities, diverse intellectual interests and hobbies, and an addiction to texting. I am so deeply proud of the young women that Mara and Anya are becoming, and I look forward to the ways in which they will shape the world.

The Great War in Russian Memory

1

Introduction · The Great War in Russian Memory

The Moscow City Fraternal Cemetery (also known as the All-Russian War Cemetery) was one of the most visible war memorials created in imperial Russia during World War I (figure 1.1).[1] First proposed by the Grand Duchess Elisaveta Fedorovna, it was organized by prominent Moscow civic leaders and dedicated with great solemnity and fanfare in the village of Vsekhsviatskoe on the outskirts of Moscow on February 15, 1915. The architect of the cemetery, P. I. Klein, directly linked the site to civic, national, and patriotic goals: he hoped that "future generations will here learn love of the motherland and will carry away in their hearts the steadfast resolution to serve for the benefit of the fatherland."[2] These national goals were to be realized through an Orthodox Christian religious idiom of memorialization. First a temporary chapel was erected at the cemetery in 1915; then the prominent architect A. V. Shchusev's memorial Church of the Transfiguration was consecrated three years later. The cemetery eventually held 17,500 dead from World War I, including Allied troops and enemy prisoners of war. After revolutionary disturbances began in 1917, ten thousand of the revolution's victims (both Reds and Whites) were also interred in the cemetery. Buried together with the World War I dead of several nations were revolutionaries killed by tsarist troops in March 1917, cadets from Moscow military schools who fought *against* the Bolsheviks in November 1917, Soviet Civil War commanders, and victims of the Red terror executed by the Soviet secret police.[3]

Klein's hope that the site would instill patriotism in future generations was not fulfilled. In 1925 burials in the cemetery ceased, its administrative offices

FIGURE 1.1. Moscow City Fraternal Cemetery. From S. V. Puchkov, *Moskovskoe gorodskoe bratskoe kladbishche* (Moscow: Gorodskaia tipografiia, 1915).

were closed, and it was turned into a park. Relatives of the dead no longer knew where to turn to request permission to repair graves or erect monuments, and gradually the graves began to "fall into decline and lose their inscriptions." Soon, no one knew where to find the graves of their relatives or of the revolutionary martyrs buried in the cemetery. Openly abandoning their responsibility for the upkeep of the cemetery, Moscow city authorities enlisted the help of a voluntary organization, the Old Moscow Society, to "take the graves of outstanding public figures under its protection."[4] The society, which likely included relatives of those buried in the cemetery, protected the site to the best of its abilities. But, before it ceased meeting in 1929, when the Soviet government disbanded many voluntary societies, it had been unable to obtain 10,000 rubles from the Sokol district soviet to build a fence around the cemetery that would protect it from the students of a nearby school.[5] Deprived of both civic and financial support, the cemetery was left to its fate.

Information about the destruction of the cemetery is shrouded in urban legend. According to the testimony of some local residents, the All-Russian War Cemetery was desecrated and "neighboring urchins . . . played football with skulls that they dug up from the ground."[6] The grave markers were supposedly destroyed in 1932 on Stalin's personal orders.[7] In another account, it was the building of the Moscow metro that precipitated the cemetery's destruction, and afterward, the People's Commissariat of Internal Affairs (NKVD) used the site to execute and bury victims of Stalin's purges.[8] What is certain is that sometime in the 1930s or 1940s, the Church of the Transfiguration and all monuments and grave markers were demolished, with the exception of one.

The unique exception to this general destruction was a monument to Sergei Aleksandrovich Shlikhter, a Moscow University student who was wounded at Baranovichi on June 20, 1916, during the Brusilov offensive and died on June 25, 1916. The monument mixed the personal and the political. Inscribed on a sculpted stone tablet in new orthography was a quotation from his war diary: "How good is life. How good it is to live."[9] On the base of the monument were also inscribed the words "To a victim of the imperialist war." While the first inscription pointed to the irony of war taking the life of this particular exuberant young man, the second inscription set Shlikhter's death within a Soviet anti-imperialist context. How can one explain the survival of this lone Soviet-era monument to a "victim" of World War I, the last remaining physical evidence of war memory in the former territory of the Moscow cemetery?

The dead soldier was the son of Aleksandr Grigorievich Shlikhter, Soviet Russia's first People's Commissar of Provisioning in 1917 and later the vice president of the Ukrainian Academy of Sciences. According to S. A. Shlikhter's nephew, the youth had joined the tsarist army against his revolutionary father's wishes. Sometime in the early Soviet period, Shlikhter honored his son with a monument carved by the famous sculptor S. D. Merkurov.[10] When the cemetery was being destroyed, legend has it that Shlikhter lay on the gravestone and protested "You will have to destroy me as well."[11] A more prosaic conjecture is that Merkurov's almost two-ton granite block was left by chance, because it was too heavy to move.[12] Whether or not Shlikhter actually intervened in such a dramatic way to save his son's grave, this particular gravestone was preserved from the Stalin-era bulldozers and allowed to remain standing in the park, continuing to give voice to the tragedy of World War I (figure 1.2).

In the late 1940s, as Moscow expanded well beyond the boundaries of the former village of Vsekhsviatskoe, residential and commercial building began in earnest on the cemetery site, the area around today's Peschanaia Street. Ur-

FIGURE 1.2. Monument to World War I victim S. A. Shlikhter, a Moscow University student wounded at Baranovichi who died June 25, 1916. Moscow City Fraternal Cemetery. Photograph taken by author.

ban legend tells us that the Leningrad Movie Theater was built in 1956 at the location of the Church of the Transfiguration. A portion of the All-Russian War Cemetery remained a park (Leningrad Park), but almost all of the cemetery's memorial features had disappeared.[13] Soviet authorities had first adopted a utilitarian stance toward the memorial cemetery, burying its heroes and enemies indiscriminately. Later they practiced demolition of both tsarist and Soviet graves by neglect. And ultimately they almost, but not quite, erased the cemetery from the Moscow landscape.[14]

The fate of the cemetery demonstrates a dramatic contrast between the Soviet Union and much of the rest of Europe. Between 1918 and 1939 Europeans built tens of thousands of World War I memorials. They engaged in intense cultural and political activity as they commemorated and reinterpreted the catastrophic events of the war, honored the dead, and connected the war to future political and social agendas. European opinion makers of all persuasions competed to define the war in ways that forwarded their particular social and political goals. At the same time, as local communities and millions of mourning families tried to come to terms with the loss of their loved ones, they constructed more intimate memorials and remembered the war in highly personal ways. As the successor state to the Russian Empire, the Soviet Union was unique among the combatants in the virtual absence of public commemoration of World War I at the level of the state, community, and civic organizations, or even individual mourning.

Scholars generally agree about this erasure of memory. Daniel Orlovsky has observed that the major scholarly works about European intellectual and social responses to World War I do not include "a single word about Russia and Russian memory about the fallen."[15] This absence has largely been explained by the Soviet leaders' rejection of World War I (in contemporary Soviet terminology "the world war" or "the imperialist war") as an illegitimate imperialist war and their conscious refusal to commemorate the sacrifices of Russian soldiers and civilians in the service of the tsar.[16] Peter Gatrell argued that the Bolsheviks "discouraged public reflection on the war as a compelling human struggle and did nothing to sustain its commemoration." Aaron Cohen showed that the marking of World War I anniversaries in the Soviet press contained "few depictions of the actions of individuals, the details of battles, the suffering of soldiers or civilians, or the experience of Russia and the Russians." And Richard Stites suggested that "the absence of a real historical memory [of World War I] in Russia" is "one of the many historical phenomena that have divided Russia from the West psychologically in our century."[17] It is true that World War I, as an "illegitimate" and "imperialist" war, remained largely outside of official myths and on the margins of Soviet culture. The Soviet government generally ignored the war and instead poured its energies into creating a myth of the revolution, constructing Sovietness through a conscious process of forgetting imperial Russia's last war.[18] The dead of World War I, according to Catherine Merridale, were displaced by "millions of more important bodies—red heroes of the civil war—for the new state to honor." While to some extent this is true, the example of the All-Russian War Cemetery suggests that even these Red heroes were only sporadically honored in an official Soviet milieu that was generally resistant to creating a cult of the dead.[19] World

War I was also pushed to the background of Soviet consciousness because of the much greater physical devastation of the Civil War, with a population loss nearly twice as great as that of World War I due to military engagements, general lawlessness, famine, and disease in the years 1918–1922.[20] Personal commemoration of both World War I and Civil War dead was made extraordinarily difficult by the daily struggles for survival during the Civil War years, and few had the wherewithal to honor their own dead. There were a variety of reasons, then, both political and personal, why World War I receded from a central place in Soviet life.

Yet, I argue that the absence of official commemoration did not mean the absence of war memory itself. The 18.6 million men of the Russian Empire who had been in uniform during World War I, the families mourning the 2 million (or more) dead, the 5 million hospitalized for wounds or disease seeking to recover their health or learning to cope with their disfigurements, and the 5 million who endured the hardships of prisoner of war camps simply did not forget about their war experiences in the decades after World War I.[21] The marginalization of World War I in Soviet culture and the lack of centralized myth-making or official commemoration does not signify an absence of memory or the failure of Russians to see the war as a compelling human struggle. When one analyzes the broader discourse of World War I beyond the official press, one finds a complex and varied discussion of individual war experience. Remembrance of and reflection on World War I occurred quite regularly in Soviet interwar culture, even if World War I often appeared as mere "prelude" to the revolution or its foil. This book examines the myriad depictions of World War I to recover the Soviet discourse about the war that has hitherto remained largely outside of historical view.

Because analysts have tended to focus on "official" commemorations and pronouncements and have privileged the accounts of the "main attraction" of the revolution over extant sources about the "opening act" of World War I, they have often overlooked the considerable attention to World War I that emerged on the margins of Soviet culture. By excavating and analyzing this rich and complicated discourse at the margins, we can learn much about the centers of Soviet ideology and Soviet culture. In comparison to the other European combatant countries, the Soviet state maintained much tighter control over all cultural production and was much more active in shaping World War I discourse. But in spite of some state actors' conscious attempts to control, to marginalize, and in effect to "forget" certain interpretations of World War I, treatments of the war nonetheless addressed many aspects of war experience in candid, compelling, and sometimes subversive ways.

By Soviet World War I discourse, I mean all public and media representations of World War I during the interwar period including print, visual sources, music, commemorative practices, and public events and interactions. This book focuses broadly on this discourse to consider the implications of the absence of Soviet World War I "myths." In his groundbreaking study of World War I memory, George Mosse examined "the myth of the war experience," prominent especially in Germany and other "defeated nations." In this myth, "the memory of the war was refashioned into a sacred experience which provided the nation with a new depth of religious feeling."[22] Although the Russian Empire was "defeated," no such legitimating myth could emerge in a Soviet context.

My work explores Soviet understandings of World War I in a country where millions of individual memories and experiences of the war generally lacked an overarching mythic narrative within which they could be organized.[23] In the Soviet Union, there was not a singular and agreed upon World War I "memory." Without overarching myths to guide the process, the contest to construct or to obstruct cultural memory of World War I was far more fragmented and more open-ended than the creation of European World War I myths or the Soviet myths of the October Revolution and Civil War. Because this notion of contestation is central to my understanding of how all memory works, I see memory as "an outcome of the relationship between a distinct representation of the past and the full spectrum of symbolic representations available in a given culture."[24] The relationships among such representations were constantly changing; by acknowledging that all memory is "unstable, plastic, synthetic, and repeatedly reshaped," I hope to provide insight into the ever-shifting contours of World War I memory and identify the forces behind its reshaping.[25]

Various Soviet World War I memories gained or lost prominence in relation to other memories of World War I as well as in interactions with the dominant Soviet myths of the October Revolution and the Civil War. This notion of contest makes it imperative to define the creators of these distinct representations of the past.[26] The actors engaged in the battles over World War I memory include individual writers, artists, historians, military theorists, and museum curators; the critics, publishers, and journalists who vetted their works; the government institutions that provided financial support for the production of the works; censorship agencies; and the readers/viewers who responded to the works. Mourners, clergy, civic organizations, and individual veterans or groups of veterans also engaged with various Soviet institutions in their efforts to carry out acts of remembrance that did not leave a literary or artistic trace. These acts are much harder to document, but nonetheless constitute an important component of World War I memory.

The marginalization of World War I was not accomplished by some kind of overarching directive from top Soviet authorities. Changes in the nature of World War I memory occurred over decades through thousands of individual bureaucratic, personal, or institutional contests in which memory of the war was both intentionally and unintentionally protected or undermined. Engaged in these contests to promote particular kinds of World War I remembrance were thousands of individuals, such as the members of the Old Moscow Society who donated their time to the upkeep of the All-Russian War Cemetery, A. G. Shlikhter, who may have fought to preserve his son's gravestone, and the military theorist A. A. Svechin, who was a prominent member of the Red Army's commission to study war experience in the early 1920s. Although the Old Moscow Society, which disappeared in 1929, and Svechin, who was shot as an enemy of the people in 1938, both ultimately failed in their efforts to promote their visions of World War I memory, their struggles are worthy of our attention. The lone gravestone left standing in the Moscow memorial cemetery is symbolic of the persistence of particular visions of World War I memory in spite of considerable efforts to destroy them.

Remembrance of World War I evolved in the interwar period (like many other Soviet interwar social phenomena) for a variety of reasons, including the curtailment of civil society in the late 1920s, Stalinist repressions, power struggles in the Red Army, the complex efforts to define a new Soviet proletarian literature, and the inherent difficulty of creating a heroizing narrative about the lost war of a toppled empire. But throughout the entire interwar period, World War I was decentered rather than forgotten. As some types of World War I memory were destroyed, idiosyncratic new ways of remembering the war appeared. It is the persistent efforts of individuals (and institutions) in interwar Russia to interpret, consider, and reflect on World War I that have truly been forgotten by generations of Soviet citizens and historians alike.

TRANSNATIONAL CONTEXTS AND RUSSIAN WAR MEMORY

Just as Russian and Soviet wartime mobilization and state-building need to be considered within the context of "the common European deluge" of 1914–1921, Russian and Soviet literary and cultural responses to the calamity of war must also be situated among the European cultural responses to the World War I era.[27] European historians of World War I have vigorously debated the extent to which World War I was a complete break with the past. They have discussed the balance between modern, ironic sensibilities and traditional, heroic sensibilities in postwar Europe. While some authors such as Paul Fussell, George Mosse, and Modris Eksteins emphasized the transformations in intellectual and social life wrought by the war, and the creation of a distinct "modernity" that could variously be defined as ironic or violent, other scholars, notably Antoine Prost and Jay Winter, have instead pointed to the way that traditional structures of religion and community provided continuity and a compelling framework within which to understand the war. They have debated whether the memory of World War I challenged or strengthened the ideal of the heroic warrior and have queried the extent to which the memory of the war bolstered patriotism and nationalism. These debates have profound implications for the analysis of World War II as well. Was it the experience of World War I that led directly to the violent lawlessness of the interwar period, the rise of fascism, and the second war? Or did the origins of the second conflict emerge from divisions within European society that existed long before 1914? This work engages these debates by returning the Russian Empire and the Soviet Union to their rightful places in the cultural history of interwar European memory of World War I.

The Soviet situation also had significant commonalities with the experiences of the new Eastern European states that, like the Soviet Union, succeeded a defeated and humiliated empire.[28] Also, like the Soviet Union, these countries developed historical narratives about the complex period of the "common European deluge" to bolster the legitimacy of their fledgling states; but their narratives were often contested. At times, the Soviet Union's discussion of World War I was comparable to that of Germany, Austria, and the East European successor states; at other times it reflected the key issues addressed in British, French, and American wartime memory, and sometimes Soviet views of the war remained distinctive.

Like Prost and Winter, I emphasize continuity over rupture in my analysis of Soviet war memory. While there is no doubt that the vast cataclysm of war, revolution, and civil war fundamentally reshaped the Russian state, the intensive Soviet efforts to create "the New Soviet Man (and Woman)" often disguised essential continuities between tsarist and Soviet *mentalités*, and between tsarist and European wartime mobilizations and Soviet peacetime rule.[29]

Continuities in World War I discourse were double-edged swords; in the interwar period, Russians and Soviets used traditional religious and moral values to question warfare and heroism in powerful ways, but also drew on belligerent tsarist tropes extant before World War I in the building of a new Soviet militarism. As the threat of a second war drew closer, the balance between these two trends began increasingly to shift away from questioning and toward belligerence.

Failing to recognize Russia as a part of Europe has historical as well as historiographical implications. Along with excluding Russia from modern debates about World War I and memory, historians of both Europe and the Soviet Union have underestimated the extent to which Russian and Soviet memory interacted with contemporary Russian émigré and interwar European war memory. In the dislocation of the postwar years, Russian war participants remembered World War I not only in Moscow, Petrograd, and Kiev, but also in the Russian diaspora in such places as Paris, Berlin, Sofia, Belgrade, Harbin, and San Francisco. Following Aaron Cohen, who compared remembrance of World War I in the diaspora with the anniversaries of World War I in the Soviet press and demonstrated that émigrés' collective remembrance of the war highlighted their honorable behavior to construct "a non-Soviet Russian past," this book contextualizes Soviet works within the larger rubric of diasporic Russian war memory.[30]

It is also critical to remember that Russian-language printed materials crossed international borders. Until the end of 1923, the Soviet government allowed selected materials published abroad about Russia's World War I and the Russian Revolution to be distributed in the Soviet Union, after the Main Administration for Literary and Publishing Affairs (*Glavlit*) carefully vetted them.[31] The literary publishing house Gelikon in Berlin, for example, identified its place of publication as "Moscow-Berlin" to signal its loyalty to the Soviet Union and facilitate the importation of its books into the Soviet Union.[32] Soviet books were, of course, also sold abroad. The boundaries of knowledge between the diaspora and the metropole were thus somewhat porous in the early Soviet years, creating multiple vectors of memory in the Soviet Union and Europe.

Furthermore, Soviet publishing houses, like publishers around the world, actively sought out "suitable" literary works about World War I to translate into Russian. Writers such as Henri Barbusse, Jaroslav Hašek, Ernest Hemingway, T. E. Lawrence, Erich Maria Remarque, Romain Rolland, and Arnold Zweig all appeared in Russian translation at various times in the interwar period. Publishers also translated the memoirs of key military and political figures, such as David Lloyd George, Raymond Poincaré, Kaiser Wilhelm, and

Paul von Hindenburg. Meanwhile, the memoirs of General Aleksei Brusilov, the World War I works of such Soviet writers as Il'ia Erenburg, Sof'ia Fedorchenko, Kirill Levin, Mikhail Sholokhov, and of filmmakers such as Boris Barnet circulated in English, French, German, Spanish, Dutch, Yiddish, Serbian, Czech, Danish, and Japanese translations in the interwar period. During World War II, when Russia became the ally of Britain and the United States, the World War I novels of Sergei Sergeev-Tsenskii were also translated into English. Remembrances thus crossed borders in multiple directions.

Scholars have been quick to recognize the Soviet Union's uniqueness in its failure to commemorate the so-called "Great War," but they have not so readily acknowledged Soviet awareness of and even participation in some European trends, such as in the stormy reception of Erich Maria Remarque's *All Quiet on the Western Front*.[33] By emphasizing the Soviet Union's separateness from European culture, scholars have underestimated the extent of the Soviet Union's participation in a pan-European dialogue about World War I.

Soviet authors in the early 1920s were keenly aware of European remembrance of the war and highly cognizant that the Soviet approach to World War I differed sharply from that of its European neighbors. They engaged with and responded to the phenomenon of memorialization in Europe, often by consciously rejecting it and seeking to undermine the sacred nature of European World War I monuments. A 1931 novel by Vladimir Lidin, *The Grave of the Unknown Soldier* (*Mogila neizvestnogo soldata*), proposed that the body underneath the Arc de Triomphe in Paris belonged not to a heroic and patriotic Frenchman but to a Russian-Jewish legionnaire who was killed "like a bandit" for refusing to follow orders. The Frenchmen who thought they were venerating a "legendary" soldier, a character in the "tale of the greatness of France," were in fact revering a revolutionary mutineer.[34] The novel symbolically overturned both the meaning of the monument and the French interpretation of the war.

No Soviet writer, however, was more scathing about Europe's drive to memorialize the war in the 1920s than Il'ia Erenburg. In the 1924 foreword to the first Soviet edition of his World War I memoir, *The Face of War* (*Lik voiny*), he implicitly defended the Soviet Union's lack of commemoration by attacking the prevailing European obsession with World War I memory.[35] Erenburg is so well known for his powerful anti-Nazi propaganda during World War II that the pacifism of his early writing is often overlooked. Erenburg was living in Paris when the war broke out. He became a newspaper correspondent on the Western Front after he tried to volunteer for the French Army but was rejected for physical infirmity. In the midst of covering the war for the Russian newspaper *Birzhevye vedomosti* (Stock Exchange Gazette) Erenburg suffered a nervous breakdown, but he recovered to continue his reportage of life in the trenches.[36] In *The Face of War,* Erenburg spoke eloquently of war's insanity, pointlessness, and human suffering. He wrote as a "moral witness," an "individual with a terrible tale to tell," based on his "direct and personal" experience of the horrors of war.[37] In the foreword to the memoir, he expressed a different kind of outrage as well: the horrors of capitalism and the vulgar commemoration of the war that he experienced in interwar Europe:

> "The renowned Morte-Homme! Here more than forty thousand people perished," yelled out the conscientious guide. And behind him they turn curiously: forty thousand! . . . It would be good to send a postcard from this very place.
>
> On the lousy ground invalids crawl—pieces of meat, without arms, without legs, often without eyes or face, burned to a hot liquid or half-suffocated by gas. They sell postcards with views of the places where they left their arms, legs, or eyes. But I'll give them what-for. And chasing away the cripples, the waiter from the café brings iced cocktails. . . .
>
> The bones of the unknown soldiers are dug up and then buried again in the middle of the Place de l'Étoile in Paris and Congress Square in Brussels. Delegations, flags, wreaths. Today the Shopkeepers' Society of Vincennes, tomorrow the war attaché of Uruguay, the day after tomorrow, Mr. Poincaré himself. Here there are so many vulgarities that it becomes magnificent. In Brussels, for example, they have led gas pipes to the bones. An inextinguishable icon-lamp. What do you want: the shopkeepers of Vincennes are poets at heart.
>
> Near Verdun a guide exclaims:
>
> "Attention! Up to eighteen thousand skulls. The bones of the defenders of Fort Demoine!"
>
> The curious approach. "And why don't they smell?"
>
> "Oh, mister, everything is perfectly arranged. And then . . . four years have already passed. . . ."
>
> . . . The European tradesman, ready to sell skulls! . . .
>
> And so, everything is in order. It can all begin again from the beginning. There are enough cities not destroyed and people who are not crippled.[38]

In his memoir, and also in his fictionalized, satirical, and highly irreverent version of his experiences of war and revolution, the 1922 novel *The Extraordinary Adventures of Khulio Khurenito and His Disciples . . . .* (*Neobychainye pokhozhdeniia Khulio Khurenito i ego uchenikov. . . .*), Erenburg excoriated battlefield excursion bureaus for profiting from the suffering and death of millions.[39] He expressed his concern about the increasing trivialization of the war at newly built monuments all across Europe. He claimed that these commercialized and trivializing forms of memory "sold" Europeans on patriotism once again by allowing them to forget the horrors of war. This re-envisioning of World War I paved the way for the remilitarization of Europe for the next war, but Erenburg insisted on reminding Europeans about the horrors of war that they were trying to forget. He offered his writings as an antidote to both the forgetting of the realities of war and to its mindless and vulgar glorification.

Erenburg's description of commemoration is striking because it contained features of both official Soviet ideology and typical European treatments of the war. His authorial voice overflowed with the irony that has been noted as a key characteristic of a "modern" consciousness, and Erenburg's firsthand account of World War I shares much in common with the British writers that Paul Fussell featured in his landmark study *The Great War in Modern Memory*. Erenburg directed his irony squarely at those who sought to use the memory of the war for their own personal profit or to ignite another war. He consistently questioned why men had to be turned into "pieces of meat" and resisted frameworks of comfort that defined a purpose for the soldiers' sacrifices. Erenburg, in ironic detachment, asserted that he did not have his own agenda in writing about the war; in the foreword to the first edition of the work, he claimed not to be "for" or "against" the war but aimed to describe "the hundreds of different faces of war, while war's true face remained invisible to me."[40]

Erenburg showed himself to be fully a member of the European intellectual community struggling to find direction in the postwar world. His writings demonstrate the penetration of the Soviet public sphere by the common European quest to understand the "Great War" and prevent the next one, and also by European uncertainty, irony, and unwillingness to arrive at definitive conclusions in the transformed postwar world. The Soviet Union may not have officially recognized World War I as part of its own founding myth, but in the 1920s, it nonetheless took part in the pan-European intellectual movements that interpreted the war and coped with its aftermath.

SOVIET MOBILIZATION FOR WAR

While integrating the Soviet Union into the pan-European history of the memory of World War I is a central goal of this work, I also illuminate a second, specifically Soviet story, about the role of World War I memory in the mobilization of an already war-traumatized population to prepare for the next war. I define mobilization broadly, as the Soviet state's attempts to shape the cultural attitudes of its citizens not just to facilitate such concrete military activities as conscription, military training, and preparation for civil defense, but also to influence citizens' understandings about the nature of war itself and to enable them to envision their potential roles in prosecuting the next war.[41] Soviet leaders in the 1920s and 1930s believed that war was the norm for international relations in the era of capitalism, and so they rejected liberal pacifist thought as both naïve and potentially dangerous to national security.[42] At a time when Bolshevik attitudes during World War I were uncompromisingly antiwar, Lenin urged soldiers not to lay down their arms, but rather to turn the imperialist war into a civil war. My book explores the interaction of World War I memory with other Soviet myths of heroism and patriotism to understand the broad cultural foundations of Soviet military mobilization and attempts to make war "thinkable" in the Soviet interwar period.[43]

World War I's marginalization by the Soviet state and its persistent association with the Russian Empire's military failure and ineptitude makes it, in some ways, a more intriguing object of study than the Civil War in regard to military mobilization. Because of the very exclusion of World War I from official myth-making, representations of the war did not have to adhere as closely to official narratives as did depictions of the October Revolution or Civil War. The marginal location of World War I (and likely of the Russo-Japanese War as well, though this must be the object of future study) provided an intellectual and political space in which Soviet writers could discuss wartime experience in complex ways. While many, though far from all, Civil War accounts described military events in black-and-white terms, World War I was often represented in various shades of gray.[44] A substantial portion of the postwar public discussion about World War I by Soviet veterans, journalists, historians, artists, film directors, and writers contested the glorification of warfare and the veneration of the male warrior hero by depicting the ugliness, horrors, and ambiguities of war.

World War I narratives defied Soviet conventions because of a series of inherent contradictions in Soviet ideology: between the Soviet government's rejection of World War I as a tsarist and capitalist war and its need to inspire military prowess, heroism, and sacrifice among the war-weary Soviet population in the 1920s; between the communist narrative of the internationalist and proletarian brotherhood of all soldiers and the need to develop a national-patriotic ethos in defense of the Soviet motherland; between the pacifist elements inherent in depicting the horrors of war and the need to make the next war "thinkable"; between heroizing the revolutionary refusal to fight an imperialist war and the need to inspire obedience and perseverance among Soviet soldiers.

The way in which World War I memory dealt with these contradictions evolved over the course of the interwar period, and this evolution sheds light on the ongoing scholarly debates about "The Great Retreat." Ever since 1946, when sociologist Nicholas Timasheff first introduced the term, there has been a vibrant debate about the relationship between early Soviet cultural policies and the cultural trends of the 1930s and 1940s.[45] Timasheff pointed to the rise in Russian nationalism, the return to traditional education, concessions given to religion, and the diminishing of women's rights to suggest that Stalin had abandoned the revolutionary policies of the 1920s in favor of conservative but popular norms. Other cultural analysts have also neatly divided the early Soviet period into two "cultures," positing a sharp division between the liberating and experimental culture of the New Economic Policy era in the 1920s and the monumental, conservative, and repressive Stalinist culture of the 1930s.[46] It is very tempting to tell the story of World War I memory within this context, because there is much corroborating evidence. In such a narrative, World War I memory challenges Soviet heroism, nationalism, and masculinity during the freer 1920s and then becomes renationalized, reheroized, and remasculinized in the repressive 1930s. But, in fact, both patriotic and pacifist, nationalist and internationalizing, masculine and "feminizing" rhetoric coexisted throughout the entire interwar period.

Like Katerina Clark in her recent work, I argue that the chronology of "The Great Retreat" obscures key aspects of Soviet World War I memory.[47] First of all, it would be a mistake to argue that all World War I remembrance in the 1920s contested Soviet heroic and patriotic narratives; from the revolution onward, a portion of World War I discourse echoed heroic tsarist tropes and facilitated their integration into Soviet discourse in ways that augmented and reinforced representations of new Soviet heroes. One of the key aspects of Soviet culture in the 1920s was thus its unstated reliance on the tsarist culture that it claimed to have destroyed. Likewise, it would be a mistake to view the 1930s solely as the decade of reheroization, renationalization, and remasculinization. Internationalist and pacifist ideas and moral critiques of the violence of war survived throughout the interwar period. There was always a counterpoint between heroism and antiheroism, though the heroic voices became much louder and the antiheroic voices grew fainter as time passed. This was not so much a shift away from socialist ideals, but a partial reconfiguration of how these ideals interacted with preexisting Russian cultural "building blocks."

THEMES AND METHODS

Religion, Gender, Violence, Nationality

Because I am interested in the public representation of World War I, the most crucial sources for this book are those that were produced or displayed in the Soviet Union between 1917 and 1945. I was continually surprised by both the quantity of such sources and, in many cases, their high artistic quality. Although it would be impossible to view every single Soviet World War I source, I have endeavored to survey as much Soviet cultural production about World War I as possible. I have examined visual works such as films, graphic art, architecture, and painting; literary works such as novels, short stories, and poetry; publicistic works such as memoirs, journalism, and criticism; museum exhibits, histories, and document collections written or edited by professional historians; and military and strategic histories by officers of the Soviet general staff, many of whom were active participants in the events they sought to explain. Each of these genres provides a different kind of insight into key aspects of Soviet war memory and the culture of Soviet military mobilization in the interwar period, and I have sought out the most prominent, popular, and resonant sources in each genre.

I use the literary method of close analysis of texts and the anthropological method of thick description to analyze the ways in which Russian and Soviet citizens interpreted World War I and the nature of war in general.[48] While it is much more difficult to trace people's deeds than their words, wherever possible I analyze concrete events and interactions that occurred during the interwar period as evidence of particular kinds of World War I memory. To the extent possible, I also focus on the reception of books and film to determine what kind of criticism they received in the Soviet press and to gauge the reaction of Soviet readers. Analyzing the dialogue of authors with censors and critics allows me to establish the range of opinions about the important philosophical and ethical issues raised by warfare.

Because artistic literature and literary memoirs had the greatest influence on the general Soviet population, they constitute the most significant segment of my source base, though the works of the military-history establishment for military specialists and for the general public are also considered. I have sought out published works with multiple editions and the broadest circulation. One of the key works featured in this book is perhaps the most popular Soviet novel of the interwar period, *Quiet Flows the Don (Tikhii Don)*. While this novel has hitherto been considered primarily a "Civil War" novel, I show its equal significance as a World War I novel. As a well-known blockbuster among Soviet novels, *Quiet Flows the Don* is the exception among my sources. My research calls attention to a variety of other significant pieces of Soviet World War I literature, many of which were quite popular in the interwar period but are now relatively unknown, usually because they fell out of favor with Soviet authorities and were not rediscovered until the 1980s or 1990s. Some of the featured works have still not been brought out in new editions. Very prominent Soviet writers such as Il'ia Erenburg, Dmitrii Furmanov, and Aleksandra Kollontai authored a number of these relatively unknown works. The names of other talented World War I authors—Sof'ia Fedorchenko, Sergei Klychkov, and Lev Voitolovskii, among others—are less familiar because their careers were cut short by repression. This study restores such works to their rightful place in the interwar literary landscape by examining them alongside canonical Soviet literature such as Mikhail Sholokhov's *Quiet Flows the Don*. The literary landscape also contained many other figures—little-known authors whose works were more ephemeral. For example, despite the fact that the peasant writer Moisei Georgievich Gromov's World War I novella *For St. George Crosses (Za krestami)* came out in ten editions between 1927 and 1935, there is scarcely any information available about him (figure 1.3).[49] The "rediscovery" of these authors is relevant to the mapping of the interwar political and cultural landscape, if not its literary landscape.

Four key themes emerge in the contested World War I discourses between 1914 and 1945: religion, heroic masculinity, violence, and patriotism. European historians of World War I have emphasized the importance of religion in coming to terms with the meaning of war;[50] religion also plays a very significant and heretofore unrecognized role in the Soviet case. Official tsarist rhetoric as well as popular piety defined World War I as an Orthodox Christian Holy War. This notion aided tsarist mobilization of the Orthodox population, even as it may have impeded the mobilization of the non-Orthodox citizens of the Russian Empire. After the revolution, the atheistic Soviet state challenged the idea of Holy War by rejecting the existence of God. Yet to perpetuate the Soviet myth of the patriotic warrior, state ideologists had to come to terms with heroic deaths in both World War I and the Civil War outside of a religious context. Soviet treatments of heroic death reflected the difficulties in constructing notions of heroism in the absence of an afterlife. Despite the new atheist "orthodoxy," religious discourse continued to provide meaning for those facing death and mourning their losses in the Soviet Union as well as in the rest of Europe. The imagery of resurrection and redemption, so important in tsarist Russia, remained crucial to the Soviet discourse of war.

The mechanized warfare and mass slaughter of World War I posed a formidable challenge to traditional definitions of the male warrior hero all over Europe. In Russia, the revolutions of 1917 destabilized gender norms as first the Provisional Government and then the Soviet state articulated radical notions of gender equality and citizenship. Despite these changes in official policy, notions of innate gender differences still remained absolutely crucial in the process of defining the warrior and justifying participation in war. In the Soviet Union, as in the rest of Europe, there continued to be a powerful connection between manliness, honor, and the willingness to commit violence in the name of one's country.[51] I use Soviet military literature and memoirs to demonstrate how depictions of the horrors of war destabilized prewar notions of Russian masculinity. This argument counters the suggestion that while the trauma of World War I shattered the image of the glorious and heroic warrior all across Western Europe, in Russia this male heroic ideal survived.[52] The challenging of heroic manliness was a significant aspect of interwar culture, as was the response to this challenge in Soviet efforts to remasculinize war and redraw gender boundaries to repair the image of the heroic warrior.

Recent works about World War I contend that historians have long had difficulty coming to terms with the sheer violence of warfare and have tended to sanitize wartime trauma.[53] My book confronts violence directly by comparing how World War I combatants and Civil War combatants described the violence that they perpetrated and witnessed. Their definitions of "just killing," their reactions to killing other soldiers in combat, and their violent interactions with the multiethnic civilian population on the frontlines provide a picture of warfare that is full of moral ambiguities. Soldiers' attempts to define when and against whom it was permissible to commit wartime violence did not easily correspond to Soviet notions of the class enemy or to the Soviet emphasis on exterminating all enemies of the state without mercy. Soviet representations of wartime killing, raping, and marauding during World War I

FIGURE 1.3. *Facing page.* Cover of Moisei Georgievich Gromov's World War I novella *For St. George Crosses* [*Za krestami*] (1927).

М. ГРОМОВ

ЗА КРЕСТАМИ

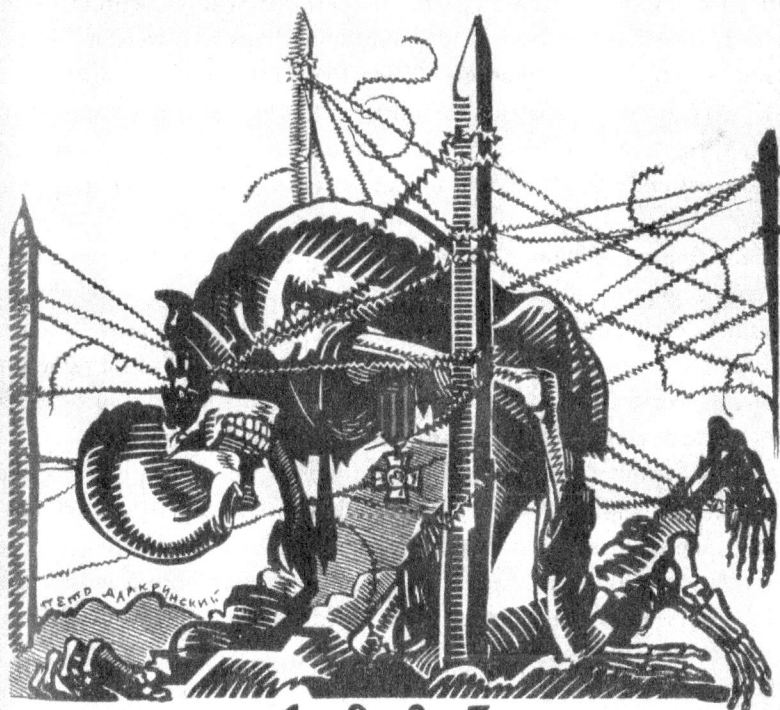

1927
ГОСУДАРСТВЕННОЕ ИЗДАТЕЛЬСТВО

revealed the toll that violence took on the perpetrators as well as the victims and repeatedly called the morality of wartime heroism into question.

Interwar representations of World War I also challenged notions of nationalism and patriotism. There has been lively scholarly debate about the extent to which the Russian Empire was able to mobilize its multiethnic and peasant population to identify with the Russian nation. Recent scholarship demonstrates persuasively that whatever the state of patriotism in 1914, by the mid-1930s, official Soviet culture had embarked on promoting a national and patriotic myth.[54] Representations of World War I reveal the battle between an incipient Soviet patriotism, drawing on Russian national identity, and the ideology of international class solidarity in the 1920s and 1930s. One crucial aspect of World War I identity was the delineation of "the enemy." Were German workers, for example, viewed as proletarian brothers or historic enemies of the Russian state? How was patriotism defined in the clash of the multiethnic Austro-Hungarian Empire with the Russian Empire? What was the significance of wartime ethnic violence perpetrated by Russian and Cossack soldiers against Jewish, German, and Polish civilians who were subjects of the same country? Representations of World War I illuminate competing national, international, and patriotic identities in this formative period and demonstrate the power of ethnic distinctions to undercut both pacifistic and internationalist notions of brotherhood and overarching imperial and Soviet identities.

The themes of religion, heroic masculinity, violence, and patriotism are not merely of great significance to twenty-first-century analysts; censorship officials in the early Soviet period were preoccupied with them as well. Glavlit sent directions to popular libraries in late 1923 or early 1924 about removing undesirable works from their shelves. According to the instructions, "the libraries had to be cleansed of books arousing 'animal and antisocial feelings,' . . . superstition, nationalism, and militarism (*militarizm*)." Soviet officials were most concerned with removing materials "disseminating patriotic, religious, and monarchistic ideas."[55] I contend that despite the anxieties of officials about the circulation of these themes, they remained constantly in play in World War I discourse (as well as in other Soviet discourses) during the interwar period. The continued circulation of these ideas was facilitated, in part, by their family resemblance to new Soviet themes such as the creation of a Promethean New Soviet Man, the love of the socialist fatherland, and militarization (*voenizatsiia*) in defense of this fatherland.

Tracing the Disappearance of World War I Discourse

While the first half of this book explores the rich fabric of World War I discourse in the interwar period, the second half examines shifts in the emphasis of this discourse over time. This analysis sheds light on Soviet censorship, revealing the boundaries of permissible Soviet discourse and pinpointing what could or could not be said at particular moments in the interwar period. As long as a book remained in favor, it was likely to be reprinted. The publication dates and print runs of the various editions of a single work provide us with valuable information not only about how much exposure the ideas in the book received, but also about the time period in which the work was considered acceptable. The appearance of only one edition of a work was usually an indication that something about the work displeased Soviet authorities almost immediately after its publication. When multiple editions of a work about World War I do exist, I compare them to determine if anything has been added or removed. This method, modeled on the scholarship of Herman Ermolaev and other literary scholars, enables me to produce a detailed chronology of various key ideas in Soviet discourse, and document the rhythm of their appearance and disappearance over time. The painstaking research of literary scholars on changes in various editions of Soviet literary works provides key additional data that I incorporate into this study.[56]

One of the most useful tools in analyzing Soviet publications is the "editor's preface." Forewords informed readers about which parts of the book the editors did not consider ideologically sound. By indicating that they published such ideas "against their better judgment," editors tried to inoculate themselves against criticism. These critical editorial remarks formed a counterpoint to the book in question, indicating particularly contentious issues, and revealing the multivalent nature of Soviet ideology. When Erenburg's *The Face of War* was published in 1928 as part of his *Collected Works,* literary critic L. Averbakh, the head of the Russian Association of Proletarian Writers (RAPP), wrote the preface. Somewhat predictably, Averbakh criticized Erenburg's lack of attention to class relations between soldiers and officers, one of the predominant themes in many contemporary Soviet works about World War I. On the theme of officers and soldiers, Averbakh instead recommended to readers Henri Barbusse's *Under Fire* (*Ogon'*; in French *Feu*) as a work that captured the essence of officer-soldier relations. Averbakh's singling out of this famous example of Western European war literature for praise is an example of the pan-European nature of World War I discourse and the penetration of left-wing Western European ideas into the Soviet Union.[57]

Although Erenburg claimed to be neither for nor against war, his memoir contained significant pacifist elements and, in fact, he had nearly been expelled from France during World War I because of his pacifist writings.[58] Averbakh criticized the antiwar aspects of the memoir, noting that "Erenburg does not understand the differences between imperialist war, civil war, revolutionary wars. . . . For him any war was diminished according to the philistine ethics of the 'young philologist' . . . 'I cannot kill. It is a sin. Against whom, against what?'"[59] Averbakh, like many other Soviet authors, made a sharp distinction between justified killing during a revolutionary war and immoral killing in the midst of an imperialist one. Averbakh's attack on Erenburg created a dialogue in Soviet culture about the ethics of wartime violence. While Averbakh left no doubt which interpretation was the "correct" one, Soviet citizens could nonetheless reflect on the moral issues raised by Erenburg and come to their own conclusions. Given the Soviet impetus toward militarization, even countenancing such questions was subversive of the imperative to ready the male population for participation in the next war.

Although the sharply critical introduction to Erenburg's work revealed the ways in which he was writing against the Soviet grain, the memoir was nonetheless included in his collected works, allowing for the possibility of debate about the causes and costs of war. The existence of such debates permits us to trace the fate of contested ideas during the Soviet era. When *The Face of War* was published for the first time in the Soviet Union in 1924 (its third edition) and again in 1928, there were more than thirty pages missing from the 1923 Berlin edition. The omissions tended to fall into two main categories: political deletions and those addressing moral and religious issues. Predictably, the 1928 edition omitted Erenburg's unflattering discussion of Bolshevism among the Russian soldiers in France, his depictions of the Russian soldiers' lack of revolutionary will, and his characterizations of the total breakdown of discipline among the mutinying Russian troops.[60]

While the Soviet editors permitted the publication of some pacifist passages in Erenburg's 1928 work, they omitted other religious and philosophical episodes. Taking advantage of Erenburg's ambivalence about religion (while living in France before the war, Erenburg, a Jew, had nearly converted to Catholicism), the editors included his moments of cynicism toward religion and censored his admiration of religious faith. They excised, for example, Erenburg's meditation on the contradiction between the Lord's commandment "Thou shalt not kill" and the notion of "holy war" propagated by "abbots and philosophers, diplomats and poets," even though this formulation echoed the themes of Soviet antireligious tracts about World War I. Erenburg had written, "Only in the ancient book, not effaced by anything, and somewhere in the depths of each of our souls, not completely trampled, lives the prohibition 'Thou shalt not kill.'"[61] Erenburg's acknowledgment of the enduring power of the Judeo-Christian scriptures made this passage doubly objectionable to Soviet editors. While it was possible to acknowledge the existence of pacifism in the late 1920s, it was problematic to recognize the strength of religion.

By studying specific contestations within World War I discourse and documenting particular deletions and additions, I provide insight into the chronology of the battles for survival, the adaptations, and the extinctions of certain ideas in the Soviet "ecosystem."[62]

RUSSIA'S WAR (1914–1921)

The general outlines of the dominant narratives about World War I constructed both during and after the war, as well as current historical debates about the events of World War I, provide useful background for an analysis of Russian and Soviet remembrance of World War I. Wartime discourse in Russia (as in all of the belligerent countries) was shaped by military censorship. While the Russian military censorship directives promulgated in 1914 were extremely broad in scope, according to the eyewitness account of M. Lemke, an officer attached to the tsarist general staff, they were put into practice in typical bureaucratic fashion: "on the one hand systematically ignored, and on the other hand interpreted in an extremely arbitrary way."[63] Despite the attempts of Russian censors to facilitate the enthusiastic and optimistic representation of warfare by trying to eliminate war news that "seemed depressing," sober acknowledgment of the costs of the war did find its way to the pages of Russian newspapers and journals.[64] Although restrictions tightened in early 1916, by then the "legal press had lost its credibility in favour of uncensorable hectographs and hand written news."[65] The Russian population saw glimpses of the horrors of war even as they were occurring.

Some public discourse was implicitly critical of tsarist policies, though not openly critical of the war effort. The newspaper *Russkoe slovo* (Russian Word), for example, published a series of articles on the desperate plight of civilian refugees in the Western territories, displaced by the advance of the Germans and the Russian military's scorched earth policies.[66] Representations of war that were produced in the Russian Empire thus contained a broad range of images, symbols, and tropes. While epic and heroic tropes dominated, especially during the first year of the war, other images obliquely called heroism into question and acknowledged the costs of war.

Post-1917 writers and memoirists drew on all phases and all types of tsarist discourse in their representations of war. While they sometimes mocked and critiqued these pre-revolutionary representations of war, at other times they drew direct inspiration from tsarist heroes in the creation of Soviet heroes. Soviet memory of the war was a multivocal and complex mix of Russian and European influences. While Soviet cultural leaders sought to distance themselves from tsarist culture and tsarist ideology, there were myriad continuities in personnel and ideas that shaped early Soviet culture as dramatically as did revolutionary ideology. Soviet thinkers also took émigré and "enemy" accounts of the war on the Eastern Front very seriously. While Soviet ideologues were intentionally silent about Soviet debts to tsarist culture and while they systematically underestimated and denied continuities, the tsarist legacy is an important aspect of Soviet life that deserves scholarly attention.

While I argue that there was no overarching Soviet mythology of World War I, and no heroic or mythic World War I narratives that were separate from larger revolutionary narratives, there were nonetheless certain standard tropes that commonly appeared in Soviet World War I accounts. These include the evils of imperialism and the role of capitalist powers in forcing tsarist Russia to provide cannon fodder (in Russian the even more graphic "cannon meat") in exchange for capitalist gold. Other key themes include the brutality and senseless training of the tsarist barracks, the mistreatment of soldiers by officers, a wave of enthusiasm for war at its outbreak followed by disillusionment and, of course, a happy ending in the finale of revolution. What made World War I discourse so interesting, however, was that these standard themes were intermingled with a wide variety of highly individualized and idiosyncratic interpretations of the war that both undermined the standard themes and went far beyond them to probe "the face" and "the footsteps" of war.[67]

Many interwar myths of the Russian Revolution and the Civil War, on the other hand, were even more explicitly militaristic. Graphic depictions of White atrocities revealed the suffering of the soldiers and the population, often within a trope of revenge that justified violent retribution enacted by the warrior hero. After the Bolshevik victory in the Civil War, this war became the focal point of military mobilization and the cornerstone of myths about Soviet military strength. After 1921, there was an increasing tendency to glorify the Red Army while denigrating tsarist war efforts. In the 1920s (and to some degree the 1930s) there still remained some room for ambiguity about the nature of the Civil War and the horrifying destruction that it wrought.[68] The costs and moral complexities of the Civil War are palpable in the works of such early Soviet authors as Isaak Babel', Aleksandr Fadeev, Fedor Gladkov, Nikolai Ostrovskii, and Mikhail Sholokhov. These works formed the backdrop against which the early Soviet works about World War I were written.

In both Western and in Soviet and Russian historical literature, Russia's participation in World War I suffers relative neglect in comparison with the Russian Revolution.[69] Surprisingly, though, there is a great deal of consistency in Soviet and émigré accounts of events from the outbreak of the war until the February Revolution. Émigré, Soviet, and contemporary narratives only definitively diverged when recounting events after the economic and political strains of fighting the war toppled Tsar Nicholas II in March 1917.

The generally agreed-upon narrative started with the Russian general staff changing its war plans at France's request to begin simultaneous offensives against Germany and Austria-Hungary in July–August 1914. The Russian generals Samsonov and Rennenkampf bungled their advance into East Prussia due to poor generalship and failures in communication and intelligence, and they endured a devastating and costly defeat at the hands of the Germans at the Battle of Tannenberg. Although the Russians successfully engaged the Austro-Hungarian army in the fall of 1914 and early 1915, capturing L'vov and later the fortress at Przemysl, the imperial army was forced into a disastrous and disorderly retreat in the late spring and summer of 1915 due to inadequate firepower, manpower, and transport. The Austrians regained all of occupied Galicia and the Russians lost all of Russian Poland, the provinces of Grodno, Vilno, Kovno, Kurland, and parts of Belorussia. By August 1915, there were even fears of German occupation of Petrograd, Kiev, and Odessa.[70]

Due to various government efforts at the end of 1915 and throughout 1916, the Russian army rallied; conscripts were better trained and armed and morale improved. The Russian army went on the offensive again in 1916 in response to French requests to relieve the pressure at Verdun. In June 1916, the Russian army scored its greatest victory in the war when General Aleksei Alekseevich Brusilov led a brilliant offensive against the Austrians at Lutsk. The

Russians broke through a fifty-mile stretch of the front and captured 200,000 men, half of the Austrian forces on the Eastern Front, though it cost the Russian army half a million of its own men. Contemporaries (and Brusilov himself) claimed that the offensive "had relieved Verdun and rescued the British and French position in the west, saved Italy, and forced Austria-Hungary to consider a separate peace." Ultimately, however, Generals Aleksei Evert and A. N. Kuropatkin failed to advance in order to consolidate Brusilov's victory and the Russian army could not capitalize on this opportunity to knock Austria out of the war.[71]

In discussions of the military aspects of the war, émigré/Western and Soviet narratives shared a great deal of common ground. They blamed France for insisting that the Russian Empire begin its offensive against the Germans in East Prussia when it was not yet ready in order to relieve pressure on the Western front. The Soviet version emphasized French "imperialism" using Russian peasants as cannon fodder for the benefit of French capitalists, while the émigré/Western versions emphasized Russia's noble sacrifice for France and England. Both Soviets and émigrés bemoaned the bungling of the thoroughly incompetent officers of the Russian general staff and other senior army officers while recognizing to varying degrees the individual skill and bravery of lower ranking officers or those who were not favored because of their lack of connections. Both narratives saw the shell shortage and lack of heavy artillery early in the war as a failure of Russian planning and a sign of the economic weakness that doomed the war efforts to failure, while they admired the raw talents of rank-and-file soldiers who would likely have won if properly armed. Finally, both narratives raised the suspicion of pro-German treachery and the betrayal of the war effort among the members of the tsarist court and generals with German names.

Soviet and émigré narratives emphasized the disasters of the first year of the war. The two narratives blamed the Russian monarchy for its inability to provide effective strategic leadership and for failing to adequately supply the army during the critical first year of the war, when up to a quarter of the troops were sent to the front unarmed and instructed to pick up weapons from the dead.[72] Soviet narratives were probably even more sensitive than émigré accounts to the traumas endured by civilians in the occupied territories and the plight of millions of refugees. Many of these refugees, including especially Jews and Germans, but also Poles, Lithuanians, and Roma were mistreated under Russian occupation or forcibly deported from the shifting frontlines by an army in a "pogrom mood" during the great retreat of 1915.[73] These narratives highlighted the disaster, destruction, and humiliation of Russia's war from beginning to end.

Both sets of narratives about World War I acknowledged, however, the significance of the Brusilov offensive, while viewing the general himself with some ambivalence. Émigrés acknowledged Brusilov's military talent but held him in contempt for later joining the Red Army, while some Soviet narratives pointed out the massive casualties in a campaign that yielded no tangible results, and they noted the growing numbers of desertions and instances of fraternization with enemy troops in 1916.[74] Both sides tended to see Brusilov's efforts as doomed to failure given the incompetence of the high command and/or the rising revolutionary movement.

Recent Western scholarship about the Eastern Front in World War I has challenged the pessimistic view of these narratives, suggesting that the catastrophe at Tannenberg was "more than balanced by the real victories scored against Austria in the south" and that the disasters of the retreat of 1915 were the impetus for the creation of the War Industries Committees and other measures that effectively mobilized Russia's economic resources for war. Scholars point to the military recovery of the tsarist army between September 1915 and February 1917 and its relative success in offensive operations during this period, and argue that the tsarist military "compares favorably with those of the other major powers, while the tsar's government proved to be relatively effective in organizing the war effort."[75] They have also demonstrated the many similarities between European and Russian approaches to mobilization and their parallel strengthening of the "total war state" to respond to the fundamental problems engendered by the war, noting that in Russia, successful mobilization efforts called forth the social forces that orchestrated the downfall of tsarism.[76] This scholarship suggests that the tsarist government's efforts to rectify the mistakes of the disastrous first year of the war were as politically damaging to the tsarist government as the mistakes themselves.

There is a second, analogous debate among contemporary historians that is even more closely intertwined with the main themes of this book: a fundamental disagreement about the mood of the population of the Russian Empire during the war and the extent of its patriotism. Some scholars suggest that the enthusiastic war discourse of 1914 lasted for little more than a year, and had disappeared entirely by the end of the great retreat in autumn 1915.[77] This notion that the population mentally abandoned the war effort in the fall of 1915 lends credence to émigré and Soviet depictions of the inevitable failure of the tsarist military effort. Furthermore, some contemporary scholars affirm émigré claims about the fatal absence of national consciousness among the Russian people during World War I, and reject the notion that Russia could even be called a "nation" at the time. These scholars argue that the Russians had a clear picture of the enemy, focusing on German atrocities such as the "rape" of Belgium, and likening Kaiser Wilhelm II to Satan, but they lacked a notion of "for whom and for what" they fought and failed to "imagine" their nation as a "community."[78]

These negative views have been challenged by a number of historians who have demonstrated how historic and competing definitions of Russian nationhood shaped both the war effort and the outbreak of revolution. This new historiography encourages reconsideration of the strength and efficacy of Russian patriotism and Russian nationalism in the ongoing war effort, arguing that publishers, artists, and censors did attempt "to articulate a national and patriotic identity around various themes and symbols" and that it was the inability of publishers to produce an optimistic message after 1915 rather than the rejection of the national themes that led to the halt in patriotic publications.[79] These scholars argue that the war led to new possibilities for citizenship because "in wartime Russia, patriotism, citizenship, and membership in the nation became powerfully entwined." National belonging became "inclusive and participatory, since every individual, regardless of faith or class or ethnicity, could (at least theoretically) be a patriot and *demonstrate* patriotism."[80]

But the growth of national consciousness did not always serve to strengthen the war effort or to preserve order. The expectations of quick victory raised by patriotic propaganda in the early days of the war may have contributed to popular antagonism against the Romanovs as traitors to the nation.[81] Notions of the equality of sacrifice and the entitlements owed the citizen-soldier were double-edged concepts that could work both for and against the imperial and later the Provisional Government.[82] Studies of wartime dissent suggest that the opposition of rural Russians to the war effort was framed in "national" terms. The fall of the monarchy, therefore, could be understood as a sign "of the tangible presence of the Russian nation, not of its absence."[83]

Although everyone could theoretically be part of the nation, those who were perceived as disloyal or failing to sacrifice were nonetheless targeted for exclusion.[84] The campaign against "enemy aliens" during World War I included the spontaneous popular expression of a particular form of economic nationalism in which Russians took revenge on the non-Russians in the empire whom they perceived as economically dominant, particularly Germans and Jews. This anti-German and anti-Jewish sentiment produced ethnic riots and popular disorder that was against the interests of the tsarist state. The Russian image of "the enemy" was thus much more variegated than those scholars denying Russian nationhood have allowed, and Russian national identity was developing in a complex dialogue with other nationalities, especially with Germanness and Jewishness. Soviet World War I memory counterbalanced this developing Russian identity with its acknowledgment of Jewish victimhood and its proposition that workers in the German army were "us" and not "them." Nonetheless, underlying suspicions about Germans and Jews bubbled beneath the surface of this new discourse. My analysis of the continuities between Russian military and patriotic discourses and Soviet discourses relies on the arguments of the scholars who maintain that there indeed existed notions of national community, even if these notions were contested and sometimes contradictory. These notions were perpetuated across the divide of war and revolution.

The structure of this book reflects my dual goals of integrating Russia's World War I memory into the history of European war memory while also mapping the constantly shifting constellation of military-patriotic ideas that appeared, disappeared, and sometimes appeared again, in tsarist World War I culture and Soviet memory of World War I. Part 1 comprises four thematic chapters that explore religion, heroic masculinity, violence, and patriotism.

Part 2 pinpoints how the treatment of these four themes changed over time; it investigates what ideas drew public criticism and when they did so, what themes the censors challenged, and what new ideas about religion, gender, violence, and national identity appeared in Soviet World War I discourse. Chapter 6 presents case studies of the fate of key figures and institutions engaged in the production of World War I memory. These individual cases demonstrate the complex processes by which, both because of intentional erasure and also because of the unintended consequences of various Soviet policies, the complexity of earlier World War I discourse became muted and key elements of that discourse were eventually transformed. Chapter 7 undertakes a textual analysis of earlier and later editions of the same texts to examine what themes were omitted and when they disappeared. It also investigates new trends introduced into World War I discourse in the 1930s and 1940s and their relation to earlier trends. The conclusion provides a brief overview of World War I memory from 1945 to the present before its final consideration of the book's arguments. World War I discourse deserves to be excavated from historical obscurity, not just because it is inherently interesting, but because it reveals much about the Soviet Union's relation to interwar Europe and about the rhythm of transformations in all Soviet discourse in the interwar period.

2

Spirituality, the Supernatural, and the Memory of World War I

In the classic *The Great War and Modern Memory*, Paul Fussell identifies the desire to create "myth, ritual, and romance" about World War I as one of the key elements of wartime memory. Among his most noteworthy examples of myth is the "Golden Virgin" atop the ruined basilica at Albert in France. The statue of the Virgin and Child leaned precariously from the top of the basilica without falling. Rumors abounded that the war would end when the statue fell, or that whoever knocked it down would lose the war. This was but one example of "dozens of miracle-rumors of crucifixes and Madonnas left standing amid chaos. In a few cases the image dripped blood or spoke words of prophecy concerning the duration of the war."[1] One of the ways in which World War I participants dealt with the inhumanities of war and the experience of death was through this turn to the supernatural.[2] "The bizarre and unnatural world" of the battlefield turned out to be "the perfect environment for the spread of tales of the supernatural,"[3] particularly in the Catholic and Orthodox countries that had a strong native tradition of popular spiritualism.

Historians' analyses of bereavement in postwar Europe also demonstrate that Europeans attempted to come to terms with war grief, in part, by drawing on religious notions of sacrifice, death, and resurrection.[4] The creation of tombs of the unknown soldier in several European capitals in the early 1920s demonstrates that the symbol of the fallen soldier played a crucial social and political role in coming to terms with the tragedy of mass death in Western European nations. Europeans engaged in civic rites and traditional religious practices to comprehend the fates of their loved ones, and they also explored means such as séances to communicate with the dead. In the context of mass death and mass mourning, the imaginative boundaries between the natural and the supernatural and between the living and the dead remained porous.

There has been little study of Russian spirituality during wartime (1914–1921) or of the spiritual aspects of coping with the consequences of war in the postwar period. My work places World War I spirituality in a comparative framework that is cognizant of revolutionary and Soviet myths as well as European ones. Though the notion of analyzing spirituality and World War I memory is a conscious borrowing from the European historiography, there is no doubt that this analysis is pertinent to the Russian context. World War I produced a torrent of spiritual discourse in the Russian Empire. Religious institutions and rhetoric played a key role in mobilizing imperial Russia for war;[5] at the same time, popular notions circulated in both the front and the rear that the war was God's punishment for the people's sins.[6] Soldiers employed religious and spiritual idioms to discuss their actions, misfortunes, and relationships to their dead comrades both during the war and afterward. Lenin himself acknowledged the "growth of religious feeling" that the war produced. He noted, "Again the churches are crowded, the reactionaries joyfully declare. 'Wherever there is suffering there is religion,' says the arch-reactionary Barrès. He is right, too."[7] This wartime turn to the mystical did not suddenly evaporate with the founding of an atheist state in October 1917. The study of World War I memory illuminates Russian and Soviet attitudes toward death and the afterlife and provides insight into how the spiritual realm was imagined between 1914 and 1945.[8]

Although World War I did not figure positively in the mythology of the Soviet state, the Soviet government nonetheless had to come to terms with the wartime loss of millions of its people despite the fact that the Russian Revolution had dramatically overturned the spiritual order along with the political order. While tsarist militarism was supported by the idea that fighting for the tsar was a sacred duty, this notion was challenged by Soviet atheism and a postrevolutionary scientific discourse that emphatically rejected the existence of God and, therefore, religious justifications for war. Soviet authors argued that the clergy of all countries were tools of "the bourgeoisie and landowners" who cunningly used the name of God to trick the soldiers into going "submissively into battle."[9]

As an "official" atheistic worldview replaced an "official" Orthodox Christian one, Soviet propagandists sought to create an alternative philosophical framework that would make military and revolutionary deaths meaningful in the absence of an afterlife and without the promise of a heavenly reward for the heroic soldier.[10] Despite its radical new ideology, the Soviet Union nonetheless followed the European pattern of sacralizing its Civil War soldiers. Russian revolutionaries followed the French revolutionary precedent in which "the new religion was the love of the fatherland as an expression of popular sovereignty," and the revolutionary state "nationalized" its dead revolutionary soldiers.[11] Drawing on nineteenth-century Russian revolutionary traditions as well, Soviet thinkers found meaning in revolutionary deaths through the notion of sacrifice for the revolutionary cause; the fallen were to serve as an inspiration to the living to continue the fight. While death was final, the revolutionary cause (and the revolutionary state) lived on.[12] In this new context, however, World War I deaths were meaningless, because they occurred in the service of an unjustified imperialist war and a tsarist national ideal that had ceased to exist. Soviet rhetoric tended to mock those who sought comfort in religion, while simultaneously denying the families of the World War I dead the alternative of heroic sacrifice for the cause.

The denial of spirituality in favor of a materialist and scientific worldview was a key theme of Soviet World War I memory (and Soviet culture generally) in the 1920s. During that decade, it was widely argued that science and technology rather than religion held the key to "abolishing death."[13] Many Soviet writers persistently associated religion with a series of negative attributes: ignorance, backwardness, greed, drunkenness, gluttony, cowardice, and so forth.[14] Paradoxically, Soviet-era attacks on religion and the supernatural reproduced the ideas of popular spiritualism so that it could attack them and prove them false. As a result, the discourse of war was rich with religious allusions, however contested they may have been.

But the attitudes of Soviet writers and cultural leaders toward spiritual matters were much more complex and diverse than these frequent and crude attacks on religious belief might lead one to believe. The work of proletarian writers in the revolutionary period was suffused with notions of the sacred and Christian religious imagery, whether the writers were Orthodox believers or atheists.[15] After the revolution and the reestablishment of the patriarchate under Tikhon, the revival in religiosity and the renaissance of Russian Orthodox thought that had begun in the late nineteenth century continued, due not only to the upheavals of revolution and civil war, but also, in my view, to the legacy of World War I.[16] Despite the official Soviet emphasis on the rational and the material, the spiritual and the mystical also made its way into sanctioned Soviet representations of World War I and commemoration of its he-roes. After discussing tsarist religious imagery and the Soviet backlash against it, this chapter analyzes the various places in Soviet culture of the 1920s in which the spiritual emerges, particularly in terms of the concept of the after-life and the resurrection of the dead. In depicting the confusion and horror of war and its tragic aftermath, Soviet rationalism could not succeed in van-quishing the competing religious, spiritual, and mystical worldviews, and so it absorbed them instead. After a brief discussion of spirituality in the World War I years, this chapter examines Soviet attacks on religion and then explores the persistence of spirituality in Soviet discourse. The chapter ends with reflec-tions on how the broad attacks on religion called forth popular-spiritual re-sponses from the suffering population, responses that also mirrored the myths of World War I.

TSARIST RELIGIOUS IMAGERY

Russian propagandists used domestic and imported religious imagery in the mobilization of the population for the war effort, sending the clear message that God was on the side of Russia and its allies, and millions of Russian sol-diers found inspiration in this idea. The French legend of the Madonna of Albert traveled to Russia in the guise of war news. In December 1916, the illus-trated weekly journal *Niva* (Field) published two photographs of the statue atop the ruined Cathedral, "hanging on by a miracle," and "falling over France, blessing the country with the sign of the cross—the figure of the baby Jesus with outstretched arms."[17] The captions of the pictures declared the position of the statue to be a supernatural rather than a natural or coincidental occur-rence. Furthermore, the photographs suggested that the destruction wrought on the cathedral by the Germans only intensified God's blessings on Russia's French allies.

While the theme of holy war was less pronounced in World War I *lubki* (popular prints) than in the depictions of earlier wars, lubki still "appeal[ed] to Russian Orthodoxy as a source of identity," alongside other notions of the loyal *muzhik*-soldier dedicated to "tsar" and "fatherland" as well as to "faith."[18] One print called on Russians to pray that God would lead the Russians to vic-tory while He allowed the "damned enemy [to] die."[19] And Cossack war hero Koz'ma Kriuchkov proclaimed that accomplishing his famous exploit (fell-ing eleven Germans single-handedly) was simply doing God's will.[20] Both the stark contrast between the righteous and the damned and the notion that kill-

FIGURE 2.1. "The Appearance of the Holy Mother from the Heavens to the Russian Troops before Battle, an Omen of Victory" [*Iavlenie Bozhei Materi na nebe pered srazheniem russkomu voinstvu, predznamenovavshee o pobede*] (Moscow: M. N. Sharapov, n.d.). From Hoover Institution Poster Collection.

ing the enemy was enacting God's will provided unambiguous justification for wartime violence. Popular prints and literature represented Russian Orthodox clergy as important participants in the war effort; they showed priests at the front urging troops into battle, "inspiring the troops by blessing them," risking danger, and sometimes even sacrificing their lives for others.[21] Soviet interpretations of the war later seized upon the notion of the clergy exhorting violence to discredit both the clergy and the war.

Tsarist wartime propaganda also appealed to mystical elements in Christianity. One popular print, "The Appearance of the Holy Mother from the Heavens to the Russian Troops before Battle, an Omen of Victory," drew on the supernatural to combat the uncertainties of war, as did the Albert legend (figure 2.1). According to the print, the apparition of the Mother of God was a harbinger of Russian victory. One variant of this poster was produced in an enormous print run of 320,000 copies, suggesting that the publishing house believed that this theme would strike a popular chord. In other popular prints, Christ and the Mother of God appeared on the battlefields to heal the sick and comfort the dying.[22] Prints such as "I Shall Manifest Myself to Him" emphasized the intensity of the soldiers' Christian beliefs at the moment of death. The poster showed a dying soldier, who had already demonstrated his heroism and earned the St. George cross, with Jesus reaching out his hand to comfort him. A quotation from the Gospel of John praised the soldier for demonstrating his love of God and neighbor by laying down his life for his friends.[23] Another wartime article told of a dying soldier who requested to hold the cross and pray as he died.[24] While the apparition of the Mother of God provided hope of success, these posters offered comfort in the case of loss. The pious and brave soldiers who gave their lives for the tsar were Christ-like and beloved of God; they would be rewarded in heaven with salvation. Many popular conceptions of the war effort thus understood notions of justice, victory, and sacrifice within an explicitly Orthodox Christian framework. Miraculous apparitions, wartime miracles, and the eternal life of the fallen became part of the common discourse of war.

Official memorialization of the war and the commemoration of the fallen also took place within a Russian Orthodox context. Perhaps the most important site of national commemoration of World War I was the Moscow City Fraternal Cemetery, designed in part to enhance patriotism and motivate Russian citizens to sacrifice themselves for their country. The site defined Russian national identity in unambiguously religious terms. In S. V. Puchkov's original proposal, "the words of the Savior: 'Greater love hath no man than this, that a man lay down his life for his friends,'" were to be inscribed at the entrance to the cemetery, linking the sacrifice of the dead soldiers to the sacrifice of Christ.[25] In commemoration of the great love of the martyred soldiers, the cemetery became a pilgrimage site for the wider public during Easter week in 1916; city authorities ran special trains that brought visitors to pay their respects both to the honored dead and to the ideal of a national community. The site was also to include a war museum to highlight the military achievements of the nation, but the plans for the museum were not realized.[26]

Although the cemetery was imagined as a site of national mourning, the memorial church that was actually built on the site was shaped by the grief of a particular family. The couple A. M. and M. V. Katkov donated money for the erection of a church in honor of their two sons who were killed in battle in August 1914, on the eve of the feast of the Transfiguration. Architect A. V. Shchusev designed a memorial Church of the Transfiguration in the Russian

FIGURE 2.2. A. V. Shchusev's design for the memorial Church of the Transfiguration, Moscow. From S. V. Puchkov, *Moskovskoe gorodskoe bratskoe kladbishche* (Moscow: Gorodskaia tipografiia, 1915).

style, including elements of northern architecture, in a conscious evocation of the "truly Russian" architecture of the pre-Petrine era (figure 2.2).[27] The side-chapels of Shchusev's church were dedicated to the Archangel Michael and Saint Andrew the Apostle, in honor of the patrons' dead sons, Michael and Andrew. On the first anniversary of their deaths in August 1915, after a prayer service and a religious procession, the cornerstone of the church was laid. The two side-chapels were consecrated in January 1917, and the main altar in 1918. Thus both the ritual practices surrounding the memorial and its form were directly linked to the commemoration of particular individuals and the mourning process of a specific family.[28] As in other European countries, mourners imbued memorial sites with multiple, overlapping, and sometimes contradictory meanings.

While individual mourning shaped the Church of the Transfiguration, a second monument projected on the site went beyond the nation to memorialize the suffering of the entire world. When, in 1916, sculptor I. D. Shadr heard about the Moscow City Duma's competition for a monument to the victims of the *Portugal,* a Red Cross hospital ship torpedoed by the Germans in the Black Sea, he proposed instead a grandiose "monument to world suffering," convinced the Moscow Duma to broaden its vision, and won the competition. The All-Russian War Cemetery was thus the planned location of a religiously inspired universal monument to all victims of war.[29]

In 1918, at roughly the same time that Shchusev's church was dedicated, the early Soviet journal *Tvorchestvo* (Creative Work) published Shadr's plan for the "monument to world suffering," despite what editor V. Friche called its "religious-Christian color" (figures 2.3 and 2.4). Friche was willing to overlook the religious nature of the design because of its "grandiose monumentality," its aspiration to combine nature with "all kinds of art—architecture, sculpture, painting and words," and because the sculptor Shadr was "a son of the people." According to Shadr's plan, the visitor entered the monument through the "gates of eternity—tall granite walls inscribed with biblical utterances about the eternity of life." Four large statues flanked the entrance to the garden, two on either side of a narrow door cut into the stone, representing Birth, Courage, Wisdom, and Eternity. The statues held their bowed heads in mournful reflection or prayer. An inscription reminded the visitors "we are strangers and wanderers on earth"; the words above the narrow door read: "There is one entrance into life and one end for all."

The visitor took the metaphorical journey into life by passing through the narrow passageway into the memorial garden. Here the visitor found two lines of tall and well-proportioned poplars on either side of an open courtyard, and between them a pool of stagnant water, the "lake of tears." In front of the pool a snow-white marble statue personified Mercy, with the mournful inscription: "The human being born of woman is short of days and surfeited with sorrows. Like a flower he blossoms and fades. He runs away like a shadow and does not stay." On his way to the colossal pyramid at the far end of the courtyard, the visitor passed a statue of a dying youth lying on a granite slab with Death (a woman) at his head and his mourning mother at his feet. The pyramid itself was adorned with an ancient stone cross and the figure of Job, signifying humanity's "Golgotha with its innumerable steps of suffering."

In the pyramid, the visitor metaphorically descended into the "bottom of the grave." Then "with trembling hand" he opened the last doors and was "enveloped in an unusual light." In front of him was the chapel of the Resurrection. Above the visitor's head was a golden cupola with a mosaic fresco, "Praise

FIGURE 2.3. *Above.* Sketch for plan of entrance to I. V. Shadr's monument to world suffering. From O. Voronova, *Shadr* (Moscow: Molodaia gvardiia, 1969).

FIGURE 2.4. *Left.* Sketch for plan of interior of Shadr's monument to world suffering. From O. Voronova, *Shadr* (Moscow: Molodaia gvardiia, 1969).

Eternity." Inscribed in "fiery" letters on the wall were the words "Your dead will revive; the bodies of the dead will rise." This powerful message would transform the visitor: "Contented, with a soul joined with destiny and open to goodness, as if having grown sighted and wise, the person returns to the Gates of Eternity."[30] In Shadr's conception as he communicated it in a Soviet publication in 1918, the promise of resurrection alone made human suffering bearable.

After the February Revolution, first the Provisional Government and then the Soviet government created new memorial sites such as Petrograd's Mars Field and Moscow's Red Square where the revolutionary dead were buried in a new kind of "sacred ground" that was civically rather than religiously defined. Only a few years after the dedication of his Church of the Transfiguration, and while this church still stood in the Moscow City Fraternal Cemetery, Shchusev was commissioned to design the most important Soviet memorial building: Lenin's Mausoleum. Shadr also went on to prominence in the Soviet Union as a sculptor who immortalized both socialist leaders and new Soviet men and women. There were distinct continuities in the personnel and the conceptualization of memorialization across the revolution, even if the built projects differed in form and were stripped of overtly Orthodox trappings. Soviet commemorative practices and the founding myths of the Soviet state sprouted from Orthodox roots.

Russian Orthodoxy was only one of several sources of supernatural belief during World War I. Wartime occult publications foretold the destruction of Germany and the death of Kaiser Wilhelm and predicted ultimate victory for Russia. These works were translated from the English and the French in the early months of the war.[31] Like Orthodox religious symbolism, the occult prognostications about the war offered encouragement to the Russians and gave them an opportunity to envision victory. In the course of the war, however, spiritualism and the occult lost ground to Orthodox Christian supernatural manifestations in the Russian popular imagination.[32] Nonetheless, later Soviet authors had access to the vocabulary of the occult as they sought to understand the meaning of the war.

Tsarist discussions of wartime sacrifice sometimes combined the material and the spiritual. In an article titled "The Meeting," in *Niva* in January 1916, war correspondent M. Domanskii recounted his interactions with a grieving widow who traveled to the front to retrieve the body of her fallen husband, an ensign in the reserves. The story is notable for its lingering emphasis on the material nature of the dead body of a fallen officer. The widow's tale began with a premonition as she kissed her husband goodbye. It was as if someone whispered to her, "You won't see your Serezha any more. You will never see him again." Although she and her children prayed for the safe return of her husband, "apparently we were sinful; our prayers did not reach God."[33] In the widow's tale, premonition and prayer coexisted. Religious faith, however, did not prove efficacious in warding off the violence of war or preventing the widow's personal loss. The widow did not blame this failure on God, but rather on her own sinful nature.

In trying to explain their father's death to her young children, the widow did not make reference to the afterlife; she told them that their father was "sleeping" in a far away place. The son replied, "It is better for him to sleep near us. We won't make noise! We won't wake him up!"[34] The pathos of the innocent child misunderstanding death underscored the importance of retrieving the body for the mourning family.[35] The widow set out to get her husband's body not specifically out of concern for a proper religious burial, but because she wanted her beloved husband's new home to be physically close to hers. After many difficulties, the widow and the correspondent bought a coffin and found the husband's grave. The correspondent described the horror of the material decomposition of the body after death. "The process of decomposition was fully under way. As horrible as the appearance of the deceased, was the excruciating smell that came from him. I literally lost consciousness from this smell." The correspondent held the widow back, fearing she would jump forward to embrace the putrefying corpse.[36] Tsarist-era readers were thus not shielded from the gruesome details of wartime death.

The story further emphasized the physical and the physiological in an unexpected conversation between the widow and the correspondent. The widow shocked the correspondent by saying:

> I've heard more than once that the love between a man and a woman, between a husband and a wife, is primarily a physical feeling. . . . Just now I tested myself. Indeed, after what I saw today, all physical feeling toward my deceased husband should have disappeared. . . . And even memories about physical attraction should be excruciating! . . . But I feel that I love Serezha as before, even more than before. My soul is full of him.

This candid admission underscored the widow's suffering and an emotional and physical bond with her husband that transcended death. The widow sought to reject death by denying the power of its effects on the body.[37]

When the correspondent met the widow several months later, she was unrecognizable. She had become a nurse, and, although she was still grieving, she consoled herself that "in a sea of suffering, my personal grief is a minute droplet."[38] This story demonstrated that one path to successful mourning was bringing home the physical remains of the dead. In the chaos of revolution and civil war, it became virtually impossible to bring home the bodies of the dead, and millions of families were denied this comfort. In Europe, local war monuments served as physical spaces to mourn the dead who could not be recovered. Such monuments did not exist in the Soviet Union, denying Soviet citizens both spiritual and material processes of mourning. The widow's story also offered a second path to mourning: the willingness to serve others. This notion of service as an antidote to the meaninglessness of war also appeared in later European and Soviet depictions of war.[39]

Tsarist representations of the war sometimes embraced supernatural myth and emphasized religious faith, particularly in the early period of the war. As the war dragged on, however, more complex reactions to the sorrows of war could be found in the Russian press. It was not until after the Russian Revolution, however, that the outright rejection of faith became part of World War I discourse.

THE SOVIET AND THE SUPERNATURAL

There is no doubt that the dominant Soviet approach to religion was to mock and denigrate it, but even those who questioned religious faith were sometimes captivated by its power to motivate and to mobilize. Due to the didactic and "scientific" nature of much Soviet discourse on religion, which sought to "prove" that there was no God and that religion was a tool of the ruling classes to keep the population in thrall, many Soviet ideologues engaged religion head-on. In explicitly combating religious discourse, they reproduced and disseminated it, and at times even presented religious faith in positive or neutral terms. In addition to the theme of religious faith, notions of the occult, ghosts, and the practice of magic also appeared relatively frequently in World War I discourse. Soviet hostility to the practice of religion and the eagerness of Soviet authorities to show their success at debunking and dispelling "superstition" often focused the attention of Soviet writers on the very religious and supernatural beliefs that they sought to undermine. For example, Boris Kandidov's 1929 antireligious tract *Religion in the Tsarist Army* (*Religiia v tsarskoi armii*) featured a postcard illustrating "the appearance of the Holy Mother from the heavens" during the battle at Avgustovo. Even though the text mocked the notion of the Mother of God appearing as the "heavenly commander" of the Russian troops, Kandidov nevertheless introduced into

Soviet circulation one of the most popular religious images of the first year of World War I (figure 2.5).[40]

Other Soviet historians of World War I reproduced the religious discourse of the soldiers during the early months of the war in their efforts to illustrate the transition from "unconscious 'hurrah-patriotism'" to "a conscious rejection of the 'bourgeois war.'" In 1932, archivists in the Tatar Republic, in close co-operation with the head of the Tatar Oblast' Party Committee's Department of the History of the Party (*Istpartotdel*), commenced publishing a regular series of "archival documents of historical-revolutionary content" to coincide with the twentieth anniversary of the beginning of World War I.[41] In the first volume, they deliberately included letters from their archive that had been excerpted by the Kazan District Military Censorship Committee in the first three months of the war because they were "highly patriotic." These soldiers' letters were suffused with religious and eschatological language, speaking of the soldiers' "faith in the Lord God" by whose will they defended "Holy Russia." One letter proclaimed that those who laid down their lives for Holy Russia would live in "eternal memory." Another letter boasted that the Russian soldier wasn't afraid of "Satan himself."[42] These letters clearly expressed the idea that the "holy" status of the warrior allowed him to overcome evil and defy death.

On September 20, 1914, the soldier I. Ignat'ev wrote a letter to a male relative in the form of a prayer: "I live. I do not grieve. I serve the White Tsar through the true faith and I am ready to die for faith, tsar, and fatherland, and for our brothers of the same faith, if the Lord contrives for me to perform this holy exploit (*podvig*). My life is in your power Lord and may your will be done. Amen."[43] The editors contextualized the letters by admitting that the peasant soldiers had been temporarily "seized" by patriotism promulgated from above, but they did not comment at all on the Orthodox Christian religiosity articulated in the letters. They did not challenge the soldiers' view of the war as an Orthodox Christian war; nor did they denigrate the faith in God that the letters contained, and they allowed the prayers to stand as prayers.

The volume also included one September 1914 letter from a Muslim soldier who evinced faith in God. The soldier Mukhametov wrote to a female relative in the town of Menzelinsk: "Soon I will go into battle. Perhaps I will not return home. Fatima, ask for God's mercy that I will return a conqueror with the giaours."[44] This letter not only acknowledged Muslim religious faith but articulated the ambivalence of the Tatar soldier toward the war. On the one hand, he prayed to return home a victor, but on the other hand, he called his

FIGURE 2.5. Cover of Boris Kandidov, *Religion in the Tsarist Army*
[*Religiia v tsarskoi armii*] (Moscow: Bezbozhnik, 1928).

fellow soldiers "giaours," a derogatory word for non-Muslims, thus setting himself apart from the Orthodox Christians with whom he served. His religion was actualized both in his prayer and in the way he defined himself.

These letters also touched on one of the most important philosophical questions engendered by the war: the role of God in allowing the war to occur. Some soldiers' letters reflected the notion that the war was a battle of "Good" and "Evil" in which the Russians were called by God to take part in order to defeat "satanic" enemies. An alternate interpretation of the war was that it was a scourge from God to punish the Russians for their sins. This notion appeared in a 1916 letter from a soldier to a "dear" female relative that was published in the journal *Krasnyi arkhiv* (Red Archive) in 1934. The soldier counseled her to reject the notion that the war was inevitable. He wanted her to have "a correct understanding of the war, and not to think that the war is sent by God. The war is a deed of the hands and minds of cunning people . . ."[45] While this soldier embraced a notion of the causality of the war that was consistent with Soviet ideology, he also acknowledged that many at home understood the war to have been caused by the hand of God.

Il'ia Erenburg also addressed the cause of the war in *The Extraordinary Adventures of Khulio Khurenito and His Disciples. . . .* This outrageous novel appeared in a Soviet edition (omitting key scenes that featured Soviet leaders) due only to the intervention of Erenburg's schoolmate Nikolai Bukharin.[46] In *Khulio Khurenito,* Erenburg blamed the war not on capitalist imperialism but on supernatural forces and proposed that it was not the hand of God that produced war, but the devil's manipulation of human frailties. Several years before Mikhail Bulgakov invented his satanic "foreigner" Professor Woland, who wreaked havoc in Moscow in *The Master and Margarita,* Erenburg's mysterious Mexican "Teacher" Khulio Khurenito gathered disciples to unleash both war and revolution on an unsuspecting world.

While this satirical narrative poked fun at religious thought, it simultaneously allowed readers to dwell on the notion of war as a manifestation of pure evil that unmercifully destroyed the innocent. In the months leading up to the outbreak of war, the narrator of the novel (one of Khurenito's disciples actually named Il'ia Erenburg) described how the body of the Teacher showed the strain of his efforts to foment catastrophe: His face grew "drawn, his shoulders stooped and his temples [were] marked with grey." On the very morning of the assassination of the Austrian Archduke, Khulio Khurenito appeared to have second thoughts about his actions. When a passing baby stretched out its hands toward Khurenito: "The Teacher stepped back to the wall and began to babble helplessly, as if he were a child himself: 'I can't! Grown-ups, all right, but children, why children? Perhaps better not? Drop it! Run, run! A bullet in the head!'" But Khurenito recovered at once and reassured his disciple, "It's simply weakness. Pay no attention. I'm overtired, and then there's this heat."[47] Khurenito did not succumb to the temptation of remorse, and so the war began. Erenburg's novel blamed the war not on capitalist imperialism but on evil incarnate, elucidating, if not embracing, a worldview in which diabolical supernatural forces interfered in human events to cause calamity.

Along with the battle of good and evil, another recurring theme in Soviet war discourse was the power of God to intervene in the lives of individual soldiers. It was common in Soviet memory of World War I for authors to attack the soldiers' faith in miracles and in supernatural forces that could save them from death. Erenburg's memoir *The Face of War* showed his familiarity with the miracle stories about crucifixes and Madonnas circulating in France during the war and his disdain for such stories. His description of a ruined churchyard in France served as a conscious counterpoint to the romantic myths of the supernatural that abounded during wartime:

> A square in Bapaume. Here there was a church. A statue of the crucified Christ, the head knocked off. It lay resembling a corpse. Soldiers' helmets, a broken rifle. Saucepans of some kind. The skulls of priests once buried here, pulled out of the earth by a shell. And above everything, a chamber pot, surely thrown out of the neighboring house.[48]

Erenburg deromanticized this scene of desolation. Jesus was not a holy figure but an ordinary corpse mixed together with the bones of long-dead priests and the detritus of war. The statue of Jesus was not miraculously intact like the Virgin of Albert, offering hope for the swift conclusion of the war. Instead, the focal point of the scene, standing "above all," was a chamber pot. Erenburg's European-style irony was melded with a typically Soviet skepticism about religion. Erenburg clearly doubted whether religion could offer a real path to understanding or to winning the war. This passage also shows his doubts about whether the war could be assigned any meaning at all; he presented the war only as a catalyst for unleashing the random and senseless destruction of man by man.

While Il'ia Erenburg was skeptical, even cynical, about the efficacy of religion in wartime, he was aware that the mystical nonetheless held a powerful appeal for the soldiers going into battle. He recounted how French soldiers were offered medals with the depiction of the Lourdes Madonna. One free-thinking anarchist metal worker could not decide whether to take the Lourdes medal. His comrade talked him into it, telling of a soldier who was shot right in the heart, but the bullet was miraculously stopped by the soldier's religious medal. The metal worker decided to take a medal after all. Erenburg's disappointment in the behavior of the supposedly "conscious" worker became evident when he described another medallion that supposedly stopped bullets, one that a Senegalese soldier had given him. The African bestowed upon Erenburg a "'gri-gri'—three German teeth in a case."[49] Erenburg equated the Virgin of Lourdes with a "pagan" talisman, denying any difference between African and European "superstition." In Erenburg's view, the soldier in battle had no control over life or death, and the claim that any religious faith could control fate was a cruel delusion.

Mikhail Sholokhov's 1928 *Quiet Flows the Don* contains a fictional scene of soldiers discussing talismans that is reminiscent of Erenburg's memoir. One of the most popular Soviet novels of the 1920s, *Quiet Flows the Don* directly addressed the issue of religious faith and fate in the context of World War I. In the early days of the war, as the Cossacks prepared to go into battle, they met an old veteran of the Russo-Turkish war who offered them advice about how to stay alive through practicing "human righteousness." The old man counseled the soldiers, "In war you must never take anything that doesn't belong to you—that's one thing. And never touch women, heaven forbid. And besides that, you've got to know a certain prayer."[50] The soldiers mocked the man, especially for advocating celibacy, but he insisted that the soldiers would come to harm if they succumbed to war's temptations of looting and sexual conquest. While most soldiers copied down the tattered old prayer to carry with them, one soldier suggested that the paper the prayer was written on would only attract lice. Thus in dialogic form, Sholokhov presented the mystical point of view while attacking it.

Nevertheless, Sholokhov dedicated an entire page of the novel to reproducing three prayers: the prayer against arms, the prayer against assault, and the prayer in attack. Like the crosses and native soil the soldiers carried, the prayers reflected a mixture of pagan and Christian beliefs. The prayers called on the Father, Son, and Holy Ghost, the Immaculate Virgin, Saint Dmitrii of Salonica, and a "man of iron" in the sea of Buian who "charmeth all iron, steel, blue tin, lead, and all who shoot them," with the words, "Go thou, iron, into your mother-earth away from the slave of God and past my comrades and my horse. The arrow that is made of wood, go thou into the forest, and the feather, into its mother-bird, and the glue, into the fish."[51] Sholokhov conveyed an image of soldiers who coped with the fear of death by a desperate appeal to spiritual and supernatural forces. By listening to the advice about "human righteousness," and by copying the prayers, the soldiers tried to regain a measure of control over their own fates, control that the war had taken from them.

Sholokhov demanded the last word on the matter by conveying the sorry outcome of those who wore the prayer:

> The Cossacks carried away with them under their shirts the prayers they had copied. They tied them to their crosses, to their mother's blessings and to the little bundles of their native soil that they carried, but death struck down even those who carried these prayers.
> Their bodies rotted on the fields of Galicia and East Prussia, in the Carpathians and Romania, wherever the flames of war lit the sky and the earth was marked by the hooves of Cossack horses.[52]

Sholokhov's attack on superstition was followed by an articulation of one of the defining themes of European World War I literature, that the killing was indiscriminate and that there was no logic or reason to explain who would survive and who would die. The notion that World War I soldiers were powerless to control their fate in battle became part of the Soviet understanding of the war. The Soviet "official" theme of the mockery of religion simultaneously conveyed "the pity of war."

The scene from Sholokhov (as well as the story in *Niva*) emphasized the failure of prayer in determining who would live and who would die in wartime. While the officer's widow blamed herself for the failure of her prayer, Sholokhov suggested that prayer could never be efficacious. Kirill Levin's frequently reprinted memoir about Russian World War I prisoners of war also addressed the power of prayer to heal the wounds of war. *Notes from Captivity* (*Zapiski iz plena*) described Levin's experiences as a World War I POW and medic in two prisoner of war camps in Austria-Hungary and Germany. The main theme of the memoir was the suffering endured by the prisoners of war, but, in true Soviet style, Levin also seized every opportunity to criticize class differences among the prisoners and to mock religious belief (figure 2.6). He noted with disdain how a POW icon painter gained privileges by producing icons for the commander of the prison camp. The violin-maker Shvandin, one of the more well-off prisoners, also purchased icons, but Levin treated him with a mix of contempt and compassion.

Shvandin had been shot in the genitals. He had "ceased to be a man" and was "gradually turning into a eunuch." Levin believed that Shvandin had be-

FIGURE 2.6. Russian prisoners in POW camp in Austria. Personal collection of Kirill Levin, Russian State Archive of Literature and Art.

come devout because of the torment of his bodily transformation.[53] Here Levin conceded that religious faith might provide consolation and spiritual healing. He described Shvandin's prayers in detail:

> He, delicately crying, sat with his legs spread and his shirt raised. Lighting himself with the icon lamp, he looked at his mutilated body. Then he got the icon of Saint Nicholas, and having poured a few drops of lamp oil onto it, he held it to his groin. He did the same with the icon of the Mother of God. While doing this, he blushed, quickly crossed himself, and some kind of niggardly hope shone on his swollen face.[54]

The point of Levin's tale is that prayer can never heal Shvandin's wounds and his false hopes could never be realized. The memoirist juxtaposed the impotence of religion with the physical impotence of the wounded man. In doing so, he also documented that warfare, so often depicted as the ultimate act of manliness, could rob the soldier of both his physical integrity and his masculine self.

Levin ended the vignette with a few words about Shvandin's fate. Rather than returning home, Shvandin found a new place for himself, running a home for blind invalids who could not see "his mutilation, his womanish hair-less face."[55] Shvandin thus permanently exiled himself from his home to be among other unfortunates whose disabilities masked his own. Like the griev-ing widow in the wartime story, Shvandin found consolation in serving oth-ers who were suffering, demonstrating a method of coping with his loss of self that was not necessarily tied to religious belief.

Not every Soviet depiction rejected the efficacy of prayer. Leonid Sobo-lev's 1933 novel *The Big Refit* (*Kapital'nyi remont*), set aboard the Russian im-perial battleship *Generalissimo Count Suvorov-Rymnikskii*, treated the issue of prayer in the context of two centuries of Russian imperial naval tradition. Sobolev offered a lyrical description of the silence before the daily hoisting of colors from the point of view of a naval cadet:

> On a distant voyage, when even a foreign shore was not in sight; when the day rose from the ocean bed, strange, hostile and treacherous; when the ocean was so wide that the villages, estates, and towns of home, and all that was dearest in them, were hidden by the round earth—these minutes were surrendered wholly and reverently to the inner self, to God and family. The voiceless calm unlocked *simple naval hearts,* men remembered their friends and kindred, without word or prayer (even slightly ashamed) they turned to the Most High, for the per-ils of the sea are inexhaustible—"Who hath not been at sea, hath never prayed to God!" Cleansed and enlightened by this moment of concentration, at peace with one another, the men began their day at sea, ready for the eternal conflict with the elements.[56]

While Sobolev then undercut this poetic description by revealing that some of the officers were thinking about their sordid personal affairs and career ad-vancement, and that the lowly stokers were thinking about protesting their abuse by officers, he nonetheless acknowledged the possibility of spontaneous appeal to the "Most High" in times of danger and when separated from loved ones. Sobolev did not debunk the tradition of praying to preserve one's life while fighting the elements in the same way that Sholokhov mocked the "prayer in attack"; whatever the thoughts of the officers and stokers at this moment of reverie, the proverb about the power of prayer at sea was left standing. The spirituality of sailors at sea became a part of Soviet 1930s discourse.

While it was possible to find sympathetic depictions of prayer in Soviet World War I discourse, it was more difficult to find positive views of clergy. Soviet authors attacked clergy for their active support of an imperialist war and blamed them for luring innocent soldiers to their deaths. One analyst even suggested:

The concern of the church for the living manifested itself in [the desire] that the soldier should sooner perish, since that is what the interests of militarism required. But then, the clergy displayed touching solicitude toward the corpses, in honor of which they built temples, decorated fraternal cemeteries, and recorded the names of the dead on special plaques in churches. All of this was so the soldier—cannon meat—did not understand the true meaning of his dog's fate—to suffer and die for the interests of his class enemy.[57]

This ironic interpretation mocked the very idea of memorialization because of the priests' prior indifference to the fate of the soldier while he was still alive, and perhaps even their murderous complicity in providing anonymous "cannon meat" to the imperialist war.

In her acclaimed documentary film *The Fall of the Romanov Dynasty* (*Padenie dinastii Romanovykh*), which was produced in 1927 to celebrate the tenth anniversary of the October Revolution, director Esfir Shub utilized film footage from 1912–1917 to construct a chronicle of the downfall of the tsarist government.[58] Shub demonstrated the various ways in which the tsarist government attempted to manipulate the soldiers into waging war and sought to prove that religion played a key role in perpetuating the war. She used the image of a priest blessing the troops in the trenches to show how "the 'holy fathers' tried to prop up the troops' fighting ability with 'the word of Christ.'" By dwelling on the Orthodox clergy's support for World War I, Shub reversed the polarity of images that were originally captured on film as a way of strengthening the Russian war effort. Thirteen years later, Shub employed these images to highlight the hypocrisy of a religion that urged people to kill.

Priests appeared regularly throughout the film, blessing soldiers at patriotic rallies, in the trenches, and in mass graves. The film juxtaposed the spiritual with the material, moving directly from a shot of a priest blessing a mass grave to a shocking image of a dead body being unceremoniously dumped into an open grave. This graphic image of the material nature of death called into question the efficacy and purpose of the priestly blessings. Shub's film associated the spiritual symbol of the cross with the dead soldiers in their mass graves. She created a symbolic reversal in her treatment of religion: rather than Christianity rescuing people from death, it led people to their deaths. Rather than serving as moral arbiters, the clergy sanctioned the senseless violence of an imperialist war.

Il'ia Erenburg's memoir also made a direct connection between the role of clergy and the perpetuation of wartime violence. He described spending Christmas with French troops near Verdun and waiting for their Christmas mass to begin. One "red-faced corporal" described his activities in an attack on the previous day. "We really put in some work! It's too bad that I had to leave my rifle behind. I drove my bayonet into a Boche. It struck high, and it wouldn't slip out again. I put one leg on the stomach and pulled, but it still wouldn't come out. So I was forced to leave it." When Erenburg wondered out loud why the mass hadn't started yet, this very corporal announced that he was the priest. He put his cassock on over his soldier's overcoat and began the mass. Erenburg noted: "The mouth that had just recalled the ripped-open stomach now proclaimed, 'Pax in terra!'"[59] Once again, Erenburg tendentiously pointed out the ironies of war and the hypocrisy of clergy who promoted the war or took part in killing all the while preaching about the brotherhood of mankind. Religion was impotent both in otherworldly and worldly ways. Prayer failed to save people from their violent fates, and clergy failed to promote morality and peace when they took sides in a bloody war. The critical approach to the clergy adopted by both Shub and Erenburg was implicitly pacifist as they both portrayed wartime killing as inherently illegitimate. Both works created ironic tension by showing how the clergy violated the biblical commandment "Thou shalt not kill."

Not just priests but also mullahs were depicted in Soviet war memory as glorifying death and urging soldiers to sacrifice their lives. In a document collection published in 1932, a letter from a Tatar soldier in the 105th Artillery Regiment described how, with the permission of the commander, a mullah gathered the Muslim soldiers together to pray and exhorted them: "Be happy lads, said the mullah, that God himself brought you here to die the death of the prophets for your fatherland, for your future children, and for the tsar. Fight with the enemy to the last drop of blood. This is the bidding of our great prophet Mohammed and you should carry it out to the letter."[60] Soviet war memory thus depicted all clergy, whatever the religion, as promoting loyalty to the tsar and convincing soldiers that battle was a holy cause, and death a desirable outcome.

Mysticism and folk religion also made their way into Soviet works about World War I. One notable work that described folk religion was Sof'ia Fedorchenko's ethnographic account of the war through the eyes of the soldiers, *The People at War* (*Narod na voine*), originally published in Kiev after February 1917. Fedorchenko included hundreds of vignettes purportedly overheard while she was at the front as a nurse in 1915 and 1916. This work was republished several times in the 1920s to great critical acclaim, though it was not republished between 1928 and 1990 due to a controversy about its authenticity.[61] Before 1928, however, and even afterward, Fedorchenko's work was perceived as revealing the authentic voice and worldview of "the people."

The anecdotes in *The People at War* emphasized the magical power of the forest in folk belief.[62] One soldier told of a mysterious being whom he met while marching through the forest in the pitch dark. He felt something pull at his sleeve and he thought he was caught on a stump. He became separated from the rest of the soldiers and discovered that he was not alone. The male being who had dragged him, "silently . . . emptied a bottle down my throat. I drank boldly, and it was rum . . . I finished drinking and that one disappeared as if never there. I walked up to my fellow-countrymen and they asked me, 'Why are you in such a good mood?'"[63] The soldier offered no explanation for this mysterious episode and Fedorchenko did not make an effort to debunk it or explain it away. The anecdote acknowledged the supernatural possibilities of the forest.

Fedorchenko also included a conversation between two soldiers about supernatural beings in the forest; the first explained, "I looked, it was as if a small flame was dimly visible. I followed it straight across country. And the small flame continued to be dimly visible about a *verst* away. I walked toward the light but it was no use. It must have been a wood goblin (*leshii*)." Fedorchenko then gave the response of another soldier: "You have a dark forest in your head, and in such a forest, that's where you find wood goblins. But when you have light in your head, that light extinguishes any spirits."[64] As in Sholokhov's prayer scene, an "enlightened" soldier immediately challenged folk belief and asserted that education would make supernatural forces disappear. Nevertheless, the notion of the forest as a magical, mysterious, and frightening place was clearly evident in Soviet war discourse. This was particularly true in the uncensored 1917 and 1923 versions of Fedorchenko's work, where many anecdotes dealt with supernatural phenomena such as the dead on the battlefield mysteriously coming back to life.[65] Another legend that appeared in Soviet sources was that of the "White Horseman," a "ghostly rider who surveyed the Russian lines at night and who granted survival in forthcoming battles to those whom he looked in the eye."[66] Soviet atheism had to counter both organized religion and strongly held folk beliefs about the natural and supernatural world.

Aleksei Tolstoi's 1922 novel *Purgatory* (*Khozdenie po mukam*), was written and first published in emigration after Tolstoi, initially sympathetic to the Whites, left Russia in 1918. Once he had reconciled with the Soviet government and returned in 1923, the novel was published in the Soviet Union.[67] This novel detailed the lives and loves of two intelligentsia sisters, Katia and Dasha, in war and revolution. In the novel, there is a debate between two minor characters (a proletarian father and son working in a Petrograd armament factory) about the spiritual aspects of the war. In dialogic form, Tolstoi used the differences between Ivan Rublev and his son Vas'ka to contrast a hybrid spiritual-revolutionary worldview with a more orthodox socialist view of revolution. The father, an Old Believer, was described as "a believer" (*veruiushchii*) but not particularly God-fearing (*ne bogoboiaznennyi*).[68] In a scene that was set in late 1916, he explained his view of the war:

> At home . . . in the Perm forests, in the hermitages, it's all written down in the books—all about this very war, and the ruin that will come to us out of the war—how our whole land will be ruined—and how many of the people will survive—there won't be many—and how a man will come from a hermitage in the forest, and how he will rule the earth, and rule it with the terrible word of God.

His socialist son replied disdainfully, "Mysticism."[69] Tolstoi recounted the mystical ideas emanating from mysterious hermitages in the forest and then showed how they were met with revolutionary skepticism. He also faithfully reproduced the folk opinion that the war was preordained as a scourge on the Russian land.

Ivan Rublev went on to question his son's socialist identity, calling him instead a Cossack who was eager to engage in fighting for fighting's sake. He demanded "'Rise up for battle' . . . Fight against whom? For what? You blockhead, you!" The father suggested that the freedom that his son Vas'ka sought was illusory and told him: "Your sort has no humility—you never think of that. You don't understand that in our days everyone must be meek at heart. . . ." Vas'ka accused his father of being muddle-headed and an anarchist, and pointed out that Ivan had contradicted himself because he had recently called himself a revolutionary too. Ivan replied that he did not support the tsar and would be the first to join the revolution with his pitchfork. "'I need land, and not these damned nuts and bolts.' He kicked a pile of shrapnel on the floor with his boot . . . 'Of course I'm a revolutionary! Do I want to save my soul, or don't I?'"[70]

Tolstoi here described the complex ways in which World War I and the revolution could be understood. For Ivan Rublev, the war was a calamity that could only be conquered by the return of human righteousness, "the terrible word of God," and the meekness and humility of mankind. Ivan believed there was to be a revolution of the soul that would bring justice to the earth and salvation to mankind. He embraced the possible overthrow of the tsar and the taking of the land, but simultaneously rejected the passion of battle and the shrapnel that destroyed lives. While Ivan's contradictory ideas certainly can be characterized as a "muddle," this passage nonetheless showed the melding of the mystical and the revolutionary, articulated an apocalyptic view of the war, and offered a counter-narrative to the militancy of revolution. The way to salvation for Ivan was through meekness and humility, not battle and bullets: Tolstoi thus sketched out an alternative utopian future that embraced revolutionary transformation without violence.

While Soviet treatments of religion in World War I tended to reject religion and show its failures, they also articulated many of the important themes of both European World War I literature and nineteenth-century Russian literature. Discussions of religion underscored the senselessness of war, the soldier's lack of control over his own fate, war's destruction of masculinity, and the moral ambiguity of killing; it offered possibilities of a nonviolent response to war through meekness and humility.[71]

DEATH AND RESURRECTION

In the 1919 French film *J'accuse,* directed by Abel Gance, the World War I dead arise from the battlefield and go home to see if the sacrifice of their lives has created a better world or if they have died in vain.[72] One of the ways in which Europeans in the 1920s coped with the war's aftermath was by imagining the "return of the dead" who would determine whether those who survived were living up to their ideals.[73] Interwar Europe was preoccupied by the relationship between the living and the dead, and the fate of the soul or spirit after death. In Russia, as the intense spiritual climate of the late tsarist era gave way to the putatively materialist and scientific Soviet era, there were a number of competing notions of resurrection as society coped with millions of violent wartime deaths in World War I and the Civil War.

Before World War I, some Russian proletarian writers imagined the reunion of the dead and the living in a new millenarian and revolutionary era. One of these, Aleksei Gastev, described how the fallen revolutionaries would arise again to take part in revolutionary struggle.[74] After 1917, traditional Russian Orthodox notions of resurrection and salvation through the sacrifice of Christ persisted, even though they were flatly rejected by the Soviet state. Soviet attacks on religion coincided with the circulation of revolutionary-religious imagery that replaced God with man and frequently imagined man's victory over death.[75] As in interwar Europe, the boundaries between life and death were imagined as permeable in the interwar period.

Alongside messianic and millenarian rhetoric about resurrection, there existed in Russian and Soviet culture a less spiritual interpretation of eternity that was consistent with the rejection of the afterlife. In this interpretation, the memory of the dead would spur people to build the revolution, and in the success of the cause, the fallen would become eternal. The deceased would inspire others to action and would hence live on in "eternal memory" (*vechnaia pamiat'*). These words were used universally in prerevolutionary radical culture, in Soviet culture, and in Orthodox Christian funeral ritual to commemorate the fallen. During the Orthodox funeral the words were chanted many times; they were sung in the church "when mourners filed past the coffin to give the corpse a farewell kiss."[76] The final repetition of the hymn usually occurred when the coffin was being lowered into the grave. In this context of Orthodox ritual, eternal memory conveyed a promise of eternal life and resurrection and a perpetual connection between the living and the dead through the medium of memory and commemoration of the soldiers' or revolutionaries' sacrifice. In the transition from the funeral service to revolutionary rhetoric, these words gained new meanings, without necessarily completely shedding the older transcendent meanings. In the revolutionary and Soviet context, these words articulated a duty of living Soviet citizens to honor the memory of the dead by continuing their deeds. Thus the antireligious state allowed for a ritual of remembrance that had unmistakable echoes of Orthodox Christianity, even while denying the existence of the Orthodox Christian God. In adapting the forms of Christianity, the Soviet state unintentionally absorbed some Orthodox content as well.

Because they died in the service of an imperialist war, World War I soldiers were often depicted as helpless victims rather than revolutionary heroes; in the Soviet context, they were caught between the religious and the secular versions of eternal memory. In *The Fall of the Romanov Dynasty,* Shub showed the World War I dead being treated without individual dignity as they were tossed into crowded mass graves. She later depicted the honor and respect bestowed upon the fallen revolutionaries who were buried on March 23, 1917, in Petrograd's Mars Field, showing the coffins of the fallen being carried with ceremony to the burial site.[77] Although contemporary coverage of the funeral in such newspapers as *Pravda* (Truth) and *Rabochaia gazeta* (Workers' Gazette) urged mourners not to "weep over the bodies of the fighters" and not to "sing mourning poetry for them,"[78] Shub's film emphasized precisely this moment of personal mourning as she focused on a woman weeping over the bodies of the fallen revolutionaries. Individual sorrow at the loss of loved ones was acknowledged, and the greatness of the revolutionary cause was offered as the only comfort; there was no appeal to a higher power. Shub edited the scene so that no priest or cross was visible, though in reality some of the coffins were inlaid with Orthodox crosses underneath the red banners, and Orthodox imagery appeared in the actual funeral procession.[79] While Shub gave these deaths revolutionary significance that made them meaningful, and therefore more bearable, the film suggested that the dead of World War I had been pointlessly sacrificed.

Shub's 1927 reworking of the funeral footage denied any connection between the revolutionary funerals and World War I; however, contemporary readings of the funeral in March 1917 directly linked the dead martyrs to the cause of victory in World War I, suggesting that through their sacrifice, Russia would be resurrected.[80] The dead on Mars Field served as patriotic inspiration; the Women's Battalion of Death, for example, marched to Mars Field to honor the revolutionary dead before they set off for the front.[81]

Historian Thomas Trice has analyzed the press's reaction to the funeral:

The popular daily *Peterburgskii listok* (Petersburg Leaflet) relied on a fictional exchange between the dead and their mourners to sound the call to arms. These zombies declared that they had done their duty by toppling the tyrannical old regime, but refused to depart this world for "[their] trenches at Mars Field" until they were sure of Russia's survival. "Do not think that burying us means paying us *last* respects. Your duty is to assure us that we have not died in vain. . . ." they exclaimed. The dead patriots ordered mourners to vanquish that "tyrant of tyrants," that "apostle of militarism," Wilhelm II. Frontline soldiers responded with a pledge to stay in the trenches indefinitely without demanding an eight-hour day, vacation time, or higher pay. By contrast, workers (for whom this phantasmagoric tale was clearly intended) remained silent. Angered, the apparitions derided the workers for their notoriously low productivity. . . . They closed with the cry "Workers, to your lathes, for those are your trenches!"[82]

Predating Gance's *J'accuse* by two years, this newspaper story threatened the return of the revolutionary dead to haunt the living if Petersburg workers did not sacrifice for the nation. The vengeful dead who were laid to rest in Mars Field demanded more than burial; they insisted that they could only rest in their own "trenches" if Germany were defeated and the Russian nation, to which they were eternally linked through sacrifice, were saved from German aggression. In the period of upheaval between the February and October revolutions, the notion of resurrection took on a threatening tone. While the connection between revolution and World War I victory was severed by the October Revolution, the notion that the dead could arise to observe and to influence the living continued into the Soviet period.

The March 1917 funeral and burial in Mars Field, which drew 800,000 participants, was a significant mass phenomenon that appealed to all social strata in Russian society.[83] The victims of the street fighting in Moscow after the October Revolution, who were likened to light-giving Easter candles in the Social Democratic press, were also buried with great ceremony in the Kremlin Wall to the strains of the hymn "Eternal Memory."[84] But Mars Field and the Kremlin Wall were the exceptions. After 1918, the Soviet state tended to discourage spontaneous participation in mass burials. Cemeteries were de-emphasized in Soviet culture throughout the 1920s and 1930s; many Orthodox cemeteries, including the All-Russian War Cemetery, were neglected, turned into parks and workers' clubs, or destroyed.[85] The Soviet state did not tend to call attention to burials and burial places as sites of civic commemoration in the interwar period because of the persistent association of burial with traditional forms of religion, the tightening of control over public demonstrations, and an increasing tendency to hide death from public view.[86]

Instead, the Soviet government tended to turn to science; utopian Soviet notions of the power of science led to some rather idiosyncratic views of the afterlife. Some Bolsheviks, following the nineteenth-century philosopher N. F. Fedorov, believed that technology would overcome death and mankind would achieve immortality and be able to resurrect ancestors. Fedorov opined that resurrection "is the personal business of each man, as a son and descendant."[87] Part of the impetus for the embalming of Vladimir Lenin after his death in 1924 and putting him on display in his tomb on Red Square was to preserve the body in the hope that one day Lenin could be resurrected by technology.[88] Other Soviet writers placed the resurrection of Lenin in a decidedly Christian context. They described Lenin as a Christ figure who would first himself rise up and then resurrect all of the dead.[89] Thus the central legitimizing symbol of the Soviet state at the physical and geographic center of Soviet power was a body that was dead but not putrefying. Lenin's body both "scientifically" defied the physical attributes of death and conformed to the Orthodox Christian notion that the body of a saint was incorruptible.

Like the World War I dead in Abel Gance's film, some myths about Lenin suggested that he arose from his mausoleum to judge the work of the living. A legend from Viatka province explained that Lenin had only pretended to be dead because "he was worried about how the country would fare without him." In the tale, he secretly left the mausoleum to check on the progress of socialism. When he saw the growing number of Communists, and the "Lenin corner" in place of the icon corner, he peacefully returned to the mausoleum, satisfied with the progress of Soviet civilization. The tale went on to explain that Lenin "has been sleeping for many days now. He will probably awaken soon."[90] Yet in this reassuring tale, the boundary between death and life was crossed; the implication of such resurrection stories was that the unhappy dead might take revenge on the living for their failures.[91]

The idea that the World War I and revolutionary dead haunted the living appeared in two crucial scenes in Tolstoi's *Purgatory*. In the novel, the interaction with the dead destroyed the lives of two important characters. In one scene, Bessonov, the amoral antihero of the novel and the love interest of both Katia and Dasha, was brutally murdered at the front by a deserter who had lost his mind. The crazed soldier heard a unit marching by and "took a look at them from the ditch: there they were, all marching in shrouds, there was no end to them. . . . Like a cloud they were. . . ."[92] Unhinged by the war and the appearance of the ghostly soldiers, the deserter strangled Bessonov and then hoped that he himself would be torn to pieces by a pack of wild dogs. Here the horrific killing of war robbed men of sanity, leading to a cycle of ever more pointless violence.

In a second scene set in early 1918, Dasha was attacked on Mars Field. She gave birth prematurely and lost the baby on the third day. The dead child thus served as a mirror image of Christ who arose on the third day. Tolstoi described the attack rather ambiguously:

> Dasha was attacked on the Mars Field by two superhumanly tall figures muffled in shrouds. They were probably those "leapers" who in those fantastic times fastened special springs to their feet and held all Petrograd in fear. They whistled and gnashed their teeth at Dasha and she fell to the ground. They tore off her coat and disappeared in long leaps over the Swan Bridge.[93]

On the one hand, Tolstoi offered a possible real-world explanation for the event, suggesting that the figures were "probably" thieves with an ingenious method of frightening their victims. Tolstoi's use of the word "probably" opened up the scene to other supernatural interpretations, however; he situated the attack on Mars Field, the place where the dead of the February Revolution had been buried, and he described the attackers as covered in shrouds and making inhuman noises. While stealing an overcoat could be a human action, it also was a ghostly one in Russian literary tradition; the ghost of Nikolai Gogol's poor clerk Akakii Akakievich stole overcoats from unsuspecting bureaucrats in revenge for his own lost overcoat. The incident also recalled Bessonov's murder by the repetition of the image of terrifying shrouded figures. Whether a ghostly revenge of the revolutionary martyrs on the Russian intelligentsia or a real event, this incident robbed Tolstoi's protagonist of her future by leading to the death of her child. She was unable to cope with this loss and became nearly insane, separating from her husband and losing her ethical moorings. Sometimes the dead thus arose to torment the living.

These examples reveal the rich and variegated figurative discourse about the death and resurrection of both World War I and revolutionary dead throughout early Soviet culture. The images functioned in a variety of ways: they could comfort mourners and inspire other fighters to heroic action; they could promote the legitimacy of the Soviet state by the veneration of a resurrected leader; but they could also could create a sense of unease and guilt because of the notion that the dead were unhappy with the living and might take revenge upon them. While some notions of the afterlife facilitated the mourning of those left behind, other images were not in the least bit comforting.

Orthodox, Soviet, and Occult Believer: The Case of General Brusilov

World War I memory was embedded in Soviet cultural practices as well as in Soviet texts. Descriptions of the 1926 Soviet funeral for the World War I hero Aleksei Brusilov provide insight into the texture of Soviet World War I memory as practice, as well as illuminating its contested nature and the various contingencies that influenced its creation. On March 17, 1926, Brusilov died in Moscow. His funeral serves as a case study of the syncretic nature of early Soviet culture and the ways in which various contradictory notions of resurrection and the afterlife co-mingled in one commemorative event. Brusilov occupied a unique position in Soviet culture as a military hero of the past who could still be celebrated in the Soviet present. He was the most internationally well-known World War I general, the architect of the famed "Brusilov breakthrough." But Brusilov was also one of only a few World War I generals who was "in favor" in the Soviet context because he joined the Red Army during the Soviet–Polish war. He threw in his lot with the Bolsheviks because he believed that they represented the best hope for preserving the Russian nation. In May of 1920, he publicly called for other former tsarist officers "to forget all grievances" and "to work for the benefit, the freedom, and the glory of our native mother Russia."[94] Beginning in 1920, Brusilov worked on the Military-Legislative Council of the Revolutionary Military Council (Revvoensovet) and then as a cavalry inspector until his retirement due to ill health in 1924.[95]

Brusilov's funeral in March 1926 revealed the attempts of the Soviet military establishment to co-opt certain aspects of his military glory. In the death announcement in *Pravda* on March 18, 1926, Kliment Voroshilov, People's Commissar for Military and Naval Affairs, wrote:

> The workers and peasants of the Soviet Union will not forget A. A. Brusilov. In their memory, his image will be surrounded by a bright halo, as a commander of the old army who was able to understand the significance of the social transformation that was occurring, and to elevate comprehension of the enthusiasm for the revolutionary defense of the Republic of Workers and Peasants.

Voroshilov argued that Brusilov would "live on" in the memory of workers and peasants, and in this way gain immortality in a Soviet civic context. He also used the religious image of the "halo" to suggest the people's veneration of Brusilov as a sacred figure for his defense of the country. The article also noted that the Revvoensovet would arrange for a personal pension for the Brusilov family and would pay funeral expenses. Brusilov was thus embraced as a member of the Soviet establishment who would be buried with official Soviet military honors. Although a 1918 decree prohibited the Soviet state from paying for religious funerals, "regardless of the status of the person involved," this rule seems to have been bent if not broken in the case of Brusilov.[96] A devout Orthodox believer, Brusilov had earlier sought and received M. V. Frunze's permission to be buried at the Novodevichii Monastery. He was buried there in full accordance with Orthodox rites and traditions.[97]

Brusilov's obituary recalled his connection to the tsarist past. He was described as "one of the most outstanding commanders of the Russian army," and it was noted that "the name of Brusilov is connected to the summer offensive of 1916 that led to the breakthrough at Lutsk." Although Brusilov worked for the Soviet government, many of his close friends and associates from the old tsarist army did not. The official state funeral of Brusilov accommodated his status as a World War I hero and a tsarist officer as well as his position as a Soviet military official. The funeral was to take place in an Orthodox cemetery, yet Voroshilov had suggested that the best way to commemorate Brusilov's memory was to serve the nation by participating in its "revolutionary defense."

On the day after his death, Brusilov's body lay in state in his own apartment. Members of the Revvoensovet and the army visited the apartment to

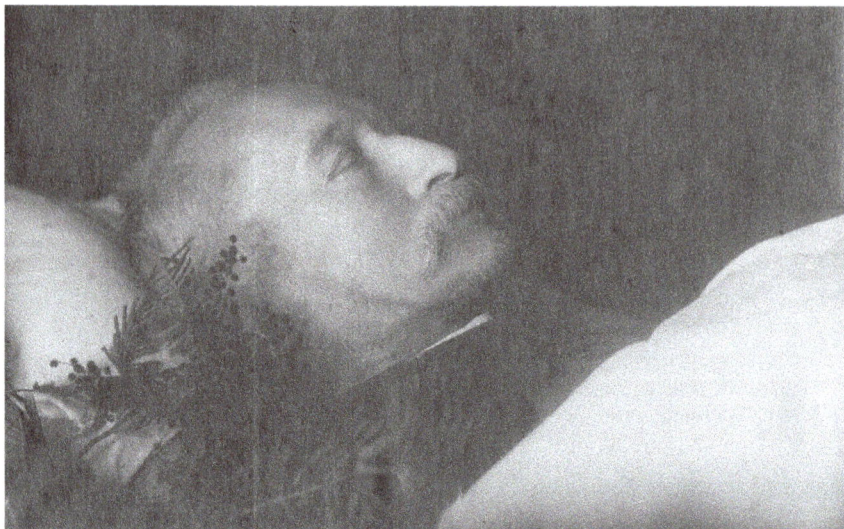

FIGURE 2.7. General Aleksei Brusilov in his coffin. Collection of
Aleksei A. and Nadezhda V. Brusilov, Bakhmeteff Archive.

pay their last respects (figure 2.7).[98] Brusilov's wife Nadezhda Vladimirovna
Brusilova stated in her unpublished memoirs that "[n]o authorities interfered
in any way," and the Orthodox Christian requiem was recited twice daily.[99]
On the third day, as is customary in Russian Orthodoxy, a priest, family, and
friends, including many former tsarist officers, accompanied Brusilov's coffin
from his apartment to church for Orthodox funeral services. Former officers
served as pallbearers at the church. There the liturgy for the repose of the soul
was completed, and afterward the coffin was brought back to Brusilov's apartment.[100]

Next the "Soviet" part of the ritual commenced. A military honor guard,
including a company of infantry, a squadron of cavalry, and a half-battery of
artillery, arrived at Brusilov's home to accompany the funeral procession to
Novodevichii Cemetery. The delegation from Revvoensovet laid a wreath on
the coffin to emphasize Brusilov's service to his country. It was inscribed: "To
an honest representative of the old generation, who placed his battle experience at the service of the USSR and the Red Army. To A. A. Brusilov from the
Revvoensovet."[101] Yet the Revvoensovet's wreath was not the only decoration
on Brusilov's coffin. The casket was also covered with "wreaths of white flowers

with ribbons of the Order of St. George." An article in a Russian émigré news-paper noted with satisfaction: "This was very likely the first time after the October Revolution that St. George ribbons appeared openly on the streets of Moscow."[102] Brusilov's military successes in the tsarist period were publicly acknowledged, and the procession was allowed to display both his tsarist and Soviet honors. He was buried in 1926 explicitly as a military hero of both the prerevolutionary and revolutionary eras.

The Soviet troops accompanied Brusilov's coffin to the gates of the Novodevichii Cemetery. The priest who had earlier accompanied Brusilov's coffin to church did not accompany the Soviet troops to the cemetery. Outside the cemetery gates, the procession halted and three Soviet military officials—Aleksandr Egorov, representing the Revvoensovet; Semen Budennyi, representing the People's Commissariat of Military and Naval Affairs; and G. Gai, representing the Frunze Military Academy—gave formal speeches about Brusilov's contribution to the Soviet military.[103] Although the Soviet government organized a state funeral, Voroshilov did not attend; Brusilov was valued by the Soviet state, but was not honored by the top Soviet military official. G. Gai said, "Sleep peacefully, outstanding general. Your victorious saber, covered with laurels, is now in trustworthy hands."[104] Gai thus publicly identified the Red Army as the legitimate heir to the tsarist army. Brusilov's success in World War I would be followed by the heroism and victory of the Red Army.

After the official Soviet speeches that appropriated Brusilov's achievements as Soviet, there was once again a split between the public and private rituals, and the geography of the burial continued to reflect the hybrid nature of Brusilov's hero status. The coffin was taken inside Novodevichii Monastery, but Egorov, Budennyi, and the Soviet troops remained standing at attention outside the gates. Gai, along with Brusilov's relatives and friends, accompanied the coffin to the grave. At the graveside, relatives and friends gave speeches that were not for Soviet public consumption; one speech expressed gratitude to Brusilov "in the name of the Slavonic peoples, for his battle against the Austro-Hungarian army."[105] Another funeral oration celebrated Brusilov's relationship with rank-and-file Russian soldiers. "The simple Russian soldier remembered his father-commander and forgetting himself, through a truly noble awakening, brought his labor to his father-commander."[106] Both of these speeches demonstrate the persistence of unofficial and non-Soviet remembrances of World War I. Soviet ideology explicitly rejected the notion that the significance of the war was national liberation for Slavs; likewise the official narratives of the war almost unanimously condemned the tsarist officer corps for its brutality toward the "simple Russian soldier." The memory of Brusilov as a paternalistic and benevolent father-commander who could awaken the soldiers to loyalty and noble labor was a subversive reading of Brusilov's life in the Soviet context. While Soviet officials took great care to prevent these ideas from being expressed in print as part of the official report of Brusilov's funeral, they nonetheless gave Brusilov's friends and relatives the time and space to remember him and the war in this most unofficial way.

After the speeches, the priest completed short prayers, and the funeral service ended with the singing of the words "eternal memory" three times as Brusilov's coffin was lowered into the grave. Outside the cemetery, Budennyi gave a signal and soldiers fired off a three-shot salvo after each repetition of "eternal memory." Brusilova reported that this ritual took place "exactly as in old times."[107] The Soviet army thus actively participated in a religious-military tradition from prerevolutionary times in honor of Brusilov, though not without a certain amount of anxiety. Brusilova noted in her memoir that the commandant of the Soviet troops wanted reassurance that the priest would not come to the gates of the cemetery to meet them. He also worried that there might be bell-ringing that would call attention to the religious nature of the funeral.[108] In honor of Brusilov, Soviet officials were willing to permit and even actively participate in a religious ritual, as long as they were not caught doing it in public.

The remarkably hybrid nature of this ceremony and the active cooperation between Soviet officials and the church reveal the complicated relationship of the Soviet government toward Brusilov's military achievements as a tsarist general. Because Brusilov supported the Soviet state, his glorious military career could be celebrated both as a Soviet career but also on its own terms as a reflection of an honorable tsarist career. Because Brusilov passed his "laurel covered saber" to the Soviet state, in fact, he *had* to be recognized as an outstanding tsarist general who had brought honor to the tsarist military in an otherwise disastrous war. Brusilov's legacy of tsarist military success was so valued by some members of the Soviet military establishment that they allowed Brusilov to be buried as a tsarist general, with the ribbons of the Order of St. George in full sight, and in an Orthodox cemetery in accordance with full Orthodox rites. They even participated in the tsarist military tradition of a gun salvo at the moment of interment at the end of the Orthodox funeral service. Religion was allowed as long as it stayed behind the gates of the cemetery and separated from the Red Army. No priest could be seen walking with an honor guard of Soviet soldiers in the streets of Moscow, even though the priest publicly accompanied the coffin when the honor guard was not present. Brusilov was remembered publicly as a heroic tsarist and Soviet general, but the Soviet state would not publicly recognize him in Soviet public space as an Orthodox believer.

While Brusilova was successful in burying Brusilov in the manner he would have wished, she also had to exert vigilance to preserve his grave marker. Like A. G. Shlikhter, who may have intervened to prevent the destruction of his son's grave, Brusilova arrived at the Novodevichii Cemetery one day in 1930 to find "a whole army of Godless-hooligans" systematically destroying grave markers in the cemetery. The crashing of the collapsing gravestones sounded to her like "artillery fire." She immediately contacted Robert Petrovich Eideman, head of the Frunze Military Academy and editor of the journal *Voina i revoliutsiia* (War and Revolution), in an endeavor to protect the cross on Brusilov's grave. He sent his secretary to the cemetery right away and assured her "in the name of the authorities" that the grave would not be touched. He later wrote her a letter in which he wondered "if the dark force would overcome" the cross on Brusilov's grave.[109] The struggle to preserve evidence of Brusilov's religious faith was ongoing.

The attention to the wishes of Brusilov's widow at his funeral (and even afterward) might be explained by the Soviet government's pursuit of another kind of memory of World War I. Brusilov had promised Soviet officials that his memoirs would be published first in Russia, and Soviet military officials were anxious for Brusilov's widow to allow them to publish the memoirs rather than sending them abroad.[110] The officials were successful in their endeavors, and Brusilov's memoirs appeared in 1929. These negotiations with Brusilova seem to have resulted in the memoirs appearing in virtually their original form.[111] Brusilov's memoirs are striking in their frank discussion of his religious faith, his involvement with the occult, and his belief in the afterlife.

As was typical of Soviet publications in the 1920s, the introduction to Brusilov's memoirs described Brusilov's mistaken understandings of war and revolution, noting that the memoirs had to be read as a "historical document, reflecting the relationship between the progressive military bureaucracy and Nicholas II. . . ."[112] This "historical document" also reflected Brusilov's religious convictions in an unmediated way. Brusilov described in detail the death of his first wife in 1908:

> In the last instant before death, her face, distorted from suffering, suddenly was transfigured: a joyful, happy smile appeared on her face. She completely lit up

and stretched herself forward, stretching out her arms as if she saw someone toward whom she was striving, and she died. This was so real that it implanted in me the conviction that there is no death, but only an alteration of our mode of life.[113]

Thus the memoir of the most famous tsarist general included both wartime and personal experiences that affirmed the existence of an afterlife.

Brusilov's Orthodox belief and his conviction that there was an afterlife also led to his involvement in occult practices, such as séances to talk to the dead. His memoirs described several of these events, expressing his sincere belief that the mediums were indeed communing with the dead. He first became interested in the occult while serving in the Caucasus in 1879–1880. During one séance, the medium announced that a particular staff officer had died. According to Brusilov, there was no way that anyone in the regiment could have heard this news, but they received a telegram announcing the death the next day. At another séance, mysterious words appeared that no one could understand. They turned out to be a message in Persian for an officer (and Persian prince) from his long-dead grandmother. She "reproached him for leaving the ways of his ancestors, drinking wine, and so forth."[114] This episode emphasized the importance of keeping religious traditions and also suggested that the dead judged the living and sought to interfere in their affairs.

According to Brusilova, her husband's fascination with the supernatural continued after the revolution and they attended some séances shortly before Lenin's death. The medium predicted that "Lenin would soon die (this was the only thing that then came true) and that afterward, Budennyi would organize a vast Jewish pogrom and Brusilov would be declared dictator." Brusilova believed that the séances were a provocation by the Soviet secret police, hoping to "draw out the feelings and ideas of [her] husband."[115] Given the highly politicized nature of these predictions at a time of leadership instability, she may have been right. However, the form of the "provocation" reveals the continuing appeal of spiritualism in uncertain times, and the persistence of private practices directly contradicted the Soviet "scientific" worldview.

Brusilov's discussion of spiritualism and the afterlife in his memoirs was followed by an acknowledgment of guilt about the nature of his relationship with his dead son Aleksei. Brusilov confessed, "I loved him passionately, but as a father I was mediocre. My mind was engrossed only with work and I did not know how to bring him nearer to me, I did not know how to guide him. I consider that this is a great sin on my soul." Brusilov's memoir claimed that his son made a disastrous marriage and fled his home by joining the Reds during the Civil War, but the younger Aleksei Alekseevich may have joined the Red Army to convince the Cheka (secret police) to spare his father. He then went missing without news, but Brusilov was convinced that Denikin had executed his son after discovering his identity.[116] Brusilov, tormented by guilt, acknowledged, "And in Russia I am not the only father grieving for a lost son. We are many."[117] Brusilov here acknowledged the demographic tragedy of a generation of young men who ought to have outlived their fathers, but were lost in the violence of war. Brusilov's memoirs also reveal emotional aspects of grief in an Orthodox Christian context. His admission that he failed his son served as a confession of a sin that he must acknowledge in order to receive healing and absolution. Brusilov not only mourned his son's death, but he grieved that he would now never be able to establish the intimacy between father and son that he should have created earlier. Brusilov, though perhaps more deeply implicated in his son's death than many fathers, articulated the kind of grief and guilt that was shared by many of the mourning fathers of Russia.

Both the funeral and the memoirs of Brusilov revealed the ways in which the revolutionary era accommodated the heroes and the ideas of the tsarist era. While the Soviet reader (or witness to the funeral) was encouraged to view Brusilov through a Soviet lens, his prerevolutionary deeds, honors, beliefs, and ideals were made visible to Soviet audiences who could reflect on mourning and eternal life in both prerevolutionary and Soviet ways. Organizers of Soviet commemorations, like their tsarist predecessors, embraced the notion of eternal memory and sometimes even used religious imagery, but also promoted the secular idea that service to the country was an appropriate response to death.

The Soldier Resurrected

The image of Lenin as a resurrected hero was disseminated in Soviet culture beginning in the middle of the 1920s. The connection between military heroism and resurrection also appeared in various other Soviet literary and artistic works. By studying these contexts, we can probe the meanings of death and mourning in the Soviet cultural milieu. While revolutionary-era newspapers admonished the Russians not to grieve for fallen heroes who had sacrificed their lives for the revolution, Soviet culture offered opportunities to explore the grief experienced by the families of the fallen. Fedorchenko's *The People at War* contained a vignette of a soldier mourning his dead brother. He found the communal grave where his brother was buried and constructed an individual cross. On the cross, he wrote the words of a poem that he had written:

Sleep, my older brother.	Spi moi brat starshoi,
Here, I, your younger brother,	Zdes' ia, brat tvoi menshoi,
Am sent to you with a bow	Ot otsa i selian
From our father and our neighbors.	Ia s poklonom poslan.
You lay down in a foreign land,	Leg v chuzhom ty kraiu
But you will wake up in paradise . . .	A prosnesh'sia v raiu . . .[118]

These heartfelt words and simple rhymes underlined some of the most important elements of the mourning process. Although the soldier's father and the other villagers could not visit the grave, the soldier's younger brother would stand in for the family and village, thereby affirming the deceased's membership in the community. This commemoration was thought to be essential for facilitating a smooth passage into the afterlife for those who died violent deaths. While the mourning process was complicated because the body lay "in a foreign land," the individual cross and the promise of salvation would both console the family and assure that the soldier rested in peace. Such a scene represented the religious worldview of the common soldier and his notion of resurrection in a clear and simple way.

Other discussions of mourning were more complex. In *Quiet Flows the Don*, Mikhail Sholokhov allowed both his readers and the family of Grigorii Melekhov, the main protagonist, to believe that Grigorii had been killed in battle. The scene that followed illuminated the family's grief for their lost son, husband, and brother. Twelve days later, mourning turned to joy when the family received the news that Grigorii was still alive. In metaphorical terms, Melekhov died and was resurrected from the dead.

The heart-rending scene of the receipt of the news of Grigorii's death demonstrated the depth of the family's despair. Grigorii's sister Duniasha, the only literate member of the family, could not finish the official letter. "'I have to inform you . . .' Duniashka began, then slid off the bench, howling with grief. 'Oh Father! Father! Oh, Mother! Our Grisha . . . Oh! oh! oh! He's been killed.'" The entire family was consumed with grief. Grigorii's mother Il'inichna was "lying in inconsolable grief," his wife Natasha wanted to kill herself, and his father Pantelei "went to pieces all at once . . . His memory began to fail, his mind became clouded." Pantelei forced his daughter to read the letter about Grigorii over and over, and he lost control of his physical urges, becoming "gluttonous, eating huge amounts and carelessly."

On the ninth day of mourning, a significant day of remembrance in Orthodox ritual, the village priest counseled Pantelei to get hold of himself:

Grigorii had died a "holy death" and "wore a crown of thorns for the tsar and the fatherland." If Pantelei were not to accept this sacrificial death, the priest believed that he would anger God. The image of the dead soldier as a Christ-figure, sacrificing himself for the nation, thus crossed into Soviet discourse. This imagery offered Grigorii the promise of spiritual resurrection because of his holy death. The interaction with the priest proved to be the catalyst that allowed Pantelei to move through his grief. Pantelei "broke into a violent flood of tears," but then "overcame himself and recovered his spirit."[119] Profoundly disturbed by the loss of his son, Pantelei found comfort in the image of his son's Christ-like sacrifice and in the traditions of Cossack military heroism. While this passage once again connected the Orthodox clergy to the promotion of the war effort, the scene did not demonize the priest, but demonstrated the way in which religious faith eased the suffering of war's victims. As in Kirill Levin's description of the "eunuch" Shvandin, religion might possibly heal the spirit, if not the body.

Sholokhov's depiction of the Melekhov family also depicted the gendered nature of grief. Pantelei, tied to the hypermasculine Cossack military tradition, employed self-control to overcome his grief eventually. The women of the family, particularly Grigorii's wife Natasha, who was "gnawed by a wasting sickness," continued to suffer. Although Pantelei had begun to come to terms with Grigorii's violent death, "[a]n invisible corpse haunted the Melekhov house and the living breathed the cornflower-sweet smell of its decay."[120] In these passages the Christian imagery of resurrection competed with a reminder of bodily corruption and the folk notion of a corpse that could not rest quietly because of its violent death in battle, but instead haunted its home.

Yet another image of resurrection was added to this mix when Grigorii's brother Petro sent a letter from the front, announcing that Grigorii had been injured rather than killed, and had been decorated and promoted. Pantelei went around the village spreading the news and shedding tears of joy. Yet this episode of grieving had robbed Pantelei of some of his manliness. He thought to himself, "Ah, Pantelei, Pantelei, you're not the man you were! You used to be hard as flint. . . . But now? Grishka's knocked the stuffing out of you."[121] Like Brusilov's memoir, *Quiet Flows the Don* focused on the relationship between a father and his dead adult son; seven years of warfare had produced millions of such fathers grieving for their grown sons. The novel thus acknowledged the painful costs of war and depicted the mourning for a dead warrior in sympathetic terms as a traditional Christian and religious act. This scene placed

Pantelei's response to Grigorii's purported death in a spiritual framework that competed with Soviet notions of transforming grief into service for the revolutionary cause.

It is instructive to compare this episode of mourning and release with the final scene in Aleksandr Fadeev's Civil War novel *The Rout* (*Razgrom*), in which the Red partisan commander Levinson wept until "the tears ran down his beard" for his young protégé and second-in-command Baklanov who was killed in battle. Levinson regained control over his own emotions only after viewing peasants laboring in a glorious natural world, in "fields radiant with the beautiful golden crowns of the fat haystacks, resounding with a joyful busy life of their own." He then "ceased crying; it was necessary to live, and a man had to do his duty." Nature and labor gave to Levinson the comfort and the determination that religion had given Pantelei.[122]

Death and resurrection are also a recurring theme in the only Soviet full-length feature film about World War I in the interwar period, Boris Barnet's remarkable 1933 film *Borderlands* (*Okraina*).[123] The heroes of the film are the proletarian shoemaker Kadkin, his elder son Kolia, and Sen'ka, the younger son. Throughout the film, Barnet made a series of distinctions between the heroic Kolia and the comically inept Sen'ka. Both brothers went to the front together and were together in the trenches under fire. After they both came under attack, Kolia played a trick on Sen'ka by pretending to be dead. Sen'ka, in a panic, tried to wake him up, but then Kolia "awoke," teasing his brother while playing on the notion of death and resurrection. The other soldiers laughed at Kolia's jest while Sen'ka wept in humiliation. This scene combined tragic and comedic elements to demonstrate how soldiers coped with fear in battle.[124] It revealed Kolia's desire to belittle and defy the possibility of death.

But neither Kolia nor Sen'ka was fated to cheat death. Sen'ka died a senseless death as his officer dragged him unwillingly into his first battle, and Kolia was to become a martyr for the revolution. After Sen'ka's death, the action of the film jumped forward from 1914 to October 1917 and showed Kolia still fighting in the trenches. But Kolia had had enough of the war and followed Lenin's call for fraternization at the front. He risked his life to walk to the German trenches with the white flag of surrender as he tried to organize fraternization among the troops. Kolia's bravery in defying the officers cost him his life. He was sentenced to death and shot by firing squad. Like Sen'ka, Kolia would not be returning home; but Barnet imbued Kolia's death with great significance, while Sen'ka's death was utterly meaningless. Kolia did not die alone. His mentor, an older soldier and a father figure, comforted him. The scene shifted back and forth from the dying Kolia to the revolution that was taking place in Kolia's hometown. When the old soldier announced that "some Winter Palace" had been taken, Kolia smiled and died a death that was given meaning by the revolution. The old soldier, like Sen'ka in the earlier trench scene, pleaded with Kolia to get up. For a fleeting instant in the last frames of the film, Kolia's eyes seemed to open, enacting a second "resurrection." Kolia thus lived again through the revolution. While the World War I dead remained unredeemed, the revolutionary dead rose again.[125]

Even as late as 1939, *The Great Soviet Encyclopedia* (*Bol'shaia Sovetskaia Entsiklopediia*) included a striking woodcut of gruesome death in World War I and the metaphorical resurrection that was possible through revolution. Accompanying the lengthy article titled "The First World Imperialist War" were woodcuts by the Flemish antifascist and antiwar artist Frans Masereel. The series of four images depicted the gruesome suffering of war, featuring skeletal dead and collapsing soldiers, some with dismembered heads and others strangling on barbed wire (figure 2.8). The title of the work was "Dead, Rise Up!"[126] Even on the eve of the Second World War, images of World War I conflated resurrection and revolution as the dead of World War I were called upon to "rise up" in revolution against the old order and build a new revolutionary and millennial order.

Soviet memory of World War I in commemorations, literature, memoirs, and film thus contained a complex and variegated discourse about death and resurrection. Eternal memory was represented in a variety of ways—from the traditionally religious to the metaphorical—and the treatments of World War I devoted attention to problems of mourning, the meanings of heroic death, the impact of death on the living, and the ultimate fate of the dead. While some Soviet works frontally attacked religion and the afterlife, it is clear that the spiritual searching of Soviet society could also be found in religious and occult idioms. Wartime suffering, mythology, and religiosity were not forgotten; they simply emerged in unexpected ways and in unlikely places as Soviet society coped with the calamities of seven years of war.

RELIGION AND POPULAR UNREST

This chapter has provided vignettes from the conceptual landscape of death and mourning in late imperial and early Soviet Russia but, with the exception of Brusilov's funeral, has not dealt with actual Soviet events. How, then, can we begin to assess the significance of religiosity and religious discourse in a

Мазереель Ф. Из сюиты «Мертвые, восстаньте».

Гравюры на дереве.

Soviet context? I would like to end the chapter with an epilogue that returns us to the Golden Virgin discussed in the chapter opening. A scene from Kate Brown's *A Biography of No Place,* about the western borderlands of the Soviet Union in the twentieth century, allows us to consider the real world implications of the religious discourses and mythologies discussed in this chapter. Even if these discourses were teeming under the surface of Soviet society and rarely bubbled up, they nonetheless had real-life effects. Despite the attempts of Soviet officials to assert that religion was a part of the past, Soviet officials had to deal with popular resistance to their policies in the form of religious manifestations.

Brown describes a scene reminiscent of the legend of the Golden Virgin of Albert. The event, which took place in 1923 in a Podillian village in Right Bank Ukraine, demonstrates the influence of wartime legends in the Soviet period. The influence of wartime publicity about Marian apparitions in lubki and other forms of Russian popular culture became evident not only in postwar discourse, but also in postwar social relations. According to the Podillian legend, three Bolsheviks were riding through the countryside when they came upon a wooden figure of Christ. One Bolshevik shot at the statue seven times and missed each time.

> The eighth bullet, however, punctured the figure of Christ just below the second rib. Blood gushed from the wound and flowed down Christ's body onto the ground. The Virgin Mary appeared, weeping from grief, and began to cleanse the wound with her tears. . . . From Mary's tears, a spring emerged with miraculous healing powers, and news of the holy site spread rapidly.[127]

This site became the focal point for an apocalyptic popular religious movement in Right Bank Ukraine that encompassed between ten and twenty thousand pilgrims a day in the fall of 1923.[128] In this tale, the tears that were proof of a mother's grief became a wonder-working substance, inspiring people to gather together as a religious community at the pilgrimage site.

In the 1923 myth, the notion of "war" had been transformed from the World War to the Bolshevik war against religion, as the wounds in the crucifix were caused on purpose by Bolsheviks attempting to destroy belief in God. Despite

FIGURE 2.8. *Facing page.* F. Mazereel' (Masereel), "Dead, Rise Up!" Woodcut from the suite "Mertvye, vosstan'te," illustration for the article "The First World Imperialist War" in *Bol'shaia Sovetskaia Entsiklopediia,* vol. 44 (Moscow: Sovetskaia Entsiklopediia, 1939).

the transformation in the notion of war, the spiritual essence of the myth remained the same: that the power of God was ultimately stronger than the power of the enemy, and that God would intercede on the side of the righteous to bring victory. The experience and memory of World War I thus continued to play a significant role in the ideological battles between Soviet atheism and popular religion.

This analysis of religion and Soviet war memory emphasizes continuities in religious discourse across the revolutionary divide. Despite the radical break between tsarist and Soviet religious policy, there were strong currents of religious thinking that traversed the revolution to make their appearance in Soviet culture. As in Europe, spirituality offered Soviet mourners opportunities to come to terms with the death and destruction of war and revolution.

The persistence of religious thinking in this radically new environment underscores similarities between Soviet and European responses to the war, and the way in which seemingly dramatic ruptures obscured a bedrock of cultural continuities. The Soviet case reinforces European historians' arguments for the continuities underlying even the most intensive transformations and demonstrates the complex interaction of the traditional with the modern in the interwar period.

Despite the Soviet state's vigorous efforts to introduce a "modern" and "scientific" worldview, Soviet memory of World War I shows that religious and folk responses to the suffering of war were quite vibrant in the early Soviet period. Traditional attitudes and religious imagery could even infiltrate "official" Soviet commemorations, though such elements were usually accompanied by a Soviet vision of "eternal memory" that emphasized service to the Soviet Union instead of eternal salvation. The Soviet state was much more successful in creating a hybrid of new and old than it was in eradicating the old.

3

The Paradoxes of Gender in Soviet War Memory

Just days after World War I began, the Russian press glorified its first individual hero, the soldier who was awarded the first St. George cross of the war. In a decidedly uneven skirmish with the German cavalry (twenty-seven Germans to four Cossacks) on August 12, 1914 (Old Style), the Cossack Koz'ma Kriuchkov single-handedly killed eleven Germans in battle while suffering no fewer than sixteen wounds. One lubok explained that Kriuchkov upheld the "military glory of the Russian Cossacks": when "the Germans struck with lances, he first repulsed them with his rifle, when his rifle gave out, then he began to fell them with his saber, and then he wrested a lance from a German and put it to use."[1] The "good-looking . . . tall, agile, and muscular" but ever-modest Kriuchkov was always pictured fighting on horseback (figure 3.1).[2] He was the latest in a long line of Russian military heroes, celebrated in Russian popular literature for their military prowess, bravery, and endurance in battle. He was the direct descendant of the *bogatyr'*, the heroic warrior of Russian medieval epics, as well as of earlier military heroes such as General Skobelev and Admiral Makarov.[3]

Kriuchkov's fame spread far and wide "in circus and variety shows, in the movies, and particularly on postcards and lubki" that depicted him skewering "German soldiers like kebab on his lance" or slicing off their heads with his saber.[4] He appeared in more popular prints than any other individual except the villainous Kaiser Wilhelm.[5] Kriuchkov was an icon of Russian national masculinity and the first and most potent emblem of the death-dealing capacity of a Russian military that fought bravely and effectively while showing no mercy

FIGURE 3.1. "Heroic Struggle of the Cossack Koz'ma Kriuchkov with Eleven Germans" [*Geroiskaia bor'ba kazaka Koz'my Kriuchkova s 11 nemtsami*] (Odessa: M.S. Kozman, 1914). Hoover Institution Poster Collection.

to enemies. The Cossack soldiers of the Russian Imperial Army were symbols of one strain of Russian military masculinity, reprehensibly violent and at-tractively heroic at the same time, as Cossack mythology portrayed them.[6] So-viet writers later found that early tsarist bravado and hypermasculine Cossack heroes such as Kriuchkov made an easy target for Soviet propaganda.

Kriuchkov's seemingly inexhaustible courage and derring-do led to vic-tory over the Germans in an ideally heroic cavalry battle: mounted warriors in hand-to-hand combat employing sword and lance. This ideal image of battle did not, however, correspond to the new realities of mechanized warfare where artillery barrages prevented the combatants from meeting each other at close range and cavalry battle tactics were rendered nearly obsolete (figure 3.2). One Russian émigré cavalry officer commenting on Kriuchkov's exploit in his mem-oirs admitted that he did not "remember a single case when the lance was

Guerre 1914-1915. — EN POLOGNE — Établissement d'une tranchée par les Soldats Russes.
Visé Paris 200   IN POLANDE — Trench establishment by the Russian Soldiers.
J. Courcier, 8, rue Simon-le-Franc, Paris.

FIGURE 3.2. "In Poland—Trench Establishment by
the Russian Soldiers" (Paris: J. Courcier, 1915).

thus used in actual fighting."[7] Soldiers all over Europe discovered in the first
weeks of the war that battles, which they thought would prove their manliness through the display of heroism, initiative, and courage, dehumanized and
destroyed them instead. In the catastrophe caused by four years of war, "[a]n
aesthetic and ethical code of heroism, courage, and battle violence vanished."[8]

One of the common tropes of European World War I literature was the
recognition of the irony that the flower of European youth destroyed itself
without achieving heroism or glory. British poet Wilfred Owen famously proclaimed, after describing the suffering of soldiers under artillery and gas attack, that if one could witness the actual warfare, "My friend, you would not
tell with such high zest / To children ardent for some desperate glory, / The old
Lie; Dulce et Decorum est / Pro patria mori."[9] Yet, both during the war and

afterward, this ironic vision of wartime heroism was always in dialogue with (as Owen showed) and contested by war literature that continued to define the sacrifices of war as heroic and glorious. There is still no consensus among European historians about whether nineteenth-century norms of masculinity were destabilized by the horrors of war or survived into the interwar period; whether the ruptures of war or the continuities of the gender order should be stressed.[10] Though comparatively little has been written about the masculinity of Russian soldiers in World War I, historian Catriona Kelly has argued that the image of the heroic masculine warrior emerged intact in Soviet culture.[11]

Owen's poem separates the experience of the soldier at the front from that of the "friend" at home exhorting the "children" to fight. While many Western scholars have emphasized this tension between front and the "male and female jackals" of the rear in their discussions of World War I, more recent scholarship has focused attention on the sustaining intimate relationships of soldiers and their families during wartime.[12] While the soldiers' letters in the Russian archives await a future researcher, it is clear from materials in the public sphere that the continued exhortations to heroism from those safe in the capitals produced a strong potential for alienation of soldiers from the home front, as did perceptions of immoral behavior back home. As the author of one 1917 revolutionary tract explained, the soldiers at the front were indignant at the failure of civil authorities to control the "Bacchanalia that had taken hold in the rear, especially among those who most frequently and loudly celebrated the war and called for continuing the war to a victorious conclusion."[13]

The European scholars who emphasize the divide between front and rear often argue that an intense camaraderie among the men at the front compensated for the soldiers' alienation from the home front. Analysts agree that an essential component of the "myth of the war" in most combatant countries was that the camaraderie of the frontline soldiers transcended class boundaries and produced a brotherhood of soldiers and officers sharing a common vision and common goals. Some analysts are more skeptical than others about the efficacy of this mythical camaraderie in erasing real class differences, but whatever the potency of the myth, the distinct social conditions in Russia constrained possibilities for both mythic and real camaraderie.[14]

A fourth debate about wartime masculinity has to do with the effect of the war on the bodies and minds of soldiers and on their sense of themselves as men. The imagery of Owen's poem emphasized the suffering of the male body under a gas attack, the "white eyes writhing in his face," and "the blood / Come gargling from the froth-corrupted lungs." Analysts of Russia such as

Catherine Merridale, on the other hand, have argued that soldiers' individual trauma and suffering was downplayed, while "the Soviet experience of war was narrated with a particular emphasis on survival and endurance."[15]

My study of gender in Soviet World War I discourse challenges the conclusions of Kelly and Merridale by demonstrating that indeed there was a reexamination of heroic masculinity evident in the Soviet interwar discussion of World War I, and that the traumas of World War I were not always narrated with an emphasis on "survival and endurance." One of the most striking aspects of Soviet World War I discourse was its candid examination of the toll that war took on the manliness of the warrior.

The second goal of this chapter is to demonstrate the ways in which Russian gendered discourse was similar to that of the other European combatants, as well as where it differed radically from its European counterparts. While Russian and Soviet representations of the relationship between front and rear often bore a strong similarity to European discourses, both Russian and Soviet ideas of camaraderie differed markedly from their European counterparts.

GENDER AND WAR IN RUSSIA AND THE SOVIET UNION

Gender analysis is particularly appropriate to military culture because the warrior is the quintessential masculine hero.[16] All the belligerent countries in World War I deployed notions of ideal masculinity to mobilize men to fight for the nation.[17] Russian and Soviet military mobilization inextricably intertwined gender identity and the Russian national project. In his wartime writings before the revolution, Vladimir Lenin had deliberately severed the connections between valorous military service and Russian citizenship, between patriotism and masculinity, arguing that "the Great Russians cannot 'defend the fatherland' otherwise than by desiring the defeat of Tsarism in any war."[18] Once in power, however, Lenin was eager to reestablish those very connections between male citizenship and soldiering. Soviet writer Dem'ian Bednyi recalled a conversation in 1918 in which Lenin said, "Before, there was the so-called 'damned scoundrel [*rasprokliataia zlodeika*] tsarist service,' and now there is service to the worker-peasant Soviet government; before, [serving] under the knout and lash, and now consciously fulfilling the revolutionary-popular debt; before, they went to fight for devil knows what, and now for their own."[19] While the conditions of tsarist and Soviet military service may have been quite different, there was a profound continuity in this connection between male military service and male citizenship. Although early Soviet rhetoric often depicted soldiers in the tsarist army as humiliated victims who had been denied their manhood "under the knout and lash," Lenin had anticipated that the military and psychological lessons learned by these brutalized soldiers would harden them for future revolutionary battles.

A significant complicating factor in this equation of military service and citizenship was that World War I had destabilized gender roles in many of its combatant countries as women took on new activities at home that had previously been defined as male.[20] Russian women in particular defied military traditions and gender norms by taking part in combat operations; while there were women volunteers who disguised themselves as men and joined the Russian army individually as early as 1914, it was the February Revolution of 1917 that profoundly transformed Russian understandings of gender roles, citizenship, and soldiering.[21] The Provisional Government was quite radical in its offer of liberation and citizenship to women in exchange for their military service. It was the first modern state ever to officially sponsor organized units of women in combat roles in the army. While one goal of the women's units was to raise morale by demonstrating the devotion of volunteers to the war effort, the organizers also intended for the units to shame the wavering men into doing their duty. Fighting women volunteers challenged the masculinity of men who were unwilling to fight.[22]

Like female warriors, military failure also challenged the masculinity of the defeated. As the Russian war effort during World War I collapsed, revolutionary rhetoric called into question the masculinity of key actors such as the tsar, Provisional Government leader Aleksandr Kerenskii, and the bourgeoisie in general. Then and afterward, enemies of the Provisional Government pointed to its efforts to recruit women in the armed forces as evidence of its weakness and lack of masculine power and popular support (not to mention the women's lack of revolutionary consciousness). Revolutionaries made much of the fact that the Women's Battalion of Death defended the Provisional Government at the Winter Palace on the night of the October Revolution when the Bolsheviks "stormed" it.[23] After Kerenskii escaped the Bolsheviks, rumors spread that he was disguised in women's clothing to evade capture.[24] Bolshevik rhetoric thus repeatedly feminized the losing side in the revolutionary struggle.[25]

Gender roles were in flux during the 1920s in the Soviet Union, just as they were all over the rest of Europe, in the United States, and beyond.[26] Nowhere did women gain more legal rights in the post–World War I era than in the new Soviet state, since the Communists embraced women's equality as a key aspect of their ideological agenda. The first Soviet law codes granted women full legal rights; they made acquiring divorce easy, so that women would be able to escape bad marriages, and they legalized abortion. Despite the unprecedented legislative equality for women in the Soviet Union, persistent beliefs in the innate differences between men and women continued to shape notions of military service and heroism.

During the Civil War, the Soviet state had actively recruited thousands of women into the Red Army in support positions, but they did not organize women's combat units or promote women's participation in battle the way that the Provisional Government had done between February and October of 1917.[27] The association between the bearing of arms and citizenship in revolutionary Russia continued to prioritize male belonging to the Soviet community, and men acquired rights in exchange for military service. The Soviet Union "nationalized" masculinity, linking a physically aggressive masculine identity with membership in the political community.[28]

Russian literature also emphasized the masculine as the Russian Revolution offered a powerful opportunity for restoring masculine honor that had been tarnished by the debacle of World War I. Soviet literature of the revolutionary era was characterized by a masculine ethos that marginalized women, domesticity, and the feminine in its quest for "a new, masculinized society." This literature imagined the new Soviet society as a utopian brotherhood of men, ready at any time to pick up arms in the defense of the Revolution and Soviet society.[29] Soviet heroism and masculinity also cannot be divorced from issues of class in the revolutionary period. To be a Soviet man was to be a hero who had overturned the class order, replacing heroic and virile proletarian masculinity for the effete and questionable masculinity of the upper classes and the intelligentsia.[30] Yet one must be extremely careful when associating Soviet masculinity with one particular kind of masculine image. Rather than conceiving of "the Russian Revolution as a culminating moment in the creation of a new masculine identity," it is important to recognize that Russian and Soviet masculinity were "always in the making" and that throughout the interwar period there were several "competing or coincidental" Soviet masculine identities.[31]

In addition to paying attention to multiple masculine identities, we must also consider the relationship between masculine norms and the lives of real men.[32] To the extent that my sources permit, I will attempt to analyze how autobiographical writing and fiction depict the individual experiences of soldiers. These works cannot, however, be viewed as unmediated sources of subjectivity, since the soldiers' stories are situated within set tropes of tsarist and Soviet military culture.

The collapse of the tsarist army in the midst of revolution, combined with continuities in notions of manliness and citizenship across the revolutionary divide, created contradictions in all Soviet World War I accounts of soldiering. If the soldier displayed the traditional masculine qualities of courage and heroism in World War I, he demonstrated a lack of political consciousness by fighting for the victory of tsarism; if, on the other hand, the soldier was a helpless victim, or if he evaded fighting and shirked his military responsibilities, he undermined the amalgamation of military service, manliness, and citizenship that underlay the Soviet as well as the tsarist military ethos. Traditional World War I heroism thus remained problematic in the Soviet period, while Civil War heroes could excel as both men and patriots.

Many Soviet depictions of World War I emphasized revolutionary consciousness and the rejection of tsarism at the expense of soldierly heroism. These Soviet memoirs differ from European memoirs of the same period in their skepticism about heroic masculine behavior in World War I. In European war literature, ideals of normative military masculinity even "informed the attitudes of those who asserted their hatred of military conflict." Former German soldier Erich Maria Remarque's famous antiwar novel *All Quiet on the Western Front* actually celebrated the virtues of male camaraderie at the front, and "even a left-wing journal (*Die Weltbühne*) described the book as 'pacifist war propaganda.'"[33] The work of Remarque, like that of German nationalist writers such as Ernst Jünger, who was only nineteen when World War I began and served as a lieutenant, "radiates generational conflict, a sense of alienation between front and *Heimat,* and a distrust of the leadership behind the front, all the while extolling the virtues of 'comradeship.'"[34] Issues of manliness, comradeship, and heroism are often depicted in much more ambiguous ways in Soviet treatments of World War I.

HEROISM AND WORLD WAR I

As the example of Koz'ma Kriuchkov demonstrates, tsarist war culture contained many works that glorified the war and celebrated the joys of combat in an unproblematic way. Like many Europeans of that time, some Russian writers took seriously the notion that it was "sweet and proper to die for one's country." Their works contained no hint of the disillusion and ironic consciousness that became a hallmark of many Western European works about World War I.

In his wartime dispatches for *Russkie vedomosti* (Russian Gazette) in 1914 and 1915, Aleksei Tolstoi described Russian soldiers as incredibly courageous and fearless in battle.[35] Tolstoi suggested that the Russian bravery on the battle-field stemmed from the fact that the soldiers saw death only as an "unfortunate chance" and they spoke "about their lost comrades as simply as they speak about losses at cards."[36] Tolstoi participated in the creation of a sanitized war and fervently denied the impact of death on the common soldiers. The soldiers did not suffer emotional pain or mourn for their missing comrades, conquering fear through their fatalistic belief in chance.[37]

Military documents submitted for promotions and for honors such as the St. George cross revealed a language of heroism that was not quite as exaggerated as the newspapers' and broadsheets' celebration of the bloodthirsty Koz'ma Kriuchkov and the soldiers who calmly accepted fate. Soldiers and officers received accolades for more mundane activities if they carried them out under enemy fire; these included saving wounded comrades, repairing telephone lines, remaining at observation posts, taking reconnaissance aerial photographs, and leading men into attack. Officers were particularly praised when they emboldened their men to carry out attacks despite enemy fire, when they put themselves at personal risk in the frontlines, and when they remained in the ranks despite their injuries.[38]

These commendations revealed a great deal about the ways in which the officer corps dealt with the new circumstances of a modern war. One letter praised a certain Sotnik (Lieutenant) Pelepeiko, whose forces were reluctant to move forward in an attack under heavy fire. To embolden them, Pelepeiko "leapt out in front of the line [of soldiers] and under strong rifle and machine-gun fire began to dance the *lezginka* [a folk dance]. This bold action so strongly affected the Cossacks that they, with a shout of 'Hurrah,' threw themselves on the Austrian trenches."[39] Military officials appreciated reckless acts of bravery that exposed oneself to harm as the epitome of heroism. Another commendation described the actions of Staff-Captain Solov'ev, who, "with selfless bravery and selfless courage in spite of a hurricane of strong artillery, machine-gun, and rifle fire, led his company in a bayonet attack, dislodging the enemy from the first line of trenches and continuing forward, beating back the enemy." This attack came at a heavy cost: only one soldier in the first platoon of the company remained uninjured. The rest of the platoon lay dead or wounded.[40]

These exploits reveal one of the ideal traits of a tsarist officer: he could get his men to follow him into extraordinary danger. The quixotic nature of both of these exploits clearly demonstrates the paradoxes of heroism in World War I. The bayonet attack—the ideal heroic exploit—was extraordinarily risky because of the "hurricane" of artillery fire directed at the Russian troops. None-theless, officers attempted such attacks, incurring a costly sacrifice of soldiers' lives. Such reckless actions were, however, the ones that promised officers rec-ognition and promotion (if they survived). "Insane" bravery did indeed seem to be a trait that could be found among the real men and officers of the Rus-sian army, as well as depicted on posters and in the newspapers.[41]

In a letter that was copied by the censors, an officer on the Southwest-ern Front of the tsarist army declared that decorations were very important to the Russian soldier. He suggested that "vodka and praise can compel this person [the Russian soldier] to work wonders."[42] While the public representa-tions of the war enthusiastically depicted soldiers winning medals and hon-ors, they were decidedly more circumspect about the role of vodka in mo-tivating the soldier. Induction in the army had long been accompanied by alcohol consumption, and disorder at recruitment points often included the looting of liquor stores.[43] Russian depictions of the war, on the other hand, went out of their way to proclaim that the heroism and endurance of the Rus-sian military had nothing to do with the consumption of alcohol. Both Tol-stoi and the prominent poet and founder of Acmeism Nikolai Gumilev, whose episodic memoir *Notes of a Cavalryman* (*Zapiski kavalerista*) was published in *Birzhevye vedomosti* in 1915–1916, emphasized Russian sobriety in their dis-patches. Tolstoi described meeting a wounded soldier whose leg had just been operated on in a Moscow hospital. When the nurse offered the soldier a second helping of wine for the pain, he refused, saying, "If I don't stop, then they'll say I'm a drunkard." Instead of drinking, this soldier wanted to "become as clean and as quiet as possible." Tolstoi argued that it was this emerging cleanliness of spirit that would lead to victory.[44] He emphasized the endurance and stoicism of the soldier who would rather experience pain than be seen as a drunkard. He also envisioned the war as purifying the nation.

Tolstoi claimed that officers, too, were moderate in their use of alcohol. Describing a scene at a restaurant in L'vov after the Russians captured it, Tol-stoi noted that "to the very end of the evening, I didn't hear one drunken exclamation that might have cast even the slightest shadow on the officer's uniform." The only drunk in the restaurant was "a thin girl in a white ball dress" who suddenly leapt up from her chair and began smashing dishes on the floor.[45] Here Tolstoi used gender to emphasize the contrast between the disci-plined and upright behavior of Russian military officers and the frivolous and unbridled comportment of civilian women. Perhaps as a defensive response to accusations of Russian soldiers' abuse of the Polish population, Tolstoi projected charges of drunkenness and impropriety away from soldiers and onto civilian women.[46]

Gumilev, on the other hand, identified a different drunken group: enemy soldiers. He witnessed German troops marching and singing "two or three alternating notes, with ferocious and gloomy energy." Gumilev "did not understand right away that the singers were dead drunk," but he watched as the Russians mowed them down.[47] Here Gumilev suggested that German bravery in battle was due not to spirit but to spirits.[48] Both writers implied that the courage of the Russians never came from a bottle, but from their emotional and spiritual strength as a manly nation. Both Tolstoi and Gumilev celebrated Russian soldiers' bravery in combat, their sobriety, probity, and modesty. They actively glorified the Russian soldiers and heroized their participation in war, becoming agents in the production of a pro-war discourse that valorized the soldiers of the Russian Empire, denigrated its enemies, and obscured the participation of soldiers in wanton destruction.

Ia. Okunev was a self-described "non-believing *intelligent,* positivist and atheist" who nevertheless wrote enthusiastically about the war effort.[49] Okunev's 1915 memoir also celebrated the individual soldier's participation in warfare. Okunev described the intoxication of going into battle and even defined "battles, attacks, and skirmishes" as "holidays."[50] This memoir, which was openly published in the tsarist era, also actively criticized the way that newspapers represented the war. The populist Okunev protested that what the newspapers wrote was "an invention. And they invented the soldier as though he were a hero and not the simple and gray private . . . who fulfills his business here as successfully and adroitly as he plowed the fields at home."[51] Okunev called for a less exalted and more honest portrayal of the frontline soldier. He also objected to the depiction of the Austrians "as some kind of rabble and not an army" with "cannons that shoot poorly" and undergoing "full demoralization." Okunev felt that the newspapers' insecure boasting about the unworthiness and weakness of the enemy was "an offensive evaluation of our sacrifices, our gigantic labor."[52] The Russian press, with its unrealistic black-and-white depictions of both enemies and heroes, alienated even those who were enthusiastic about the war effort.

One of the key aspects of the pan-European myth of World War I was the notion of the special status of the combatant at the front in relation to those in the rear. The notorious tensions between the frontline soldier and the army brass and civilians in the rear were often cast in gendered terms with the front as the hardened and masculine arena and the rear as a feminized, despised, and soft locale. Ernst Jünger, for example, wrote in his memoir *Storm of Steel,* "Though I am no misogynist, I was always irritated by the presence of women every time that the fate of battle threw me into the bed of a hospital ward. One sank, after the manly and purposeful activities of war, into a vague atmosphere of warmth."[53] The writings of World War I veterans who became part of the German right-wing paramilitary Freikorps also tended to erase women from their works. These writers defined themselves as warriors and men in an exclusively masculine milieu.[54] This binary between front and rear was a crucial element of the German myth of the "stab in the back," but it flourished in other European countries as well. The Russians had their own expressions of this myth.

Russian writers gendered the front masculine and the rear feminine and developed a moralizing discourse about the weaknesses of the latter. Aleksei Tolstoi's discussion of drunkenness in L'vov demonstrated this trope. He also described a street scene among the Jewish residents of Kovel shortly after the beginning of the war. "The crowd (chiefly made up of excellently dressed young ladies) walks from the movie theater to the Belle View. . . . All of this distressed us—indeed only the other day, seventy versts away, a battle unparalleled in history occurred."[55] Tolstoi chose well-dressed Jewish ladies hedonistically enjoying themselves at the cinema to symbolize the rear's lack of concern for the events at the front and to imply that the non-Russian population was not engaged with the war effort.

The knee-jerk association of the rear with immoral women was not Tolstoi's alone. A particularly striking example of the association of women in the rear with debauchery can be found in the memoirs of Mariia Bochkareva, published in emigration. Bochkareva was allowed to enlist in the army in early 1915 because of the tsar's direct intercession and later founded the Women's Battalion of Death. When a regimental commander offered her the opportunity of enlisting as a Red Cross nurse or in some other auxiliary capacity instead, Bochkareva said, "I rejected his proposal. I had heard so many rumors about the women in the rear that I had come to despise them."[56] According to Tolstoi and Bochkareva, while men at the front gave their lives for the cause, women in the rear unconcernedly went to the movies and lived a life of sexual promiscuity. The trope of the battlefield as a manly and heroic space and the rear as a feminine and immoral one thus can be found in Russian as well as European discourse.

Although Bochkareva associated nurses with immorality, there was a rival wartime discourse that praised nurses' selfless service in hospitals in the rear, where they tenderly cared for invalid soldiers. Newspaper articles and lubki celebrated the heroism of nurses who saved the wounded under fire at the front. One such lubok showed a motherly woman in a nurse's uniform reaching out to hold the hand of a wounded soldier, gazing into his eyes, and comforting him with her hand resting on his back. The lubok proclaimed, "When men are at the front, this is your place, women!"[57] Another poster singled out nurse E. P. Korkina for her "exploit," and depicted her bravely tending the wounded and arranging for their evacuation as a fierce battle raged nearby (figure 3.3).[58] Public discourse in newspapers, posters, and pamphlets also honored the few exceptional women who either disguised themselves as men or gained special permission from the authorities to go to war.[59] One pamphlet recounted the achievements of volunteer Tychinin, who turned out to be a female student from a Kiev high school in disguise. On September 21, 1914 (Old Style), under fire she delivered ammunition to the troops, tended the wounded, and carried them from the battlefield until she was seriously wounded herself. She was awarded the St. George cross (4th class) before her superiors knew her true identity.[60] Russian imperial discourse thus associated women with virtue and heroism as well as with immorality, though neither of these discursive extremes represented the experiences of the vast majority of real women.

At the start of World War I, tsarist military culture emphasized patriarchal relations in which father-commanders benevolently watched over their soldier-sons. The male relationships across rank in the Russian army, were, therefore, not usually imagined as an egalitarian "band of brothers" engaged in male camaraderie and communalism that transcended class divisions.[61] Tsarist posters figured the soldier-sons as extremely loyal to their beloved father-commanders. A 1914 poster titled "Russian Soldier" showed a soldier carrying his wounded officer from the battlefield to safety. On the one hand this poster reinforced hierarchical relations by demonstrating the loyalty of the lower ranks to their officers. On the other hand, the boldly striding rank-and-file soldier exhibited his superior strength while the frail and diminished wounded officer lay passively in his arms.[62] In either reading of the poster, the relationship was not one of easy and casual camaraderie.

A celebration of cross-class camaraderie similar to what is more typically found in Western European memoirs and literature was present, however, in the memoirs of the woman warrior Mariia Bochkareva. She noted that before a major battle, "[m]en and officers mixed, joking about death. Many expected not to return and wrote letters to their dear ones. Others prayed. Before an of-

FIGURE 3.3. "The Exploit of Sister E. P. Korkina" [*Podvig sestry E. P. Korkinoi*] (Moscow: I. D. Sytin, no. 86, 1915). Hoover Institution Poster Collection.

fensive the men's camaraderie reached a climax. There would be affectionate partings, sincere professions by some of their premonitions of death and the entrusting of messages to friends."[63] Ironically, an image of male camaraderie emerged most clearly in the writings of a woman, who, as an outsider, valued and admired (and perhaps idealized) the close relationships of the men to one another.

A different representation of cross-class unity appeared in the memoir of the populist intellectual Okunev. Unlike most official representations of the war, which celebrated the superior qualities of officers as leaders, Okunev romanticized the simple *muzhik* (male peasant) and fantasized about shedding the baggage of the intellectual and becoming one with the people. He wrote that during the war, "we somehow became simpler, we merged. We organically grew together, soul to soul, body to body, with the golden-bearded muzhiks striding side by side with us on Austrian soil. . . . In our soul it became spacious and clean because the usual labels and formulas for things, ideas and feelings were no longer there."[64] The dream of creating unity across class in wartime was most clearly expressed by a member of the radical intelligentsia, a group that had been struggling to find a common language with ordinary Russian workers and peasants for more than half a century in order to achieve their revolutionary goals. Okunev believed that unity in the war effort could close the gap separating intelligentsia and people. While Tolstoi believed that the war was a catalyst for cleansing some of the inherent weaknesses of the ordinary Russian people, Okunev thought that it was the intelligentsia who would be cleansed in the crucible of war. The memoir described inequality that interfered with camaraderie, even though Okunev reversed the hierarchies and saw the peasant-soldier as the superior figure.

How did the unprecedented violence of seven years of war affect the bodies and the minds of Russian and Soviet soldiers and veterans? Soviet socialist realist literature contains at least two contradictory models of the male body: "the overly healthy, virile, and productive male body" and the "wounded, mutilated, long-suffering 'mummy'" exemplified by the character of Pavel Korchagin in the semiautobiographical novel *How the Steel was Tempered* (*Kak zakalialas' stal'*). A blind and paralyzed Civil War veteran, Korchagin could only actively participate in building socialism by dictating his inspirational novel as he lay bedridden.[65] These two tropes about the male body are also extant in tsarist and early Soviet representations of World War I. The soldier hero exhibited his virility and strength in defeating the enemy, while the bodies and minds of wounded and traumatized soldiers revealed their sacrifice in the name of the tsarist state.

While heroic images of World War I tended to sanitize and minimize the impact of violence, some war posters did call attention to the wounded in the process of gathering aid for them. A 1914 poster by S. Vinogradov titled "Help for War Victims" showed a wounded soldier who had returned to his village. The entire village gathered around him as he sat on a bench with his arm in a sling and a crutch lying at his feet. Other than these markers of injury, the soldier looked alert and vigorous. He met the gaze of the villagers directly and gave an impression of dignity. The suffering depicted in this poster was minimal, and the poster suggested that local communities would warmly welcome and tenderly care for their wounded men.[66]

A 1914 poster by Leonid Pasternak, the father of the famous novelist, was also captioned "Help for War Victims"; it depicted a soldier clearly in distress (figure 3.4).[67] The poster showed a wounded soldier in full uniform holding his rifle and bayonet. The soldier leaned against the wall dejectedly and held a bloody handkerchief to his head, looking as if he might fall at any moment. The colors of the poster were muted except for the bright red of the blood on the soldier's handkerchief, sleeve, and in a puddle at his feet. According to Pasternak's memoir, the poster was popular beyond his wildest expectations. "Crowds gathered before it and women burst into tears." Hundreds of thousands of postcard reproductions were sold. It was imitated on candy wrappers, labels, and even trademarks. Pasternak received word, however, that the tsar was dissatisfied with his poster and had declared that "*his* soldiers conducted themselves bravely, and not like this!"[68] The tsar's reputed response to Pasternak's poster revealed a tension in Russian depictions of men at war similar to the diverging models of the male body in socialist realism. On the one hand, the population was extremely moved by the plight of wounded soldiers and appreciative of their sacrifices, and did not expect all soldiers to conform to the ideal of the brave and hypermasculine hero. On the other hand, some feared that realistic depictions of men suffering in wartime might demoralize the troops and weaken their will to fight.

A poster from late 1916 titled "From the Merchants of Moscow to the Soldier-Invalids" demonstrated the possibilities for depicting wounded manhood during the third year of the war.[69] The poster invited patrons of Moscow to their shops on September 24, 1916, because on that day, 5 percent of the sales would be donated to the hospital for invalids. The poster showed two soldiers in full uniform with several medals pinned upon their chests. The first soldier was on crutches and had one leg amputated just below the knee. The other walked with a cane and had one arm amputated at the elbow. The latter soldier gazed into the distance, while the former looked directly at the viewer. This poster contained several elements visible in other posters. What was most noticeable about these men was their dignity; despite their wounds they stood tall and appeared as soldiers. Unlike Pasternak's soldier, their wounds had not weakened them. On the other hand, the men's bodies visibly revealed the permanent costs of war, and the composition of the poster drew the viewers' attention to their missing arm and leg. In late imperial Russia, a rare and somewhat sanitized acknowledgment of dismemberment did become part of public culture, although the dominant tropes of tsarist masculinity continued to privilege the courageous, strong, and physically intact male warrior.[70]

SOVIET DEPICTIONS OF HEROISM

Soviet treatments of heroism in World War I were often in dialogue with the tsarist discourse that they replaced. Although later Soviet ideologues claimed a strict separation between tsarist culture and Soviet culture, in reality the Bolsheviks actively borrowed certain aspects of tsarist culture. Heroic imagery of World War I posters, such as "the depiction of one's own side as a mounted warrior impaling tiny opponents on his lance, or the representation of the enemy as a mythological monster surrounded by skulls," found its way into Soviet Civil War posters.[71] The Bolsheviks also embraced Leonid Pasternak's popular image of the wounded soldier. The very first poster issued by the Bolsheviks in August 1918 was a replica of "Help for War Victims" with the new pacifist caption "The Price of Blood" (figure 3.5).[72] Having kept their promise to pull out of World War I in March 1918, Bolshevik leaders endorsed public reflection on the costs and the suffering of the war.

Soviet World War I discourse engaged in a sustained critique of the ways in which the tsarist newspapers represented the war and its heroes, seeking to uncover "the truth" about the war that tsarist newspapers concealed. Aleksei Brusilov's 1929 memoirs criticized the tsar and his military advisors for their ineptitude and cronyism, and accused the tsar's favorites of creating false and self-serving accounts of the war. He charged that certain generals received high accolades in the press while more talented generals (himself among them) were denied honors. Brusilov described, for example, how the ambitious General Ruzskii did nothing to correct the press's inaccurate depiction of the conquest of L'vov. While the press described "the brave troops of General Ruzskii marching through the streets up to their knees in blood," in actuality General Ruzskii entered the town by car, "made an excellent lunch at the George Hotel, and bought some cake at a confectioner's."[73] Brusilov felt that official representations of heroism thus advanced the careers of certain fortunate military officers at the expense of the truth.

Unlike Brusilov, most other Soviet writers rejected the war. These works contained even more scathing attacks on the way that the war was portrayed in tsarist newspapers. One Soviet-era memoir that is particularly noteworthy for its complicated and nuanced depiction of the war, and especially of the relationship between soldiers and officers, is *In the Footsteps of War* (*Po sledam voiny*) by Lev Naumovich Voitolovskii. A Social-Democratic psychiatrist and literary critic who edited the literary section of the liberal newspaper *Kievskaia mysl'* (Kievan Thought), Voitolovskii was conscripted into the tsarist

На
помощь
жертвамъ
войны
20го–21го авг.
Москва.

FIGURE 3.4. *Facing page.* Poster by Leonid Pasternak, "Help for War Victims" [*Na pomoshch' zhertvam voiny*] (Moscow: A. A. Levenson, 1914). Hoover Institution Poster Collection.

FIGURE 3.5. *Above.* Drawing by Leonid Pasternak, "The Price of Blood" [*Tsena krovi*] (Petrograd: Petrogradskii Sovet Rabochikh i Krasnoarmeiskikh Deputatov, 1918). Hoover Institution Poster Collection.

army during both the Russo-Japanese War and World War I (figure 3.6).[74] He also volunteered for the Red Army during the Soviet-Polish War. He was an anomalous figure—a revolutionary and a Jew with a tsarist officer's rank. His memoirs, like many Western writings about World War I, recorded his deep disillusionment with both the war and the heroic rhetoric of the newspapers. Calling the war a "bloody garbage pit," he excoriated the "journalists of the rear" for creating an imaginary war. In his opinion, the false representations of the war were not only the fault of the journalists themselves. He also blamed the intelligentsia for lacking confidence in itself and "being more interested in someone else's opinions than one's own." The result was that "we constantly have two histories, one written in ink and the other in blood."[75] Voitolovskii's description of Russia's two histories captured an essential truth of both the tsarist and Soviet eras.

In his depiction of the difference between the real war and the newspaper war, Voitolovskii set up a sharp opposition between the virtue of the front and the immorality of the rear. Like Wilfred Owen in "Dulce et Decorum Est," Voitolovskii directly addressed the civilian audience of the newspaper war in the rear: "All of you who are sitting at the other end of the world from the battlefield and thirstily swallowing striking communiqués about victories with your morning tea, you want to see courage and heroism everywhere. But they don't exist." While Voitolovskii acknowledged brief moments of "death-dealing enthusiasm" on the battlefield, he rejected the notion that this phenomenon was glorious; it led only to "piles of human corpses on the earth" and "a spirit of devastation and grief that fills the heart."[76]

Voitolovskii deeply resented both the journalists and civilians who constructed, consumed, and perpetuated images of a glorious imaginary war. Those in the rear who supported the war condemned others to fight and die in hellish conditions at the front. Since he did not believe that such a thing as heroism existed at the front, Voitolovskii directly challenged the newspapers' creation of mythic larger-than-life heroes such Koz'ma Kriuchkov. He wrote pointedly about finding a blood-spattered letter from home in a trench near the dead body of its recipient. The letter read, "My dear little brother! I am proud that you are standing up in the defense of our motherland against the German villains, and I wish that you may fight with the enemy as bravely and boldly as Koz'ma Kriuchkov who covered his name in immortal glory." One of the other officers threw down this letter in disgust, saying that he would prefer it if the letter writer lay in the place of his fallen little brother.[77] Voitolovskii suggested that relatives, friends, and journalists in the rear were complicit in

FIGURE 3.6. Photograph of L. N. Voitolovskii (far right) at the front.
Personal collection of L. N. Voitolovskii, Russian State Archive of
Literature and Art.

the deaths of soldiers at the front. It is likely that Voitolovskii's perceptions of wartime betrayal fueled his desire to overturn the tsarist order.

Mikhail Sholokhov also chose to include the Cossack Koz'ma Kriuchkov as a character in *Quiet Flows the Don*. In contrast to the tendency in a great deal of Soviet war literature to equate "Cossack" with reactionary, Sholokhov explored the political divides within the Cossack community and the nature of both "White" and "Red" Cossacks.[78] He began the action of the novel in the years immediately preceding World War I because he realized that "the average reader had no knowledge of the Don Cossacks" and would not understand why Cossacks took part in attempts to suppress the revolution or fought against the Bolsheviks in the Civil War.[79]

Sholokhov's novel directly engaged with Cossack mythology in the wake of the events of 1914–1921. The historical record of actual soldiers' behavior on the Eastern Front during World War I had intensified the myth of the violent Cossack. The Cossacks were blamed, and very often justifiably so, for war atrocities including the looting, rape, and murder of the local population, especially in the Jewish borderlands of the Russian and Austro-Hungarian empires. Notions of Cossack brutality also played more than a figurative role in Soviet culture as they explicitly divided the Cossacks from the rest of the Soviet population and placed them in the category of "other." During the 1919 de-Cossackization campaign, Cossacks were targeted for elimination as "an entire social collectivity."[80] Although this policy was in force only briefly, it demonstrated the complexity of Cossack status in the Soviet Union. Cossacks could be seen as a caste, a class, or an ethnicity; as keepers of order in the Russian Empire; as lawless marauders victimizing the civilian population and engaging in pogroms; as "instinctive counterrevolutionaries" despite the fact that some served in the Red Army; and eventually as partially Sovietized heroic adventurers in the novels of Mikhail Sholokhov and Dmitrii Furmanov.

Sholokhov focused on the origins of the 1914 myth about the Cossack Kriuchkov in a conscious attempt to contest the tsarist narrative of Kriuchkov's superhuman achievements and redefine the nature of heroism in World War I. Yet Sholokhov's treatment of Kriuchkov's exploit contained ambiguities that undermined these goals. The multivalent nature of the novel may explain why Sholokhov faced persistent rumors of plagiarism from the late 1920s onward. Although the most recent computer and textual analyses have demonstrated Sholokhov to be the author of the novel, some who accused him of plagiarism suggested that the author was actually a Cossack officer who joined the Whites during the Civil War. In other words, the doubters believed that the novel had actually been written from the point of view of a loyal tsarist officer.[81]

Sholokhov, who had himself seen combat in the Red Army during the Civil War, interviewed Mikhail Ivankov—one of the other Cossacks involved in the skirmish that made Kriuchkov famous—and incorporated eyewitness details about Kriuchkov's life and deeds into the novel to challenge Kriuchkov's status as hero.[82] Sholokhov showed Kriuchkov to be a sadistic noncommissioned officer who "had just received his corporal's stripes" and who enjoyed whipping the new recruits with his belt buckle "for every trifling offense."[83] Rather than exemplifying heroism, Kriuchkov illustrated the arbitrary authority of tsarist functionaries who brutally disciplined the bodies of rank-and-file soldiers.

Sholokhov's account emphasized that Kriuchkov did not accomplish his exploit single-handedly. Rather, he was one of several Cossacks sent out to in-

tercept a German patrol. When the Germans surrounded the Cossack Ivankov, Kriuchkov and several other Cossacks raced to assist him. Yet Sholokhov's
narration of Kriuchkov's deeds echoed and recapitulated the hyperpatriotic
tsarist rhetoric of 1914. First he described how Kriuchkov saved Ivankov's life
by killing a German with his lance before the German could draw his carbine
to shoot Ivankov. Then, "about eight dragoons surrounded Kriuchkov, trying
to capture him alive. But he reared his horse and, swinging his body from the
waist, fought them off with his sabre. When it was knocked out of his hand, he
snatched a lance from the nearest German and wielded it as if at exercises."[84]
Sholokhov here conceded that Kriuchkov was a brave, strong, and skilled warrior who fought vigorously against the Germans. His tone abruptly changed,
however, as he described how the fight continued: he showed how the Cossacks
and Germans were "brutalized by fear" as they "stabbed and hacked at anything they saw." All of the participants panicked and took flight after the Cossack Astakhov shot and killed the German commanding officer.[85]

Sholokhov contended that because Kriuchkov was the "squadron commander's favorite" he received the St. George cross, while his comrades "were
left in the shade." Then, "the hero was transferred to divisional headquarters,
where he loafed till the end of the war. . . ."[86] Sholokhov depicted Kriuchkov
as a fraud, undeserving of the honor bestowed upon him. He had betrayed
notions of wartime camaraderie by allowing himself to be elevated above his
comrades and had achieved his supposed exploit simply by taking part in an
ordinary and rather inglorious battle. Depictions of him with Germans skew-
ered on his lance were a tsarist fantasy.[87]

Sholokhov used this episode to emphasize the dehumanizing influence
of war; the novel's narrator declared that during the skirmish, the men had
been "overcome by animal fear, had charged and battered one another, striking blindly and maiming themselves and their horses." This description of the
transformation of men into animals is similar to the protagonist Paul Bäumer's narration of battle at close quarters in Erich Maria Remarque's *All Quiet
on the Western Front*. Bäumer said, "We have become wild beasts . . . we can
destroy and kill, to save ourselves, to save ourselves and to be revenged . . .
crouching like cats we run on, overwhelmed by this wave that bears us along,
that fills us with ferocity, turns us into thugs, into murderers, into God only
knows what devils."[88] Both novels depict their protagonists as losing the human capacity of moral judgment in the chaos of battle. Sholokhov's narrator
claimed this directly when he stated that after the skirmish both sides had "ridden away morally crippled."[89]

Sholokhov's view of a morally crippling war, however, contradicted his earlier descriptions of Kriuchkov. Sholokov acknowledged that Kriuchkov chose to risk his own life to rescue Ivankov. If Kriuchkov had ridden away to safety instead, leaving a companion to die, would he not also have been "morally crippled"? Furthermore, Sholokhov's description of Kriuchkov wielding his lance "as if at exercises" demonstrated the warrior's composure. This description contradicted Sholokhov's idea that animal fear motivated the battle. In this scene, as in many others in the novel, Sholokhov presented multiple and contradictory ideas about the morality and justice of war. In Sholokhov's treatment of Kriuchkov, the reader could see both the war's injustices and the inherent appeal of tsarist rhetoric glorifying battle.

Yet Sholokhov's rejection of frenzied killing in battle could also be read as a pacifist trope. This scene's similarity to Remarque's explicitly pacifist text places it within the bounds of European pacifist writing. Soviet critics, however, connected the pacifist tone to Russian literary tradition. They singled out this passage for criticism, accusing Sholokhov of stooping to "mechanical imitation" of the famous Russian writer Lev Tolstoi. Although he was later attacked for it, the critic I. Mashbits-Verov claimed that the novel adopted Tolstoi's style of interrupting the novel's action to cast moral judgments, and that it embraced Tolstoi's ideology.[90] Another critic noted Sholokhov's borrowing of "Tolstoi's moralistic relationship to war."[91] Thus the pacifist moments in Sholokhov's novel emerged at the same time as contemporary European antiwar sentiment, but they were likely inspired, at least in part, by Russian intellectual traditions.[92]

Sholokhov further explored the psychology of the Cossacks and the nature of heroism through the fictional Grigorii Melekhov, a brave and daring Cossack warrior who wavered between devoted service to the tsar and revolutionary ideas, and then between the Whites and the Reds. *Quiet Flows the Don* was published as a serial, and between 1928 and 1940 it was unclear whether Melekhov would turn out to be a hero or an antihero. At the end of the second installment Melekhov joined the Whites, but many readers expected him to switch sides once again and turn out to be a committed revolutionary and a Soviet hero. One fan of the novel who was a former Red partisan predicted in a letter to the State Literature Publishing House, erroneously as it turned out, that Melekhov would become a Red and live happily ever after with his lover Aksin'ia because of his fine moral fiber. The partisan wrote that Melekhov was "an honest and firm person" who, while "serving in the army did not permit the taking of other people's things or pillaging. And he related to women as human beings with special feeling."[93] In other words, Melekhov deserved a happy ending because he lived up to ideals of prerevolutionary military honor.

In the third part of the novel (1932), Sholokhov was pressured by censors to draw Melekhov as an increasingly negative character, and at the novel's end (1940), Melekhov could not reconcile himself to the Soviet regime. The protagonist was so popular among Soviet readers that Stalin himself asked Sholokhov to transform Melekhov into a Red Cossack. Sholokhov refused to comply, however, because he felt it would ruin the "artistic credibility" of the character.[94] Melekhov remained an unusually attractive antihero, a tragic figure with "excellent human potential" who was doomed because he had "lost touch with the people."[95] Some Soviet readers ignored or misinterpreted Sholokhov's intentions, however; in a 1950 interview for the Harvard Project on the Soviet Social System, one forty-year-old Ukrainian male informant proclaimed that *Quiet Flows the Don* was "not a subversive book, because even though it isn't the picture of a man who was always a Communist, it's a picture of a search for Communism, and that's what the man [Melekhov] finally finds."[96] Melekhov remained a hero to at least some Soviet readers.

In *Quiet Flows the Don,* Melekhov also won the St. George cross, but under very different circumstances than Kriuchkov. Severely wounded in a battle with Hungarian hussars, Melekhov regained consciousness on the battlefield and was struggling to return to his unit when he encountered a wounded officer. "Grigory helped the officer to his feet and they walked on together. But with every step the wounded officer leaned more heavily on Grigory's arm. As they climbed out of a hollow he seized Grigory's sleeve and said through chattering teeth, 'Leave me here, Cossack. I'm wounded in the stomach.'" Melekhov disobeyed this order. As "the eyes behind the pince-nez grew dull" and the officer fainted, "Grigory carried him, falling, pulling himself up and falling again. Twice he abandoned his burden, only to go back and pick it up, and then struggle on, as if in a waking dream."[97] One could read Melekhov's determination to save the wounded officer as a lack of class-consciousness because he failed to recognize that the officer was an "enemy," but one could also read it as a sign of his humanity, compassion, and determination to save life; for this exploit he received the St. George cross, 4th class. In this episode, Melekhov doggedly pushed himself to the limits of his strength in order to save another, becoming a war hero who did not shed blood to earn a medal and a promotion to corporal. He jeopardized his own life to save the officer, even after he received permission to leave him behind. At the same time, like the soldier in a tsarist-era poster titled "Russian Soldier," he asserted his masculine superiority over the weak and fainting Russified German officer with a pince-nez.

There is a similar scene of Paul Bäumer's heroism in *All Quiet on the Western Front* that is based on Remarque's real-life experience of carrying a wounded friend on his shoulders to a dressing station while under fire, though in Remarque's novel both protagonists were soldiers.[98] Unlike Melekhov, who received recognition and honor for saving a life, Bäumer's efforts were futile. "'You might have spared yourself that,' says an orderly. I looked at him without comprehending. He points to Kat. 'He is stone dead.'"[99] In Remarque's ironic narrative, even the noblest expressions of honor and comradeship were powerless in the face of the war's destruction.

By giving Melekhov the distinction of earning a St. George cross for heroism, Sholokhov, on the other hand, depicted World War I as a possible breeding ground for heroism in which the true hero mitigated the effects of the brutal killing around him. Yet Sholokhov depicted wartime honors as a double-edged sword; the St. George cross, Melekhov's reward for bravery and human decency in wartime, ultimately led him away from revolutionary ideas. Because of "the honour that the village people accorded to their first winner of the St. George cross," he succumbed to the "subtle poison of flattery" and forgot "the seeds of truth" that the revolutionary Garanzha had earlier planted in his mind. Receiving this honor renewed Melekhov's willingness to perform his duties as a Cossack warrior despite the fact that he was "inwardly unreconciled to the senselessness of war."[100] Sholokhov depicted tsarist military honors in ambiguous ways, revealing them as sometimes unjust and at other times well deserved, sometimes repulsive and at other times seductive.

After consciously debunking Koz'ma Kriuchkov's superhuman ability to kill Germans, Sholokov transformed Melekhov into the model Cossack, endowing him with mythic strength to save life and extraordinary devotion to authority. This model of the life-saving war hero was also prefigured in the tsarist discourse of 1914 which celebrated, alongside Koz'ma Kriuchkov, the dutiful soldier-hero prepared to give his life to save his officer.[101] While harshly criticizing the bloodthirsty celebration of the unworthy Kriuchkov, Sholokhov acknowledged and even foregrounded the existence of heroism, loyalty, devotion, and cross-rank solidarity in the tsarist army. Sholokhov's depiction of war made both Melekhov and certain aspects of the tsarist military appealing. Both Remarque and Sholokhov evoked the romance of certain elements of war even as they revealed its horrors.

While Sholokhov's critique of heroism remained ambiguous, other writers pursued a frontal attack on the notion of heroic wartime masculinity. In Moisei Gromov's novella *For St. George Crosses,* the protagonist's peasant mother advises him: "You, sonny, don't be particularly brave. Don't stick yourself into the thick of battle; you'll be better off on the side."[102] Her son's survival was far more important to her than his demonstrating courage under fire.

Dmitrii Os'kin was a soldier who eventually rose through the ranks to become first a tsarist officer and then, during the Civil War, a Red commander.[103] Os'kin also sought to debunk the myth of the simple Russian soldier happily and willingly going into battle. In *Notes of a Soldier (Zapiski soldata),* he recounted how he and the other soldiers in his unit spent the hours before an attack in "somber meditation."[104] Furthermore, he showed that Russian courage did sometimes come out of a bottle. After drinking some liquor captured from the Austrians, Os'kin described how "one feels intoxication and at the same time an impetuous boldness, the desire to accomplish some kind of exploit that would discharge pent-up energy."[105] On another occasion, while repulsing an Austrian attack, the Russians focused primarily on overpowering the Austrian soldiers who were carrying flasks of rum.[106] After imbibing a considerable amount of rum himself, Os'kin left his trench in search of more rum and was seriously wounded.[107] Os'kin saw alcohol not as the basis of group solidarity but as a way of coping with the miseries of war. Behavior that seemed heroic was actually induced by a desperate craving for alcohol to soothe the pain of war.

Depictions of evasion and desertion also posed a fundamental challenge to notions of wartime heroism, and there was a fundamental disagreement among Soviet writers about whether desertion was a humiliating and unmanly act or, as L. Averbakh suggested in 1928, "desertion from the ranks of the bourgeois divisions is valor (*doblest'*).[108] One particularly interesting scene in *In the Footsteps of War* revealed Voitolovskii's relationship with his servant and the question of desertion. In the first days of the war, during a battle in which the Russian troops were forced to beat a hasty retreat, Voitolovskii became separated from his unit while under fire and was trapped in a ditch. Luckily, his servant, Konovalov, turned out to be nearby, and called out, "Is that you [formal], Your Worship?" Voitolovskii was cheered and said, "You [informal] are here, Konovalov?" He replied, "Of course I'm here. Would I really abandon you?"[109] Konovalov's response affirmed the official tsarist (and common Western European) vision of harmonious officer-soldier relations in which the soldier was devoted to his officer. Konovalov made himself suspect in Soviet terms by willingly enacting the subservient masculinity of the lower classes under tsarism.

Voitolovskii then reproduced the following conversation between them, faithfully conveying Konovalov's Ukrainian dialect:

> "Let's run away, Your Worship. Let's run away."
> "How can we abandon our unit?"
> "What do we need our unit for?"
> "We would become deserters, you know."
> "And what of it?"
> "If everyone deserted, then who would fight?"
> "Is this really war? Your Worship, let's run away before they kill us."

Voitolovskii was able to convince Konovalov that "it was still far from the hour of their deaths" and they returned to their unit. As they traveled together in the dark night, Voitolovskii feared that "strange thoughts crept into Konovalov's head."[110] This scene brings to the fore the complicated and contradictory notions of Bolshevik consciousness, class, and wartime heroism.

In a reversal from the usual Soviet trope of class and heroism, it was the officer who bravely continued to carry out his duties while calming the fearful (and misguidedly subservient) rank-and-file soldier. Voitolovskii demonstrated both bravery and concern for the welfare of the soldiers in his unit. Later in the memoir, Voitolovskii also expressed guilt at leaving his soldiers at the front when he received a month-long assignment at a veterinary base in the rear.[111] He expressed his revolutionary solidarity with the lower-class soldiers he commanded through his desire to remain with them at the front. On the other hand, although Voitolovskii detested the war, he nonetheless urged the faithful Konovalov back into harm's way at the front and exposed the other soldiers he commanded to danger as well. Voitolovskii perceived that his actions made him a class enemy, and he feared that Konovalov's "strange thoughts" might turn him from a loyal servant into a potentially murderous one. The scene, reminiscent of some Western European accounts, revealed the ethical dilemma of an officer conscientiously carrying out his duties while fighting a war he considered immoral. In the Soviet context, neither the reluctant Konovalov nor the brave Voitolovskii could be models of ideal behavior.

After failing in his attempts to evade mobilization, Bolshevik worker Aleksandr Pireiko became a soldier in the tsarist army, and he, too, contemplated desertion. When some Jewish civilians whom he protected from a pogrom suggested that he hide in their basement until the Austrians came, and "then you will stay a prisoner of war and you'll be fine," Pireiko "flatly rejected such a suggestion."[112] Thus Pireiko revealed the complexities of a good Bolshevik's behavior: he did not volunteer for tsarist service, but also did not voluntarily become a prisoner of war because surrender to the enemy was ignominious. Unlike Voitolovskii (and various Western European authors), however, Pireiko did not emphasize his bonds of comradeship with the other frontline soldiers, and, as long as he did not give himself to the enemy, he felt no pangs of guilt at the idea of absenting himself from the front without leave. After he was sent to Kiev as an escort to a group of soldiers who had gotten separated from their unit, Pireiko stowed away on a train to Petrograd, hiding among the civilian refugees. His stay in Petrograd was brief, however, because he could not find a place to sleep, and he returned to his unit, planning a future escape by preparing forged documents. Pireiko thus demonstrated great cunning in evading military service. A good Bolshevik, according to Pireiko, could break the rules and employ every possible stratagem to evade tsarist service, but he could not allow himself to fall into enemy hands. Bunchuk, the fictional officer-turned-revolutionary in *Quiet Flows the Don*, also exhibited this pattern of behavior by deserting and then using forged papers that invalided him out of the army so that he could foment revolution in the rear.[113] These narrations of World War I elided the Soviet project with the tsarist nationalist project in that the model Bolshevik could not capitulate to a foreign power.

While some Soviet World War I accounts suggested that the revolutionary soldier should not allow himself to be captured by the Germans or Austrians, other treatments acknowledged that "unconscious" soldiers might express their spontaneous protest against the tsarist war effort by turning themselves over to the enemy. In his autobiographical novel *Through Captivity* (*Skvoz' plen*), the novice proletarian writer Leonid Katsov brought his own war experience in World War I to life through the thinly fictional character of Mendel, a poor Jewish worker who surrendered to the Austrians.[114] Mendel's desertion was the product of unfortunate circumstances rather than premeditation. While trying to return to his unit, he became lost in the forest and hid in a trench with two others soldiers who had been cut off from their unit by the sudden appearance of Austrian troops. The two soldiers realized that they should warn their unit that the enemy was advancing by shooting their rifles, but they did not have the courage to do so, for fear of being shot by the enemy. As even more Austrians approached, one of the other soldiers suggested surrender. When he saw the indecisiveness of his companions, Mendel took the initiative to save their lives. Mendel said, "We must not delay. . . . We have to get out of the trench," and he threw down his rifle and was first to climb out of the trench. When the Austrians began firing, all three soldiers put their hands in the air and yelled, "*Pan, vash* (Sir, yours)."[115] Neither Mendel nor the other two soldiers were willing to risk their lives on behalf of their comrades, and Mendel did not show regret at leaving his comrades at the front to continue the fight. For the unconscious soldiers, desertion was an individual act to save individual lives.

V. Dmitriev's memoir *Volunteer: Remembrances about War and Captivity* (*Dobrovolets: vospominaniia o voine i plene*), which appeared in 1929, stands in stark contrast to the others in that he narrated his surrender to the enemy as a heroic and revolutionary act, just as Pireiko placed his attempts to evade mobilization within a heroic frame. Although Dmitriev was promoted to lance-corporal and then to platoon commander, he fell afoul of authorities because of his "soft relations" with the soldiers. A scribe warned him that after one more infraction he would be shot as unreliable. He therefore decided to voluntarily give himself over to the enemy, but he did not do it alone. In a way reminiscent of many revolutionary memoirs, Dmitriev recalled the moment when "for the first time in my life I appealed [to my platoon] with a speech." He proclaimed, "We are not fools to wage war without bullets and shells and allow ourselves to be slaughtered. And what is the use, dear brothers, of them killing us like cattle in this war? We don't need the war. What are we fighting for?" One bearded militiaman from Kaluga threw himself at Dmitriev and cried, "Is it possible that I will now live? You see I have six children."[116] The entire platoon decided to surrender; Dmitriev waved a white shirt on the end of his bayonet, attracted the attention of Austrian scouts, and informed them that the platoon wanted to surrender. He recounted, "At first roughly and then in formation, we boldly stepped toward the Austrian trenches."[117]

Dmitriev narrated his actions heroically and within the revolutionary context of "boldly stepping" forward into the future. Like Voitolovskii, he did not abandon the men for whom he was responsible; he took them with him, showing leadership and the value of collective action. The soldiers did abandon the tsarist cause partly out of fear for their own lives, but Dmitriev implied that they would have kept on fighting had the tsarist army supplied them with ammunition, and if it hadn't been threatening him with unjust disciplinary action. Dmitriev and his platoon thus fought injustice by their conscious decision to desert. Dmitriev reversed the polarities of honorable masculine military behavior by aligning cowardice with fighting, and bravery with surrender. Yet, in the rest of the memoir, Dmitriev recounted the hunger and cold that he and his men suffered as prisoners of war and their humiliation at the hands of the civilian population. Dmitriev showed how the soldiers had in fact traded "submissive, weak-willed, obedience" to the tsar for perhaps an even worse submission to their enemies.[118] No "wonders of bravery" could occur in captivity, and the soldiers' masculinity was diminished whether they fought for the tsar or surrendered to the enemy. As helpless victims of the war, they could not develop into heroic and fully masculine warriors until they took their roles on the revolutionary stage.

The memoirists all had great difficulty in framing their actions as heroic. Voitolovskii's work had much in common with that of some Western European officers who shared his anguish over the necessity of doing one's duty even in a senseless war. Voitolovskii's position was made even more complex by his own fear that he was betraying the class that he hoped to champion. Pireiko and Bunchuk displayed cunning in the evasion of their duties, but their actions could be read as models of how to evade Soviet authorities as well as tsarist ones. Mendel was depicted as a possible future hero who displayed weakness in the present because he had yet to realize his revolutionary potential. Dmitriev, who started off as the most "patriotic" of the memoirists, surrendered his platoon to the enemy and caused his companions tremendous misery as prisoners of war. Where, then, was a model for Soviet heroism? Whether they were fearful, submissive, and dominated, or cunning and disrespectful of military authority, or compromised as leaders, the men in the memoirs and novels could not serve as effective models for the New Soviet Man. In the 1930s, censors and editors addressed this problem by eliminating or explaining away any behavior that might seem cowardly. Dmitriev's memoir was never republished; Katsov's editor had to justify his desertion, and Pireiko's narrative was altered to soften the desertion. Soviet censors in 1933 even burnished Melekhov's heroic image by excising a scene in which he showed fear in battle.[119]

All Soviet sources criticized tsarist heroism as false and destructive. While some authors, like Sholokhov, simultaneously demonstrated that heroic rhetoric nonetheless had enduring appeal, others virulently rejected tsarist heroism in its entirety. In doing so, however, the latter authors also revealed masculine weaknesses. The fearful, submissive, alcohol-dependent and captive soldiers they described could not serve as effective models for the New Soviet Man.

Sholokhov's "unconscious" but heroic Melekhov represented a far more appealing masculine ideal than the victimized and miserable soldiers in other Soviet works.

"WAR BETWEEN FRONT AND REAR, BETWEEN MEN AND WOMEN": THE FRONT AND THE REAR AS GENDERED ZONES

The representations of women in the tsarist era made sharp distinctions between the front and the rear and were prone to associating the feminized rear with immorality. The Soviet depiction of women in wartime offered a broader array of images of women. While women continued to be persistently associated with the "rear," they were also represented as the mothers and wives of soldiers, and they were shown working in munitions factories and nursing the wounded. Women were also sometimes depicted as victims of war and in relationships with frontline soldiers.

In *The Fall of the Romanov Dynasty*, Esfir Shub represented war in classically gendered terms.[120] She showed how war tore families apart and depicted women as war's passive victims. In several scenes of the film, the camera lingered on the tearful farewells of women who escorted their men to induction points. Women also wept amidst the destruction of war. While men carried the burden of fighting, women suffered the emotional and physical losses of war. Women also appeared in the film as nurses and wives supporting wounded soldiers and husbands and caring for their needs. Shub depicted the homecoming of soldiers as enormously joyful and included a striking image of a young wife sitting next to her wounded husband's bed and smiling radiantly at their reunion.

In addition to reflecting women's traditional roles, Shub also documented the changes in women's lives during wartime. The film showed women hard at work in munitions factories, explaining that the government replaced the mobilized men with women workers. This formulation indicated that it was the government that determined the fate of the women rather than the women themselves. This image of women working was followed by a caption that announced that the country was being ruined and the population was suffering from shortages. Women's work during the war was not represented as heroic or liberating in any way, yet women retained a positive moral valence in Shub's depictions of them.

A more enthusiastic appraisal of women's participation in the war effort came from Brusilov, who acknowledged in his memoirs "the unremitting, devoted and heroic services rendered by the enormous majority of them [nurses], who would not allow enemy bombs to distract them from their painful and exhausting duties as they bent over our blood-stained, suffering soldiers. How many of them, too, were wounded or killed!" Yet Brusilov offered this praise to contradict the "dirty-minded tittle-tattle [*navetov i griaznykh rasskazov*]" that was circulating about the nurses.[121] Brusilov's protest acknowledged a persistent association between nurses and sexual misconduct in both the front and rear. He fought to defend the "enormous majority" of women who engaged in self-less and heroic behavior in the primarily masculine and heroic sphere of the front. Attacks on the sexual morality of these women diminished the celebration of their achievements.[122]

Many other Soviet analysts were far less charitable toward women's wartime activities. In his writings about the French home front, Il'ia Erenburg highlighted the tensions developing between men and women because of increased economic opportunities for women workers during the war. Because of their high-paying factory jobs, new public spaces such as cafés, cinemas, and casinos became accessible for women. Women in factory towns could afford to purchase fashionable clothing and perfumes. Erenburg depicted the new independence of French women as leading to women's alcoholism, their participation in casual sex with foreign guest workers, and the spreading of syphilis from town to countryside. He uncharitably described the women's fears about what would happen when the war was over and "they" (their husbands) came home. Like Aleksei Tolstoi, Erenburg envisioned the rear as a place of women's hedonism and vice.

Erenburg's discussion of women's behavior also considered the soldiers' point of view. When the husbands returned home on leave, they were dissatisfied with what they saw: "We are dying like animals in the trenches and you are enjoying yourselves." The men imagined chasing women out of the workforce and back into their traditional roles at war's end. Erenburg concluded: "The war gave birth to a war between front and rear, between men and women."[123] Although Erenburg was not describing Russian society, he nonetheless reinforced a gendered interpretation of the conflict between front and rear, and he articulated male resentment of women's perceived freedoms during wartime that resonated with the experience of at least some Russian men. As in much other Russian discourse, the rear was associated with vice and disease. Implicit in Erenburg's view was the notion that the frolicking wives wronged the long-suffering soldiers. Erenburg hinted that because of men's suffering in wartime, they deserved to return to a dominant role in postwar society.

Other Soviet-era memoirists were particularly keen on exposing what they saw as the immorality of the rear, and they did so in explicitly gendered terms. Voitolovskii believed that in the rear, "falsehood—official and newspaper, took possession of all minds and actions." The result, in Voitolovskii's opinion, was prostitution. "The rear becomes the purveyor and nursery of unprecedented mass prostitution."[124] Voitolovskii then conflated this metaphorical prostitution with the actual kind. He described a lurid scene of soldiers in the rear cavorting with local peasant women. When he asked a soldier whether he minded that he would be neither the first nor last soldier to have sexual relations with a particular woman, the soldier replied, "A *baba* is not soap; she doesn't get used up."[125] To Voitolovskii, war was a site of universal corruption— violence at the front and lies and licentiousness in the rear. His use of prostitution as a metaphor implied that revolution, as a purifying force, would have to cleanse both political falsehood and the morals of loose men and women.

When Os'kin was sent to recuperate from a serious leg wound in a Moscow hospital, he received excellent care in a private infirmary. It was when his leg had healed enough for him to return to the "recovering detachment" that he encountered the pernicious influence of loose women in the rear. Os'kin discovered to his horror that most of the other soldiers in the detachment were recovering not from war wounds but from gonorrhea. Os'kin recounted how these soldiers, safely stationed in the rear because of their own immoral behavior while other men fought and died, organized orgies with local gonorrhea-infected prostitutes. An acquaintance of Os'kin's even offered to help him stay in Moscow by introducing him to "a particular [person], so that you will land straight in our company."[126] Os'kin noted that after the venereal company was sent to the front to dig trenches, there remained "a multitude of 'widowed' girls of easy virtue" around the barracks. Despite Os'kin's warnings to his men, some of the healthy soldiers became infected within a couple of weeks. In Os'kin's writing, venereal disease was the main metaphor with which he described the rear. Some soldiers willingly infected themselves to remain in the rear, while others were seduced by the easy availability of rearguard temptresses. Tsarist society was a source of infection and corruption, and the reserve soldiers were morally and physically weaker and less manly than their counterparts at the front. Both tsarist-era and Soviet-era texts envisioned the rear as a site of immorality and diminished masculinity. Interestingly, while Soviet texts consistently associated sexuality and pollution with the females in the rear, censors grew uncomfortable with expressions of soldiers' sexual prowess. Anecdotes in Fedorchenko's *The People at War* that dealt with lusty or violently jealous soldiers were systematically omitted after 1923.[127]

CLASS AND MASCULINITY

One of the prevalent Western European myths of World War I was that in the crucible of war, class difference between officers and soldiers disappeared and all warriors embraced common notions of duty and a common vision of brotherhood. One paradigmatic example is from Ernst Jünger's *Storm of Steel*. Jünger recalled, from his perspective as a young lieutenant, how the conditions of battle could and did create camaraderie across class lines. He spoke about how, in a lonely trench, an officer could talk to an NCO "like a brother." In another scene, alcohol cemented the army's cross-class camaraderie as an officer "circulated a bottle of 98% without distinctions of rank."[128] *Storm of Steel,* the mirror image of standard Soviet memoirs, was conspicuously silent about the tensions between officers and those of lower rank.

Soviet memoirs, on the other hand, repeatedly called this possibility of cross-rank solidarity and common masculinity into question. Because the Russian Revolution of 1917 pitted soldiers across the Russian Empire against their officers, the injustices and brutality that the Russian soldiers experienced at the hands of their officers during World War I was a crucial leitmotiv in Soviet memory of World War I. The war itself was often reduced to a backdrop against which the class struggle between the soldiers and the officers was played out. Soviet authors reinterpreted the brutal training that soldiers received to desensitize them to violence and make them ready to kill the enemy as evidence of the abuse of the lower classes by the upper classes.[129] While it is clear that the image of the cruel officer and the abused soldier appeared very frequently in Soviet depictions of the war, it would be a mistake to suggest that all officer-soldier interactions followed this one trope. We will first examine the contest for masculinity between officers and soldiers and then explore the possibilities for camaraderie.

Soviet depictions of the tsarist army emphasized that upper-class participants in the war effort were less than real men. In *The Fall of the Romanov Dynasty*, Shub directly attacked the masculinity of the tsarist troops by employing images of gymnasium students being drilled in military exercises. The film footage showed these young bourgeois men marching in formation; the caption demeaned them as "toy soldiers," who lacked the manliness to win the war. Shub also depicted the vast divide between tsarist soldiers and officers by juxtaposing two scenes recording daily life on a tsarist naval vessel. First she showed sailors in spotless white uniforms cleaning the deck without being allowed to kneel on it. They swabbed the deck while squatting, moving forward with an awkward swaying motion. This image of men prevented from rising to their full height visually encoded the humiliation of the sailors by their officers. The scene immediately shifted to the wardroom where the officers ate an elaborate dinner on fine china and played leisurely with a small lap dog. This juxtaposition was a commentary both on class and on masculinity. Temporarily, the effete officers were able to force the sailors into a subordinate and servile masculinity, but the officers' own indolence and fondness for luxury compromised their ability to lead and to fight. Shub contrasted the officers' inactivity and softness to the vigorous physical activity of the humiliated sailors. It is clear who would be victorious when the sailors rose up to their full height.

Six years later, Leonid Sobolev's novel *The Big Refit* similarly depicted the compromised masculinity of naval officers, emphasizing both the mutiny of rank-and-file sailors and the navy's ineffectual preparation for the coming of World War I. After Austria delivered its ultimatum to Serbia on July 23, 1914, the *Generalissimo Count Suvorov-Rymnikskii,* a ship that was "obsolete before her launching," underwent its "big refit." It was discovered that the masts, two "huge trellised towers of steel tubes" as tall as the "Alexandrine Column," were useless in directing fire power but might give away the ship's position to German gunners, and, if shot down, crush their own men. The commander-in-chief ordered them to be taken down, and Lieutenant Levitin, one of the book's central characters, organized the shearing off of the masts with an acetylene torch.[130] To prepare for the coming war, the crew symbolically emasculated the ship and metaphorically tore down a tsarist monument; tsarist naval efforts were as feeble as tsarist officers with their "white, delicate bodies."[131]

The Soviet-era memoirs of both Voitolovskii and Os'kin repeatedly denied the possibility of cross-rank solidarity. Os'kin's memoir is punctuated throughout with scathing attacks on cowardly, abusive, and drunken officers who hid in trenches while ordering soldiers into battle, punished soldiers arbitrarily, and did not share the dangers and discomforts of war with their men.[132] Voitolovskii recounted how he had to eavesdrop on the soldiers in order to hear what they really thought about the war because they would not express themselves freely in front of an officer.[133] He lamented that "the soldier strides with great steps by our side, he does everything that is ordered, he is obliging, he is quick, but in his eyes there is not the tiniest spark of brotherly sympathy."[134] These authors suggested that on the Eastern Front, male camaraderie could not transcend class divisions. Like many other members of the radical intelligentsia, Voitolovskii recorded the distance between himself and the soldiers with regret. His memoir provides little evidence of common ground for masculine or heroic ideals. The scene in which Voitolovskii prevented his batman from deserting shows Voitolovskii's awareness of the ambiguities of his position.

While much of *Quiet Flows the Don* can be understood as developing the theme of class struggle, Sholokhov's depiction of World War I is particularly striking because of the evenhandedness with which he presented the relationships between officers and soldiers.[135] Of course there are episodes showing the callousness of officers, the "criminal negligence of the high command," and the "insurmountable wall" separating the officers from the soldiers,[136] but there are other episodes that demonstrate the officers' responsiveness to their men and the men's dedication to the officers.[137]

The actions of Melekhov provided a distinct variation on the trope of war as a contest between soldiers and officers, since he gained military honor by saving an officer; this officer was not cruel, even urging Melekhov to leave him to die so that Melekhov could save himself. Pince-nez and all, this officer both maintained authority and showed compassion to a common soldier, living up to tsarist ideals of the father-officer. This relationship that Sholokhov created between Melekhov and the wounded officer demonstrated that military loyalties and male bonds could cross class boundaries, creating camaraderie that facilitated military endeavors.

Sholokhov's novel also depicted several other officers who had sympathy for their men and protected them. In an episode reminiscent of the famous mutiny on the battleship *Potemkin,* the soldiers in Melekhov's unit protested when they were fed rotting meat: "Puffy white maggots lay limply beside a blood-red lump of meat amid the greasy blobs of fat on the floor."[138] The outcome, however, of this incident was quite different from the *Potemkin* mutiny. When the soldiers symbolically "arrest[ed] the soup" and marched it to the squadron commander, he was immediately responsive to them, asking "What's the matter, lads?" After "the uproar had died down, [he] then said sharply, 'Quiet there! Silence! That's enough. The quartermaster will be changed today. I shall appoint a commission to investigate his activities.'"[139] Like the lieutenant in *All Quiet on the Western Front* who overruled the cook and allowed the soldiers to have their dead comrades' rations, this squadron commander immediately acceded to his soldiers' demands to protect them from corrupt army officials.[140] Furthermore, the soldiers trusted him enough to bring him their complaint and to raise objections about how they were being treated. The officer's use of the word "lads" suggested his paternal relationship to them. In this scene, hierarchical relations were modeled on family relations and built on mutual trust.

Another event that took place shortly after the rotten meat episode further demonstrated the compassion of officers in Melekhov's unit. The Cossack Uriupin, a violent and pitiless man, was caught pillaging barley from a Romanian village by the troop officer. When the troop officer demanded that he return the grain, he yelled, "Court-martial me! Shoot me! Kill me on the spot! But I won't give you the barley! Why should my horse starve to death?" The officer "stood staring silently at the animal's horribly jutting ribs, then nodded and said, 'Why are you feeding a hot horse?' There was a note of embarrassment in his voice."[141] Because the officer recognized that Uriupin's insubordination was justified, he allowed him to break the rules and did not punish him for his disobedience or his insolence. The officer respected Uriupin's outspokenness for a just cause. Sholokhov's depictions of the interactions of World War I officers and soldiers demonstrated that good relations were possible if not always likely. The memory of World War I that he created did not reduce the war to a titanic class struggle.

While literary critics have often pointed out that *Quiet Flows the Don* treated Cossacks of all classes objectively during the Civil War, they have devoted less attention to the depiction of class during World War I. Here Sholokhov's contribution to the memory of World War I is significant, because he constructed a narrative that preserved and disseminated key elements of the tsarist and European mythology of the war, including definitions of heroism and masculinity and the acknowledgment of male camaraderie across ranks. Sholokhov's World War I demonstrated that strong male bonds could and sometimes did cross class boundaries. Yet, the wartime bonds of affection between men of any class in Sholokhov's work do not possess the same lyrical quality that Remarque's descriptions of Paul and his mates do. For Sholokhov, literal and figurative familial relationships remained crucial. Melekhov, for instance, could only confess his guilt about killing to his brother. The generational conflict caused by war, a major theme in Remarque's work, played out quite differently in *Quiet Flows the Don*. Melekhov's service in the military actually helped him to heal the breach with his father caused when he abandoned his wife to live with another woman. Military hierarchies and masculine relationships remained couched in a patriarchal discourse.[142]

The notion of the benevolent World War I father-commander persisted in Soviet discourse well into the 1930s. In 1934, the journal *Krasnyi arkhiv* published excerpts from soldiers' letters that had been recorded by the military censors in their systematized surveys of soldiers' opinions. The editor selected letters that illustrated the common Soviet theme of the strained relations between officers and soldiers. In one letter, a soldier from the Smolensk infantry reserve battalion complained bitterly about the "really evil person, sick and short-tempered" who was the assistant commander of his detachment. In contrast, he praised the detachment commander: "He is a soul-person. He will tell you everything. You can go to him for any kind of advice at any time. He is like one's own father [*rodnoi otets*] and he loves everyone as if they were his children."[143] The letter revealed that the sadistic officer, ever ready to "knock the soldier in the teeth," was not the only model of leadership that existed in the tsarist army. The traditional ideal of the father-commander could be discerned even among documents that were selected to highlight the mistreatment of the soldiers in the tsarist army.

Another letter, written by an officer in the 410th Usmanskii Regiment, revealed his despair about the "ruling conviction that only fear of the authorities can move the soldiers." Because this officer felt differently, he reported "terrible loneliness, especially when I see the sidelong glances and hints all around that an officer with humane views is superfluous."[144] This ostracized officer simultaneous proved the mistreatment of the soldiers and the existence of "humane" officers who sought to construct relationships with their men that were not based on fear. It must be noted, however, that even the most sympathetic depictions of officer-soldier relations in the Russian and Soviet case did not measure up to the European myths of male fraternity. Russian and Soviet depictions of wartime brotherhood in World War I were attenuated and fragile, and positive depictions of officer-soldier relations tended to emphasize paternalism.

WAR AS MAIMING RUSSIAN MASCULINITY

Both Aaron Cohen and Catherine Merridale have suggested that the memory of World War I in the Soviet press and Soviet society tended to ignore the trauma and suffering of individuals either by focusing on the collective or by casting the war as an abstract "European" and "imperialist" endeavor.[145]

Yet a variety of sources published in the 1920s provide a radical alternative to this vision. Instead of hypermasculine heroism à la Kriuchkov, Voitolovskii described the piteous sight of wounded Russian soldiers who had been unloaded onto the bare cement floor of the railway platform: "They collapsed, tossed about, and shouted out incomprehensible words. Their teeth chattered spasmodically. Their eyes were exhausted, their faces were ash-gray. . . ."[146] As Voitolovskii and the other medics dressed their wounds, "they cursed us, shoved us, and begged in a plaintive voice. . . . Helpless fingers slid over our faces, snatched at our coats, tried to grasp our necks. And the quantity of gray overcoats and moaning throats did not lessen."[147] Voitolovskii's vivid prose revealed the costs that Russian manhood paid for the imperialist war. The Russian men on the railway platform were no longer in control of their own bodies. Their actions were helpless, and they were reduced to begging. Worse yet, they were transformed from individuals into a never-ending line of gray overcoats and groaning mouths. In Voitolovskii's memoir, war was not a place to prove one's masculinity; rather, war caused the destruction of masculinity and selfhood.

One of the preoccupations of European war literature was the question of what the people "in the rear" owed to the soldiers who had sacrificed their lives, bodies, and health to the war. Wilfred Owen's poem "Disabled" dealt with the plight of a young man who was "legless, sewn short at elbow," totally dependent on others for his care. He had joined up in part to please a woman, a "giddy jilts" who had now abandoned him. Old before his time, having thrown "away his knees," the disabled man "noticed how the women's eyes / Passed from him to the strong men that were whole."[148] The anguish of the soldier revealed a gendered resentment against the woman who had encouraged him to become a soldier to enhance his manly status and then rejected him when the war robbed him of any hope of performing a normative masculine role in society.

This resentment was played out in a dramatically different way in at least one Soviet-era war diary, that of Dmitrii Furmanov, the author of the famous Soviet novel *Chapaev*. Furmanov worked during the war as a medic (*brat miloserdiia*) in the Union of Zemstva medical services. His diary was published posthumously in 1929 in only one edition; it was likely not reprinted because it was far too candid and because it spotlighted the bourgeois class identity that preceded Furmanov's radical transformation into a disciplined Soviet commissar. Furmanov described a scene that took place at the Kursk railway station in Moscow in January 1916. Three soldiers who had been awarded

St. George crosses were brought in and propped against the railway station wall. The soldiers "had neither arms nor legs,—their legs were amputated all the way to the groin, and their arms at the shoulder." When their three wives recognized them, the women did not embrace them and refused to take them home, even after they were offered three hundred rubles a year to care for the invalids. The wives answered: "We don't need a thousand rubles. . . . We are better off working ourselves day and night. We don't need your money or the cripples." The unfortunate men sobbed and were taken to the workhouse.[149]

Furmanov recorded the disapproving reaction of the grumbling crowd. Given that these women were violating traditional expectations of their roles as caregivers, one might imagine that Furmanov would also be critical of their actions. However, he defended the women, because if they took their husbands home, their lives would have been "forcibly cut short"; he appreciated their honesty about their "inability to sacrifice themselves to their crippled husbands." Furmanov celebrated the actions of a mother who embraced and cared for her crippled son with "tender solicitude," but did not condemn these wives for abandoning their husbands to whom they were tied only by "official marriage" and not by love. Instead, Furmanov blamed the doctors who should have allowed such men to die on the battlefield rather than trying to save them.[150] Furmanov's diary revealed several bitter truths about war. Some of the returning soldiers were no longer men but "cripples," unable to do anything but lean against the wall, sob, and be dependent on others. Not only were they themselves mutilated and useless to society, but their injuries stole the "strength, hopes, and wishes" of the wives and mothers forced to care for them. The tragedy of war did not stop when the battle had ended, but destroyed the futures of the wounded and of their families.[151] Furmanov's horrifying conclusion at the time was that doctors on the battlefield should have honored the soldiers' dignity and saved the women's lives by practicing euthanasia rather than medicine.

Although Kirill Levin had enlisted in the tsarist army voluntarily, he wrote *Notes From Captivity* in the late 1920s as an ardent revolutionary whose story substantially conformed to official Soviet narratives; he rejected the war as imperialist, emphasized the common plight of the multiethnic prisoners of war and the ordinary soldiers guarding them, identified certain Russian prisoners as "class enemies," and attacked religion vigorously. Because Levin illuminated class struggle and his memoir ended with his escape over the Russian border to fight for the revolution, some Soviet critics in the early 1930s celebrated it as an antidote to the pessimism and the pacifism of Remarque's

All Quiet on the Western Front.[152] Soviet narratives did not end in the stasis of captivity; their heroes all escaped to fight once again for the revolutionary cause.

Yet Levin's tale took place in a "bourgeois" and "imperialist" prisoner of war camp; therefore his account also lingered on the tragic victims of war, their individual sufferings, and how war, disease, and death ravaged their bodies and minds. His widely read memoir offered its readers perhaps the most gruesome and disturbing images of wartime suffering available in Soviet discourse. While the memoir's overall narrative may not have been pacifist, the unvarnished details of soldiers' agony focused readers' attention on the horrifying effects of war on men's bodies.

One scene in the memoir recounted in excruciating detail the transformation of a bearlike bogatyr' of a man into a "living corpse" due to smallpox. Pieces of the patient's body fell off when his attendant tried to change bandages, and pus dripped onto the floor, "forming a four-cornered frame of pus in the shape of the bed." The narration of the bogatyr' stoically enduring "the most terrifying death imaginable" took the reader vicariously through the horror of the complete disintegration of a living human body.[153] While Levin acknowledged the stoic heroism and endurance of the bogatyr' and linked him to Russian epic heroism, he lingered on the details of how disease and death had overpowered this particular hero. Levin did not link the tragic and gruesome death of the hero to any higher cause.

The fate of the body after death was another theme of Levin's memoir (figure 3.7). When the widow of a Hungarian soldier came to the POW camp to exhume his body and bring it home, she witnessed the horrible effects of death on the human body.[154] After smelling "the unbearable stench," the wife saw that "a moustache still proudly stuck out from the black unraveling face of the lance-corporal. Shreds of hair from his head along with skin collapsed on his forehead and in the ruin of his nose small maggots the size of grains of rice thickly swarmed." When they tried to pick up the body, it crumbled in their hands.[155] Nothing remained of the soldier's proud manhood except his moustache. In both of these cases, Levin documented that the cost of war was the annihilation of manhood and the manly body. Heroism and stoicism could not halt the disintegration of war, death, and disease.

Levin's memoir also detailed the impact of war on the minds of the soldiers. While an early Soviet study of Russian prisoners of war had suggested that captivity itself produced a mental illness that the Germans called "barbed-wire psychosis," Levin focused primarily on those who had lost their reason

FIGURE 3.7. Cemetery in POW camp in Austria. Personal collection of Kirill Levin, Russian State Archive of Literature and Art.

due to the violence of war itself.[156] One notable section of the memoir (thirteen pages or about five percent of the text) was devoted to the discussion of "patients whom the war punished with particular cruelty: the epileptics, idiots, and lunatics." Levin explained that "the shocks they experienced destroyed their brain. They were no longer fully valued people, and an unhappy future awaited them."[157] In these pages Levin sympathetically recounted the individual cases of the various shell-shock victims living in the camp hospital and explained how these men had come to be ill.

In the late imperial period, some psychologists linked the phenomenon of shell shock to individual weakness and vice, because "it menaced a cherished national myth about heroism."[158] Russian (and later Soviet) psychologists and psychiatrists sought physiological reasons for war trauma such as physical damage to the central nervous system; many were reluctant to acknowledge its psychological origins. The army censored the few psychiatrists who sought to make the link between psychological trauma and shell shock during World War I, though there were some psychiatrists who readily acknowledged the ability of war to "induce fear in normal men."[159] There was continuity between Levin's depiction of insanity and the late-tsarist notion that shell shock was a "normal" phenomenon. Levin made it explicit that it was the War itself that had destroyed men who were not particularly weak and were in no way to blame for their sad predicaments. Rather than emphasizing "survival and endurance," he focused on the individual suffering of the mentally ill. Levin showed that just as bullets could destroy a soldier's body, so could the trauma of war destroy his mind. The shell-shocked men simply could not endure the horrors that they experienced as a result of war and went mad. They were even more victimized by the war than those with physical injuries.

Levin explained that there were several dozen shell-shocked men who passed through the camp, but that most were moved to a special hospital. Only those who were not considered dangerous were allowed to stay in the POW camp. He described eight men and explained in detail how five of them had lost their sanity. Perhaps the most chilling tale was that of Armiakov, a scout who went out of his mind after falling into a pit filled with Austrian corpses. No matter how hard he tried, he could not climb out of the pit and remained there all night. "What he experienced that night was too much for him." When they pulled him out, he had "a flaccid face, a mouth somehow strangely slanting to the side, and white eyes."[160] His officer noted that he refused to carry a rifle and that he had human flesh, skin, and hair on his clothes. When questioned, he bleakly told the officer that "devils caught him and forced him to eat human flesh all night, and human flesh tastes like buckwheat porridge gone sour." This soldier then refused to take cover in battle and waited at the barbed wire barrier with his head in his hands until the Austrians took him captive. Armiakov's abrupt loss of sanity turned him temporarily into a flesh-eating monster. This horrifying experience of being trapped with the very men that his Russian comrades-in-arms had killed may have led him to cannibalism, but it also made him refuse to fight any longer. His response to the horror of death was to stop killing. Armiakov would no longer do his soldierly duty and increase the number of enemy corpses by his own actions.

Levin also described the plight of a Russian prisoner of war named Goldberg, a Jewish lawyer from Borisov who was an inmate of the mental ward, suffering from shell shock. Goldberg did not become unhinged during the military struggle against the Austrians or Germans. Instead, he lost touch with reality after witnessing a pogrom by the advancing Cossacks on a poor Galician town. Levin highlighted the "reprehensibly violent" side of the Cossacks as they terrorized innocent women and children in the occupied territory; they were about to rape a Jewish woman in front of her children. The Jewish soldier Goldberg tried to protect the woman, and for his efforts the Cossacks "brutally beat him and then mockingly put him half-dead on top of the woman, with the intention of forcing him to rape her." This episode proved too much for him to bear, and he went out of his mind. When they took him out of the room, he believed that he stood before "a severe and just court and that he should expound on the grave crime that he had witnessed."[161] Nicknamed "the orator" by the other inmates in the POW camp, he constantly gave speeches protesting the trampling of human rights. The only way to stop him was to bang a spoon on a glass and announce, "Orator, your time has run out." Levin presented the shell-shocked men sympathetically, as victims of the brutality of war. Within their insanity, the shell-shocked men were free to criticize war by refusing to take part in it and by detailing its injustices. In an ironic twist, some of the shell-shocked exhibited more sanity than those of sound mind.

Goldberg's fate also demonstrates the complex nature of masculinity in wartime. His story contrasts two opposing types of masculinity, each of them flawed. The violent soldier fought bravely and heroically in battle but had no scruples whatsoever about enacting ethnic and sexual violence on helpless women and children; the moral soldier was imbued with notions of human rights and chivalry but was too weak in body and mind to stop violence against civilians. Each wartime encounter, and the war itself, was a contest for masculinity in which our sympathies do not always lie with the victor. Class, ethnicity, and gender were all intertwined in this battle in which the Jewish intellectual was left to fight a fruitless war of words against the physically superior Cossack common soldier. The memory of World War I in the interwar period offers rare insight into the construction of dominant forms of masculinity—the uncontrolled violence inherent in the masculine ideal and the many ways that war could destroy this ideal.

WOUNDED VETERANS

Alongside the discursive reminders of the trauma of war provided by memoirs like Levin's, the living veterans of both World War I and the Civil War also constituted an important part of Soviet interwar remembrance. While powerful civic organizations such as the British Legion and the *Union Nationale des Combattants* developed in many European countries to fight for veterans' rights, the nascent veterans' associations of Soviet World War I and Civil War combatants had negligible strength and longevity due to the lack of official government patronage and Soviet controls on the public sphere.[162] But issues such as veterans' pensions produced popular discontent nonetheless. In 1925, secret police informers recorded the following antigovernment outburst by peasant Filipp Panchuk at an election rally:

You ought to know that the peasants curse you usurpers in their morning prayers. . . . You are stealing our last cow, our last meager belongings. You won't pay the peasant invalid who lost a leg defending your revolution even a ruble, but you've found 300 a month for the tsarist general Brusilov. Where is truth? Where is justice? Why did you fool us with words such as freedom, land, peace, and equality? Now we understand that Kerenskii's government was better for us.[163]

Historian David Brandenberger cited the peasant's bitter diatribe against the state to show that there was "a lack of allegiance to the Soviet cause among the peasantry." This speech shows much more, however, than simply peasant discontent. Panchuk's protest reveals the contradictory actions of a militarizing but impoverished Soviet government that heroized Brusilov to emphasize continuities between tsarist military successes and the prowess of the Red Army. Brusilov's military expertise and his association with national honor trumped his class identity in the allocation of scarce resources, especially since he had voluntarily joined the Red Army in 1920. Panchuk openly criticized this state policy of promoting tsarist-era national glory at the expense of disabled Civil War veterans.

The honor and monetary benefits given to Brusilov contrasted sharply with the neglect of other invalid veterans from both World War I and the Civil War. The disabled from both conflicts were entitled to receive pensions if they met state and local requirements of being "needy."[164] Due to the severe economic crises of the Soviet state in the 1920s, however, the central government could not afford to provide relief for perhaps over two million mentally and physically disabled veterans from both wars.[165] Although both the number of war invalids eligible for pensions and the size of the pensions increased steadily throughout the 1920s and 1930s to almost 200,000 pensioners in 1939, only a small fraction of war invalids received pensions or placement in invalid homes and work cooperatives. The rest, including those with "psychological disorders" and "severe nerve trauma," were left by and large to fend for themselves or to draw on traditional sources of support in the family and peasant commune. In the late 1920s, official war invalid aid committees at the regional and district levels even organized a voluntary society, Friend of the Invalid, to help fill the void left by insufficient state funds.[166]

The Soviet state's failure to live up to its obligations to soldiers did not escape the notice of the military. As the commander of the Moscow garrison and the Moscow military district wrote in a secret report to the Central Committee: "The position of disabled persons cannot but affect the morale of the Red Army. Invalids appearing on crutches without hands, legs, starving and ill-clad as a result of being denied legal aid produces a painful impression and comprises a significant agitator against Soviet power."[167] Although officials were concerned that inadequate aid to war invalids would threaten current Red Army morale, the majority, if not the vast majority, of disabled veterans were nonetheless denied compensation.

The millions of emasculated veterans suffering from physical wounds and psychological trauma were painful evidence of aspects of war that the Red Army would rather forget, but the Soviet state did not have the resources to keep these human reminders of war off the streets. The interests of veterans would continually be sacrificed in the name of building up the tactical strength of the current Soviet military. Yet as Filipp Panchuk's outburst and the secret report of the commander of the Moscow garrison show, the choices of the Soviet leadership had negative consequences, producing both general discontent and the potential to stir up demoralizing memories of both World War I and the Civil War that were embodied by the neglected veterans. The Soviet project of constructing military pride and national loyalty in the 1920s was a work in progress that required constant reinforcement by selected remembrance of certain aspects of war and a planned forgetfulness of others. The economic neglect of invalid veterans, may, paradoxically, have made them more visible.

Wounded or psychologically traumatized veterans were thus commonly encountered in the social landscape of the Soviet Union in the 1920s as the living embodiment of war memory and a powerful and daily reminder of the costs of war. While disabled veterans may have been physically present in villages and cities, their plight was not often the subject of public discussion. Soviet publications, while generally silent about the difficulties facing their own disabled veterans, criticized the treatment of returning veterans in "imperialist" countries. In V. Lidin's *The Grave of the Unknown Soldier* a Swiss World War I veteran who lost an arm fighting for France declares in despair, "France doesn't need invalids."[168] Thus the idea of the mistreated World War I veteran entered Soviet discourse.

Isaak Babel''s 1935 play *Mariia* was an exception to the trend of silence about disabled veterans in the Soviet Union. The fate of the play indicates both the continuation of antiheroic tropes into the mid-1930s and their curtailment. In 1935, the play was published both in the journal *Teatr i dramaturgiia* (Theater and Dramaturgy) and in book form by the State Literature Publishing House and was therefore accessible to the reading public, at least until Babel''s arrest in 1939. Although *Mariia* was chosen for the repertoire at the celebrated Vakhtangov Theater, it was banned while still in rehearsals and never opened. A. M. Gorkii's private reaction to Babel' provides insight into the play's fate: Gorkii complained about Babel''s "Baudelairean predilection for rotting meat." He told Babel', "All the characters in your play, starting from the invalids, are putrid."[169]

The play, set during the Civil War, opens with a conversation among three disabled World War I veterans turned smugglers and the organizer of their smuggling ring. Babel' highlights the double tragedy of these soldiers; because their health and livelihoods were stolen from them in an "imperialist" war not embraced by the revolutionary authorities, they have no place in the construction of the new society, and must resort to shadowy criminal activities. The three veterans personify the lasting physical effects of World War I on Russia's soldiers. Evstignevich is "a stout man with a large red face" who "has had both legs amputated above the knee." Bishonkov has "an empty, pinned-up sleeve." Half of Filip's face "is scarred with burned flesh." Although other Soviet works described the fate of World War I invalids, Babel' pushed the issue a step further by giving the legless invalid Evstignevich a voice with which to describe his own plight and that of the other disabled veterans.

The stage directions describe two of the veterans (Evstignevich and Bishonkov) as "wearing medals and a St. George Cross on their chests." This detail reveals the paradox of the wounded soldiers. The medals attest to the soldiers' personal valor, bravery, and achievements on the battlefield, but because they were earned fighting for the tsar, they also raised the possibility of the men's disloyalty to the new Soviet state. Despite the fall of the autocracy, Evstignevich and Bishonkov continue to wear their medals, perhaps to raise their current status, since valor on the battlefield was prized both before and after the revolution, even if fighting for the tsar was not. To survive, the invalids have turned to smuggling food and vodka, with the hope that their disfigurements will inhibit the Soviet guards from searching them as they travel to Petrograd. Their previous honors—military medals and St. George crosses—have become a part of their "disguise" as disabled veterans, ruses they use to evade Soviet authorities. This process degraded both the disabled veterans and their medals.

As the Civil War goes on, however, the invalids discover that the Soviet authorities are increasingly likely to search them, in spite of their evident disabilities. In an encounter with Soviet authorities it becomes clear that the invalid Filip, a noticeably "big, strong man" with a disfigured face, also suffers from invisible psychological wounds. When the smugglers encounter gunfire at a train station, Filip falls apart. Evstignevich suggests that they should move to a different checkpoint to evade authorities, but Filip confesses, "I'm afraid to go." Evstignevich tells him: "Vodka smuggling is no big deal, you'll just get a kick in the pants, so what are you worried about?" But Filip collapses from the strain; "he was already lying there flat on his belly." Evstignevich complains that "he's got no guts, his insides are weak."[170] The shell-shocked Filip manifests both the mental and physical wounds of war, showing that some of the devastating effects of warfare could be invisible to witnesses. Demonstrating a distinct lack of camaraderie, Evstignevich and Bishonkov abandon Filip, who is captured and tortured.

The veterans complain about how the revolution has worsened their plight. Bishonkov says, "Before the Revolution you could live quite well as a crippled veteran, but now. . . ." Evstignevich continues, "Now you can forget it—it's all about education! In the past, soldiers got a hell of a lot of respect—now it's zilch." He recounts how a Soviet guard threw him off of a train. Evstignevich explains to the guard that "a shell blew both my legs off," and the fellow replies, "What's so special about that? . . . Your legs got blown off right away without no suffering. You didn't have no suffering. . . . you were chloroformed when they took your legs off, you didn't feel nothing. It's just that you can't come to grip with your toes—your toes kind of act up, itch, even though they've been chopped off, that's the only problem." The guard then announces, "We're throwing you off [the train] because goddamn Russia's sick and tired of all the cripples!"[171] Babel' depicts the new "educated" Soviet man as utterly lacking in compassion and completely inured to the suffering of others. Tired of witnessing the tragedy of war, the New Soviet Man callously pushes the cripple out of sight.

The Bolshevik's desire to remove the cripple from his sight rather than assist him revealed one of the tragic realities of the early Soviet period. The disabled World War I veterans continued to confront the ironies of having sacrificed their health and vitality for a state that no longer existed, and they continued to struggle to obtain the respect that they felt they deserved. And Civil War invalids were not much better off.[172] As late as 1935, the play called attention to the ways in which war destroyed the masculinity of soldiers, robbing them of arms and legs, disfiguring them, and causing them unseen trauma. Worse yet, these soldier-invalids had additional wounds inflicted on them by Soviet society when they were cast aside instead of respected for their earlier sacrifices. Babel' depicts ordinary men in tragic circumstances who find no relief for their suffering in the Soviet social order.

Of course, the play *Mariia* is fundamentally a tale of the Civil War era. The title character, a Bolshevik soldier, is often discussed by the other characters of the play, but she herself never appears, an action that highlights the separation from loved ones that war produces. Mariia is so dedicated to the Bolshevik cause, and perhaps to her Bolshevik lover, that she abandons her aristocratic family to its fate while she fights at the front. When her father sends her a telegram to return home because he needs her, she sends him word that she is in battle, and supplies him with a sack of boots. A family friend then asks the soldier to convey to Mariia that her father is dying and her sister has been arrested, adding, "Tell Maria Nikolayevna that we wish her all the best, and that she mustn't feel remorse about not being here with us in our hour of need."[173] Mariia has abandoned her family, just as the state has abandoned the wounded veterans. Babel"s account of the wounds, the displacement, and the sorrow of war is all the more striking because it emerged in 1935 and was contemporaneous with a number of artistic works that began to sanitize and valorize warfare.

The horrors of World War I and its human costs were also part of the spectrum of Soviet memory of the war. While the Soviet press may have represented World War I as an abstraction, Soviet memoirs like Levin's personalized the war and showed its devastating effects on the bodies and minds of the Russian soldiers. While the dominant discourse about war in the 1920s and 1930s may have emphasized endurance, sacrifice on behalf of the Soviet Union, and an unproblematic heroism, a counter-discourse about the war as a disfiguring and dehumanizing experience also emerged. Memoirs and literature presented the idea that war was a mutilating event that robbed soldiers of their manhood and of their identities. The focus on the human costs of war made little distinction between the suffering that took place in an illegitimate "imperialist" war and the trauma of a just and righteous Soviet war. These images of suffering soldiers could be interpreted in opposition to all war even when they appeared in works that explicitly rejected pacifism.

REVOLUTIONARY CONSCIOUSNESS AT THE EXPENSE OF HEROISM

Most Soviet depictions of World War I tended to emphasize revolutionary consciousness at the expense of heroism. Unlike European works from the same period that tended to construct ideal images of masculine heroism and camaraderie even when they rejected war, many Soviet treatments of the war denied any possibility of heroism. They suggested that Russian bravery was produced by alcohol consumption and that it was as heroic to surrender as to fight. These works charged that heroic rhetoric produced only death and destruction, and that wartime behavior could never be called glorious. They demonstrated how men in combat did not gain honor but instead lost their minds.

Like many of the European treatments of the war, Soviet depictions of war were quite attuned to the distinctions between the actual experience of battle at the front and the way it was represented in the rear. The jingoistic depictions of bravery in the newspapers were easily disproved and dismissed by the soldiers themselves. Even patriotic memoirists like Brusilov and Okunev objected to the "lies" in the newspapers. Those who rejected the war were virulent in their attacks on the falsehoods used to promote the mobilization for war in tsarist Russia.

For many of these memoirists (both Russian and Soviet), the drawing of distinctions between the front and the rear relied on gendered language and gender distinctions. Many memoirists agreed that those remaining in the rear were immoral. The population in the rear (especially the women) disgraced the war effort by loose behavior that spread moral and physical disease. This commonality suggests that a gendered understanding of the nature of war had a powerful grip on all classes and ranks. While the political order was completely overturned by revolution, significant aspects of gender relations remained intact and continued to influence depictions of war.

Although the gendering of front and rear was similar in Russia and Europe, the myth of male camaraderie was not. Russian Imperial representations of war continued to emphasize the patriarchal over the fraternal, and while many Soviet depictions of the war expressed class hatred against officers that made camaraderie impossible, there were notable exceptions to this rule. While both tsarist and Soviet rhetoric often emphasized the barriers that separated men rather than the experiences that drew them together, some authors such as Sholokhov and Brusilov presented the cross-class solidarity of the tsarist army in a somewhat positive light. These sources served as a conduit for notions of military honor and glory that later reappeared in Soviet culture.

Depictions of military masculinity in World War I possessed irresolvable tensions and contradictions. There were multiple and contradictory notions of heroism and class embedded in discussions of World War I masculinity. As war once again threatened in the middle to late 1930s, pacifist and internationalist visions of war, which often denied the possibility of heroism, lost ground to a renewed vision of hypermasculine wartime heroism and honor.

The antiwar vision was challenged from the outset by the ongoing needs of the Soviet state to mobilize Soviet manhood for military purposes, and by the fact that the older visions of honorable manhood had never disappeared from Soviet discourse. While the discourse of pacifism may have resonated with the experiences of millions of men, tsarist militarist discourse appealed both to former soldiers and to officials seeking to mobilize Soviet manhood. As the international situation changed, military mobilizing discourses regained the prominence that they had held in the tsarist era.

4

Violence, Morality, and the Conscience of the Warrior

The French historians Stéphane Audoin-Rouzeau and Annette Becker have suggested that the historical profession may be complicit in mythologizing and sanitizing war because, when it comes to describing wartime violence, "'memory serves to forget.'" The testimony of combatants was largely silent about transgressing the "fundamental taboo . . . not to kill." Few Western Europeans were as candid as the French veteran who wrote in 1936 about taking pleasure in killing, in jumping on the enemy and enjoying the enemy's terror "like those unfortunate drug addicts who know the magnitude of the risk but can't keep themselves from taking more poison"; and historians have often failed to seek out evidence about the willing perpetration of violence.[1]

By focusing on Soviet depictions of wartime violence from the point of view of both perpetrators and victims, this chapter sheds light both on the question of brutalization and on the extent and nature of the "mythologizing" of violence that took place in the Soviet Union in the interwar period. The issue of brutalization is particularly important, because the Soviet regime was considerably more violent toward its own citizens in "peacetime" than any other European government. The normalization of war was also an important part of the Soviet Union's preparation of a militarized citizenry to fight what its leaders saw as the inevitable coming war against capitalism. How, then, did Russian combatants, literary and cultural figures, and propagandists represent the violence of World War I and the soldiers who perpetrated it in the interwar period? To what extent did Soviet treatments of World War I normalize and glorify the violence of war, and to what extent did they reveal an unsanitized view of the violence? What kinds of violence remained central to Soviet notions of citizenship and manliness?[2]

Historians of World War I have sought to understand the impact of wartime violence on postwar European society. Some have argued that the effect of the extensive exposure of millions of European men to violence was a brutalization of politics in interwar Europe and a growing indifference toward mass death. George Mosse argued that the "myth of the war experience" was "central to the process of brutalization because it had transformed the memory of war and made it acceptable."[3] Other analysts of Germany and Italy have likewise linked war experience and memory to a heightened willingness to commit violence. They cite German Freikorps literature and the Italian Fascist writer Gabriele d'Annunzio to show the appeal of racial and sexual violence in mobilizing men to fight for their nation. In 1935, for example, d'Annunzio invited fellow Italians to join the Ethiopian campaign: "Do you want to fight? To kill? See rivers of blood? Great heaps of gold? Herds of female prisoners? Slaves?"[4] Such appeals both aestheticized and normalized violence.

In contrast to these scholars, Jay Winter has rejected the notion of World War I as a rupture and has emphasized soldiers' ability (especially in England and France) to overcome the horrors that they faced through traditional modes of mourning and commemoration and to resume relatively normal lives. He argues that "whatever was true in Nazi Germany, Fascist Italy, and (after June 1941) the Soviet Union, the rest of European society greeted war as the abomination that it was."[5] Winter's line between the "nonviolent" and the "violent" also marks the line between interwar democracy and dictatorship, suggesting a peculiarly violent Southern and Eastern European path that separated the Germans, Russians, and Italians from the rest of Europe because of their inability to overcome the traumas of war.

In his World War I–era writings, Vladimir Lenin himself speculated about the effects of battle on the Russian soldier and hoped that "horrors of war would not only intimidate and repress [the semi-proletarians and petty bourgeoisie] but enlighten, teach, arouse, organize, steel and prepare [them] for the war against the bourgeoisie of their 'own' country and 'foreign' countries."[6] The violence of World War I could thus productively lead to the violence of revolution. Modern analysts have argued in a similar vein that "the revolutions of 1917 had woven together an ethos of violence emerging out of the

First World War with a belief in the revolution's promise to remake the world," making violence an integral part of peacetime political culture.[7]

While there is still scholarly disagreement about the extent to which Bolshevik terror stemmed from revolutionary ideology, the specific conditions of the Civil War, or the overall experience of seven years of warfare, the unprecedented level of violence in the Soviet Union in the interwar period cannot be denied.[8] Both during the Civil War and afterward, violence played a central role in propelling the Soviet population along its forced path to modernity. In early Soviet World War I and Civil War memory, while enacting violence on behalf of the state was a central attribute of male citizenship, there nonetheless existed a complex dialogue about the effects of violence on the manhood of the perpetrators.[9] While there were attempts to justify violence in public Soviet discourse, framing it as retribution for White or German "atrocities,"[10] and there were general calls to exterminate the class enemy without mercy, between the end of the Civil War and the eve of World War II there was little evidence in public discourse of the overt glorification or aestheticization of violence such as in the works of d'Annunzio or in Freikorps literature.

One trend in Soviet discourse condemned the excesses committed by soldiers of the Russian Empire by deflecting the blame onto already suspect groups such as "Cossacks" or "officers," and in some sense this vilification of class enemies (like tales of German atrocities during World War I or White atrocities during the Civil War) implied a justification for violence against them. But Soviet war memory also consisted of a reflective discourse in which soldiers examined their consciences and acknowledged the psychic costs of war. Such representations of violence often depicted its enactment as a tragic necessity just as likely to take away manliness as to bestow it; those who engaged in violence for the sake of manliness often deeply regretted their actions. This reflective discourse revealed the toll that violence took on the perpetrators as well as the victims, called the morality of heroism into question, and recognized that virtually all combatants bore responsibility for the violence.

While tsarist-era depictions of violence were overwhelmingly cast in a patriotic mold, even before the October Revolution some authors acknowledged the sorrow of having to kill. In accounts published after the October Revolution, some Russian soldiers who killed the enemy and interacted violently with the multiethnic civilian population at the front acknowledged the moral ambiguity of their own actions. Once again the Soviet leadership was caught in a paradox. On the one hand, sober reflection seemed to be an appropriate response to violence in a war that the Soviet leadership considered unjust. On the other hand, the Soviet leadership virulently rejected any pacifistic or religious notion of nonviolence. Expressions of ambivalence at killing contradicted the Soviet ideal that citizens must be prepared to fight mercilessly against enemies of the state. The ideal Soviet wartime use of force was controlled, coldly calculating, merciless violence against the known enemies of the Soviet state. This targeted revolutionary violence was epitomized by Iakov Protazanov's melodramatic 1927 Soviet film about the Civil War, *The Forty-First* (*Sorok pervyi*), based on Boris Lavrenev's novella, in which a female Red sharpshooter and a dashing White lieutenant are shipwrecked alone together and fall in love. When they are about to be rescued by Whites, the sharpshooter claims her forty-first victim by killing the man she loves.[11] Will overcame emotion to allow the exercise of methodical violence against the enemy.

Depictions of violence in World War I were much more multivalent than this ideal Civil War violence. Some Soviet sources tried to exculpate "ordinary" workers and peasants by blaming the violent excesses of World War I on class enemies alone. Alongside the confessions of anguished perpetrators and the demonization of enemies, echoes of the righteousness of patriotic killing remained audible in Soviet discourse and grew louder as the threat to national security grew in the 1930s.

WARTIME KILLING IN THE TSARIST ERA

The honor code of the Russian military made a clear distinction between the legitimate and honorable killing of enemy soldiers in battle and committing violence against the unarmed, the wounded, prisoners of war, and civilians. As one Cossack officer explained in 1915: "God forbid I should raise my hand against a defenseless person. I, a Cossack, consider that to be an eternal indelible stain."[12] Russian World War I rhetoric extended the officers' honor code to the Russian soldier in general, who was described as "an eagle, a lion, and a tiger in battle but an angel of light and a good dove to his dying enemy," helping the wounded and prisoners of war of all nationalities.[13] Observers lauded this compassion for the defeated enemy as a positive attribute of the entire Russian nation. Likewise, Russian soldiers were depicted as being kind, generous, and just in their dealings with POWs and the civilian population.[14]

The Russian honor code was similar to officers' codes of ethics all over Europe and to the code of the White officers in the Civil War. Ernst Jünger explained that he strove to "treat the enemy as enemy only in battle and to honour him as a man according to his courage."[15] White Russian officers fighting in the Civil War believed that "[b]ecause honour is a matter for knights, and not for others, there is no honour to be won from attacking civilians, killing prisoners and so forth, only from fighting other knights."[16] While combatants clearly articulated honor codes, they had much more difficulty putting them into practice.

Ernst Jünger, for example, acknowledged that his ideals were sometimes difficult to achieve. He noted that the desire to kill unarmed prisoners was "base but understandable."[17] The commission of atrocities by one side breaking this honor code often led to the other side responding in kind. In one chapbook, the famed Cossack hero Koz'ma Kriuchkov advocated harsh treatment for German prisoners of war: "Why should you look after them, they won't do it for us! If you fall into their mitts, they'll slice you to pieces."[18] The constant threat of danger led soldiers of all nations to repeatedly break honor codes. Representations of war described violence against other human beings within a context that justified it or, alternatively, they exposed the ways in which combatants violated the rules of humane conduct. Tsarist-era reflections openly discussed killing the enemy, but tsarist censorship generally prohibited recollections of specific violence against noncombatants.

Nikolai Gumilev was unique among Russian intellectuals in embracing "war for the sake of war" and for his "vision of the fighting as a personal adventure and a 'grandiose spectacle' wherein he discovered the 'mystery of the soul.'"[19] In *Notes of a Cavalryman*, Gumilev described his mental state in battle as he was poised to kill, placing violence in the context of adventure and a highstakes game in which he gambled his life. He vividly described his thoughts as he encountered an enemy soldier on patrol in the course of one of his scouting missions: "I had only one thought, alive and mighty like passion, fury, ecstasy: I will kill him or he will kill me."[20] By defining battle as passion and ecstasy from which he could be released by killing, Gumilev eroticized war. Gumilev also defined the contest with the enemy in terms of his privileged aristocratic experience. From the very beginning of the memoir, Gumilev described himself as a hunter. When he saw two German soldiers within shooting range, he noted that "[o]nly hunting for big game animals, leopards and buffalo, have I experienced the same feeling, when anxiety for oneself suddenly changes into dread of losing magnificent spoils."[21] Gumilev then described how he killed one of the men but the other escaped. The metaphor of the hunt was one that identified Gumilev as part of a long-standing upper-class and masculine tradition. Gumilev made the act of killing familiar and natural by transforming Germans into big-game animals and war into safari. Though Gumilev's interpretation of the war was a singular one, this kind of glorification of violence became one of the many interpretations of the war available to the Russian public.[22]

While Gumilev identified killing with the sporting life of an aristocrat, he called it "work" for the lower classes, and thereby naturalized it. Gumilev described one regiment that calmly "goes into battle as if it were ordinary field work."[23] In his wartime dispatches, Aleksei Tolstoi asserted that Russian artillery excelled because of "the Russian soldier's unconquerable composure and his attitude toward battle that is like his attitude toward work."[24] The populist intellectual Ia. Okunev also equated war with work. He introduced the figure of Laptev, a peasant from Olonets, who symbolized the virtuous peasantry in a way reminiscent of Platon Karataev in Lev Tolstoi's *War and Peace*. Laptev himself "calls hand-to-hand combat 'work'" and, when his unit was relieved for the night, "crosses himself broadly and steadily just as he had recently been shooting and says, 'Glory to you Lord, we put in some work [*porabotali*]. What will God send tomorrow?'"[25] The intelligentsia on both the left and right maintained an idealized image of the peasant soldier as a noble laborer, now mowing down enemies as naturally as he had mowed his fields in peacetime. Killing was a task sent by God and as virtuous an activity as labor.

The popular prints that poured off printing presses in unprecedented numbers during the first year of the war depicted many battle scenes in which large quantities of red ink represented the spilling of enemy blood in righteous battle. While some showed fierce fighting and mounting numbers of enemy dead in matter-of-fact ways, others represented the death of the enemy as terrifying. One poster depicting the 1914 battle for L'vov, for example, included a dying enemy soldier with a horrified facial expression as he choked out his last breath, with blood streaming copiously from his empty eye socket.[26] Viewers could have read such posters in varying ways, either as normalizing and heroizing violence or perhaps making it seem repulsive.

The identity of those to be killed also played a role in how killing was represented. In Aleksei Tolstoi's work, there was a marked difference in tone depending on whether the enemy soldiers were Europeans or Turks. Tolstoi depicted the Russians as expert killers, but he also praised Austrian courage. He wrote that the Austrian soldiers "courageously go to their deaths. Whole regiments are mowed down."[27] Tolstoi described the violence enacted on Turks in much greater detail and without metaphors. He recorded the words of an artillery officer in the Caucasus who recounted his experience of killing Turks:

> Turks began to pour across the mountaintop. They threw their weapons down and began to slide down themselves. I opened fire as did the artillery behind me. All the Turks remained lying on the bottom. Right at that moment I see a second group climbing. They see that the ravine is crowded full, but they make a racket and jump down like devils. We finished them off too. We showered them with machine-gun fire and that's that. Then they poured out in an unbroken mass. And it was like that until it got dark. I feel that I cannot kill anymore. I'm in such a state that my hair was standing on end.[28]

The officer's matter-of-fact language about his own actions contradicted his expression of dismay at killing so many men. The seemingly unending slaughter of men who did not have weapons capable of responding to the Russian attack may have troubled and exhausted the officer, but the notion of killing Turkish "devils" did not. Tolstoi also described how the lips of a "boy-volunteer" quivered because "he was so happy that he had fought with a bayonet and killed a genuine Turk."[29] This young boy seemed to be living out his childhood play fantasies.[30] While both Gumilev and Tolstoi celebrated the Russians' appetite for killing, Tolstoi emphasized the particular pleasure that Russians got from killing their "historic" enemies, the Turks. Both Tolstoi and Gumilev valorized and celebrated killing, the desire to kill, and the willingness to risk one's own life in battle.

While the Russian honor code did not call for introspection or conscious reflection about the killing of bona fide enemies, regret at killing the enemy emerged as a possibility even in the generally bloodthirsty early phase of the popular discourse of World War I. One could find in popular culture the image of an ideal soldier who killed the enemy with honor but also recognized that he was changed by the experience. As a lover of all humanity, this soldier loved the enemy as well. For example, the prominent author of lubok literature Khristofor Shukhmin recounted the exploits of the Don Cossack Semen Iakontov in *A Dozen Germans on One Cossack Bayonet*. As literary critic Ben Hellman notes, not only did Iakontov best Koz'ma Kriuchkov by killing one more enemy, he was also superior to Kriuchkov because he demonstrated sorrow at killing: "He felt that every [fallen enemy] was a person close to him. And then he received many revelations for his soul, and gloomy and heavy thoughts dug into his brain and even provoked tears in the eyes of the hero." Like a classical hero, the soldier felt the sorrow of war but continued to fight honorably.[31]

A SOVIET PACIFIST ALTERNATIVE?

Because of tsarist censorship, the notion of nonviolence was rarely articulated in public between 1914 and 1917.[32] Even after 1917, however, notions of nonviolence were not widespread because of the Soviet belief that war was a necessary and inevitable aspect of the advent of world revolution; while Soviet ideologues rejected World War I as a capitalist and imperialist war, they embraced the necessity and inevitability of war itself. In 1917, however, the Bolshevik slogan of "peace" might have been interpreted by at least some segments of the population as opposition not just to World War I in particular, but against war in general. Many in the Russian population viewed war as a calamity sent as punishment from God and as an evil in and of itself, and they did not necessarily make a distinction between a "just" and an "unjust" war.[33] While non-Orthodox religious sects such as the Molokans, Dukhobors, Baptists, Evangelical Christians, Mennonites, and Tolstoians had long practiced nonviolence, there were also a few voices espousing civic (secular) pacifism in late-imperial Russia. During World War I, the number of conscientious objectors gradually began to rise but still numbered only in the hundreds.[34] Refusal of service was neither widespread nor popular, but it was nonetheless increasing during the war years.

Despite their strong belief in the necessity of war to create revolution, the Bolsheviks, paradoxically, expanded opportunities for "conscientious objection" to military service during the Civil War. While members of Russian Protestant sects had made up approximately half of those who refused tsarist service on religious grounds during the war, this total number was very small and most Protestants fulfilled their military service without question. But at the end of World War I, the situation changed. In order to attract peasants, engage sectarians as revolutionary allies, and fight against the Orthodox Church by favoring its enemies, on January 4, 1919, the Bolshevik government issued a decree allowing for alternative military service or complete exemption for religious conscientious objectors. This new legal possibility emerged at a time when evangelical pacifism was gaining adherents because of soldiers' experiences in World War I and the ongoing Civil War. As a result of the new rules, the refusal to bear arms became very common among evangelicals, and various evangelical groups "declared themselves to be opposed to the bearing of arms."[35] The Soviet state thus inadvertently promoted religious pacifism and advanced "the Christian conviction that [one] could not participate in the spilling of blood."[36]

The wartime experiences of the evangelicals of the tsarist Empire led to a deepening of religious pacifism and to a public rejection of bearing arms that was highly subversive of prevailing Soviet notions of identity and citizenship. One Soviet official objected to the 1919 decree, telling Lenin, "He who does not wish to defend the land from the robbers of imperialism does not have a right to make use of [the land], he cannot elect or be elected to Soviet institutions and enjoy the social service law." This official pondered the possibility of exile for this "anti-social element."[37] During the Civil War some local authorities went even further, rejecting the religious exemptions and summarily executing the objectors.[38] By 1925, the Soviet government placed restrictions on those who could request alternative service, allowing only those who were born into sects that forbade military service before 1917 to claim exemptions. Recent converts who might have been attracted to evangelical groups because of their pacifist stance were no longer exempt from service.[39] This episode demonstrates that the early 1920s in Russia provided fertile ground for the spreading of a popular religious pacifist discourse that emerged out of the horrors of the Russian war experience. Soviet officials considered this pacifist discourse to be extremely dangerous; they repressed it by changing the permissive 1919 law and by putting pressure on evangelical leaders to renounce their opposition to military service. The Soviet state silenced World War I's legacy of evangelical pacifism, obscuring the extent to which pacifist movements were flourishing in the 1920s. When the adherents of these movements followed their consciences in opposing the Soviet military establishment, their very actions could be construed as remembrance of World War I.

The memoirs of Iakov Dragunovskii, a Tolstoian pacifist who was shot in 1937 for preaching nonviolence in a Stalinist prison camp, revealed the seminal role that his World War I experience played in nurturing his Tolstoian convictions. Though these memoirs remained unpublished until 1988, they reveal the motivation for Dragunovskii's political action in the Soviet period. While in the hospital recovering from a foot wound sustained during the summer of 1915, he described the horrifying aftermath of his first battle in November 1914. He walked among German trenches that were "filled with dead men, most of them shot through the head, and some of them with their heads blown off." He was assisting a severely wounded comrade when he heard cries from wounded Germans and shared his water with them. Though "full of pity" for the wounded Germans, Dragunovskii could not bind their wounds, since his Russian comrade also urgently needed his help. Then, "[a]nother wounded German asked me for water, and I gave him a drink, and I gave another drink to my wounded comrade. I do not know how I came by so much water: I gave a drink to so many men and still had some left." The unlimited water supply in Dragunovskii's canteen implied divine intervention in, and approval of, human compassion to all of Dragunovskii's "brothers" on the battlefield. Yet Dragunovskii admitted that even after these events, he was brutalized by the war and did not feel pity when he shot at the Germans, acting "as a dumb sheep."[40]

On the Thursday before Easter in March 1915, Dragunovskii had another experience that raised questions in his mind about the war; ten Germans left their trench and began fraternizing with the Russians. He wrote, "For us it was a joyous miracle. I too ran over to find out how this peace had taken place." For a whole day and night the soldiers fraternized and peace reigned in the sector. "'Why should we kill each other?' they said on both sides. 'Let's get along with each other!'" Soon, however, the Russian officers took measures to end the fraternization. Dragunovskii concluded that the rank-and-file soldiers would have gladly "made peace," but the officers "only got in the way of this good work." Corroborating the Bolshevik view of officer-soldier relations, he depicted the rank-and-file soldiers on both sides of the conflict as advocates against the senseless violence of war while Russian and German officers forced soldiers to fight "like wild animals."[41]

The final war experience that drove Dragunovskii to embrace nonviolence was a particularly horrific battle in May 1915, during which the Germans fired more than a thousand shells at the Russian trenches. After a German bomb fell on one of the Russian dugouts and it collapsed, Dragunovskii rushed to the scene, bravely defying the shells that were exploding around him. He began digging and saved one wounded soldier while unearthing one dead comrade. A few minutes later, he was called upon to save the same wounded soldier again after German shells buried the soldier for a second time as a medic tended to his wounds. When he returned to his own unit, he discovered that his "good comrade, with whom [he] had almost finished reading *Anna Karenina*," had been struck by a piece of shrapnel and was dying. This night was a turning point for Dragunovskii who wrote, "That terrible night is one I will never forget."[42]

When Dragunovskii was wounded a month later, he sought ways to evade returning to the front and even engaged in self-mutilation, hindering his wound from healing and making himself deaf in one ear. Only in the Soviet era, however, did Dragunovskii consciously refuse military service because of his belief in Tolstoian nonviolence. He was arrested in 1920 and interrogated by the

Cheka after he voluntarily announced to a Soviet court that he intended to re-fuse military service, even though he had not yet been called up. The inter-rogators called him a "blockhead," astonished by his principled declaration against military service, in the absence of actual conscription. Dragunovskii made clear to Soviet officials that he refused to kill on behalf of the Soviet or any other government and revealed that he had learned about Tolstoian non-violence at the front in May and June 1915.[43] Dragunovskii's lifelong practice of Tolstoian pacifism expressed the remembrance of World War I in practice rather than in words. It is difficult for the historian to capture this kind of World War I memory, and while Dragunovskii was one of a tiny minority of vocal pacifists in the Soviet Union, his testimony affirms how former soldiers could be driven to pacifistic deeds as a direct result of their war experience.

To be sure, some Soviet-era written accounts about religious pacifists saw them as peculiar outsiders and depicted them with a certain lack of sympa-thy. In his 1926 memoir *The Barracks* (*Kazarma*), Sergei Grigor'ev complained about the constant proselytizing of a Baptist pacifist soldier during military training. Grigor'ev considered the Baptist less than a man because of his "fe-male" romance with Christ. This soldier refused even to answer questions about the military oath, let alone take the oath. The unit's sub-ensign treated the Baptist with a tolerance uncharacteristic of the typical noncommissioned officer, saying, "Don't force him. They do everything, only they don't take the oath and they don't carry weapons." Grigor'ev looked forward to the time when the pacifist would stop proselytizing and be taken away to become a medical orderly, a function that conscientious objectors often carried out in the tsarist army.[44]

Dmitrii Furmanov wrote about Mennonites as orderlies in the Union of Zemstva medical services. Without addressing their pacifism directly, Fur-manov spoke in glowing terms of Mennonites carrying out their alternative service in the tsarist army. He claimed that "you will not find better medical orderlies than the Mennonites" and declared that Mennonites were beloved by the soldiers because of their "innate goodness, their gentleness, and their calm, solicitous assiduousness" in caring for the needs of the wounded.[45] Fur-manov depicted the conscientious objectors as unselfish and dedicated men who, by ministering to war's victims, immeasurably helped the war effort with-out ever bearing arms.

Pacifists and Tolstoians were, however, sometimes satirized in the Soviet period. In Il'ia Erenburg's *The Extraordinary Adventures of Khulio Khurenito and his Disciples* . . . two characters addressed the issue of Tolstoianism from opposing points of view. Khurenito, the devil incarnate, was dedicated to promoting and extending the destruction of war. He rejected outright the idea that life in the trenches could be a "school for altruism or a breeding-ground of Tolstoians," and he averred that war had "already struck root" in the "peaceful bodies [of the soldiers], it's become their own trade. They'll never lose their liking for the job."[46] Through Khurenito, Erenburg presented the argument that the soldiers were permanently brutalized by the war and that they would desire to fight and to kill long after World War I was over. Khurenito denied that the horrors of war could create a true desire for peace.

Aleksei Spirodonovich Tishin, Erenburg's comical exemplar of the Russian intelligentsia, represented the opposing point of view in the novel. Aleksei Spirodonovich was fighting in the French Army and had been sent to Senegal to put down a "Negro revolt." He shot and killed a Senegalese man who turned out to be the brother of Aisha, one of Khurenito's other disciples. The act of killing unhinged him and he bemoaned his fate: "I wanted to save Russia and humanity, sacrifice myself, defend Christ, and instead of that all I've done is to kill a Negro. Why? What for?"[47] After this episode, he began to read books by Lev Tolstoi and decided to become a vegetarian. After being interned in a German POW camp, Tishin grew depressed, and he "hesitated between three possible courses of action: hanging himself, becoming an out-and-out Tolstoian—which would mean forgiving his tormentors all and perhaps even inviting the sergeant to beat him to death—or changing his name to Tishenko and being moved to the Ukrainians' camp, where things were considerably better." In the end, he simply "went sick as the best way out."[48] Aleksei Spirodonovich's contemplation of his options revealed both the impracticality and the improbability of the Tolstoian solution and the ways in which it was contradicted by human nature. Erenburg, always paradoxical and skeptical, denied the efficacy of Tolstoian nonviolence while he catalogued the pointlessness of the war and decried the tragic violence of the Russian Revolution.

There were also rare instances of secular pacifist thought appearing in Soviet works, as in the 1925 edition of Lev Voitolovskii's *In the Footsteps of War*. Voitolovskii's rejection of war was quickly censored and did not reappear in later editions of the work.[49] While some Soviet sources treated religious pacifists admiringly and some treated them with disdain, the widely acknowledged presence of people who held so strongly to their religious convictions not to bear arms nonetheless raised questions about God and about the nature of all soldiers' moral obligations.

THE ACT OF KILLING

While the act of killing remained an important theme in Soviet-era memoirs of the 1920s, these works did not romanticize killing in the way that Aleksei Tolstoi, Gumilev, or Okunev had done before the October Revolution. Soviet memoirists often sought to debunk the trope of heroic killing, as demonstrated by their negative treatment of the tsarist hero Koz'ma Kriuchkov. Most Soviet sources depicted killing during World War I as a senseless and illogical act that morally wounded or metaphorically killed the perpetrator as it actually killed the victim.

In the fictionalized ethnography *The People at War,* Sof'ia Fedorchenko included the account of a soldier who described killing at close range with his bare hands:

> Close at hand a fire blazed up. A sturdy German had lit a primus, and was boiling coffee—and the scent of it! "Oh Lord!" I thought, "if one only had that, how good it would be!" My mouth was full of saliva. I crept on; he sat waiting for his coffee and looking at the fire. I fell on him from behind, to strangle him quickly. He died silently, evidently from fright. I took the coffee and drank it, burning myself in my haste. I drank it up, and carried off the coffee-pot and his helmet.[50]

While the victim was an enemy combatant, and therefore the killing did not violate the rules of war, the motivation for the murder was not strategic; nor was the killing committed because of imminent danger to the soldier or a moment of fear or passion. This soldier admitted to killing casually, for a cup of coffee. The style of killing was not mechanized and impersonal but immediate and physical as the soldier strangled the German with his bare hands, surprised at how easy it was to accomplish his task. The soldier did not show any remorse; he simply recounted his actions in a matter-of-fact way. Thus Fedorchenko showed the brutalization of the soldiers in wartime and the way in which the indifferent, deprived, and traumatized soldiers were driven to commit senseless violence by the circumstances of war. Fedorchenko's vignette undercut received notions of heroism and honor in warfare. Fedorchenko did not deflect the blame for killing onto "Cossacks" or "officers," since this confession came from an anonymous soldier representing the Russian everyman.

The culminating scenes of Sergei Klychkov's semiautobiographical novel *The Sugary German* (*Sakharnyi nemets*) deal with the psychic cost of killing the enemy. A "peasant" writer in the Esenin circle, Klychkov first published his highly original novel in 1925; it appeared again under the title *Poslednyi lel'* in 1927 and was issued in a revised second edition in 1929.[51] Klychkov, the educated son of a tradesman, was promoted to the rank of officer and called upon to command his fellow villagers during the war. His protagonist, the officer Zaitsev, known by his men as "zaichik" or "little rabbit," is autobiographical. Like the character Zaitsev, Klychkov's war poetry was published during the war and he was heralded as a "front poet." The novel moves easily back and forth between fantasy fairytale kingdoms, tales of the village that the soldiers had left behind, and scenes of soldiers at the front. One of the central themes of the novel is a debate about whether God and the Devil exist.

Klychkov explored man's motivation to commit evil in the culminating scenes of the novel in which the mild Zaichik impulsively killed a German soldier who had left his trench to fetch water from the river. When Zaichik saw the soldier he "leapt up and completely caught fire," grabbed his rifle, loaded it, and killed the soldier.[52] Afterward, some of the soldiers felt sorry for the German and were unhappy with the commander's action. During their debate about whether the killing was justified, one of the soldiers told a parable about a robber who stabbed a holy man in the desert; at the moment of the stabbing, the holy man hit the robber with his cross. The two delivered their death blows simultaneously and died in each other's arms. The devil arrived and couldn't decide whose soul to take to hell, so he gathered up both of them. In the parable, killing in self-defense turned out to be as fatal for the soul as deliberate murder.[53]

While the soldiers were disquieted by Zaichik's action, he himself was driven near to insanity. He was tortured by guilt and lamented how it could have happened that his "white angel" did not "deflect his hand in time and did not push him under her white wing?"[54] At the moment at which he was buried alive in his trench by a German bombardment, Zaichik saw a redemptive vision of a miniature riverbank seemingly covered with sugar instead of snow. The German soldier that Zaichik had killed, now toy-sized, appeared on the sugary bank with a toy gun and told him to pray. The German then said, "Don't be afraid Rus', don't be afraid. I don't have a real weapon, and the bullet isn't a bullet but a sugary sweet gumdrop, but human blood is sweeter than the gumdrop." As he lost consciousness, Zaichik imagined himself in a purifying river.[55] In a final chapter that Klychkov added to the 1929 edition, the unconscious Zaichik was rescued by his devoted sergeant-major. The novel ended with the sergeant-major carrying Zaichik out of the trench into the cleansing first snowfall and dreaming of getting a medal for saving his officer. Redeemed and alive, Zaichik could hope to save his soul.[56]

Not surprisingly, given its pacifism, this novel met with severe criticism. In *Krasnaia nov'* (Red Virgin Soil) in 1925, V. P. Pravdukhin attacked the character of Zaichik for his religiosity, and his "dedication to the idea of the non-resistance to evil" that reflected the "one-sided 'womanly' element in the general national type of the Russian person."[57] The Tolstoian Zaichik was clearly not man enough to be a character in Soviet literature. In *Novyi mir* (New World) in 1926, A. A. Divil'kovskii complained about the contents of the novel: "Where is there even a shadow of the fighting revolutionary mood ripening among these very same peasant soldiers long before the revolution? There is not a trace of it. The maximum is only some kind of Tolstoian, ruminant, vegetarian pacifism, the protest of bulls to the slaughter."[58] In the minds of these critics, remorse and revulsion at the idea of killing was a characteristic of women, animals, and vegetarians, but not of true Soviet men. The novel, however, survived these scathing reviews and appeared in several new editions until Klychkov's arrest in 1937. The image of the wavering "womanly" officer who questioned killing remained available in Soviet public discourse for at least another decade.

One of the central themes of *Quiet Flows the Don* is the effect of killing on the psyche of the warrior. Grigorii Melekhov's initiation as a killer was one of the first scenes of the novel that Sholokhov wrote. In an early draft, Sholokhov's protagonist "saw the enemy soldier through a wood eating blackberries, and shot him while he was engaged in this innocent activity."[59] In the published version, Melekhov's first murderous acts occurred in the context of a battle. His reaction to his first kills shaped his wartime moral philosophy. In his first cavalry battle, Melekhov killed an Austrian who had fired a gun at him with a lance blow "so powerful that the lance went right through him, burying half its length in his body. Grigory was unable to withdraw. He felt the convulsions of the falling body coming up the shaft."[60] Melekhov thus was trapped in a desperate coupling with his dying victim. Not sated by his first kill, Melekhov became "inflamed by the madness that was going on all around him" and next slaughtered an unarmed man. "Their eyes met. The Austrian's were flooded with the horror of death. . . . With half-closed eyes, Grigory swung his sabre. The long, swinging stroke split the skull."[61] Horrified by his action, Grigorii dismounted in confusion and stared at the man he had killed. The dead Austrian was "holding out a dirty brown palm, as if for alms. Grigory looked into his face. It seemed to him small, almost childlike, despite the drooping moustache and the stern twisted mouth, tortured by recent suffering or perhaps by the joyless life it had known before." Grigorii honestly and directly confronted his begging, childlike victim in an attempt to come to terms with his own violent actions. A Cossack officer rode by at this moment and interrupted Grigorii's reflections.[62]

Several of the 1930s illustrated editions of *Quiet Flows the Don* emphasized Grigorii's violation of the honor code while "inflamed by madness" rather than his repentance afterward. These artistic choices were in keeping with the trend toward depicting Grigorii in a negative light. A 1934 edition of the novel with engravings by A. Kravchenko showed Grigorii on a charging steed. He awkwardly twisted backward in the saddle with his sword raised over his shoulder ready to strike the cowering Austrian. The latter appeared with his hands defenselessly at his sides and his knees already buckling in anticipation of the fatal blow. Grigorii was rendered in profile as the quintessential Cossack with cartoonish emphasis on the forelock sticking out of his Cossack cap, his prominent nose, moustache, and epaulettes (figure 4.1).[63] Grigorii's strength was acknowledged as far superior to that of the unarmed Austrian, whom he should have spared.

Many later editions of *Quiet Flows the Don* reproduced an illustration of this scene that first appeared in 1935. A lithograph by S. G. Korol'kov showed a fierce and sharp-nosed Grigorii on horseback gritting his teeth and raising his sabre high over his head in preparation for landing a merciless and powerful blow on the hapless Austrian (figure 4.2). The dwarfed Austrian was almost pushed out of the frame of the picture by the commanding figure of Grigorii and his charging horse. The unarmed soldier cowered meekly in the corner of the drawing, with one hand raised over his head and the other in front of his face to emphasize his helplessness. In this version, the Austrian was depicted as an older soldier with a worn face and a gaping mouth open in horror at death.[64] The scene underscored Grigorii's senseless brutality and the pitiful nature of his victim.

While these artists placed their emphasis on Grigorii's act of violence, the text of the novel also dwelt on Grigorii's reaction to the experience of killing. A fan letter from a white-collar worker and war veteran, who claimed to have lived through some of the same experiences as Melekhov, admired Grigorii for his "pure heart to which he always gave free rein." The letter writer claimed that the scene in which Grigorii killed the Austrian was "carved in his memory" and that he sympathized with Grigorii during his moment of repentance. Believing in Grigorii's (and perhaps his own) "pure heart," this war veteran viewed the scene through the lens of class, explaining that when Grigorii stood over the Austrian and began to repent, "the officer riding by did not allow him to lay out his thoughts and think about why he killed this soldier" or to ask "to whom was imperialist war and war in general useful?" The writer saw Grigorii as good-hearted rather than brutal and blamed the officers for preventing soldiers from contemplating the moral implications of their actions and of war in general. The novel's discussion of unjust killing clearly struck a chord with at least some of its readers.[65]

Sholokhov went on to explain that after Grigorii shed blood, he had "a nagging inward pain" and was disturbed by nightmares in which he relived these episodes:

> Often on the march and while resting, asleep or dozing, he dreamed of the Austrian he had cut down by the iron railing. Time and again he relived that first encounter, and even in his sleep, pursued by memories, he felt the convulsion that the lance had transmitted to his right hand; when he awoke, he would try to banish the dream by pressing his eyes until they hurt.[66]

When his brother arrived at the front, he confessed his distress: "My conscience is killing me. At Lesznjow I stuck my lance right through a man. That was in battle. It was the only thing to do. But why did I cut down that other one?"[67] Despite his anguish and misgivings, Melekhov continued to give his utmost effort to every battle and did not avoid fighting. Although he hated the war, his duty as a Don Cossack overrode his personal disillusionment. Sholokhov defined Melekhov as a warrior hero who continued to follow orders and kill armed men on the battlefield.

Melekhov, like Zaichik, gave voice to the anguish of the warrior with blood on his hands, and both novels explored the inner thoughts of a guilty soldier repulsed by killing. While Zaichik came to reject violence itself, Melekhov's guilt prompted him to define the just warrior as one who killed the enemy in battle but protected the lives of unarmed prisoners and civilians. At least until the last volume of the novel appeared in 1940, and probably beyond, Melekhov remained a model for Soviet masculinity. He defined acceptable wartime violence in a way that corresponded to the ethos of Jünger and Cossack and White officers, and this ethos also appealed to Soviet readers who admired Melekhov for his purity of heart.

Melekhov's acknowledged trauma at perpetrating gratuitous violence showed that he believed in an honor code, even though he failed to live up to it in his first battle. Uriupin, a particularly violent Cossack in Melekhov's unit, gloried in killing both the armed and the unarmed. When Melekhov was

FIGURE 4.1. *Facing page.* Grigorii's first kill, wood-
cut by A. Kravchenko, in Mikhail Sholokhov's
Quiet Flows the Don [*Tikhii Don*], Book 1 (Moscow:
Gos. izd-vo khudozh. lit-ry, 1934).

FIGURE 4.2. *Above.* Grigorii's first kill, lithograph
by G. Korol'kov, 1935, in Mikhail Sholokhov's
Quiet Flows the Don [*Tikhii Don*] (Moscow: Gos.
izd-vo khudozh. lit-ry, 1941).

heartsick with guilt, Uriupin mocked him for having a "sniveling" soul.[68] Uriupin told Grigorii, "Cut a man down boldly. He's soft as dough, a man is. . . .
Don't think about what it's all for. You're a Cossack. It's your duty to cut people
down without question. It's sacred work to kill a man in battle. God pardons
one of your sins for every man you kill, just the same as for a snake."[69] Uriupin's brutality, his misanthropy, and his articulation of the idea that killing
was God's work all stood in contrast to Melekhov's belief that the only just killing was that of an armed enemy. Melekhov, however, expressed anguish not
only at having killed the unarmed Austrian, but also the armed man whom he
killed in battle. A killing that was "just" according to Russian Orthodox and
Cossack codes tormented Melekhov; he was repelled by the act of killing itself. As the war continued, Melekhov lost these scruples. Sholokhov wrote: "at
last the pain of human compassion that had tortured him in the first days of
the war seemed to have gone forever . . . Grigory's heart had become impervi-
ous to pity." Now Melekhov "knew that when he kissed a child it was hard for
him to look into those clear eyes." He understood that "his row of crosses and
his promotion" had come at the cost of his humanity.[70]

The notion of just and unjust killing played a pivotal role in the novel at
the crucial moment when Melekhov rejected the Bolsheviks after witnessing
them massacre unarmed White officers. Melekhov's notion of honor meant
that any unarmed prisoner, no matter what his class, deserved protection and
fair treatment. Melekhov had long suppressed the notion that killing itself was
wrong but still defined proper and improper killing in accordance with prerevolutionary codes of honor. Early Soviet critics of Sholokhov's work attacked
him because of Melekhov's compassion for all classes: "This sickly-sweet po-
tion of religious-tasting and hypocritical all-forgiveness and of the vilest kind
of humanism is clearly an expression of the influence on Sholokhov of inimi-
cal class forces."[71] Tsarist codes of military honor clashed with the Soviet dic-
tum to exterminate class enemies. As pressure built on Sholokhov to paint
Grigorii in an increasingly negative light, Sholokhov did so, in part by having
Grigorii betray the code of honor that he had espoused in the first two books
of the novel. In revenge for his brother's death in book 3 of the novel, Grigorii
ordered the slaughter of unarmed Red prisoners.[72] Thus Sholokhov's positive
vision of the military honor code remained constant even as both the Reds and
the Whites disregarded it.

To probe the vacillation of *Quiet Flows the Don* between the rejection of
killing that transgressed the honor code and the rejection of all killing, it is

instructive to compare the scene of Grigorii's first kill with a similar scene in *All Quiet on the Western Front*. Remarque's description of the horror of killing bears a striking similarity to Sholokhov's. Paul Bäumer was lying in a shell hole when a French soldier fell on top of him. He explained, "I do not think at all, I make no decision—I strike madly at home, and feel only how the body suddenly convulses, then becomes limp, and collapses. When I recover myself, my hand is sticky and wet."[73] Sholokhov and Remarque, like Gumilev, gave killing at close range explicitly erotic overtones. They both focused on the frenzied passion of the moment of killing and the victims' vulnerability to the warriors' thrusts in an acknowledgment of the protagonists' complete loss of self-control when faced with the danger of combat.

After Bäumer and Melekhov were released from the grip of passion, both men also carefully examined their victims. Bäumer's victim was still alive; he tried to alleviate the suffering. After the soldier died, Bäumer, like Melekhov, described the face of the individual whose life he had taken and imagined what that life might have been like. Unlike Melekhov, Bäumer explicitly asked his victim for forgiveness and explained, "Comrade, I did not want to kill you. If you jumped in here again, I would not do it, if you would be sensible too."[74] Bäumer then made a promise to fight against a future war if he should survive: "I will fight against this, that has struck us both down; from you—taken life and from me—? Life also."[75] Remarque and Sholokhov each described how war took life from both the perpetrators and the victims of killing. Sholokhov has Melekhov explain to his brother, "I feel like a man who's been not quite killed."[76] Despite this realization, Grigorii continued to fight bravely and to kill when necessary. When, however, Melekhov fell to the ground after being seriously wounded in battle, Sholokhov recorded his thoughts: "'It's all over!' The soothing thought slithered through his mind."[77] Unlike Bäumer, Melekhov's remorse did not lead him to reject war or to promise his victims that he would work toward pacifism. Both warriors were exactly alike, however, in their acceptance of death as a release from the torments of war.

This question of what constituted a "just killing" and how a soldier should feel after killing the enemy under battle conditions also engaged the Soviet readers of *All Quiet on the Western Front*. One Red Army soldier mentioned that he appreciated in particular the scene with the French soldier. Another reader, a veteran of the Russo-Japanese war and a World War I POW who identified himself as I. A. Belov, "a private in the tsarist army and a St. George Cavalier three times over," wrote a letter to the State Literature Publishing

House in Moscow with his critique of *All Quiet on the Western Front*. He questioned Remarque's realism in the scene between Paul Bäumer and the Frenchman: "As though a person could be dispirited by what he carried out; as though he would repent before the corpse. In his action, the preservation of his own life would always be at the forefront."[78] Belov disputed Remarque's depiction of the mentality of the soldier after killing, denying the possibility that the soldier would feel regret at a justified killing to save his own life. Belov's defensiveness on this issue reveals the struggles of the millions of veterans who came home with blood on their hands. They had taken part in "just" killing under battle conditions and did not feel guilty about it, or did not want to feel guilty about it. Yet the fictional Melekhov and Bäumer reminded them that even justified killing took a toll on the perpetrator.

In scenes depicting the Civil War in *Quiet Flows the Don,* Sholokhov also showed how Il'ia Bunchuk, the staunch Bolshevik revolutionary who served as a counterpoint to Melekhov, reacted to his work on the tribunal of the Don Revolutionary Committee. Each night he and a squad of Red Guards took the condemned out of town, dug a grave, and then Bunchuk ordered the Red Guards to shoot "at the enemies of the revolution." This task had an immediate impact on Bunchuk: "In one week his face grew gaunt and black, as if he had been buried under ground. His eyes hollowed out and the nervously twitching lids failed to hide their anguished brightness." Killing enemies of the revolution "buried" Bunchuk as well as the condemned men. Despite the fact that he hated the killing, Bunchuk justified it: "Before you plant out the flowerbeds and the trees, you've got to get rid of the filth! You've got to manure the ground! You've got to get your hands dirty!"[79] But the tragic necessity of having to do the revolution's dirty work wreaked havoc on the mind and body of this loyal revolutionary.

In a scene that was edited for sexual content by puritanical Soviet censors in the mid-1930s, but that nonetheless remained in the novel, Anna, the woman whom Bunchuk loved, offered herself to him for the first time.[80] He could not consummate the relationship, however, because he was impotent as a result of his horror at being an executioner. When the two finally did have sex, Anna explained that the first time, she thought Bunchuk had been with another woman: "I thought you'd spent it all before. I didn't realise it was the work that had taken it out of you."[81] Sholokhov once again showed how perpetrating violence took away the life force and the very manhood of its perpetrators. By repeatedly raising questions about the human effects of war, even a just Soviet war, the novel broke new ground in memorializing war's pain and trauma. In the 1920s, anguish at committing violence was permitted into Soviet discourse, although expressing joy at killing was not.[82]

CLASS, ETHNICITY, AND COSSACK IDENTITY

The typical Soviet depiction of the war emphasized the cruelty, depravity, and incompetence of the tsarist officers leading the war effort. Many World War I accounts included scenes in which sadistic officers brutally beat soldiers, even wounded ones, for trifling infractions such as failing to salute properly.[83] They also showed officers straying far from any kind of honor code by despoiling the civilian population and engaging in lewd and drunken behavior. This vilification of the officers unambiguously cast the events of the war as part of the larger class struggle, preventing the war itself from occupying center stage. It also rather conveniently deflected the blame for the horrors and atrocities of war from the potentially Bolshevik rank and file to the unredeemable class-alien officers.

Class trumped everything else in these depictions, but class identity was established by gendered behaviors. One key aspect of the symbolic shorthand for characterizing the inherent depravity of tsarist officers was their treatment of women. The decadent and hedonistic masculine drives of tsarist officers could only be satisfied by the sexual abuse of innocent women and children. Fedorchenko's *The People at War* contained several vignettes about tsarist officers who raped local women or forced them into prostitution. In one such vignette, a soldier met a woman being treated for venereal disease. She told him, "The officer called me to come one evening to collect the laundry. I went, and three of them tormented me right up until midnight. They let me go and gave me three rubles, but since that time I have been ill."[84] Not only did the staff officers gang rape this servant woman, but they infected her with venereal disease, ruining her life and health. Gender divisions reinforced class divisions, as Fedorchenko defined tsarist commanders by their callous abuse of lower-class females.

In the 1930 novella *In the Trenches (V okopakh)*, author Tat'iana Dubinskaia told the story of Zina, a sixteen-year-old girl who ran away from home to volunteer for the tsarist army. In this first-person narrative, Zina recounted her development from deluded tsarist volunteer to conscious revolutionary. She also recalled how, while on a scouting mission, her officer promised to nominate her for a St. George cross in exchange for intimate relations. When she refused, the officer raped her with the assistance of a noncommissioned officer who held her down. The officer promised the NCO that he could also rape Zina, but then reneged on his offer. Zina was not in a position to scream for help, because if she did, she would endanger her fellow soldiers by giving away their position to the enemy. The novella also included Zina's feelings the day after the rape when she looked in the mirror and saw eyes that were "like someone else's, not mine." Even in retrospect, however, Zina concluded that protecting the safety of her comrades was more important than protecting her virtue. In later editions of the novella, Zina did not have to face this choice as a revolutionary soldier rescued her in the nick of time.[85]

Dubinskaia associated the tsarist officer with deep moral corruption and the abuse of the young and innocent soldiers in his care, not with any notion of "honor." The officer's lack of manly restraint over his sexual appetites identified him as a representative of a hated class. Yet it is also worth noting that the officer's name was Zambor, not a typical Russian name. This appellation perhaps denoted that this depraved officer was also somehow foreign, hinting at a positive link between Russianness, lower-class status, and honorable behavior.

Soviet World War I discourse had a much more difficult time contextualizing ethnic violence. How could ethnic violence be explained given that nationality, in theory, was not supposed to matter? Soviet sources often blamed ethnic violence, such as the murder of German prisoners and the plundering of Polish and Jewish civilians, on officers, reimposing a class framework over the national one; however, there was also an extremely strong tendency for Soviet sources to ethnicize the ethnic violence by naming the Cossacks in particular as its perpetrators. This tendency, of course, stemmed from the actual participation of Cossacks in a substantial amount of ethnic violence during World War I and the Civil War. Accounts of wartime violence themselves reinforced ethnic difference and constituted the Cossacks as ethnic "others," recognizable by their brutality. Soviet interwar depictions of ethnic hatred perpetrated by Cossacks could be read either as grounded in fact, as a blanket attack on all Cossacks, or as the continuation of the myth of the simultaneously violent and heroic Cossack.

Soviet explanations for violence moved fluidly back and forth from Cossack exceptionalism to an acknowledgment that the circumstances of war and the training and battle experiences that desensitized soldiers to violence produced impossible ethical situations.[86] Some Soviet discussions of the war acknowledged that soldiers of all classes and ethnicities were prone to making ugly choices in their treatment of enemy soldiers and civilians, whatever *their* own class or ethnicity. In these latter Soviet accounts, which mirrored European indictments of the universal brutality of war, the nature of war itself trumped both class and ethnicity as the prime cause of horrifying violence.

Not all of the raw material from which Dmitrii Furmanov created his novel about the famed Red Cossack hero Chapaev came from his experiences as a commissar in the Civil War; Furmanov also encountered Cossacks during his World War I service. In his diary, Furmanov consistently distinguished between Cossacks and other soldiers, emphasizing Cossack brutality. His descriptions laid bare both the intense ethnic hatred of the enemy in World War I and the excesses of war. Furmanov recorded a conversation with a Cossack officer in his diary entry of October 31, 1915, revealing the mutual hatred of the Germans and the Cossacks. The Cossack officer stated, "I fight the German because he is a German. And indeed the German will fight the Cossack because he is a Cossack. And let it be. We do not ask for mercy. To hit a German in the teeth gives me enormous satisfaction." When Furmanov objected, "But you are beating a defenseless person," the Cossack answered: "If you can imagine, my conscience is calm. . . . It is quiet." Despite the Cossack's acknowledgment that attacking defenseless people was a sin, he forthrightly appealed to ethnic difference to justify ignoring his own code.

The Cossack officer was not embarrassed to admit the grossest violations of Cossack honor codes. The officer hated the Germans so much that he could not "look at a German snout." The officer recounted how a German prisoner of war refused to salute him and he stabbed the POW in the stomach with his bayonet.[87] He also told how he and his soldiers stabbed a German woman and her children to death "in the heat of the moment." He concluded, "No, brother, I sincerely hate the German, and to give it to him in the snout—is pure satisfaction."[88] Furmanov's diary revealed to Soviet readers the connection between powerful national hatreds and wartime atrocities that broke all codes of ethical behavior. The officer's frank admission of his willingness to annihilate any German, be it a soldier in arms, a defenseless prisoner, a woman, or even a child, linked the image of the Cossack to the extreme ethnic brutality that became the hallmark of twentieth-century warfare.[89] The Cossack officer defined his Russian patriotism, in part, as the willingness to brutalize the German enemy. The ethics of war became obsolete; all that remained was the satisfaction of violence against a hated ethnic enemy. Furmanov's disapproval of the officer's actions was made explicit by his question about the defenseless victim; this passage thus provided Soviet readers with a critique of Cossack violence as it perpetuated the myth of the courageous Cossack warrior who asked for no mercy and gave none.

Furmanov recounted a lengthy conversation with a second Cossack officer in an entry from August 10, 1916. The officer defended Cossack honor by categorically rejecting the rumors that Cossacks "smashed the heads of small children in Galicia against the wall." This Cossack claimed that a Cossack's love for a child outstripped that of the child's own mother. He was incensed by such rumors and suggested, "You have to smash the head of the one who says such things."[90] He claimed that the Cossacks were free people who had no need for revenge, while the infantry was full of oppressed people who might take out their frustrations on others—though he also admitted that there might have been individuals who "shamed Cossack honor." Later on in the conversation, the officer explained that he personally had witnessed German atrocities: Cossacks with their eyes plucked out and their arms chopped off at the elbows. He suggested that in such cases there was nothing exclusive or surprising about Cossack brutality in demanding "an eye for an eye."[91] He further admitted that war created intractable ethical situations. He described taking away all of the fodder from a Galician woman for his own hungry horses, leaving her animals to starve. He then asked the ethical question: "Is that marauding? No, gentlemen, here the borders between violence and necessity were so washed away that your head spins and you try not to think."[92]

In reporting this speech, Furmanov allowed the Cossack officer repeatedly to undermine his own words. The speaker began by denying brutality and finished by acknowledging how the wartime context produced it. He contextualized the brutal treatment of Polish and Jewish non-combatants by describing how wartime circumstances erased the ethical and practical boundaries between "violence" and "necessity." Furmanov thus demonstrated the pressure placed on a normative code of honor by the horror of the war itself. Wartime conditions pushed individual Cossacks into dishonorable acts so that they had to threaten violence to defend their already tarnished honor. While the Cossacks pledged to deal fairly with civilians, they were forced to abuse them because of the difficult conditions of warfare. The passage revealed the fragility of honor codes and implied that honorable behavior during wartime was an impossible goal. The Cossack officer also justified excesses against Germans by pointing to atrocities perpetrated against Cossacks. Furmanov's diary thus revealed how ethnicity served as a primary factor in intensifying the violence of war, overshadowing class hatred and class distinctions. He challenged the overarching Soviet interpretation of World War I as an "imperialist" struggle of capitalist powers; instead his memoir depicted war as a mortal conflict between rival nations.

The relation of the Cossacks to the civilian population in occupied Galicia was also a topic of discussion in former tsarist officer Fedor Stepun's epistolary novel *From the Letters of an Ensign-Artillerist* (*Iz pisem praporshchika-artillerista*). In a letter to his wife in November 1914, the fictional ensign described the nature of looting in Galicia. He opined that the Cossacks were "professional marauders" and explained that "the difference between Cossacks and soldiers in this regard consists only in that the Cossacks carry away everything with a clean conscience: what they need and what they don't need. The soldiers, always experiencing a few pangs of conscience, take only the things they need."[93] Stepun, who was not a Bolshevik, concurred with the predominant Bolshevik view that the Cossacks should be singled out for their brutality to civilians.

In addition to emphasizing Cossack predilections for looting and marauding, Soviet World War I discourse often also identified the category of "Cossack" with sexual abuse and rape. In his memoir *In the Footsteps of War*, Lev Voitolovskii recounted one Russian officer's negative assessment of Cossack scouts: "The Cossack is an excellent horseman, good in an attack and in battle, but if you send him out for reconnaissance, he goes around to the poorest peasant huts and feels up [*shupaet*] the girls."[94] Fedorchenko's work featured a soldier's testimony about a horrifying Cossack gang rape of a seven-year-old child. "That Cossacks spoil women, that is the truth. I saw how they tore apart a seven-year-old girl just as if she were a whore. One . . . , and three stomp their feet impatiently and neigh. I thought she was already dead under the second one, but all four proved themselves. I cried out in shame and rage, but they did not hear. I didn't succeed in dragging them off, they finished. . . ."[95] World War I discourse thus associated Cossacks with the most heinous crimes imaginable against a defenseless civilian population. On the one hand, the association of Cossacks with pogroms and rape likely had considerable justification; extant contemporary reports from the Collegium of Jewish Social Activists linked the instigation of pogroms to Cossack units 80 percent of the time and mentioned rape in one-third of the reports.[96] On the other hand, "Cossacks" were a convenient Soviet target.

Cossacks were also associated with other kinds of corruption. Although open discussion of homosexuality was rare in Soviet sources, another World War I memoir also accused Cossack officers of same-sex sexual violence against their own recruits. *Soldiers* (*Soldaty*), by the Bashkir writer Afzal Tagirov, described the life of the soldier Vaniuk, who had been with the army since he was ten years old and who was raped repeatedly by two Cossack officers.[97] The hero of *Soldiers* met poor Vaniuk in the hospital where he was suffering from venereal disease. Cossack officers were thus also tied to the most extreme abuse of young and vulnerable rank-and-file soldiers, and the spread of disease.

As in the Fedorchenko vignette above, in the 1920s, rape was often described from the point of view of the male bystander who was attempting to protect women from his marauding compatriots. These men are portrayed as ancillary "victims" of rape who suffered a loss of masculinity because of their failure to defend the innocent. In the extreme case of the soldier Goldberg, discussed in chapter 3, his inability to prevent the rape of a Jewish coreligionist, and the Cossacks' attempts to force him to rape her, unhinged his mind. Both his masculinity and his very identity were undermined by the traumatic episode.

In *Quiet Flows the Don,* Sholokhov revealed Grigorii Melekhov's personal revulsion at the Cossack propensity to rape when Grigorii inadvertently witnessed the gang rape of a Polish housemaid by other Cossack recruits. When he walked in on the terrible scene, his fellow Cossacks beat him and tied him in a sack, leaving him unable to stop their violent actions. Melekhov then became complicit in the rape to some degree because he did not report it to his superiors. Later at drill, when the troop officer noticed a missing button from his greatcoat that he had lost in the scuffle, Grigorii "for the first time in years . . . felt like crying."[98] Both Goldberg's and Melekhov's intervention against rape led to physical humiliation, and neither was able to prevent the sexual abuse of an innocent civilian woman. Melekhov also suffered from guilt because he allowed the Cossacks to get away with the rape. The violent ethos of the Cossacks as a group seemed to overwhelm the consciences of individual Cossacks.

THE ABUSE OF CIVILIANS

Judging from contemporary reports, Cossacks may indeed have taken the lead in instigating particular kinds of ethnic violence, but systematic displacement of civilians and looting were carried out by a large number of both Cossack and non-Cossack army units. In Soviet World War I discourse, the army's mistreatment of civilians was sometimes framed as ethnic conflict and at other times generalized as a military-civilian problem. Some descriptions of the abuse of Jewish or Polish civilians did not emphasize the ethnic tensions inherent in the conflict, focusing instead on the plight of the soldier-perpetrators who were forced by circumstances to use force against harmless civilians. Given that soldiers often had to provision themselves, there were an enormous number of tense interactions between soldiers and civilians. Voitolovskii described the soldiers' indifference to the tearful plea of the wife of a Russian soldier that if they took her grain there would be nothing left to sow in the spring: "Let them cry," the soldiers said. "Moscow does not believe in tears." Voitolovskii also described how one soldier frightened some wailing women into feeding him by threatening to put a cross on each house where there wasn't any bread for Russian troops so that the "authorities" would know.[99] These episodes, which took place at the very beginning of the war, indicate how easy it was for soldiers living off of the local population to develop adversarial and threatening relations even with citizens of the Russian Empire, not to mention those in occupied territories.

In the first year of the war, various units of the Russian army indiscriminately removed civilians of all ethnicities from the frontlines and pursued what amounted to a scorched earth policy in Galicia that deprived local populations of their homes and livelihoods.[100] German colonists and Jews experienced particularly brutal treatment because of suspicions that they were aiding the German enemy, and in some cases the army took Jewish hostages "as insurance" against the hostile behavior of Jewish communities. In January 1915, Chief of Army Headquarters N. N. Ianushkevich sent a "circular to army commanders throughout the front zone authorizing the expulsion . . . of 'all Jews and suspect individuals.'"[101] According to one estimate, "more than 600,000 Russian Jews were displaced even before the mass deportations began in the summer of 1915" as the Russians retreated from Poland.[102] The soldiers of the Russian army thus actively participated in the forced resettlement of hundreds of thousands of innocent people. Fedorchenko's work contained a vignette of a soldier whose job it was to deport the civilian population of unstated ethnicity from the front area:

Oh, what a terrible time it was! When the first wagon arrived, Semen Ivanovich alighted from it and said to the woman, "Gather your children and your most necessary things, you are being evicted." A crowd assembled in an instant; it was as if a thunderbolt had struck the village, and all were crying. Some were striking their heads against the ground, others tearing at their hair. One old woman fetched out a young heifer, put her arms around her neck, and howled; and so did all the dogs, for company. Well, they had to be loaded into the wagons by force, as they could not be persuaded. Most of them barefoot—rain, mud, cold, a terrible, terrible time at its very worst.[103]

The narrator of this terrible scene had difficulty in acknowledging his own part in it. He used the passive voice at the crucial moment of intervention; the soldier-narrator may have forcibly loaded the crying, barefoot, and cold women and children onto the wagon, but he shielded himself from guilt by hiding his role in the violence. The detailed description of the village at the moment of its deportation offered Fedorchenko's readers a glimpse of the dislocation and misery that destroyed civilian lives during wartime. Fedorchenko made visible to the Soviet public the massive movement of internal refugees, primarily women and children, displaced by tsarist military policy during the war. The soldier's description revealed the trauma of the resettlement of these entirely innocent victims, and acknowledged that he and his fellow soldiers were responsible for their suffering. A key aspect of the tragedy of war as it was represented in Fedorchenko's work was the toll that violence took on both the rank-and-file soldiers who created the catastrophe of wartime dislocation and on its defenseless victims.

Another boundary that was frequently fraught with tension was the line between the "legal" procurement of food from the civilian population and looting. The words of the ensign in Fedor Stepun's epistolary novel suggested that the cause of marauding was the nature of war itself combined with the wealth of the Austro-Hungarian lands. The ensign explained that he could not react to looting severely because "you cannot begrudge a person who is ready to give up his life the prosperity of the Galician and the lives of his calves and chickens. A person experiencing the most extreme violence cannot help but become an aggressor." He then recalled that when people complained to Kutuzov about marauding, Kutuzov said, "When you fell timber, the chips fly."[104] The ensign recognized that the experience of violence had changed his soldiers, making them ready to enact violence not only on other combatants but also on the helpless civilian population. While he regretted the extreme "Cossack" version of marauding, he did not enforce discipline on his own troops or seek to halt the process of "the prosperity of the Galician" changing hands in wartime circumstances. The troops, themselves miserable and constantly under the threat of violence, wreaked havoc on other innocents to compensate for their own suffering. Stepun showed that the constant violence experienced by the soldiers undercut possibilities for "honorable" wartime behavior and that ethical codes of conduct lost their meaning in wartime circumstances.

Not all of those involved in looting and other crimes against civilians were remorseful. One of Fedorchenko's narrators justified his own participation in looting: "And to be honest, it wasn't a sin. It's all the same. If we didn't [take things], then others would, because the owners were not there." This soldier's explanation had an ethnic undercurrent to it since the "owners" of the house in question—terrified Jewish civilians—had fled for their lives from the approaching Russian army. By casting blame on the terrorized Jews for leaving their homes, this soldier justified looting as a morally neutral action. The soldier also cast blame on any Jewish men who left their women behind; from this soldier's point of view, it was only to be expected that the soldiers would rape any Jewish women they found because of the lack of sexual partners at the front: "Lord, when you catch sight of a woman, you neigh like a stallion. . . . Whether she's weeping or not, you get down to it."[105] According to the ethical scheme of this warrior, both material possessions and women who were left behind by fleeing or absent men belonged to the occupying army and could be taken at will without any regrets.

The soldier's narrative made clear that because of pervasive anti-Semitism, most soldiers engaged in the looting of Jewish homes with special enthusiasm. The Jews who served in the Russian army were placed in a particularly unpleasant position of witnessing their comrades' gleeful harassment of Galician Jews. The soldier who felt that looting was "not a sin" described an encounter that took place in a wealthy Jewish home. As the men of the company were dividing up the linens, they were interrupted by one of "their Jews" who said, "Lads, we shouldn't act this way." When his angry shouts brought in the company commander, the commander laughed, but ordered them to drop the goods. While this Jewish soldier was able to prevent this particular act of looting, his success came at a high cost to him: both the men in the company and the company commander beat the "yid" so severely that he ended up in the hospital.[106] This scene revealed some of the darkest aspects of the tsarist army in wartime. Although soldiers were supposed to be regulated by a strict ethical code, when they broke it, neither the soldiers nor their commander saw the violation of the code as a "sin," particularly if the victim was a rich, Jewish "enemy." The Jewish soldier, on the other hand, served as the voice of conscience in decrying the injustices being done to the Jewish civilian population in the occupied territories. For his righteousness, however, the soldier himself became a victim to ethnic violence within the army. The tsarist army was revealed to be an amoral breeding ground for harassment, theft, ethnic violence, and violence against women enacted by both the officers and the rank-and-file soldiers.

BYSTANDERS AND PROTECTORS

The narrator of the deportation scene placed himself at "the scene of the crime" even if he studiously avoided representing his own actions, while the second narrator justified his own participation in looting and rape. Many other inter-war narrators presented themselves as innocent bystanders who described the effects of violence only after it had already occurred. These narrators articulated a much more benign relationship to the victims, whom they sought to comfort and aid. One of Fedorchenko's soldiers represented himself as such a bystander and described the actions of "soldierdom" (*soldatnia*) on a poor Jewish family, not specifying the identity of the soldiers in question. Since he did not refer to the perpetrators as "the enemy," or narrate the scene in the trope of "atrocity," he implied that "soldierdom" consisted of his compatriots in the Russian Imperial Army, though he did not say it directly.

> How many ruined children I have seen here! There is one little Jewish boy that I cannot forget. Think of it! In a single hour, soldierdom completely orphaned him. They beat his mother to death, hanged his father, and tortured and outraged his sister. And this boy was left, not more than eight years old, and with him a baby brother not yet weaned. I tried to give him bread as gently as possible, and to stroke his head. He cried out like some kind of vampire, and with that cry, set off running over anything that lay in his way. After he was out of sight, one could long hear him squeal like a beast from grief and orphanhood.[107]

This scene revealed the intensity of the violence against the Jewish population in areas of the Austro-Hungarian Empire occupied by the Russian army. Soviet readers could learn that the inevitable looting and the scorched earth and resettlement policies of a defeated and retreating Russian army were sometimes accompanied by extreme violence. This violence was directed not only against males who were potential Austrian or German soldiers, but against their wives and children. The speaker depicted the aftermath of a spree of rape and murder by describing the plight of an orphaned child who had been transformed into a "vampire" or "beast" by the actions of the soldiers.

The narrator described his own actions, on the other hand, as humane. He did not discuss his own whereabouts during that "single hour" in which the murders took place. Instead he explained his failed attempt to assist the victims. The little Jewish boy's transformation from a normal child into a feral animal made assistance impossible. The boy, made wild by grief, rejected the soldier's tenderness and nourishment. The child and his infant brother were now beyond all help, which made it unlikely that they would survive. This scene brings into relief the tragedy of all of the participants: the murdered Jews, the survivors of the original attack who were nevertheless lost, and the compassionate bystander who could not ameliorate the evil acts whose aftermath he witnessed. There was no heroism or redemption for anyone in this particular wartime episode.

Fedorchenko included another painful anecdote about a soldier's feeble attempt to help the victim of a heinous crime that he had failed to prevent. In this case, a young girl was the victim of rape:

> And there she is, a slip of a girl. They are all like this. And who takes such girls? I do not say. This one is nine years old, not more. . . . Well, come here. Come here. Don't be afraid. . . . You are ashamed? . . . Oh how gaunt you are. . . . Here is half a ruble for you, now money is cheap. . . . Oh you Akul'ka! . . . Betia? That is also a name. There you are Betia, you did not pray much to your angel, and they hurt you, Betia. . . . Go on your way, dear one. . . . War, war. . . .[108]

This shocking vignette revealed the depraved behavior of Russian soldiers who abducted refugee children and sexually abused them. The narrator emerged on the scene after others had already raped the girl. He described her as small and gaunt, likely malnourished. The narrator made a point of saying that he would not identify who had committed such an outrage, but he indicated that the girl was not alone in her plight. She was one of many "Akul'kas" and "Betias" and perhaps other girls whose names started with the rest of the letters of the Russian alphabet. The narrator thus implied that many soldiers were guilty of the sexual abuse of the vulnerable displaced population, yet he chose not to reveal specific perpetrators or call them to account. Instead, he even shifted some blame onto the girl, pointedly asking her if she was ashamed, and accusing her of bringing about her own misfortune by not praying hard enough to her guardian angel.

This soldier was ineffectual in his attempts to aid the girl. He offered her money, but then admitted that money was now "cheap," and so giving her money was neither a great sacrifice on his part, nor a great help to her. His advice to the girl to "go on her way" also rang hollow amidst the massive dislocations of the war. How could a defenseless and starving nine-year-old make her way alone through a war zone? What could be her destination or her fate on her own, as one of the estimated six million refugees, or nearly 5 percent of the total population of the empire, who became "a whole empire walking," across Russia?[109] The soldier revealed his own compassion for the child, but an inability to save her from her fall into prostitution. All of these protagonists and narrators failed to live up to the masculine role of protecting women and children. Instead, they helplessly watched the innocent suffer and die at the hands of their own compatriots. This was the tragedy of "War, war . . ." revealed in Soviet World War I memory. Soldiers who desired to uphold an honor code repeatedly experienced defeat, frustration, and humiliation.

Other Soviet-era accounts of World War I recorded violence and looting against non-Russian civilians from the point of view of a moral soldier who attempted to protect the civilian population. For example, the committed Bolshevik Pireiko described how he shielded some Jewish civilians from a Cossack pogrom in Rava-Russkaia as the Russians were retreating from the town. Pireiko agreed to spend the night with a Jewish family with whom he had earlier boarded. At nightfall, the Cossacks came to the door yelling, "Open up, Jew-bird (*zhid parkhatyi*)!" When Pireiko, "a Russian soldier," opened the door, they left that house in peace, only to wreak havoc on other Jewish homes in the town, plundering, killing, and "tormenting innocent people and even children" just because they were Jewish.[110] Pireiko's tale cast himself as hero, the Jews as victims, and the Cossacks as villains in a story that bemoaned ethnic violence, while, paradoxically, setting off the Cossack as a barbaric other. A significant aspect of Pireiko's description of his wartime experience was the recording of his earnest attempt to enforce the honor code that protected the civilian population. Yet the scene ultimately showed Pireiko's weakness. His actions only deflected the violence from one Jewish family to another, without being able to stop it. Pireiko framed his own actions as honorable, but also revealed that they were ultimately ineffectual in preventing "Cossacks" from marauding.

In the first two volumes of *Quiet Flows the Don*, Grigorii Melekhov also attempted to follow the honor code and showed distress because he was repeatedly unsuccessful in intervening when injustice was being committed against unarmed civilians and prisoners of war. He wanted to kill the brutal Cossack Uriupin to revenge a young Austrian prisoner of war whom Uriupin had shot in cold blood. Grigorii attempted to shoot Uriupin but missed. Grigorii threatened to try again, but Uriupin sneered, "Bullshit! You won't kill me," and he was right. Grigorii did not make a second attempt, revealing his own hatred of the act of killing.[111] Here Melekhov took on the same "heroic" role as the conscious Bolshevik Pireiko, determined to protect the innocent, but failing to do so. This repeated failure to protect the innocent compromised the masculinity of the narrators and protagonists in World War I discourse and showed the ways in which war forced the soldiers to operate beyond the boundaries of accepted moral codes.

In discussions of the violent nature of war, Soviet censors of the 1920s were most comfortable with the presentation of ethnic and gendered violence against civilians from the point of view of the victims or of horrified bystanders who were unable to intervene. Sof'ia Fedorchenko's representations of violence from the point of view of common soldiers who themselves looted, raped, and murdered civilians were often, though not always, censored both after 1925 and even into the post-Stalin period.[112]

CIVIL WAR VIOLENCE

The literature about violence in World War I must be seen as part of the continuum of the literary depiction of violence during the Civil War. Civil War literature dealt with many of the same themes: the atrocities of the enemy, the behavior of "Red" Cossacks toward the civilian population, rape, looting, and the frustration of bystanders unable to protect civilians from their own troops or from the enemy's. Soviet writers often designated rape as an "atrocity" committed only by Whites. The gifted Soviet-Jewish writer Isaak Babel' was a political officer at the front during the Soviet–Polish War of 1920, and he witnessed the aftermath of one of the many Civil War–era pogroms in which Whites robbed and terrorized the Jewish population in retribution for their supposed support for the Reds.[113] He wrote about White attacks on Jews in a September 17, 1920, newspaper article in *Krasnyi kavalerist* (Red Cavalryman) unambiguously titled "Murderers Who Have Yet to Be Clubbed to Death." The article described in horrific detail the actions of the White Cossack captain Iakovlev during a pogrom in Komarow: "Seventy-year-old men with crushed skulls lay naked in pools of blood, infants, often still alive, with fingers hacked off, and old women, raped, their stomachs slashed open, crouched in corners with faces on which wild, unbearable desperation had congealed." Babel' continued, "Two hundred women were raped, many of them tortured to death. To escape the rapists, women had jumped from second- and third-floor windows, breaking limbs and necks."[114] This piece, written as the Soviet forces were retreating from Poland in disarray, demanded that the Soviet soldiers enact violence to take their revenge for inhuman acts against Polish-Jewish women. In a familiar gendered trope, Babel''s wartime writings sanctioned the men of the Red Army to kill in the defense of all civilian women as well as old men and infants. Fedor Gladkov's *Cement (Tsement)*, one of the most significant Soviet novels of the 1920s, also detailed the rape of the heroine Dasha Chumalova by White officers and the torture and execution of her comrades.[115]

While World War I accounts did not describe rapes to the level of detail that Babel' did in his newspaper article, they admitted that rape was an action that could be perpetrated by one's own soldiers. In Babel''s unpublished 1920 diary, on which he based his *Red Cavalry* stories, Babel' also acknowledged that rape was not an exclusively White phenomenon. His terse observation spoke volumes about a masculinity out of control in the context of war and engaged in terrorizing the Jewish civilian population: "All our fighting men—velvet caps, rape, forelocks, battles, revolution and syphilis. All Galicia is infected."[116] Babel''s published work was also highly unusual, if not absolutely unique in the Soviet context, because his *Red Cavalry* stories described both metaphorical violence and actual violence enacted by Red soldiers.

After the war, however, Babel' constructed the *Red Cavalry* cycle of short stories with multiple narrators who espoused multiple and dialogical points of view on the enactment of male violence. While some of the narrators openly espoused and excused violence, the central narrator, the Jewish intellectual Kirill Liutov (the same pen name Babel' used in his newspaper articles), reflected on the male desire to commit violence and its consequences in a story titled "My First Goose." Anxious to be accepted by his Cossack comrades despite his university education and his spectacles, Liutov demanded dinner from a half-blind old woman. When she refused to oblige, he grabbed a saber and killed her goose: "I caught the goose and forced it to the ground, its head cracking and bleeding. Its white neck lay stretched out in the dung, and the wings folded down over the slaughtered bird."[117] With this "ritual reenactment" of murder, Liutov gained the acceptance of his Cossack comrades.[118] Yet he also recounted the effect of his action; the story ends with his admission that "I dreamed and saw women in my dreams, and only my heart, crimson with murder, screeched and bled."[119] The goose was his own heart.

In another story, "Salt," the narrator Balmashev offered a justification for rape in his verbal attack on a woman who had pretended that she was traveling with a small infant so that she would be allowed on the train with the Red Cossacks, when in fact the "baby" was a sack of salt that she was smuggling. When she begged for forgiveness he said:

> Address yourself to these two girls, who are now crying for having suffered under us last night. Address yourself to our women on the wheat fields of Kuban,

who are wearing out their womanly strength without husbands, and to their husbands, who are lonely too, and so are forced against their will to rape girls who cross their paths! And you they didn't touch, you improper woman, although you should have been the first to be touched. Address yourself to Russia, crushed by pain![120]

According to Balmashev, rape was an inevitable part of being a lonely soldier torn from his domestic happiness, and the soldiers regretted raping innocent girls but were forced to do so. Balmashev saw rape as a suitable punishment for the woman's immoral behavior, but treated her even more severely, throwing her off the moving train and then shooting her to death. Along with such works by Babel', World War I memory was one of a very limited number of places in Soviet culture that alerted readers to the wartime sexual violence against women perpetrated by the "good guys." Such accounts acknowledge that sexual violence was an inevitable accompaniment to war and not the action of a few depraved or vicious individuals.

The Soviet Union cannot be easily categorized along with Germany and Italy in terms of the brutalization of the soldiers and the normalization of violence, since Soviet accounts of war generally framed violence as un-Soviet, a response to enemy atrocity, a regretful necessity, or an unfortunate spontaneous act. The notion of violence as an unambiguously purifying or manly act was generally absent from Soviet sources until the very end of the interwar period. Soviet authors reflected on violence by acknowledging the existence of religious pacifists and others who consciously refused to commit violence. They also included the agonized points of view of those who spontaneously committed acts of violence and later regretted their thoughtless and instinctive actions.

While Soviet depictions often blamed wartime violence on un-Soviet "others" such as officers and Cossacks, many examples of violence revealed that "ordinary men" could easily engage in the abuse of unarmed prisoners and civilians due to the circumstances of the war itself.[121] Given the brutal realities of war, soldiers were often unable to fulfill the masculine duty of protecting the innocent against the depredations of their fellow soldiers, and were sometimes either compelled to or even voluntarily took part in raping, looting, and murdering civilians and evicting them from their homes. Soviet World War I discourse displayed the entire spectrum of soldiers, from those who refused to engage in violence, to those who were reluctant killers, to those who killed quite willingly. It depicted war as producing the circumstances in which spontaneous and senseless violence could and did routinely occur; war was understood in these texts as producing senseless tragedy as much as it created heroism.

The Soviet example certainly upholds the notion that the enactment of violence is central to conceptions of wartime masculinity and male citizenship, but in Soviet World War I discourse, violence did not always build masculine identity. It was equally possible for violence to unman and haunt its perpetrators, sapping away their lives and killing them as they killed. Literary renderings of violence in the Soviet Union were particularly sensitive to the possibility that violence destroyed its enactor, and they dwelt on the negative consequences of violence in shaping the warrior's identity. While willingness to defend the nation through violence may have sometimes been seen as a virtue, Soviet authors also understood that those who enacted wartime violence could be morally compromised by it as well.

5

World War I and the Definition of Russianness

Notions of religious faith, the construction of heroes and enemies, representations of manhood and womanhood, justifications of wartime violence, and
articulations of national identity are all inextricably intertwined. Although
the previous chapters have focused primarily on the themes of religion, gender, and violence, they have also touched upon many aspects of national identity. Religious interpretations of World War I understood death in combat as
a sacrifice on behalf of the nation that would bring the soldier eternal memory
and an eternal reward. While Soviet ideologists may have contested this idea,
it nonetheless remained resonant in Soviet World War I and revolutionary discourse. Notions of military service on behalf of the nation and representations
of heroic conduct in warfare were a constituent part of both tsarist and Soviet "nationalized masculinity" and gendered depictions of citizenship more
generally. The violence of war was often intensified by ethnic hatred, rivalry,
and distrust; despite Soviet efforts to emphasize class over ethnicity, Soviet
war memory revealed that ethnic difference heightened the violent nature of
encounters among soldiers and between soldiers and civilians and that some
ethnicities (Cossacks, for instance) were understood to be violent by their very
nature. Building on these discussions of national identity, this chapter considers the nature of "Russianness" in the late tsarist and Soviet period. It focuses
on moments of self-mobilization to fight for the nation, instances of refusal
to bear arms for the nation, the dilemmas of internationalism, and the role of
ethnicity in defining external and internal enemies.

World War I was greeted with a wide variety of emotions across Europe. Descriptions of the various nations' enthusiastic reactions to the outbreak of war almost immediately became part of the process of national mobilization in the guise of "the myth of war enthusiasm."[1] Of course, the realities of mobilization were much more complex than the myth of the population rising as one in a blaze of patriotism to defeat the perfidious enemy. In all combatant countries, reactions to the war varied substantially along class, ethnic, regional, and gender lines.[2] Throughout the war, both pro- and antiwar advocates constantly attempted to measure morale and to assess the strength of their particular point of view. The extent of the population's enthusiasm for war and its opposite, the famed civilian "stab in the back" that sabotaged the war effort, became key elements of contestation both during the war itself and in the European postwar order.

In the Russian Empire, the patriots and the internationalist "defeatists" were mirror images of one another in their assessments of the mood of the population: patriots tended to emphasize and exaggerate the enthusiasm of the people for the war, while "defeatists" tended to emphasize workers' strikes and riots during mobilization to demonstrate lower-class opposition to the war from the start. Each side also admitted, however, that the *narod* (the people) did not always behave in the way that their side desired. Analysts from both sides had a ready explanation for the population's actions: the supposed "backwardness" of the Russian people. "Backwardness" was used to explain both the narod's failure to embrace a patriotic national identity, and its unfortunate propensity to do so when "intoxicated" by chauvinism. Because of these countervailing tendencies and conflicting contemporary interpretations, historians have sharply disagreed about the strength of patriotic identification with the Russian national project during World War I.

In recent years there has been lively scholarly debate about the extent to which the Russian Empire was able to mobilize its multiethnic and peasant populations to identify with the Russian nation. Some scholars continue to uphold the older historiography's claims that there was no Russian national consciousness or Russian nation during World War I. Others push the antinational argument even further, arguing that there was an "absence of an articulate sense of national identity" not only during World War I, but all throughout the 1920s, and even as late as the mid-1930s when a "Russo-centric étatism" emerged.[3] A number of historians have recently challenged this antinational historiography, arguing that because Russia was one of the "old, continuous nations," it could draw on elements of "proto-national identity" and put them to new wartime uses.[4] They argue that Russian cultural figures and the Russian public produced and consumed a variety of patriotic discourses and adopted patriotic identities throughout the war. The growth of national consciousness did not, however, necessarily enhance the war effort or bolster the tsarist state. The war called forth national sentiments that created civil disorder and destabilized the monarchy.[5]

My analysis of national identity in World War I remembrance engages various aspects of this debate, including the extent of Russian national identity during World War I, the timing of the development of a particular Russo-Soviet national identity, and continuities between tsarist and Soviet national identities. The contests in the 1920s and 1930s pitting an incipient Russian/Soviet patriotism against the ideology of international class solidarity illuminate a Russian/Soviet nation in the process of being constructed.

NATIONALISM IN THE TSARIST ERA

Like writers in many Western European countries, Russian literary figures saw the war as the beginning of a new age, or as a purifying fire that would lead to salvation. As it became clear that Russia would have to make great sacrifices to wage the war, writers depicted wartime sacrifice as Christ-like suffering that would lead to national redemption. Aleksei Tolstoi envisioned the war as a phenomenon that cleansed both the souls of men and the spirit of the Russian nation. He wrote that, at the beginning of the war, "The revolution occurred in a single day. Toward evening we became a strong, decisive, pure people."[6] Both Tolstoi and Nikolai Gumilev pointed to the strength of spirit (*dukh*) as a key element in fighting the war. Tolstoi argued that Russians possessed "the greatness of spirit" to defeat the Austrians, who were "dead in spirit" and tried to make up for this failure by "technology and iron discipline."[7] Gumilev described the spirit of the individual warrior as being "as real as our body only infinitely stronger."[8] It was Russian spirit that would overcome material obstacles such as superior numbers of better-armed forces. Implicit in both accounts by these aristocratic writers was that "spirit" was something that could unite all the Russian people: officers and conscripts, middle-class students and peasants. These authors argued for a national revival among all classes in the crucible of war and a breaking down of the social barriers that had previously kept these groups apart. After "the great retreat" in 1915, however, the Russian educated classes were much less optimistic about this mystical unification of Russians into a powerful spiritual and physical entity.[9]

While it may have been muted after autumn 1915, this idea of Russian fighting spirit was not entirely lost. In their analysis of the "mood" (*nastroenie dukha*) of the army, the military censors attached to the command staff of the armies of the Southwestern Front revealed that a portion (though by no means all) of the private correspondence they reviewed in late 1916 still articulated a vision of holy purpose and Russian strength and unity.[10] One letter from a soldier in a Tambov infantry detachment exhibited Russian bravado by complaining that Russia's "damned" enemies were as prideful as Napoleon, but with God's help, "Russian eagles would give it to the German and the Turk good and hot" (*zadadut' nemtsu i turku khoroshago pertsu*).[11] A national discourse of heroism thus persisted well beyond "the great retreat."

Soldiers' letters connected the glorious future of the nation to the sacrifices of the Russian military. One soldier from the 15th Siberian Rifle Regiment dreamed of a future time of peace and freedom when "a heroic and mighty Russia would be renowned in the whole universe and would remember our heroes who laid down their lives for Faith, Tsar, and Fatherland."[12] The reward for the soldiers' sacrifices would be the grateful memory of a powerful Russian nation.

Many letters tried to give meaning to loss of life by connecting the individual to the nation. One no doubt formulaic letter, written by an officer to the sister of a fellow officer killed in action, stated that in his bravery and heroism the recipient's brother was a "true-Russian officer." While "serving as a valiant example" to his subordinates, this officer "showed how one must die defending the holy faith and the Russian land. Your brother is one of the brave . . . for whom all Russia prays in its numerous churches."[13] This letter sought to comfort the family of the fallen not only by praising the courage of the officer, but by underscoring his Russianness, his dedication to the Orthodox faith and the Russian land that was repaid by all of Russia remembering him in its prayers. The letter envisioned a Russian community of faith to which the officer belonged and through which his memory would live on and the suffering of his family would be relieved.

Other letters likewise linked the concept of the Russian nation with destiny, sacrifice, and memory. As one poorly educated artillerist wrote to his brother in Vologda province in the fall of 1916: "Do not be angry with your fate. Such is our lot, for which we were born. To stand up for our Tsar and motherland, we may have to lose our young heads for this holy cause, but for centuries they will remember us with a good word."[14] The writer of this letter was engaged in dialogue with a brother who was angry about the role he was forced to play in the war effort. This dialogue showed that even as late as the end of 1916, some common soldiers envisioned fighting as a sacred duty for which they were destined by fate. This destiny required them to be willing to sacrifice their lives for both tsar and mother country, but in return, they would gain immortality through memory. And while rank-and-file soldiers of the Russian Imperial Army may have increasingly rejected this soldier's sentiments, his engagement in this dialogue preserved the idea of a holy war on behalf of a national community who would remember its soldiers for centuries with a "good word."

These examples show that tsarist nationalistic discourse did not simply die out at the end of 1915 but was a continuous presence all the way throughout the war, even as it was contested by revolutionary rhetoric. While the February Revolution overturned the ideal of fighting for the tsar, notions of Russian military prowess, motherland and fatherland, national spirit, holy war, and personal sacrifice rewarded by the memory of the nation flowed unimpeded into the Soviet era.

THE PARADOX OF THE SOVIET VOLUNTEER

In Western European literature memorializing World War I, the volunteer holds pride of place as the quintessential hero. This soldier, caught up by war enthusiasm, voluntarily offered his life as a solemn and holy sacrifice for his country.[15] Russian scholars have likewise pointed to enthusiastic patriotic demonstrations in many cities and towns at the beginning of the war involving wide swaths of the Russian population from leading political figures and intellectuals to ordinary workers and shopkeepers.[16] While this kind of war enthusiasm tended to fade along with Russian hopes of military success, the letters from the front in late 1916 show that it never entirely disappeared. Recent scholarship has suggested, however, that the most prevalent reaction to mobilization in Russia was not enthusiasm but quiet and personal grief, and that there was also "active public opposition" to mobilization in the form of draft riots and evasion.[17] At the outset of the war, there were some already sympathetic to the antiwar position of the Bolsheviks, though this stance did not substantially capture the popular mood until after the tsar was overthrown in February 1917.

Some later Soviet accounts emphasized this oppositional response and downplayed the notion of war enthusiasm altogether. An illustrated documentary history titled *1914*, created by the writer Il'ia Feinberg and the constructivist artist Solomon Telingater to commemorate the twentieth anniversary of the outbreak of the war, sought to help "unmask" the contemporary "instigators of war" by using the events of 1914 as an "object-lesson." The work was a unique "artistic composition of documentary material on the basis of the organic combination of text with photograph."[18] It included a picture of Russian workers reading the mobilization order "with downcast arms and gloomy faces." The work also cited evidence that "on the day the reserves were mobilized, as a sign of protest against the war, more than twenty St. Petersburg enterprises went on strike. In some places workers met the reservists with shouts of 'Down with the War.'" Feinberg also quoted Aleksei Brusilov's lament that the men in the trenches went into battle without "any elevation of spirit whatsoever" because they had no idea why they were fighting.[19] In this interpretation, it was compulsion and not enthusiasm that propelled the tsarist war effort.

But some of the tsarist soldiers-turned-Bolsheviks, who later wrote memoirs or appeared in novels, had willingly gone to war. After the fact, these postwar Soviet memoir and literary accounts had to justify and contextualize the acts of these individual volunteers and to explain their protagonists' motivations for serving willingly after conscription. Western European–style war "enthusiasm" was transformed by Soviet ideology into "ecstasy" or "intoxication" from the noxious fumes (*ugar*) of chauvinism. Soviet analysts blamed the ruling classes, "Great-Russian nationalists," "reactionaries," and the clergy for releasing the "chauvinistic fumes" that "enveloped the army." The editors of a 1932 document collection asserted that peasant-soldier patriotism was only temporary and that it was not innate "spontaneous monarchism." It was the "unconscious repetition of age-old, old-fashioned traditions that had been inculcated by the landowner-bourgeois elites." The editors did acknowledge that some of the patriotic sentiment came from the soldiers themselves and was a reflection of their "warlike ardor" and their desire to show their boldness.[20] Tsarist patriotism, in this sense, was a positive attribute that could be seen as a reflection of the peasant soldier's innate bravery and martial potential.

Ol'ga Chaadaeva (a Soviet historian and editor of several document collections on the revolutionary era) wrote in 1935 that chauvinist influence was class-dependent and was most notable among the privileged petty-bourgeois stratum of workers.[21] Chaadaeva conceded, however, that "a part of the proletariat was attracted by fraudulent words about the protection and defense of the fatherland," subjected to an "attack" by the "blood-thirsty despoiler" Germany. Chaadaeva also argued that thousands upon thousands of soldiers obediently went to the front because they could not avoid going and because they felt peace would be declared only after victory.[22] Soviet analysts resorted to a combination of alien class attitudes, fatalistic passivity, and false consciousness in explaining soldiers' attitudes toward the outbreak of war, while still acknowledging the existence of innate martial instincts among the lower classes.

Innate desire to fight seemed, however, to be concentrated among Orthodox and Slavic lower classes. In their introduction to a collection of letters written by Tatar soldiers, editors claimed that while the Tatar bourgeoisie and Muslim clergy supported the war wholeheartedly, the Tatar workers and peasants were resistant to war enthusiasm. The editors claimed that "a significantly smaller portion of Tatar soldiers yielded to the chauvinistic fumes than did Russians," and they explained that Tatar soldiers "endured a double oppression in the Tsarist army." If officers were "simply brutes" in relation to the Russian soldiers, they were "fierce brutes" in relation to the Tatars. Furthermore, the "unconscious portion" of the Russian soldiers participated in the humiliation of the Tatars, "mocking Tatars as Turks and infidels." Soviet authors pointed to lack of consciousness to explain not only the desire of Orthodox soldiers to fight the war, but also their abuse of their non-Orthodox peers. This intense abuse hindered the development of patriotism among non-Russians and explained in turn non-Orthodox peoples' (such as Tatars' and Jews') lack of inclination to fight for the tsar at all.[23]

Those authors admitting to the existence of any war enthusiasm at the beginning of the war demonstrated its temporary and fleeting nature. Once soldiers began to experience war, argued Soviet analysts, the patriotism of the Russian soldier was destroyed "without a trace" by military failures, interruption of supply "leading to sheer starvation, senseless regimentation, discipline of the rod, . . . unbridled mockery of the defenders of the motherland, getting beaten in the face, flogging, and so forth. . . ." The mistreatment of soldiers not only led to the disappearance of patriotism, but also to mass suicide, desertion, refusal to follow orders, and the hatred of officers.[24] The soldiers refused to fulfill their innate military potential under the unbearable conditions of the tsarist army. These conditions, however, laid the foundation for revolution and the creation of the glorious Red Army.

But what about those soldiers who were already conscious revolutionaries when the war began? Bolshevik doctrines produced paradoxes for "conscious" warriors, creating ethical situations and moral choices that were difficult to explain to a Soviet audience. In 1915 Lenin wrote enthusiastically about the revolutionary possibilities offered by mobilization, if not voluntary service:

> Today you are given a ballot paper—take it, learn to organize so as to use it as a weapon against your enemies. . . . Tomorrow your ballot paper is taken from you and you are given a rifle or a splendid and most up-to-date quick firing gun— take this weapon of death and destruction, pay no heed to the mawkish snivelers who are afraid of war; too much still remains in the world that must be destroyed with fire and sword for the emancipation of the working class; if anger and desperation grow among the masses, if a revolutionary situation arises, prepare to create new organisations and use these useful weapons of death and destruction against your own government and your own bourgeoisie.[25]

The ideal Bolshevik had to walk a very fine line in his attitude toward the tsarist war effort as it was in progress. On the one hand, he should probably not volunteer before being "given" his rifle. Nor should he be enthusiastic about going to war on behalf of the tsarist government, since he should reject Great Russian chauvinism and Russian imperialist ambitions and ought to have recognized from the outset that the war was illegitimate. Adopting the "revolutionary defensism" of some socialists was also a serious ideological mistake, because it erroneously lent support to the class alien autocracy and bourgeoisie. On the other hand, refusing to be mobilized was not acceptable either, because the good Bolshevik was certainly not a "mawkish sniveler" who feared war, but a brave and capable soldier. So, the good Bolshevik had the illogical task of fighting skillfully and bravely while learning to shoot his "splendid" new weaponry at his German and Austrian proletarian brothers. He fought, paradoxically, for a cause he explicitly rejected, preparing to eventually turn his guns against his own government.

One Soviet-era character who attempted to explain his motivation for going to war in a strictly Leninist framework was the Bolshevik Il'ia Bunchuk in Mikhail Sholokhov's *Quiet Flows the Don*. Bunchuk was a volunteer who chose to enlist during World War I in order to train himself for future combat with the upper classes. He announced to his lieutenant, "I'm interested in the art of war. I want to learn it." Going to the front and serving in a machine-gun platoon provided Bunchuk with the military experience necessary for a revolutionary leader. He learned how to use the most modern weaponry in the service of the future revolution. Bunchuk was a Leninist through and through, demonstrating an interest in modern mechanized killing where technology efficiently produced the death of the enemy. Furthermore, Bunchuk was so skilled at his job that he earned the rank of cornet, a commissioned officer.

In a scene set in October 1916, Bunchuk's Leninism was underscored by his reading of an article written by Lenin to other officers in his unit. Implausibly, Bunchuk shared his revolutionary ideas with these officers, affirming that he was a defeatist who espoused Lenin's slogan of "turning the imperialist war into a Civil War." Bunchuk read aloud the passage cited above and also quoted another of Lenin's articles, in which he asserted that the horrors of war will "enlighten, teach, awaken, organize, harden and prepare for the war against the bourgeoisie."[26] One of the other officers (Lisnitskii, who also seduced Grigorii Melekhov's beloved Aksin'ia) immediately pinpointed the contradiction in Bunchuk's position, saying, "The man is against war, against the destruction of his—what do you call them?—his class brothers, and suddenly he becomes an officer. . . . How many German workers have you and your machine-gunners disposed of?" Bunchuk, of course, cannot adequately answer this question, saying that he volunteered because he would have been called up anyway. Not only did Bunchuk have to justify volunteering, he also had to provide a rationalization for killing his "class brothers." He explained, "The knowledge I've gained here in the trenches will come in useful in the future," and then he quoted Lenin's praise of the tsarist army for its organization of the millions.[27] The scene revealed that preparing for the revolution required learning how to kill Germans and Austrians as efficiently as possible—whether they were fellow workers or not. While Bunchuk's military service revealed his bravery and his talent as a machine-gunner, his activities also suggested his failure as an internationalist.

Bunchuk soon remedied this failure and solved the contradiction by deserting. He disappeared from the front immediately after his conversation with the other officers, leaving copies of a revolutionary leaflet behind him. The leaflet bemoaned the killing of workers by other workers and encouraged the soldiers to turn their guns against the Russian tsar, industrialists, and landowners. It demanded that the troops "fraternize with the German and Austrian soldiers. Reach out through the wire fences with which they have caged you off from one another like wild beasts. You are brothers in toil. . . ." Having learned sufficiently about weaponry and organization, it now was honorable for Bunchuk to desert the tsarist cause so that he could avoid killing any more Austrian and German brothers.[28] Desertion and fraternization thus became heroic acts.

Actual Bolshevik leaflets reproduced and discussed in interwar histories of World War I also expressed ambivalence about Russians having to go to war and to commit violence against their proletarian brothers. One leaflet published by Tver' Bolsheviks in August 1915 noted that if "subordinated by force, it was necessary to take up arms, then it was also necessary to remember that in the enemy trenches there were brother-proletarians, also taken violently and living by the same thought."[29] The pamphlet seemed to suggest that front-line soldiers should try to avoid killing the so-called enemy. Orthodox Bolsheviks remained in a practical and moral bind in which no action that they took could be fully revolutionary. It was difficult for the conscious Bolshevik to explain his stance on the war whatever his involvement.

The memoirs of Bolshevik worker Aleksandr Pireiko also confronted the inherent contradictions in the stance of Russian revolutionaries toward mobilization. Pireiko, a conscious worker and Social Democrat, refused to go off to war voluntarily and proclaimed, "To the devil with you and your motherland (*rodina*); let the one who has a motherland go and defend her."[30] He explicitly rejected the Russian national idea in his refusal of military service and articulated the notion that tsarist Russia could never be the motherland of the proletariat.

Following Lenin's defeatist position, Pireiko also rejected the "defensist" Mensheviks and Socialist Revolutionaries who feared German victory. He noted derisively that "among these fervent defensists one did not meet a single person voluntarily going off to war."[31] Pireiko here made a clear distinction between Bolsheviks who did not volunteer for war because of their principled stand against it, and the Mensheviks and SRs who supported the war but were too cowardly to volunteer for combat. While volunteering implied a lack of Bolshevik consciousness, not volunteering for a war that one supported revealed the far worse trait of cowardice. Pireiko accused the non-Bolshevik revolutionaries of being "warriors at someone else's expense until mobilization concerned them." Then they suddenly became "defeatists-Bolsheviks." Pireiko admitted that cowards were attracted to Bolshevik defeatism even as he strove to justify his own status as a conscious revolutionary rather than a coward. Yet to the outside observer, evasion was perceived as cowardly no matter what the motivation.

Pireiko next recounted in detail his unsuccessful attempts to evade mobilization by moving from Riga to Ekaterinoslav. When he was called up in Ekaterinoslav, he admitted that he was "seduced by Menshevism," and paid an invalid to appear with his documents at the mobilization point. Unfortunately for Pireiko, his invalid was "pronounced fit" for military service and he was conscripted into the army.[32] Pireiko attempted to narrate his decidedly unheroic efforts at evading service as part of his heroic tale of acquiring Bolshevik consciousness. He also justified his status as a soldier by demonstrating that he had no choice but to serve, and by documenting his unwillingness to fight for the tsar. Significantly, a later edition of Pireiko's memoir recast Pireiko's tales of evasion to remove any hint of cowardice.[33]

Other Soviet-era testimonies frankly acknowledged the earnest desire of some of the "unconscious" narod to go to war after they had been conscripted. These accounts often emphasize the youth and inexperience of the participants, who would not have wanted to leave their homes and their families had they known better. Sof'ia Fedorchenko recorded the words of one such soldier in *The People at War:* "And I went very willingly, even. My family simply covered me with tears, but I stood like a statue, and hemmed and hawed in shame. My only thought was to go as quickly as possible. I love a sensational life, something different. War suits me well."[34] The experience of Artur (Artem) Vavilov was extremely similar to that of Fedorchenko's soldier. He did not think about the fate of his elderly parents but was "just a childish little boy (*mal'chishka-mal'chishkoi*). My relatives are crying all around me, and only I am laughing, as if the call-up has nothing to do with me, as if it were some kind of joke and I do not understand for whom they are crying and why."[35] Vavilov further admitted that he was attracted to the idea of being a soldier because he had always thought, "The devil take it, how brave the soldier is when he returns from service, as if he were a completely different person from a different kingdom, from a different power."[36]

Some peasant men did not even wait to be called up, but volunteered. The title of V. Dmitriev's 1929 memoir *Volunteer: Remembrances about War and Captivity* openly proclaimed that Dmitriev was eager to become a member of the tsarist army. Although he gradually did develop revolutionary consciousness as a prisoner of war, Dmitriev did not show the slightest evidence of consciousness at the beginning of the war. In retrospect, Dmitriev offered personal reasons for his decision to enlist: he did not get along with his father, a prosperous peasant, and he received encouragement from an uncle at the front who had already earned a medal. He thus headed off to war, in his own self-mocking words, as a greenhorn (literally a milk-sucker—*molokosos*) "to experience the fate of a hero."[37] All of these testimonies reinforced the connection between manliness and warfare. Each of these lower-class men saw the military as a sphere of glamorous adventure, as an opportunity to escape everyday life, to shed their boyish ways, and to mature into "real men." War was an opportunity to experience new sensations and to demonstrate individual worthiness by becoming a brave hero in battle. These accounts show the attraction that military life held for young Russian peasants. While this attitude was not specifically patriotic, it nonetheless mobilized Russian youth to the defense of the fatherland.

Other Soviet-era texts about World War I revealed the explicitly patriotic sentiments of peasant soldiers at the beginning of the war. In 1935, Chaadaeva selectively quoted from letters that had been first published in 1932 in a collection of documents from the archives of the Tatar Republic. One peasant soldier, according to Chaadaeva, "repeated the patriotic press and the authorities" in 1914, by declaring, "[W]e defend the Tsar and Fatherland and, no matter what happens, we strive to finish off our criminally intentioned enemy, who planned to capture us. Under no circumstances do we think of submitting to him, but we will finish him off for good, so that he knows the meaning of a four-sided Russian bayonet." Another such letter proclaimed, "I strive, like every soldier, for the quickest possible victory over the enemy of our motherland, and when we are victorious, only then will we return."[38] It should be noted that Chaadaeva slightly edited the letters that she reproduced, choosing to omit references to "Holy Russia" and the "savage" enemy. While Chaadaeva dismissed the soldiers' letters as mere "repetition" of the chauvinistic press that aimed to "deceive" the population, the documents nonetheless reveal that some lower-class Russians spoke about the war using a common language of patriotism with educated society. These peasants explicitly identified themselves as defenders of the Russian nation.

The 1932 documents included many more references to the Russian nation than Chaadaeva reproduced. The letters spoke of Holy Rus', and they called the tsar "Little Father," and Russia the "motherland Little Mother." The writers sought to prove the prowess of "mother's little sons—Russian warriors" who vowed "to wipe [the enemy] from the face of our native land." These letters employed a language of family that acknowledged the possibility of powerful bonds of affection between warrior-sons and their beloved mother/fatherland.[39] The familial metaphors did not extend, however, to the enemy, whom soldiers most certainly did not see as a brother. The Russian warriors planned to "smash the snotty nose of the German devil," "beat the German like a son of a bitch," and "give what for to the cursed German kielbasa."[40] The faithful reproduction of language that the Kazan censors had identified as "highly patriotic" allowed Soviet readers to see how peasant-soldiers spoke of themselves as part of the tsarist family and how they distanced themselves from the reviled and "cursed" Germans. A few "chauvinistic fumes" thus reached Soviet noses along with the revolutionary themes of international brotherhood and hatred of the tsarist army.

The words of both the patriots and the youthful adventurers showed that, at the outset of the war, the tsarist empire had willing lower-class warriors at its service. Soviet analysts sought to remove accountability for this enthusiasm from the soldiers by emphasizing how they were deceived, how the tsarist state took advantage of the youth and inexperience of its impressionable population, and how quickly the soldiers abandoned these sentiments. Writing in the Soviet era, the memoirists looked back and critiqued their younger "greenhorn" selves. They had been correct that the war would mature them, but it did not do so in the heroic way that they had expected. The authors acknowledged in hindsight that they had been mistaken in their appraisal of war. Now Vavilov and the unnamed soldier understood from experience what their elders had been trying to express to them through their floods of tears: that war was a "misfortune," a "popular (or national) calamity" brought upon them by forces outside of their control, and that having to go off to war was a personal tragedy.[41]

In *Volunteer* Dmitriev recounted how he had matured quickly under fire, and within four months of going to war, his "heroism was as if sunken, and [he] forgot to think about it."[42] Dmitriev explained that he had joined the army because he expected "unusual adventures," but he was deeply disappointed because the tsarist army didn't require "bravery and deftness" but only "submissive, weak-willed obedience." He complained that "instead of battles and engagements where wonders of bravery occur, there are dirty and stinking trenches, lice, and the senseless slaughter of thousands of people."[43] Dmitriev's disillusionment led him to surrender to the Austrians. He then recounted how he eventually escaped to Russia and joined the Bolshevik revolution. In the last line of the memoir Dmitriev was once again a "volunteer," but this time in the Red Army.[44]

Dmitriev's account is striking because of his candid and unapologetic description of his enthusiasm for going to war and his desire for heroism, attributes that many memoir accounts either suppressed or explained away. Dmitriev's memoir combined the trope of the developing revolutionary with tropes found in canonical "ironic" war accounts of educated Western Europeans, depicting initial enthusiasm and a thirst for heroism followed by the shock of disillusionment.[45]

Whether ardently revolutionary or not, whether real or fictional, World War I participants in Soviet narratives had great difficulty in becoming ideal heroes because of the contradictions in Bolshevik ideology. Bunchuk was too willing to kill his international brothers; Pireiko was tainted by cowardice;

Dmitriev, Vavilov, and the other peasant soldiers were stained by chauvinism. No heroic or national narrative could be sustained.

PACIFISM, INTERNATIONALISM, AND LENINISM

Along with narratives that probed the problem of patriotism and identification with the Russian state, World War I discourse also considered the dilemmas of internationalism. In the last chapter, I discussed the strain of Russian pacifism that embraced nonviolence as a moral imperative. But there were also other kinds of pacifism that did not refuse violence per se; instead they rejected the idea of the nation and demanded class loyalty across national lines. An internationalist point of view raised complex issues such as the agony of having to fight a war against one's class brothers and sisters, the proper role of socialists and "bourgeois pacifists" in preserving the peace, and the relationship between pacifism and militant revolutionary struggle. Soviet treatments of World War I have to be understood against the backdrop of Leninist teachings. At the 1912 International Socialist Congress in Basel, delegates embraced the slogan "a war on war." But as Lenin's widow Nadezhda Krupskaia later explained, as early as 1907 Lenin had argued that "the battle against war must set itself the goal not only of struggling for peace" but also of "replacing capitalism with socialism."[46] While Lenin did not oppose socialist desires to prevent imperialist war, he believed that once such a war had begun, it could become a powerful catalyst for revolution. Not surprisingly, when World War I broke out, he advocated "defeatism" to hasten revolution and he urged the combatants to "transform the imperialist war into civil war."

The treatments of pacifist-internationalism in Soviet depictions of World War I did not always share Lenin's emphasis on revolution over peace. In her 1914 diary (published in 1925) Aleksandra Kollontai embraced a pacifist ethos, rejecting national allegiances in favor of international proletarian solidarity. She was in Germany at the time the war broke out, and she and her twenty-year-old son spent an anxious seven weeks there from July 24 to September 6, 1914, when they were permitted to leave the country for Scandinavia.[47] In addition to chronicling the German detention of Russian nationals as enemy aliens, the memoir delivered a blistering critique of the actions of most of Kollontai's German Social Democratic colleagues. Kollontai was horrified by their "chauvinism" and their approbation of a war to "free Russia from tsarism" or to defend German social democracy "from the danger of an invasion by 'dark' Russia."[48]

She wrote approvingly of Karl Liebknecht, one of the few German Social Democrats who sought to "pierce the shroud of national hypnosis" and affirm worker solidarity across national lines.[49] Kollontai was frustrated by her German friends' failure to understand that she did not wish for the victory of Russia simply because she was Russian. Karl Liebknecht teased her about her impossible position: "If you wish for the defeat of Russia—you are a bad internationalist. The defeat of Germany is no less desirable. So will you hope for the defeat of both of them? How can that be done?"[50] Kollontai attempted to escape the suffocating grip of national allegiances by rejecting the war itself. Right before leaving Germany, Kollontai and some of her Social Democratic colleagues decided to take inspiration from the Basel manifesto of 1912 and work for "a war on war."[51]

At times, Kollontai's arguments against war slipped out of a strictly class rubric into a universal vision of peace based on the gendered notion of motherhood. She approvingly quoted the words of a German laundress whose son had been sent to the front: "I am sorry for you and for all mothers whether they are German or Russian. Isn't it all the same? Who is suffering now? Mothers." She told Kollontai, "Your son and my son are both alike. They are both tall and thin. And they have eyes like innocent children. For what reason would they hate each other? Why would they kill one another?"[52] Kollontai's diary attacked the nationalist militarism of the day and rejected the war in universal terms. This pacifist vision became part of Soviet discourse in the 1920s as Kollontai's diary faithfully reflected her beliefs during the early days of the war, before she became an adherent of Lenin's slogan to turn the imperialist war into a civil war.[53]

Pacifist ideas also appeared in the visual arts. The bottom third of a 1929 poster, "To the Struggle against Imperialist Wars," was covered with the corpses of those killed in World War I, reminding its viewers that the war caused ten million dead, twenty million wounded, and four million invalids (figure 5.1).[54] The battle against war was symbolized at the top of the poster by a giant red hammer, wielded by two enormous red hands, preparing to crush the weapons of imperialist war. The cast of characters promoting war in this poster, however, was somewhat unusual. Ghosts of White generals hovered above typical capitalists, but the poster also decried fascism and attacked German Social Democratic "compromisers" for their actions during World War I. The poster depicted a German Social Democrat proclaiming in 1914: "In the struggle for its independence and national honor, Germany is united, and will remain united to the last drop of blood." This poster thus linked the destruction of

FIGURE 5.1. Poster, "To the Struggle against Imperialist Wars"
[*Na bor'by s imperialisticheskimi voinami*] (Moscow-Leningrad:
Gosizdat, 1929). Hoover Institution Poster Collection.

World War I to Germany in particular, tarring fascism and German Social Democracy with the same imperialist brush. Only the Soviet Union (and, presumably, the German Communist Party) would put an end to the horror of
imperialist wars.

In commemoration of the twentieth anniversary of the war in 1934, Feinberg's *1914* put the word "pacifist" in a positive light in a variety of different
ways. For example, he chronicled the assassination of the "magnanimous pacifist" Jean Jaurès on July 31, 1914, at the hands of a "half-witted fanatic of patriotism."[55] Feinberg also reminded his readers about the Basel manifesto's slogan
of "a war on war" and the Second International's betrayal of it. Feinberg's *1914*
featured "A War on War" as a section heading, and quoted Stalin's critique of
the Second International for failing to live up to this "menacing" slogan. Although Soviet critics often attacked the notion of "bourgeois-pacifism," in 1934
Feinberg invoked the possibility of a non-bourgeois pacifist movement in positive tones.

The foreword of *1914* also quoted Stalin's speech to the Seventeenth Party
Congress in early 1934 saying that the Soviet Union "held firmly and stead-
fastly to its peaceful positions, fighting the threat of war, fighting to preserve
the peace, going halfway to meet those countries who in one way or another
stand for preserving the peace, and unmasking those countries who prepare
for and provoke war." While Stalin may have mocked "bourgeois pacifism" for
its ineffectual "chatter about disarmament," in the mid-1930s he himself sometimes used rhetoric that could very easily be confounded with "bourgeois"
antiwar discourse. Soviet propaganda also clearly identified the forces that
would ignite a future war. In commemoration of the twentieth anniversary of
the outbreak of World War I, poster artists produced threatening images of
imperialist rearmament in large print runs; these images implicitly contrasted
the war-mongering capitalist-imperialists with the Soviets who wished to prevent war.[56] Nationalizing and antiwar elements thus coexisted in the Stalinist
political lexicon (figure 5.2).

Kirill Levin even participated in the international antiwar movement, con-
tributing a short story to a British collection titled *We Did Not Fight: 1914–
1918 Experiences of War Resisters* edited by the British poet Julian Bell and including contributions from such prominent figures as Bertrand Russell and
Siegfried Sassoon. The foreword by Canon H. R. L. Sheppard, the founder of
the Peace Pledge Union, explained that some of the writers in the volume were
Christian and humanitarian and others were socialists and reformers, but they
all agreed that "war must be abolished if civilization is to endure, and they

FIGURE 5.2. Poster, Deni and Dolgorukov, "The Kitchen of War"
[*Kukhnia voiny*] (Moscow-Leningrad: OGIZ-IZOGIZ, 1934).
Hoover Institution Poster Collection.

believe that it is the duty of all honest and thoughtful men to resist war and the preparations and policies that make war imminent."[57] Levin contributed a short story titled "The Wild Battalion" chronicling the mutiny of a mixed band of Russian and Austrian soldiers who commandeered a train engine to take their battalion away from the front because they had "decided not to fight anymore."[58]

When the Russian army pursued them, one of the soldiers framed their dilemma for the others: "We left the front, so as not to fight any more, and now they are hunting us. Decide what to do now. Shall we fight, or shall we fight against fighting?" The answer was, of course, a union of Russians and Magyars to fight against fighting. While most of the mutineers were killed by the Russian imperial troops, four soldiers escaped into the forest "like hunted animals . . . hiding within themselves the embryo of a great revolt, preparing the war against war."[59] Levin's story thus explicitly advocated taking up arms in order to prevent war, while appearing alongside the work of Christian and humanitarian pacifists as a contribution to the peace pledge movement in Britain.

But, at the same time, the internationalism of Levin's story was undercut by the way in which he described the Russian imperial troops that put down the mutiny. In the well-worn Soviet trope, tsarist officers would always be more than willing to annihilate the mutineers, but why would lower-class soldiers of the Russian Imperial Army willingly kill their brethren? The title of Levin's story played off the nickname of a well-known Caucasian unit, "The Wild Division," known for its loyalty to the tsarist government. Levin described how the mutinous soldiers' train was surrounded by "hundreds of swarthy, hooknosed men with rifles and hand grenades." These soldiers were led by a "tall officer in Caucasian jacket and Caucasian soft shoes" who "ran to the engine which was being uncoupled in a very unskilful way by hook-nosed soldiers who were laughingly watched by the driver." While the episode may have reflected real historical events, Levin nonetheless articulated an ethnic and racial distinction between the mutineers and the "unskilful hooked-nosed" lowerclass Caucasians who remained loyal to the tsar.[60] While the European soldiers were brothers, the swarthy Caucasian soldiers were depicted as the politically unconscious and violent "other." This hint of racism portended ill for Caucasian populations who were deported en masse during World War II.[61] Furthermore, this detail revealed how inflections of Russian nationalism emerged in internationalist works of the 1930s just as inflections of pacifism emerged in the militarizing works of the 1930s.

Internationalism

Leninist definitions of internationalism were much more straightforward. Class was the primary determining factor; nationality was irrelevant. Dmitriev, for example, emphasized the commonality of the soldiers when he observed the Austrian soldiers who were taking him into captivity as a prisoner of war: "Enemies? They walked side by side, with the same unshaven faces, weather-beaten and coarse. Only perhaps they were a little cleaner than we were, and had a different uniform."[62] Dmitriev focused on a distinguishing feature of common manliness, the beard, in order to assert a unity among men of many different nationalities. Despite minor differences in clothing and hygiene, all soldiers were fundamentally the same. Both Kollontai's and Dmitriev's descriptions of their experiences asked Soviet readers to place themselves in the shoes of the so-called "enemy" and to understand that the German and Austrian people were just like them.

Another work that focused on the plight of the German soldier was the 1931 short story by Konstantin Finn called "Borderlands" (*Okraina*). This story emphasized the tragedy of the German prisoners of war confined to a barracks in a Russian provincial town.[63] In the short story, two lonely people, the German prisoner of war Friedrich Raskotten and the thirty-five-year-old Russian "old maid" Maria Greshina, fall in love. Greshina was so miserably alone that she imagined herself to be a soldier's wife, waiting for her husband to come home. She fantasized, "Let him come home crippled, she would still love him."[64] But, alas, her imaginary husband never came home. Instead she met the prisoner Raskotten. The narrator asserted that the German prisoners of war were innocents who "never committed any crimes. They did not feel pangs of conscience," and in the summer when the trees hid the barbed wire, they "sometimes forgot they were in prison."[65] These prisoners were depicted as victims of war, as were the provincial Russian townspeople.

Although Maria's father Greshin and his best friend Filov initially rejected Raskotten because of his Germanness, when they discovered that he was a shoemaker, a skilled craftsman like them, the four of them eventually became "one family."[66] Commonality of labor trumped nationality. Since Greshin considered the Germans to be an intellectually superior people, he began to welcome the idea of a German son-in-law. Unfortunately for all four of the main characters, the war-weary townspeople harbored more malevolent stereotypes of the Germans. When the local cabdriver lost his livelihood because of wartime conditions, he blamed the Germans for the war and his personal misery. "The Germans are the ones putting the pressure on. They want to beat everyone. That's the kind of people they are."[67] Other townspeople grumbled that the Germans were taking Russian women, and also complained, "Bread is taken away from us and given to them."[68] The frustration caused by three years of war, which crippled the men at the front and the economy at home, was expressed in gendered terms. The male townspeople were enraged because of their impotence in preventing Germans from eating "their" food and consorting with "their" women. The war was an emasculating experience for Russian men who held the Germans to blame.

The anger boiled over into mob violence. A crowd gathered around the German prisoner of war. The shoemaker Kadkin, who had lost his own two sons in the war, hit Raskotten in the face. Someone then yelled, "Beat the Germans." Filov defended Raskotten by saying that he was a shoemaker, not a German. Raskotten calmed the crowd by demonstrating his skill in bootmaking. Although the crowd dispersed, Filov told Raskotten that he'd better not come back; next time, "They might really kill him."[69] The shoemaker Kadkin apologized for his act of violence toward Raskotten, saying that "among laboring people, among our brother workmen, there can be no nationality of any kind because we are all equal." He attributed the mob's reaction to "ignorance" and "darkness."[70] The story ended with Filov realizing that he loved Greshina and marrying her. Raskotten despaired at being trapped in the barracks once again and committed suicide.

This story articulated a fully internationalist and implicitly pacifist message complete with an attack on Russian nationalism and an acknowledgment of the costs of "Russian darkness." The laboring people eventually recognized each other as brothers across national lines, and they did so without the tutelage of the Bolsheviks or the Communist Party. They were powerless, however, to change the prevailing societal attitudes of national chauvinism or even to offer Raskotten protection from the townspeople who might riot at any moment. The chauvinistic attitudes of the townspeople seem to be stronger and deeper than a mere temporary "intoxication." The author provided no revolutionary uplift at the end of the story, and the fate of the German prisoner of war was tragic. While Greshina and Filov might find consolation in each other, perhaps even undercutting the internationalist message of the story by reaffirming the Russian man's right to the Russian woman, there was no alleviation of the pain of the frustrated townsmen, the grieving father Kadkin, or the cabby who lost his livelihood. The wartime social order remained bleak; the workers, immobilized and helpless. The war brought nothing but misery, and there was no way to make international solidarity a reality.

When Finn's story was turned into the feature film *Borderlands* in 1933, Finn and his coauthor, the director Boris Barnet, changed the entire structure of the story and made the shoemaker Kadkin and his two sons Kolia and Sen'ka the central figures in the film. The film did not eliminate the internationalist theme of the novella, and the plight of the German POW also remained integral to the plot. Instead of ending with the tragic suicide of the German prisoner of war, however, the film culminated in the revolutionary martyrdom of the young worker Kolia Kadkin and the victory of the October Revolution, in which the now hopeful German POW took part.

While the short story emphasized the bleakness of the war, the screenplay restored the notion of heroism and redeemed the characters by the addition of an implicitly militaristic revolutionary narrative. A positive review of the film *Borderlands* by A. Dubrovskii in *Izvestiia* (News) in April 1933 noted that the film had improved upon the short story because "the short story was written in particularly somber tones, but the film was imbued with optimism." The substance of the change had primarily to do with the outcome of the story. The depiction of a senseless war by itself was no longer desirable; now the characterization of World War I was accompanied by the portrayal of a meaningful revolutionary battle for which the hero willingly sacrificed his life. Death in battle was made meaningful once again.

In the same review, Dubrovskii asserted that *Borderlands* was a good film about the world war because it was different from "bourgeois pacifist books and films. Remarque and his comrades-in-arms are overwhelmed by the war. They see its senselessness, but do not see a way out of it. In *Borderlands,* the imperialist war is contrasted to the idea of international struggle and the solidarity of the proletariat." As a result "people do not just perish in the war, they also develop" revolutionary consciousness. While Remarque's war was only a "senseless slaughterhouse," Barnet's war looked forward to a glorious revolutionary future.[71] It is notable that the critic chose to frame *Borderlands* in an international context, comparing it not only with Remarque's book but also with the 1930 American Academy Award–winning film by Lewis Milestone.[72]

A. Erlikh reviewed the film *Borderlands* in *Pravda* the same week. While his review was also generally very positive, Erlikh disliked the film's conclusion: "The end of the film is confused. The authors did not succeed in portraying October in the borderlands. The unsuccessful ending, cut off from the fundamental theme of the international meaning of the revolution, somewhat lowers the quality of this restrained, politically true and intelligent film."[73] The ending that one critic applauded for rescuing the film from the dangers of pacifism was rejected by another as a diversion from the main theme of internationalism.[74] *Borderlands,* true to its title, hovered at the juncture between militaristic and internationalist discourse.

The decidedly multivalent *Borderlands* culminated in a celebration of class warfare in the October Revolution, but it also definitively proclaimed the international solidarity of the German and Russian workers. Like other works of this era, the film *Borderlands* set out to show the transformation among soldiers who were at first swayed by patriotic rhetoric, but later developed into conscious revolutionaries. Kolia became a soldier after listening raptly to the warmongering speech of the misguided "defensist" socialist leader at the factory. He thus "mistakenly" volunteered due to his proletarian solidarity with the other workers in his factory and their betrayal by non-Bolshevik socialists. Sen'ka decided to prove his courage and show that he was no less a man than his brother by also going to war as a volunteer. Kolia laughed at the idea of Sen'ka enlisting and his father called him a fool, saying that one son at the front was enough. These demeaning actions called Sen'ka's masculinity into question and underlined the reason that Sen'ka desired to go to war in the first place. Sen'ka was susceptible to patriotic enticements in part because he saw the battlefield as an arena in which he could prove his masculinity. When his father and brother tried to stop him from going to war, Sen'ka called them cowards. His desire to volunteer, on the other hand, remade him temporarily into the brave one. But Sen'ka was to pay dearly for his desire to prove himself in the tsarist army.

Throughout the film, the elder, quintessentially proletarian son Kolia did not show much patience or compassion in his dealings with the vulnerable Sen'ka. In contrast to the classic myth of male comradeship, the shared dangers of the trenches did not seem to increase Kolia's affection or respect for the brother who had so foolishly volunteered instead of remaining in his rightful place at home with their elderly father. Kolia continued to mock Sen'ka for his ineptitude and lack of personal courage. That the proletarian hero led the other soldiers in tormenting his own brother sent a powerful message that weakness, ineptitude, and cowardice would be punished by exclusion from the Soviet brotherhood.

The call for the brothers' unit to attack the enemy came when Sen'ka was suffering from a toothache; Sen'ka's inability to withstand pain also clearly indicated that he could not be a Soviet hero. The commanding officer, a stereo-type of brutal tsarist authority, dragged an unwilling Sen'ka into a battle in which he was killed almost immediately. Kolia saw his brother fall, and though he hesitated momentarily, he continued into battle nonetheless. Historian Denise Youngblood notes that "Sen'ka's death is a perfect example of the kind of brutal realism that inspirationalist Socialist Realism intentionally ignored: his fear as he is dragged whimpering to his death is visceral and very difficult to watch."[75] This brutal scene demonstrated the pointlessness of Sen'ka's war-time death. There were no redeeming features here, no heroism or sacrifice, no cause to celebrate, and no hope for "eternal memory" of any kind.

This ambiguous scene criticized the brutality of the tsarist officers who hounded the sick into battle and forced them to die, but it also demonstrated that there was a right way and a wrong way to go into battle. Kolia remained the exemplary fighter, not allowing his personal grief to prevent him from do-ing his soldierly duty. Despite the film's internationalist message, the repre-sentation of Kolia valorized courage and the willingness to engage in battle and do one's duty in the face of death, even in a misguided "imperialist" war. Sen'ka's unreflective patriotism, his weakness, and his cowardice led him to a meaningless death.

In the same attack in which his own brother was killed, the proletarian hero Kolia Kadkin fought with the young German Mueller in hand-to-hand combat and disarmed him. After the two men huddled together because of an exploding shell, Kolia was happy to discover that the German was alive and comforted him, laughing and saying, "No more war. You are a prisoner now." Although Kolia asserted his superiority over the German by capturing him, he was kind, reassuring, and even affectionate to the German soldier. Kolia was able to exercise immense (and improbable) control over raw battlefield emotions to overcome his hatred and desire for revenge against the Germans. Within minutes of his own brother's death before his eyes, Kolia was able to perceive that the young German was also his brother.

Mueller, now a prisoner of war, coincidentally was sent back to Kolia's town, employed by Kolia's father, and befriended by a young girl named Man'ka. The German now literally as well as figuratively took the place of Kadkin's dead son, becoming a member of an international proletarian family. Yet the film suggested that overcoming national prejudice was not easy or automatic. After Kadkin received official word that Sen'ka was dead, and another friend of Kadkin's returned home maimed by the war, the townspeople gathered and viciously attacked the young German POW. A chauvinistic popular print in-citing hatred of the Germans was clearly visible on the wall of the building in which the POW was beaten, and the townspeople were, no doubt, affected by its poisonous presence.[76] At first, only Man'ka stepped in to defend the German POW from the mob attack, and the elder Kadkin, embittered by his son's death, allowed the beating to continue. After a few moments, however, he conquered his grief and hatred and intervened to save Mueller. By rejecting the opportunity to enact revenge against Mueller simply because he was German, Kadkin also denied that his own son's death was a sacrifice for the Russian nation. He showed that "chauvinism" against Germans could be overcome by the suppression of grief, great personal courage, and profound empathy for other workers.[77] Despite the fact that the German army had inflicted a grievous wound on the Kadkin family, neither Kolia nor his father condemned the German proletarians.

In the film's final montage, as Kolia was executed for organizing fraternization among the troops, the elder Kadkin, Mueller, and Man'ka marched joyfully, carrying out the October Revolution. Mueller was no longer a prisoner but was fully integrated into the revolutionary movement. The new battle lines had been drawn, and they erased any consciousness of national difference while justifying warfare on the basis of class differences. The film narrative transformed the short story by eliminating Mueller's suicide and resurrecting him as a revolutionary. It even supplied a romantic happy ending for the POW who won both the girl and new status as a free Soviet worker.

Soviet interwar depictions of internationalism embraced international class solidarity but did not always explicitly articulate the Leninist ethos of class warfare. War itself sometimes remained the problem and was not embraced as the solution to social injustice. These examples existed side by side with more orthodox Leninist depictions of internationalism that identified the toiling peoples of the combatant countries as "brothers," and also introduced the notion of a future war against a new set of enemies: the upper classes of all nations. For example, a minor character in *Quiet Flows the Don,* the worker Knave (*Valet*), exhibited orthodox proletarian internationalism. When he found an unarmed man in a German dugout, he first held him at bayonet point and then, "uttering a strange throaty sound, something between a cough and a sob, he stepped toward the German . . . 'Run! German! I've got no grudge against you. I won't shoot.'"[78] Despite the language barrier, both men identified themselves as Social Democrats, and the German noted, "In the coming class battles we shall be in the same trenches."[79] This scene is notable in two ways. First of all, the fear and other emotions commonly found in the heat of battle, which Sholokhov depicted so forcefully in other scenes of the novel, were entirely absent here. Knave dispassionately judged that he had no grudge against the German and made a conscious decision to spare him. Secondly, the spared German turned out to be not only a proletarian like Knave but a conscious revolutionary Social Democrat. The path to brotherhood across national lines and to participating in future class warfare was depicted as rational, uncomplicated, and direct. While Remarque's protagonist Paul Bäumer promised the Frenchman he had killed that he would join a universal brotherhood against war, Knave's release of the German worker defined a new war waiting to be fought.

DEFINING THE ENEMY

In stark distinction to tsarist patriotic discourse, these internationalist works all made it clear that enemies could not and should not be defined by nationality alone. The Russian elites were to be viewed as enemies while German and Austrian rank-and-file soldiers should be considered brothers. To harbor hatred against all Germans was tragically misguided. The cause of the war was not German national ambition but economics; capitalism, in its advanced form of imperialism, ignited the world war in its competition for world markets. French bankers then forced the Russian Empire into the war, exchanging capital for cannon fodder. Such abstractions, however, were hard for the Soviet public to comprehend. In *The Fall of the Romanov Dynasty,* Esfir Shub used subtitles to blame capitalism and imperialism for triggering a war that caused the death or injury of thirty-five million people. She made the impersonal forces of war visible by bombarding the viewer with scene after scene of advanced weaponry wielded by the various armies, without singling out any country as aggressor. She also directly addressed the terrible irony of World War I from the socialist point of view: rather than uniting, the workers of the world were actively engaged in killing one another. She included a shot of munitions workers preparing artillery shells. The title read: "The hands of the workers were preparing death for their brothers." Workers thus figured as pawns in a tragic de-nationalized fratricidal war caused by capitalists.[80]

Yet the scene in the story "Borderlands" in which the townspeople nearly beat the German prisoner of war to death made clear to its Soviet audience that anti-German sentiment was an integral part of the Russian wartime landscape. Soviet treatments of World War I had difficulty explaining the endurance of widespread ethnic prejudice within their internationalist framework. One Soviet analyst of anti-German prejudice turned to a familiar trope by explaining ethnic enmity as a quality peculiar to the upper classes. He argued that anti-German sentiments of "animal hatred . . . emanated only from representatives of 'civilized' Russia." He cited as evidence the letter of an ensign from the 53rd Infantry Regiment who declared in the early months of the war that he would give the "cursed Germans" no quarter and "even if I have no arms and legs, I will gnaw with my teeth and await the moment with impatience when I can get revenge on them for all of their evil."[81] Yet the same author revealed that lower-class soldiers also wanted to "smash the snotty nose of the German devil." Not just "class enemies" saw the Germans as representing diabolical evil.

Other Soviet representations of World War I also suggested that ethnicity was relevant to understanding the destruction of war. The seven disciples in Il'ia Erenburg's *The Extraordinary Adventures of Khulio Khurenito and His Disciples . . .* each portrayed an ethnic stereotype. In a scene set in April 1914, just before Khurenito set off to Paris, Germany, Vienna, and London to ignite World War I, "the Teacher" proclaimed that the Jews had always been different from all of the other nationalities because of their willingness to destroy, to say "no," and to insist on "terrible, naked, destructive justice."[82] Chillingly prescient, Erenburg has Khurenito recount various episodes of violent anti-Semitism throughout the ages and predict "the Destruction of the Tribe of Judah" in the twentieth century. The notions of the Jews as a people apart who were hated for being different, and the Jews as simultaneously the catalyst for violence and its victims were thus vividly expressed in Soviet World War I discourse.

The main ethnic opposition that Erenburg constructed in the novel, however, was between the philosophizing Russian intellectual Aleksei Spirodonovich and Karl Schmidt, the unrelentingly disciplined German student. Aleksei Spirodonovich's attitudes toward World War I echoed both Soviet and Western European tropes of initial enthusiasm followed by disillusionment. When the war broke out in July 1914, Aleksei Spirodonovich expressed a Pan-Slav view of the war, hyperbolically declaring, "This is the day of redemption, bright and pure! Russia! Messiah! The cross of St. Sophia! Brother Slavs!" He enthusiastically embraced Russia's role as savior and redeemer of the Orthodox Slavs. It was immediately clear to Aleksei Spirodonovich that this messianic mission made him the enemy of the German Schmidt. He rushed to Schmidt and embraced him saying, "My foe! My brother! I love you, and just because I love I must kill you! Do you understand? I do not kill, but as I kill I die, sacrificed; we shall defeat Germany! Christ is risen!"[83] Schmidt pushed Aleksei Spirodonovich politely out of the way, ignoring his comically impossible and illogical synthesis of foe and brother, love and hate, killing and dying. Aleksei Spirodonovich's determination to kill on behalf of the Russian idea did not last; he eventually embraced the equally Russian stance of Tolstoian nonviolence.

Erenburg, on the other hand, repeatedly associated the willingness to kill with German national identity. In one telling scene set during World War I, the character Il'ia Erenburg became preoccupied with various methods of killing and explained that he "began to have a real, physical sense of killing." He then reported that he "began to doubt whether [he] wasn't, perhaps, a German." In the novel, the German student Schmidt was a symbol of the willingness to use force to produce change. Schmidt believed that the world "must be organized by means of force," and he had no qualms whatsoever about killing. He declared unapologetically, "Between killing one weak-minded old man and ten million people for the good of mankind there's only an arithmetical difference. Yet killed they must be, or else the whole world will continue on its stupid, senseless way." He explained that he "would not hesitate for an instant" to "sink all the *Lusitanias* and send hundred of thousands of human beings to their death" for "the success of a campaign today—which means for the good of Germany tomorrow and of humanity the day after."[84] Daring even to criticize the Russian Revolution, Erenburg eventually had Schmidt embrace the revolution as another means of organizing the world through force. Though the novel must be read as satire employing the method of comic exaggeration, it nonetheless created a vision of World War I as an ethnic conflict between bloodthirsty machinelike ethnic Germans and the rest of Europe. The seeds of Erenburg's famous anti-German World War II writings were already planted, and the shoots of anti-German ethnic hatred were sprouting even in the Soviet Union's internationalist phase.[85]

Depictions of ethnicity that engendered or justified hatred, however, were only one part of understanding the enemy. Russian soldiers also implicitly assessed and affirmed their own national character through comparisons to their enemies. Lev Voitolovskii's *In the Footsteps of War* quoted an infantryman who asserted with bravado at the beginning of the war, "What is an Austrian anyway? Are Austrians really a people? They are a worthless, loose people like free-flowing sand. All you have to do is touch him and he runs out like water from a wash-stand."[86] The soldier's questioning of Austrian national identity suggested that the Russians were a "real" and a "brave" people. The implied contrast between the bravery of the Russians and the cowardliness of the Austrians shows that this soldier's notions of ethnicity and masculinity were intertwined. Russian masculinity was defined not only by soldiers' willingness to defend the national community but also in contrast to soldiers of other nationalities who were lesser men in their cowardice, their ineptitude, or their bestiality.[87] While official Soviet manhood was associated with fighting for the multinational socialist fatherland in the 1920s and 1930s, the notion of a dominantly Russian national masculinity persisted into the Soviet period and appeared regularly in Soviet depictions of tsarist Russia's last war.

Representations of World War I enemies in the interwar period revealed both ethnically based patriotism and internationalism. Soviet authors and editors wanted to emphasize the progression of the soldiers from misguided tsarist patriots to conscious revolutionaries. As the war proceeded, therefore, authors emphasized the rise of two antinational trends: fraternization with the enemy, and refusal to follow orders to take the offensive. Fraternization could be seen as concrete evidence of the soldiers' abandonment of patriotic thinking and as a way in which the soldiers could redeem their earlier chauvinistic mistakes. Many soldiers' letters published in the early 1930s recalled Easter 1916 as a catalyst for fraternization. It was an occasion for friendly greetings and the exchange of Easter kisses, tea drinking, trading presents such as Easter eggs, bread, potatoes, liquor, and cigarettes, and the performance of music and dancing. These soldierly exchanges did not always go smoothly. Sometimes Russian officers broke up such meetings, and at other times soldiers from one side or the other voluntarily gave themselves up into captivity. On one occasion, a Russian officer used a supposedly friendly meeting as a ruse to capture an Austrian officer.[88] Nonetheless, Soviet authors used these popular descriptions of fraternization to demonstrate a fundamental change in the definition of the enemy and to illustrate the spread of internationalism among the Russian troops.

The publication of letters that described soldiers refusing to take the offensive was another way of showing that the soldiers' perceptions of their "true" enemy had changed. As one letter put it, "one hears that regiments don't want to go on the offensive. In general, it is time to end this fratricidal war. The enemies are behind our back, not in front of us."[89] Clearly, this letter writer was well on his way to being ready to "turn the imperialist war into a civil war." In seeking to show the imminence of revolution, many representations of World War I articulated the notion that "chauvinistic intoxication" had been thoroughly routed and replaced by fraternal internationalism.

THE ENEMY WITHIN?

The transformation from patriotism to internationalism in World War I was, of course, not as simple as the revolutionary narrative sought to portray it. The most significant complication was that popular "chauvinistic" sentiment had been directed not only at external enemies, but also at non-Russians within the Empire, especially, but not exclusively, at Germans and Jews. Despite some attempts by particular groups of non-Russians to promote their positive participation in the war effort,[90] the war spurred intense anxiety about the danger of traitors and internal enemies within the Empire. The execution of Lieutenant Colonel S. N. Miasoedov for espionage in March 1915 intensified the epidemic of spy mania that eventually led to the arrest of General V. A. Sukhomlinov, the former minister of war. Given the early defeats at Tannenberg and later "the great retreat," many in tsarist military circles were all too willing to believe that the Russian army had been routed because of German espionage and traitors in high places rather than because of more mundane failures and mistakes.[91]

The military disasters of 1915 also gave rise to widespread rumors that the tsar's court was "a hotbed of Germanophiles and defeatists" led by the German-born tsarina and the dangerous Rasputin.[92] Building on the devastating rumors that had helped to deal a fatal blow to the legitimacy of the Romanov dynasty in 1917, Soviet treatments of World War I displayed an overlapping discourse of class and ethnic hatred in attacks on Russian-German elites.

One August 1915 letter from a soldier of unidentified class origins to a recipient in Moscow, published in 1934, allowed Soviet readers a clear view of ethnic hatred within the Russian Empire. This letter assiduously deflected the blame for Russian military failures from the native Russian people to the Russian-Germans:

> We learned about the Minister of War, what the scum did, how he sold out all Russia. Here it is the same. If in Russia the chiefs were all Russian, we would have defeated the enemy long ago . . . but now everything will drag out for a long time. . . . If we wait for peace, and are alive, then we will not keep even one German, even if he is a Russian citizen [*poddannyi*]—it was only for this reason that they became citizens.[93]

Although the letter was likely included to illustrate the rising interest in internal affairs and revolutionary discontent, it revealed much more. The hyper-nationalist letter writer advocated ethnic cleansing of all Russian-Germans in order to solve Russia's political problems. Despite the fact that it was antithetical to official Soviet positions on both class and internationalism, the idea that one could improve domestic conditions by Russifying the population and excising all classes of such traitorous ethnicities as the Germans thus traveled from the World War I era into interwar discourse. Such policies were actually adopted by Soviet authorities beginning in the late 1930s, when the Soviet Union deported the Korean population from its borders as it engaged in military conflict with Japan.

Voitolovskii spoke eloquently about the obsession with traitors on the frontlines even before the reverses of 1915. He revealed how ethnicity became shorthand for determining who might be a spy. Voitolovskii saw ethnic prejudice as a "classed" phenomenon, with tsarist officers to blame for unjustified accusations against non-Russians. In his account of events from September 1914, he claimed that Russian common soldiers were not ruled by ethnic "hatred," so the officers competed with one another in their "fabrication of the horrors of treachery" in order to mobilize the soldiers against their enemies.

Voitolovskii told of a Georgian lieutenant in the tsarist army (a cousin of the Menshevik Duma deputy I. Tsereteli) who was suspected of spying because his orderly, a Latvian, spoke Russian with a "foreign" accent. The day after the lieutenant passed through Voitolovskii's unit, the telephone was damaged and the barbed wire was cut for a stretch of several yards. The commander exclaimed:

> Not for nothing did the physiognomy of this scoundrel seem so suspicious. What kind of Georgian was he? He was a Turk. A typical Turk. . . . And his head was entirely shaved, like a Turk's. And the leader, of course, was not him, but the second one, the German. You understand what blackguards: right from here they jumped into the forest, cut the barbed wire and went further along.[94]

The other officers tried to convince the commander that the enemy gained no tactical advantage from cutting this particular barbed wire, but the commander insisted that spies were abroad. The episode showed the complexity of a multiethnic empire at war. Even before the Ottoman Empire formally declared war on the Russian Empire, a Georgian citizen of the Russian Empire could be distrusted on sight and imagined as a "Turk," the "traditional" enemy of the Russian Empire. And, following the twisted logic of seeking the enemy within, the seemingly subordinate Latvian orderly was transformed into a "German" master spy.

Voitolovskii explained that instead of instilling "vigilance among the young officers" and "kindling hatred of Germans," spy mania produced unintended consequences: "a conviction of the internal rottenness of the military apparatus and a deep distrust of the population. They didn't trust the inhabitants, insulted and oppressed them at every step."[95] Here, Voitolovskii tacitly acknowledged that the constant fear of treachery coarsened even the rank-and-file soldiers' interactions with the non-Russian population, and that the ethnic prejudices he attributed to the officers also influenced the actions of lower-class soldiers.

The Jews living on the border between the Russian Empire and the Austro-Hungarian Empire were particularly vulnerable to charges of espionage because of their cross-border ties with Jews in the Austro-Hungarian Empire and because the Yiddish language was so closely related to German. Both Jewish and an officer, Voitolovskii shed light on the army leadership's anxiety about "Jewish" spying; he reproduced army directives warning about female Jewish spies and advocating the arrest of any and all "suspicious" Jews.[96] Voitolovskii also documented countless scenes of anti-Semitism, but he did not find fault with ordinary Russian soldiers for this ugly phenomenon. Instead, he identified Cossacks as the instigators of pogroms against the Jews and the perpetrators of random violence against Jewish (and Polish) civilians. He blamed army leaders for inciting hatred against Jews and for their failure to intervene when "Cossacks" were abusing the Jewish population.[97]

Finally, Voitolovskii documented the anti-Semitism of the Russian home front—suggesting that the attitudes of Russian educated society produced the anti-Semitic actions of the army. In one telling scene, Voitolovskii recounted a conversation with two "Russian bureaucrats" while he was on leave in the rear. One was an elderly priest and the second was the director of a teachers' training college. Not recognizing Voitolovskii as a Jew, the two spoke "about the perfidy of the Jews; they tried to persuade me to hate and fear Jews as the most ferocious and crafty traitors."[98] Voitolovskii's interpretation of ethnic conflict as caused by class hatred was somewhat inconsistent, considering that he himself ethnicized the Cossacks in his analysis of wartime atrocities; he also demonstrated that Russian soldiers could deal callously with the civilian population without any incitement from their officers. The pervasiveness of wartime ethnic conflict was thus visible in his account.

Wartime letters from Tatar soldiers also revealed ethnic tensions between Russians and non-Russians in the tsarist army. Although there were a couple of letters describing a Russian factory worker who treated Tatars as equals, or a Russian soldier going out of his way to rescue a wounded Tatar soldier on the battlefield, other letters bemoaned the treatment of the Tatars at the hands of the Russians, and not just Russian officers. One desperately lonely soldier, the only Tatar in his company, explained, "If there were a few [Tatars] we could stand up for ourselves, but now there is only ridicule. True, our platoon commander is not a ruffian, but he mocks me terribly." Another soldier wrote that the soldiers were prohibited from speaking their own language: "As soon as we start to speak, they immediately shout, 'Hey, you Turks, non-Christians are not allowed,' and that is why being in the detachment is a thousand times worse than being a prisoner of war." Because the Russians feared that the Tatars were more likely to give themselves up voluntarily, some units designated a Russian soldier to watch over every Tatar soldier. These letters all suggest that while the army leadership set the tone for abuse, ordinary soldiers were complicit in isolating and denigrating their non-Christian peers.[99]

At the same time, the letters reveal that the Muslim soldiers viewed the Russians as others, calling them giaour and kiafir—both words to denote nonbelievers or infidels. While some of the letters emphasized the common plight of the Russian and Tatar soldiers, others openly pointed to the ethnic and religious differences that prompted the abuse, humiliation, and resentment that kept the groups apart. On the other hand, the abuse that Muslim soldiers experienced drew them closer together as they "lived as one family" in self-defense when possible.[100] These phenomena openly called into question the universal brotherhood of the working classes and shed light on the potential for ethnic violence.

For all their internationalist rhetoric, Soviet sources revealed that long before the onset of "Russo-centric étatism," Soviet readers were acquainted with and susceptible to an ethnic discourse in which prejudices and stereotypes both determined and explained the course of events. While in some cases Soviet sources explicitly criticized this discourse, they sometimes did so by resorting to ethnic stereotypes of Cossacks as the perpetrators of ethnic prejudice. Furthermore, the creators of Soviet memory of World War I widely reproduced ethnic thinking and circulated it alongside internationalist thinking, at times implicitly endorsing the ethnic stereotypes they presented.

Soviet readers were not shielded from the brutality of national hatred in World War I. They were made aware that national identity could breed the most extreme hatred on the part of officers, enlisted men, and civilians. Yet, Soviet readers and spectators were also encouraged to view working-class Germans as innocent victims and as allies in the fight against the upper classes. Notions of patriotism in the 1920s and early 1930s were extremely complex as national prejudice was both condemned and reinforced by images of World War I. In the 1920s and early 1930s, Russianness was viewed negatively through a Cossack lens and positively through the notion of worker solidarity. Non-Russians likewise could appear as proletarian brothers or as inferior and suspect ethnic others. An ethnicizing worldview and the outlines of anti-Semitism were clearly expressed in World War I discourse despite several layers of internationalist rhetoric.

Still, the very existence of powerful internationalist rhetoric that challenged notions of patriotism is striking. While Kollontai rejected war itself, Sholokhov rejected the patriotic notion that what was "Russian" was good while what was "German" was bad. Furmanov demonstrated how wartime conditions destroyed the boundary between ethical and unethical conduct, creating horrifying violence against the innocent. These depictions of war showed the problematic nature of the patriotic hero and demonstrated how war destroyed the traditional codes of honor and heroism on which the ideal of the nation was built.

This discourse of nationality did indeed undergo transformations in the mid-1930s, but patriotism did not suddenly reappear in the middle of the 1930s; it had been present all along. Beginning in the 1930s, unproblematic notions of military honor and heroism, earlier usually connected to the Revolution and Civil War, increasingly encompassed World War I as well. Patriotism became an essential attribute of the future Soviet soldier before he ever became Soviet. As the Russo-centric worldview strengthened, an ethnic divide grew up between the enemy and the Soviet soldier, gradually overcoming international notions of class solidarity that linked proletarians across borders. In the late 1930s Polish pans, Teutonic knights, and Japanese samurai were depicted as both class and ethnic enemies. This conflation of class and ethnicity had serious and sometimes fatal consequences for Soviet diaspora nationalities such as Poles, Germans, Latvians, Koreans, and Jews in the late 1930s and during World War II.[101] But only under the actual combat conditions of World War II did ideas of fraternization and international solidarity disappear almost entirely. Internationalism and ethnic nationalism coexisted in an uneasy way all throughout the interwar period.

6

Arrested History

Even though World War I was never officially commemorated in the Soviet Union, there was a vibrant and multifaceted discourse about the war in the 1920s and the first half of the 1930s that explored the moral, psychological, and physical world of the soldier, his actions, his conscience, and the devastation that war brought to both soldiers and civilians. As in the rest of Europe, the number of novels and memoir publications increased during the second half of the 1920s as participants began to be ready to reflect on the war. While some aspects of this discourse revealed bitter truths about war, other war memory recapitulated tsarist heroism, articulating both Russian nationalism and international rivalries. As a researcher, I was continually surprised by the quantity, quality, and variety of Soviet approaches to the war, and also by the depth of early Soviet analysis of "the face of war." Yet this rich and varied discussion of World War I was all but unknown to Western and Soviet scholars alike. The post–World War II generations were generally unaware of both the Soviet challenge to militarism and the penetration of tsarist World War I tropes into the early Soviet period. The second half of this book explores why, when, and how World War I discourse disappeared from Soviet public consciousness.

This section of the book is a study of the mechanisms of censorship in the Soviet Union, emphasizing both the timing and processes of discursive change. It also maps the transition from a largely antiheroic and antimilitaristic discourse to a largely heroizing, nationalizing, and militarizing discourse and explores the grounds for this change. The new militarizing discourse emerged in the mid-1930s from elements in the 1920s "ecosystem," grew stronger in the late 1930s, and reached fruition during World War II.

To uncover the particularities of the operation of Soviet censorship of World War I discourse, this chapter will begin with a discussion of the nature of Soviet censorship and an analysis of the reasons for the movement toward a heroizing and militarizing discourse that reshaped the image of both heroes and enemies in more and more national terms. This analysis of discursive transformation will be followed by five case studies that show in detail how and when changes in World War I discourse came about. They are: 1) The rise and fall of the Moscow Military History Museum; 2) The fate of the Red Army Staff's project for a twelve-volume document collection on World War I; 3) Vicissitudes in the representation of General Aleksei Brusilov; 4) Critical and popular response to Erich Maria Remarque's *All Quiet on the Western Front*; 5) The fate of three compelling World War I works of exceptional quality during the twentieth anniversary of the war's outbreak in 1934. I chose these case studies because of the availability of archival documents and other evidence that took me "behind the scenes" to explore conflicts in decision-making processes; they allow me to identify some individual historical actors and to show their participation in promoting or curtailing the memory of the war. These instances show that the study of World War I was sponsored and promoted by state institutions such as the People's Commissariat of Enlightenment (*Narkompros*) and the Red Army in the immediate aftermath of the war. Within and between these institutions there were ideological conflicts and disagreements over the allocation of scarce resources, leading to a decreasing emphasis on World War I by the end of the 1920s, just as some of the most thoughtful works about the war were beginning to appear. The study of World War I was only resumed in the late 1930s as a new war with Germany loomed.

THE NATURE OF CENSORSHIP

While conducting research for this book, I examined the Russian translation of *All Quiet on the Western Front* from the collection of the former Lenin Library, now the Russian State Library in Moscow. When I opened the book to the title page, I saw that the editor of the 1929 Land and Factory edition was Dm. Umanskii. Beneath his name there was a heavy black line obscuring the name of the foreword writer: Karl Radek. Radek's name was no doubt removed from the book after his arrest in 1937. As my research continued, I found a copy of the 1932 volume *The Tsarist Army in the Period of World War and* the February Revolution (*Tsarskaia armiia v period mirovoi voiny i Fevral'skoi revoliutsii*) with three photographs (presumably featuring purge victims) obviously cut out by hand, and a copy of the 1923 edition of Sof'ia Fedorchenko's *The People at War* with one single sentence of the text blacked out. I was able to locate Fedorchenko's offending sentence in another edition; it turned out to be a fairytale episode in which a male soldier and a male demon have sex "from the front and from the rear" all night long. Censorship by altering the physical reality of a book after its publication could thus be political or puritanical, and prompted by government dictates or by local sensibilities.[1]

The physical removal or defacement of a previously published work was either a last-ditch censorship effort to correct an earlier mistake or evidence of the changing nature of what was considered permissible. Most Soviet censorship occurred before publication by preventing a work from being published at all, by prohibiting republication of a work, or by permitting publication only when inadmissible themes and ideas had been removed or with a critical foreword identifying the author's mistakes. Public criticism after publication often led to the censorship of the next edition. In the following section, I explore all of these types of disappearances from World War I discourse. While it is extremely difficult to trace when and if books were removed from general library circulation, there is substantial evidence to be gained from analyzing the chronology of public criticism and alterations in various editions of the same book.

My research also suggests that the erasure of certain World War I themes allowed for some new topics to emerge. To the extent that is possible, I will try to locate these transformations within a changing Soviet ideological environment, though documenting causation for such changes is difficult to do. For the most part, the changes themselves are the only evidence to which I have access. Though the timing and quality of these changes offer hints about motivation, it is often difficult to make definitive statements about how and why these changes were made.

The archival records of the agency that oversaw censorship—the Main Administration for Literary and Publishing Affairs (*Glavlit*)—are incomplete, and it is clear from notations in the files that some of the most pertinent documents, such as lists of banned books, were destroyed. Nevertheless, the extant Glavlit files from 1938 to 1941 offer clues into the psychology of Soviet censorship that enable us to better understand the fate of World War I discourse. Perusal of these files reveals the censors' preoccupation with military secrecy and the suppression of any kind of economic, technical, or military data that would aid foreign powers in planning an attack on the Soviet Union.[2] This anxiety about revealing information that could allow enemies to penetrate Soviet borders shaped the writing of military history about the tsarist empire during World War I. For example, the Military-Historical Department of the Soviet general staff did not permit the publication of documents about the Russian Empire's fortification of Warsaw in 1914, despite the fact that Warsaw was not even part of the Soviet Union![3] The Soviet paranoia about guarding military secrets became an impediment to researching and writing about the Russian experience in World War I.

Another of Glavlit's primary concerns in the late 1930s was the removal from libraries of the works of those who had been arrested as enemies of the people. Glavlit files contained lists of authors who had been purged and recommendations that all literature by these authors be removed from libraries. The works of Sergei Klychkov were recommended for removal from libraries, for example, not specifically because *The Sugary German,* his daring and original novel on World War I, transgressed the boundary between realistic war fiction and fairy tale, or because of his autobiographical depiction of a sympathetic tsarist officer, but because of his arrest in 1937 for supposed anti-Soviet ideological activities as a member of the Laboring Peasant Party.[4] The disruption of the purges played a powerful role in shaping all Soviet discourse, including World War I discourse.

While Glavlit endorsed the removal of all works authored by "enemies of the people," they encountered a serious problem if they included all the works edited and translated by purge victims or mentioning the names of purge victims. One Glavlit report indicated that 20 percent of all Soviet books had been published with the participation of "enemies" as editors or translators and bemoaned the fact that many useful and important works were ending up in libraries' restricted sections. In 1939, Glavlit tried to restrain libraries from prohibiting the circulation of valuable works simply because they had been edited by an "enemy of the people" or because one article in a journal issue was authored by or made reference to an "enemy of the people."[5] Hence the recourse to blacking out the name of Karl Radek in the Lenin Library's copy of *All Quiet on the Western Front* or cutting out pictures of former military heroes turned enemies. Nonetheless, the extensive purges of the Soviet publishing establishment limited the circulation of World War I discourse when its particular editors and translators became purge victims.

The archival files of the Scientific Military-Historical Department of the general staff of the Red Army did include at least one list of military history books recommended for withdrawal from libraries in October of 1937.[6] The memorandum was addressed to the head of cultural and mass work (the Fifth Department of the Political Administration of the Red Army) and contained a long list of books about World War I and the Civil War with recommended actions and specific explanations of why each book needed to be removed from circulation. Most books were designated for removal because the authors or editors had been arrested or unmasked as enemies of the people. The list did not automatically demand removal of a work simply because it contained the name of an enemy. In the case of works that were still deemed valuable to the military-historical enterprise, the books could be physically altered instead of removed. For example, the list recommended that the recently published Russian translation of Hans Delbrück's *History of Military Art within the Framework of Political History* (*Istoriia voennogo iskusstva v ramkakh politicheskoi istorii*) be allowed to remain on the shelves after its foreword by Marshall Mikhail Tukhachevskii was removed.[7] The list also recommended that Lenin's *About Imperialist War* (*Ob imperialisticheskoi voine*), published in 1929, be examined to remove any mention of enemies of the people and the names of the arrested editor and compiler.[8] Thus even the promulgation of Lenin's canonical interpretation of World War I was challenged by the haphazard and unpredictable mechanisms of the purges.

Works designated for exclusion also fell into a third important category. These were works that were considered by the military history authorities to have become "antiquated" or "out of date" (*ustareli*). This category was, of course, a euphemism for the dramatic changes in ideology or policy toward certain kinds of historical works about World War I, the very changes that this book is trying to pinpoint. Many of the works in the "antiquated" category happened to be translations from the German, such as the 1923 Soviet translation of Erich von Falkenhayn's *The [German] High Command* or H. Kuhl's *Memoirs of Peacetime and the Experience of War*.[9] Given that it is hard to imagine how any eyewitness memoir could suddenly go out of date, the reason for the decision to pull these books from library shelves in 1937 clearly had much more to do with the growing xenophobia and anti-German sentiment of the purge era than with the texts themselves becoming antiquated.

The anxious Soviet leadership began to fear works that interpreted World War I from the German point of view or demonstrated the extent of German military strength. G. S. Isserson's 1926 *Cannae of the First World War: The Destruction of Samsonov's Army* (*Kanny mirovoi voiny: Gibel' armii Samsonova*) was also pulled from library shelves in 1937. Isserson's work likened the German success against the Russian army of Samsonov at Tannenberg to Hannibal's defeat of the numerically superior Roman army in the Punic Wars. Even when the work was first published, its editors warned readers that Isserson was "too carried away by German military sources that excessively extol the leaders of the German army." They felt that the Germans' resounding victory was caused in large part by the German interception of radio-telegrams that informed them of the precise locations and plans of Russian units, and by the "most serious of mistakes" on the part of the Russian command. Yet the editors also conceded that "the superiority of German strategic thought proclaimed itself not just in the East Prussian operation, but during the course of the entire imperialist war."[10]

In 1937 both such an admission on the part of the editorial board and the tone of the work itself made military authorities uncomfortable. The work was curtailed because it was perceived as "a laudatory hymn to Germany" whose author was "held captive by German operational ideas."[11] Any positive evaluation of German military strength in comparison to tsarist Russia during World War I was now outside the bounds of Soviet military discourse. Documentation of German military effectiveness was "antiquated" because of its forthright acknowledgment of the strength of the enemy.

In the political climate of 1937, praise of Germany's effectiveness could very easily be read as traitorous to the Soviet Union. The 1936 work *Engagement at the Border of the Western Front*, published by the staff of the Kiev military district, was pulled from library shelves in 1937 because it was "the work of enemies of the people and it was compiled only from German data."[12] These two accusations mutually reinforced one another. To employ German data indicated an underlying untrustworthiness.

While many commentators have noted the xenophobic anti-German slant of the purges, and attributed it, justifiably, to the growing Nazi military threat, I argue that Soviet anti-German sentiment was also nurtured and shaped by World War I experience and is, in effect, a type of World War I memory. While all of the "imperialist" powers, including Germany, were suspect in the late 1920s and early 1930s (the war scare of 1927 focused on Britain; three Germans were defendants in the 1928 Shakhty trial; and the French were the purported enemies in the 1930 Industrial Party trial), the concern with German "enemies" in the mid-1930s had deep cultural roots. Long before World War I, there were tensions between the Germans living in Russia and the Russians themselves.[13] During the cataclysm of World War I, broad segments of the Russian population believed that generals with German-sounding names, Rasputin, and the German-born tsaritsa were all secretly working for German victory. The persistent suspicions of German infiltration of the highest levels of leadership during the purges recalled this World War I notion of a "German clique" in the Russian government. "Germans" such as General P. K. Rennenkampf were blamed for the disasters at Tannenberg, just as traitors supposedly working for the Germans were accused of "wrecking" during the purges.

World War I produced a paranoid mindset among army leaders, who thought that spies were everywhere and that all non-Russians were suspect, but especially German and Yiddish speakers. Spy mania emerged in the irrational anxieties of key World War I Russian army officers, including not only Ianushkevich but also the then commander of the Petrograd military district, M. D. Bonch-Bruevich, later an important figure in the Soviet military leadership. Key components of anti-German World War I discourse reemerged in Soviet 1930s purge discourse. World War I spy fever and adventure narratives about the capture of spies emerged as a popular phenomenon in the jingoistic Russian press; spy mania reappeared as a common trope in Soviet adventure literature of the 1930s.[14] The accusations of collaboration with the Germans were also reproduced in the discourse of the purges as the indictments in the Moscow show trials accused Lev Trotskii and other prominent former Soviet leaders of working with secret police agents of the Gestapo to topple Stalin and his government.

The widespread fear of Germany as a formidable military opponent also emerged in both World War I and purge discourse. Given both the historical precedents of military defeat of tsarist Russia by Germany in World War I and the ignominy of the treaty of Brest-Litovsk, as well as the contemporary realities of Nazi rearmament and the Spanish Civil War, it was hardly surprising that Germany would be a major focal point of Soviet anxiety and Soviet bravado. Yet it is worth noting how this anxiety was shaped by contemporary events as well as by lingering popular perceptions of Germany and the memory of World War I.[15]

In the 1920s and 1930s some Russians thought of World War I not as "the Second Patriotic War," as the tsarist government had dubbed it, nor as the "imperialist war," as it was called by Lenin and Soviet officials, but as "the German war." The naming of World War I as "the German war" and Russia's "western" front as "the German front" occurred in both official reports and museum catalogues as well as in the letters of ordinary Soviet readers, identifying Germany (rather than the Austro-Hungarian Empire) as the most dangerous and formidable adversary of the World War.[16] As a letter from a fellow prisoner of war to Kirill Levin put it in the early 1930s: "Yes, I had to endure quite a bit by the will of the thick-skulled tsaritsa and the damned Fritz."[17] This soldier identified as German the dual causes of his suffering. And a fictional female volunteer at the front claimed in a 1930 novella: "The Germans seem to me to be terrifying and brutal. I am afraid." It is noteworthy that this open expression of ethnically based fear was excised from later editions of the novella.[18]

Interwar sources also described World War I–era court cases against Tatar peasants who "insulted His Majesty" by making favorable comparisons between the Germans and the Russians. A peasant elder in Mamadyshskii uezd, for example, was reportedly visiting friends when he "praised German weaponry, German resourcefulness, and excellent military tactics. He remarked about the sovereign [Tsar Nicholas II]: 'He doesn't know anything, and only puts the people under German fire. He ought to be killed himself.'" In this case the articulation of respect for the power of the German military (and the desire for violence against the tsar) came from a non-Russian whose loyalty Russians doubted because of his nationality.[19]

At a meeting of the Military-Historical Department of the general staff on December 28, 1937, Colonel A. D. Pulko-Dmitriev[20] explained why it was essential to counteract the "falsification" of World War I in the German military historiography:

> As a result of the absolute horror of World War, the impressions from this war among segments of the population of the USSR are not overcome to this day. The German heavy artillery created the common opinion that, in battle, Germany knows how to use all means of fighting and all its forces very well. This pernicious influence has very likely penetrated the milieu of the rising generation as well.

He complained that contemporary Red Army commanders seemed like "pygmies" in comparison to the "powerful and prepared" German commanders.

Pulko-Dmitriev proposed to offset this exaggeration of German success through study of the history of the imperialist war, in which could be found "a series of examples when whole German corps ran from the field of battle in panic."[21] This candid admission that "segments of the Soviet population" who had experienced German bombardment during World War I still feared the Germans is as close to a "smoking gun" about the reasons for the change in tone of military propaganda as I could find in the Soviet archives. Pulko-Dmitriev suggested that the way to counteract multiple Soviet generations' awe of German power was to foreground battles in which the tsarist army stood up to the Germans. The absence of a narrative of tsarist prowess against the Germans had allowed popular perceptions of German military invincibility to develop unchecked. It was belatedly realized that this myth challenged the honor of the Red Army, and so military authorities began to seek ways to contest this myth by recasting World War I.

The growing acknowledgment of the population's fear of Germany suggests a strong motivation for the transformations in World War I military discourse evident in the middle to late 1930s. The Department of Special Purpose (*fakul'tet osobogo naznacheniia*) of the Drama Section of the Union of Soviet Writers briefed its members about the events of World War I and also about German relations "with the Slavs and Peoples of Russia," making prominent mention of the victories of Aleksandr Nevskii and the later inability of Germans to defeat Moscow's centralized government. According to this account, Muscovites and Tatars joined together "to whip the Germans like swine."[22]

Since the Red Army had failed to defeat the Germans in 1918, military historians and playwrights were encouraged to invoke earlier historical examples of Russo-German combat, such as Prince Aleksandr Nevskii against the Teutons, to reassure the population that the contemporary army had precedents for beating the Germans. The most brilliant example of such a work is, of course, Sergei Eisenstein's unforgettable cinematic depiction of this victory in *Aleksandr Nevskii*. As new Soviet myths about Russian military prowess emerged, such victorious World War I episodes as the Brusilov breakthrough received new attention while internationalist and reflective World War I tropes were muted or disappeared altogether.

This new narrative was framed on multiple levels, pointing to the superiority of the Soviet military, the strength of the centralized state, the unified efforts of Slavs and non-Slavs, and of course, the aggression of the Germans.[23] In the late 1930s, the historical profession went out of its way to correct earlier interpretations of the World War I era that did not single out Germany for war blame. While in 1928 Marxist historian M. N. Pokrovskii had criticized E. V. Tarle for "ententophilism" and blaming the outbreak of World War I primarily on the Germans, in the late 1930s historians made a concerted effort to attack the Pokrovskii school for its failure to understand Germany's malevolent role in the coming of World War I.[24] In both military and historical works, any hint of "sympathy" with Germany was unacceptable. Even during the Molotov-Ribbentrop pact, a historical article by A. Manusevich, "Toward a History of the Versailles Treaty," was held up by the censors because it seemed to justify the German annexation of Austria.[25] In the 1930s, this new wariness of the Germans accompanied a new willingness to study and to valorize tsarist military prowess.

MEMORY CASE STUDIES

As one might infer from this discussion about Germany in the late 1930s, the current perception of World War I as a "forgotten war" does not adequately capture the ebb and flow of Soviet war memory. The robust early Soviet attempts to understand and describe the war and the various reasons for the subsequent loss of focus on World War I merit serious attention alongside the Soviet recasting of World War I in the late 1930s. In the early years of the Soviet Union, there were many civilian and military historians who took the experience of World War I seriously and conscientiously documented it. A flurry of World War I–related memoirs and monographs appeared as early as 1920, and throughout the 1920s and 1930s there were debates about technical aspects of World War I such as food supply, fuel supply, and military transport on the pages of journals such as *Voina i revoliutsiia*. It is also likely that World War I made a frequent appearance in officer training materials throughout the interwar period.[26] These proponents of studying the war and preserving its artifacts, however, often complained of fighting an uphill battle against those who believed that the Red Army's victory in the Civil War made World War I irrelevant.[27] The following five case studies examine these battles and, to the extent possible, the individuals involved in both constructing World War I memory and prohibiting it. It also considers the extent to which the military culture and ethos of the tsarist army endured into the 1920s and influenced Soviet military culture.

The Rise and Fall of the Moscow Military History Museum

One of the earliest Soviet struggles over World War I memory and the tsarist military legacy in general took place over the creation of a Moscow museum to document prerevolutionary Russian military history. During World War I, trophy museums and war archives opened in Moscow, Petrograd, Minsk, Warsaw, and Kiev, among many other Russian cities. The tsarist government, like the British and German governments developing their own war museums, imagined such sites as incubators of patriotism and as places to preserve war trophies and relics that might otherwise be lost. The British Imperial War Museum opened in 1920, and while it struggled for space and financial support in its early years, it survived and eventually grew into an important national institution memorializing World War I.[28] In the Soviet Union, on the other hand, Narkompros appropriated the inventories of many local Russian war museums and dispersed them among military-history museums, deliberately shifting the main focus of the exhibits away from World War I and toward military history more generally.[29] Narkompros did not want to allow the "imperialist" war a central place in its museums.

In Moscow, plans for the creation of a new Military History Museum, a branch of the State Historical Museum, got under way in 1921. This museum focused on Russian military history up to the October Revolution; its goal was "the study of all of the achievements and the mistakes of the old in order to better get to know and learn the new."[30] The Red Army simultaneously developed its own museum in Moscow, focusing on the creation of the army during the Civil War. The Military History Museum first opened its doors in September 1923; it inaugurated its permanent exhibit dedicated to the "development of Russian military art from the eighteenth to the twentieth centuries" on Red Army Day in 1925, and it added several rooms devoted to World War I in 1926. In that year, its staff reported that it was receiving a thousand visitors a month.[31] In 1923–1927, the museum was housed in a highly sought-after space, in part of a Petrine-era palace once the residence of Prince G. D. Iusupov. This prominent location revealed that at least some early Soviet decision makers highly valued the enterprise of preserving the Russian military heritage, including the history of World War I. This desirable space caused the museum difficulties, however, as during its short existence it was always under threat of being evicted. Throughout the early 1920s, Narkompros forced the collection to move nine different times.[32]

The exhibits in the Military History Museum came primarily from the disbanded regimental museums of the former tsarist army, and its exhibits reflected this heritage. The museum dedicated an entire room to military banners; in this part of the collection visitors could view a photograph of World War I soldiers proudly gathered around their regimental banner, as well as World War I–era banners prominently displaying the icon of "Christ Not Made By Hands" and adorned with St. George ribbons. The museum also devoted an entire room to early twentieth-century tsarist jubilees in honor of the victory at Poltava, the defeat of Napoleon, and the three hundredth anniversary of the Romanovs.[33] In short, the accoutrements and symbols of tsarist military valor in World War I (and in earlier wars) were openly on display for visitors to observe.

As it was constituted in 1926, the exhibition cautiously embraced certain aspects of tsarist military heritage. The curators put General A. V. Suvorov's death mask on display and praised this general "educated in the best traditions of the previous [Catherinian] era" for his protest against the brutal military innovations of Paul I. While the exhibit called Paul I's minister of war A. A. Arakcheev an "evil genius," it noted that "strangely enough" the tsarist government was indebted to Arakcheev for the fact that the Russian artillery of this era "yielded little to the superlative artillery of Napoleon." The exhibit went on to evaluate the post-Crimea military reforms in a positive light and to recognize the talents of General M. D. Skobelev, hero of the Russo-Turkish war.[34] Mixed in with these qualified but positive interpretations of tsarist military history, the exhibit also introduced countervailing revolutionary narratives, noting, for example, that the siege of Sevastopol during the Crimean War was Russia's first encounter with English imperialism. The exhibits on the Russo-Japanese War emphasized the Russian military leadership's mistakes and overconfidence as well as the outbreak of the Revolution of 1905. The museum also included a "regimental corner" with a display in memory of the regiment's "hero-general" killed in the Japanese war.[35]

The World War I exhibit was similarly multivocal—including heroic moments, revolutionary moments, and realistic depictions of the nature of war. The museum exhibited colorful World War I–era popular prints and patriotic leaflets that were "unsuccessful attempts to raise the spirit of those sent to the slaughter without rifles or shells" in order to contrast them with revolutionary appeals to the soldiers. The exhibit emphasized the high number of Russian casualties, the many strategic mistakes, and the increase in illnesses among the troops. A central theme of the exhibit was the new technology of warfare, underlining the potential dangers of a new imperialist war. Visitors could find out about battle communications, poison gas, armored defense, and the air war. They could see gas masks, artillery shells, mortars, bomb-throwers, rockets, cannons, helmets, shields, and diagrams of positions with barbed wire. This exhibit was unlike prerevolutionary military exhibits in its emphasis on the ordinary soldier. Visitors learned about the misery and boredom of the soldier's life in the trenches and could see everyday items like mess tins and aluminum spoons, as well as objects that soldiers in the trenches had made from rifle cartridges.[36]

But, reinforcing the messages conveyed by patriotic prints, visitors could also look at trophies and banners captured from the enemy, including unique, historically significant trophies of tsarist World War I victories: the banner of the captured Austro-Hungarian fortress Przemysl (1915), and the keys to the Turkish fortress at Erzerum (1916). The exhibit also gave voice to another familiar World War I trope: one display case in the exhibit was devoted to "German atrocities—in reports, denunciations, and photographs."[37] The exhibit thus also articulated a notion of national glory and constructed Russian identity in opposition to German identity.

The heroic and nationalistic trope evident both in the World War I exhibit and the Brusilov funeral of the mid-1920s is one that historians more frequently associate with the "great retreat" of the mid-1930s, when many aspects of "traditional" Russian culture were reintroduced into Soviet ideology, rather than with the Marxist historiography in the 1920s; yet Soviet institutions and leaders in the 1920s also positively framed Russian military heroes and Russian technical prowess and acknowledged them as the heritage of the Soviet state while defining the Germans as enemy. The museum exhibit also served as a transmission belt for the continued circulation of tsarist symbols and the tsarist language of valor in Soviet Russia. Of course, like the appropriation of tsarist history in the 1930s, the museum's approach to the prerevolutionary period was selective, qualified, and accompanied by contradictory narratives that challenged the notion of tsarist military glory. However short-lived the exhibit, it nonetheless reveals that the impulses to nationalize, heroize, and militarize were present throughout the interwar period.

Alongside these heroizing elements, the museum also emphasized one of the most popular revolutionary tropes about the World War I experience: the vast distance between the common soldier and his officer, and the misery and injustice of barracks life. The Military History Museum illustrated this distance in a clever and tangible way, counterposing the "soldier's corner" with the "officer's corner." In the soldier's corner was displayed "a pitiful bunk, a crudely made table and stool with materials all around for drilling the soldier: 'the obligatory knowledge for the rank and file soldier,' prayers, inventories of one's 'kit,' tables of shoulder-straps and decorations, and all that was usually hung on the walls in the old barracks." The officer's corner, on the other hand, displayed the "regimental museum," with lavish gifts from the tsar to the regiment, and a gala ceremonial table, set with prize silver and cards laid out on a gambling table.[38] The scene crisply contrasted the officers' decadence with the soldiers' lack of freedom in the barracks. The museum thus exemplified all aspects of the multifaceted discourse of World War I in the mid-1920s.

The Military History Museum faced tremendous pressures from all sides, however. The most obvious pressure was ideological, due to the museum's exclusive focus on tsarist history and achievements. In the heady days of the early revolutionary period, when many in Narkompros and other Soviet institutions advocated the complete rejection of history and a total break with the tsarist past, the museum's association with the old order made it vulnerable. While Narkompros repeatedly demonstrated a lack of support for the museum, the military newspaper *Krasnaia zvezda* (Red Star) and members of the military establishment publicly defended its existence. In the summer of 1925, after Narkompros ordered the museum to move without allocating it a new space, one defender of the museum in *Krasnaia zvezda* sadly acknowledged that there were some who thought "to whom is this museum still necessary or interesting?" He pointed to the special "administration for the study of the experience of past wars" under the auspices of the Red Army staff as evidence that some contemporaries were keenly aware of the importance of military history. Another letter writer reminded the readers of *Krasnaia zvezda* that Napoleon and Suvorov relied on military history, adding, "There is no basis to think that now the situation has changed and the significance of history has decreased. . . . No other field of history has such pressing significance as precisely military affairs."[39] These pleas revealed the hostile ideological environment facing not only those who valued the history of World War I, but also those who saw utility in tsarist military history generally.

The museum was also under pressure because of the grinding poverty and general disorder of New Economic Policy (NEP)-era Moscow. Like the Old Moscow Society seeking to protect the graves of World War I dead from hooliganism, the Military History Museum staff struggled with issues of security. The museum was burglarized in mid-June 1926. In one ironic twist among many, the most appealing target to burglars was the very exhibit that the museum used to remind its viewers of the decadence of the old order: the officer's corner. *Rabochaia Moskva* (Worker's Moscow) reported that "the thieves penetrated the 'officer's corner,' where they gathered around two poods [seventy-two pounds] of silver and crystal tableware from tsarist tables." In the difficult conditions of the mid-1920s, the museum could not even fulfill its basic function of protecting the historical inventory entrusted to it. In another incident, after the museum was already formally closed, one of the cannons located in the courtyard mysteriously disappeared. The authorities were puzzled as to how this could have happened despite the twenty-four-hour surveillance of the courtyard entrance.[40] NEP lawlessness contributed to both the demise of the museum and the destruction of the artifacts that the museum had been trying to preserve.

Finally, the museum was under pressure because of the fierce competition for resources among Soviet institutions during the NEP era. One letter writer in *Krasnaia zvezda* lamented publicly that the museum was the victim of "interdepartmental friction." The director of the museum suggested that ideological attacks on the museum were motivated by the prospect of material gain. He cynically noted that among the many institutions that coveted the museum's comfortable quarters, there frequently arose the "idea of the complete lack of necessity for a museum of the tsarist army to exist."[41] The ideological battles raging in the 1920s became all the fiercer because of the dearth of material resources.

Narkompros's notion that the museum was unnecessary eventually held sway at the upper echelons of the Soviet government. After only four years of existence, on July 6, 1927, the Council of People's Commissars liquidated the museum and transferred its inventory to the State Historical Museum. Mikhail Rosenfel'd, an investigative reporter for *Komsomol'skaia Pravda* (Komsomol Truth), wrote that despite protests from the civil defense voluntary organization Osoaviakhim and the General Staff and Political Administration of the Red Army, Narkompros engineered the closing of the museum. The reporter blamed Narkompros for systematically destroying the museum in order to claim its space for a research institute and to provide private apartments for Narkompros staff.[42] Despite the fact the contemporary observers knew that military history museums were flourishing both in Europe and in "the provinces" and felt that Moscow was lagging behind, the museum lost its battle for existence.

As many historians have already noted, World War I memory was rejected by some Soviet ideologues who valued their new revolutionary history over the history of the past, including tsarist military history. However, what has not been recognized was that in the 1920s there were historians, archivists, curators, and educators actively working to include the memory of World War I in Soviet discourse. Their failure and the subsequent absence of World War I memory was caused in part by Soviet ideological rejection of the tsarist past, but World War I memory was also shaped by the brutal bureaucratic competition and the grim economic circumstances of the 1920s. Conceptualizations of World War I memory were actively emerging in the first half of the 1920s before they were arrested both by ideology and by material circumstances. A return to the comprehensive exhibition of tsarist military history did not occur until after World War II had thoroughly transformed the context of the tsarist legacy.

Compiling a Documentary History of the First World War

In the first years after World War I in all of the combatant countries, military historians compiled documents, wrote narratives, and began to analyze the course of the war to educate the soldiers who would be responsible for fighting the next war. The Soviet Union was no different. In August 1918, six months after the founding of the Red Army, the general staff created the Commission on the Research and Use of the Experience of World War I. This commission was devoted to the serious study of the strategic, tactical, and technological aspects of the recent wars. Its goal was to facilitate the "rapid use of the experience of the World and Civil Wars by studying these events, the transformations in military-technical means used to conduct the wars, and examples of military art that occurred in the course of these wars." The commission was also charged with collecting documents and materials connected with the wars and with popularizing its results. In early 1925, World War I was removed from the title of the commission, which was now charged to study "the experience of war" in general, but the commission nonetheless continued to focus primarily on the study of World War I.[43]

The commission attracted the attention of prominent Red Army leaders, and in its early years Lev Trotskii was an active member. In the mid-1920s, the commission relied heavily on the expertise of at least seven former generals of the old army who had received higher military education at the elite academy of the tsarist general staff. Led by these men—the *"genshtabisty"*—the commission was particularly productive in the first half of the 1920s and published the seven-volume *Strategic Outline of War, 1914–1918*.[44] The eminent military historian A. M. Zaionchkovskii wrote the most authoritative single-volume summary of the war in 1924, accompanied by detailed maps drawn by A. N. De-Lazari. In 1926, Zaionchkovskii's final scholarly work was published, detailing tsarist Russia's preparation for war. A variety of other strategic and tactical works appeared in the late 1920s and in 1930, including the memoirs of former tsarist officers such as K. Gil'chevskii and A. A. Svechin. In short, in the first decade after the war, the military history commission of the Red Army staff was extremely active in documenting and analyzing the war. As in the case of the Military History Museum, World War I was emphatically not forgotten.[45] At the highest levels of the Red Army, both Commissar for Military and Naval Affairs Kliment Voroshilov and military reformer M. Tukhachevskii also emphasized the importance of World War I as the model to study in preparation for a future war.[46] It is therefore difficult to agree with Soviet historian I. A. Korotkov, who wrote in *The History of Soviet Military Thought* in 1980 that "incommensurately more attention was devoted to the world imperialist war in the 1930s."[47] In fact, the military study of World War I almost completely disappeared from sight in the first half of the 1930s, reappearing in the late 1930s primarily in the guise of very specialized works analyzing particular military operations.

The story of the never-completed project to compile World War I documents reveals much about study of the war in the 1930s. In late 1929, B. M. Shaposhnikov, a former tsarist colonel and genshtabist serving as the Red Army chief of staff, proposed that the military history department undertake an ambitious new project: a six-volume document collection, to be put out in two to three thousand copies, focusing primarily on the war of movement. The first five volumes were to be organized chronologically, while the sixth volume focused thematically on the economic preparation and prosecution of the war. This systematic documentary project was to take the place of the historians' ongoing work on "individual historical moments of the war." Each volume was to consist of 80 percent original documents and 20 percent explanatory text. The chosen authors included senior historians of the Red Army staff trained before the revolution as well as young specialists from the Military Section of the Communist Academy. These younger Soviet-trained specialists were to "guarantee a politically consistent approach to the analysis of events."[48]

This project was shaped by the ideological and political struggles within the Red Army. The orientation against tsarist military history that was visible in the mid-1920s in Narkompros seemed to gain some ground in the Red Army at the end of the 1920s. The professional tsarist-trained military specialists increasingly clashed with more politically oriented figures who tended to prioritize Civil War experience. This politicization of military history and military doctrine eventually led to the downfall of the military specialists; many of the most prominent became victims of the purges.[49] The inclusion of explicitly Communist historians in this documentary project hinted that, from the very outset, it was shaped by the simultaneous dependence on and distrust of the military specialists.

The ideological tension is also evident in the format of the World War I project. On the one hand, this project can be seen as advancing military knowledge, since the World War I archives were still in a poor state and the compiling of critical but unknown documents would enable future historians and army commanders to make their own conclusions about important events. On the other hand, the decision to focus on compiling documents instead of writing monographs limited the opportunities for the military historians themselves to interpret events. This project recast their professional duties toward archival research and source study and away from analysis.

Over the next several years, the World War I documentary project was reorganized several times, and although four volumes of documents eventually appeared between 1936 and 1940, the project was never fully realized. The trials and tribulations of the World War I documentary project, though somewhat murky, provide some insight into the forces that curtailed the Red Army staff's pursuit of the study of World War I, beginning roughly in 1930. That year is also notable for the publication of the first volume of military specialist A. A. Svechin's memoir *The Art of Leading a Regiment* (*Iskusstvo vozhdeniia polka*), a work that was criticized after its publication for its lack of attention to class contradictions in the tsarist army. No doubt as a result of this criticism and other attacks on Svechin as a "bourgeois" theorist, the second volume of Svechin's memoirs was never published. It was also in 1930 that the State Publishing House declined to put out a second edition of Brusilov's memoirs, despite the success of the first edition.[50] While Moscow's Military History Museum and the Moscow City Fraternal Cemetery began their struggles for survival in the mid-1920s, the turning point for World War I memory within the institutional structure of the Red Army occurred around 1930, when the tide increasingly turned against the military specialists, both because of internal doctrinal struggles and personnel changes in the Red Army and because of the ascendance of "Marxist" historiography. Yet the sea change in ideology did not immediately undermine official plans to complete an ambitious World War I documentary project. In March 1932, the project was expanded and reorganized to encompass twelve thematic volumes. At that point, the editorial team, approved by the Presidium of the Central Executive Committee of the USSR, consisted of E. Z. Barsukov, M. D. Bonch-Bruevich, A. E. Gutor, Iakubovskii, Iakimichev, A. N. Lapchinksii, F. E. Ogorodnikov, A. A. Svechin, P. Sytin, and B. B. Zherve.[51]

There are some clues about the nature of the struggle over the documentary project available in the unpublished memoirs of E. Z. Barsukov, a former tsarist officer and the editor-in-chief of several volumes of the World War I documentary history project that were never published. He wrote his memoirs in the mid-1950s, when he was one of the few participants in the World War I project who was still alive. While it is difficult to verify his rather partisan account, it is still worth considering in light of the dearth of other evidence. He blamed changes in personnel at the Red Army staff for impeding the progress of work on the documentary collection, specifically the appointment of F. A. Anulov (a specialist on the Civil War) as the head of the Military History Department and A. I. Egorov (a former tsarist colonel) as the chief of staff. Barsukov complained that Anulov was "psychologically ill" and began "to hamper the compilation of the sixth volume of the collection." In Barsukov's opinion, Egorov, who had become chief of staff in 1931 after Shaposhnikov fell into temporary disgrace for praising Trotskii, "evidently did not recognize scholarship, especially history. (It seems that in the past he was an operetta singer) and he ordered that the compilation of the collection be stopped."[52]

Furthermore, Barsukov's team of researchers was not paid for the work that they had already completed (8–10 rubles per printer's sheet) and they took the Red Army staff to People's Court. After Barsukov served as a witness for the aggrieved historians, his relations with Egorov became "intolerable"; Egorov reprimanded him and threatened to dismiss him, but didn't have the right to do so since Barsukov was an employee of the Central Directorate of the Red Army, and not the Red Army staff. Barsukov eventually retired from the Red Army on a personal pension in 1934 but continued to publish his own scholarly work on the history of Russian artillery. In Barsukov's account, it was personality rather than ideology that shaped events.

The records of the Red Army staff's Commission for the Study of War Experience confirm that the World War I documentary project faced severe problems regarding funding, logistics, and leadership, but they do not specifically name Anulov and Egorov as the key decision makers in determining the fate of the project. One document from 1932 or 1933 included a list of reasons why work on the World War I collection was not moving forward: the editors were overworked and could not find time for archival research, they were not given money or ration cards, and they could not continue their work without typists and paper.[53] Somewhere between 1930 and 1932, the General Staff's commitment to provide material support for the project had clearly evaporated, leaving the project completely bereft of finances and leadership. This lack of support demonstrates the turn away from both the tsarist past and the Soviet military specialists trained under the old regime.

In November 1933, a new directive from V. N. Levichev of the Chief Directorate of the Red Army changed the format of the collection by declaring that the documents should be published with a brief introductory sketch of the featured operation, but no other commentary at all. The new plans for the document collection also limited the scope of the volumes to documents that concerned only "the command and management of troops." These decisions limited the interpretive powers of the historians even further. Now, they were simply supposed to unearth the documents and publish them with the barest amount of contextualization. One of the volume editors, Korol'kov, protested that the new head of the Army's Fifth Department wouldn't allow him to publish "descriptions of the most interesting battles" in order to "illustrate the important staff documents being published." He warned that without narratives or commentaries, "a naked skeleton of only documents remained. In order to understand the events illuminated by the documents, a reader who was unfamiliar with the operation would have to study the entire publication; the reader would be charged to carry out work beyond his strength." But the pleas of Korol'kov and other historians that contextualization was integral to the success of the volumes fell on deaf ears. Furthermore, the new schema that narrowly focused on the command of troops entirely excluded volumes that had been in progress for years, such as Barsukov's volume on the economic aspects of the war.[54]

In February of 1934, the Military History Department determined that only 15 percent of the work on the document collection had been completed and that the compilers were doing a poor job. They completely reorganized the project for the third time in June 1934, scaling it down from twelve volumes to "two or three." Now, the works were to "reflect those positive and negative sides of the operational art of the Russian command . . . that should be studied by our Red Army commanders for the development of operational thought." They drew up new publishing agreements in June 1934, leaving those who had worked on the earlier edition in limbo. The old publication plan had been stopped, evidently without paying those who had worked on it, and there was no money yet allocated to start the new plan. The new leadership of the Military History Department distrusted the historians and eliminated their interpretations of events. They were wary of narratives by a single author that might not be "objective."[55] The leadership feared the work of individual historians, no longer prioritized the general study of World War I, and sought to focus only on the narrow topic of operational art. Furthermore, they did not even make the funds available to carry out the work that they had mandated. As a result, serious historical study of the war was both circumscribed and stalled. Five years of work on the documentary project had not produced a single publication.

In early 1934, Bonch-Bruevich (a former tsarist officer) and V. Lazarevich had already completed their volume on the Lodz Operation and submitted it to the publisher. It was rejected, however, because it did not comply with the new format. Colonel A. Kh. Bazarevskii was asked to reorganize the volume, and it finally appeared in print in 1936, without any indication that Bonch-Bruevich or Lazarevich had been the ones who had done all of the research on which the volume was based. The foreword to the Lodz collection, the first volume of the series, announced that the publication of documents from the "World Imperialist War 1914–1917" would give readers "concrete military-historical material characterizing the work of the chief, front, and army commands in the formation of strategic plans and in putting them into effect."[56] The volume itself consisted of a ten-page introduction discussing the Russian and German operational plans and the extent to which they were realized, followed by almost five hundred pages of documents. Thus only 2 percent of the book was made up of explanatory material.[57] Three other volumes of similar format followed, without commentaries and with the identities of their original compilers and editors likewise erased.[58] The group of historians who advocated serious work about World War I and their conceptions of how this work should be carried out were pushed aside.

In 1937, as anxiety about the German threat increased, the historians of the General Staff of the Red Army regretted that Russian military historians had not completed a history of World War I, because the French history was not yet finished and the German and Austrian histories had to be discounted because of their "bias." These historians felt that the most urgent need, not surprisingly, was an analysis of operations on the western border of the Russian Empire. The department decided on a fourteen-volume chronology of the war, but this new project's editorial board was destroyed in the purges before the project could get under way. Leaders of the Military History Department also recognized the urgency of completing the document collection that they had initiated in 1929. In March of 1938, I. F. Nefterev complained to Chief of Staff Shaposhnikov that "enemies of the people" had impeded work on the history of World War I and, despite all their efforts, there were only four volumes of the World War I document collection either published or soon to be in press.[59] In the end, the Military History Department of the General Staff produced no fourteen-volume chronology of the war and only four volumes of the projected twelve volumes of documentary history. Such ambitious long-term projects could not be fully sustained during the upheaval of the purges. In the mid-1930s, however, a number of single-author monographs about particular

World War I operations did make their appearance under the auspices of the Ministry of Defense and the Frunze Military Academy.[60] Systematic study of the war in general gave way to the analysis of the operations that were perceived as the most strategically important, but certain historians were once again entrusted with narrating, interpreting, and analyzing events.

The convoluted fate of the World War I documentary history project, like the demise of the Moscow Military History Museum, reveals the ways in which early Soviet attempts to take World War I seriously were curtailed in the face of the rejection of the tsarist past and "bourgeois" military theory and the institutional struggles of competing Soviet agencies and competing departments within an institution such as the Red Army. For a time in the early to mid-1930s, the abilities and the expertise of the tsarist-trained military historians of the Red Army staff were devalued. And then the purges of the military swept up both those genshtabisty who, like Svechin, seemed to be promoting the study of World War I and those who seemed to be discouraging it, such as Egorov. Yet in the years before World War II as the Nazi threat loomed, it became more and more important for the Red Army staff both to plan for new battles against the Germans and to celebrate past successes against them. As a result, selected episodes from World War I began to gain new prominence in the late 1930s. The four extant volumes of the World War I document project emerged at that time as a result of this heightened concern with the German threat, as did other narrative operational histories. This ebb and flow of attention to World War I in the interwar period demonstrates the active efforts of many Soviet military historians to "remember" the war despite myriad institutional, logistical, and economic difficulties. And their efforts should not be forgotten.

Brusilov's Zigzags

The transformations in Soviet public recognition of Brusilov, like the twists and turns in the World War I documentary project, illuminate the contested nature of World War I memory and the various contingencies that influenced its creation. Before his death in 1926, Brusilov's status was tenuous. On the one hand, he was awarded a state pension and allowed to go abroad for medical treatment, and he won permission from the chair of the Revvoensovet M. V. Frunze to be buried at Novodevichii Monastery. On the other hand, his historical works were not accepted for publication, he was engaged in a bitter feud with some representatives of the Soviet military-history establishment such as his former protégé Zaionchkovskii, and he had been unable to intervene to prevent the arrests of some of his friends and associates among the former tsarist military.[61]

From the point of view of the Soviet state, the death of Brusilov resolved some of the ambiguities and allowed the Soviet military establishment enhanced control over Brusilov's legacy. Soon after his death, Brusilov's reminiscences were published under the auspices of the official Soviet publishing apparatus. Excerpts of his memoirs about World War I appeared first in the journal *Voina i revoliutsiia* in 1927.[62] In 1928, the State Publishing House sought to publish Brusilov's memoirs in a freestanding volume, and the Museum of the Revolution also pursued N. V. Brusilova to acquire documentary materials related to her husband's career. The State Publishing House paid Brusilova at least 3,000 rubles for the memoirs alone.[63] All five thousand copies of the first edition of Brusilov's memoirs were sold out in 1929, and the book was an international success, appearing in English and French translation in 1930.

The State Publishing House planned to reprint the book in 1930. Sometime during that year, however, the publishing house changed its mind, and the book did not appear in print again until after the outbreak of World War II.[64] The decision not to reprint Brusilov's memoirs occurred at roughly the same time that Shaposhnikov charged the younger Communist historians working on the World War I documentary project with monitoring the historical analysis of the older military experts. Given this timing, one can speculate that the intensifying suspicion of "experts" and "former people" during "the great break"—the series of radical policies between 1928–1932 including forced collectivization, rapid industrialization, and aggressive promotion of working-class cadres at the expense of the "bourgeoisie"—might have produced the authorities' reluctance to promulgate the views of even a "progressive" member of Nicholas II's military bureaucracy. But there might have been other factors at play as well. In late 1929 and early 1930, Nadezhda Brusilova applied to leave the country to go to Czechoslovakia for medical care, and her request was denied three times. In mid-1930, however, Robert Eideman persuaded Kliment Voroshilov to allow Brusilova to go abroad to receive medicine and treatment not available in the Soviet Union, following the long-standing tradition of such privileges for the military. Since authorities probably presumed she was returning, it seems unlikely that Brusilova's attempts to leave the country had a decisive influence on the State Publishing House's 1930 decision regarding Brusilov's memoirs. Brusilova's later resolve to stay in emigration, however, most likely reinforced the downplaying of Brusilov's legacy in the 1930s.[65]

Between 1930 and 1938, Brusilov's class alien status came to matter more than his patriotism, and his military achievements were not necessarily viewed as successes. While 1934 is often seen as a key turning point in Soviet attitudes toward the tsarist past, the twentieth anniversary of the start of World War I did not result in a positive evaluation of Brusilov or the republication of his memoirs. In the mid-1930s, analysts tended not to value the effects of the Brusilov offensive. In 1934, historian Ol'ga Chaadaeva emphasized the catastrophic losses incurred during the Brusilov offensive—half a million men dead, injured, or captured. She assessed the results of the offensive by noting that it "led to new losses and new defeats," and "definitively undermined the faith of the soldiers in the impending conclusion of the war by means of victory."[66] Chaadaeva depicted the Brusilov offensive as a stepping-stone on the path to inevitable revolution rather than an object of national pride. At the moment of the "about-face" toward Russian state-centered nationalism in the mid-1930s, when tsarist military heroes of the more distant past gained prominence in Soviet culture,[67] Brusilov was not celebrated as an example of military prowess the way that he had been in the 1920s.

Positive references to Brusilov were largely absent from Soviet publications until the end of the 1930s when anxiety about the Nazi threat increased. In 1938, a pamphlet titled *The Lutsk Breakthrough* by M. Rozhdestvenskii was published by the People's Commissariat of Defense for wide distribution among the commanders and chiefs of the Red Army. Rozhdestvenskii's assessment of the offensive at Lutsk criticized historians who denied the influence of the breakthrough on further developments in the Russian theater of war. The author called the operation "brilliant," arguing, "It proved to everyone that the Russian army had not collapsed after the difficult trials of 1915. In 1916 the Russian Army was still strong, for it had smashed the strongest opponent and gained successes not enjoyed by any other army in the period of the world war."[68] Rozhdestvenskii credited the "Russian soldier" with this great victory but acknowledged Brusilov for his faith in the strength of the Russian army and his ability to convey this faith to his subordinates. By 1938, the memory of the "breakthrough" became an important aspect of military education even if the recognition of Brusilov's role remained limited.

In 1939, Iu. Veber's story "Breakthrough" was published in *Artillerists* (*Artilleristy*), an agitational volume produced by the Komsomol for a wide readership. Like *The Lutsk Breakthrough,* this story emphasized the success of the offensive without mentioning Brusilov in the title. Veber, repeating Rozhdestvenskii's assessment for a wider audience, suggested that Brusilov's significant achievement was that he was the one general who "believed in the success of the operation and in the battle-worthiness of the Russian soldier."[69] While both of these works celebrated the performance of tsarist-era soldiers during the Brusilov offensive, they stopped short of heroizing General Brusilov personally.

While it is difficult to discern the specific impetus for the change, it is possible to document a further rise in Brusilov's status between 1939 and 1940. After having lost a tremendous amount of time in chronicling the experience of World War I, the military historians of the Red Army staff began to examine the Russian offensive at Lutsk. In a textbook published by the Academy of the General Staff of the Red Army, the military historian L. V. Vetoshnikov provided an "operational-strategic study" titled *The Operation of the Breakthrough on the Southwestern Front in 1916*. One year later, after war had already broken out in Europe, the Commissariat of Defense published a second edition of this work under the title *The Brusilov Breakthrough*. The change in the title revealed a renewed willingness to acknowledge Brusilov personally for his successes against the Germans and to recognize him as a predecessor on the family tree of the Red Army.

The invasion of the Soviet Union largely ended Soviet squeamishness about celebrating the achievements of a member of the tsarist elite as propagandists eagerly sought to publicize any circumstances under which the Russians had militarily defeated the Germans. The outbreak of war propelled Brusilov into the spotlight as a hero once again. V. V. Mavrodin's short biography of Brusilov was first published in 1941 and then reprinted several times throughout the war in large print runs. He praised Brusilov as a "talented, educated, decisive, and energetic commander" who "brilliantly" carried out "the breakthrough of the Austro-German troops in 1916 that has received the appellation 'the Brusilov Breakthrough.'"[70] The Ministry of Defense Publishing House put out new editions of Brusilov's own memoirs in 1941 and 1943. I. L. Sel'vinskii's play *General Brusilov* premiered in 1942, and, in 1943, Sergei Sergeev-Tsenskii published a full-length novel about the Brusilov breakthrough.[71] The new rhetoric about Brusilov will be examined further in chapter 7.

Brusilov's new popularity did not go completely uncontested, however. There were still a few Soviet writers who spoke against the rehabilitation of a World War I general as a popular hero. In a May 1944 letter to the Central Committee's Agitation and Propaganda Department, historian A. M. Pankratova decried Brusilov's new popularity, arguing that the heroization of Brusilov was confusing to schoolchildren because "this World War I general's claim to fame was based on his defense of a regime that Lenin would soon overthrow."[72] Thus, even during the patriotic fervor of World War II, there were voices raised against the figure of Brusilov and the rehabilitation of the heroic memory of World War I. Revolutionary and internationalist interpretations contested the ideological soundness of the new patriotic and heroic discourse. During World War II, however, such voices were in the minority, in contrast to the end of the 1920s and the beginning of the 1930s when such opinions had been influential in circumscribing the study of World War I.

The Reception of All Quiet on the Western Front

Although there is a tendency to imagine the Soviet Union as separated from European cultural and social trends in the 1920s, the Soviet Union actively participated in one of the most significant episodes of international World War I remembrance: the highly contested reception of Erich Maria Remarque's blockbuster war novel *All Quiet on the Western Front*. The appearance of this novel was an international phenomenon in which Russian-speakers actively participated. The novel appeared in translation within six months of its original publication in German. A very short summary of the entire novel appeared in the journal *Molodaia gvardiia* (Young Guard) in July 1929, a forty-five-page illustrated edition came out in *Roman-Gazeta* (Novel-Newspaper) in early 1930, and this shortened edition was reprinted as a pamphlet by the Soviet Worker publishing house that year. The book appeared in full in 1929 in *Vestnik inostrannoi literatury* (Bulletin of Foreign Literature), and in a variety of editions by Federation, Red Proletarian, and Land and Factory. The latter two publishing houses offered large print runs (of as many as 100,000 copies) at low prices, producing a "cheap library" edition that cost only 35 kopeks. The work also appeared in Georgian and Ukrainian translations, and there were Soviet editions in the German language with a foreword by Karl Radek and a special school edition with a Russian-German glossary for language learners.[73]

Many Soviet critics warmly received *All Quiet on the Western Front*. The hundred thousand copies of the Land and Factory edition reproduced glowing reviews from the Soviet press on the cover leaves. These reviews came, not surprisingly, from the two journals directly involved in publishing the book, but also from the official government newspaper *Izvestiia* as well as *Literaturnaia gazeta* (Literary Gazette), *Krasnaia zvezda,* and *Vecherniaia Moskva* (Evening Moscow). The review quoted from *Molodaia gvardiia* read: "The portrayals that Remarque developed in his novel are so significant that one can speak of this book as one speaks of an event. No other work has captured the immediacy of war material with such breadth or with such tragic significance." *Vecherniaia Moskva* wrote, "This book is terrifying, like the most implacable face of war. It is like a song; you cannot throw anything out if it."[74] In 1929, then, Soviet readers and critics were avid consumers of Remarque's novel and took part in building its international acclaim.

The most striking excerpt on the cover leaf of the novel came from *Izvestiia,* the official bulletin of the Central Executive Committee of the Soviet Union. After noting that *All Quiet on the Western Front* had sold a million and a half copies in Europe and the United States, the reviewer proclaimed:

> He [Remarque] allows the reader to understand, to feel, almost to touch that horrible state of mind that a person experiences in the environment of contemporary slaughter, with all of its technological means for the annihilation of people, with all of the brutality that spontaneously arises in the soldier, with its mass conversion of human bodies into a bloody mash, with all of its madness, the imprint of which to a greater or lesser degree almost always remains on a person who has been in battle, who has been exposed to the danger of being killed and killing. . . . Remarque depicts this person–wild beast [*chelovek-zver'*] in his book.[75]

The *Izvestiia* reviewer lingered on Remarque's description of the horrors of modern war, acknowledging that all soldiers become "wild beasts" in the midst of battle and that virtually all of them return home bearing the stamp of the insanity of war. This candid discussion of war stood in stark contrast to the usual tropes of Soviet militarization; it seems almost as if the *Izvestiia* critic was articulating a pacifist rejection of war itself.

The tone and vocabulary of some of the positive reviews of *All Quiet on the Western Front* hinted at some underlying ambivalence, however. *Literaturnaia gazeta,* for example, applauded Remarque for recording only "the facts" and for avoiding "arguments and unnecessary humanitarian emotionalism."[76] The adjective "humanitarian" held the key to understanding some Soviet critics' unease with Remarque. In the late 1920s, Soviet ideologues attacked "bourgeois" humanism and humanitarianism for valuing the fate of individuals above the well-being of the toiling classes. This individualistic and class-blind attitude could erroneously lead to compassion for the class enemies of the Soviet state or to a rejection of the use of violence to achieve revolutionary goals.

While many early reviews of the artistic qualities of Remarque's book were extremely positive, some of the early praise was qualified because of the novel's nonproletarian nature and its pacifist opposition to all wars. In an August 1929 article in the journal *Na literaturnom postu* (On Literary Guard), Z. Lippai called Remarque a petty-bourgeois "humanist and pacifist" who wanted to write an apolitical pacifist novel, and who completely ignored the class aspects of the war. Yet Lippai went on to say that, despite Remarque's intentions, the book was extremely valuable to the proletarian reader because it unwittingly broke out of the bounds of petty-bourgeois literature and no longer served bourgeois class interests. "Thanks to its high artistic truthfulness, it is hard to make this book a means of disseminating pacifism, with whose help it would be possible to distract the attention of the masses from the threat of a new war." Lippai asserted that instead the book was a "brilliant foundation for political agitation against the preparation for imperialist war as well as against imperialist war itself."[77] Instead of interpreting the book as a tragic tale of a lost generation destroyed by the war, Lippai saw the book as a call to action to the proletariat to prevent imperialist war and if necessary turn imperialist war into civil war against the bourgeoisie.

Lippai's reading of the novel against the grain of its own class nature demonstrated the powerful impact that the novel had on this Soviet critic who sought to rescue it from its potential political defects. The article clearly admitted the dual nature of Remarque's work and the fact that it might be read as an attack on all war instead of as a call to class war. This kind of "apolitical" pacifism thus passed into Soviet discourse along with the novel. The initial participation of the Soviet Union in the world reception of the novel revealed both genuine enthusiasm and a desire to adopt the novel into a Soviet framework.

One of the key elements to Sovietizing the novel was to recast the ending from a focus on tragedy to a focus on action. No generation could be "lost" in a Soviet context. Remarque's realism (Lippai pronounced Remarque to be an even finer realist than Zola) was extraordinarily attractive to Soviet writers and critics, but Remarque's decision to have Paul Bäumer die rather than join the revolution contradicted the fundamental principles of both Soviet literature and Soviet politics. Bäumer's pointless and ironic death only weeks before the armistice, on a day "that was so quiet and still on the whole front," denied him personal revolutionary development and deprived the reader of the promise of a revolutionary future.[78]

While critics between the years of 1929 and 1931 praised Remarque for a novel that, despite its class blindness, could still be interpreted as a proto-revolutionary book, after publication of the 1931 sequel *The Road Back,* Soviet critics distanced themselves from Remarque. In the novel, he did not portray Communists favorably and did not embrace revolution as salvation for the returning veterans.[79] *The Road Back* was not translated into Russian, and *All Quiet on the Western Front* was not reprinted after 1931, though the more than one hundred thousand copies still circulated and the book remained popular with readers.

In the 1930s, *All Quiet on the Western Front* captured the imagination of Soviet writers who sought to address Remarque's revolutionary deficiencies by writing adaptations of the novel. Internal reviewers at the State Literature Publishing House, however, were not at all impressed with two dramas based on Remarque's novel that were submitted to them, and so both remained unpublished. Nonetheless, these works tell us a great deal about the Soviet literary establishment's perceptions of Remarque and of World War I in the early to mid-1930s.

The first work was an early 1930s radio-play based on *All Quiet on the Western Front* by Nikolai Sokolovskii. I can find no evidence that any of this author's other work ever appeared in print in the Soviet Union. Within a year or two of the publication of Remarque's novel, it was clear to even an amateur writer that ideological trends demanded that traces of "bourgeois humanism" and rejection of war should be removed from the novel, while additional scenes of class struggle should be added. For example, Sokolovskii included the pivotal scene in which Paul Bäumer killed a Frenchman in the radio-play, but unlike in the novel, Bäumer did not promise "to fight against this, that has struck us both down."[80] The end of all wars was not the answer.

Instead, in a scene set in the beer hall in Bäumer's hometown while he was on leave, a radicalized Paul prophesied about a new war. Like any true revolutionary, he revealed his desire to turn the imperialist war into a war against the bourgeoisie. But this was to be a war of a peculiar sort: "The days, weeks, years we spent at war will return again. Our dead comrades will rise up then and will march with us. Our heads will clear up and we will have a goal in front of us. Our dead comrades will walk alongside us. We will destroy you." In Sokolovskii's macabre vision, the dead would rejoin the living, not to see if the survivors were carrying out their legacy as in *J'accuse* and not to witness the success of the cause as in *Borderlands*, but to annihilate their enemies—the bourgeoisie. This radio-play envisioned the revolution as a supernatural event, enabled by the participation of the now clear-sighted living who could finally see who their true enemies were and the raised dead who could turn back the clock to fight a new war. This particular image of resurrection was not found suitable, however, for a Soviet audience in the 1930s.

In the same beer hall scene in Sokolovskii's radio-play, a German worker and mother discussed her vision for her son at war. This German mother was the antithesis of the one described by Kollontai in her 1924 memoir. This mother said, echoing Lenin, "They will give you a weapon. Take it and learn to kill. Get to know this science, not to kill your brothers as your father did, but to destroy the masters, those who made the war."[81] This radio-play eliminated any trace of Remarque's pacifism and instead called for the use of violence against the "masters" in retribution for the war. In Sokolovskii's play, Paul Bäumer took up this call to fight against the bourgeoisie. He died as a martyr to the revolution, not as a helpless victim in a senseless war. According to Sokolovskii's revised ending to Bäumer's story, he was killed at the barricades on May 1, 1918, proud of his party card in the Union of Revolutionary Front-Line Soldiers of Germany.

Despite this new revolutionary twist in Bäumer's biography, the reviewer for the State Literary Publishing House felt that the play did not sufficiently illuminate the tensions between soldiers and officers, or the soldiers' lack of desire to fight and their growing antiwar mood. The critic felt that Sokolovskii had failed to capture the tension between the front and the rear that was central to Remarque's novel and that the beer hall scene was unsuccessful. He complained that what in Remarque was "magnificent in its brevity and clarity was here dragged out" and turned into "sentimental melodrama." The critic's evaluation reveals both the clumsiness of the attempt to repair Remarque's faulty ideology and the reviewer's real appreciation of Remarque's achievement. This reviewer was willing to overlook the ideological faults in Remarque's novel and let it stand as written because of its exceptional strength in depicting the war. Of course, by rejecting the radio-play, the critic also limited the population's exposure to the novel.

The second play, *The Traitor,* which was reviewed and rejected by the critic Kir'ianov on behalf of the State Literature Publishing House in October 1936, took a different approach. It was a biographical play about Remarque in the 1920s that carried on a polemic with the ideas of Remarque. The dramatist of the rejected play was likely Mikhail Borisovich Zagorskii, the author of several actors' biographies and works on theater history, including *Gogol and the Theater* and *Pushkin and the Theater*.[82]

Zagorskii's play was written sometime after 1931 when Soviet critics perceived Remarque as betraying the revolutionary promise they saw in *All Quiet on the Western Front*. The play was set in Berlin after the novel's publication; it featured Remarque's interaction with his frontline comrades, the well-known characters from his novel, some of whom were rescued from their fictional deaths to appear in the play.[83] Zagorskii depicted Remarque as a miserable neurasthenic, torn between a life of fame and fortune and the ideals of class struggle embraced by his lower-class war comrades, especially Katczinsky, now a conscious revolutionary.

A new character in the play was Jeanne Duval, the daughter of the French printer that Paul Bäumer killed in *All Quiet on the Western Front*. When Jeanne Duval sought out Remarque to find out more about her father's death, he admitted, "I promised him that I would become a typesetter and live the life of a simple worker near you, to replace your father and to fight against the war that destroyed both him and me." Duval then accused Remarque of deceiving her father.[84] Zagorskii depicted Remarque as betraying his working-class comrades by accepting fame and fortune and aligning himself with the Germans who had sat the war out in the rear. He also disappointed his comrades by failing to depict the true class nature of the imperialist war.

Kir'ianov's 1936 review of this play reveals a great deal about Soviet critics' admiration for Remarque's style and about changing tides in the Soviet literary scene. Kir'ianov felt that the play had some merits: "Zagorskii succeeded in avoiding Remarque's pacifism. He succeeded in sharpening scenes and filling them with class content." Like Sokolovskii, Zagorskii sought to repair Remarque's known defects while showcasing his novel. Nonetheless the critic found fault with Zagorskii's adaptation: "but for Remarque's readers, the choice of scenes will seem unconvincing, for the majority of them are the least characteristic of the original. And then, for those who have not happened to read the original, these scenes will seem insufficiently connected and illogical."[85] Kir'ianov thus faulted Zagorskii for not remaining true to the novel and failing to successfully convey the essence of the original to audience members who had not read it. He felt that the spirit of the original novel should remain accessible to Soviet audiences.

The conclusion to Kir'ianov's review offers important insight into transformations in Soviet ideology: "As for polemics with Remarque—this time has passed. Similar conversations have been removed from the order of the day. The play was intended for a certain moment and done in a cultured way (*kul'turno*), but this moment has passed. Now there is no longer any reason to publish it."[86] By 1936, the issues of "turning the imperialist war into a civil war" and rejecting "bourgeois" pacifism in favor of revolutionary militarism were passé. On the one hand, Soviet autarky had lessened the need for world revolution. On the other hand, after the National Socialist takeover of Germany in early 1933, the Soviet Union's recognition by the United States later that year, and the Soviet entrance into the League of Nations in November 1934, Soviet ideologues no longer lumped the Western powers together in the same undifferentiated category of "imperialist." Soviet leaders, including Stalin, began to develop their own language of pacifism in response to the bellicose rhetoric of Nazi Germany. The few years that elapsed between the writing of the play and its review destroyed its relevance and eliminated the possibility of its publication, even though it was ideologically correct for its time and "cultured." Even though Soviet ideologues found *All Quiet on the Western Front* acceptable for only a very brief time, these two plays demonstrate that the novel captured the admiration and respect of Soviet authors and critics in the mid-1930s, and it continued to have resonance in Soviet intellectual life despite the fact that it was not reprinted between 1930 and 1959.

Although the American film adaptation of *All Quiet on the Western Front* directed by Lewis Milestone for Universal Pictures was not shown publicly in the Soviet Union, Soviet readers learned about its notoriety.[87] In 1931, the journal *Proletarskoe kino* (Proletarian Cinema) reported on the stormy reception of the film. A brief article chronicled how around this "patriotic" film "genuine militaristic passions flared up." It reported that copies of the film were stolen from a movie theater on the border of Germany and Holland and burned because it was "not to someone's taste" that hundreds of Germans were crossing the border daily to see a film that was banned in Germany proper. The article also mocked fifteen members of the British Parliament for their protest of the German ban on the film. The MPs asserted that the film "did not lower the honor and prestige of Germany but rather showed her heroic struggle against the allies." The author of the article then commented, "As they say, 'What wouldn't comfort a child [*chem by ditia ne teshilos'*]?'"[88] The article revealed the author's disdain for both the film and its militaristic critics, but also showed that the European scandals surrounding the reception of both the novel and the film were of interest to the Soviet public.

There is another aspect of the film that connects it to war memory in the Soviet Union—the biography of the director. The son of a successful manufacturer, Lewis Milestone was born Lev Milstein in Odessa, and attended Jewish schools in Kishinev. Sent to engineering school in Germany by parents trying to discourage his love of theater, Milestone ran away to seek his fortune in the United States. When the United States entered World War I, Milestone volunteered for the army and served in the Photographic Division of the United States Signal Corps, becoming a photographer and then a filmmaker and editor. Although he did not see combat, Milestone "witnessed the impact of war when he had to preserve, photograph and catalogue limbs that had been sent from the battlefield to Washington."[89]

Milestone began his career in Hollywood after the war, and when asked to direct *All Quiet on the Western Front*, he took inspiration from the work of Sergei Eisenstein, borrowing from Eisenstein's pioneering montage methods to create "some of the most realistic and horrific battle scenes in cinema history."[90] Bringing the butchery of war to the screen in this innovative way carried a pacifist message. Contemporary American reviewers believed that the film "preach[ed] the doctrine of peace." In his later life, Milestone told an interviewer that he "didn't believe in war and was against violence." He claimed that his war films were a success because he "tried to expose war for what it is and not glorify it."[91] Milestone, raised and educated in a Russian-Jewish milieu and influenced by early Soviet filmmaking, shaped both the style and the message of this classic "American" film.

The Nazis cast aspersions on the film version of *All Quiet on the Western Front* by calling it a "Jewish" film because of Milestone and Carl Laemmle, its producer.[92] While of course rejecting the Nazi racism that this formulation implied in the early 1930s, I would nonetheless like to consider the film alongside the work of other Russian-Jewish witnesses of war. Many of the most powerful Soviet voices that explored the morality of violence and forcefully depicted the tragedies of war—Erenburg, Voitolovskii, Babel', Levin, and Katsov—were all Russian-Jewish writers. This controversial film that some called pacifist and some called patriotic, then, could be seen as part of a transnational Russian-Jewish tradition of interpreting the impact of war. The poignancy of these accounts was enhanced by the dual identities of the writers witnessing atrocities committed against "their" people (the Jews) by "their" people (the Russian and Red armies). Jewish writing was tinged with the trauma of being a victim who was ostensibly on the same side as some of the perpetrators.

Both before and after the attacks on Remarque heated up in 1931, Soviet readers, like readers all over the world, tore through *All Quiet on the Western Front* "like a shot."[93] Some readers were engaged enough to write to the publishers in Moscow with their opinions of the book. These letters, written mostly in Russian but also in Ukrainian between 1929 and 1937, demonstrate the popularity of *All Quiet on the Western Front* as well as the Soviet readers' predominantly positive responses to the work. One Stalingrad worker explained in a 1931 letter that the novel was hard to find and "did not ask" but "ordered" the publishing house to put out the book "in innumerable quantities" so that everyone could read it. Another wrote a review of the novel "from a dark little corner" of the Soviet Union and wanted to know if her letter had reached the center.[94] These letters demonstrate that the more than one hundred thousand copies of the novel were dispersed across the Russian, Belorussian, Ukrainian, and Kazakh Soviet republics and in demand.

Many of the letter writers described the novel in glowing terms. One librarian from the Belorussian Republic argued that the book deserved the Nobel Prize because "the author is full of such passionate tender sympathetic love for man, in spite of his protestation that he is only 'accustomed' to killing." This call to give Remarque the Nobel Prize echoed European calls for Remarque to receive this high honor. Another letter from a joiner who was a Komsomol member at the model construction project at Magnitogorsk explained that he had read the novel over and over again. He suggested that the "authorities" should give the publishing house a thousand-ruble prize for putting out the novel and that every honest citizen of the Soviet Union should read *All Quiet on the Western Front*. The novel was clearly appreciated by some members of the Soviet public as something out of the ordinary, written by an author who possessed the "will, courage, and nerves of steel" to depict these "terrifying events."[95]

As might be imagined, the novel struck a chord with World War I veterans. A thirty-five-year-old boilermaker from Rostov on the Don, who had been wounded twice in World War I, declared after reading the novel that Remarque "became a brother" to him because the novel showed the "suffering of the human soul." In his 1931 letter, he wrote: "Finally I am satisfied that I found a person who recounted to the world the suffering, the torments of the gray trench soldier of the 1914–1918 war. . . . [Remarque] has become valuable not only to me, but I think to the million-strong mass of frontline soldiers whom he reminded about the horrors of the meat-grinder of the human body." Another Russian veteran stated that the novel made him "live through the war a second time," and a younger writer acknowledged that the book confirmed his father's war stories.[96] The World War I veterans living in the Soviet Union were paradoxically grateful to Remarque for reminding them of the horrors that they had experienced. Given that they had few public outlets to express their feelings and opinions about the suffering they had endured, especially in comparison to Civil War veterans, Remarque's stirring up of memories gave them the opportunity to reflect on their experiences and share them with others, while the novel also validated their own suffering.

Not all of the letters were uniformly positive. Some readers, like the professional critics of the novel, raised the issue of Remarque's lack of class-consciousness in his explanation of the war. One sixteen-year-old letter writer complained that Remarque had failed to portray "that class which still and now thirsts for war," and another letter writer would recommend the novel to former soldiers of the German front, but "hardly believes" that there would be any among them "who understood the reason for this war less than Remarque."[97] The absence of an explicit class framework in the novel lessened its value in the eyes of these Soviet readers.

Other criticisms of the novel were more idiosyncratic. One former soldier from the Ukraine accused Remarque of "a tint of chauvinism" in the last pages of the novel when he "justified the defeat of the Germans as their being overwhelmed by well-fed enemies, forces who were superior in number and better supplied with shells." The letter writer feared that such a description of events "might arouse patriotic feelings in the German reading it."[98] This interpretation of the novel revealed the former soldier's continuing distrust of the Germans and his unwillingness to allow them any excuses for their defeat. It also underlined the multivalent nature of the novel that was criticized from all sides as either unpatriotic or too patriotic.

None of the letter writers that I surveyed, however, echoed the language of public criticism by attacking Remarque as a "bourgeois pacifist." The notion that the book could be an effective tool in the struggle against war was widespread, though how exactly it would serve this function remained in contention. Some readers placed the book within an orthodox framework of militant world revolution; a sixth-grade girl who read the novel as a school assignment declared, "I now understood that until we destroy the capitalist world . . . there will be bloody slaughter and millions of workers will perish, especially youth." As one former soldier framed it, only a war against capitalism would defeat imperialist war: "The proletariat of the entire world will have to once again drain the cup of sorrow in a battle for proletarian revolution."[99] These Soviet interpreters of Remarque's novel believed that one had to fight another war to end imperialist wars.

Other readers (including a Red Army recruit and the ardent Komsomol from Magnitogorsk) were inspired to direct military action by the novel, promising to "go cheerfully to the defense of the border of the Soviet Union" and "to really study soldiering" to be "a defender" of the Soviet Union.[100] In this case, the future war would be prevented not so much by revolution but by proactive defensive action on the part of the Soviet Union. Yet, the novel was still interpreted within the context of military mobilization. These readers' interpretations of the novel strayed rather far from the dominant interpretations of the novel as pacifist.

Readers who projected the horrors of the past onto a future imperialist war did not all see the novel as motivation for militarization. The Stalingrad worker who demanded "innumerable" copies of the book wanted workers to read it because "in a future war [they] would have to turn into pieces of rotten meat." This worker then revealed his distress at this idea, writing, "Answer me. What then is life if we await, as they say, this unavoidable fate?" The novel led this person to despair about the horrors of the future rather than to volunteer "cheerfully" to fight in a future war. Other letter writers spoke about stopping war more generally, hoping that people would "wake up" and that "the new generation would not tolerate war." A twenty-six-year-old peasant who had "lived through the horror of war" wrote in 1933 that in war,

> workers become crippled, are poisoned by gases, are dying by every possible means of modern warfare made by the hands of these same people, who, as a result of the fear of death caused by these same weapons, reach insanity, and all the time do not understand that war is the greatest of the greatest insanities of the human race, against which it is necessary to fight with all the forces and all the means that can be applied.

This letter writer regretted that Remarque had not offered any explanation of how war could be stopped or how the people "perishing in this devil incarnate" reacted to it.[101] His reaction to the work clearly articulated a pacifist response that advocated the end of war without using "the greatest of the greatest insanities" as a means to that end. Readers' letters revealed that *All Quiet on the Western Front* struck a chord with Soviet readers and that they interpreted it in a wide range of ways. This range shows that the novel opened up dialogues about the nature and causes of war, about militarism and pacifism; and that, as in Europe, there were profound disagreements about whether there was a way to avoid "the unavoidable" and ever-looming imperialist war without engaging in war to do it. These reactions show that the Soviet government had cause to be concerned about pacifist ideas spreading among the population.

Twentieth Anniversary Discourse

In the field of literature, the turning point for the curtailment of World War I memory seems to be somewhat later than in the historical and military fields. For example, although *Quiet Flows the Don* underwent a thoroughgoing overhaul by censors in 1933, it continued to be printed in attractive editions and large print runs throughout the 1930s. Typical of Soviet cultural practice during the 1930s, there was a flurry of publishing about World War I in honor of the twentieth anniversary of the start of the war in 1934.[102] These extremely interesting works featured a complex view of World War I. This case study examines the fates of three particular books during the 1934 anniversary. All three works stand out for their compelling nature and their extraordinary literary and artistic qualities, but only two of the three could be published during the anniversary, and 1934 marked the last time that each work could be published for fifty years. None of them was reissued until the 1980s.

Two of the works appeared in the mid-1920s (Sof'ia Fedorchenko's *The People at War* and Lev Voitolovskii's *In the Footsteps of War)* but were attacked by critics at the end of the 1920s or in the beginning of the 1930s. Despite being subject to criticism, Voitolovskii's work appeared in a new edition in 1934, while Fedorchenko's work did not. Il'ia Feinberg's *1914* was published for the first time during the twentieth anniversary of the outbreak of war in 1934; the book was well received, but when the Union of Soviet Writer's Defense Committee later recommended that the work be reissued in honor of the Red Army's twenty-fifth anniversary, this proposal was rejected.

The People at War

Sof'ia Fedorchenko's *The People at War* was one of the most influential Soviet works about World War I in the 1920s, and it offered readers a very frank and compelling discussion of the brutal nature of war. In the introduction to the 1917 edition, Fedorchenko, a nurse at the front, claimed that she had collected the material for the book in 1915 and 1916 by listening to the soldiers speak to one another and recording what she heard (figure 6.1).[103] The book was reprinted in a substantially expanded edition in 1923, the only complete edition. The 1925 edition underwent thoroughgoing censorship and many anecdotes from both the 1917 and 1923 editions disappeared. A second volume, about the revolutionary months between February and October, appeared in 1925; fragments of a third volume, about the Civil War, appeared in the periodical press in the late 1920s, but the volume was not published in full until 1983.[104]

In the mid-1920s the work received much acclaim and warm praise from Soviet writers such as Maksim Gorkii, V. V. Veresaev, and others. But Fedorchenko had her critics as well. On the one hand, some questioned whether the work could be called art or whether it was merely stenography. Ethnographers, on the other hand, doubted the soundness of her methodology. Answering these challenges, Fedorchenko confessed to a journalist that she was neither an ethnographer nor a stenographer; rather, she had written the book based on her own impressions of men at war.[105] In an essay written in 1927 but not published until decades later, Fedorchenko explained that the idea for the book emerged only when she returned home to the rear and saw the "lies" that were being written about the war. She then decided to tell "the truth about the war, and only the truth, even if [she] could not succeed in writing the whole truth." She chose the soldiers' narrative point of view because she felt it was the simplest way to convey her impressions.[106]

The timing of Fedorchenko's confession was unfortunate; as the struggle to define proletarian literature was escalating, her admission cast doubt on the authenticity of the soldiers' voices in her work. She opened herself up for criticism as an intellectual pretending to speak in the voice of the people. Proletarian writer Dem'ian Bednyi viciously attacked her in a 1928 *Izvestiia* article calling her a "falsifier" and a "hoaxer," accusing her of fabricating the entire work and slandering "the people." Bednyi's vicious attack destroyed her career as a writer. Fedorchenko became ill afterward, and neither *The People at War* nor any of Fedorchenko's many children's stories were reprinted after 1930.[107]

In a 1952 autobiography, Sof'ia Fedorchenko claimed that Maksim Gorkii "highly valued [*The People at War*], called it 'epoch-making,' and proposed issuing it in full for the twentieth anniversary of the imperialist war."[108] But the State Literature Publishing House refused to comply with Gorkii's recommendation, even though they were seeking works to commemorate the anniversary. This rejection may have had multiple causes. No doubt Dem'ian Bednyi's accusations of falsification still clung to the work, but the nature of the work itself may also have influenced the publishing house's decision. *The People at War* contained an exceedingly dark view of the soldiers' behavior and of human nature. It described the soldiers' widespread belief in the supernatural

FIGURE 6.1. *Facing page*. Sof'ia Fedorchenko during World War I. Personal collection of Sof'ia Fedorchenko, Russian State Archive of Literature and Art.

and examined marauding, rape, violence, and murder from a first-person perspective. While this kind of depiction was marginally acceptable as the unvarnished truth constructed out of the soldiers' own words, it became unacceptable as the invention of a class-alien woman writing about the vices of the peasantry. Because of her social position, her gender, and her status as a non-combatant, Fedorchenko was not permitted to seek the greater truth of the war through fiction. Thus, one of the most interesting pieces of World War I literature disappeared from the Soviet publishing world after 1927, not primarily because of changing visions of World War I, although Fedorchenko's negative view of the war certainly played a role, but because of the complex literary and identity politics of the era.[109]

In the Footsteps of War

The authenticity of the memoirs of Lev Voitolovskii was never in doubt; he spent three years serving in the tsarist army and carefully preserved his campaign diaries. Voitolovskii's daughter Adda recounted in her memoirs that the family's safety deposit box contained only one thing: her father's war notebooks.[110] Like Fedorchenko, Voitolovskii made a special effort to understand the peasant soldier and recorded as much peasant speech as he could. His account is also, to some degree, ethnographic. As a doctor and literary critic from Kiev, Voitolovskii was an outsider in relation to the peasants and presented his analysis of their thoughts and ideas from this point of view, never attempting to speak for them. And while his account did not gloss over the brutality of war, he distanced himself from the violence and did not admit to perpetrating it the way that Fedorchenko's soldiers did.

The first two volumes of Voitolovskii's account covering the first two years of the war appeared in 1925 and 1927 respectively, and met with substantial critical acclaim when they first appeared. Publishers advertised a third volume describing the course of the war in 1916 and including the breakthrough at Lutsk (the Brusilov breakthrough) and the February Revolution at the front. It was never completed, however, due to Voitolovskii's ill health and the loss of his sight.

In December of 1925 Maksim Gorkii wrote to Voitolovskii from Italy with extravagant praise for the first volume of *In the Footsteps of War*. Gorkii congratulated Voitolovskii for

> a work remarkably successfully done and indisputably having the most profound historical importance. Big words? Don't be afraid. For me your book completely

surpasses Fedorchenko's *The People at War,* a work highly esteemed by me. And in general it is the most valuable work that has been written in Russia and everywhere about the *muzhik* at war, about how, precisely, he pulled down the army.

The objectivity with which you write is almost the objectivity of an artist. Certain places made me remember Tolstoi's *War and Peace.* I salute your courage, because the book, apart from all its many virtues, is written courageously, something that isn't often done now. Its truth is blinding and teaches a great deal. Handsome indeed is the Russian writer when he watches with sharp-sighted and honest eyes.

He wrote a second letter in January of 1927 to tell Voitolovskii that he thought the second volume was as good as the first, and to inquire when the third volume would appear.[111]

The second volume of Voitolovskii's *In the Footsteps of War* included scenes that emphasized the tragedy of war for civilians: the plight of refugees and a pogrom that took place in Molodechno in August 1915. Gorkii praised Voitolovskii for speaking out about these brutal events, commenting, "Some day brutality ought to provoke organic disgust toward itself, it really should. One cannot be afraid of it, if we want to fight it and overcome it."[112] Gorkii's warm and enthusiastic response to Voitolovskii, whom he did not know well, indicated that Soviet Russia's most famous literary champion assessed Voitolovskii's work as significant both nationally and internationally.[113] Gorkii's ranking of Voitolovskii's firsthand account above Fedorchenko's ethnographic account suggests the primacy that Gorkii placed on actual war experience and on a narrative that might help to humanize the brutality of war.

The first two volumes of *In the Footsteps of War* were republished several times in various combined editions. The 1931 edition, however, differed substantially from the previous editions and contained a considerable number of deletions.[114] Some of these deletions were made simply to shorten the work, as they contained literary descriptions of landscape and scenery that were not particularly pertinent to Voitolovskii's interpretation of the war. There were numerous substantive deletions as well, in which topics such as anti-Semitism, violence against civilians, ethnic conflict, and pacifism were omitted.

One's gut instinct about Soviet censorship would suggest that once materials had been deleted for ideological reasons, they would never again see the light of day. This was not the case with *In the Footsteps of War.* While the desire to produce works in honor of the twentieth anniversary of the war could not convince publishers to allow Fedorchenko back into print, the anniversary edition of Voitolovskii in 1934 restored virtually all of the material that had been removed from the 1931 edition. This edition was also handsomely bound and printed on high-quality paper. Voitolovskii's heartfelt reflections on the nature of war's destruction thus emerged relatively unscathed in the early 1930s.

Although Voitolovskii's work was republished virtually intact in 1934, it did not meet the approval of critics at the Defense Committee of the Union of Soviet Writers. The committee's 1934 survey of Soviet writing about World War I did not cite *In the Footsteps of War* among the best works for future Soviet writers to emulate—instead giving the place of honor to *Quiet Flows the Don* because of the "Marxist-Leninist-Stalinist" views of the characters Garanzha and Bunchuk. The critic claimed, rather, that *In the Footsteps of War* was among the works that "manifested pacifist tendencies, wishing to seek the truth about war to expose the 'great mystery out of which war is born' (Lenin)."[115] Voitolovskii's philosophical musings on the impact of war took the focus away from a concrete Marxist analysis of the specific economic and political underpinnings of "imperialist" war that could only be thwarted by revolution.

Yet it was not the charge of "pacifism" that led to Voitolovskii's disappearance from the literary scene, but his family situation. Voitolovskii lived in Leningrad and members of his extended family fell victim to the wave of purges after the Kirov assassination. First, three of Voitolovskii's sons-in-law were arrested, and then his own three daughters were imprisoned. According to the memoirs of one of his daughters, the police came to arrest Voitolovskii himself on two occasions in 1937 and 1939, but "his blindness and a disorder of the nervous system saved him from confinement."[116] He died in 1941, a victim of the siege of Leningrad. Voitolovskii's powerful account of World War I did not appear in circulation again until after the fall of the Soviet Union because of Stalin's purges. This particular erasure of World War I memory was an unintended consequence of the terror.

1914

While the two previous works were written in the 1920s, the experimental artistic and literary work *1914,* released in commemoration of the twentieth anniversary of the outbreak of war in 1934, created its own new genre of "documentary pamphlet-lampoon." Il'ia Feinberg and Solomon Telingater artfully combined text and images, carefully choosing materials for their phraseology and style. The formatting of *1914* was original and elaborate; it contained two fold-out montages, several color photographs, text printed in both red and black ink, and quotes from Lenin and Stalin imprinted on sheets of tissue paper and strips of red velvet.

Particular episodes leading to the outbreak of the war received emphasis in *1914*: the Balkan conflicts and the assassination of Franz Ferdinand; Raymond Poincaré's visit to St. Petersburg in late July 1914; Kaiser Wilhelm's thirst for war and the ultimatum to Serbia; English and German imperial rivalry for their "places in the sun"; the initial war enthusiasm in all nations and the patriotic socialists' betrayal of the working classes; revolutionary responses to the threat of war and to the war itself. The work spread the blame for the war among all of the imperial powers, including Russia. It closely chronicled the events leading to the war but did not include any material on the frequently cited "turning point" when Nicholas II ordered Russia to mobilize.

The collaborators playfully mixed images and text to convey the essence of abstract historical forces and complex events. One creative and satirical juxtaposition in the work illustrates a quotation from Lenin discussing World War I as the outcome of Germany's imperial rivalry with England and Russia to gain control of territory and colonies. The citation is accompanied by an image of two pairs of battling dinosaurs superimposed over a projection of the globe. Although doomed to extinction, the imperial powers battled on, seeking to dominate the entire world through brute force (figure 6.2).

Another visual satire attacked socialists for supporting their countries' war efforts. A color photograph titled "August 4, 1914" showed two military-style medals hung on colorful orange, brown, and white–striped ribbons. In response to Karl Kautsky's declaration that all socialists "have the right and the obligation to defend their fatherland," Lenin had avowed that the best answer would be to "order a medal with the figures of Wilhelm and Nicholas II on one side and Plekhanov and Kautsky on the other." Feinberg and Telingater dutifully fulfilled Lenin's order, showing the two sides of the medallion with the portraits of all four men (figure 6.3).[117] The work used visual humor to articulate the depth of the "defensist" socialists' betrayal of the international proletariat.

Among the members of the Defense Committee of the Union of Soviet Writers, *1914* met with great critical acclaim. Literary critics such as Viktor Shklovskii and others praised the originality of the work for its creation of a new genre by bringing the technique of montage into literature, thereby demonstrating the influence of cinematography on the creation of new literary

FIGURE 6.2.
"Fighting Empires," in
Il'ia Feinberg, *1914-i:
Dokumental'nyi
pamflet,* illustrated by
S. Telingater (Moscow:
MTP, 1934).

„4 АВГУСТА 1914 г."

FIGURE 6.3.
"Two Medals," in
Il'ia Feinberg, *1914-i:
Dokumental'nyi
pamflet,* illustrated by
S. Telingater (Moscow:
MTP, 1934).

forms. The Union of Soviet Writers promoted the work by organizing a special exhibition based on its content.[118] Feinberg and Telingater's interpretations of World War I thus circulated broadly among the Soviet literary establishment. In the mid-1930s, an acclaimed work dedicated to the memory of World War I gained a prominent place in Soviet intellectual life and stood on the cutting edge of Soviet artistic and literary development.

Members of the Defense Committee of the Union of Soviet Writers wrote to the State Military Publishing House in early 1937 to advocate that a second edition of the book be published in honor of the twenty-fifth anniversary of the Red Army. But it was not to be; in an undated reply, the editors at the Military Publishing House unequivocally rejected the work, stating that "the majority of the photographs, in our opinion, are inexpedient to publish today. The text of the book is very unsuccessful and can call forth only bewilderment among the readers."[119] Given the rapidly changing political situation in Europe, and Soviet commitment to "collective security" against the growing Nazi threat, the book's irreverent tone and its blanket condemnation of all of the European powers had indeed become inexpedient.[120]

Feinberg's scathing treatment of the former French prime minister Poincaré was a case in point. Using a quote attributed to the former French president Paul Deschanel, Feinberg called Poincaré "the initiator of the war." The accompanying visual images emphasized Poincaré's association with the deaths of millions. A photograph of Poincaré walking determinedly and chatting with a colleague on a 1930 visit to a war cemetery sported the incendiary caption: "Poincaré smiles at war." Worse yet, Feinberg and Telingater used photomontage to superimpose this smiling image of Poincaré onto a contrived cemetery backdrop showing rows of crosses above the ground and piles of skulls beneath the ground. Now, Poincaré cheerfully strode forward onto the forehead of a giant decomposing corpse with a grotesquely open mouth and an oozing neck wound. Feinberg and Telingater's daring attacks on European imperialism had been permissible in the political climate of the early 1930s, but now they overstepped the boundaries of prudence. Due to this negative assessment by editors at the Military Publishing House, this extremely innovative work about World War I disappeared from Soviet consciousness.

CONCLUSIONS

These case studies reveal clear trends in the Soviet memory of World War I. First of all, World War I memory was an integral part of Soviet culture in the 1920s, even if the war was often viewed as mere prelude to the Revolution. The tsarist army's achievements were acknowledged and its symbols were displayed in such venues as the Moscow Military History Museum and at Brusilov's funeral. The grand plans of the Red Army staff for a documentary project on World War I history revealed the army leadership's belief in the war's continued relevance. Although emphasis on World War I was contested throughout the 1920s, sometime around 1930 (and in the case of the museum run by Narkompros, earlier), World War I fell victim to the competing views of ideology and history that devalued both the tsarist legacy and former tsarist officers. Active study of and publications about the war disappeared for half a decade and the military expertise of the professional military historians was not utilized. Study of the war only resumed at the end of the 1930s, when the fear of another conflict with the Germans made coming to terms with the successes and failures of World War I an urgent necessity. Ultimately, World War I was not a "forgotten" war. It was remembered, then forgotten, then remembered once more, and finally forgotten again after the cataclysm of World War II became the defining moment of Soviet military history.

The causes for the disappearance of World War I were multiple and contingent. Some had to do with personal rivalries inside institutions such as the Red Army, pitting former tsarist officers against commanders who rose to prominence only during the Civil War. Other disruptions were caused by disagreements among institutions, such as the ideological struggle between Narkompros and the Red Army about the importance of prerevolutionary military history. When ideological differences occurred in an environment of scarcity, the fight over resources sharpened the effects of ideological disagreements. The upheavals of the First Five-Year Plan and the Great Break contributed to the disappearance of some elements of World War I discourse while enabling the spread of other elements. On the one hand, the wave of internationalism in the Great Break temporarily enhanced the status of some World War I works, such as *All Quiet on the Western Front, In the Footsteps of War,* and *Notes from Captivity,* while severely limiting the dissemination of the works of "former people" such as the tsarist general Brusilov and the "bourgeois" Fedorchenko. The iconoclastic attacks on religion during the Great Break meant that the physical landscape of World War I memory was also in great danger of destruction, and once destroyed, there were no mechanisms in the 1930s to rehabilitate the physical markers of wartime remembrance.

The purges also shaped World War I discourse in a variety of predictable and unpredictable ways. Individual World War I works disappeared when their authors fell into disgrace, and a number of the highest quality World

War I works—ones that were published with pride in 1934 as a part of the twentieth anniversary commemoration of the war—could never be published again because of the personal circumstances of their authors as purge victims. Finally, in the mid-1930s and the post-purge era, the tables turned in the ideological struggles over the use of the tsarist history of war. As "defense literature" became an important component of mid-1930s culture, some internationalist authors who had been "winners" in the early 1930s now were seen as "outdated." This change enabled the emergence of new kinds of military history about World War I at the same time that it forced the removal of certain kinds of earlier works. To understand Soviet militarizing culture in the 1920s and 1930s, one must have a great appreciation for both the simultaneous existence of different cultural trends and the contingencies that shaped their appearances and disappearances.

7

Disappearance and Reappearance

In a World War I battle scene from Mikhail Sholokhov's *Quiet Flows the Don*, Grigorii Melekhov, the archetypically brave Cossack warrior, suddenly became fearful before an attack on German trenches in November 1916. Sholokhov wrote: "Now as never before he was afraid for himself and for his men. He wanted to throw himself to the ground and weep, pouring his troubles out childishly to the earth as if she were his mother."[1] This passage showing the momentary vulnerability and fear of the warrior-hero is not at all unusual in war literature. It is significant, however, because it was excised from all Stalin-era editions of *Quiet Flows the Don* after 1933, while the World War I battle scenes in which Melekhov performed heroically were left virtually untouched. Why did the Stalinist censors of the 1930s approve of representations of bravery in World War I battles while targeting this moment of fear for deletion? Why was Melekhov's acknowledgment of his own weakness and loss of manhood during battle, expressed through his childlike fantasy to retreat to his mother's bosom, no longer permitted in Stalinist discourse after 1933? This omission is particularly striking because Melekhov was not a Bolshevik hero at the time the battle took place and the scene was not in any way connected to revolutionary action or doctrine. Furthermore, after the publication of book 3 of *Quiet Flows the Don* in 1933, Melekhov was increasingly viewed as an antihero. Why was it not even permissible for the flawed antihero to show fear in battle?[2]

The first half of this chapter seeks to answer this question by analyzing conscious deletions from World War I texts in order to explore the contours of changing discourses about religion, gender, violence, and the nation in a militarizing Soviet Union. Chapters 2 through 5 of this work explored these four themes through textual examples that remained constant through all Soviet editions of the same work. The first part of this chapter analyzes the same four themes, using textual references that editors deliberately erased from later editions of previously published works. This method allows us to trace specific changes in World War I discourse and the exact chronology of change.

Historian David Brandenberger has identified an important trend in the evolution of Soviet thought in the mid-1930s, arguing that the Soviet leadership engaged in an "ideological about-face" from internationalism to a "russocentric étatism." My analysis of World War I memory suggests, however, that his image of a sudden "about-face" does not adequately capture the intellectual trends of the 1920s and 1930s.[3] As Brusilov's funeral and the publication of his memoirs show, the project of nationalization was part of the Soviet "ecosystem" in the 1920s, even if it was not a dominant feature of the landscape. Former tsarist officers such as Barsukov, Bonch-Bruevich, Gil'chevskii, Svechin, and Zaionchkovskii explored positive aspects of the military heritage of the tsarist Army, as did Sholokhov. Hints of the earlier Russian anxieties about "Germanness" and about the debacle of the "German" war also emerged in the 1920s. Thus, the building blocks of a patriotic, national, and military mobilization were always available within the early Soviet context and did not just suddenly reappear in the mid-1930s.

Nonetheless, Brandenberger is correct in pointing to the new ways in which Soviet writers began to conceptualize the history of the Russian Empire in the mid-1930s. The reconfiguring of tsarist participation in World War I was one important aspect of this transformation. In World War I discourse of the 1930s and 1940s, transformations in national identity were tightly intertwined with changes in gender identities, the heroic military ideal, and representations of spirituality. The second half of this chapter examines all of these changes together. To complement the first half of the chapter, it will proceed chronologically rather than thematically in order to foreground an analysis of the causality of transformations.

In documenting these changes it is tempting to construct rigid divisions, with Hitler's rise to power as an obvious turning point. Anxiety about capitalist encirclement flared up periodically in Soviet discourse—for example, during the war scares of 1923 and 1927—and Soviet leaders believed from the birth of the Soviet state that a future war with capitalism was inevitable. But Soviet interpretations of how to react to a future war did not remain consistent over time. While Soviet critics continued to attack "bourgeois pacifism," by 1934 a new language of Soviet-style pacifism emerged. This formulation, too, was short-lived, and was replaced by an increasingly militarized mobilizing discourse. Nonetheless, there is no doubt that the trends of the 1930s in general demonstrate the Soviet leadership's heightened concern with *voenizatsiia*, the mobilization of the population for a future war effort. Grigorii's fear was excised from *Quiet Flows the Don* in 1933 because of a shift in the balance of Soviet discourse toward nationalism, militarism, and masculinity. Questioning the meaning of war and the definition of heroism, as had been common in the 1920s and early 1930s, became rarer in the mid-1930s. World War I (and Civil War) discourse in the 1930s tended to excise ambiguities in manliness and heroism to recreate and recuperate an unproblematic male heroism and the glorification of warfare. The vision of war in the 1930s tended not to dwell on morality, ethics, or belief in the supernatural. It tended to sanitize violence and to glorify the heroic will of the warrior-hero.

The culture of the 1930s offered a simultaneous discursive renationalization, reheroization, and regendering of Soviet culture that sought to find positive meaning in events that had previously been rejected as worthless and demoralizing. One might liken these trends in 1930s memory of World War I to other efforts to remasculinize heroic culture after defeat.[4] The frank acknowledgment of military defeat, the problematization of warfare, and the emphasis on international rather than national identities were all overtaken by a militaristic, patriotic, and sentimental discourse that glorified the masculine soldier at war.

It is essential to keep in mind that the changes discussed here were not absolute; a shift in the balance of antiheroic to heroic tendencies does not mean that the antiheroic tendencies completely disappeared. In the 1920s, the discourse was weighted toward the antiheroic, but in the 1930s and 1940s, the majority of the weight shifted from the antiheroic to the heroic, forcing the scales to tip, but not necessarily to hit bottom on the heroic side. There were still, therefore, published works up to 1941 that questioned the heroism of World War I, highlighted the loss of masculinity caused by war, and questioned the nature of the enemy. The start of World War II marks an obvious turning point in the history of military mobilization. After the war began, the heroic vision of World War I became dramatically sharper and clearer, and even religion could once again be spoken of in lyrical terms. Nonetheless, even during and after World War II, voices skeptical of heroizing the tsarist war effort could still be heard.

MISSING IN ACTION

The Vanishing Discourse about Religion

As we have seen in chapter 2, the theme of religion was richly represented in World War I memory, despite censorship pressures. The penetration of ideas about God and the supernatural into an ever more restricted discourse revealed the centrality of these themes to any understanding of the war. The 1917 and 1923 editions of Sof'ia Fedorchenko's *The People at War* not only articulated an intense Orthodox Christian religious sensibility, but also demonstrated a wide range of belief in the supernatural. Fedorchenko offered readers many different anecdotes on supernatural forces, God, death, and the soul. By 1925, however, Fedorchenko's discussion of wartime spirituality became a central target of Soviet censorship. Soviet editors or Fedorchenko in self-censorship removed dozens of soldiers' anecdotes on the topic of religion from the new 1925 editions of her book.

Several of the censored anecdotes deal with the theme of the dead haunting the living. These stories bear a striking similarity to the scenes from Abel Gance's *J'accuse* and Aleksei Tolstoi's *Purgatory* discussed in chapter 2. For example, one soldier, separated from his unit and resting in a ditch, spoke of the wonders (*chudesa*) that occur in times of war. As he lay, he recounted,

> I heard them marching, marching. Night was going, morning was near; but I was powerless to move. I heard them tramping, tramping, nothing but infantry; their boots stamped regularly in time. I thought, "Lord! There are not so many of us around here. Suppose they are the Germans!" I raised my head a bit and looked. So far as I could see, the place was full of the dead. They were disposed in companies, in white winding-sheets. I could hear the tramp, but these seemed to lie flat, like a mist. I lay still as death.[5]

Unlike the deranged soldier in Tolstoi's novel, the narrator did not seem to have been harmed by his vision of the dead. Although he was fearful at the time, in retrospect he even seemed to be happy to have been a witness to such a miracle or wonder. It is unclear from this tale why the dead were marching or where they were going. The dead do seem to have retained their soldierly nature, as their march was precisely synchronized and in formation. They had achieved a perfect orderliness that most likely had eluded them while they were alive.

Other religious texts were also censored. While readers of the 1923 edition of Il'ia Erenburg's *The Face of War*, which was most likely available in

Russia, could read Erenburg's diverse musings on faith in wartime, the readers of the later editions could not.[6] The censorship of the 1924 and 1928 editions distorted Erenburg's complex characterization of religion by including only the passages in which his treatment of religion was ironical and doubtful. The editors omitted Erenburg's philosophizing on the meaning of life and death and cut vignettes that reflected Erenburg's attraction to Catholicism. Erenburg's ambivalence toward religion and his sharp swings between cynicism and devotion were an essential part of the writer's character. The Soviet editions of the work distorted Erenburg's literary legacy by recognizing only his cynical side.

Erenburg's discussion of the heroism of the French clergy was erased from the text. Soviet readers could no longer learn about the heroism of the nuns of the city of Arras, who fought fires while the city was being shelled and saved antique artifacts from the church. Nor could they learn about the brave abbot Monsieur Dellet who was to be shot at dawn by the Prussians for hiding partisans, and who spent his last night finishing a chapter of his saint's life of St. Redigonda; or about the church watchman in Belgium who was killed by drunken Prussian soldiers when he refused them entry into his beloved church.[7] The Soviet editions erased Erenburg's recurrent theme of the heroism of the faithful.

Erenburg's discussions of morality, the meaning of death, and the nature of the afterlife were also systematically removed from the texts. In a passage about All Saints' Day, Erenburg described how the French put flowers on the French graves but applauded when a woman spit on the German graves as she passed by. Erenburg lamented, "Even after death there is no reconciliation; even these crosses can seem to be enemies." Then a grandmother and her granddaughter arrived on the scene. The granddaughter asked whose graves these were, and the grandmother answered that one was her father's grave and one was a German grave. She then instructed the granddaughter to put flowers on all of the graves. Erenburg concluded the scene by exclaiming, "For the sake of ten righteous people, O Lord, you promised to spare Sodom."[8] Erenburg's praise of the righteous grandmother was likely objectionable on many counts: the appeal to Judeo-Christian morality, the implicit pacifism, and the final prayer to spare France from destruction in spite of its sins.

The final passage of Erenburg's collection was also censored. In it, an Indian told Erenburg that he did not pray properly because he cursed some things while blessing others. The Indian on the other hand, blessed everything: "The weeping mother and the inventor of poison gas, the smiling child and the tank. You do your deeds. You build and destroy; you sow and you reap. . . . Blessed is His wise will." Erenburg concluded with the thought that he never prayed like the Indian, but he often repeated "Job's eternal lament: 'Why are you fighting with me? Your hands toiled over me and now you destroy me! . . . Reveal your will to me! . . .'" Erenburg's expression of the incomprehensibility of war through a religious idiom, and his conclusion of the book with a prayer, did not suit the Soviet censors. Soviet ideologues searched for the cause of war not in the spiritual plane but the material one: war was the inevitable outcome of capitalist imperialism, and only the destruction of capitalism through revolution would lead to the end of war. Erenburg's religious sensibility was out of step with Soviet doctrine and was, therefore, eliminated.

Pacifism

As discussed in chapter 1, Soviet critics attacked Il'ia Erenburg's *The Face of War* for espousing pacifism, and Soviet editors removed many passages that advocated religious or pacifist nonviolence from Soviet editions of the text.[9] Other memoirs were also purged of religious and moral pacifistic thinking, or simply were not republished because of their protagonists' antiwar views.

One work that appeared in at least three editions, the latest in 1924, before entirely disappearing was *Notes of a Militiaman (Zapiski opolchentsa)* by N. Stepnoi, the pseudonym of Nikolai Aleksandrovich Afinogenov. Purportedly the diary of an ordinary soldier in a "gray overcoat," the notes repeatedly questioned why the soldier had to kill. Although the soldier rejected the Tolstoian path of refusing military service because "in the present century, one or another struggle is necessary," he lamented his own violent actions and pondered what in the makeup of his own personality allowed him to become a "hardened" killer. He repeatedly acknowledged that military training and service had robbed him of his selfhood and recounted a harrowing moment of stabbing an Austrian in battle and being unable to remove his bayonet from the man's body after looking into the reproachful eyes of his victim. It took both the soldier and his company commander to pull the bayonet from the Austrian's stomach. This soldier with blood on his hands repeatedly wanted to cry out, "Murder is always murder, the worst and most inhuman deed." By the late 1920s (and perhaps even earlier), this explicit rejection of wartime killing was no longer permissible.[10]

There were also substantial changes made to Lev Voitolovskii's memoir *In the Footsteps of War* between the first editions in 1925 (vol. 1) and 1927 (vol. 2) and the second edition in 1931. In the latter edition, many of Voitolovskii's reflections on the effects of war on the soul of the soldier were deleted. In one omitted passage, Voitolovskii quoted "trench wisdom": "He who preserves his soul in war is not a soldier," and asserted that the war needed "only the soldier armed with bayonet and machine gun, the person who knew how to pillage, rape, and kill. All of the others are replaced because they are useless."[11] Voitolovskii's passage emphasized the wartime ascendancy of cold-hearted killers who had already destroyed their souls.

The 1934 edition of Voitolovskii was unusual in the context of Soviet censorship in that it restored practically all of the passages missing from the 1931 edition, including the material described above about the destruction of the soldier's soul and the cultivation of heartless killers. However, one of the few deletions *not* restored in 1934 consisted of the passages right before and right after the discussion of the effects of war on the soldier. Voitolovskii defined war as "the greatest obstacle to and the most repulsive exterminator of culture. It is the destruction of all that has been accumulated by the centuries in hearts and minds—and now hurled wastefully under the feet of the armed soldiers." According to Voitolovskii, "On every military banner, on the eagles, on the shoulder boards, the secret motto is imprinted: Down with culture, long live destitution and the poverty of the spirit." War demanded of "the cultured person" that he abandon his "theories" and "commandments" and provide only "vacant endurance and uncomplaining submissiveness."[12]

Voitolovskii saw war as a cataclysmic destruction of the heritage of humanity, out of which no good could come. He did not embrace Soviet doctrine that revolutionary battle was just and necessary and argued that all war destroyed the very humanity of the combatants, demolishing their culture, their spirits, and their souls. While Voitolovskii's ambivalence about the impact of war could be tolerated in the 1934 edition, his complete rejection of the concept of war was excluded from the memoir.

Censoring Violence

One of the many complexities of Soviet censorship in the 1920s was that at the same time that censors began to prevent the expression of religious pacifism and ethical nonviolence, they also began to prohibit the depiction of certain kinds of violence committed by World War I soldiers. Soviet censors eschewed nonviolence because they believed that war, with its inherent use of force, was necessary. Ideal revolutionary violence, however, was to be carried out only by conscious revolutionaries (like Bunchuk in *Quiet Flows the Don* and the sharpshooter in the film *The Forty-First*) who hated committing violence and did so reluctantly, only when it was absolutely necessary for the revolution. Although it was not carried out as systematically as the censorship of religious or pacifist content, censors began to remove some depictions of violence that did not fit this conscious revolutionary model. The idea that soldiers in war might enjoy killing the enemy or the fact that some soldiers knowingly and unapologetically committed atrocities against helpless civilians were sometimes suppressed. These images were troublesome, in part, because scenes of such violence could lead to the conclusion that war itself was immoral and that it corrupted the warrior. While it was possible in Soviet discourse to depict a reluctant warrior who killed only because it was his (or her) duty, it was more problematic to portray rank-and-file soldiers with a lust for killing, raping, and looting. The censors at times tried to clean up the image of war to minimize scenes of corruption perpetrated by ordinary soldiers. These sanitizing revisions protected the image of the moral warrior and paved the way for a new heroization of wartime violence.

In the revisions to the 1928 version of Erenburg's memoirs, one finds a desire to suppress the ugly effects of wartime killing on the character of the warrior. One vignette that did appear in the 1924 Soviet edition but not in the 1928 version dealt with the indifference of French soldiers to killing the enemy. Erenburg recorded their words:

-We are lying down and watching: they run out of the trenches—and onto the ground. The machine guns are working. And all of their hands are thrown up, as if they were dancing. And how we laughed! . . .
-You laughed?
-Of course. It was funny to watch.
-But they were dying, you know.
-They were dying. *Je m'en fous* [I don't give a damn].

Erenburg showed how the circumstances of wartime killing made the perpetrators completely indifferent to the suffering of their victims. The actions of the machine-gunners had become detached from the consequences of the actions, and the death of another human being could be viewed as humorous rather than as tragic. When the realities of their actions were pointed out to them, the soldiers responded not with remorse but with the recognition that they had grown completely indifferent to the suffering they caused others. Logic, conscience, and compassion were all victims of war, along with the "dancing"

German soldiers. The toll that war took on the killers, however, was not a subject that Erenburg's editors wished to air in public in 1928.

The acknowledgment of the brutality of rank-and-file soldiers toward civilians also began to be excluded from discourse about World War I. As we have seen in chapter 4, the vast majority of the descriptions of Russian wartime violence against civilians that appeared in the 1925 edition of *The People at War* were narrated either as "atrocities" committed by Soviet-era internal enemies such as officers or Cossacks, or from the point of view of an innocent bystander. The presence of this moral bystander who had not lost his moral compass in the midst of war showed that honor and decency during wartime were possible.

The first two editions of Fedorchenko's *The People at War* contained several scenes of ethnic violence and rape told from the standpoint of the perpetrators. One anecdote about the looting of Jewish homes was edited in the 1925 edition to omit the narrator's glee at his company's mistreatment of Jewish civilians. In the paragraph missing from the 1925 edition, the speaker made fun of local Jewish leaders, one of whom "bellowed," another lay down on the floor as if dead, and a third stealthily approached the officers and "whispered." The soldier-narrator noted that despite these various entreaties, the soldiers proceeded to loot wealthy Jewish homes in any case.[13] By 1925, the censors were not comfortable with the framing of this ethnic conflict—they were possibly unsettled by the open mockery of the Jewish leaders' attempts to save their community or perhaps even by the association of Jews with wealth.

Along with ethnic hatred, violence against women was a theme that was more and more curtailed in later Soviet editions, even when it was described from the point of view of the innocent and suffering victim. A first-person and detailed description of rape by an officer in Tat'iana Dubinskaia's *In the Trenches* was changed in the 1936 and 1939 editions. In the later publications, the officer with a foreign-sounding name (Zambor) attempted to rape the protagonist Zina, but a fellow soldier saved her.[14]

If rape from the point of view of the victim could be problematic, describing such violence from the point of a perpetrator was even more so. As we have seen in chapter 4, *The People at War*, along with Isaak Babel''s *Red Cavalry*, was one of the few places in Soviet discourse that presented rape from the point of view of the perpetrator. In an anecdote censored from the 1925 edition of her work, Fedorchenko presented an even more disturbing picture of male soldiery than did Babel'. Babel''s Red Cossack narrator claimed that the lonely soldiers could not help molesting women, while some of Fedorchenko's rank-and-file soldiers participated in wartime rapes and abductions simply to amuse themselves. One soldier in a Fedorchenko vignette described how he now "gave no quarter" in battle and no longer asked for anything but simply took it. When he arrived in the destroyed town of Oprisheny there was nothing left to loot, so he seized a plump woman as his war booty: "Three days I kept her with me and amused myself. And I shared her with my platoon commander. Like I would share tobacco, I shared the woman. And then I became afraid and let her go in the field."[15] This soldier acknowledged that his behavior might be considered wrong—he feared punishment if he did not release the woman—but he did not express any remorse for his actions. The platoon commander was not likely to punish the soldier, because he participated in the same immoral behavior. Both men viewed the woman as spoils of war, and both used and discarded her at will. The soldier was not concerned about the fate of the woman whom he took away from her home and then abandoned in a field. Such intentional abuse, narrated without remorse, no longer sat well with the censors.

Gender Relations in a Masculinizing World

In the Russian heroic vision of war, as in that of other nations, the soldier's personal behavior at the front is impeccable. He treats all civilians with courtesy and does not view war as an opportunity for sexual adventure. In reality, and in depictions of this reality in early Soviet World War I discourse, there were many aspects of the relationship of men and women in wartime that were fraught with difficulty. War separated families and opened up the possibility for infidelity both on the frontlines and in the rear. The front, meanwhile, offered a variety of sexual possibilities, including prostitution, casual sex with the local female population, and rape. Many Soviet treatments of World War I acknowledged sexual violence, like other gratuitous violence, by displacing it onto enemies of the Soviet state, particularly officers and Cossacks. The sexual violence of the common soldier and the sexuality of soldiers in general were aspects of war that made Soviet censors uncomfortable. The Soviet heroic vision of war generally preferred chaste heroes.

Soviet discomfort with sexuality was evident in the editor's foreword to Ernest Hemingway's 1929 novel *A Farewell to Arms* when it was translated into Russian in 1936, after a delay of several years. S. Dinamov wrote: "Hemingway is poisoned by sexuality; he continuously returns to the erotic theme." Dinamov felt that "the romance of the hero with Miss Barkley occupies too much space in the novel and doesn't allow the writer to turn to more significant phenomena." Despite this fault, the novel was nonetheless valued for its depiction of the "senselessness of the imperialist war," and was published in a print run of ten thousand—sexuality, romance, and all.[16]

Scholarship on censorship in Soviet literature has illustrated the course of Soviet prudery, documenting the disappearance of sexual details from many early Soviet novels; and in the early Soviet period, public health officials defined "healthy sex almost entirely in terms of absence and restraint."[17] Keeping with these trends, much Soviet World War I literature showed only "abnormally" violent Cossacks and depraved aristocratic officers indulging in sexual activity with innocent women and children. While it is commonplace in analyses of Soviet society to comment upon the large disjuncture between Soviet rhetoric and the actual living conditions of the Soviet people, there is little theorization of the impact of this contradiction on Soviet sexual relations. It is highly unlikely that sexual practices were fundamentally altered as soon as people began to speak about them in new ways or refrained from speaking about them at all. By investigating the anecdotes and images that disappeared in the mid-1920s, one can gain a sense of a very different kind of sexuality among World War I soldiers. While these representations are sometimes as stylized as the depictions of brutal Cossacks or degenerate officers, they nonetheless offer insight into popular conceptions of sexuality that did not disappear from people's minds and actions as quickly or as completely as they disappeared from public discourse.

There is a long and complex history of the connection between sexual prowess and soldiering. During World War I, particularly in France, there was a celebration of the sexuality of French soldiers as an integral aspect of their masculine and military identities.[18] Although sexual prowess was not an attribute of the heroic soldier in the Russian imperial press during World War I, the idea of the soldier as a sexual being, seeking out sexual contacts and easily winning conquests among the female population, emerged clearly in the work of Sof'ia Fedorchenko. In the 1917 and 1923 editions of *The People at War*, she related several anecdotes from the point of view of soldiers who bragged about their sexual activities or articulated their sexual needs. One soldier proclaimed, for example, "If you are going to give me bread, give me a woman too. It is not possible for a healthy person to live without bread or without a woman."[19] Other soldiers stressed the ease of their sexual conquests: "I am very handsome. Women swarm around me like bees round a flower, and I'm not one to refuse them; but I am always waiting for it to be different. For what is it like?—just like dogs or cows, who smell one another and are mated."[20] Both soldiers suggested that "normal" sexuality included regular sexual intercourse, perhaps with multiple partners and not necessarily within the bounds of marriage. Furthermore, the latter soldier stressed the naturalness of "mating" even while he searched for something more profound. His anecdote also indicated that women were active in choosing partners and initiating sexual contact.

Another soldier explained his success in seducing virgins: "For some reason women love me. I can butter up whichever one you like, however strict. And I can corrupt a lass very easily, all because I am affectionate. And our woman is not used to affection. I lure her with laughter, and when she becomes accustomed, I share her sorrows and shed a few tears. Then take her with your bare hands. She's all yours. . . ."[21] Fedorchenko here suggested that soldiers were amoral in their sexual relations, indifferent to the harm they might cause by "corrupting" girls, and engaging in sexuality as a form of sport. This image of the freewheeling soldier engaged in irresponsible behavior, along with the other images of soldiers' sexual needs, desires, and habits, were all excised from Fedorchenko's 1925 text.

The gender tension between the front and the rear was an aspect of wartime social relations often explored in European war literature, and as we have seen, both Russian and Soviet writers metaphorically linked the rear with immoral women, prostitution, and venereal disease. One vignette included by Fedorchenko in the 1917 and 1923 editions of *The People at War,* but missing from the 1925 edition, reinforced this linkage by describing a soldier's response to his wife's infidelity. The soldier arrived home unexpectedly, since the letter he sent in advance had not been received, and looking through the window, he saw how "Mariia sits and next to her is some stranger. And incidentally, he had thrust his hand into her bosom, and she sits so quietly." When the offended husband knocked at the window, his wife "stood up so calmly that it was evident that everyone already knew about it, that this situation had been going on for a long time. She came to the window . . . saw me, and trembled. And I was so glad at their fright that I shook all over." Mariia told her "fancy man" to run "but I struck her a mortal blow, and in the morning I drove away to the town and spent all my money with girls there."[22]

It is not clear whether Mariia survived this incident; whether she lived or died, the narrator's decision to leave home the next morning revealed complete indifference to her fate. The soldier's enjoyment at instilling fear and his physical retribution against his wife suggested his "brutalization"; he gained satisfaction from his extremely violent treatment of his wife and lacked re-morse for what he had done. It remained unclear whether his World War I ex-perience produced this extreme violence or if he had always engaged in such behavior. The absence of this passage from the 1925 edition eliminated two problematic images. The first disappearing theme was the unfaithfulness of the soldier's wife while her husband was away fighting for his country, quite a touchy subject in a militarizing society. Secondly, the later edition omitted the soldier's cruel and possibly murderous treatment of his wife. The "darkness" of the soldier, his cruelty, and his misogyny were no longer deemed appropri-ate subjects for Soviet discourse. Backwardness could be acknowledged in a general way, but dwelling on unpleasant details that might cast doubt on the population's future transformation into new Soviet men and women was dis-couraged. Furthermore, any suggestion that wartime violence brutalized and corrupted the soldier, making him even more likely to enact violence within his own family, was also not helpful in the military mobilization of Soviet society.

A comparison of the various versions of Fedorchenko's work reveals the systematic removal of the themes of sexuality and sexual violence, either by squeamish editors or by the author in self-censorship. While the 1917 and 1923 editions of *The People at War* explored the sexual desires of soldiers, their ro-mances, and their exploits, virtually all sexual anecdotes were missing from the 1925 edition. Not only was sexual violence now taboo, but sexuality in any form became suspect. The 1925 edition of Fedorchenko foreshadowed the growing anxiety about sex among Soviet editors; by the early 1930s both sexu-ality and other "earthy" descriptions of bodily functions had disappeared from many other works of Soviet literature.

In the Soviet period, wartime images about women remained sharply bi-furcated. Alongside the well-developed trope about women's disgraceful be-havior in the rear, there was a tendency to depict women as the quintessen-tial symbols of the sorrows of war. Women appeared in Soviet remembrances of war as they bade farewell to beloved family members, mourned their dead, and suffered as innocent victims of violence. Soviet sources, on the other hand, were relatively silent about the participation of women in the tsarist war effort. Mariia Bochkareva, the founder of the Women's Battalion of Death, published her memoirs only in emigration, and the Women's Battalion became notorious not for their role in World War I but for their defense of the Provisional Gov-ernment during the October Revolution.[23]

With the exception of the three different versions of Dubinskaia's novella about Zina, a young woman who disguised herself as a boy to volunteer at the front, first published in 1930 as *In the Trenches,* there were very few depictions of nurses, female soldiers, or other women actively working for the tsarist war effort. Zina spoke often of her personal life and detailed her emotional response to various events at the front. One literary critic on the Defense Committee of the Union of Soviet Writers, writing in response to the 1936 version of the novella called *Woman Machine Gunner (Pulemetchitsa),* expressed discomfort with Zina's circumstances as the only woman among men long-separated from their families. He also complained that the novella was "littered with personal experiences that were not in keeping with the general style, cluttering the primary background." Less charitable critics called Zina a "female gymnasium student" reminiscent of the pulp fiction of Lidiia Charskaia.[24] There was clearly a disjuncture between "women's writing" and "war writing" that Dubinskaia had difficulty bridging.

In each successive version of Dubinskaia's tale more and more personal details were edited out, so that while the 1930 version had 190 pages, the 1936 version contained only 150 pages, and the 1939 version but 100.[25] Details of Zina's romance with another soldier in her unit, for example, became sparser in each successive edition. Though Zina did receive the St. George cross (fourth class) at the end of the novella,[26] heroic women created by male authors such as Anka in Dmitrii Furmanov's *Chapaev*[27] or Anna in *Quiet Flows the Don* played a much more significant role in Soviet Civil War discourse than any woman at the front played in World War I literature.

War without Fear?

In earlier chapters I have highlighted the ambivalent ways in which Soviet writers dealt with the tricky issues of the evasion of military service and desertion from the ranks. Some works described these decidedly "unheroic" actions in neutral terms or sought to redefine them as positive revolutionary acts. This section explores the transformations in depictions of Soviet heroism by documenting the narrowing of permissible actions for a "positive" Soviet character.

Key changes in later editions of works by Leonid Katsov and Aleksandr Pireiko demonstrate a growing uneasiness with antiheroic rhetoric and the refusal to bear arms. A second edition of Katsov's novel *Through Captivity* about the war experience of a poor Jewish POW named Mendele came out in 1934 with a new preface, but virtually no changes to the text itself. In the foreword to the first edition in 1930, Soviet journalist Mikhail Kol'tsov did not make any reference to Mendele's desertion from the ranks of the tsarist army.[28] In his 1934 introduction to the second edition, Karl Radek felt obliged, however, to explain Mendele's behavior. According to Radek, he sought to escape the "rain of fire and steel" at the front after he had "gotten it in the teeth" from his officer:

> He deserted, speaking without embellishment, to the Austrians. This was not a heroic action in the least, but Mendele did not have the slightest desire to be a hero for the tsar. And he could not even think that the front could become a forge of Bolshevik consciousness for the workers and peasants dressed in grey overcoats, since he did not even know about the existence of the Bolsheviks.[29]

In Radek's view, the fictional Mendele had correctly rejected Russian chauvinism, had not considered the Russian Empire to be his fatherland, and would not fight for it because of Russian brutality to Jews: "In his ears still sounded the cries of the violated women, the dying moans of his murdered brothers, the roar and whooping of the pogrom organizers."[30] Radek vividly reminded Soviet readers of the terrifying ethnic violence perpetrated against Jews in the tsarist period.

Yet the patent failure of the Russian Empire to be a fatherland for the Jews was not a sufficient excuse for Mendele's capitulation to the enemy. Radek further justified Mendele's failure to remain on the frontlines by explaining that Mendele had never heard of the Bolsheviks when he deserted, and therefore he could not transform himself into a revolutionary fighter. Mendele later redeemed himself by becoming a Bolshevik, and after he returned to Soviet soil he "vowed . . . to work on this very land and defend it from enemies."[31] What seemed like cowardice was merely ignorance, and Mendele was transformed into a model Soviet citizen who would never desert his fatherland. Radek affirmed the integration of Jewish citizens into the Soviet Union, and proclaimed their heroic duty to defend their country.

A substantially reworked edition of the memoirs of Bolshevik A. Pireiko was published in 1935 with a new title. The 1926 edition had been called *In the Rear and at the Front of the Imperialist War: Memoirs of a Rank and File Soldier* (*V tylu i na fronte imperialisticheskoi voiny: Vospominaniia riadovogo*); the later edition was titled *At the Front of the Imperialist War: Memoirs of a Bolshevik* (*Na fronte imperialisticheskoi voiny: Vospominaniia bolshevika*). The revised title not only emphasized Pireiko's status as an Old Bolshevik (it was published by the soon-to-be-disbanded Society of Old Bolsheviks) but it elevated the significance of frontline experience over events in the rear. In the 1935 edition, Pireiko (and/or his editors) systematically reframed and even erased his less heroic and ambiguous moments.

In the 1926 memoir, Pireiko had mocked the socialists who changed from "defensists" to "defeatists" when mobilization concerned them.[32] The idea that "defeatism" could be appealing not only to orthodox Bolsheviks devotedly following Lenin's line, but also to cowardly Mensheviks who wanted to avoid going to war altogether, is conspicuously absent from the 1935 edition.[33] In both versions of the memoir, Pireiko explained that many Mensheviks sought to evade mobilization by paying an invalid to appear at the inspection point in their places. In the 1926 text, Pireiko wrote that this Menshevik method of evading service was "seductive" to him (*soblaznitel'nyi*), while in the 1935 text he was "infected" by it (*zarazitel'nyi*). This striking change in vocabulary reveals much about transformations in *mentalité* in the intervening eleven years. In the first text's sexual metaphor, the feminized Mensheviks caused Pireiko to lose his manly willpower in seeking to avoid war. The language of sickness permeates the second text, depriving Pireiko of agency. He was "infected" with this disease, he explained, especially since "he had never called upon anyone to defend 'the fatherland' and, on the contrary, considered that the defeat of the autocracy in war would lead to revolution."[34] He may have avoided mobilization because he desired the defeat of tsarism, but at least he was not hypocritical like the Mensheviks. Pireiko's new self-justification revealed that by 1935, Soviet editors considered evasion of even tsarist military service or any hint of unwillingness to take up arms as negative traits that had to be contextualized. Yet, Pireiko's justification continued to highlight the paradox of the conscious World War I soldier. He had to be willing to fight a war he hoped he would lose. More ominously, while seductive Mensheviks could be overcome by willpower, infectious Mensheviks had to be quarantined from healthy society.

Once mobilized, Pireiko sought to evade his military duties, and he took advantage of circumstances to escape from the front and return to Petrograd. Though Pireiko rationalized his evasion of mobilization in the 1935 edition, he could not justify desertion, and so he falsified his memoir. The 1935 version included a new explanation for his absence from the frontlines: "Verbally, I was permitted to travel from Kiev to Petrograd to see relatives."[35] Pireiko made this fictional new order a "verbal" one because otherwise his extended adventure narrative of stowing away on a train to Petrograd was inexplicable. While in the first memoir he returned to the front because he could not find a safe place to stay in Petrograd, in the second memoir he returned because he felt that he would be more useful to the revolution in the army than in Petrograd.[36] The 1935 memoir strengthened Pireiko's status as a dedicated revolutionary, but it also expunged his failures as a soldier, or softened them with excuses and explanations. Although the desertion of the fictional Bolshevik Bunchuk in *Quiet Flows the Don* remained unchanged throughout the era, the flesh and blood Bolshevik Pireiko either chose to varnish the truth or was compelled to do so. Paradoxically, by 1935, lack of commitment to the tsarist army was a problematic attribute for a revolutionary whose goal was to overthrow the tsarist state.

Toward a New Definition of the Nation?

Although many Jewish writers told of their war experiences in World War I, and it might be argued that they had a unique perspective because of the extent of the victimization of the civilian Jewish populations of the Russian and Austro-Hungarian empires, Soviet censorship did not encourage these writers to speak of their experiences as Jews. By 1934, "Jewishness" was implicitly linked to "backwardness" to explain the willingness of Leonid Katsov's Jewish soldier to desert from the tsarist army. Even in the 1920s, however, Soviet editors were not keen to highlight particularly Jewish experiences. In March 1925, A. Kadishev reviewed Sergei Grigor'ev's story "In the Tsarist Barracks" for the Military Publishing House.[37] Kadishev expressed concern in part about the Jewishness of the main character. "The personal history of a Jewish volunteer (his call-up, his privileged position, and so forth) might give negative results for the mass reader." The editors recommended: "It is necessary to remove (*vytravit'*) the personal history of the Jewish volunteer in the tsarist barracks" and to add more "phenomena of a mass character."[38]

When the piece was published in 1926 as *The Barracks*, there was no hint that the main character was Jewish. The diary was said to belong to an anonymous friend of the author who went missing and probably died in July 1917 on the southwestern front. This soldier was not a "volunteer" but someone who chose not to use his "educational qualifications and societal position to in any measure evade the burdens of war and barracks life." This man chose to remain a private for the duration of the war.[39] The published story thus erased ethnicity altogether and recast the class nature of the protagonist. He was not a middle-class "volunteer," but an educated man who refused the privilege of deferral and rejected officer status to be one with the people. While the reviewer seemed concerned about both class and ethnicity, Grigor'ev acknowledged the protagonist's social status in the story's foreword, while completely effacing his Jewishness.

Grigor'ev's protagonist in *The Barracks* was also antinational, candidly admitting in his war diary that it was impossible to love Russia in an open, simple-hearted way (*prostodushno*).[40] It is noteworthy that although Grigor'ev had a decades-long career, primarily as a juvenile author, *The Barracks* was never reprinted after 1926.

THE RETURN OF THE NOT-ENTIRELY REPRESSED

In the mid-1930s, there was a new mode of Soviet writing about warfare as epic struggle. Authors began to look to the Russian military past for models of courage and prowess to inspire Soviet military achievements. Aleksei Tolstoi, for example, placed the state-building and military actions of Peter the Great in a new and positive light. The novelist Sergei Sergeev-Tsenskii, the son of a Crimean War officer who was himself a veteran of World War I, published more than a dozen military-historical novels in the 1930s and 1940s, including the very popular *Ordeal of Sevastopol'* (*Sevastopol'skaia strada*, 1939–1940) set during the Crimean War. These works highlighted the brave actions of Russian tsars and officers, introducing a new set of heroes on the Soviet stage.[41]

It was far more complicated, however, to portray heroic officers in the Russo-Japanese War and World War I because of the coexistence of revolutionary narratives with military narratives. It was exceedingly difficult, if not impossible, both to portray warfare as epic struggle and to follow the ideologically correct line of Leninist "defeatism." Some of the earliest attempts to combine both national and revolutionary history came in historical fiction about the tsarist navy. Writers and critics openly addressed the contradiction between the national and the revolutionary in an attempt to determine the best way to "navigate" these troubled waters.

In his novel *Tsusima*, written in 1932–1933, Aleksei Novikov-Priboi emphasized the incompetence of tsarist naval commanders and the suffering of the sailors during the Russian navy's devastating 1905 defeat at the hands of the Japanese in the Tsushima straits during the Russo-Japanese War.[42] In *Tsusima*, revolutionary rhetoric and heroic visions of the past were palpably in tension with one another. In a review of *Tsusima* in the journal *Literaturnyi kritik* (Literary Critic), writer Vs. Vishnevskii put his finger on the contradiction that military-historical writing had to overcome if it was to be true to the Leninist line of "defeatism." He wrote, "I want to ask myself and others: how, through what methods, do we combine a defeatist stance with a subjective relationship to the mass of suffering and dying soldiers and sailors?" He noted that Novikov-Priboi failed in his attempt to combine the idea "I am here, I fight on this, the Russian side" with the notion "It is necessary for this situation to be even worse. The worse the better." According to Vishnevskii, Novikov-Priboi could not sustain his defeatism and introduced episodes into the novel that reflected "old fleet valor."[43] Novikov-Priboi inadvertently glorified the tsarist order while anticipating its overthrow.

There were several novels about World War I in the mid-1930s that were fraught with the same kinds of ambiguities as *Tsusima*. Leonid Sobolev focused on the inept preparation of the tsarist navy for war in *The Big Refit* (1933). Sergeev-Tsenskii's series *The Transfiguration of Russia: An Epic* (*Preobrazhenie Rossii: Epopei*), which explored the transformation of the Russian intelligentsia during the revolutionary era, included several World War I novels. *Reserve Regiment* (*Zauriad-polk*, 1934) focused on a militia regiment in the rear during the fall of 1914. *Masses, Machines, Elements* (*Massy, mashiny, stikhii*, 1935) followed the fate of an infantry regiment at the Galician front during the difficult winter of 1914–1915.[44] The most well known novel of the trilogy, *Brusilov's Breakthrough* (*Brusilovskii proryv*), published in 1943 under the radically different political circumstances of World War II, examined Brusilov's successful spring offensive in 1916. All of these novels negotiated the terrain between revolutionary rejection of the tsarist military and admiration of its traditions and accomplishments, between revolutionary and militarizing tropes.

OFFICERS AND SOLDIERS

One key aspect of militarizing discourse in the Soviet Union (and elsewhere) is the presentation of positive role models of military leadership and the articulation of harmonious relations between officer and soldier, with the latter unquestioningly accepting the authority of the former. In the Soviet interwar period, the process of creating a militarizing discourse was complicated by the fact that the revolutions of 1917 were fueled in large part by the rebellion of soldier against officer. In the years after the revolution, typical depictions of officer-soldier relations in World War I as class struggle undercut the creation of positive leadership models and the depiction of trust and cooperation between soldiers and officers. The formulaic tsarist officer in Soviet World War I discourse in the 1920s and first half of the 1930s was a typical class enemy—cruel, depraved, and incompetent—and certainly not a role model for the next generation of Soviet officers.

But, as demonstrated in earlier chapters of this work, the image of the brutal officer was not the only model of officer available in Soviet World War I discourse. There were also some early Soviet works that presented images of intelligent, effective, and responsive tsarist officers. In Brusilov's 1929 memoirs, he represented himself as a patriotic and skilled leader in opposition to the Romanovs. Bolshevik psychiatrist and literary critic Lev Voitolovskii portrayed himself in his memoirs as an officer who was compassionate to his soldiers but nevertheless followed the orders of his superiors and did his duty. These examples suggest that it was possible in the culture of the 1920s to find heroism and leadership among carefully selected members of the tsarist privileged classes. It is thus very important not to draw the distinctions between the 1920s and the 1930s too sharply.

Another trope in early Soviet discourse, especially in literature about the Civil War, emphasized the tragic failure of tsarist officers and the Russian intelligentsia generally to adapt to revolutionary times. Sholokhov allowed for the *possibility* of sympathetic officers in *Quiet Flows the Don* and depicted Melekhov as a skilled warrior and leader; Melekhov, however, was not the only tragic White officer of his era. In *The Days of the Turbins* (*Dni Turbinykh*, a dramatic adaptation of his novel *The White Guard* [*Belaia gvardiia*] about the Turbin family) Mikhail Bulgakov told of the struggle of White officers against the Ukrainian nationalist forces of Petliura in 1918–1919 and detailed the crushing defeat of the White movement. Censors forced Bulgakov to remove scenes that showed the heroism of White officers from the play, so that his upper-class and intelligentsia characters appeared militarily ineffectual and helpless in the face of popular upheaval. But *The Days of the Turbins* nonetheless told its tale from the Whites' perspective and did not uniformly vilify the former tsarist officers. Despite its controversial nature, the Moscow Art Theater performed *The Days of the Turbins* "a record 987 times" between 1926 and 1941.[45] Thus the potentially sympathetic tsarist/White officer who was doomed to failure also became part of the Soviet literary landscape.

Some World War I literature of the 1930s offered variants of this model, tsarist officers who possessed some attractive traits but who were ultimately doomed. In Sobolev's *The Big Refit*, the educated but not wealthy Lieutenant Levitin demonstrated both the positive and negative qualities of a tsarist officer. He possessed intelligence, competence, dedication, and an awareness of the need for the radical transformation of tsarist Russia, but he was also gripped by cynicism, condescending to the rank-and-file sailors, and a womanizer. When he was an idealistic young officer, he drew up ambitious plans for modernizing the navy, for which his superiors reprimanded him. By 1914, he was no longer willing to "beat on the bulkheads with [his] bare fists." Adopting a proto-Bolshevik stance, Levitin did not believe that the creation of a republic through revolution would prevent war, because he thought that those at the government's helm would continue to profit from war.

Levitin lacked the will to fight for a socialist rather than bourgeois revolution, and his refusal to fight led to passivity, resignation, and his acquiescence to the defeat of the tsarist fleet and his own death. He advised the revolutionary-minded engineer Morozov to follow in his footsteps of debauchery and egocentrism rather than bloodying his knuckles in a fruitless battle.[46] Sobolev depicted Levitin in the tradition of the nineteenth-century "superfluous man," frustrated by the lack of a creative outlet for his talents. His character in the novel revealed the heroic potential of the navy that could never be fulfilled under the Romanovs.

Sergei Sergeev-Tsenskii, on the other hand, introduced his readers to a junior officer from the intelligentsia who was a Bolshevik in the making in his novel *Reserve Regiment,* published first in the last four issues of *Znamia* (The Standard) in 1934 and in book form in 1935. Ensign Liventsev, an unmarried thirty-seven-year-old mathematics student of modest means, was writing a dissertation on "function theory" when he was drafted into the tsarist militia. Coming from a family that was neither prosperous nor poor, Liventsev, despite his rank above the soldiers, revealed sympathy for them and a willingness to fight against injustice.[47] Unlike the stereotypical "debauched" tsarist officer, Liventsev displayed the much more desirable characteristics of probity and celibacy. Moral rectitude and near-poverty made him an excellent candidate for future conversion to Bolshevism.

Sergeev-Tsenskii's approach to creating a potentially heroic tsarist officer did not please everyone. E. Usievich, writing in the journal *Literaturnyi kritik* in 1935, severely criticized the writings of Sergeev-Tsenskii, including the recently published *Reserve Regiment.* Usievich complained that the character Ensign Liventsev was "an angel, not a person" and that the novel depicted rank-and-file soldiers as "slaves, devoid of a sense of human dignity, cowardly and pitiful."[48] In other words, by making the actions of Ensign Liventsev the foundation of heroic and moral action in the novel, Sergeev-Tsenskii had neglected the "real" proletarians and portrayed them only as pathetic victims. Usievich called attention to Sergeev-Tsenskii's attempt to blur class lines as he created a military role model from the tsarist officer class. He was caught red-handed between militarizing and revolutionary tropes.

Any good hero needs something to fight against, and Sergeev-Tsenskii's attempts to define an antagonist for Liventsev were even more problematic in the eyes of the critic Usievich than the nature of Liventsev as hero. *Reserve Regiment* took place in the rear, so that military battles with the enemy were not an option. Instead, the struggles in the novel took place between the competent and democratic Liventsev and the rest of the officer corps. Nonetheless, Liventsev's main antagonist was a German, lieutenant-colonel Genkel'. This German enemy was not an officer in the German or Austro-Hungarian army, but rather a Russified-German officer in the Russian army. Sergeev-Tsenskii depicted the native Russian officers in the novel as incompetent but good-natured, while portraying Genkel' as the cause of real misery among the soldiers. As Usievich put it, Genkel''s arrival brought "on the one hand, an idiotically precise execution of the idiotic regulations, and on the other hand attempts to become rich off the soldiers." Although Usievich overstated the case by suggesting that Sergeev-Tsenskii thought German intrigue rather than tsarism or capitalism "corroded the tsarist army" and was the source of all evil in tsarist Russia, she was certainly correct in pointing out the peculiar yet familiar ethnic component of the plot development in the novel.[49]

Why did Sergeev-Tsenskii use ethnicity to differentiate between heroes and villains in the novel? The novel itself seems to hearken back to the language and mindset of 1914, when popular anti-German sentiment swept the Russian Empire and talk of German traitors and spies was ubiquitous. *Reserve Regiment* seems to have absorbed some of the atmosphere of the time about which it was written. And while Usievich may have been off the mark in suggesting that Sergeev-Tsenskii was defending tsarism and capitalism, she was certainly warranted in her claim that Sergeev-Tsenskii engaged in ethnic stereotyping and scapegoated Germans for the failures of the Russian army. Sergeev-Tsenskii was a pivotal figure in the renationalization of Soviet discourse, and this 1934 novel indeed represents a turning point. Usievich's objections show that Soviet critics actively pointed out ideological contradictions as they occurred, and publicly objected to the new elements emerging in Soviet discourse that emphasized nation over class. Over the next decade, Sergeev-Tsenskii continued to write in this new patriotic vein, and Usievich continued to criticize him.[50]

RUSSIA'S MILITARY PROWESS

Significant transformations in Soviet memory of World War I were evident as early as the middle of 1939, months before the start of World War II. These changes could be traced both to the tense military-diplomatic situation after the Nazi annexations of Czechoslovakia and Austria, and to the atmosphere of the purges which revived the World War I–era specter of German traitors and spies everywhere. In 1939, a markedly defensive and nationalistic tone about tsarist military achievements could be detected in Soviet military literature. For example, the journal *Morskoi sbornik* (Naval Collection) attacked Novikov-Priboi's depiction of Tsushima for dismissing "the Russian gunnery as hopeless, and for [its] portrayal of the sailors as potential or actual mutineers rather than as Russian seamen capable of acts of heroism."[51] While in 1935 Novikov-Priboi was criticized for introducing "old fleet valor" into his novel, in 1939, he was condemned for his insufficient attention to the patriotic heroism of the sailors.

The 1939 Komsomol volume *Artillerists* celebrated the military prowess of Muscovite, Imperial, and then Soviet artillerymen beginning in the pre-Petrine period. Such a timeframe clearly sought to demonstrate the continuity between tsarist military achievements and the prowess of the Red Army. The work included two articles on World War I: a descriptive article that recounted the activities of World War I artillerists in detail, and a piece of historical fiction about the Brusilov breakthrough.[52] Both pieces sought to demonstrate the superior skill and bravery of Russian World War I artillerists in spite of the overall failure of the war effort. The artillerists were now depicted as military heroes to be emulated by Soviet artillerists.

E. Z. Barsukov, a top specialist on the history of the Russian artillery, was one of the former tsarist generals who left the staff of the Red Army in the early 1930s over disagreements about the shape of the World War I documentary history project. He wrote a survey article for the 1939 Komsomol volume called "Artillerists of the World War," arguing that the ineffective use of artillery in World War I could be traced to "the blind worship of foreign military thought." Barsukov sought to glorify Russian military successes, such as the invention of the 76-millimeter rapid-firing cannon, while explaining the reasons why native talent could not produce successful results. In his narrative, tactical errors by a penny-pinching Russian General Staff that was too dependent on French theory and not attentive enough to its own experiences in the Russo-Turkish and Russo-Japanese Wars cost the Russian army its success.[53]

In its defensiveness about the checkered past of the Russian Imperial Army, the volume prefigured many of the prevalent themes of World War II and post–World War II militaristic and Cold War discourse. These themes include the valorization of specialists, whatever their class origin; the superiority of the Russians as inventors and innovators; and the huge debt that Britain and France owed to Russia for its military actions during wartime. Furthermore, this discourse hearkened back to the earlier patriotic discourses of the Russian Imperial Army at the turn of the century, emphasizing the intellectual superiority and outstanding courage of the soldiers of the Russian army while pointing to the inferiority and cowardice of non-Russian opponents. Thus the 1930s discourse, which in this case was actually written by a prominent former tsarist artillerist, was a stepping-stone for national ideas and a link in the transmission belt of Russian and Soviet national identity from the tsarist period to the Cold War era.

Barsukov's article recognized the existence in the Russian Empire of "not a few outstanding and talented specialists [like himself] who understood perfectly well what tasks stood before artillerists in a contemporary war." Unfortunately, they wasted their energy "in battle with the stagnation, sluggishness, and rottenness of the governmental and military machine of tsarist Russia."[54] Like the white-collar middle class of the late Stalin period, the artillerists were lauded for their technical knowledge, skill, and professionalism. Only under Stalin, so went the ideological line, could the talent of the population be recognized and brought to fruition. The class identities of tsarist-era "specialists" and of the author himself were glossed over in the urge to document and praise their technical expertise.[55]

The article claimed that Russian rank-and-file artillerists were superior to the Germans in "high marksmanship, bold initiative, and courageous heroism" not to mention inventiveness. The author even alleged that the Germans' famous and powerful gun "Big Bertha" was copied by the Germans from a previously invented Russian model.[56] Lapsing into the prerevolutionary genre of "war episodes," the essay described a number of specific battle scenes in which artillerists made up for their numerical inferiority through their marksmanship, training, and inventiveness in the field. As in Cold War discourse, despite the material advantages of "the West," Russian skill and ingenuity could save the day as, for example, one Russian battery destroyed six German batteries. Furthermore, while the Russians were extremely brave and did not leave their positions even when wounded, the Austrians enduring a Russian artillery attack "lost their heads in terror" and were "seized by general panic."

German pilots dropping bombs were pronounced to be ineffectual because they were "timid" and "uncertain."[57] The hero remaining on the field of battle while wounded and the association of bravery or cowardice with particular national identities were both popular tropes in military propaganda generally and in late tsarist military propaganda in particular.[58] The treatment of heroic Russians and inept Germans and Austrians in the Soviet discourse of the late 1930s was virtually indistinguishable from the tsarist discourse of 1914–1915; depictions of Russian prowess also shared common tropes with Cold War Soviet discourse. As we have seen in chapter 6, the reasons for the hearkening back to World War I discourse were multiple. One reason was the continuity in personnel; the few remaining generals who had been working assiduously throughout the 1920s and struggling against the current in the 1930s to foreground the lessons of World War I were finally allowed to do so. The Red Army General Staff finally realized that while they had deemphasized the "imperialist war" and muted its memory, the soldiers and civilians in territories formerly occupied by the Germans had not forgotten German prowess. Popular perceptions of "the German war" had to be countered with assurances that the Germans were not, after all, invincible.

The earlier internationalist World War I discourse contained not only characterizations of Russians and their enemies but also references to Russia's allies. This discourse had nothing but disdain for Russia's allies who had created the conditions for war through their competition for capitalist markets. Russia was depicted as the victim of French bankers who demanded cannon fodder in exchange for French loans. Iu. Veber's story "Breakthrough," on the other hand, suggested a radically different role for Russia: military savior of Britain and France, although such a claim has not held up to the scrutiny of more recent military historians.[59] According to Veber, the Russian military council decided on the offensive in April 1916 because "[i]t was necessary to divert German forces from Verdun, and Austrian forces—from the Italian front."[60] While the breakthrough ultimately did not bring Russia victory, it nonetheless accomplished crucial goals:

> The Russian soldier saved France from the threat of the exhaustion/attrition of its forces, and Italy—from complete and utter defeat. The Russian soldier also defined the behavior of Rumania. Immediately after the breakthrough on the Southwestern front, Rumania declared war on Germany and its allies.
>
> And, of course, it was not the fault of the Russian soldier that the high command, made up for the most part of untalented and indecisive individuals, could not make complete use of the fruits of this most prominent victory.[61]

The rehabilitation of the Brusilov offensive was coupled with a new Soviet conceptualization of Russia's relationship to the West that echoed prerevolutionary discourse about Russia. It was the sacrifices and the successes of the Russian military that proved decisive in the Allies' ultimate victory in World War I. This trope of sacrifice for Europe (in its prerevolutionary form, Russia saved Europe from the Mongol hordes and later Napoleon) was already reemerging before the events of World War II strengthened Russian and Soviet perceptions of their unique military role. Once again, in 1930s discourse, prerevolutionary tropes reemerged as precursors to Cold War tropes.

The conclusion of "Breakthrough" made a sharp distinction between "the Russian soldier" and the high command, and in both World War I pieces there was an ambiguity regarding the class status of the new heroes. Often the "rank and file" was singled out for praise, but at other times the pieces discussed the superior education of Russian artillery officers, the careful planning of an unnamed "chief of artillery," and the achievements of both "junior officers" and "noncommissioned officers."[62] Thus the class lines of heroism were somewhat blurred. While the author deployed the trope of the heroism of the Russian rank-and-file soldier as fully as any 1914 author, in 1939 Veber remained unwilling to elevate an individual tsarist general to hero status. Brusilov remained a minor character in a celebration of his own greatest military endeavor.

The emphasis on tsarist-era skill and efficiency by specialists, if not by the high command, also led to a transformation in how this new World War I discourse portrayed the effectiveness of the tsarist army in killing the enemy. In "Artillerists of the World War," Barsukov lauded the effective use of weaponry to kill the enemy without any reflection on the class or ethnic identity of that enemy or the act of killing itself. Barsukov approvingly described the Russian army's 76-millimeter cannon by its nickname, "the scythe of death," thereby valorizing the technology of killing.[63] Veber's "Breakthrough" described the Russians attacking the Austrians with poison gas in almost lyrical terms:

> It was three o'clock when from the right flank of the Russian positions appeared a big greenish-yellow cloud. A light wind moved this cloud . . . toward the strongly fortified redoubt of the enemy. The cloud slowly crept along the land, shrouding the barbed wire and barricades and filling every little hole and depression. Noiselessly and ominously it crawled through the morning silence, stealing its way closer and closer to the Austro-Hungarian redoubt.

This description of a gas attack transformed this horrifying weapon into a natural phenomenon propelled by a light breeze into pastoral quiet. The killing of the men in "every little hole and depression" was aestheticized, and death-dealing celebrated. As soon as the men left their trenches to flee the gas, the Russian artillerists opened fire, using a second technological means to bring death to the Austrians.[64] While earlier descriptions of poison gas in World War I emphasized its inhumane nature, and earlier depictions of killing the enemy framed killing either as brutality and/or as an unavoidable sorrow, new World War I discourse emphasized that mass killing through technology was the desired and desirable outcome of war.

In the late 1930s, authors retelling the events of World War I employed a jingoistic discourse of Russian messianism, national heroism, wartime prowess, and the glorification of violence that recapitulated tsarist World War I propaganda. This renewed patriotic discourse was soon put to the test in extremely harsh wartime circumstances.

THE SECOND WORLD WAR

Heroism and Enemies

While the transformations in World War I discourse in the mid- to late 1930s require contextualization and explanation, it is obvious why World War I discourse dramatically changed after the German attack on the Soviet Union on June 22, 1941. In the midst of another war with Germany, the Russian experience of World War I suddenly became a mobilizing tool rather than an embarrassing episode that needed to be explained away. All aspects of World War I discourse experienced significant changes; themes of religion and morality required radical reinterpretation as Soviet citizens struggled with the real life-and-death issues of an even more devastating war. In line with other Soviet war propaganda, World War II–era depictions of World War I emphasized the need for total dedication to the national cause and merciless hatred of the enemy. Post-1941 World War I discourse foregrounded heroism and manliness against a backdrop of transformed images of Soviet womanhood, the nation, and spirituality.

The tension between nationalist and internationalist discourses tended to be resolved on the side of the national. Whereas it had earlier been argued in World War I discourse that the tsarist workers had no motherland, and therefore they did not have to fight in World War I, now tsarist Russia was reclaimed as the extension of the Soviet motherland, and it was traitorous not to fight for her. After June 1941, authors describing World War I could no longer recognize evasion of duties and Lenin-sanctioned fraternization as evidence of Russian soldiers' advanced revolutionary consciousness. Earlier texts were edited to remove depictions of revolutionary internationalism. For example, a comradely encounter between the worker Knave and a German Social Democratic soldier was excised from Sholokhov's *Quiet Flows the Don* between 1945 and 1953.[65] Nationality now trumped class, and Russians could no longer refuse to fight for Russia.

Needless to say, World War II–era authors also rejected religious or moral inclinations toward fraternization. In one scene in Sergeev-Tsenskii's 1943 novel *Brusilov's Breakthrough,* the divisional commander Gil'chevskii mocked a cowardly and inactive colleague by quipping, "What was Yakovlev doing here all week, I'd like to know? Preaching non-resistance to evil?"[66] The narrator made clear that Tolstoian pacifism had no place at the front. Sergeev-Tsenskii's attitude toward Orthodox Christian moral precepts was more complex. On the one hand, Sergeev-Tsenskii participated in the World War II trend toward the incorporation of Orthodox religious belief as a component of Russianness by having his hero Ensign Liventsev fondly remember the Easters of his childhood. Liventsev blended reminiscences of happy times with his love of nature:

> The day-long, week-long, pealing of the bells in all the churches; the bright colours of the Easter eggs, dyed pink and red; the Easter kiss; the blissful idleness; going visiting; people merry with drink on every side, many of them even drunk; the women's bright new dresses; the song of the lark in the fields; the tender, shrinking willows fringing the ponds.

Nothing in this text detracted from the lyricism with which Easter was described. Absent was the undercutting or mocking of religion itself that was common in many prewar texts. But Sergeev-Tsenskii's narrator then made clear that this appreciation of Easter did not include any tinge of pacifism. The narrator pointedly noted, "But no one could forget that the words, 'Let us then embrace, and cry, "Brother!" and forgive our enemies,' were confined to the walls of the churches in which they were sung on Easter morning."[67] Easter memories of home and childhood encouraged the soldiers to pursue military successes rather than reminding them of their common humanity with the enemy. Renewed attention to spirituality was not intended to weaken Soviet resolve to kill.

Whereas in earlier World War I discourse desertion and surrender to the enemy was viewed as something that was understandable and possibly even heroic, during World War II, Soviet authors reacted harshly to desertion and surrender to the enemy. Surrender was redefined as a supremely unmanly and cowardly act. In *Brusilov's Breakthrough,* Sergeev-Tsenskii made it clear that the only proper course for a man to follow in defending Russia was identical in World War I and World War II. Just as in July 1942 Stalin had ordered "not one step back" without orders from higher command, Sergeev-Tsenskii's Brusilov asserted in a June 1915 directive:

> I therefore order that no mercy be shown to cowards who abandon the lines or yield themselves prisoner, that rifle and artillery fire be directed against capitulators, even if this should involve ceasing fire against the enemy, and that the same measures be taken against any who attempt to retreat or flee. If necessary, they are to be shot down to a man.[68]

Before the war, this brutal order might have been cited as evidence of the class antagonism between the officers and the rank-and-file soldiers. Now it was introduced as an example of the proper behavior of an officer in battle, indicating that every Soviet man must be ready to fight or he would face death at the hands of his own compatriots.

Throughout *Brusilov's Breakthrough,* Sergeev-Tsenskii contrasted the brave Ensign Liventsev with the cowardly Ensign Obidin (from *obidnyi* or offensive). Their definitive interaction came when, during a battle with the Hungarians, Liventsev saw:

> Ensign Obidin—it was he, unmistakably—and a group of his men stood with their hands in the air, surrounded by Hungarian soldiers.
> "Platoon, fire! Kill the traitors!" shouted Liventsev, beside himself, forgetting that there were but a few men around him.

Liventsev's men succeeded in wounding Obidin and preventing the Hungarians from capturing the Russians.[69] Sergeev-Tsenskii made it clear that cowardice must be severely punished and that it was the duty of a hero to kill his own comrades if they succumbed to the desire to surrender. The Soviet narrative of heroism in World War I had completed its transformation, moving from the 1929 memoirs of V. Dmitriev, who represented his own surrender as heroic, to the uneasy justification of Mendele's surrender in the foreword to Leonid Katsov's *Through Captivity* in the mid-1930s, to the 1943 fictionalized Liventsev who gained heroic stature precisely because he tried to kill the "traitors" who wanted to surrender. The final iteration of the World War I hero not only had no mercy for the enemy, he also brutally punished his own comrades for their cowardice.

The patriotic discourse of the World War II era also included new attention to ideal soldier-officer relations. V. V. Mavrodin's wartime biography of Brusilov implied a return to the tsarist ideal of the officer as a father to his troops: "Brusilov believed in the Russian soldier and loved him." Mavrodin then quoted Brusilov: "The soldiers were Russians. I looked upon them as my own family." Mavrodin neatly tied together the veneration of the father as officer and the articulation of the soldiers as a family—here, tellingly, a specifically Russian family. And the father in the family must exert his authority lovingly. Mavrodin went on to explain that "Brusilov demanded discipline, not the German regimentation and discipline of the rod under which soldiers turn into automatons, but conscious discipline in which the old rule of Suvorov ('every soldier must know his maneuver') received new strength."[70] While interwar remembrance of World War I routinely associated "regimentation and discipline of the rod" with the tsarist officer corps, Mavrodin defined Brusilov's "conscious" discipline in contrast to the abusive Germans rather than to abusive tsarist officers.

Ideal Gender Norms Reestablished

Although there are a few exceptions, the image of the female soldier or nurse is largely absent from Soviet World War I discourse in the interwar period. Images of the female in World War I reemerged, however, after the outbreak of World War II. In *Brusilov's Breakthrough,* Sergeev-Tsenskii offered his readers both desirable and undesirable female models engaged in the tsarist war effort. When the hero Ensign Liventsev arrived at the front, he met "a Cossack in a jaunty Circassian coat" who assigned Liventsev to the 9th company of the battalion. Liventsev was puzzled by the notion of a Cossack as battalion commander in an infantry regiment and "was struck by the absence of any hair on the round white face." He soon met the "real" commander of the battalion, Lieutenant-Colonel Kapitanov, a man who "gave an impression of helpless weakness." Kapitanov introduced the Cossack in the Circassian coat as his wife, and their orderly then admitted to Liventsev that it was "the Lady" (*barynia*) who gave orders to the battalion. Liventsev's impression of this woman in command was extremely unfavorable as, in his view, she both lacked tenderness and charm and she also weakened the fighting capability of the army. Kapitanov's wife was vehemently opposed to Brusilov's plan for an offensive because, like a cat, she did not want to leave the "hearth and home" she had created in her comfortably fitted-up dugout.[71]

When the offensive commenced, the Kapitanovs' battalion behaved disgracefully by halting their advance to raid a wine cellar and get drunk on the "Lady Cossack's" orders. The enraged division commander Gil'chevskii then banished her to the rear because she was "spoiling officers and men."[72] In this depiction of the tsarist war effort, Madame Kapitanova, the female warrior, became symbolic of everything that was wrong with the tsarist army. Furthermore, Liventsev was appalled as much by her lack of true womanliness as by her leadership of the battalion. The presence of this woman at the front seemed to be subverting the natural order of things. Given that the problem of officers' wives masquerading as Cossacks was not a major cause of Russian defeat in World War I, this episode reveals a misogynistic undercurrent in Sergeev-Tsenskii's work, and the articulation, during World War II, of a desire for limitations on women's wartime roles.

This appearance of the negative female "officer" in Sergeev-Tsenskii's work was balanced by the appearance of the ideal female role model. Sergeev-Tsenskii's thirty-seven-year-old bachelor hero Ensign Liventsev went through two years of war (and two novels in the trilogy) without revealing an attachment to any woman except his elderly mother. In *Brusilov's Breakthrough,* however, Sergeev-Tsenskii introduced a romance between Liventsev and a virtuous and modest librarian by the name of Natal'ia Sergeevna Verigina, whom he met when his regiment was stationed in Kherson. Her surname was derived from the word for the chains worn by ascetics, and it was also reminiscent of the Latin word *virgin*. She was thus the living representation of chastity and restraint and the polar opposite of the cross-dressing, officer-spoiling Kapitanova.

In describing the budding romance, Sergeev-Tsenskii forced Verigina to carry an even broader symbolic significance than that of all womanly goodness. He described Liventsev's feelings about Verigina in the following way:

> In those eyes he had found the solicitude of a mother, the tenderness of a sister, the responsiveness of the one person nearest to his heart.
> This was not a case according to Schopenhauer's theory of palingenesis. No, it was something immeasurably greater: Motherland! . . .

Sergeev-Tsenskii elided Liventsev's love for Verigina with his love of country a second time a few pages later when he had Liventsev hesitate before opening a letter from Verigina. "Whatever this letter might actually contain, he wanted it now to echo in his soul as the one password: 'Russia!'"[73] In both of these passages patriotism, romance, and maternal love were fused together into an overwhelming emotional force.

Unlike early revolutionary rhetoric that merged masculinity with Soviet patriotism by emphasizing the belonging of the soldier to the all-male community, Sergeev-Tsenskii built his patriotism on an ideal of community in which the feminine was essential. The soldier's mother, his female love object, and the land that required defending were one and the same. As *Song of the Motherland* (*Pesn' o rodine*), the unofficial prewar Soviet national anthem, put it in 1936, "We love the motherland as we would our bride. We protect her as we would our affectionate mother."[74] Patriotism now required the presence of a chaste love object.

The ideal of a beloved and virtuous woman on the home front "keeping the home fires burning" while the male soldier endured the horrors of war gained new strength during World War II. A second exemplary role for women was as "healers of wounded souls" who were to nurse their shattered men back to health.[75] In Sergeev-Tsenskii's depiction, there was no question about the relative status hierarchy of the military zone and the home/healing zone. When Verigina decided to become a nurse herself, "she did not even write [to Liventsev] that she was attending courses for Red Cross nurses. . . . She felt that it would be purposeless, even boring, to write of herself and of the work she was doing. . . . The fate of Russia, the fate of all humanity, was being decided out there, on the fighting line."[76] Verigina thus emphasized the insignificance of her work in relation to Liventsev's and also laid the groundwork for the "surprise" plot twist of her appearance at the very hospital in Dubno where Liventsev was taken after being seriously wounded.

After successful surgery to save Liventsev's wounded leg, Liventsev and Verigina dwelled on the prospects of a happy future together and the narrator defined the role of "Woman":

> Woman carries eternity within herself, even when she is unaware of it. Woman gives birth; woman protects and preserves life. There had been no need for Liventsev to fear degradation in Natalia's eyes had she watched the doctors cutting his unconscious, half-dead body, or seen the pus and ichor and blood oozing out of his swollen leg.[77]

Verigina represented all women as a life-giving force and a healer who would not turn away from Liventsev's wounded body no matter how repulsive it was. This kind of womanliness represented dedication, love, and service, with the

eroticism removed. This woman was markedly different from the sexual crea-
tures with whom Fedorchenko's soldiers interacted. By 1925, these women had
disappeared from Soviet discourse through censorship, and by 1943 they were
replaced by the ascetic Natal'ia, who did not fear the bodily disfigurement of
her love.

Though women warriors appeared in Soviet Civil War discourse and in
civil defense training for women (not to mention the realities of World War II),
Sergeev-Tsenskii's work denigrated the notion of women at the front. While
Soviet interwar gender policies and official rhetoric certainly opened up possibilities for "model" women to employ violence in the defense of their country,
Sergeev-Tsenskii's novel is an example of a new current countervailing these
trends.[78] Recapitulating traditional themes in a rather heavy-handed manner,
Sergeev-Tsenskii defined "Woman" as giving life rather than taking it, and
serving as a symbol of what was to be protected rather than protecting anything herself. This kind of discourse added yet another layer of complexity to
the postwar struggles of returning male and female soldiers, nurses, and those
who remained in the Soviet rear.

FULL CIRCLE?

This discussion of Soviet World War I remembrance during World War II
seems to suggest that Soviet discourse had come full circle. Orthodox religion
was the object of nostalgia rather than criticism. Eschewing women's equality,
the wartime novels articulated separate spheres and roles for heroic men and
their nurturing women. In no way questioning violence, the wartime remembrance valorized and justified killing both enemies and traitors within one's
own army. Now the upper-class commander of the troops was a father to his
disciplined lower-class soldier-sons, and Germanness was a marker of evil while
Russianness was an indication of innate goodness. While it is tempting to accept this picture of a clean break with earlier trends in Soviet World War I remembrance, to do so would be far too schematic. As in the 1920s and early
1930s, when echoes of tsarist patriotic discourse resounded despite the dominance of revolutionary and internationalist interpretations of the war, in the
mid-1940s voices were raised against this reinstatement of a patriotic mascu-
linizing discourse.

Chapter 6 detailed historian A. M. Pankratova's opposition to the heroization of Brusilov because of the general's loyalty to the old regime. Sergeev-
Tsenskii also came under criticism for his nationalistic-patriotic mode of

writing. A November 1945 review of *Brusilov's Breakthrough* by E. Usievich in *Znamia* challenged Sergeev-Tsenskii's nationalizing views of the war in a continuation of a decade-long feud between writer and critic. Usievich's review demonstrates the ways in which the earlier internationalist discourse remained in tension with new patriotic tropes, even after the events of World War II had radically transformed the Soviet ideological landscape. Before Usievich embarked on a discussion of the few (in her view) merits and many faults of Sergeev-Tsenskii's novel, she offered her readers a thumbnail sketch of Russian participation in World War I. This brief survey of the war revealed that by 1945 Usievich was obliged, to some degree, to accommodate new interpretations of Russian military history. Like Veber's immediately prewar interpretation of the Brusilov offensive, Usievich's critique emphasized the way in which the unexpected breakthrough "saved France, Paris from an immediately impending threat," by weakening German pressure on Verdun and allowing the Allies time to prepare an offensive on the Somme. Speaking from the confidence of 1945, Usievich added that the Brusilov offensive "foreordained the defeat of Germany in the First World War."[79]

Usievich's analysis of the Brusilov offensive differed from Veber's 1939 interpretation in that she dealt explicitly with the role of patriotism in producing the unexpected victory. Usievich argued that the Brusilov breakthrough was a "significant historical event" that revealed the "fundamental tendencies of social forces." She proposed that "the military steadfastness [*stoikost'*] of the people is not possible without patriotism, without the attachment of the people to their country."[80] Usievich then struggled to fit this notion of patriotism into the class framework of prerevolutionary Russia, and to reconcile her argument with previous historical traditions that had associated patriotism with the bourgeoisie and derided it as "national chauvinism."

Usievich tried to retain her class analysis at the same time that she embraced national categories by asserting that true patriotism, now a positive quality, could only be found among the lower classes; the court, aristocracy, and capitalists only participated in the war due to "self-interest." She admitted, however, consistent with earlier interpretations of the war, that the "petty-bourgeoisie" were caught up by "chauvinist intoxication" in 1914, but were soon "sobered" by the realities of war. In another creative revision of earlier interpretations, Usievich claimed that most workers, under the strong influence of the Bolshevik Party, were against the war from the beginning. But, in a paradoxical turn of events, these same workers who opposed the war performed "wonders of bravery" and "brought about the steadfastness of the Russian army."

Usievich created this contradiction by her refusal to abandon class as the foundation of all positive developments; she exaggerated the party-mindedness of the workers at the same time that she insisted on the significance of their contribution to tsarist military success. Usievich thus created an impossible soldier who was a conscious opponent of the war while bravely risking his life because of love of country, a sentiment markedly different from petty-bourgeois "chauvinist intoxication."[81]

When she turned to criticism of *Brusilov's Breakthrough,* on the other hand, Usievich attacked Sergeev-Tsenskii because his novel fell prey to the same contradiction between patriotism and Leninist doctrine that she herself had just attempted to smooth over. Like the critic Vishnevskii, who in 1935 faulted Novikov-Priboi for introducing "old fleet valor" instead of defeatism into his novel *Tsusima,* Usievich accused Sergeev-Tsenskii of failing to conform to the Leninist line because the hero of the novel—the patriotic Ensign Liventsev—was a "defensist" at best, and at worst an advocate of "war to a victorious conclusion," who believed that the goal of the war was to transform Russia. Usievich also suggested that Ensign Obidin, the novel's cowardly antagonist who hoped for a separate peace and eventually tried to surrender to the enemy with his men, was the only character in the novel exhibiting "defeatism," though she recognized that Obidin's cowardly brand of defeatism was, of course, not the same as true revolutionary Leninist defeatism.[82]

Sergeev-Tsenskii responded to Usievich's review in an angry 1946 letter to the editorial board of *Znamia* that somewhat distorted her views. He threatened to sue Usievich for slander because she suggested that he had been intending to create "a principled Leninist" when he introduced the "self-seeker and coward" Obidin into the novel.[83] Although Sergeev-Tsenskii mischaracterized Usievich's words to some degree, their dispute demonstrated once again the complexity of portraying Leninist defeatism during World War I without admitting that the actions of "defeatists" bore a strong resemblance to cowardice, while "defensist" and pro-war actions could be perceived as heroic. Even before World War II, it had been tricky to portray orthodox Leninist defeatism in a positive light, but given the exigencies of the second war, it became almost insurmountably difficult. Nonetheless, Usievich took Sergeev-Tsenskii to task for portraying Liventsev in the only way a military hero could possibly be portrayed in 1942–1943.

Sergeev-Tsenskii vigorously defended the patriotic thrust of his novel. He explained that it had been written as "defense literature" in 1942 when it was important to "unmask the myth that the Germans were invincible." Because of this vital mobilizing task, Sergeev-Tsenskii explained that he "would be the first to censure himself if he had introduced defeatism and defeatists into the novel." Sergeev-Tsenskii candidly admitted that *Brusilov's Breakthrough* was shaped by the context of World War II, and that Leninist defeatism could not play a positive role in the mobilizing effort. Sergeev-Tsenskii continued in a more conciliatory vein, suggesting that in any case "defeatism" only occurred after the Brusilov offensive, and he was planning to include it in his next novel.[84] Depictions of World War I continued to be fraught with ambiguities, and authors who braved the topic faced the danger of being denounced for ideological missteps that were impossible to avoid.

In his defense of *Brusilov's Breakthrough,* Sergeev-Tsenskii also boasted that he received letters from the front during World War II in which young officers "communicated to me that they took my Ensign Liventsev as a model for how they should act as the commander of a company. In this manner, this novel stood in defense of the motherland in the same way as did the *Ordeal of Sevastopol'*."[85] Sergeev-Tsenskii thus acknowledged that the writing of defense literature required the depiction of the tsarist officer corps in a heroic light. Liventsev could be a model for Red Army commanders only if he was willing to fight to the death for his motherland and only if he earnestly desired "her" victory in World War I.

The transformations in Soviet discourse of World War I remained contested and incomplete, yet the trends were very clear. Depictions of heroic action in World War I in the late 1930s and during World War II repeatedly contradicted revolutionary rhetoric and socialist precepts of atheism, defeatism, class struggle, gender equality, and internationalism, but they were nonetheless embraced by most Soviet editors, authors, and critics as an essential part of voenizatsiia and war mobilization. While the voices of dissenters justifiably pointing out these myriad contradictions were still audible, by World War II the memory of World War I had been predominantly recast in the image of tsarist World War I rhetoric. This trend portended ill for postwar gender equality, for the status of non-Russian nationalities, for nonviolence, and for egalitarianism.

8

Legacies of the Great War

WORLD WAR I MEMORY—1945 TO 1991

The cataclysm of World War II forever changed the meaning and also the name of World War I in the Soviet Union as in the rest of Europe. In the last years of Stalin's reign, the overwhelming task of rebuilding the country despite the loss of perhaps as many as twenty-seven million people overwhelmingly eclipsed the remembrance of World War I. Furthermore, soon after the war, the Stalinist authorities opted to minimize the public commemoration of even the heroes and the victims of World War II, never mind those of World War I. In 1947, Stalin "demoted" Victory Day from a state holiday to a regular working day. Plans for a memorial cemetery honoring those who died in the blockade of Leningrad were halted in 1949 because of purges of the local party organizations. It was only during the Khrushchev and early Brezhnev eras that the major monuments to the World War II dead—including Leningrad's Piskarevskoe Memorial Cemetery (1960), Moscow's Tomb of the Unknown Soldier (1967), and Volgograd's memorial complex (1967)—were dedicated.[1] In this "forgetful" atmosphere, the already marginal World War I receded even further into the background. While the first edition of the *Great Soviet Encyclopedia* in 1939 had included over 125 pages detailing the social, political, and economic causes and effects of World War I, the post–World War II second edition of the encyclopedia dispensed with the entire war in a mere five pages.[2]

One exception to this effacement of World War I memory in the immediate postwar period was the continued heroization of Brusilov. After the war, Brusilov was still recognized as a precursor of Soviet military prowess in World War II and an example of the talent that was wasted because the tsarist army had a "criminally inactive general command," in contrast to the brilliant Generalissimo Stalin.[3] In the late 1940s several works celebrated the Brusilov "breakthrough." Two new editions of Brusilov's memoirs appeared in 1946 and 1950; I. L. Sel'vinskii's wartime play came out in book form in 1947, and Iurii Slezkin's novel *Brusilov* also appeared that year.[4] In contrast to the 1943 novel *Brusilov's Breakthrough*, Brusilov himself was the title character of Slezkin's 1947 novel and the author relied heavily on Brusilov's own memoirs in expressing Brusilov's interior thoughts. Slezkin's dedication of the novel showed, however, that World War II had changed the frame of reference for all historical writing about war. It read: "To my son Lev Slezkin, participant in the Great Fatherland War. To a decorated tank crewman—about the war of my generation."[5] World War I was now the "prelude" to a new narrative, the tale of how in twenty-four short years the Soviet Union prepared itself to beat the Germans.

The epilogue of *Brusilov* depicted the general as a loyal servant of the Soviet Union writing his memoirs in the early 1920s. On the one hand, Slezkin used Brusilov's own words to evaluate his military actions, and Brusilov emerged as a hero in the novel. On the other hand, Slezkin openly declared that Brusilov lost importance as a historical figure as soon as the breakthrough was over. He explained in the epilogue that he ended the novel in the summer of 1916 because "the great task that had fallen to Brusilov was completely fulfilled. The later course of the history of his motherland required different people, and the further development of the novel's plot, other heroes."[6] Slezkin conceded ground to those who did not want to valorize Brusilov at all by rushing him off the stage in July 1916.

But even Brusilov's role as a respected precursor to Soviet military glory was short-lived. Amid the suspicions and paranoia of Stalin's last years, the figure of Brusilov experienced yet another turn of fortune. A memoir describing Brusilov's life in the Soviet Union was discovered in the émigré archive in Prague. Although specialists working in the Khrushchev era later asserted that Brusilov's widow Nadezhda had actually penned the volume, the discovery of a "strikingly anti-Soviet" memoir led to Brusilov's sudden fall from favor for the second time.[7] Between 1950 and 1962 Brusilov was not heralded as the heroic ancestor of the Red Army who had demonstrated that Russians could decisively beat Germans, and World War I receded even further into the background of Soviet historical narratives.

The death of Stalin brought a change in World War I discourse as in virtually all other areas of Soviet discourse. The memory of both World War I and World War II began to reemerge during the period christened "the Thaw" by none other than the pacifist turned antifascist Il'ia Erenburg. Brusilov's memoirs reappeared yet again, and many works that had been rejected for publication in the Stalin years now entered the public realm. Former tsarist officer Mikhail Bonch-Bruevich, whose name had been erased from the Red Army staff's World War I documentary project, had also been prevented from publishing his own memoirs in the mid-1930s. His account of war and revolution, *All Power to the Soviets*, which had been circulated to publishing houses in 1936 and rejected by them, was finally released in 1958.[8]

The Russian Revolution and Civil War gained new prominence in this period as the Soviet government sought sources of legitimacy that were independent of Stalin's legacy. In 1957 director Sergei Gerasimov filmed a lavish epic production of *Quiet Flows the Don*. In keeping with the Thaw's preoccupation with private and family life, the passionate romance between Grigorii and Aksin'ia was the centerpiece of the production.[9] Given this new focus on private life, World War II's preeminence in the category of wartime remembrance, and cinematic constraints, it is perhaps not surprising that the Russian experience of World War I was largely omitted from the film.

Gone from *Quiet Flows the Don* was any reference to Koz'ma Kriuchkov as a World War I cultural icon. Grigorii's experiences in World War I battles were also truncated. While the novel depicted the physical interaction of Grigorii and his first victim on the battlefield in vivid detail, the film showed Grigorii merely throwing his lance at the enemy. Grigorii was thus one step removed from the killing. The critical episode of Grigorii killing an unarmed Austrian and gazing at him in confusion was present in the film, but there was no dialogue exploring the nature of Grigorii's guilt. After showing Grigorii looking at the dead man, the director cut immediately to Aksin'ia betraying Grigorii by allowing herself to be seduced by the nobleman Lieutenant Lisnitskii. The following scene shifted to Grigorii, wounded in the hospital. The emotional wound that Aksin'ia inflicted on Grigorii appeared in the film, while the physical horrors of war did not.

Unlike the novel, which carefully described the heroic actions that earned Grigorii a St. George cross, the film showed members of the royal family awarding Grigorii the medal without any explanation of how he received it. In this scene, the film emphasized a key revolutionary moment in the novel: the instant in which Grigorii acted on the revolutionary ideas he had learned about from another wounded soldier in the hospital. He behaved boorishly to the royal family, abruptly announcing that he needed to urinate while in their company. The themes of wartime heroism, ethics, and morality took second place both to passion and betrayal and also to revolutionary consciousness in the 1957 film adaptation of the novel.

There were limits on what could be said about World War I, even during the relatively free era of the Thaw. In the 1950s, when some of Sof'ia Fedorchenko's literary works were again published, she also submitted *The People at War* to the State Literature Publishing House in the hope that it would appear in a new edition. In 1956, the Publishing House commissioned M. M. Skuratov to review the manuscript; he was disturbed by Fedorchenko's portrait of the ugly behavior of the soldier at war. He wrote, "And the brutality, and the unconscious violence of the soldier against innocents, often against his own brother, and the chaos in his head and murk in his soul, and dark religious prejudices, and national narrow-mindedness, and his brutal relationship with women, toward his own wife and girlfriend, all of this is given in the book."[10] Fedorchenko failed to idealize the common soldier, and her portrait of "the people" was therefore not terribly attractive.

Skuratov recommended publication of the book with some excisions to make the book more suitable for a 1950s Soviet audience. He complained about "the frequent references in the book to the Lord God, as if this were necessary. This [idea] no longer lives." The many brutal scenes in the book also needed, according to Skuratov, "considerable selection and sifting." He believed that a gang rape scene and other rapes should be taken out of the book because they "are being told as if in the name of the people." Skuratov also criticized Fedorchenko for presenting sexist and misogynist remarks without comment and for using the word "zhid," an ethnic slur on the Jewish people.[11] Skuratov's anxiety about religion, national prejudice, and violence mirrors the concerns of Glavlit circulars in the early 1920s.[12] There was consistent pressure from the 1920s through the 1950s to suppress both the ugly side of human behavior in war and the turn to spiritual comfort that the horrors of war inspired. The horrifying experiences of World War II and the turn to spiritual comfort during that war only intensified the need to sanitize war in the post–World War II period; yet, despite this pressure, such themes persisted within World War I memory. Fedorchenko's work, however, was not fated to be published again before her death in the late 1950s. The remembrance of World War I in *The People at War* exceeded the limits of Thaw discourse. Only in 1990, during the last year of *glasnost'*, was the censored 1925 edition republished. Fedorchenko was not alone in this fate—neither the works of Voitolovskii nor Klychkov again saw the light in the Soviet Union until after glasnost'.

The post-Stalin period opened up the possibility that literary works that could not pass censorship within the Soviet Union could be published abroad, although their authors suffered severe consequences for such publications. For example, Nobel Laureate Boris Pasternak's masterpiece *Doctor Zhivago* was first published in Italy in 1957. The chapter of *Doctor Zhivago* set during World War I contains a kaleidoscope of familiar Russian and Soviet World War I images: a brave lieutenant brandishing a pistol and shouting "Hurrah!" as he led his men into battle; the incompetent tsar at the front; a horrifically injured soldier with a mutilated face; and Cossacks abusing Jews for sport.[13] The upheavals of the war also played a critical role in advancing the plot of the novel. The circumstances of war brought together the army doctor Iurii Zhivago with Lara Antipova, a young woman who fascinated him, and who was serving as a nurse at the front after the disappearance of her husband in battle. While the war may have facilitated Iurii's meeting with Lara, the philosophical center of Pasternak's novel addressed the shape, scope, and dilemmas of the revolution; the events of World War I remained instrumental.

While Pasternak's vision was focused on the revolution, a second Nobel Laureate, Aleksandr Solzhenitsyn, was eager to allow World War I to take center stage. Solzhenitsyn's father was an "artillery officer on the German front" who "fought throughout the war." Solzhenitsyn never knew his father, who was killed in a hunting accident in the summer of 1918, six months before the author was born, but World War I fascinated the young Solzhenitsyn. In 1937, in his first year at Rostov University, he "chose to write a descriptive essay on 'The Samsonov Disaster' of 1914 in East Prussia and studied material on this." The young Solzhenitsyn planned his first novel as a grand epic of World War I, the Revolution, and the Civil War. He wrote the first chapters in the late 1930s but did not complete the work until 1970.[14] The novel *The Red Wheel, Knot 1* (*Krasnoe koleso, uzel I*, translated as *August 1914*) was first published in Paris in 1971. The other "knots" in the four-volume epic were November 1916, March 1917, and April 1917. The work did not appear in Russia until the 1990s.

Solzhenitsyn's narrative drew on both émigré and Soviet elements. It was objectionable to Soviet censors in 1970 both for its open discussion of religious faith and for its recapitulation of the viewpoint of White émigrés. Solzhenitsyn's heroes were the officers of the General Staff Academy, led by F. F. Palitsyn and Grand Duke Nikolai Nikolaevich, who had fought to modernize the tsarist military in a "military renaissance" after tsarist Russia's humiliating defeat in the Russo-Japanese War. In the first month of World War I these well-trained and dedicated officers were thwarted at every turn by the cowardice, ignorance, and incompetence of the tsarist general staff and thoroughly inept generals such as Samsonov and Rennenkampf.[15] The dedicated officer was personified in the novel by the fictional character Colonel Vorotyntsev of the general staff. The novel culminates in Vorotyntsev's blistering report to the general staff, revealing all of the many mistakes that led to the disaster at Tannenberg.

In addition to valorizing military expertise, the novel also possessed a strong populist streak, praising the "staunchness of the Russian infantry and the superb standard of their rifle fire," as well as heroizing the Russian peasantry à la Tolstoi in the character of the good-natured, intelligent Blagodarev. Vorotyntsev was so taken with Blagodarev, a brave soldier with "a hint of clumsiness about him—the clumsiness of excessive strength," that he invited him to be his orderly.[16] Vorotyntsev and his servant traveled from battle site to battle site, together witnessing the devastation of war. Both characters exemplified class ideals of national and patriotic masculinity, but like Tolstoi before him, Solzhenitsyn saw these two kinds of heroisms as distinct from one another, allowing class to undermine the unity of nation. While Vorotyntsev and Blagodarev are unambiguous in their desire to serve their country, two of Solzhenitsyn's other characters struggle with their wartime roles in ways that recapitulate tensions in interwar Soviet discourse. The main character Isaakii Lasynitsyn, representing the author's father, began the novel as an avowed Tolstoian, but surprised himself with his contradictory determination to volunteer for the front because he "felt sorry" for Russia. Another character, the revolutionary Lieutenant Lenartovich, did not want to "die a pointless death for the *wrong* cause," yet felt elation after a battle for "having had a part in a victory which had not been merely scored in verbal debate but won with his body, his own arms and legs."[17] His elation did not last long, and he decided to save himself by deserting the platoon he was leading. Both characters reflected the complexity of wartime morality, but Solzhenitsyn depicted Lasynitsyn in a positive light and portrayed Lenartovich negatively. Like other earlier Soviet authors, Solzhenitsyn portrayed pacifism as an improbable ideology and marked those who refused to fight and die for Russia as somehow untrustworthy. *August 1914* was a hybrid work, hearkening back to the principles of the old tsarist army with an added dose of Tolstoian populism and a touch of Soviet-style militarism.

Although the Thaw produced some memoir and artistic literature depicting World War I, the most compelling Russian works about World War I were "tamizdat," or works published abroad, outside of the constraints of the Soviet censors. Both Pasternak and Solzhenitsyn saw World War I as prelude to the revolutionary events, but while Pasternak mostly used the war as backdrop, Solzhenitsyn sought to reinscribe World War I into Russian national narratives of heroism, bravery, and military ability. Solzhenitsyn's attention to World War I and the brave tsarist officers who fought for their nation envisioned a prerevolutionary legacy that was "dissident" in a Soviet context. Solzhenitsyn's work presaged the valorization of tsarist officers in particular that emerged after the fall of the Soviet Union.

While Russian memory of the war and revolution emerged primarily outside of the Soviet Union in the post-Stalin period, this was startlingly not the case in Armenia. In the early 1960s, the Armenian population increasingly put pressure on the leadership of the Armenian SSR to memorialize the Armenian genocide at the hands of the Turks in 1915, an event that had not been publicly commemorated during the Stalin years. Armenian officials blamed this lack of commemoration on Stalin's "cult of personality." As the fiftieth anniversary of the genocide approached, officials from the Armenian Communist Party and the Academy of Sciences, with the approval of the Central Committee in Moscow, made plans to hold a scholarly conference about the genocide with published proceedings, to erect an obelisk "symbolizing the rebirth of the Armenian people under Soviet rule," and to organize a closed official commemoration at the opera house in Erevan on April 24, 1965, the fiftieth anniversary of the genocide.[18]

On the anniversary, however, thousands of unofficial demonstrators gathered in several places throughout the city, including on Lenin Square, the symbolic center of Soviet power in Armenia, "demanding the return of the historical Armenian lands." In the evening, a small number of demonstrators became disorderly and the police were eventually called in. This outbreak of disorder caused the Armenian Communist leadership to have to justify their decision to allow the commemoration, and they did so by explaining that they were hoping to channel the national feelings of the intelligentsia and students in the "right direction." In 1967, official attempts to guide national feelings were realized in a monument to the victims of the genocide at Tsisernakaberd in

Erevan. The opening of the monument took place on November 29, 1967, the forty-seventh anniversary of the founding of the Armenian Soviet Republic.[19] This development suggests that the resonance of World War I–era events in the non-Russian republics, and especially in Armenia and among the Yiddish-speaking and other non-Russian populations on the warfronts, is a topic that deserves much more consideration in the future.

WHAT DOES SOVIET WORLD WAR I MEMORY TELL US?

One of the major goals of this book has been to demonstrate that *there was* World War I remembrance that developed and evolved within the Soviet Union in the first decades after the war. Much to the author's surprise, she discovered that she was on a mission of recovery of long-forgotten works as well as emphasizing aspects of familiar works long ignored by other scholars. One goal of this book, then, has been to raise a submerged island of interwar discourse and bring it to light. The recovery of this discourse places the Soviet Union back into European interwar debates and struggles about the meaning of World War I rather than segregating the Soviet Union into a separate category because of its "failure" to reflect upon the traumas of war European-style. The mere existence of World War I remembrance serves to recast the Soviet Union's place in European interwar debates, including discussions about faith, the challenges to contemporary manhood, violence, and the nature of national versus international identities.

This work suggests that religious discourse was quite resonant in early Soviet culture as people of faith retained, developed, and nurtured a religious world view despite attempts of "the Godless" to promote an atheist state. Soviet literature of World War I shows that understandings and depictions of the war were very often framed in terms of the supernatural, whether it be the power of God or the power of dark forces, demons, witches, and the like. The battlefield was a place where the "uncanny" held sway, and later depictions of war also reflected this tendency toward the supernatural.[20] Even ideologically correct Soviet movies such as *Borderlands* could easily slip into a Christian religious framework by imagining the revolutionary sacrifice of the soldier-hero as resurrection.

Although it is difficult to find volumes of evidence because of the disproportionate power of the state to the individual in early Soviet times, my work also suggests that there were many individual battles stemming from the experience of World War I in which people of faith struggled to preserve the attributes of their faith in the face of state atheism. Religious pilgrimages to the Madonna unharmed by bullets, the declarations of Tolstoians that they would not fight for the Red Army, and the battles of Nadezhda Brusilova to give Brusilov a proper Orthodox burial and preserve the cross on his grave-marker are, in my opinion, only the tip of the iceberg in terms of individual struggles to insist on a religious understanding of World War I and its aftermath. While additional evidence may be hard to find, it is important that future researchers be attuned to this aspect of interwar Soviet experience.

Despite radical transformations in gender and ethnic policies in the 1920s and 1930s, older discourses of the inferiority of women and non-Russians continued to operate on a linguistic level and to affect social reality as well. Both tsarist and Soviet authors, for example, saw women in the rear as carriers of corruption and contagion. Both alluded to the cowardliness of the Jews and the Tatars, the perfidy of the Germans, and sometimes the brutality of the Cossacks. In these cases, there were often very strong continuities between tsarist and Soviet discourse. The persistence of notions of gender and ethnic inferiority in the country most avowedly determined to eradicate such inequalities suggests that such continuities in mentalité were likely to be even stronger among the other European combatants. The cataclysm of war caused rapid political and economic change, but did not as quickly accelerate changes in attitude about race, ethnicity, and gender.

Soviet transformations in class discourse were much more extreme than elsewhere in Europe and produced more of a rupture as the heroic officer of prerevolutionary discourse was replaced by the heroic revolutionary of Soviet discourse. Even here, there were some moments of continuity as the occasional officer showed decency despite his class. Notions of class caused the most difficulty for the increasingly militarizing Soviet state as it moved toward restoring discipline and hierarchy in the army. The awkward figure of the "déclassé" officer somehow turned revolutionary revealed the tensions between the Soviet discourse of class struggle and the need for effective officers in the 1930s. This problem was a uniquely Soviet dilemma.

Although there were great continuities in the use of gendered and national discourses to denote hierarchies, Soviet interwar remembrance of World War I also challenged the heroic, national, and manly nature of warfare. Especially in the first decade after World War I, many Soviet depictions of war emphasized the sorrows of war, disfigurement of male bodies, physical diseases, moral corruption, and psychological trauma that were produced on the battlefield and in violent interactions with the civilian population. Such works revealed to Soviet readers the ugliness of war—its naked ethnic hatreds, casual violence, and wanton abuse of women and children. While the Soviet government may have been unprecedented in its peacetime use of brutality against its own citizens in the 1920s and 1930s, World War I and some Civil War discourse showed that at least some Soviet authors reflected openly on the costs of violence to its perpetrators. This disruption of official or traditional narratives about militarism, heroism, and gender was extremely hard to sustain, and this is, no doubt, why there is still so much ambiguity about the extent to which the war transformed notions of masculinity all over Europe. Challenges to masculinity in all combatant countries were constantly being countered by reassertions of masculinist, militarizing, and heroizing discourse.

These attacks on the national warrior hero at times rent the fabric of Soviet heroic discourse, calling into question traditional notions of the male warrior fighting for his fatherland or motherland. During the 1930s, Soviet ideologues mobilizing the population for war sought to patch up this ideal warrior image, but many of the tears in the fabric were still visible when the national emergency of World War II radically transformed how warfare and national sacrifice were understood.

The second part of this book has explored the complex circumstances under which Soviet World War I discourse was formed, suppressed, revised, rehabilitated, and sometimes suppressed again. It is a tale with many twists and turns, but there are two key aspects of World War I memory that should be highlighted. The first is that many aspects of World War I remembrance were actively developing in the first years after the war and that there was considerable official attention paid to the World War I experience in the early Soviet years. But by the end of the 1920s, when discussion and reflection of the war had really begun to blossom across Europe, there were many bureaucratic and ideological forces and economic constraints within the Soviet Union pushing against continued emphasis on World War I. These included intense competition for economic resources in general; changes in the personnel of the Red Army after Trotskii's exile and the growing preeminence of the Civil War in the Red Army's imagination; the hostility of Narkompros toward prerevolutionary military history; the rising antireligious campaigns that made suspect all memorialization of the dead; the attacks on civil society and on "remnants of the past" during the Great Break; and, eventually, the purges. These forces hindered Soviet participation in the pan-European World War I discourse in which they had actively participated up to that point. The success of these various factors in substantially suppressing World War I remembrance has led to the mistaken impression that there was not any remembrance in the first place.

Second, it is important to underscore that the marginalization of World War I was not the result of some overarching *diktat* from the top, but was instead the result of thousands of individual struggles between myriad Soviet institutions and various social actors working alone or in groups. "Forgetting" World War I required the active participation of thousands upon thousands of individuals, both winners and losers in contests for meaning, and forgetting World War I was never completely accomplished. Unlike the other major combatants, the Soviet state harbored an ideological predisposition to ignore World War I; it had rejected the war from the outset, and it was natural that any state would prioritize its own founding events, such as the October Revolution and Civil War, over the embarrassing military defeat that led to those events. But World War I discourse was nonetheless actively developing in the early years of the Soviet state. It was a combination of ideological hostility to World War I and other unrelated and unpredictable historical forces, such as the purges and the struggles over military doctrines in the Red Army, that caused World War I to disappear from public discourse.

The vitality of some aspects of World War I discourse revealed itself in the late 1930s when some of the actors who had been actively engaged in the "forgetting" of World War I suddenly realized that any example of Russians defeating the German military could be employed to bolster the confidence of Soviet troops. A new military strand of World War I remembrance developed in the late 1930s and came to fruition during World War II. After World War II, attention to World War I was sporadic—neither the systematic focus of Soviet ideologists, nor entirely neglected. Yet by the 1990s, the passing of generations had accelerated the process of forgetting that various ideological pressures had put into motion in the early Soviet period and that had only been temporarily reversed by the exigencies of World War II. When historian Catherine Merridale, in 1997 and 1998, asked Russian adults to recall the three most deadly wars in Russia's twentieth century, "almost no one even mentioned the war of 1914. To some, indeed, my [Merridale's] mentioning it came as a surprise— 'Oh, that!'"[21]

THE MOSCOW FRATERNAL CEMETERY REVISITED

As Merridale was conducting her interviews in 1998, a new memorial to World War I was under construction in Moscow. Battles over the remembrance of

World War I that began in 1914 are still being played out in the Russian Federation today; this remembrance remains contested and multivocal. These contemporary contests for memory are, of course, shaped by their own particular cultural, political, and social contexts, in circumstances radically different from those of tsarist Russia or of the interwar Soviet Union; these contexts include the rise of glasnost' in the Gorbachev era and the emergence of oppositional civic groups, the fall of the Soviet Union, the search for new legitimizing symbols for the Russian Federation, and the struggle of citizens in post-Soviet Russia to come to terms with the complex Soviet legacy. Where the All-Russian War Cemetery once stood in Moscow, today there is the Memorial Park Complex of the Heroes of the First World War. The history of the restoration of this site is as complex as the history of the cemetery's destruction, illuminating the extent to which World War I memory continues to be controversial.

The ceremonial opening of the memorial complex in Moscow's Leningrad Park was modeled after the original opening of the cemetery in 1915 and took place on August 1, 2004, to mark the ninetieth anniversary of the outbreak of World War I. The city of Moscow spent 95 million rubles to create attractive fencing and to provide a variety of memorial steles, columns, and plaques. An article written the day before the ceremony anticipated that the opening would be attended by Prime Minister Mikhail Fradkov, Minister of Defense Sergei Ivanov, and the mayor of Moscow, Iurii Luzhkov; the top Russian official actually present at the opening was the vice mayor of Moscow, V. Shantsev.[22] The cemetery was not, however, deemed top priority at either the national or local level. To explore the ambiguous place of the cemetery in Russian civil life, we will first explore the memorial geography of the site as it now stands, and then highlight the roles of the various actors in the process of rebuilding the site.

There are currently twelve eclectic monumental pieces spread throughout the territory of the park, including the Shlikhter gravestone, the only monument surviving from the original cemetery. Six of the twelve pieces, including a chapel, are adorned with the Orthodox cross, indicating the centrality of Orthodoxy and the active engagement of the Orthodox Church in Russian national and civic projects of memorialization in the post-Soviet period.

The most prominent element in the memorial complex is the 1998 chapel of the Transfiguration of the Savior (also sometimes called "Reconciling the Nations"), created in honor of the destroyed Church of the Transfiguration that had once stood in the cemetery. The very small red brick chapel, in which a requiem is celebrated every afternoon at one o'clock, is decorated with a white concrete emblem of St. George (figure 8.1). The tradition of building churches as war memorials dates all the way back to Byzantium, and until the eighteenth century, "the only war memorials built in Russia were churches."[23] The decision to build a chapel on the site of the Moscow War Cemetery was thus in keeping with a millennium-long tradition of war memorials in Russia and a vibrant post-Soviet church-building boom.[24] The memorial chapel to World War I thus reestablishes the age-old connection between wartime heroism and spiritual salvation. Part of the former cemetery is once again consecrated as hallowed ground.

The chapel of the Transfiguration of the Savior is a church in miniature, consisting of one lone cupola decorated in the Muscovite style with *kokoshniki,* arches in the shape of the traditional head coverings of women in the pre-Petrine period. The size of the church no doubt reflects the limited resources available for its erection in the economically tumultuous 1990s. Like Shchusev's original Church of the Transfiguration, it is an example of neo-Muscovite architecture and represents a double revival. It recapitulates the Russian style of the last decades of the tsarist era, itself a rejection of the Western classical styles of the eighteenth and early nineteenth centuries.[25] This late-twentieth-century church restored the memory of World War I by reclaiming the Russianness that had first been obscured by the Westernizing Peter the Great and then again by the imposition of atheistic Marxism.

Other religious markers are scattered throughout the park. One antique-looking monument in the shape of a cross seems to be a salvaged grave marker from an Orthodox cemetery; in prerevolutionary orthography and using archaic language, it praises those "leaders and soldiers" who gave their lives for "faith and fatherland." The use of the word "vozhd'" and the absence of the word "tsar" in the formulation of "tsar, faith, and fatherland" suggests, however, that this "old" orthography was inscribed in post-Soviet times. A new stone and stucco pillar carved in the outline of the domes of an Orthodox church, reminiscent of Shchusev's original design, commemorates the location in the park where a chapel once stood.[26] The new stele in honor of Russian nurses also sports a stylized church dome and cross. In post-Soviet Russia, wartime sacrifice in World War I was definitively situated within the Christian context of eternal memory and eternal reward that had been markedly out of favor during the Soviet period.

In addition to Christianity, another recurring theme in the complex is the articulation of the national: the double-headed eagle with St. George slaying the dragon nestled between its wings, once associated with the Romanov dynasty but now the central image of the coat of arms of the Russian Federation, crowns a memorial obelisk at the south end of the park. Another large ornamental wall prominently displays an engraving of the Russian coat of arms. This monumental wall also evokes nationality in its inscription "to fallen Russian soldiers." While many of the inscriptions honor "fallen heroes" in general, this wall and the monument to World War I nurses emphasize the Russianness of the dead. Other monuments in the park use the more fluid language of motherland and fatherland to evoke patriotism without specifying either the entity engaged in warfare or the nationality of the warriors.

Although the park is dedicated to the "heroes" of World War I, the complex serves multiple memorial functions, and there is a great deal of flexibility in the definition of its honorees. The park contains one stone marker, similar to a gravestone, specifically remembering the "fallen heroes" of World War II. Given the dominance of World War II in both the post-Stalin Soviet mindset and the post-Soviet world, no memorial site could be complete without an acknowledgment of World War II.

There are also multiple ways of defining which World War I dead are honored. One of the most prominent monuments in the complex is a marble column topped by a soaring bronze eagle, inscribed "to the fallen in the World War 1914–1918." The classical form of the column and the symbol of the eagle are not specific to Russia and imply a dedication to all of the World War I dead. On a square tablet superimposed on the column there is an "all-seeing eye," staring out at the viewer, set within a triangle and surrounded by rays of light. This European Enlightenment or Masonic element suggests a universal definition of the fallen. It also stands in contrast to the Orthodox and national imagery of many of the other monuments.

The memorial white stone obelisk at the south side of the park sporting the double-headed eagle is emblematic of the syncretic nature of post-Soviet monumentalization; its four sides are made out of cinderblocks with a worn surface that looks as if it has been scraped and patched multiple times. There is a design on each of the four sides. Engraved into the stone on one side of the obelisk in a medieval-style script are the words "To those who fell for the freedom and independence of the motherland." Striking in its inclusivity, this tribute is equally applicable to virtually all of the soldiers who died in the service of either the Russian Empire or the Soviet Union.

The other three sides of the monument revealed a similar inclusivity that could also be read as a certain kind of incoherence. Two of the other three sides of the obelisk display bronze emblems of the St. George cross and the Order of St. George, high tsarist military honors that were abolished after the Russian Revolution. In the center of the four points of the St. George cross is a circle

FIGURE 8.1. *Above.* Chapel of the Transfiguration of the Savior, built in 1998 on the site of Shchusev's Church of the Transfiguration in the Memorial Park Complex of the Heroes of the First World War, Moscow. Photograph taken by author.

FIGURE 8.2. *Facing page.* Obelisk displaying bronze emblem of the St. George cross in the Memorial Park Complex of the Heroes of the First World War, Moscow. Photograph taken by author.

within which St. George slays the dragon; the rhombus-shaped star has sun-like rays projecting from the center and a central circle emblazoned with the words "For Service and Bravery." The last side of the obelisk contains an image of a five-pointed Soviet star with a hammer and sickle nestled between the two bottom points of the star. In a circle superimposed upon the star's center stands a Red Army soldier holding a rifle, surrounded by the words "Proletariat of the World Unite" and "U.S.S.R." The pillar valorized the sacrifices of both tsarist and Soviet soldiers, though the Soviet symbol was outnumbered by tsarist symbols two to one. The multivocal nature of the monument reveals the tensions between retaining Soviet traditions and defining the new heroes of the Russian Federation (figure 8.2).

The cemetery first became a point of friction between Soviet authorities and an incipient civil society in 1987 during glasnost' when Erofei Mikhailovich Levshov, an Orthodox Christian veteran of World War II, brought a cross from Solovki to be blessed by Patriarch Pimen and placed it in the center of the park. The contention that the park should be treated as "sacred ground" was one of the many battles fought by Soviet citizens who wanted to restore the Orthodox Church to a central place in their lives. In 1989, city authorities gave permission for monuments to be placed in the park. The cemetery was one of the hundreds of thousands of sites of civic activity that eroded the legitimacy of the Soviet state.

Those engaged in memorializing the park in the late 1980s and early 1990s sought to restore not only Orthodoxy, but also tsarist military traditions. They wanted to honor those Russians who fought valiantly for Russia during World War I, but against the Bolsheviks during the Civil War. Along with city and church officials, Cossacks as well as White émigrés returning from abroad participated in the planning of the memorial. The White Guard and monarchist military history clubs Volunteer Corps and Cadet Corps played an active role in ceremonies. The cemetery was an important symbolic location for this work, because young cadets from several military schools who died defending Moscow against the Bolsheviks as well as victims of the Red Terror during the Civil War were in fact buried in the cemetery. The cemetery became a site of anti-Soviet resistance.

But from the beginning, there were other civic organizations that contested this interpretation of the cemetery site. A newly active Soviet and then Russian civil society rejected this new definition of the memorial as a White Civil War site. In the late 1980s, when the idea of restoring the cemetery was proposed, the local veterans' association of Moscow's Sokol region (where the cemetery was located) opposed the plan. These World War II veterans by and large identified with the Soviet cause, and while they were tolerant of the Orthodox revival, they rejected the notion of celebrating the actions of counter-revolutionaries.

By the middle of the 1990s, the cemetery's proponents had gained the upper hand. They were able to fend off a plan to construct a commercial center on the site, and they successfully articulated the notion that the new chapel was to be dedicated in honor of "Reconciliation of Nations," and in memory of "all the defenders of Russia, who fell during wars for the Fatherland."[27] The memorial thus included the anti-Bolsheviks as well as all the war dead. On November 8, 1998, a few days before the eightieth anniversary of the Armistice ending World War I, the new Orthodox chapel, named Reconciliation of Nations, was dedicated "in memory of the victims of the two World Wars and the Civil War." For the dedication, the members of the Volunteer Corps club dressed in World War I officer and soldier uniforms and organized a religious procession from the Church of All Saints to the new chapel, followed by the presentation of military honors. An Orthodox priest then conducted funeral prayers.[28]

Yet in contemporary Russian society, there still remain sharp differences about the identities of the "victims" of these wars—about whether the White side in the Civil War, or the members of Vlasov's Russian Liberation Army, can legitimately be called "defenders of Russia" for fighting against the Bolsheviks in the Civil War or against the Soviet Union in World War II. This conflict can be seen in the many acts of vandalism that have occurred at the memorial site. The complex was vandalized in both 2000 and 2001. On March 28, 2001, vandals defiled the chapel by breaking the windowpanes and doors and throwing garbage and filth inside the church. They threw hydrochloric acid on the obelisk on the south side of the park; they tore the bronze image of the St. George cross off the obelisk and disfigured it. They also destroyed a stone cross by knocking it from its pedestal, and they tore the plaque describing the memorial zone off of the wall.[29] This attack targeted both the religious and monarchist aspects of the monument in particular. By tearing the St. George cross off the obelisk with the inscription "To those who fell for the freedom and independence of the motherland," they sought to redefine the honored fallen as only those who fought for the Soviet Union.

Between 1998 and 2004, the site was the repeated target of radical (presumably left-wing) antifascists. Because of its close association with a second memorial site within the walls of the nearby All Saints Monastery, which honors both White generals and members of the Russian Liberation Army, the Volunteer Corps has had to send its "cadets" to the memorial to guard against vandalism each year on the anniversary of the 1941 German invasion of the Soviet Union.[30] While the activists who fought for the restoration of the World War I cemetery were quite successful in imbuing the memorial site with their Orthodox vision, in recent years they have been less successful in defending their notion that the memorial should include anti-Soviet forces.

Recent commemorations at the Memorial Park have deemphasized the notion that the burial ground contains victims from both sides of World War I and the Civil War. The park is now called the Memorial Park Complex of the Heroes of the First World War, instead of Reconciliation of Nations, and the chapel is known only as the Chapel of the Transfiguration; the park's dedication to those who defended the Soviet Union is evident in the World War II monument and in the Soviet crest on the memorial obelisk. While Orthodoxy is still a critical aspect of the Memorial Park, the major pieces added for the opening in 2004 were classical and secular in nature, emphasizing the civic and national importance of memory alongside its religious significance. The current iteration of the park represents a compromise between right and left, a middle ground that prevents the introduction of specifics.

The debate about whose memory should be honored and whose memory destroyed continues in present-day Russia, as the city plans to develop a World War I museum at the site of the Leningrad Movie Theater to mark the centennial of the war in 2014. And, in the midst of these struggles, the gravestone of S. A. Shlikhter sits silently in the park, representing the persistence of memory in spite of both the rise and the fall of the Soviet Union, and still conveying the message, "How good is life. How good it is to live."

NOTES

1. Introduction

1. For a discussion of other memorial cemeteries created during World War I see M. Katagoshchina, "Pamiatniki velikoi voiny," *Voennaia byl'*, no. 3/132 (July–September 1993): 14–17.

2. N. Zubova and M. Katagoshchina, "Pamiatnik velikoi voiny," *Moskovskii zhurnal* 5 (1994): 52.

3. *Moskovskoe gorodskoe bratskoe kladbishche: Opyt biograficheskogo slovaria*, M. M. Alabin, A. C. Dibrov, V. D. Sudravskii, eds. (Moscow: Gos. publichnaia istoricheskaia biblioteka, 1992), 10, 45, 48, 52–53.

4. GIM OPI (Gosudarstvennyi istoricheskii muzei, Otdel pismennykh istochnikov) f. 402 "Staraia Moskva," ed. khr. 351, ll. 1–2.

5. GIM OPI f. 402, ed. khr. 351, ll. 13–14. The last recorded meeting of the society's cemetery commission was May 12, 1929.

6. Anna Nikol'skaia, "Geroi pervoi mirovoi," *Vecherniaia Moskva* no. 109 (23907) June 17, 2004, http://www.vmdaily.ru/old/23907/23907nikolskaya_a1.html (accessed April 12, 2006). See also http://www.vmdaily.ru/article.php?aid=976.

7. "Po kom zvonit kolokol," *Kul'tura* no. 42 (7153), November 12–18, 1998, online at http://www.kulturaportal.ru/tree_new/cultpaper/article.jsp?number=45&crubric_id=1000317&rubric_id=201&pub_id=152046 (accessed September 24, 2007).

8. Aleksandr Isakov, "Moskva skvoz' linzu ob'ektiva: Vsekhsviatskoe," December 5, 2007, at www.mosnovostroy.ru/news/lenta/4576.html (accessed July 15, 2008).

9. "Kak khorosha zhizn'/Kak khorosho zhit'."

10. Aleksandr Khokhlov, "Zapozdaloe pokaianie," *Novye izvestiia*, July 30, 2004, http://www.newizv.ru/news/?id_news=8713&date=2004-07-30 (accessed July 14, 2008).

11. "Dolg pamiati i chesti," (po materialam saita NF "Pamiat' chesti," www.white-guard.ru), *Russkii Dom* no. 10, 2004. At http://russdom.ru/2004/200410i/20041013.html (accessed July 14, 2008).

12. Nadynrom,"Po sledam bratskogo kladbishche na Sokol," http://www.liveinternet.ru/community/2281209/post107636155/ (accessed March 17, 2010).

13. Zubova et al., "Pamiatnik velikoi voiny," 55.

14. The fate of this cemetery mirrored that of many others. See I. A. Kremleva,

"Pokhoronno-pominal'nye obychai i obriady," in V. A. Aleksandrov, I. V. Vlasova, N. S. Polishchuk, eds., *Russkie* (Moscow: Nauka, 2003), 531.

15. These debates are carried out in Modris Eksteins, *Rites of Spring: The Great War and the Birth of the Modern Age* (Boston: Houghton Mifflin, 1989); Paul Fussell, *The Great War in Modern Memory* (New York: Oxford University Press, 1975); Samuel Hynes, *A War Imagined: The First World War and English Culture* (London: Bodley Head, 1990); George L. Mosse, *Fallen Soldiers: Reshaping the Memory of the World Wars* (New York: Oxford University Press, 1990); Antoine Prost, *Republican Identities in War and Peace: Representations of France in the Nineteenth and Twentieth Centuries,* Jay Winter and Helen McPhail, trans. (Oxford: Berg, 2002); Jay Winter, *Sites of Memory, Sites of Mourning: The Great War in European Cultural History* (Cambridge: Cambridge University Press, 1995), among others. Orlovsky's comment is recorded in "Velikaia voina i rossiiskaia pamiat'," in N. N. Smirnov, ed., *Rossiia i Pervaia Mirovaia Voina: Materialy mezhdunarodnogo nauchnogo kollokviuma* (St. Petersburg: D. Bulanin, 1999), 56. For a concise description of the historiographical debates see Jay Winter and Antoine Prost, *The Great War in History: Debates and Controversies, 1914 to the Present* (Cambridge: Cambridge University Press, 2005), 182–184.

16. Aaron J. Cohen, "Oh, That! Myth, Memory, and the First World War in the Russian Emigration and the Soviet Union," *Slavic Review* 62, no. 1 (Spring 2003): 79–80.

17. Peter Gatrell, *Russia's First World War: A Social and Economic History* (Harlow, UK: Pearson, 2005), 260; Cohen, "Oh, That! Myth, Memory, and the First World War," 80; Richard Stites, "Days and Nights in Wartime Russia: Cultural Life, 1914–1917," in Aviel Roshwald and Richard Stites, eds., *European Culture in the Great War: The Arts, Entertainment, and Propaganda, 1914–1918* (Cambridge: Cambridge University Press, 1999), 8.

18. This calls to mind the argument made by Ernest Renan in the nineteenth century that the systematic forgetting of the violent origins of the nation is essential to the construction of national identity. Ernest Renan, "What is a Nation?" in Geoff Eley and Ronald Grigor Suny, eds., *Becoming National: A Reader* (New York: Oxford University Press, 1996), 45. On commemoration and forgetting, see Catherine Merridale, *Night of Stone: Death and Memory in Twentieth-Century Russia* (New York: Viking, 2000); Frederick C. Corney, *Telling October: Memory and the Making of the Bolshevik Revolution* (Ithaca, N.Y.: Cornell University Press, 2004); Cohen, "Oh, That! Myth, Memory, and the First World War."

19. Merridale, *Night of Stone,* 99. The Lenin cult is a notable exception to this trend in the interwar period. Nina Tumarkin has argued that the ceremonies after Lenin's death "functioned as a cathartic experience for a population that had suffered almost a decade of war, revolution, civil war, famine, and epidemics." Only in the post-Stalin period did the dead reemerge as the focus of World War II commemoration. See Nina Tumarkin, *Lenin Lives: The Lenin Cult in Soviet Russia* (Cambridge, Mass.: Harvard University Press, 1983), 142; idem, *The Living and the Dead: The Rise and Fall of the Cult of World War II in Russia* (New York: Basic Books, 1994).

20. Demographers estimate a total population loss of 30 million between 1914 and 1923, with 11 million lost during World War I. William G. Rosenberg, "Problems of Social Welfare and Everyday Life," in Edward Acton, Vladimir Iu. Cherniaev, and William G. Rosenberg, eds., *Critical Companion to the Russian Revolution, 1914–1921* (Bloomington: Indiana University Press, 1997), 633.

21. These figures come from the meticulous work of Peter Gatrell in *Russia's First World War,* 246.

22. Mosse, *Fallen Soldiers,* 7.

23. In her study of the legacy of the siege of Leningrad, Lisa Kirschenbaum has defined the myth of the siege as a fusion of the state's "memory created from above" and "everyday" memory that helped Leningraders to turn "the 'muddle of images' that people collected in wartime into meaningful and memorable narratives." Lisa A. Kirschenbaum, *The Legacy of the Siege of Leningrad, 1941–1945: Myth, Memories, and Monuments* (New York: Cambridge University Press, 2006), 5–6.

24. This is Alon Confino's useful definition of memory. He also views memory "as the relationship between the whole and its component parts, seeing society as a global entity—social, symbolic, political—where different memories interact." Alon Confino, "Collective Memory and Cultural History: Problems of Method," *American Historical Review* 102, no. 5 (December 1997): 1391.

25. Winter prefers the term "remembrance" because it reminds us of the role of human agency. Jay Winter, *Remembering War: The Great War Between Memory and History in the Twentieth Century* (New Haven, Conn.: Yale University Press, 2006), 3–4.

26. Here I heed Jay Winter's admonition that it is necessary "to insist on specifying agency, on answering who remembers, when, where, and how." Winter, *Remembering War,* 3.

27. Peter Holquist, *Making War, Forging Revolution: Russia's Continuum of Crisis, 1914–1921* (Cambridge, Mass.: Harvard University Press, 2002), 2.

28. An important comparative source for Eastern Europe is Nancy M. Wingfield and Maria Bucur, eds., *Gender and War in Twentieth-Century Eastern Europe* (Bloomington: Indiana University Press, 2006).

29. See Holquist, *Making War, Forging Revolution,* for an in-depth discussion of these continuities.

30. Cohen, "Oh, That! Myth, Memory, and the First World War," 83.

31. Herman Ermolaev, *Censorship in Soviet Literature, 1917–1991* (Lanham, Md.: Rowman and Littlefield, 1997), 5.

32. Leonid Iuniverg, "Abram Vishniak i ego izdatel'stvo 'Gelikon.'" In *Russkoe evreistvo v zarubezh'e: Stat'i, publikatsii, memuary i esse* I (VI) (Jerusalem: M. Parkhomovskii, 1998), 165, 175.

33. The Soviet reception of *All Quiet on the Western Front* is examined in detail in chapter 6.

34. Vladimir Lidin, *Mogila neizvestnogo soldata* (Moscow: Federatsiia, 1932), 16.

35. The first Russian-language editions of *Lik voiny* had been published in Sofia in 1920 and Berlin in 1923. The Berlin edition by the publisher Gelikon was sold in the Soviet Union. The Moscow 1924 and 1928 editions contained substantial editorial deletions that will be discussed in chapter 7.

36. Anatol Goldberg, *Ilya Ehrenburg: Revolutionary, Novelist, Poet, War Correspondent, Propagandist* (New York: Viking, 1984), 30–32. Erenburg also wrote dispatches for *Utro Rossii.* See Helen Segall, "Il'ia Gregor'evich Erenburg," in Christine Rydel, ed., *Dictionary of Literary Biography,* vol. 272: *Russian Prose Writers Between the Wars* (Detroit: The Gale Group, 2003), 60.

37. Winter, *Remembering War,* 238–239.

38. Il'ia Erenburg, *Lik voiny* (Moscow: Zemlia i fabrika, 1928), 14–16.

39. Il'ia Erenburg, *Neobychainye pokhozhdeniia Khulio Khurenito i ego uchenikov . . .* (Moscow: Gosizdat, 1927), 262.

40. Il'ia Erenburg, *Lik voiny* (Berlin: Gelikon, 1923), 7–8.

41. See Kenneth D. Slepyan, "The Limits of Mobilisation: Party, State and the 1927 Civil Defence Campaign," *Europe-Asia Studies* 45, no. 5 (1993): 851–852, for an alternative definition of mobilization.

42. Mark von Hagen, *Soldiers in the Proletarian Dictatorship: The Red Army and the Soviet Socialist State, 1917–1930* (Ithaca, N.Y.: Cornell University Press, 1990), 335.

43. See Jay Winter's formulation of this question in *Remembering War,* and also his "Introduction: Henri Barbusse and the Birth of the Moral Witness," in Henri Barbusse, *Under Fire,* Robin Buss, trans. (New York: Penguin, 2003), vii.

44. For a discussion of Komsomol Civil War memoirs that address many of the same ambiguous themes as World War I memory, see Sean Christopher Guillory, "We Shall Refashion Life on Earth! The Political Culture of the Young Communist League, 1918–1928" (Ph.D. diss., UCLA, 2009), 44–87.

45. Nicholas S. Timasheff, *The Great Retreat: The Growth and Decline of Communism in Russia* (New York: E. P. Dutton, 1946). See also David L. Hoffmann, "Was there a 'Great Retreat' from Soviet Socialism? Stalinist Culture Reconsidered," *Kritika* 5, no. 4 (Fall 2004): 651–674.

46. See, for example, Vladimir Papernyi, *Kul'tura "Dva"* (Ann Arbor, Mich.: Ardis, 1985).

47. Rather than dividing the 1920s from the 1930s, Katerina Clark has identified a "series of shifts in the cultural models" that occurred in the interwar period "involving both continuity and change." Katerina Clark, *Petersburg: Crucible of Cultural Revolution* (Cambridge, Mass.: Harvard University Press, 1995, ix–x.

48. Thick description is a methodology borrowed, of course, from Clifford Geertz. See his "Deep Play: Notes on the Balinese Cockfight," in *Interpretation of Cultures: Selected Essays* (New York: Basic Books, 1973).

49. M. Gromov, *Za krestami* (Moscow-Leningrad: Gosizdat, 1927).

50. See Winter, *Sites of Memory;* Annette Becker, *War and Faith: The Religious Imagination in France, 1914–1930* (Oxford: Berg, 1998).

51. On the biological basis of sex roles, see Frances Lee Bernstein, *The Dictatorship of Sex: Lifestyle Advice for the Soviet Masses* (DeKalb, Ill.: Northern Illinois University Press, 2007). On masculinity and state violence, see Joshua A. Sanborn, *Drafting the Russian Nation: Military Conscription, Total War, and Mass Politics, 1905–1925* (Dekalb, Ill.: Northern Illinois University Press, 2003).

52. Catriona Kelly, "The Education of the Will: Advice Literature, *Zakal,* and Manliness in Early Twentieth-Century Russia," in Barbara Clements, Rebecca Friedman, and Dan Healy, eds., *Russian Masculinities* (Houndmills, UK: Palgrave, 2002), 144.

53. See Stéphane Audoin-Rouzeau and Annette Becker, *14–18: Understanding the Great War* (New York: Hill and Wang, 2003).

54. See David Brandenberger, *National Bolshevism: Stalinist Mass Culture and the Formation of Modern Russian National Identity, 1931–1956* (Cambridge, Mass.: Harvard University Press, 2002).

55. Ermolaev, *Censorship in Soviet Literature,* 6–7.

56. Ermolaev, *Censorship in Soviet Literature,* and A. B. Murphy, V. P. Butt, H. Ermolaev, eds., *Sholokhov's Tikhii Don: A Commentary in 2 Volumes,* Birmingham Slavonic Monographs No. 27 (Birmingham, UK: Department of Russian Language and Literature, The University of Birmingham, 1997).

57. A decade later Soviet critics were still singing Barbusse's praises. See O. V. Tsekhnovitser, *Literatura i mirovaia voina: 1914–1918* (Gos. izd-vo khudozh. lit-ry, 1938), 329–331.

58. Michael Klimenko, *Ehrenburg: An Attempt at a Literary Portrait* (New York: Peter Lang, 1990), 27.

59. Erenburg, *Lik voiny* (1928), 10.

60. Erenburg, *Lik voiny* (1923), 133–144.

61. Erenburg, *Lik voiny* (1923), 72.

62. In Katerina Clark's metaphor, Soviet culture is an ecosystem undergoing periodic cataclysms, and she focuses on the periods of consolidation between the cataclysms when "the surviving flora and fauna responded to new conditions; some came to dominate, others not, and others again generated mutations." Clark, *Petersburg,* ix–x.

63. Mikh. Lemke, *250 dnei v tsarskoi stavke: 25 cent. 1915–2 iiulia 1916* (Petersburg: Gos. izd-vo, 1920), 360–442, quotation on p. 371.

64. Charles A. Ruud, *Russian Entrepreneur: Publisher Ivan Sytin of Moscow, 1851–1934* (Montreal: McGill-Queen's University Press, 1990), 149; Hubertus Jahn, *Patriotic Culture in Russia during World War I* (Ithaca, N.Y.: Cornell University Press, 1995), 62–63; Ben Hellman, *Poets of Hope and Despair: The Russian Symbolists in War and Revolution (1914–1918)* (Helsinki: Institute for Russian and East European Studies, 1995), 191.

65. Historian John T. Smith argues that in 1915–1916 Russia's censorship was actually weaker than that of France and England due to "inadequate personnel, the attitude of the military and inherent weaknesses in the censorship laws." John T. Smith, "Russian Military Censorship During the First World War," *Revolutionary Russia* 14, no. 1 (June 2001): 92.

66. Ruud, *Russian Entrepreneur,* 150.

67. Here I am referring to the titles of Il'ia Erenburg's *Lik voiny* and Lev Naumovich Voitolovskii's *Po sledam voiny: Pokhodnye zapiski, 1914–1917,* I (Leningrad: Gos. izd-vo, 1925).

68. For an in-depth discussion of the cult of the Civil War, see Justus Grant Hartzok, "Children of Chapaev: The Russian Civil War Cult and the Creation of Soviet Identity, 1918–1941" (Ph.D. diss., University of Iowa, 2009).

69. Exceptions include Norman Stone, *The Eastern Front, 1914–1917* (New York: Charles Scribner's Sons, 1975); Allan K. Wildman, *The End of the Russian Imperial Army,* vols. I and II (Princeton, N.J.: Princeton University Press, 1980, 1987); W. Bruce Lincoln, *Passage Through Armageddon: The Russians in War and Revolution, 1914–1918* (New York: Simon and Schuster, 1986); David R. Jones, "The Imperial Army in World War I," in Frederick W. Kagan and Robin Higham, eds., *The Military History of Tsarist Russia* (New York: Palgrave, 2002); Mark L. von Hagen, *War in a European Borderland: Occupations and Occupation Plans in Galicia and Ukraine, 1914–1918* (Seattle: University of Washington Press, 2007).

70. Gatrell, *Russia's First World War,* 20.

71. Timothy C. Dowling, *The Brusilov Offensive* (Bloomington: Indiana University Press, 2008), xv, 163.

72. Nicholas V. Riasanovsky and Mark D. Steinberg, *A History of Russia,* 7th ed. (New York: Oxford University Press, 2005), 392.

73. Gatrell, *Russia's First World War,* 30–31; also idem, *A Whole Empire Walking: Refugees in Russia during World War I* (Bloomington: Indiana University Press, 2005), 30–32.

74. Dowling, *The Brusilov Offensive,* 176; O. N. Chaadaeva, "Soldatskie pis'ma v gody mirovoi voiny (1915–1917 gg.)," *Krasnyi arkhiv* 65–66 (1934): 119.

75. Jones, "The Imperial Army in World War I," 245.

76. Gatrell, *Russia's First World War*, 264–275; Holquist, *Making War, Forging Revolution*, 283–286.

77. Jahn, *Patriotic Culture in Russia during World War I*, 62–63. Ben Hellman argues that "by the autumn of 1915 many literary journals appeared almost without any further fictional war material." Hellman, *Poets of Hope and Despair*, 195.

78. Jahn, *Patriotic Culture in Russia during World War I*, 165, 173; Leonid Heretz, *Russia on the Eve of Modernity: Popular Religion and Traditional Culture Under the Last Tsars* (Cambridge: Cambridge University Press, 2008), 204–206; Benedict Anderson, *Imagined Communities: Reflections on the Origins and Spread of Nationalism*, rev. ed. (London: Verso, 1991).

79. Stephen M. Norris, *A War of Images: Russian Popular Prints, Wartime Culture, and National Identity, 1812–1945* (DeKalb, Ill.: Northern Illinois University Press, 2006), 161–163.

80. Melissa K. Stockdale, "United in Gratitude: Honoring Soldiers and Defining the Nation in Russia's Great War," *Kritika: Explorations in Russian and Eurasian History 7*, no. 3 (Summer 2006): 484–485.

81. Norris, *A War of Images*, 161–163. See Boris I. Kolonitskii, *Tragicheskaia erotika: Obrazy imperatorskoi sem'i v gody Pervoi Mirovoi Voiny* (Moscow: Novoe literaturnoe obozrenie, 2010), for a discussion of representations of the Romanovs in the war years.

82. Stockdale, "United in Gratitude," 485.

83. Josh Sanborn, "The Mobilization of 1914 and the Question of the Russian Nation," *Slavic Review 59*, no. 2 (Summer 2000): 289.

84. Stockdale, "United in Gratitude," 485.

2. Spirituality, the Supernatural, and the Memory of World War I

1. Paul Fussell, *The Great War in Modern Memory*, 131–132.

2. On soldiers and spirituality, see Becker, *War and Faith*.

3. Jay Winter, *Sites of Memory*, 67. While Winter takes issue with Fussell's emphasis on the "modern," both scholars emphasize the mythic dimensions of war experience.

4. See Becker, *War and Faith*, esp. 116–139; Winter, *Sites of Memory*, 7.

5. See Scott Kenworthy, "The Mobilization of Piety: Monasticism and the Great War in Russia, 1914–1916," *Jahrbücher für Geschichte Osteuropas* 52 (2004): 388–401. For a Soviet-era exposé of the role of the clergy in promoting war see Boris Kandidov, *Religiia v tsarskoi armii* (Moscow: Bezbozhnik, 1928).

6. Chaadaeva, "Soldatskie pis'ma v gody mirovoi voiny," 142–143. Gromov, *Za krestami*, 11. Heretz, *Russia on the Eve of Modernity*, 197.

7. V. I. Lenin, "The Defeat of One's Own Government in the Imperialist War," *Sotsial-Demokrat* no. 43 (July 26, 1915) in Lenin, *Collected Works*, vol. 21 (Moscow: Progress Publishers, 1964), 280.

8. For a detailed discussion of prerevolutionary and Soviet rituals of death, see Catherine Merridale, *Night of Stone;* Thomas Reed Trice, "The 'Body Politic': Russian Funerals and the Politics of Representation, 1841–1921" (Ph.D. diss., University of Illinois, 1998).

9. Kandidov, *Religiia v tsarskoi armii*, 27, 54.

10. See Jeanmarie Rouhier-Willoughby, *Village Values: Negotiating Identity, Gender, and Resistance in Urban Russian Life-Cycle Rituals* (Bloomington, Ind.: Slavica, 2008), 60–61.

11. Mosse, *Fallen Soldiers,* 36.

12. Merridale, *Night of Stone,* 86. I use the words "the fallen" here consciously with Fussell's notion of "high diction" in mind. See Fussell, *The Great War and Modern Memory,* 21–22.

13. See Irene Masing-Delic, *Abolishing Death: A Salvation Myth of Russian Twentieth-Century Literature* (Stanford, Calif.: Stanford University Press, 1992).

14. For a discussion of Soviet antireligious campaigns, see Daniel Peris, *Storming the Heavens: The Soviet League of the Militant Godless* (Ithaca, N.Y.: Cornell University Press, 1998).

15. Mark D. Steinberg, *Proletarian Imagination: Self, Modernity, and the Sacred in Russia, 1910–1925* (Ithaca, N.Y.: Cornell University Press, 2002).

16. Steinberg, *Proletarian Imagination,* see esp. 224–232; 248–256.

17. *Niva,* no. 52 (December 24, 1916): 862.

18. Norris, *A War of Images,* 146; for an early example of the theme of holy war see Daniel Rowland, "*Blessed is the Host of the Heavenly Tsar:* An Icon from the Dormition Cathedral of the Moscow Kremlin," in Valerie A. Kivelson and Joan Neuberger, eds., *Picturing Russia: Explorations in Visual Culture* (New Haven, Conn.: Yale University Press, 2008), 33–37.

19. Quoted in Stephen M. Norris, "Russian Images of War: The Lubok and Wartime Culture, 1812–1917" (Ph.D. diss., University of Virginia, 2002), 391.

20. The idea of exploit or *podvig* itself implied both chivalry and spiritual struggle. "Novye podvigi Koz'my Kriuchkova i ego tovarishchei," in *Pamiatka otdel'nykh podvigov russkikh voinov velikoi voiny 1914–1915 gg.,* II (Vyborg: Vestnika Vyborgskoi Krepostnoi Artillerii, 1915), 43.

21. Norris, *A War of Images,* 149; Heretz, *Russia on the Eve of Modernity,* 210–213. M. G. Ravitskii, "Voina Rossii s Germanii i Avstrii" (Kiev: I. T. Gubanov, 1914), Hoover Institution Library and Archives, Stanford University, Poster Collection RU-SU 307; "Podvig russkago pravoslavnago sviashchennika," (Moscow: I. D. Sytin, 1915), Hoover Institution RU-SU 343; "Smert' sviashchenika geroia," in *Nashi chudo-bogatyri v voine 1914 goda* (Petrograd: Gramotnost', 1915), 108–109; GIM OPI, f. 137 Voenno-istoricheskii muzei, d. 1189, l. 12.

22. Norris, *A War of Images,* 151. Ben Hellman, "Pervaia mirovaia voina v lubochnoi literature," in N. N. Smirnov, ed., *Rossiia i Pervaia Mirovaia Voina: Materialy mezhdunarodnogo nauchnogo kollokviuma* (St. Petersburg: D. Bulanin, 1999), 309; "Iavlenie Bozhei Materi na nebe pered srazheniem russkomu voinstvu, prednamenovavshee o pobede. . . ." (Moscow: M. N. Sharapov, n.d.), Hoover Institution, RU-SU 359.

23. "Iavliusia emy sam," (Moscow: A.D. Sazonov, n.d.), Hoover Institution RU-SU 315, quoted in Norris, *A War of Images,* 151. For a similar scene on a French postcard, see Becker, *War and Faith,* 46. Allen J. Frantzen argues that this relationship between the heroic "knight" and Christ, who are linked by their sacrifice, has roots in traditions of chivalry. Allen J. Frantzen, *Bloody Good: Chivalry, Sacrifice, and the Great War* (Chicago: University of Chicago Press, 2004), 3–6.

24. Merridale, *Night of Stone,* 98.

25. S. V. Puchkov, *Moskovskoe gorodskoe bratskoe kladbishche* (Moscow: Gorodskaia tipografiia, 1915), 4.

26. Stockdale, "United in Gratitude," 468.

27. See Richard Wortman, *Scenarios of Power: Myth and Ceremony in Russian Monarchy,* vol. 2 (Princeton, N.J.: Princeton University Press, 2000), 244–256.

28. Zubova et al., "Pamiatnik velikoi voiny," 52; Dariia Pavlova, "Vsekhsviatskoe: Pamiati pogibshikh v I Mirovoi voine," http://www.pravaya.ru/side/14/4419 (accessed July 8, 2010).

29. O. Voronova, *Shadr* (Moscow: Molodaia gvardiia [Zhizn' zamechatelnykh liudei], 1969), 48.

30. Voronova, *Shadr,* illustrations after 32; I. D. Shadr, "Pamiatnik miromy stradaniiu," *Tvorchestvo* no. 5 (1918): 21–24.

31. Maria Carlson, "Fashionable Occultism: Spiritualism, Theosophy, Freemasonry, and Hermeticism in Fin-de-Siècle Russia," in Bernice Glazer Rosenthal, ed., *The Occult in Russian and Soviet Culture* (Ithaca, N.Y.: Cornell University Press, 1997), 135–152; Hellman, "Pervaia mirovaia voina v lubochnoi literature," 310. On omens, see also Heretz, *Russia on the Eve of Modernity,* 206–210.

32. For an in-depth discussion of the occult during World War I, see Julia Mannherz, "Popular Occultism in Late Imperial Russia" (Ph.D. diss., Cambridge University, 2005), 201–226.

33. M. Domanskii, "Vstrecha," *Niva* no. 2 (1916): 35.

34. Ibid., 36.

35. Folk beliefs also emphasized the importance of the grave as a new home and as a locus of communication with the dead. See O. A. Sedakova, *Poetika obriada: Pogrebal'naia obriadnost' vostochnykh i iuzhnykh slavian* (Moscow: Indrik, 2004), 76; Rouhier-Willoughby, *Village Values,* 198–199.

36. Domanskii, "Vstrecha," 37–38. Often the illustrations on the pages of *Niva* had no relation to the written text. This discussion of the decomposition of an officer's body was juxtaposed to pictures of the tsar, his heir, and his advisors at army headquarters.

37. A similar scene of a widow disinterring her husband's decomposed body can be found in Kirill Levin's *Zapiski iz plena* (Moscow: Federatsiia, 1931), 90–91.

38. Domanskii, "Vstrecha," 38.

39. See, for example, Boris Pasternak's *Doctor Zhivago.* (New York: Pantheon Books, 1958).

40. Kandidov, *Religiia v tsarskoi armii,* 49.

41. A. Maksimov, E. Medvedev, Sh. Iusupov, eds., *Tsarskaia armiia v period mirovoi voiny i Fevral'skoi revoliutsii: Sbornik* (Kazan: Tatizdat, 1932), 3–5.

42. Maksimov et al., *Tsarskaia armiia,* 16–19.

43. Maksimov et al., *Tsarskaia armiia,* 18. The beginning of the letter rhymes: "Zhivu, ne tuzhu, Tsariu belomu sluzhu . . ."

44. Maksimov et al., *Tsarskaia armiia,* 186.

45. Chaadaeva, "Soldatskie pis'ma v gody mirovoi voiny," 142–143.

46. The first two editions of *Khulio Khurenito* were published in Berlin by Gelikon and imported into the Soviet Union; after Nikolai Bukharin interceded for his schoolmate Erenburg, the Soviet State Publishing House put out the third edition in 1927. Joshua Rubenstein, *Tangled Loyalties: The Life and Times of Ilya Ehrenburg* (New York: Basic Books, 1996), 71, 80.

47. Erenburg, *Neobychainye pokhozhdeniia Khulio Khurenito,* 104. Trans. based on Ilya Ehrenburg, *Julio Jurenito,* Anna Bostock and Yvonne Kapp, trans. (Philadelphia, Penn: Dufour Editions, 1963), 123–124.

48. Erenburg, *Lik voiny* (1928), 43.

49. Erenburg, *Lik voiny* (1928), 76. Khulio Khurenito's African disciple Aisha also

wears a "gri-gri" to protect himself from bullets. Erenburg, *Neobychainye pokhozhdeniia Khulio Khurenito,* 123.

50. Mikhail Sholokhov, *Quiet Flows the Don,* Robert Daglish, trans., Brian Murphy, ed. (New York, Carroll and Graf 1996), 223. Because of Daglish and Murphy's excellent textological work, it can be argued that this text is closer to Sholokhov's original intentions than any available Russian version. See Barry P. Scherr and Richard Sheldon, "Westward Flows the Don: The Translation and the Text," *Slavic and East European Journal* 42, no. 1 (Spring 1998): 119.

51. Sholokhov, *Quiet Flows the Don,* 224–225.

52. Ibid., 225. Soldiers may have carried native soil with them to ensure that they would rest in native soil if they were killed. I am grateful to Jeanmarie Rouhier-Willoughby for this suggestion.

53. Levin, *Zapiski iz plena,* 36. This work was first published in 1928. It appeared in at least five different editions between 1928 and 1936. Here I am using the 1931 version, with a circulation of 100,000 copies. Shvandin's name may be related to a Yiddish slang term for penis (Schwanz).

54. Ibid., 37.

55. Ibid.

56. Leonid Sobolev, *Kapital'nyi remont* (Leningrad: Gos. izd-vo khudozh. lit-ry, 1933), 70; trans. based on Leonid Soboleff, *Romanoff,* Alfred Fremantle, trans. (New York: Longmans, Green and Co., 1935; Westport, Conn.: Hyperion Press, 1975), 70.

57. Kandidov, *Religiia v tsarskoi armii,* 55.

58. Esfir Shub, *Padenie dinastii Romanovykh (The Fall of the Romanov Dynasty),* Sovkino, 1927; Kino International, 1991; Corney, *Telling October,* 184–185; I am indebted to Erika Wolf of the University of Otago, New Zealand, for recommending this film.

59. Erenburg, *Lik voiny* (1928), 78.

60. Maksimov, et al., *Tsarskaia armiia,* 187.

61. Sof'ia Fedorchenko, *Narod na voine: Frontovyia zapisi* (Kiev: Tip. Vserossiiskago Zemskago Soiuza Komiteta Iugo-Zap. Fronta, 1917), 3. Later editions include Sof'ia Fedorchenko, *Narod na voine* (Moscow: Novaia Moskva, 1923); Sof'ia Fedorchenko, *Narod na voine* (Moscow-Leningrad: Zemlia i fabrika, 1925). See chapter 6 for a discussion of the Fedorchenko controversy. Fedorchenko believed she was capturing the truth about the war, although her vignettes were not word for word transcriptions of soldiers' tales.

62. See Linda. J. Ivanits, *Russian Folk Belief* (Armonk, N.Y.: M. E. Sharpe, 1989), 64–82, for a discussion of nature spirits.

63. Fedorchenko, *Narod na voine* (1925), 26–27.

64. Ibid., 14.

65. Fedorchenko, *Narod na voine* (1917), 59–60; (1923), 39.

66. Heretz, *Russia on the Eve of Modernity,* 214.

67. Alexandra Smith, "Aleksei Nikolaevich Tolstoi," in Christine Rydel, ed., *Dictionary of Literary Biography,* vol. 272: *Russian Prose Writers Between the War* (Detroit: Gale Group, 2003), 436.

68. In other words, he was not worried about following all religious prescriptions.

69. Tolstoi's trilogy of novels has variously been translated into English as *Road To Calvary, Darkness and Dawn,* or *Ordeal.* The first and second parts of the trilogy were first published in the Soviet Union in 1929–1930, and the third part in 1942. Aleksei Tolstoi, *Khozhdenie po mukam* I (Moscow: Sovetskaia literatura, 1934), 230–231. My translations

are based on Alexei Tolstoy, *Road to Calvary,* vol. 1, Edith Bone, trans. (New York: Alfred A. Knopf, 1946), 196–197. See Heretz, *Russia on the Eve of Modernity,* 199, for a similarly apocalyptic approach to the war recorded among the Ural Cossacks.

70. Tolstoi, *Khozhdenie po mukam* I, 230–231; Tolstoy, *Road to Calvary,* 196–197.

71. In Ivan's words, there are echoes of Tolstoian pacifism and nonviolence.

72. This scene is analyzed in Winter, *Sites of Memory,* 15.

73. Winter, *Sites of Memory,* 15; Mosse, *Fallen Soldiers,* 78–79.

74. Steinberg, *Proletarian Imagination,* 239–240.

75. Ibid., 266–268.

76. Trice, "The 'Body Politic,'" 34, 274; one popular revolutionary song, "Boldly We Go into Battle" ("Smelo my v boi poidem"), proclaimed, for example, "Eternal memory to the fallen heroes; Eternal glory to those who live"; lyrics at http://www.marxists.org/history/ussr/sounds/lyrics/smelo-my.htm (accessed July 9, 2010). See also Robert A. Rothstein, "The Quiet Rehabilitation of the Brick-Factory: Early Soviet Popular Music and its Critics," *Slavic Review* 39, no. 3 (September 1980): 379.

77. For an extended discussion of the organization of this funeral, see Trice, "The 'Body Politic,'" 279–292.

78. *Pravda,* March 23, 1917, quoted in Merridale, *Night of Stone,* 85–86.

79. Merridale, *Night of Stone,* 95; Trice, "The 'Body Politic,'" 287.

80. Trice, "The 'Body Politic,'" 291.

81. Melissa K. Stockdale, "'My Death for the Motherland is Happiness': Women, Patriotism, and Soldiering in Russia's Great War, 1914–1917," *American Historical Review,* vol. 109, no. 1 (February 2004), 77.

82. Trice, "The 'Body Politic,'" 291. Trice quotes N[ikolai] G. Shebuev, "O chem krichat mertvye!" *Peterburgskii listok,* March 23, 1917.

83. Trice, "The 'Body Politic,'" 285.

84. *Sotsial-Democrat,* November 10, 1917, quoted in Corney, *Telling October,* 42.

85. Trice, "The 'Body Politic,'" 316–317; Merridale, *Night of Stone,* 136–137; Zubova et al., "Pamiatnik velikoi voiny," 55; Kremleva, "Pokhoronno-pominal'nye obychai i obriady," 531.

86. Orlovsky, "Velikaia voina i rossiiskaia pamiat'," 55.

87. Quoted in Tumarkin, *Lenin Lives,* 19; see also Masing-Delic, *Abolishing Death,* 76–104, for an extended discussion of Fedorov's ideas.

88. Tumarkin, *Lenin Lives,* 182.

89. Steinberg, *Proletarian Imagination,* 276.

90. Quoted in Tumarkin, *Lenin Lives,* 198–199.

91. The victims of war were more likely to wander the earth than the other dead; in Russian folk belief, those who died violent or untimely deaths had more difficulty making the transition into the other world. Rouhier-Willoughby, *Village Values,* 192–193; Sedakova, *Poetika obriada,* 39–40.

92. Tolstoi, *Khozhdenie po mukam* I, 200; Tolstoy, *Road to Calvary,* 170.

93. Tolstoi, *Khozhdenie po mukam* II (Moscow: Sovetskaia Literatura, 1934), 12; Tolstoy, *Road to Calvary,* 258. This scene may have been inspired by Fedorchenko's work; see Fedorchenko, *Narod na voine* (1917), 59–60.

94. *Pravda,* May 30, 1920.

95. Iu. V. Sokolov, *Krasnaia zvezda ili krest? Zhizn' i sud'ba generala Brusilova* (Moscow: Rossiia molodaia, 1994), 149–150.

96. Trice, "The 'Body Politic,'" 63.

97. GARF (Gosudarstvennyi arkhiv Rossiiskoi Federatsii) f. 5972. Personal collection of Aleksei Alekseevich Brusilov and Nadezhda Vladimirovna Brusilova, op. 3, d. 21a, l. 199.

98. *Pravda,* March 20, 1926.

99. GARF, f. 5972, op. 3, d. 21a, ll. 199; 197.

100. Many of the details of the funeral were reported in a clipping from a Russian émigré newspaper. This clipping can be found in GARF, f. 5972, op. 1, d. 12, l. 48.

101. *Nasha zhizn',* March 20, 1926. Clipping found in GARF, f. 5972, op. 1, d. 12, l. 42.

102. GARF, f. 5972, op. 1, d. 12, l. 48.

103. Sokolov, *Krasnaia zvezda ili krest?* 154.

104. GARF, f. 5972, op. 1, d. 12, l. 48.

105. GARF, f. 5972, op. 1, d. 12, l. 48.

106. GARF, f. 5972, op. 3, d. 21a, l. 209.

107. GARF, f. 5972, op. 3, d. 21a, l. 215. In the revolutionary funeral in Mars Field in 1917, each burial was accompanied by a cannon salvo. Trice, "The 'Body Politic,'" 286.

108. GARF, f. 5972, op. 3, d. 21a, l. 215. These details differ slightly from Orlando Figes's description of the funeral. He cites f. 5972, op. 1, d. 219, ll. 197–215. Orlando Figes, *A People's Tragedy: The Russian Revolution, 1891–1924* (New York: Penguin Books, 1996), 818.

109. Roger R. Reese, *Red Commanders: A Social History of the Soviet Army Officer Corps, 1918–1991* (Lawrence: University Press of Kansas, 2005), 81; Bakhmeteff Archive, Columbia University, Aleksei A. and Nadezhda V. Brusilov Collection, Box 1.

110. Sokolov, *Krasnaia zvezda ili krest?* 157.

111. A. A. Brusilov, *Moi vospominaniia* (Moscow-Leningrad: Gosizdat, 1929), 11. The abridged English translation, A. A. Brusilov, *A Soldier's Notebook, 1914–1918* (London: Macmillan, 1930), omitted the material discussed here and began Brusilov's narrative with the outbreak of the war.

112. Brusilov, *Moi vospominaniia,* 9.

113. Ibid., 35.

114. Ibid., 31. In his discussion of spiritualism, Brusilov also fervently defended E. P. Blavatskaia and believed that her writings illuminated a spiritual pathway that made life easier and brighter. He attacked Sergei Witte's depiction of her in the third volume of Witte's memoirs, 32–33.

115. GARF, f. 5972, op. 3, d. 21a, l. 24.

116. Figes, *A People's Tragedy,* 697.

117. Brusilov, *Moi vospominaniia,* 35, 37.

118. Fedorchenko, *Narod na voine* (1925), 34.

119. Rouhier-Willoughby, *Village Values,* 55; Sholokhov, *Quiet Flows the Don,* 284–285.

120. Sholokhov, *Quiet Flows the Don,* 285.

121. Ibid., 287.

122. Aleksandr Fadeev, *Razgrom,* in *Sobranie sochinenii,* tom 1 (Moscow, 1959), 145–146; trans. from A. Fadeyev, *The Nineteen,* R. D. Charques, trans. (International Publishers, 1929; Westport, Conn.: Hyperion Press, 1973), 292–293.

123. Boris Barnet, *Okraina* (released in English as *The Patriots*), Mezhrabpom, 1933; International Historic Films, 1984.

124. See Boris Barnet, "Remarques sur le cinéma comique (1954)," in François Albera and Roland Cosandey, eds., *Boris Barnet: Ecrits, Documents, Etudes, Filmographie* (Locarno: Editions du festival international du film de Locarno, 1985), 48–49.

125. Denise Youngblood points out that both Kolia and the hero from Aleksandr Dovzhenko's *Arsenal* "indubitably die but appear to live on." Denise Youngblood, *Russian War Films: On the Cinema Front 1914–2005* (Lawrence: University of Kansas Press, 2007), 219.

126. F. Mazereel' (Masereel), from the suite "Mertvye, vosstan'te," illustration to "Pervaia Mirovaia Imperialisticheskaia Voina," in O. Iu. Schmidt, ed., *Bol'shaia Sovetskaia Entsiklopediia*, vol. 44 (Moscow: Sovetskaia Entsiklopediia, 1939), after 672.

127. Kate Brown, *A Biography of No Place: From Ethnic Borderland to Soviet Heartland* (Cambridge, Mass.: Harvard University Press, 2004), 59.

128. Brown, *A Biography of No Place,* 60.

3. The Paradoxes of Gender in Soviet War Memory

1. "Geroiskaia bor'ba kazaka Koz'my Kriuchkova s 11 nemtsami" (Odessa: M. S. Kozman, 1914), Hoover Institution, RU-SU 162. For further discussion of Kriuchkov, see Karen Petrone, "Family, Masculinity, and Heroism in Russian Posters of the First World War," in Billie Melman, ed., *Borderlines: Genders and Identities in War and Peace, 1880–1930* (New York: Routledge, 1998), 103–104. Ben Hellman, "Pervaia mirovaia voina v lubochnoi literature." Kriuchkov's fame even crossed European boundaries; artist A. Pearse featured Kriuchkov's exploit on an English postcard (Frantzen, *Bloody Good,* 163).

2. *Geroiskii podvig Donskogo kazaka Kuz'my Firsovicha Kriuchkova* (Moscow: P. B. Beltsov, 1914), trans. as "The Heroic Feat of the Don Cossack Kuzma Firsovich Kriuchkov," in James von Geldern and Louise McReynolds, eds., *Entertaining Tsarist Russia* (Bloomington: Indiana University Press, 1998), 380; "Novye podvigi Koz'my Kriuchkova i ego tovarishchei," 43.

3. S. O. Makarov (1849–1904) was a naval hero of the Russo-Turkish war who was killed in action during the Russo-Japanese war; M. D. Skobelev (1843–1882) was a hero of the conquest of Central Asia and the Russo-Turkish war. See Norris, *A War of Images,* 92–93; 120.

4. Jahn, *Patriotic Culture in Russia during World War I,* 24; "Bogatyrskii boi kazaka Kuz'my Kriuchkova s nemetskimi ulanami" (Petrograd: Sodruzhestvo, n.d.), Hoover Institution, RU-SU 475.

5. Norris, *A War of Images,* 140.

6. Judith Kornblatt argues that the Soviet novels of Sholokhov and Dmitrii Furmanov represent the death of the Cossack myth as these Soviet authors subordinated the Cossack hero to Soviet strictures and transposed Cossack élan onto Bolshevik heroes. Judith Kornblatt, *The Cossack Hero in Russian Literature: A Study in Cultural Mythology* (Madison: University of Wisconsin Press, 1992), 5, 168.

7. Vladimir Littauer, *Russian Hussar: A Story of the Imperial Cavalry, 1911–1920* (Shippensburg, Pa.: White Mane Pub. Co., 1993), 4–5; 116.

8. Audoin-Rouzeau and Becker, *14–18: Understanding the Great War,* 28.

9. Wilfred Owen, "Dulce et Decorum Est," in *The Collected Poems of Wilfred Owen* (New York: New Directions Books, 1963), 55.

10. For analysis of this debate see Michael Roper, "Between Manliness and Masculinity: The 'War Generation' and the Psychology of Fear in Britain, 1914–1950," *Journal of British Studies* 44, no. 2 (April 2005): 343–362.

11. Kelly, "The Education of the Will," 144.

12. Fussell, *The Great War in Modern Memory,* 82–90, quote on 90. Hynes, *A War Imagined,* x–xi; for intimate relationships see Michael Roper, "Slipping out of view: Subjectivity and Emotion in Gender History," *History Workshop Journal* 59 (2005): 63, 67.

13. A. M. Fishgendler, *Soldaty fronta i voprosy voiny i mira* (Petrograd: Kniga, 1917), 9.

14. Skeptics include George L. Mosse, *Fallen Soldiers,* 54, 64–65; Eric J. Leed, *No Man's Land: Combat and Identity in World War I* (Cambridge: Cambridge University Press, 1979), 80–96.

15. Merridale, *Night of Stone,* 39; See also Catherine Merridale, "The Collective Mind: Trauma and Shell-shock in Twentieth-century Russia," *Journal of Contemporary History* 35, no. 1 (2000): 39–55.

16. See Graham Dawson, *Soldier Heroes: British Adventure, Empire, and the Imagining of Masculinities* (London: Routledge, 1994), 3, 24.

17. See George L. Mosse, *The Image of Man: The Creation of Modern Masculinity* (Oxford: Oxford University Press, 1996).

18. V. I. Lenin, "On the National Pride of the Great Russians," *Sotsial-Demokrat,* no. 35 (December 12, 1914), trans. from Lenin, *Collected Works,* vol. 21 (Moscow: Progress Publishers, 1964), 104.

19. Dem'ian Bednyi, "Predislovie," in L. Voitolovskii, *Po sledam voiny* (Leningrad: Gosizdat, 1925), 6.

20. For a discussion of wartime gender roles and issues of power, see Margaret R. Higgonet and Patrice L.-R. Higgonet, "The Double Helix," in Margaret R. Higgonet et al., *Behind the Lines: Gender and the Two World Wars* (New Haven, Conn.: Yale University Press, 1987), 31–50.

21. Laurie S. Stoff, *They Fought for the Motherland: Russia's Women Soldiers in World War I and the Revolution* (Lawrence: University Press of Kansas, 2006), 23–52.

22. Stockdale also speculates that if the Provisional Government had been successful in its prosecution of the war in the summer of 1917, the elevation of women to the status of full and equal citizens might have occurred in the interwar period. Stockdale, "'My Death for the Motherland is Happiness'," 79, 91, 115.

23. Sergei Eisenstein's film *October* focused on the Women's Battalion defending the Winter Palace, although he was criticized for this; see Corney, *Telling October,* 195–196.

24. Orlando Figes and Boris Kolonitskii, *Interpreting the Russian Revolution: The Language and Symbols of 1917* (New Haven, Conn.: Yale University Press, 1999), 17, 93, 171; Boris I. Kolonitskii, "Kerensky," in Edward Acton, Vladimir Iu. Cherniaev, William G. Rosenberg, eds., *Critical Companion to the Russian Revolution* (Bloomington: Indiana University Press, 1997), 148.

25. In general, they also gendered the February Revolution as feminine and the Bolshevik Revolution as masculine. See Choi Chatterjee, *Celebrating Women: Gender, Festival Culture and Bolshevik Ideology, 1910–1939* (Pittsburgh: University of Pittsburgh Press, 2002).

26. See, for example, Mary Louise Roberts, *Civilization Without Sexes: Reconstructing Gender in Postwar France, 1917–1927* (Chicago: University of Chicago Press, 1994).

27. Between 50,000 and 70,000 women served in the Red Army during the Civil War, and some did volunteer for combat roles; see Elizabeth A. Wood, *The Baba and the Comrade: Gender and Politics in Revolutionary Russia* (Bloomington: Indiana University Press, 1997), 56; Sanborn, *Drafting the Russian Nation,* 50, 153–154.

28. Sanborn, *Drafting the Russian Nation,* esp. 163–164. See also Kelly, "The Educa-

tion of the Will," and Karen Petrone, "Masculinity and Heroism in Imperial and Soviet Military-Patriotic Cultures," in Barbara Evans Clements, Rebecca Friedman, and Dan Healey, eds., *Russian Masculinities in History and Culture* (Houndmills, UK: Palgrave, 2002).

29. Eliot Borenstein, *Men Without Women: Masculinity and Revolution in Russian Fiction, 1917–1929* (Durham, N.C.: Duke University Press, 2000), 3. While I find Borenstein's readings of Babel', Olesha, and Platonov compelling, I would argue that one of the most striking things about Civil War literature (as compared to World War I or Stalinist war literature) is the prominent presence of women at the front and on the battlefield in such novels as Fadeev's *The Rout,* Furmanov's *Chapaev,* Ivanov's *Armored Train 14–69,* and Sholokhov's *Quiet Flows the Don.*

30. Borenstein, *Men Without Women,* 4–5.

31. Rebecca Friedman and Dan Healey, "Conclusions," in Clements et al., eds., *Russian Masculinities,* 232.

32. In a recent article arguing for World War I as a break from nineteenth-century norms of masculinity, Michael Roper has cautioned that masculinity studies have too often focused on "publicly circulated codes" of masculinity and not enough on how these codes "relate to the behavior and emotional dispositions of individual men." See Roper, "Between Manliness and Masculinity," 345.

33. Mosse, *The Image of Man,* 114.

34. Wolfgang G. Natter, *Literature at War, 1914–1940: Representing the "Time of Greatness" in Germany* (New Haven, Conn.: Yale University Press, 1999), 71.

35. One must note that Aleksei Tolstoi's interpretation of the war changed dramatically over the next few years. By the early 1920s, he conceived of the war as Russia's "purgatory" and no longer romanticized killing. See his 1923 novel *Khozhdenie po mukam.*

36. Aleksei Tolstoi, "Po Galitsii," in A. S. Miasnikova, A. N. Tikhonova, L. I. Tolstaia, eds., *Polnoe sobranie sochinenii,* tom 3 (Moscow Gos. izd-vo khudozh. lit-ry, 1949), 59.

37. For a discussion of the late nineteenth- and early twentieth-century constructions of soldierly fear by psychiatrists, see Jan Plamper, "Fear: Soldiers and Emotion in Early Twentieth-Century Russian Military Psychology," *Slavic Review* 68, no. 2 (Summer 2009): 259–283.

38. RGVIA (Rossiiskii gosudarstvennyi voennyi-istoricheskii arkhiv) f. 16180 (Komissiia po organizatsii narodnogo voenno-istoricheskogo muzeia voiny 1914–1918gg), op. 1, d. 472, ll. 3 ob, 7; d. 473, ll. 6, 19, 28, 63.

39. RGVIA f. 16180, op. 1, d. 472, l. 34.

40. RGVIA f. 16180, op. 1, d. 473, ll. 40–41.

41. "Bezumstvo khrabrykh," in *Pamiatka otdel'nykh podvigov russkikh voinov velikoi voiny* 1914–1915 gg., I (Vyborg: Vestnika Vyborgskoi Krepostnoi Artillerii, 1915), 84–86.

42. RGVIA f. 2067 (Shtab glavnokomanduiushchago armiami iugo-zapadnago fronta—otdelenie voenno-tsenzurnoe), op. 1, d. 2930, l. 65.

43. Sanborn, *Drafting the Russian Nation,* 30; For a discussion of male camaraderie and drinking culture among the working class, see Laura A. Phillips, *Bolsheviks and the Bottle: Drink and Worker Culture in St. Petersburg, 1900–1929.* (DeKalb, Ill.: Northern Illinois University Press, 2000).

44. Aleksei Tolstoi, "Po Volyni," in *Polnoe sobranie sochinenii,* tom 3, 13.

45. Tolstoi, "Po Galitsii," 63.

46. Thanks to Joshua Sanborn for reminding me of the wider context in which Tolstoi wrote.

47. Nikolai Gumilev, *Zapiski kavalerista*, in G. P. Struve and B. A. Filippova, eds., *Sobranie sochinenii, tom 4* (Washington, D.C.: Victor Kamkin, 1968), 457.

48. Some nations believed that alcohol improved performance; British soldiers were given a ration of rum before they "went over the top."

49. Ia. Okunev, *Na peredovykh pozitsiiakh: Boevyia vpechatleniia* (Petrograd: M. V. Popov, 1915), 45.

50. Ibid., 40, 74.

51. Ibid., 37.

52. Ibid., 75–76.

53. Ernst Jünger, *Storm of Steel: From the Diary of a German Storm-Troop Officer on the Western Front* (New York: Howard Fertig, 1975), 314.

54. Klaus Theweleit, *Male Fantasies,* vol. 1 (Minneapolis: University of Minnesota Press, 1987).

55. Tolstoi, "Po Volyni," 18.

56. Maria Botchkareva, *Yashka: My Life as Peasant, Officer and Exile* (New York: Frederick A. Stokes, 1919), 74.

57. Argus, "Kogda muzhchiny na fronte, vot gde vashe mesto, zhenshchiny!" (Russkoe Obshchestvo Pechatnogo Dela, n.d.), Hoover Institution, RU-SU 407.

58. "Podvig sestry E. P. Korkinoi," (Moscow: I. D. Sytin, no. 86, 1915), Hoover Institution, RU-SU 322.

59. Stoff, *They Fought for the Motherland,* 28–29.

60. "Vysochaishee nagrazhdenie Georgievskim krestom devitsy Tychininoi," in *Nashi chudo-bogatyri v voine 1914 goda* (Petrograd: Gramotnost', 1915), 135–136.

61. Petrone, "Family, Masculinity, and Heroism," 100.

62. "Russkii soldat," (Moscow: I. D. Sytin, no. 57, 1914), Hoover Institution, RU-SU 337.

63. Botchkareva, *Yashka,* 99.

64. Okunev, *Na peredovykh pozitsiiakh,* 83.

65. Lilya Kaganovsky, "How the Soviet Man was (Un) Made," *Slavic Review* 63, no. 3 (2004): 578–579.

66. S. Vinogradov, "Na pomoshch' zhertvam voiny" (1914), in N. I. Baburina, ed., *Rossiia—20. vek: Istoriia strany v plakate; Russia—20th Century: History of the Country in Poster* (Moscow: Panorama Publishing House, 2000), 29.

67. Leonid Pasternak, "Na pomoshch' zhertvam voiny," (Moscow: A. A. Levenson, 1914), Hoover Institution, RU-SU 1066. The poster was sometimes referred to as "The Wounded Soldier."

68. L. O. Pasternak, *Zapisi raznykh let* (Moscow: Sovetskii khudozhnik, 1975), 83–84; trans. based on Stephen White, *The Bolshevik Poster* (New Haven, Conn.: Yale University Press, 1988), 14–15.

69. "Torgovtsy Moskvy—Soldatam-invalidam" (Moscow: A. A. Levenson, August, 1916), Hoover Institution, RU-SU 70.

70. My searches on the Hoover Institution's poster database turned up no images of World War I–era amputees from any other country. See hoohila.stanford.edu/poster/index.php

71. White, *The Bolshevik Poster,* 3.

72. Leonid Pasternak, "Tsena krovi," (Petrograd: Petrogradskii Sovet Rabochikh i Krasnoarmeiskikh Deputatov, 1918), Hoover Institution, RU-SU 2284; White, *The Bolshevik Poster,* 15.

73. Brusilov, *Moi vospominaniia,* 80; trans. from Brusilov, *A Soldier's Notebook,* 31–32.

74. A. L. Voitolovskaia, *Po sledam sud'by moego pokoleniia* (Syktyvkar: Komi Knizh-noe Izdatel'stvo, 1991), 11.

75. Voitolovskii, *Po sledam voiny* I: 68.

76. Ibid., 125.

77. Ibid., 177.

78. Furmanov's *Chapaev* is another notable exception.

79. Herman Ermolaev, *Mikhail Sholokhov and His Art* (Princeton, N.J.: Princeton University Press, 1982), 17; 216–222.

80. Holquist, *Making War, Forging Revolution*, 174–175, 187.

81. See Ermolaev, *Mikhail Sholokhov and His Art*, 264–300. See "Expert analysis confirms authenticity of Sholokhov epic," ITAR TASS, October 25, 1999.

82. Murphy, et al., *Sholokhov's Tikhii Don*, 59.

83. Sholokhov, *Quiet Flows the Don*, 227.

84. Ibid., 242.

85. Ibid., 241–242.

86. Ibid., 243. Ermolaev points out that Kriuchkov actually went back to the front and continued fighting; *Mikhail Sholokhov and His Art*, 218.

87. Dmitrii Moor, "Bogatyrskoe delo Koz'my Kriuchkova" (Moscow: I. D. Sytin, no. 13, 1914), Hoover Institution, RU-SU 134.

88. Remarque, *All Quiet on the Western Front* (New York: Ballantine Books, 1982), 113–114.

89. Mikhail Sholokhov, *Quiet Flows the Don*, 243.

90. An important component of Tolstoi's ideology was, of course, the rejection of violence in any form. See I. Mashbits-Verov, "Tikhii Don," *Novyi Mir*, no. 10 (1928): 234; and for a defense of Sholokhov against these charges see D. Maizel', "O *Tikhom Done* i odnom 'dobrom kritike,'" *Zvezda*, no. 8 (1929): 189–198, cited in RGALI (Rossiiskii gosudarstven-nyi arkhiv literatury i isskustva) f. 631 Soiuz Sovetskikh Pisatelei, op. 16, d. 32, ll. 216, 219.

91. A. Dubovikov, "Mikh. Sholokov. *Tikhii Don*," *Molodaia gvardiia*, August 8, 1928, 206.

92. For a discussion of Tolstoi's influence on European nonviolence see Steven G. Marks, *How Russia Shaped the Modern World: From Art to Anti-Semitism, Ballet to Bolshevism* (Princeton, N.J.: Princeton University Press, 2002), 102–139.

93. Mashbits-Verov, "*Tikhii Don*," 229; RGALI, f. 613 Gosudarstvennoe literaturnoe *izdatel'stvo*, op. 1, d. 704, l. 140; f. 616 Izdatel'stvo Zemlia i fabrika, op. 1, d. 20, l. 167.

94. Books I and II of the novel were an immediate popular success and were reprinted in book form in five large editions of over 100,000 copies each between 1929 and 1931. The novel was also made into a film in 1931. Ermolaev, *Censorship in Soviet Literature*, 86, 97; Ermolaev, *Mikhail Sholokhov and His Art*, 20–21; The film made substantial changes to the novel and did not receive critical acclaim. See the agitational brochure: *Tikhii Don* (Moscow: Soiuzkino, 1931), 8–10.

95. Iu. Lukin, "Vstupitel'naia stat'ia," in Mikh. Sholokhov, *Tikhii Don* (Moscow: Gos. izd-vo khudozh. lit-ry, 1941), v.

96. Harvard Project on the Soviet Social System, Schedule A, Vol. 9, Case 118 (interviewer H.D), 30, http://nrs.harvard.edu/urn-3:FHCL:946680.

97. Mikhail Sholokhov, *Quiet Flows the Don*, 296.

98. Hilton Tims, *Erich Maria Remarque: The Last Romantic* (New York: Carroll and Graff, 2003), 17.

99. Remarque, *All Quiet on the Western Front,* 290.

100. Sholokhov, *Quiet Flows the Don,* 358–359.

101. This character appears, for example, in "Russkii soldat," and "Podvig riadovogo Katsa,"(Grodno: Lapin, n.d.), Hoover Institution, RU-SU 258, as well as in real-life military commendations.

102. Gromov, *Za krestami,* 10–11.

103. For the course of Os'kin's career see Orlando Figes, *A People's Tragedy: The Russian Revolution, 1891–1924* (New York: Penguin Books, 1996), 818.

104. D. Os'kin, *Zapiski Soldata* (Moscow: Federatsiia, 1929), 218.

105. Ibid., 208

106. Ibid., 274.

107. Ibid., 276.

108. L. Averbakh, foreword to Erenburg, *Lik voiny,* 1928, 11.

109. Voitolovskii, *Po sledam voiny* I: 14.

110. Ibid.

111. Ibid., 89.

112. Pireiko's memoirs were published in 1926 as part of a series on the history of the Communist Party. A. Pireiko, *V tylu i na fronte imperialisticheskoi voiny: Vospominaniia riadovogo.* (Leningrad: Priboi, 1926), 26. The manuscript version, A. Pireiko, "Iz zapisnoi knizhki riadovogo soldata epokhi imperialisticheskoi voiny, 1914–1917," is located in RGASPI (Rossiiskii gosudarstvennyi arkhiv sotsial'no-politicheskoi istorii) f. 70 Istpart TsK VKP(b), op. 3, d. 415.

113. Sholokhov, *Quiet Flows the Don,* 342.

114. Leonid Katsov, *Skvoz' plen* (Moscow: Federatsiia, 1930), 6–7 (foreword by Mikhail Kol'tsov).

115. Leonid Katsov, *Skvoz' plen* (Moscow: Mos. t-vo pisatelei, 1934), 21–22. For a sympathetic description of three soldiers who are caught trying to give themselves up to the Austrians and then executed, see Maksimov, et. al., *Tsarskaia armiia,* 199–200.

116. V. Dmitriev, *Dobrovolets: Vospominaniia o voine i plene* (Moscow-Leningrad, Gosizdat, 1929), 18.

117. Ibid., 19.

118. Ibid., 22–23.

119. See chapter 7.

120. Shub, *Padenie dinastii Romanovykh.*

121. Brusilov, *Moi vospominaniia,* 153; trans. from Brusilov, *A Soldier's Notebook,* 190. The status of nurses at the front was also a problem during the Civil War. Isaak Babel' wrote an article in the First Cavalry Army's newspaper *The Red Cavalryman* enjoining soldiers and commanders "to show respect to our nurses. It is high time we started distinguishing between the camp followers who disgrace our army, and the martyr nurses who adorn it." Isaac Babel, *1920 Diary,* ed. Carol J. Avins (New Haven, Conn.: Yale University Press, 1995), 108.

122. This trend toward sexualizing women at the front and diminishing their achievements was even more pronounced after World War II. See Vera Ivanovna Malakhova, "Four Years as a Front-line Physician," in Barbara Alpern Engel and Anastasia Posadskaya-Vanderbeck, eds., *A Revolution of Their Own: Voices of Women in Soviet History* (Boulder, Colo.: Westview Press, 1997), 215.

123. Erenburg, *Lik Voiny* (1928), 101–102.

124. Voitolovskii, *Po sledam voiny* I: 91.

125. Ibid., 92.

126. Os'kin, *Zapiski Soldata,* 316.

127. For example Fedorchenko, *Narod na voine* (1917), 118; (1923), 91; See also chapter 7 of the present work.

128. Jünger, *Storm of Steel,* 39, 173.

129. See Sanborn, *Drafting the Russian Nation,* 166–170, for a perceptive discussion of this process.

130. Sobolev, *Kapital'nyi remont,* 119, 279; trans. from Soboleff, *Romanoff,* 125, 253.

131. Sobolev, *Kapital'nyi remont,* 53.

132. See for example, Os'kin, *Zapiski soldata,* 110, 144, 167, 200–201, 215, 239, 244.

133. Voitolovskii, *Po sledam voiny* I: 43.

134. Ibid., 33.

135. Here I disagree with Brian Murphy's critical assessment of Sholokhov's treatment of strained class relations: "Introduction," in Mikhail Sholokhov, *Quiet Flows the Don,* xxxiv.

136. Sholokhov, *Quiet Flows the Don,* 304, 203.

137. Another text that describes an officer's attempts to establish good relations with his soldiers is A. A. Svechin, *Iskusstvo vozhdeniia polka po opytu voiny 1914–1918 gg.* (Moscow: Gosizdat, 1930; repr. Moscow: Assotsiatsiia voennaia kniga Kuchkovo Pole, 2005).

138. Sholokhov, *Quiet Flows the Don,* 364.

139. Ibid., 364.

140. Remarque, *All Quiet on the Western Front,* 6.

141. Sholokhov, *Quiet Flows the Don,* 365–366.

142. For a discussion of masculinity in a military context, see Sanborn, *Drafting the Russian Nation,* 132–164.

143. Chaadaeva, "Soldatskie pis'ma v gody mirovoi voiny," 126.

144. Ibid., 138.

145. See Merridale, "The Collective Mind"; Cohen, "Oh, That! Myth, Memory, and the First World War."

146. Voitolovskii, *Po sledam voiny* I: 93.

147. Ibid., 94.

148. Wilfred Owen, "Disabled" in *The Collected Poems of Wilfred Owen,* 67–68.

149. Dm. Furmanov, *Dnevnik 1914–1915–1916* (Moscow-Leningrad: Moskovskii rabochii, 1929), 218–219.

150. Ibid., 219–220.

151. A dramatic contrast to Furmanov's attitude can be found in Soviet literature of the immediate postwar years. See Anna Krylova, "'Healers of Wounded Souls': The Crisis of Private Life in Soviet Literature, 1944–1946," *Journal of Modern History* 73, no. 2 (June 2001): 307–331.

152. RGALI f. 2865 Personal Collection of Kirill Levin, op. 1, d. 65, ll. 31, 38–39. Clippings from *Viatskaia pravda,* July 13, 1930; review by M. Pasynok in *Na literaturnom postu* no. 13–14, 1930.

153. Levin, *Zapiski iz plena,* 104–105.

154. See discussion of M. Domanskii, "Vstrecha," in chapter 2 of the present work.

155. Levin, *Zapiski iz plena,* 90–91.

156. The authors of the study noted that Russian officers they visited in captivity were "obviously psychologically unbalanced." N. Zhdanov, and A. Svechin, *Russkie voennoplennye v mirovoi voine 1914–1918 gg,* I–III (Moscow: Vseroglavshtaba, 1920), 42.

157. Levin, *Zapiski iz plena,* 124.

158. Merridale, *Night of Stone,* 40–41.

159. Laura L. Phillips, "Gendered Dis/ability: Perspectives from the Treatment of Psychiatric Casualties in Russia's Early Twentieth-Century Wars." *Social History of Medicine* 20, no. 2 (2007): 339; Irina Sirotkina, *Diagnosing Literary Genius: A Cultural History of Psychiatry in Russia, 1880–1930* (Baltimore, Md.: The Johns Hopkins University Press, 2002), 153–154.

160. Levin, *Zapiski iz plena,* 126.

161. Ibid., 134.

162. On French organizations, for example, see Antoine Prost, *In the Wake of War: 'Les Anciens Combattants' and French Society 1914–1939* (Oxford: Berg, 1992).

163. Quoted in Brandenberger, *National Bolshevism,* 20.

164. Vincent Alan Comerchero, "From Outcasts to Allies: Red Army Veterans and the Soviet State from the Introduction of the New Economic Policy through the First Five Year Plan" (Ph.D. diss., Indiana University, 1997), 203; Emily E. Pyle, "Village Social Relations and the Reception of Soldiers' Family Aid Policies in Russia, 1912–1921" (Ph.D. diss., University of Chicago, 1997), 310–311.

165. According to a report cited by Catherine Merridale, more than 1.5 million World War I veterans alone were mentally disabled by trauma and "were too ill to work, or even to return to family life." Merridale, *Night of Stone,* 117. Comerchero cites conflicting figures of disabled veterans from the records of the All-Russian Central Executive Committee's aid committee for Red Army war invalids, and families of war dead (Vserokompom). One secret report sent to the Central Committee indicated that there were 1,000,000 needy disabled veterans, of whom 300,000 were cripples. The head of Vserokompom's medical department, on the other hand, estimated that there were nearly 2,000,000 war disabled. Comerchero, "From Outcasts to Allies," 212–214.

166. A. F. Zavgorodnii, *Deiatel'nost gosudarstvennykh organov i obshchestvenno-politicheskikh organizatsii po sotsial'noi zashchite voennosluzashchikh Krasnoi Armii i ikh semei v mezhvoennykh period (1921–iiun' 1941 gg.)* (St. Petersburg: Nestor, 2001), 134, 131.

167. Comerchero, "From Outcasts to Allies," 212–213.

168. Vladimir Lidin, "Mogila neizvestnogo soldata," *Novyi Mir* no. 3 (1931): 20. "The Return of the Soldier," by the African American writer Claude McKay, published in Russian in 1925, offers a variation on the theme of the unappreciated veteran. In McKay's story, a black veteran is nearly lynched because the white townspeople do not want him wearing the uniform of a U.S. soldier and acting like a "white gentleman." Klod Mak Kci (Claude McKay), "Vozvrashchenie soldata," in *Sudom lincha,* A. M. and P. Okhrimenko, trans. (Moscow: Ogonek, 1925), 44. I am grateful to Pearl James for this reference.

169. Quoted in Nathalie Babel, "Plays," in Isaac Babel, *The Complete Works of Isaac Babel,* Nathalie Babel, ed., Peter Constantine, trans. (New York: W. W. Norton, 2002), 754.

170. Isaac Babel, *Maria,* in *The Complete Works of Isaac Babel,* 801–802.

171. Babel, *Maria,* 803.

172. Comerchero, "From Outcasts to Allies," 212–216.

173. Babel, *Maria,* 835–836.

4. Violence, Morality, and the Conscience of the Warrior

1. Audoin-Rouzeau and Becker, *14–18: Understanding the Great War,* 44, 41–42.

2. This last question is inspired by Sanborn, *Drafting the Russian Nation,* 199–200, and Mosse, *The Image of Man.*

3. George Mosse claimed that it was not simply the high status of the military in the interwar period that encouraged "ruthlessness" but also "an attitude of mind derived from the war and the acceptance of war itself." He saw "the vocabulary of political battle" and "the desire to utterly destroy the political enemy," as a continuation of the violence of the First World War. Mosse, *Fallen Soldiers,* 7, 159–160, 181.

4. Quoted in Eksteins, *Rites of Spring,* 316; see also Theweleit, *Male Fantasies,* vol. 1, esp. chapter 1.

5. Winter, *Sites of Memory,* 8.

6. V. I. Lenin, "The Position and Tasks of the Socialist International," *Sotsial-Demokrat* no. 33 (November 1, 1914), trans. from Lenin, *Collected Works,* vol. 21: 40.

7. Holquist, *Making War, Forging Revolution,* 203.

8. On these debates see Sheila Fitzpatrick, "The Civil War as a Formative Experience," in Abbott Gleason, Peter Kenez, and Richard Stites, eds., *Bolshevik Culture: Experiment and Order in the Russian Revolution* (Bloomington: Indiana University Press, 1989), 57–76; Stefan Plaggenborg, "Gewalt und Militanz in Sowjetrußland 1917–1930," *Jahrbücher für Geschichte Osteuropas* 44, no. 3 (1996): 409–430.

9. Sanborn, *Drafting the Russian Nation,* 199–200.

10. Following John Horne and Alan Kramer, "atrocities" in quotation marks refers to the idea of atrocities used to construct the meaning of war rather than to actually documented atrocities. *German Atrocities, 1914: A History of Denial* (New Haven, Conn.: Yale University Press, 2001), 4.

11. Youngblood, *Russian War Films,* 23–24.

12. Furmanov, *Dnevnik,* 185.

13. Khristofor Shukhmin, *Podvig unter-ofitsera A. H. Volkova, kavalera piati Georgievskikh krestov* (Moscow, 1915), xiv, quoted in Hellman, "Pervaia mirovaia voina v lubochnoi literature," 307.

14. Tolstoi, "Po Galitsii," 51, 56.

15. Jünger, *Storm of Steel,* p. 52.

16. Paul F. Robinson, "'Always with Honour': The Code of the White Russian Officers," *Canadian Slavonic Papers/Revue canadienne des slavistes* 41, no. 2 (June 1999): 126.

17. Jünger, *Storm of Steel,* 27, 263.

18. *Geroiskii podvig,* in von Geldern and McReynolds, *Entertaining Tsarist Russia,* 380.

19. Stites, "Days and Nights in Wartime Russia," 26.

20. Gumilev, *Zapiski kavalerista,* 464.

21. Ibid., 522.

22. Soviet critic Orest Tsekhnovitser called Gumilev "the most glaring representative of Russian imperialist poetry" who "zealously served the cause of war," and emphasized Gumilev's admiration for d'Annunzio. Tsekhnovitser, *Literatura i mirovaia voina,* 103, 101.

23. Gumilev, *Zapiski kavalerista,* 473–474.

24. Tolstoi, "Po Volyni," 19.

25. Okunev, *Na peredovykh pozitsiiakh,* 111.

26. GIM OPI f. 137, d. 1189, l. 24. "Evropeiskaia voina: stychka nashego avangarda s avstriitsami pod L'vovom" (Moscow: Litografiia M. A. Streltsova).

27. Tolstoi, "Po Volyni," 32.

28. Aleksei Tolstoi, "Na Kavkaze," in *Polnoe sobranie sochinenii,* tom 3, 122.

29. Ibid., 127.

30. For a discussion of boyhood adventure literature and mobilization for war, see Graham Dawson, *Soldier Heroes: British Adventure, Empire, and the Imagining of Masculinities* (London: Routledge, 1994).

31. Khristofor Shukhmin, *Diuzhina nemtsev na odnom kazatskom shtyke* (Moscow, 1915), quoted in Hellman, "Pervaia mirovaia voina v lubochnoi literature," 307.

32. Ruud, *Russian Entrepreneur,* 151.

33. I am grateful to Mark Steinberg, who first raised the possibility of this interpretation in conversation.

34. Sanborn, *Drafting the Russian Nation,* 183, 185.

35. Heather J. Coleman, *Russian Baptists and Spiritual Revolution, 1905–1929* (Bloomington: Indiana University Press, 2005), 180–185; quote on 184. William Edgerton, *Memoirs of Peasant Tolstoyans in Soviet Russia* (Bloomington: Indiana University Press, 1993), xiii–xiv.

36. Coleman, *Russian Baptists,* 180.

37. Quoted in Coleman, *Russian Baptists,* 186.

38. Edgerton, *Memoirs of Peasant Tolstoyans,* xiii; Sanborn, *Drafting the Russian Nation,* 193.

39. Coleman, *Russian Baptists,* 188–192.

40. Yakov Dragunovsky, "From the papers of Yakov Dragunovsky," in Edgerton, *Memoirs of Peasant Tolstoyans,* 188–190. For a discussion of Dragunovskii's brutalization see Sanborn, *Drafting the Russian Nation,* 170–171.

41. Dragunovsky, "From the papers of Yakov Dragunovsky," 191–193.

42. Ibid., 194–195.

43. Ibid., 201–202.

44. Sergei Grigor'ev, *Kazarma* (Moscow-Leningrad: Zemlia i fabrika, 1926), 45–46.

45. Furmanov, *Dnevnik,* 178.

46. Erenburg, *Khulio Khurenito,* 162; trans. from Ehrenburg, *Julio Jurenito,* 190–191.

47. Erenburg, *Khulio Khurenito,* 137; trans. from Ehrenburg, *Julio Jurenito,* 160–161.

48. Erenburg, *Khulio Khurenito,* 174; trans. from Ehrenburg, *Julio Jurenito,* 205.

49. These ideas will be considered in chapter 7. See Voitolovskii, *Po sledam voiny* I: 68.

50. Fedorchenko, *Narod na voine* (1925), 19–20; trans. from Sof'ia Fedorchenko, *Ivan Speaks,* Thomas Whittemore trans. (Boston: Houghton Mifflin, 1919), online at http://books .google.com/books?id=n_UKAAAAIAAJ, 11–12.

51. Lel' is a mythological figure, analogous to Eros. The author (not the censors) was responsible for the changes in the second expanded edition. Michel Niqueux, "Kratkaia khronika zhizni i tvorchestva Sergeia Klychkova," in Sergei Klychkov, *Sakharnyi nemets* (Paris: YMCA Press, 1982; repr. of Moscow: Federatsiia, 1929), 414, 416, 419.

52. Klychkov, *Sakharnyi nemets,* 370.

53. Ibid., 378–379.

54. Ibid., 381.

55. Ibid., 385.

56. Ibid., 400.

57. V. P. Pravdukhin, "*Sakharnyi nemets*," *Krasnaia nov'* no. 2 (1925): 285–286, in Klychkov, *Sakharnyi nemets*, 445.

58. A. A. Divil'kovskii, "*Sakharnyi nemets*," *Novyi mir* no. 7 (1926): 135–137, in Klychkov, *Sakharnyi nemets*, 448.

59. Murphy et al., *Sholokhov's Tikhii Don*, 59.

60. Sholokhov, *Quiet Flows the Don*, 221.

61. Ibid.

62. Ibid., 222.

63. Mikhail Sholokhov, *Tikhii Don, Kniga Pervaia*, Graviury A. Kravchenko (Moscow: Gos. izd-vo khudozh. lit-ry, 1934).

64. Sholokhov, *Tikhii Don* (1941), 113.

65. RGALI, f. 616, op. 1, d. 20, l. 169.

66. Sholokhov, *Quiet Flows the Don*, 244.

67. Ibid., 247.

68. Ibid., 263.

69. Ibid.

70. Ibid., 361.

71. D. Maznin, "Kakova ideia—*Tikhogo Dona*," *RAPP* 1 (Moscow, 1931), 167, quoted in Richard Hallett, "Soviet Criticism of *Tikhiy Don* 1928–1940," *Slavonic and East European Review* 46, no. 106 (January 1968): 66.

72. Sholokhov, *Quiet Flows the Don*, 810; Ermolaev, *Sholokov and His Art*, 96–97.

73. Remarque, *All Quiet on the Western Front*, 216.

74. Ibid., 223.

75. Ibid., 226.

76. Sholokhov, *Quiet Flows the Don*, 247.

77. Ibid., 271.

78. RGALI f. 616, op. 1, d. 19, ll. 6, 8 ob.; 613, op. 1, d. 559, l. 25.

79. Sholokhov, *Quiet Flows the Don*, 567–568.

80. Mikh. Sholokhov, *Tikhii Don, Kniga vtoraia* (Moscow: Gos. izd-vo khudozh. lit-ry, 1933), 337.

81. Murphy et al., *Sholokhov's Tikhii Don*, 130; Sholokhov, *Quiet Flows the Don*, 570.

82. See chapter 7 of the present work.

83. See Semen Rozenfel'd, *Gibel'* (Berlin: Petropolis, 1931) 67–69; Tat'iana Dubinskaia, *V okopakh* (Moscow: Federatsiia, 1930), 74–75.

84. Fedorchenko, *Narod na voine* (1925), 25; see also 61, 62.

85. Dubinskaia, *V okopakh*, 99–103, quote on 102; idem, *Pulemetchitsa: Iz dnevnika mirovoi voiny* (Moscow: Sovetskii pisatel', 1936) 82–85; idem, *Soldaty: Povest'* (Moscow: Sovetskii pisatel', 1939), 54–56.

86. See Sanborn, *Drafting the Russian Nation*, 170–172.

87. Furmanov, *Dnevnik*, 185.

88. Ibid., 186.

89. See Eric Weitz, *A Century of Genocide: Utopias of Race and Nation* (Princeton, N.J.: Princeton University Press, 2005) for a discussion of this theme.

90. Furmanov, *Dnevnik*, 283.

91. Ibid., 284.

92. Ibid., 284–85.

93. This work was first published in Moscow in 1918 before the author's emigration. Fedor Stepun (N. Lugin), *Iz pisem praporshchika-artillerista* (Moscow: Zadruga, 1918; repr. Tomsk: Vodolei, 2000), 20–21.

94. Voitolovskii, *Po sledam voiny* I: 29.

95. Fedorchenko, *Narod na voine* (1917), 42; (1925), 41.

96. Eric Lohr, *Nationalizing the Russian Empire: The Campaign Against Enemy Aliens During World War I* (Cambridge, Mass.: Harvard University Press, 2003), 147.

97. Tagirov, an important figure in the Bashkir Autonomous Republic, was a victim of the purges. A.Tagirov, *Soldaty*, B. Kh. Cherniak and V. Ia. Tarsis, trans. (from Bashkir) (Moscow: Gos. izd-vo khudozh. lit-ry, 1934), 42.

98. Sholokhov, *Quiet Flows the Don,* 206–207.

99. Voitolovskii, *Po sledam voiny* I, 36.

100. On the Russian occupations of Galicia and the Austro-Hungarian occupation of Russian Ukraine, see von Hagen, *War In a European Borderland.* A. A. Svechin told of how he gained authority among his peasant soldiers by not following orders to burn peasant huts that were sheltering women and children near their trenches. Svechin, *Iskusstvo vozhdeniia polka,* 52–53.

101. Lohr, *Nationalizing the Russian Empire,* 144, 138.

102. Gatrell, *A Whole Empire Walking,* 15–26, quotes on 16, 18.

103. Fedorchenko, *Narod na voine* (1925), 17–18; trans. based on Fedorchenko, *Ivan Speaks,* 19–20.

104. Stepun, *Iz pisem praporshchika-artillerista,* 20–21.

105. Fedorchenko, *Narod na voine* (1917), 46; (1923), 28; (1925), 39.

106. Ibid. (all three editions).

107. Fedorchenko, *Narod na voine* (1925), 31–32.

108. Ibid., 30–31.

109. Gatrell, *A Whole Empire Walking,* 3.

110. Pireiko, *V tylu i na fronte,* 26.

111. Sholokhov, *Quiet Flows the Don,* 267–268.

112. See for example Fedorchenko, *Narod na voine* (1917), 46; (1923), 28; RGALI f. 1611 Personal Collection of Sof'ia Fedorchenko, op. 1, d. 129, ll. 14–15. See chapter 7 for a discussion of the 1920s censorship and chapter 8 for a discussion of 1956.

113. For a description of Civil War–era pogroms see Figes, *A People's Tragedy,* 677–679.

114. Isaac Babel, "Murderers Who Have Yet to Be Clubbed to Death," *Red Cavalryman,* September 17, 1920, in *The Complete Works of Isaac Babel,* 372.

115. Fyodor Vasilievich Gladkov, *Cement,* A. S. Arthur and C. Ashleigh, trans. (Evanston, Ill.: Northwestern University Press, 1980), 165–168.

116. Babel, *1920 Diary,* 41.

117. Isaac Babel, "My First Goose," in *The Complete Works of Isaac Babel,* 232; originally in *Konarmiia* (Moscow: OGIZ, 1926).

118. Borenstein, *Men without Women,* 58.

119. Babel, "My First Goose," 233.

120. Isaac Babel, "Salt," in *The Complete Works of Isaac Babel,* 275; originally in *Konarmiia.*

121. See Christopher Browning, *Ordinary Men: Reserve Police Battalion 101 and the Final Solution in Poland* (New York: HarperCollins, 1998).

5. World War I and the Definition of Russianness

1. Mosse, *Fallen Soldiers*, 7.

2. See Jeffrey Verhey's analysis of the German case in *The Spirit of 1914: Militarism, Myth and Mobilization in Germany* (Cambridge: Cambridge University Press, 2000).

3. Jahn, *Patriotic Culture in Russia during World War I*, 173; Brandenberger, *National Bolshevism*, 11, 2.

4. S. A. Smith, "Citizenship and the Russian Nation During World War I," *Slavic Review* 59, no. 2 (Summer 2000): 320.

5. Norris, *A War of Images*, 161–163; Stockdale, "United in Gratitude," 484; Sanborn, "The Mobilization of 1914," 289.

6. Aleksei Tolstoi, "Otechestvo," in *Polnoe sobranie sochinenii*, tom 3: 9.

7. Tolstoi, "Po Volyni," 32.

8. Gumilev, *Zapiski kavalerista*, 499.

9. See Jahn, *Patriotic Culture in Russia during World War I*.

10. One oppositional letter, for example, read: "I don't find it necessary to die here on the battlefield because of the idiots of all Russia." RGVIA f. 2067, op. 1, d. 2937, ll. 2, 28.

11. RGVIA f. 2067, op. 1, d. 2931, l. 188.

12. RGVIA f. 2067, op. 1, d. 2937, l. 25.

13. RGVIA f. 2067, op. 1, d. 2937, ll. 2, 5–5 ob. Technically, the censors categorized this letter under the rubric not of "mood" but of "characteristics of the officers."

14. RGVIA f. 2067, op. 1, d. 2937, l. 3 ob.

15. Mosse, *Fallen Soldiers*, 15–33; Verhey, *The Spirit of 1914*, 98–102; Samuel Hynes, *A War Imagined*, 27–28.

16. Gatrell, *Russia's First World War*, 17–18.

17. Sanborn, "The Mobilization of 1914," 272–275, quote on 275.

18. Il'ia Feinberg, *1914-i: Dokumental'nyi pamflet*, S. Telingater, artist (Moscow: MTP, 1934), i–ii.

19. Feinberg, *1914-i*, 87–88.

20. Maksimov et al., *Tsarskaia armiia*, 16.

21. O. N. Chaadaeva's works on the revolutionary movement appeared throughout the 1920s and 1930s, and in 1952 Moscow University published a collection of her lectures on the October Revolution in book form; O. Chaadaeva, *Podgotovka Velikoi Oktiabr'skoi Sotsialisticheskoi Revoliutsii: Lektsii, prochitannye na Istoricheskom Fakul'tete Moskovskogo Universiteta* (Moscow: Izd-vo Moskovskogo Universiteta, 1952).

22. O. Chaadaeva, *Armiia nakanune Fevral'skoi revoliutsii* (Moscow-Leningrad: Gos. sotsial'no-ekonomicheskoe izd-vo, 1935), 40–41.

23. The editors of the volume were archivists in the Tatar Republic with the Slavic surnames of Maksimov, and Medvedev and the Tatar surname Iusupov. Maksimov et al., *Tsarskaia armiia*, 184–185.

24. Maksimov et al., *Tsarskaia armiia*, 21.

25. V. I. Lenin, "The Collapse of the Second International," *Kommunist* no. 1–2 (1915); trans. from Lenin, *Collected Works*, vol. 21, 253–254.

26. Sholokhov, *Quiet Flows the Don*, 330. Bunchuk is quoting "The Position and Tasks of the Socialist International," *Sotsial-Demokrat* no. 33 (November 1, 1914.) Murphy et al. point out that after 1929, censors shortened the quotations from Lenin to omit his call "to raise the banner of Civil War." The remaining passages nonetheless made clear that the

proletariat was supposed to rally around "the proletarian banner of civil war." Sholokhov, *Tikhii Don* (1941), 169; Murphy et al., *Sholokhov's* Tikhii Don, 71.

27. Sholokhov, *Quiet Flows the Don,* 280, 331–332. See D. Os'kin, *Zapiski soldata,* 11–12, for an account of a real soldier who justified enlisting in the tsarist army because he was going to be called up anyway.

28. Sholokhov, *Quiet Flows the Don,* 335–336.

29. Chaadaeva, *Armiia nakanune Fevral'skoi revoliutsii,* 37.

30. Pireiko, *V tylu i na fronte,* 12.

31. Ibid., 11.

32. Ibid., 13.

33. See chapter 7 of the present work.

34. Fedorchenko, *Narod na voine* (1925), 10.

35. The introduction to Vavilov's memoir quotes this very passage from Fedorchenko's text; Artem (Artur) Vavilov, *Zapiski soldata Vavilova,* reworked by Boris Brodianskii (Moscow-Leningrad: Gosizdat, 1927), 4, 13.

36. Vavilov, *Zapiski soldata Vavilova,* 12.

37. Dmitriev, *Dobrovolets,* 3. His published justification of his pro-tsarist actions during World War I was similar to narratives in unpublished applications to join the Communist Party. See Igal Halfin, *Terror in my Soul: Communist Autobiographies on Trial* (Cambridge, Mass.: Harvard University Press, 2003), 46.

38. Chaadaeva, *Armiia nakanune Fevral'skoi revoliutsii,* 40; Maksimov et al., *Tsarskaia armiia,* 17, 18.

39. See Karen Petrone, "Motherland Calling: National Symbols and the Mobilization for War," in Valerie Kivelson and Joan Neuberger, eds., *Picturing Russia: Explorations in Visual Culture* (New Haven, Conn.: Yale University Press, 2008), 196–200.

40. Maksimov et al., *Tsarskaia armiia,* 17–20.

41. Chaadaeva, *Armiia nakanune Fevral'skoi revoliutsii,* 40.

42. Dmitriev, *Dobrovolets,* 6–7.

43. Ibid., 20.

44. Ibid., 20, 68.

45. See esp. Fussell, *The Great War in Modern Memory,* and in response, Winter, *Sites of Memory.* The wartime diary of Dmitrii Furmanov also retells war experiences through a non-Bolshevik lens, and has much in common with Western European accounts. Furmanov, *Dnevnik 1914–1915–1916.*

46. Feinberg, *1914-i,* 7.

47. A. Kollontai, *Otryvki iz dnevnika 1914 g.* (Leningrad: Gosizdat, 1924); Barbara Evans Clements, *Bolshevik Feminist: The Life of Alexandra Kollontai* (Bloomington: Indiana University Press, 1979), 84. For another work shaped by the author's internment in Germany, see Konstantin Fedin, *Goroda i gody: Roman* (Leningrad: Gosizdat, 1924).

48. Kollontai, *Otryvki iz dnevnika 1914 g.,* 34, 7.

49. Ibid., 27.

50. Ibid., 57.

51. Ibid., 79.

52. Ibid., 43.

53. Clements, *Bolshevik Feminist,* 87, 91.

54. "Na bor'bu s imperialisticheskimi voinami" (Moscow-Leningrad: Gosizdat, 1929), Hoover Institution, RU-SU 1908.

55. Feinberg, *1914-i*, 7, 84.

56. Deni and Dolgorukov, "Kukhnia voiny" (Moscow-Leningrad: OGIZ-IZOGIZ, 1934), Hoover Institution, RU-SU 567.

57. Canon H. R. L. Sheppard, "Foreword," in Julian Bell, ed., *We Did Not Fight: 1914–18 Experiences of War Resisters* (London: Cobden-Sanderson, 1935), viii.

58. Kiril Levin, "The Wild Battalion: A Story," in Bell, ed., *We Did Not Fight,* 198.

59. Ibid., 205.

60. Ibid., 206.

61. See Aleksandr Nekrich, *The Punished Peoples* (New York: Norton, 1978).

62. Dmitriev, *Dobrovolets,* 20.

63. Konstantin Finn, "Okraina," *Novyi mir* 12 (December 1931): 56–68. The text of Konstantin Finn, *Okraina* (Moscow: Gos. izd-vo khudozh. lit-ry, 1933) is virtually the same as the *Novyi mir* version. All quotations here are from the 1933 text.

64. Ibid., 191.

65. Ibid., 192.

66. Ibid., 203.

67. Ibid., 205.

68. Ibid., 207.

69. Ibid., 207, 208.

70. Ibid., 209.

71. *Izvestiia,* April 11, 1933.

72. For a detailed discussion of the reception of *All Quiet on the Western Front,* see chapter 6 of the present volume.

73. *Pravda,* April 8, 1933.

74. Both "proletarian" critics and so-called "formalists" criticized the film. M. Bleiman complained about its emphasis on the petty-bourgeoisie instead of the proletariat as the moving force of the revolution. V. Shklovskii, on the other hand, thought Barnet's realization of the film was magnificent but its politicized scenario was weak because of false notes in the depiction of both internationalism and revolution. These reviews are reprinted in Albera and Cosandey, *Boris Barnet,* 134, 137.

75. Denise J. Youngblood, "A War Forgotten: The Great War in Russian and Soviet Cinema," in Michael Paris, ed., *The First World War and Popular Cinema* (New Brunswick, N.J.: Rutgers University Press, 2000), 185.

76. I thank Stephen Norris of Miami University for this insight.

77. Denise Youngblood points out that the Kadkins' control over emotion represents the classic socialist realist victory of consciousness over spontaneity. Youngblood, *Russian War Films,* 35. See also Katerina Clark, *The Soviet Novel: History as Ritual* (Chicago: University of Chicago Press, 1981).

78. Sholokhov, *Quiet Flows the Don,* 351.

79. Ibid., 352.

80. Shub, *Padenie dinastii Romanovykh.*

81. Maksimov et al., *Tsarskaia armiia,* 16, 20. Bashkir writer A. Tagirov also attributed ethnic hatred to noncommissioned officers by having them mock Bashkir recruits, calling them "Turks" and "Tatar spades." Tagirov, *Soldaty,* 24.

82. Trans. from Ehrenburg, *Julio Jurenito,* 114–115

83. Ibid., 127.

84. Ibid., 132, 107, 199.

85. See for example, Ilya Ehrenburg, "The Justification of Hate (1942)," in James von Geldern and Richard Stites, eds., *Mass Culture in Soviet Russia* (Bloomington: Indiana University Press, 1995), 401–405.

86. Voitolovskii, *Po sledam voiny* I: 13.

87. Sanborn, *Drafting the Russian Nation*, 163–164.

88. Chaadaeva, "Soldatskie pis'ma v gody mirovoi voiny," 148–152.

89. Ibid., 156.

90. See Jahn, *Patriotic Culture in Russia during World War I*, 113; D. Chiabrov, *Voina i gruziny* (Petrograd, 1915).

91. William C. Fuller, Jr., *The Foe Within: Fantasies of Treason and the End of Imperial Russia* (Ithaca, N.Y.: Cornell University Press, 2006), 1–4.

92. Ibid., 162.

93. Chaadaeva, "Soldatskie pis'ma v gody mirovoi voiny," 133.

94. Voitolovskii, *Po sledam voiny* I, 35.

95. Ibid., 36.

96. Voitolovskii, *Po sledam voiny* I, 168; II, 30.

97. Voitolovskii, *Po sledam voiny* I, 30; II, 100.

98. Voitolovskii, *Po sledam voiny* I, 91.

99. Maksimov et al., *Tsarskaia armiia*, 188, 190, 198, 199, 201.

100. Maksimov et al., *Tsarskaia armiia*, 186, 189, 197.

101. See Terry Martin, *The Affirmative Action Empire: Nations and Nationalism in The Soviet Union, 1923–1939* (Ithaca, N.Y.: Cornell University Press, 2001), 341–343.

6. Arrested History

1. Fedorchenko, *Narod na voine* (1923), 80. For a fascinating discussion of the physical alteration of Stalin-era photographs see David King, *The Commissar Vanishes: The Falsification of Photographs and Art in Stalin's Russia* (New York: Metropolitan Books, 1997).

2. There are numerous examples of the censorship of technological and economic works in GARF f. 9425c Glavnoe upravlenie po delam literatury i izdatel'stv (Glavlit), dd. 8–18.

3. RGVA (Rossiiskii gosudarstvennyi voennyi arkhiv) f. 39352 Nauchnyi voenno-istoricheskii otdel general'nogo shtaba Krasnoi Armii; Komissiia po issledovaniiu i ispol'zovaniiu opyta i mirovoi i grazhdanskoi voiny Vseroglavshtaba, op. 1, d. 59, l. 48.

4. GARF f. 9425c op. 1, d. 6 (1938), l. 249; Natal'ia Solntseva, *Poslednii lel': O zhizni i tvorchestve Sergeia Klychkova* (Moscow: Moskovskii rabochii, 1993), 221.

5. GARF f. 9425c, op. 1, d. 7 (1939), l. 95.

6. RGVA f. 39352, op. 1, d. 60, ll. 45–71.

7. RGVA f. 39352, op. 1, d. 60, l. 46; Gans Del'briuk, *Istoriia voennogo iskusstva v ramkakh politicheskoi istorii* (Moscow: Gos. voen. izd-vo, 1937).

8. RGVA f. 39352, op. 1, d. 60, l. 48; V. I. Lenin, *Ob imperialisticheskoi voine*, F. Blumental', comp.; Ia. Berman, ed. (Moscow, Gos. izd-vo, Otdel voen. lit-ry, 1929).

9. E. Fal'kengain, *Verkhovnoe komandovanie* (1923), probably a translation of Erich von Falkenhayn, *Die oberste Heeresleitung, 1914–1916: In ihren wichtigsten entschliessungen* (Berlin: E. S. Mittler, 1920); Gans Kul', *Vospominaniia mirnogo vremeni i opyt voiny*, prob-

ably a translation of H. von Kuhl's *Der deutsche Generalstab in Vorbereitung und Durch-führung des Weltkrieges* (Berlin: E. S. Mittler, 1920).

10. G. S. Isserson, *Kanny mirovoi voiny: Gibel' armii Samsonova* (Moscow: Gos.voen. izd-vo, 1926), 1.

11. RGVA f. 39352, op. 1, d. 60, l. 47; op. 1, d. 59, l. 2.

12. *Prigranichnoe srazhenie na zapadnom fronte*, Shtab KVO, (1936); RGVA f. 39352, op. 1, d. 60, l. 49.

13. See Sheila Fitzpatrick, "The Foreign Threat During the First Five-Year Plan," *Soviet Union/Union Sovietique* 5, no. 1 (1978): 27. In *The Jewish Century*, Yuri Slezkine makes the argument that Germans held the same functional position in Russia that Jews held in Germany; Yuri Slezkine, *The Jewish Century* (Princeton, N.J.: Princeton University Press, 2004), 114.

14. Lohr, *Nationalizing the Russian Empire*, 20–21.

15. See for example fig. 5.1.

16. GIM OPI f. 137, ed. khr. 38, ll. 23, 31; RGALI f. 616, op. 1, d. 19, l. 24; f. 613, op. 1, d. 704, ll. 182, 215.

17. RGALI f. 613, op. 1, d. 42, l. 1. Leonid Heretz argues that the Russian peasantry came to hate the Germans as a result of the war and not as a result of Slavic racial consciousness; Heretz, *Russia on the Eve of Modernity*, 196.

18. Dubinskaia, *V okopakh*, 21; idem, *Pulemetchitsa*, 20; idem, *Soldaty*, 12.

19. The perceived pro-German sentiment of the Tatars was to have devastating consequences during World War II, when Tatar populations were deported due to accusations of disloyalty. Article by E. Medvedev in *Istoriia proletariata SSSR*, no. 7 (1931): 138. Quoted in Maksimov et al., *Tsarskaia armiia*, 180.

20. Pulko-Dmitriev was later promoted to lieutenant general and fought in World War II.

21. RGVA f. 39352, op. 1, d. 61, l. 31.

22. RGALI f. 631, op. 2, d. 250, ll. 21–22, 26. In 1936, writers in the Defense Section of the Union of Soviet Writers thought first-person accounts of World War I would be useful since "enemies are ready to rain down a similar slaughter on the country." RGALI, f. 631, op. 16, d. 40, l. 17.

23. As David Brandenberger rightly points out, this vision was more statist that explicitly nationalistic. Brandenberger, *National Bolshevism*, 4.

24. George M. Enteen, *The Soviet Scholar-Bureaucrat: M. N. Pokrovskii and the Society of Marxist Historians* (University Park: Pennsylvania State University Press, 1978), 87; see, for example, A. Erusalimskii, "Proiskhozhdenie mirovoi imperialisticheskoi voiny 1914–1918 gg. v osveshchenii M. N. Pokrovskogo," in B. D. Grekov, ed., *Protiv istoricheskoi kontseptsii M. N. Pokrovskogo* (Moscow-Leningrad: Akademiia Nauk SSSR, 1939), 495–517.

25. A Manusevich, "K istorii Versal'skikh dogovorov," in *Istoricheskii zhurnal*, no. 10 (1940); GARF f. 9425c, op. 1, d. 5, l. 83.

26. Further research is needed on the curriculum at Frunze Military Academy and other such institutions. Memoirs and monographs include: M. Bonch-Bruevich, *Poteriia nami Galitsii v 1915 godu*, 1–2 (Moscow: Voenno-istoricheskaia komissiia, 1920); Zhdanov and Svechin, *Russkie voennoplennye v mirovoi voine 1914–1918 gg.;* Lemke, *250 dnei v tsarskoi stavke.*

27. I am indebted to Dave Stone for his generosity in sharing his unpublished research. His ideas have informed my argument here.

28. Gaynor Kavanagh, "Museum as Memorial: The Origins of the Imperial War Museum," *Journal of Contemporary History* 23, no. 1 (January 1988): 80, 93–95.

29. Mariia Katagoshchina, "Muzei velikoi voiny," *Moskovskii zhurnal* no. 5 (1992): 39, 43–44. Local military museums likely continued to exhibit artifacts from the tsarist era. *Krasnaia Zvezda* 183/479 (August 13, 1925).

30. GIM OPI f. 137, ed. khr. 38, l. 116.

31. This figure is very small compared to the two and a half million people that visited the Imperial War Museum in its first year. Kavanagh, "The Origins of the Imperial War Museum," 94; GIM OPI f. 137, ed. khr. 38, ll. 23, 38 ob.

32. *Komsomol'skaia Pravda* 174/660 (August 3, 1927).

33. GIM OPI f. 137, ed. khr. 38, ll. 26 ob, 31; ed. khr. 47, ll. 2, 7.

34. GIM OPI f. 137, ed. khr. 38, ll. 28 ob–30.

35. V. Arendt, *Voenno-istoricheskii muzei v Moskve* (Moscow: Voennyi vestnik, 1926), available in GIM OPI f. 137, ed. khr. 47, ll. 61–64, see l. 63; ed khr. 38, ll. 118–118 ob.

36. *Krasnaia Zvezda* 171/765 (July 28, 1926); GIM OPI f. 137, ed. khr. 38, ll. 119–120.

37. GIM OPI f. 137, ed. khr. 38, ll. 31–31 ob, 120 ob.

38. GIM OPI f. 137, ed. khr. 47, l. 63 ob.

39. *Krasnaia Zvezda* 153/449 (July 8, 1925); 195/491 (August 28, 1925).

40. *Rabochaia Moskva* June 23, 1926; November 4, 1927.

41. GIM OPI f. 137, ed. khr. 38, l. 116.

42. GIM OPI f. 137, ed. khr. 47, l. 69; *Komsomol'skaia Pravda* 174/660 (3 August 1927).

43. RGVA f. 39352, op. 1, ll. 1, 6.

44. GIM OPI f. 426 Moskovskie ekspeditsii, op. 1, d. 77 (Memoirs of E. Z. Barsukov), l. 45; Reese, *Red Commanders,* 20.

45. *Strategicheskii ocherk voiny, 1914–1918,* Komissiia po issledovaniiu i ispol'zovaniiu opyta mirovoi i grazhdanskoi voiny, vol. 1–7 (Moscow: Vysshii voen. redaktsionnyi sovet, 1920–1923); A. M. Zaionchkovskii and A. N. De-Lazari, *Mirovaia Voina 1914–1918 gg.: Obshchii strategicheskii ocherk* (Moscow: Gosvoenizdat, 1924); A. M. Zaionchkovskii, *Podgotovka Rossii k imperialisticheskoi voine* (Moscow: Gosvoenizdat, 1926); K. Gil'chevskii, *Boevye deistviia vtoroocherednykh chastei v mirovuiu voinu* (Leningrad: Gosizdat, 1928); Svechin, *Iskusstvo vozhdeniia polka.*

46. Sally W. Stoecker, *Forging Stalin's Army: Marshal Tukhachevsky and the Politics of Military Innovation* (Boulder, Colo.: Westview Press, 1998), 18–19.

47. I. A. Korotkov, *Istoriia Sovetskoi voennoi mysli* (Moscow: Nauka, 1980), 93.

48. Reese, *Red Commanders,* 81; RGVA, f. 39352, op. 1, d. 48, ll. 1–4.

49. Reese, *Red Commanders,* 80–83; See also David R. Stone, *Hammer and Rifle: The Militarization of the Soviet Union, 1926–1933* (Lawrence: University Press of Kansas, 2000); Richard W. Harrison, *The Russian Way of War: Operational Art, 1904–1940* (Lawrence: University Press of Kansas, 2001). I am grateful to Bruce Menning, Roger Reese, and Dave Stone for assisting me with the historical context of the documentary series.

50. On the upheavals of the "cultural revolution," see Sheila Fitzpatrick, "Cultural Revolution as Class War," in Sheila Fitzpatrick, ed., *Cultural Revolution in Russia, 1928–1931* (Bloomington: Indiana University Press, 1978), 8–40. For a discussion of the reception of *Iskusstvo vozhdeniia polka,* see I. S. Danilenko, "Borets protiv lzhi i bezmolviia," in Svechin, *Iskusstvo vozhdeniia polka,* 23–24; Sokolov, *Krasnaia zvezda ili krest?* 158.

51. Korotkov, *Istoriia Sovetskoi voennoi mysli,* 261; RGVA f. 39352, op. 1, d. 48, l. 5.

52. GIM OPI f. 426, op. 1, d. 77, l. 48.

53. RGVA f. 39352, op. 1, d. 48, l. 50.

54. RGVA f. 39352, op. 1, d. 53, ll. 6, 8 ob. G. Korol'kov was the author of *Nesbyvshiesia Kanny: Neudavshiisia razgrom russkikh letom 1915 g.* (Moscow: Voenizdat, 1926). A similar process of removing commentaries occurred with the compilation of Pushkin's collected works during the 1937 centennial. See Karen Petrone, *Life Has Become More Joyous, Comrades: Celebrations in the Time of Stalin* (Bloomington: Indiana University Press, 2000), 140–141.

55. RGVA f. 39352, op. 1, d. 48, ll. 64, 118, 146, 152; d. 53, l. 10.

56. RGVA f. 39352, op. 1, d 53, l. 10; A. Kh. Bazarevskii, ed., *Lodzinskaia operatsiia: Sbornik dokumentov* (Moscow-Leningrad: Voenizdat, 1936), 11. Bazarevskii was also author of two World War I monographs: a 1927 work on the French and Belgian campaigns of 1918, and a 1937 work on the Ninth Army during the Brusilov offensive; A. Bazarevskii, *Mirovaia voina 1914–1918 g.g.: Kampaniia 1918 goda vo Frantsii i Bel'gii* (Moscow: Gosizdat, Otdel voennoi literatury, 1927); A. Bazarevskii, *Nastupatel'naia operatsiia 9-i Russkoi armii, iiun' 1916 goda: Proryv ukreplennoi polosy i forsirovanie reki* (Moscow: Gos. voen. izd-vo, 1937).

57. Bazarevskii, *Lodzinskaia operatsiia,* 13–22.

58. The three other volumes were edited by V. E. Belolipetskii. *Varshavsko-Ivangorod-skaia operatsiia* appeared in 1938; *Vostochno-Prusskaia operatsiia* in 1939; *Gorlitskaia operatsiia* in 1940. The Russian military archives also put out a volume on the Brusilov offensive with a similar format in 1940, edited by F. M. Borodin. It was titled *Nastuplenie Iugo-Zapadnogo fronta v mai-iiune, 1916 goda.*

59. RGVA f. 39352, op. 1, d. 59, ll. 2,4; d. 91, ll. 1–2.

60. Some examples include N. G. Korsun, *Sarykamyshskaia operatsiia: Na Kavkazskom fronte mirovoi voiny v 1914–1915 godu* (Moscow: Gosvoenizdat, 1937); *Erzerumskaia operatsiia na Kavkazskom fronte mirovoi voiny v 1915–1916 gg.* (Moscow: Gosvoenizdat, 1938); M. Rozhdestvenskii, *Lutskii proryv* (Moscow: Voenizdat, 1938).

61. GARF f. 5972, op. 1, d. 5, ll. 2–5; d. 21a, ll. 331, 336.

62. A. A. Brusilov, "Vospominaniia," *Voina i revoliutsiia* no. 4 (1927): 67–83.

63. GARF f. 5972, op. 1, g. 63, ll. 6, 10, 12.

64. Sokolov, *Krasnaia zvezda ili krest?* 158.

65. Bakhmeteff Archive, Brusilov Collection, Box 1.

66. Chaadaeva, "Soldatskie pis'ma v gody mirovoi voiny," 119.

67. Brandenberger, *National Bolshevism,* 8, 2

68. Rozhdestvenskii, *Lutskii proryv,* 39. Rozhdestvenskii clearly exaggerated here since Germany and not Austria-Hungary was the Russian Empire's "strongest opponent" in World War I.

69. Iu. Veber, "Proryv," in E. A. Boltin, L. V. Zhigarev, and M. M. Kaplun, eds., *Artilleristy: Sbornik statei i rasskazov* (Moscow: Molodaia gvardiia, 1939), 119–136, quote on 120.

70. V. Mavrodin, *Brusilov* (Moscow: Pravda, 1943), 3.

71. Brandenberger, *National Bolshevism,* 151, 156, 162; Il'ia Sel'vinskii, *General Brusilov* in *Lirika i drama* (Moscow: OGIZ, 1947), 305–376. Although Brusilov was the title character in Sergeev-Tsenskii's novel, he was not its hero. S. Sergeev-Tsenskii, *Brusilovskii proryv, I* (Moscow: Sovetskii pisatel', 1943). Sergeev-Tsenskii relied heavily on Gil'chevskii's 1928 memoir.

72. Brandenberger, *National Bolshevism,* 127.

73. Editions of Remarque's book include Erikh Mariia Remark, "Na zapadnom fronte bez peremen: Glavy iz romana," *Molodaia gvardiia* no. 14 (July 1929): 2–14; *Na zapadnom fronte bez peremen,* foreword by L. Manulskii, illustrated by V. Sbarii, *Roman-Gazeta* no. 2, 1930 and (Moscow: Sovetskii rabochii, 1930); *Na zapadnom fronte bez peremen,* Sergei Miatezhnyi and Petr Cherevin, trans., Dm. Umanskii, ed., foreword by Karl Radek (Moscow-Leningrad: Zemlia i fabrika, 1929); (Moscow: Gosizdat Krasnyi Proletarii, 1929); *Na zapade bez peremen,* Sergei Miatezhnyi and Petr Cherevin, trans., Abram Efros, ed. (Moscow: Federatsiia, 1929); *Dasavlet' is p'ronti ucvlelia,* Konstantin Gamsachurdia, trans. (Tbilisi, 1930); *Na zakhidn'omu fronti bez zmin,* Z. H. Burhardt, trans., foreword by Karl Radek (Kharkov: Ukrainskyi robitnyk, 1930); *Im Westen nichts Neues,* foreword by Karl Radek (Kharkov: Tewelew-Platz 18, Zentralverl., 1930); *Im Westen nichts Neues* (Moscow-Leningrad: Ucheb. pedagog, 1931).

74. Remark, *Na zapadnom fronte bez peremen,* back cover leaf.

75. Remark, *Na zapadnom fronte bez peremen,* front cover leaf.

76. Remark, *Na zapadnom fronte bez peremen,* front cover leaf.

77. Z. Lippai, "Roman E. Remark 'Na zapadnom fronte bez peremen': Voennaia literatura v kapitalisticheskikh stranakh," *Na literaturnom posty* no. 16 (1929): 62, 64.

78. Mak Almast, "V tupike," *Molodaia gvardiia* no. 18 (1929): 93–94. Almast finds Barbusse's depiction of the war to be superior to Remarque's.

79. Erich Maria Remarque, *The Road Back* (Boston: Little, Brown, 1931).

80. Nikolai Sokolovskii, *Na zapade bez peremen: Radio-p'esa po romany Remarka,* in RGALI f. 613, op. 1, d. 7787, l. 46–48; Remarque, *All Quiet on the Western Front,* 226.

81. RGALI f. 613, op. 1, d. 7787, l. 40.

82. M. B. Zagorskii, *Pushkin i teatr* (Moscow: Iskusstvo, 1940); idem. *Gogol' i teatr* (Moscow: Iskusstvo, 1952).

83. The cast of characters included Paul Bäumer, who was reanimated by Zagorskii as a crazed war veteran.

84. M. Zagorskii, *Predatel',* in RGALI f. 2452 Vsesoiuznoe upravlenie po okhrane avtorskikh prav, op. 3, d. 1703, l. 10–10 ob.

85. RGALI f. 2452. op. 3, d. 1703, l. 1.

86. Ibid.

87. Andrew Kelly, *Filming* All Quiet on the Western Front: *"Brutal Cutting, Stupid Censors, Bigoted Politicos"* (London: I. B. Tauris, 1998), 131.

88. "Vokrug filmy 'Na zapadnom fronte bez peremen,'" *Proletarskoe Kino* no. 4 (1931): 64.

89. Joseph R. Millichap, *Lewis Milestone* (Boston: Twayne, 1981), 26–28; Kelly, *Filming* All Quiet on the Western Front, 65.

90. James Fisher, "Milestone, Lewis," *American National Biography Online* (Feb. 2000), http://www.anb.org/articles/18/18-02053.html (accessed August 7, 2008); Kelly, *Filming* All Quiet on the Western Front, 63–64.

91. Kelly, *Filming* All Quiet on the Western Front, 103–104; 65; Millichap, *Lewis Milestone,* 38.

92. For a discussion of the reception of Remarque's novel and the 1930 film elsewhere in Europe see Modris Eksteins, *"All Quiet on the Western Front," History Today* 45, no. 11 (Nov. 1995): 29–34; idem, *Rites of Spring,* 285–299.

93. RGALI f. 613, op. 1, d. 559, l. 17.

94. RGALI f. 613, op. 1, d. 559, l. 2; f. 616, op. 1, d. 19, l.12.

95. RGALI f. 616, op. 1, d. 19, ll. 3, 10 ob–11 ob; f. 613, op. 1, d. 559, l. 13.

96. RGALI f. 613, op. 1, d. 559, ll. 10–12; f. 616, op. 1, d. 19, ll. 2, 9.

97. RGALI f. 619, op. 1, d. 19, ll. 18, 24.

98. RGALI f. 619, op. 1, d. 19, ll. 2–2 ob.

99. RGALI f. 631, op. 1, d. 559, ll. 12, 14.

100. RGALI f. 616, op. 1, d. 19, ll. 8, 10.

101. RGALI f. 616, op. 1, d. 19, l. 16; f. 613, op. 1, d. 559, ll. 2, 20, 34.

102. See Petrone, *Life Has Become More Joyous, Comrades.*

103. Sof'ia Fedorchenko, *Narod na voine* (1917), 3.

104. The missing anecdotes will be discussed in detail in chapter 7. Unfortunately, the 1990 edition of the work is a reprint of the censored 1925 edition. The third volume of the work appeared in *Literaturnoe nasledstvo* 93 (1983). See also N. A. Trifonov, "Nespravedlivo zabytaia kniga," in Sof'ia Fedorchenko, *Narod na voine* (Moscow: Sovetskii pisatel', 1990), 7, 9, 16–17.

105. *Vecherniaia Moskva* 243 (October 24, 1927), quoted in Trifonov, "Nespravedlivo zabytaia kniga," 10.

106. "*Russkaia literatura,*" 1 (1973), 153–154, quoted in Trifonov, "Nespravedlivo za-bytaia kniga," 10.

107. D. Bednyi, "Mistifikatory i fal'sifikatory—ne literatory," *Izvestiia* 43 (19 February 1928). Although some of her work appeared in journals during World War II, nothing more appeared in book form in the Stalin era. Trifonov, "Nespravedlivo zabytaia kniga," 9–11, 15.

108. "Iz avtobiografii Sof'i Zakharovny Fedorchenko," in Fedorchenko, *Narod na voine* (1990), 387. Several other Russian fictional works about World War I in circulation at the time used the same device of purportedly being actual soldiers' journals or letters and they did not suffer adverse consequences.

109. The controversy over how to interpret Fedorchenko's work continues into the present day. Fedorchenko has some modern-day champions who defend her authenticity through the use of quantitative linguistics. O. S. Porshneva and S. V. Porshnev argue that while "Fedorchenko's work cannot be called scientific-ethnographic in a strict sense, it was artistic-ethnographic." O. S. Porshneva and S. V. Porshnev, "K voprosu ob atributsii tekstov zapisei soldatskikh razgovorov S. Z. Fedorchenko," *Informatsionnyi biulleten' as-sotsiatsii "Istoriia i komp'iuter"* no. 30 (June 2002): 153. Available at http://kleio.asu.ru/aik/bullet/30/bullet30.html (accessed November 2, 2007). Using a computer, they com-pared the language of Fedorchenko's soldiers to the speech recorded by Lev Voitolovskii in *In the Footsteps of War.* They proved a strong similarity in the structure of the soldiers' speech in the two works. Porshneva defended modern historians' empirical use of Fedor-chenko as an "oral history" of the war. Porshneva used Fedorchenko as a primary source in O. S. Porshneva, *Krest'iane, rabochie i soldaty Rossii nakanune i v gody Pervoi Mirovoi Voiny* (Moscow: Rosspen, 2004). Porshneva and Porshnev, "K voprosu ob atributsii tek-stov zapisei soldatskikh razgovorov S. Z. Fedorchenko," 155.

110. Voitolovskaia, *Po sledam sud'by moego pokoleniia,* 12.

111. RGALI f. 1423 Personal collection of Lev Naumovich Voitolovskii, op. 1, d. 56, ll. 4–5.

112. RGALI f. 1423, op. 1, d. 56, l. 5.

113. Gorkii addresses Voitolovskii using the formal (*vy*) throughout the correspon-dence.

114. Unfortunately, the post-Soviet-era reprint of *Po sledam voiny,* published as *Vskhodil krovavyi mars,* used the incomplete 1931 text.

115. RGALI f. 631, op. 16, d. 40, l. 73. The quote from V. I. Lenin is taken from his "Zametki po voprosu o zadachakh nashei delegatsii v Gaage," originally published in *Kommunistcheskii Internatsional* no. 2 (1924), and reprinted in M. I. Grishin, ed., *Pomni o voine: Sbornik* (Moscow-Leningrad: Molodaia gvardiia, 1924), 346–349.

116. Voitolovskaia, *Po sledam sud'by moego pokoleniia,* 18.

117. Feinberg, *1914-i,* i–ii, 90 (foldout), 79.

118. RGALI f. 631, op. 16, d. 74, ll. 50, 54, 56.

119. Ibid., l. 50.

120. For an overview of recent historiography about Stalinist foreign policy in the 1930s, see Jonathan Haslam, "Soviet-German Relations and the Origins of the Second World War: The Jury Is Still Out," *Journal of Modern History* 69, no. 4 (December 1997): 785–797.

7. Disappearance and Reappearance

1. Sholokhov, *Quiet Flows the Don,* 366–367; Murphy et al., *Sholokhov's* Tikhii Don, vol. 1: 75–76. Murphy et al. also identify concern for "soldiers' morale" as the reason for the change. Erich Maria Remarque has a very similar reference to Paul stifling "his terror and his cries" in a female earth's "silence and her security." Remarque, *All Quiet on the Western Front,* 55.

2. Jan Plamper described two Russian military-psychiatric views of fear: the "romantics" saw fear as an aberration while the "realists" viewed fear as normal. It can be argued that the 1933 censorship of this scene marks a shift from the realistic view to the romantic. Plamper cites Voitolovskii's *In the Footsteps of War* to demonstrate the new "realistic" openness about fear in battle in the early twentieth century, but this openness did not last throughout the interwar period. Plamper, "Fear," 260, 272–274, 282.

3. Brandenberger, *National Bolshevism,* 8, 2.

4. The phenomenon of discursive remasculinization is visible in Klaus Theweleit's analysis of the literature of the German Freikorps during the Weimar Republic and also in Susan Jeffords's description of American public discourse about Vietnam in the 1980s. Theweleit, *Male Fantasies,* vol. 1; also vol. 2 (Minneapolis: University of Minnesota Press, 1989); Susan Jeffords, *The Remasculinization of America: Gender and the Vietnam War.* (Bloomington: Indiana University Press, 1989).

5. Fedorchenko, *Narod na voine* (1917), 59–60; (1923), 39; trans. from Fedorchenko, *Ivan Speaks,* 7–8.

6. Rubenstein, *Tangled Loyalties,* 71.

7. Erenburg, *Lik voiny* (1923), 27, 35–36, 53.

8. Ibid., 159–160.

9. Ibid., 72, 106–107; Erenburg, *Lik voiny* (1928), 55, 78.

10. N. Stepnoi [pseudonym of Nikolai Aleksandrovich Afinogenov], *Zapiski opolchentsa,* 3rd ed. (Kineshma: Izd-vo. kollektiva raboche-krest'ianskikh pisatelei, 1924), 5–6, 34, 12, 28, 16. N. Stepnoi was the father of the Soviet playwright Aleksandr Nikolaevich Afinogenov. No works by the elder Afinogenov were published after 1927; "Aleksandr Nikolaevich Afinogenov," in *Modern Encyclopedia of Russian and Soviet Literature,* vol. 1, Harry B. Weber, ed. (Gulf Breeze, Fla.: Academic International Press, 1977), 46.

11. Voitolovskii, *Po sledam voiny* I, 68; L. Voitolovskii, *Vskhodil krovavyi mars: Po sledam voiny* (Moscow: Goslitizdat, 1931; repr. Moscow: Voennoe izdatel'stvo, 1998), 64.

12. Voitolovskii, *Po sledam voiny* I, 68; L. Voitolovskii, *Po sledam voiny* (Leningrad: Izdatel'stvo pisatelei, 1934), 89.

13. Fedorchenko, *Narod na voine* (1917), 46; (1923), 28.

14. Dubinskaia, *V okopakh,* 99–103, quote on 102; idem, *Pulemetchitsa,* 82–85; idem, *Soldaty,* 54–56.

15. Fedorchenko, *Narod na voine* (1917), 45; (1923), 94.

16. The timing of the appearance of *A Farewell to Arms* likely had to do with Hemingway's public criticism of the U.S. government and Italian fascism in late 1935 and early 1936. S. Dinamov, "Predislovie," in Ernest Kheminguei, *Proshchai oruzhie,* Evg. Kalashnikova, trans. (Moscow: Gos. izd-vo khudozh. lit-ry, 1936), 6–7, 17–18.

17. Ermolaev, *Censorship in Soviet Literature;* Bernstein, *The Dictatorship of Sex,* 5.

18. Michelle K. Rhoades, "Renegotiating French Masculinity: Medicine and Venereal Disease during the Great War," *French Historical Studies* 29, no. 2 (Spring 2006): 298; Marie-Monique Huss, "Pronatalism and the Popular Ideology of the Child in Wartime France: The Evidence of the Picture Postcard," in Richard Wall and Jay Winter, eds., *The Upheaval of War: Family, Work, and Welfare in Europe, 1914–1918* (Cambridge: Cambridge University Press, 1988), 329–367.

19. Fedorchenko, *Narod na voine* (1917), 60; (1923), 87.

20. Fedorchenko, *Narod na voine* (1917), 114; (1923), 90; trans. based on Fedorchenko, *Ivan Speaks,* 30–31.

21. Fedorchenko, *Narod na voine* (1917), 118; (1923), 91.

22. Fedorchenko, *Narod na voine* (1917), 115; (1923), 83; trans. based on Fedorchenko, *Ivan Speaks,* 24–25.

23. See Bochkareva, *Yashka.* She was later killed while fighting for the Whites in the Civil War. See Corney, *Telling October,* 195–196, for a discussion of Sergei Eisenstein's depiction of the Women's Battalion of Death.

24. RGALI, f. 631, op. 16, d. 40, l. 8; E. Gerasimov, review of *Pulemetchitsa, Literaturnoe Obozrenie* 6 (1936): 20–21. Lidiia Charskaia was an extremely popular writer of fiction for older girls before the revolution, but Soviet critics attacked her work.

25. Dubinskaia, *V okopakh;* idem, *Pulemetchitsa;* idem, *Soldaty.*

26. Dubinskaia, *V okopakh,* 161.

27. For a discussion of Anka's role in the 1936 film *Chapaev,* see Hartzok, "Children of Chapaev," 116.

28. Katsov, *Skvoz' plen* (1930), 5–7.

29. Katsov, *Skvoz' plen* (1934), 4.

30. Ibid., 7.

31. Ibid., 5. It is notable that neither Kol'tsov nor Radek survived Stalin's purges. Katsov's fate is unclear, although a website of Moscow purge victims lists a Communist Party member Leonid Katsov as having been executed in December 1937 (http://mos.memo.ru/shot-8.htm).

32. Pireiko, *V tylu i na fronte,* 11, 13.

33. A. Pireiko, *Na fronte imperialisticheskoi voiny: Vospominaniia bol'shevika* (Moscow: Starii Bol'shevik, 1935), omissions from 12, 15.

34. Pireiko, *V tylu i na fronte,* 13; Pireiko, *Na fronte imperialisticheskoi voiny,* 16.

35. Pireiko, *V tylu i na fronte,* 29; Pireiko, *Na fronte imperialisticheskoi voiny,* 44.

36. Pireiko, *V tylu i na fronte,* 32; Pireiko, *Na fronte imperialisticheskoi voiny,* 49.

37. This piece was published as *The Barracks* by Land and Factory in 1926.

38. RGVA f. 63 Gosudarstvennoe voennoe izdatel'stvo, op. 1, d. 498, l. 4.

39. Grigor'ev, *Kazarma*, 3.

40. Ibid., 17.

41. Dmitrii Danchev, "Sergei Nikolaevich Sergeev-Tsenskii," in Rydel, *Dictionary of Literary Biography*, vol. 272, 363, 365; Brandenberger, *National Bolshevism*, 56–57, 82–83.

42. J. N. Westwood, "Novikov-Priboi as Naval Historian," *Slavic Review* 69, no. 2 (June 1969): 297–299.

43. Vs. Vishnevskii, "O 'Tsusime' Novikova-Priboia," *Literaturnyi Kritik* no. 5 (1935): 114–115.

44. S. N. Sergeev-Tsenskii, *Zauriad-polk* (Moscow: Gos. izd-vo khudozh. lit-ry, 1935). Also published in serial form in the journal *Znamia*, 1934, 9–12; *Massy, mashiny, stikhii* (Moscow: Gos. izd-vo khudozh. lit-ry, 1936). This novel was later published as *Liutaia zima*. Bibliographic information from S. N. Sergeev-Tsenskii, *Sobranie sochinenii v desiati tomakh*, t. 9 (Moscow: Gos. izd-vo khudozh. lit-ry, 1956), 725. See also P. I. Pluksh, *Sergeev-Tsenskii—pisatel', chelovek* (Moscow: Sovremennik, 1975), 134–141.

45. Ermolaev, *Censorship in Soviet Literature*, 38–39. Urban legend has it that this record run was due to the fact that Stalin liked the play.

46. Sobolev, *Kapital'nyi remont*, 304–305; trans. based on Soboleff, *Romanoff*, 276–278.

47. Sergeev-Tsenskii, *Zauriad-polk*, 3, 9–10. Liventsev was based on partially autobiographical material as Sergeev-Tsenskii himself served as a reserve officer in Sevastopol' during World War I. V. Koslov and F. Putnin, "Sergeev-Tsenskii: Tvorcheskii put'," http://scensky.ru/content/view/13/29/ (accessed 19 August 2010).

48. E. Usievich, "Tvorcheskii put' Sergeeva-Tsenskogo," *Literaturnyi Kritik* 3 (1935): 100.

49. Ibid., 100–101.

50. See chapter 8 for a discussion of Usievich's attack on Sergeev-Tsenskii in late 1945.

51. Westwood, "Novikov-Priboi as Naval Historian," 301. He cites *Morskoi sbornik* 2 (1939): 112–16.

52. E. Barsukov, "Artilleristy mirovoi voiny," in Boltin et al., *Artilleristy*, 97–118; Veber, "Proryv," 119–136. The manuscript was submitted to the publisher in May of 1939, well before the invasion of Poland.

53. Barsukov, "Artilleristy mirovoi voiny," 98.

54. Ibid., 100.

55. For the classic discussion of the "big deal" between professionals and the Stalinist government, see Vera S. Dunham, *In Stalin's Time: Middleclass Values in Soviet Fiction* (Durham, N.C.: Duke University Press, 1990).

56. Barsukov, "Artilleristy mirovoi voiny," 118, 102. This trend reached absurd proportions during the Cold War when the Russians claimed that they had invented the airplane, the radio, and even baseball.

57. Ibid., 114, 116–117.

58. Contemporaries recognized this similarity. See Kevin M. F. Platt and David Brandenberger, "An Internationalist's Complaint to Stalin and the Ensuing Scandal," in Kevin M. F. Platt and David Brandenberger, eds., *Epic Revisionism: Russian History and Literature as Stalinist Propaganda* (Madison: University of Wisconsin Press, 2006), 315–323. See also Yulia Mikhailova, "Images of Enemy and Self: Russian 'Popular Prints' of the Russo-Japanese War." *Acta slavica iaponica* 16 (1998): 45.

59. Dowling, *The Brusilov Offensive*, 163–166.

60. Veber, "Proryv," 120.

61. Ibid., 136.

62. Barsukov, "Artilleristy mirovoi voiny," 110, 112.

63. Ibid., 113.

64. Veber, "Proryv," 136, 132.

65. Ermolaev, *Censorship in the Soviet Union,* 86.

66. S. Sergeev-Tsenskii, *Brusilovskii proryv,* II (Moscow: Sovetskii pisatel', 1944), 11; trans. from S. Sergeyev-Tsensky, *Brusilov's Breakthrough: A Novel of the First World War,* Helen Altschuler, trans. (London: Hutchinson, 1945), 160.

67. S. Sergeev-Tsenskii, *Brusilovskii proryv,* I (Moscow: Sovetskii pisatel', 1943), 124–125, trans. from Sergeyev-Tsensky, *Brusilov's Breakthrough,* 80.

68. Stalin's famous Order 227 was issued on July 28, 1942. I could find no evidence of Brusilov issuing such a directive in 1915, though he did ask for the death penalty for deserters after the February Revolution. Dowling, *The Brusilov Offensive,* xx. Sergeev-Tsenskii, *Brusilovskii proryv* I, 37; trans. from Sergeyev-Tsensky, *Brusilov's Breakthrough,* 26.

69. Sergeev-Tsenskii, *Brusilovskii proryv,* I 239, 246; trans. from Sergeyev-Tsensky, *Brusilov's Breakthrough,* 149–150, 154.

70. Mavrodin, *Brusilov,* 3, 11.

71. Sergeev-Tsenskii, *Brusilovskii proryv* I, 49, 51–53; trans. from Sergeyev-Tsensky, *Brusilov's Breakthrough,* 34–38.

72. Sergeev-Tsenskii, *Brusilovskii proryv* I, 107; trans. from Sergeyev-Tsensky, *Brusilov's Breakthrough,* 123–124.

73. Sergeev-Tsenskii, *Brusilovskii proryv* I, 123, 141; trans. from Sergeyev-Tsensky, *Brusilov's Breakthrough,* 79, 90.

74. I. Dunaevskii and V. Lebedev-Kumach, "Pesnia o rodine," in *Pesni Krasnoi Armii* (Moscow: Voenizdat, 1937), 13.

75. See Anna Krylova, "'Healers of Wounded Souls'."

76. Sergeev-Tsenskii, *Brusilovskii proryv* II, 108; trans. from Sergeyev-Tsensky, *Brusilov's Breakthrough,* 220.

77. Sergeev-Tsenskii, *Brusilovskii proryv* II, 257; trans. from Sergeyev-Tsensky, *Brusilov's Breakthrough,* 315.

78. Anna Krylova, "Stalinist Identity from the Viewpoint of Gender: Rearing a Generation of Professionally Violent Women-Fighters in 1930s Stalinist Russia," *Gender & History* 16, no. 3 (Nov. 2004): 626–653.

79. E. Usievich, "Roman o pervoi mirovoi voine," *Znamia* 11 (1945): 137.

80. Ibid., 137.

81. Ibid., 137–138.

82. Ibid., 147, 142.

83. RGALI f. 1161 Personal Collection of Sergei Sergeev-Tsenskii, op. 1, d. 200, l. 17.

84. Ibid., ll. 9, 23. The novel *Zrelaia osen'* was never completed. Koslov and Putnin, "Sergeev-Tsenskii: Tvorcheskii put'," (http://scensky.ru).

85. RGALI f. 1161, op. 1, d. 200, 1. 30.

8. Legacies of the Great War

1. Tumarkin, *The Living and the Dead,* 104, 119, 127, 143.

2. There were also two full color maps. "Pervaia Mirovaia Imperialisticheskaia Voina," *Bol'shaia Sovetskaia Entsiklopediia,* vol. 44 (1939) cols. 509–759; "Pervaia Mirovaia Voina,

Bol'shaia Sovetskaia Entsiklopediia, vol. 32, B. A. Vvedenskii, ed. (Moscow: Bol'shaia Sovetskaia Entsiklopediia, 1958), 344–349.

3. Mavrodin, *Brusilov,* 9.

4. Iurii L'vovich Slezkin, *Brusilov* (Leningrad: Sovetskii pisatel', 1947). I. L. Sel'vinskii, *General Brusilov.*

5. Slezkin, *Brusilov,* 3.

6. Ibid., 455–456.

7. V. V. Mavrodin, "Predislovie," in A. A. Brusilov, *Moi vospominaniia* (Moscow: Voenizdat, 1963), 14. See also William W. Wells, Memorandum for the Director of Central Intelligence on *"Military Thought* (USSR): The Brusilov Case—How an Historical Error was Corrected," July 9, 1976, declassified December 2004. Thanks to Dave Stone for alerting me to this source.

8. M.D. Bonch-Bruevich, *Vsia vlast' Sovetam!* (Moscow: Voenizdat, 1958), online at http://militera.lib.ru/memo/russian/bonch-bruevich_md/index.html; GIM OPI f. 426, d. 79, ll. 17–18.

9. Deborah Field, *Private Life and Communist Morality in Khrushchev's Russia* (Peter Lang, 2007).

10. RGALI f. 1611, op. 1, d. 129, l. 2.

11. Ibid., ll. 14–15.

12. Ermolaev, *Censorship in Soviet Literature,* 6–7.

13. Pasternak, *Doctor Zhivago,* 90–128. Boris Pasternak felt compelled to turn down the Nobel Prize.

14. Aleksandr Solzhenitsyn, "Autobiography," in *Nobel Lectures, Literature 1968–1980,* ed.-in-charge Tore Frängsmyr, ed. Sture Allén, World Scientific Publishing Co., Singapore, 1993; available at http://nobelprize.org/nobel_prizes/literature/laureates/1970/solzhenitsyn-autobio.html (accessed June 13, 2008).

15. Aleksandr Solzhenitsyn, *August 1914,* Michael Glenny, trans. (New York: Farrar, Straus and Giroux, 1972), 112–113.

16. Ibid., 209, 241.

17. Ibid., 12, 332, 337.

18. Maike Lehmann, "Bargaining Armenian-ness: National Politics of Identity in the Soviet Union after 1945," in *Representations on the Margins of Europe: Politics and Identities in the Baltic and South Caucasian States,* Tsypylma Darieva and Wolfgang Kaschuba, eds. (Frankfurt: Campus Verlag, 2007), 181–182.

19. The First Secretary of the Armenian Communist Party, Zarobian was, however, later forced to step down. Lehmann, "Bargaining Armenian-ness," 181–182, 188, http://www.genocide-museum.am/eng/Description_and_history.php (accessed September 4, 2010).

20. See Winter, *Sites of Memory,* 64–65.

21. Merridale, *Night of Stone,* 100.

22. "Dolg pamiati i chesti" (based on materials from the website of the nonprofit foundation "Pamiat' chesti," www.white-guard.ru), *Russkii Dom* no. 10, 2004; http://www.russdom.ru/oldsayte/2004/200410i/20041013.html (accessed August 31, 2010). Aleksandr Khokhlov, "Zapozdaloe pokaianie," *Novye Izvestiia,* July 30, 2004; available at http://www.newizv.ru/news/?id_news=8713&date=2004-07-30 (accessed July 14, 2008). Aleksei Sokolovskii, "Zhivaia pamiat'," *Istoriia* 33 (753), September 1–7, 2004; available at http://his.1september.ru/index.php?year=2004&num=33 (accessed June 10, 2009).

23. Nadieszda Kizenko, "The Savior on the Waters Church War Memorial in St.

Petersburg," in Neuberger and Kivelson, *Picturing Russia: Explorations in Visual Culture,* 124–125; Aleksandr Isakov, "Moskva skvoz' linzu ob'ektiva: Vsekhsviatskoe," December 5, 2007; www.mosnovostroy.ru/news/lenta/4576.html (accessed July 15, 2008).

24. In a notable variation, the post-Soviet World War II memorial and museum at Moscow's Poklonnaia Gora (or Homage Hill) consists of an Orthodox church alongside a mosque and a synagogue.

25. Nadieszda Kizenko, "The Savior on the Waters Church War Memorial in St. Petersburg," 124; Wortman, *Scenarios of Power,* vol. 2, 244–256; I am indebted to Daniel Rowland for the notion that the church represents a double revival.

26. While some sources claim that Shchusev's Church of the Transfiguration was located at the site of the Leningrad Movie Theater at the south end of the park, this monument is located in the center of the park. The monument claims to mark the spot at which a chapel stood from 1915 to 1925. Shchusev's Church of the Transfiguration was not dedicated until 1917–1918. There was, however, a temporary wooden chapel built at the cemetery in 1915. While the cemetery was closed to burials in 1925, the Church of the Transfiguration was likely destroyed at a later date.

27. "V Moskve zalozhen kamen' na meste stroitel'stva khrama-chasovni v pamiat' vsekh zashchitnikov Rossii, pavshikh v voinakh za otechestvo," Interfaks-Religiia online, May 6, 1998, http://www.interfax-religion.ru/?act=archive&div=6657 (accessed April 12, 2006).

28. "Po kom zvonit kolokol."

29. "Oskvernena Preobrazhenskaia chasovnia na Sokole," www.zavet.ru/news/news-s010401.htm#02, March 31, 2001 (accessed July 15, 2008).

30. "Kadety okhraniaiut pravoslavnyi memorial primireniia narodov," http://www.cadetcorps.ru/News/Show.aspx?id=295 (accessed April 12, 2006).

BIBLIOGRAPHY

Archival Collections

Bakhmeteff Archive, Columbia University:
    Aleksei A. and Nadezhda V. Brusilov Collection
GARF (Gosudarstvennyi arkhiv Rossiiskoi Federatsii):
    f. 5972 Personal Collection of Aleksei Alekseevich Brusilov and Nadezhda
    Vladimirovna Brusilova
    f. 9425c Glavnoe upravlenie po delam literatury i izdatel'stv (Glavlit)
GIM-OPI (Gosudarstvennyi istoricheskii muzei, Otdel pismennykh istochnikov):
    f. 137 Voenno-istoricheskii muzei
    f. 402 "Staraia Moskva"
    f. 426 Moskovskie ekspeditsii
Harvard Project on the Soviet Social System (hcl.harvard.edu/collections/hpsss/about
    .html)
Hoover Institution Library and Archives, Stanford University, Poster Collection: (hoohila
    .stanford.edu/poster/index.php)
    Argus, "Kogda muzhchiny na fronte, vot gde vashe mesto, zhenshchiny!" Russkoe
        Obshchestvo Pechatnogo Dela, n.d. RU-SU 407.
    "Bogatyrskii boi kazaka Kuz'my Kriuchkova s nemetskimi ulanami." Petrograd: Sod-
        ruzhestvo, n.d. RU-SU 475.
    Deni and Dolgorukov. "Kukhnia voiny." Moscow-Leningrad: OGIZ-IZOGIZ, 1934.
        RU-SU 567.
    "Geroiskaia bor'ba kazaka Koz'my Kriuchkova s 11 nemtsami." Odessa: M. S. Koz-
        man, 1914. RU-SU 162.
    "Iavlenie Bozhei Materi na nebe pered srazheniem russkomu voinstvu, predzna-
        menovavshee o pobede. . . ." Moscow: M. N. Sharapov, n.d. RU-SU 359.
    "Iavliusia emy sam." Moscow: A.D. Sazonov, n.d. RU-SU 315.
    Moor, Dmitrii. "Bogatyrskoe delo Koz'my Kriuchkova." Moscow: I. D. Sytin, no. 13,
        1914. RU-SU 134.
    "Na bor'bu s imperialisticheskimi voinami." Moscow-Leningrad: Gosizdat, 1929.
        RU-SU 1908.
    Pasternak, Leonid. "Na pomoshch' zhertvam voiny." Moscow: A. A. Levenson, 1914.
        RU-SU 1066.

———. "Tsena krovi." Petrograd: Petrogradskii Sovet Rabochikh i Krasnoarmeiskikh Deputatov, 1918. RU-SU 2284.

"Podvig riadovogo Katsa." Grodno: Lapin, n.d. RU-SU 258.

"Podvig russkago pravoslavnago sviashchennika." Moscow: I. D. Sytin, 1915. RU-SU 343.

"Podvig sestry E. P. Korkinoi." Moscow: I. D. Sytin, no. 86, 1915. RU-SU 322.

Ravitskii, M. G. "Voina Rossii s Germanii i Avstrii." Kiev: I. T. Gubanov, 1914. RU-SU 307.

"Russkii soldat." Moscow: I. D. Sytin, no. 57, 1914. RU-SU 337.

"Torgovtsy Moskvy—Soldatam-invalidam." Moscow: A. A. Levenson, August 1916. RU-SU 70.

RGALI: (Rossiiskii gosudarstvennyi arkhiv literatury i isskustva)

    f. 613 Gosudarstvennoe literaturnoe izdatel'stvo

    f. 616 Izdatel'stvo Zemlia i fabrika

    f. 631 Soiuz Sovetskikh pisatelei

    f. 1161 Personal Collection of S. N. Sergeev-Tsenskii

    f. 1423 Personal Collection of Lev Naumovich Voitolovskii

    f. 1611 Personal Collection of Sof'ia Fedorchenko

    f. 2452 Vsesoiuznoe upravlenie po okhrane avtorskikh prav

    f. 2865 Personal Collection of Kirill Levin

RGASPI: (Rossiiskii gosudarstvennyi arkhiv sotsial'no-politicheskoi istorii)

    f. 70 Istpart TsK VKP (b)

RGVA (Rossiiskii gosudarstvennyi voennyi arkhiv)

    f. 63 Gosudarstvennoe voennoe izdatel'stvo

    f. 39352 Nauchnyi voennyi-istoricheskii otdel general'nogo shtaba Krasnoi Armii; Komissiia po issledovaniiu i ispol'zovaniiu opyta i mirovoi i grazhdanskoi voiny Vseroglavshtaba.

RGVIA (Rossiiskii gosudarstvennyi voennyi-istoricheskii arkhiv)

    f. 2067 (Shtab glavnokomanduiushchago armiami iugo-zapadnago fronta—otdelenie voenno-tsenzurnoe)

    f. 16180—Komissiia po organizatsii narodnogo voenno-istoricheskogo muzeia voiny 1914–1918gg.

William F. Scott and Harriet Fast Scott Soviet Military Research Collections, University of Kentucky

Journals and Newspapers

Istoricheskii zhurnal
Istoriia proletariata SSSR
Izvestiia
Kommunistcheskii Internatsional
Komsomol'skaia pravda
Krasnaia nov'
Krasnaia zvezda
Literaturnoe obozrenie
Molodaia gvardiia
Moskovskii zhurnal
Na literaturnom postu

Nasha zhizn'
Niva
Novyi mir
Peterburgskii listok
Pravda
Proletarskoe kino
Rabochaia gazeta
Rabochaia Moskva
RAPP
Roman-gazeta
Sotsial-Demokrat
Vecherniaia Moskva
Viatskaia pravda
Voennaia byl'
Voenno-istoricheskii zhurnal
Voina i revoliutsiia

Internet Sources

Interfaks-religiia (www.interfax-religion.ru)
Istoriia (www.his.1september.ru)
Kul'tura (www.kultura-portal.ru)
mos.memo.ru
nobelprize.org
Novye izvestiia (www.newizv.ru)
Russkii dom (www.russdom.ru)
scensky.ru (about S. N. Sergeev-Tsenskii)
Vecherniaia Moskva (www.vmdaily.ru)
www.cadetcorps.ru
www.frans-masereel.de
www.genocide-museum.am
www.itar-tass.com
www.liveinternet.ru
www.marxists.org
www.mosnovostroy.ru
www.pravaya.ru
www.white-guard.ru
www.zavet.ru

Reference Works

American National Biography Online. http://www.anb.org
Bol'shaia Sovetskaia Entsiklopediia. O. Iu. Shmidt, ed. Moscow: Sovetskaia Entsiklope-
    diia, 1926–1947.
Bol'shaia Sovetskaia Entsiklopediia. 2nd ed. B. A. Vvedenskii, ed. Moscow: Bol'shaia So-
    vetskaia Entsiklopediia, 1955–.

Dictionary of Literary Biography, vol. 272: *Russian Prose Writers Between the Wars.* Christine Rydel, ed. Detroit: The Gale Group, 2003.
Modern Encyclopedia of Russian and Soviet History. Joseph L. Wieczynski et al., eds. Gulf Breeze, Fla.: Academic International Press, 1976–.
Modern Encyclopedia of Russian and Soviet Literature. Harry B. Weber, ed. Gulf Breeze, Fla.: Academic International Press, 1977–.

War Memory 1914–1945

Akhun, M. I., and V. A. Petrov, eds. *Tsarskaia armiia v gody imperialisticheskoi voiny.* Moscow, 1929.
Albera, François, and Roland Cosandey, eds. *Boris Barnet: Ecrits, Documents, Etudes, Filmographie.* Locarno: Editions du festival international du film de Locarno, 1985.
Almast, Mak. "V tupike." *Molodaia gvardiia* no. 18 (1929).
Al'tman, V., ed. *Dvadtsat' piat' let pervoi mirovoi imperialisticheskoi voiny, 1914–1918.* Narkompros RSFSR, 1939.
Aramilev, V. *V dymu voiny: Zapiski vol'noopredeliaiushchegosia (1914–1917gg).* Leningrad: Molodaia gvardia, 1930.
Arendt, V. *Voenno-istoricheskii muzei v Moskve.* Moscow: Voennyi vestnik, 1926.
Arnosht, K. *Povernuvshie shtyki: Vospominaniia voennoplennogo.* Moscow: Moskovskii rabochii, 1927.
Babel, Isaac. *1920 Diary,* Carol J. Avins, ed. New Haven, Conn.: Yale University Press, 1995.
———. *The Complete Works of Isaac Babel,* Nathalie Babel, ed., Peter Constantine, trans. New York: W.W. Norton, 2002.
Babel', Isaak. *Konarmiia.* Moscow: OGIZ, 1926.
Baburina, N. I., ed. *Russia 20th Century: History of the Country in Poster.* Moscow: Panorama Publishing House, 2000.
Barbusse, Henri [Barbius]. *Ogon'.* Moscow: Goslitizdat, 1938. (*Feu*)
———. *Rechi Bortsa,* 2nd ed. Moscow: 1925. (*Paroles d'un combattant, articles et discours* [1917–1920])
———. *V Ogne.* Moscow: Akademiia, 1935. (*Feu*)
Barnet, Boris. *Okraina* (released in English as *The Patriots*), Mezhrabpom, 1933; International Historic Films, 1984.
Barsukov, E. Z. *Memoirs* (unpublished) in GIM OPI f. 426, op. 1, dd. 77–78.
Bazarevskii, A. Kh., ed. *Lodzinskaia operatsiia: Sbornik dokumentov.* Moscow-Leningrad: Voenizdat, 1936.
———. *Mirovaia voina 1914–1918 g.g.: Kampaniia 1918 goda vo Frantsii i Bel'gii.* Moscow: Gosizdat, Otdel voennoi literatury, 1927.
———. *Nastupatel'naia operatsiia 9-i Russkoi armii, iiun' 1916 goda: Proryv ukreplennoi polosy i forsirovanie reki.* Moscow: Gos. voen. izd-vo, 1937.
Bednyi, Dem'ian. "Predislovie." In L. Voitolovskii, *Po sledam voiny: Pokhodnye zapiski 1914–1917, I.* Leningrad: Gosizdat, 1925.
Berdiaev, Nikolai. *Sud'ba Rossii.* Moscow: Sovetskii pisatel', 1990. Reprint of 1918 edition.
"Bezumstvo khrabrykh." In *Pamiatka otdel'nykh podvigov russkikh voinov velikoi voiny 1914–1915 gg., I.* Vyborg: Vestnika Vyborgskoi Krepostnoi Artillerii, 1915.
Boltin, E. A, L. V. Zhigarev, and M. M. Kaplun, eds. *Artilleristy: Sbornik statei i rasskazov.* Moscow: Molodaia gvardiia, 1939.

Bonch-Bruevich, M. D. *Poteriia nami Galitsii v 1915 godu*. 2 vols. Moscow: Voenno-istoricheskaia komissiia, 1920.

———. *Vsia vlast' Sovetam!* Moscow: Voenizdat, 1958. Online at http://militera.lib.ru/memo/russian/bonch-bruevich_md/index.html.

Bochkareva, Maria. *Yashka: My Life as Peasant, Officer and Exile*. New York: Frederick A. Stokes, 1919.

Brusilov, A. A. *Moi Vospominaniia*. Moscow-Leningrad: Gosizdat, 1929.

———. *A Soldier's Notebook, 1914–1918*. London: Macmillan, 1930; repr. Westport, Conn.: Greenwood Press, 1976.

Chaadaeva, O. N. *Armiia nakanune Fevral'skoi revoliutsii*. Moscow: Gos. sotsial'no-eko-nomicheskoe izd-vo, 1935.

———. *Podgotovka Velikoi Oktiabr'skoi Sotsialisticheskoi Revoliutsii: Lektsii, prochitannye na Istoricheskom Fakul'tete Moskovskogo Universiteta*. Moscow: Izd-vo Moskovskogo Universiteta, 1952.

———. *Soldatskie pis'ma 1917 goda*. Moscow-Leningrad: Gosizdat, 1927.

———. "Soldatskie pis'ma v gody mirovoi voiny (1915–1917 gg)." *Krasnyi arkhiv* 65–66 (1934): 118–163.

Chiabrov, D. *Voina i gruziny*. Petrograd, 1915.

Del'briuk, Gans. *Istoriia voennogo iskusstva v ramkakh politicheskoi istorii*. Moscow: Gos. voen. izd-vo, 1937.

Denikin, A. I. *The Russian Turmoil. Memoirs: Military, Social, and Political*. New York, n.d.

Dinamov, S. "Predislovie." In Ernest Kheminguei, *Proshchai oruzhie*. Evg. Kalashknikova, trans. Moscow: Gos. izd-vo khudozh. lit-ry, 1936.

Dmitriev, V. *Dobrovolets: Vospominaniia o voine i plene*. Moscow-Leningrad: Gosizdat, 1929.

Domanskii, M. "Vstrecha." *Niva* no. 2 (1916): 35–38.

Dovzhenko, Aleksandr, director. *Arsenal* (feature film), 1929.

Dubinskaia, Tat'iana. *Pulemetchitsa: Iz dnevnika mirovoi voiny*. Moscow: Sovetskii pisa-tel', 1936.

———. *Soldaty: Povest'*. Moscow: Sovetskii pisatel', 1939.

———. *V okopakh*. Moscow: Federatsiia, 1930.

Dubovikov, A. "Mikh. Sholokov. *Tikhii Don*." *Molodaia gvardiia*, August 8, 1928, 205–206.

Dunaevskii, I., and V. Lebedev-Kumach, "Pesnia o rodine." In *Pesni Krasnoi Armii*. Mos-cow: Voenizdat, 1937.

Dvadtsat' piat' let Pervoi Mirovoi Imperialisticheskoi Voiny, 1914–1918 gg.: Kratkii ukaza-tel' literatury. V. Al'tman, compiler. Moscow: Nauchno-issledovatel'skii institut bib-liotekovedeniia i rekomendatel'noi bibliografii, 1939.

Edgerton, William, ed. *Memoirs of Peasant Tolstoyans in Soviet Russia*. Bloomington: In-diana University Press, 1993.

Ehrenburg, Ilya. *Julio Jurenito*. Trans. Anna Bostock in collaboration with Yvonne Kapp. Philadelphia: Dufour Editions, 1963.

Erenburg, Il'ia. *Lik voiny*. Berlin: Gelikon, 1923.

———. *Lik voiny*. Moscow: Puchina, 1924.

———. *Lik voiny*. Moscow: Zemlia i fabrika, 1928.

———. *Neobychainye pokhozhdeniia Khulio Khurenito i ego uchenikov. . . .* Moscow: Go-sizdat, 1927.

Erusalimskii, A. "Proiskhozhdenie mirovoi imperialisticheskoi voiny 1914–1918 gg. v osveshchenii M. N. Pokrovskogo." In *Protiv istoricheskoi kontseptsii M. N. Pokrovskogo,* B. D. Grekov, ed. Moscow-Leningrad: Akademiia Nauk SSSR, 1939.

Fadeev, Aleksandr. *Razgrom.* In *Sobranie sochinenii,* tom 1. Moscow, 1959.

Fadeyev, A. *The Nineteen.* R. D. Charques, trans. International Publishers, 1929. Repr. Westport, Conn.: Hyperion Press, 1973.

Fedin, Konstantin. *Goroda i gody: Roman.* Leningrad: Gosizdat, 1924.

Fedorchenko, Sof'ia. *Ivan Speaks.* Thomas Whittemore, trans. Boston: Houghton Mifflin, 1919. Online at http://books.google.com/books?id=n_UKAAAAIAAJ.

⸺. *Narod na voine: Frontovyia zapisi.* Kiev: Tip. Vserossiiskago Zemskago Soiuza Kom. Iugo-Zap. Fr., 1917.

⸺. *Narod na voine.* Moscow: Novaia Moskva, 1923.

⸺. *Narod na voine.* Moscow-Leningrad: Zemlia i fabrika, 1925.

⸺. *Le Peuple à la guerre.* Lydia Bach and Charles Reber, trans. Paris: Valois, 1930.

⸺. *Der Russe redet: Aufzeichnungen nach dem Stenogramm.* Alexander Eliasberg, trans. Munich: Drei Masken Verlag, 1923.

Feinberg, Il'ia. *1914-i: Dokumental'nyi pamflet.* S. Telingater, artist. Moscow: MTP, 1934.

Finn, Konstantin. *Okraina.* Moscow: Gos. izd-vo khudozh. lit-ry, 1933.

Fishgendler, A. M. *Soldaty fronta i voprosy voiny i mira.* Petrograd: Kniga, 1917.

Furmanov, Dmitrii. *Chapaev.* Moscow: Gos. izd-vo, 1923.

⸺. *Dnevnik 1914–1915–1916.* Moscow-Leningrad: Moskovskii rabochii, 1929.

Gerasimov, E. Review of *Pulemetchitsa. Literaturnoe Obozrenie* no. 6 (1936): 20–21.

Geroiskii podvig Donskogo kazaka Kuz'my Firsovicha Kriuchkova. Moscow: P. B. Beltsov, 1914.

Gil'chevskii, K. *Boevye deistviia vtoroocherednykh chastei v mirovuiu voinu.* Leningrad: Gosizdat, 1928.

Gippius, A. I. *Zapiski glavnougovarivaiushchego 293 pekhotnogo izhorskogo polka* Moscow: Gosizdat. 1930.

Gladkov, Fyodor Vasilievich. *Cement.* A. S. Arthur and C. Ashleigh, trans. Evanston, Ill.: Northwestern University Press, 1980.

Glaeser, Ernst. *Rozhdennye v 1902 godu.* Moscow: Molodaia gvardiia, 1931.

Grigor'ev, Sergei. *Kazarma.* Moscow-Leningrad: Zemlia i fabrika, 1926.

Grishin, M. I., ed. *Pomni o voine: Sbornik.* Moscow-Leningrad: Molodaia gvardiia, 1924.

Gromov, M. *Za krestami.* Moscow-Leningrad: Gosizdat, 1927.

Gumilev, Nikolai. *Zapiski kavalerista.* In *Sobranie sochinenii,* tom 4, G. P. Struve and B. A. Filippova, eds. Washington, D.C.: Victor Kamkin, 1968.

Hašek, Jaroslav [Gashek]. *Pokhozhdeniia bravogo soldata Shveika: Vo vremia mirovoi,* II. Leningrad: Gos. izd.-vo. khudozh. lit-ry, 1937.

Hemingway, Ernest [Kheminguei]. *Proshchai oruzhie.* Evg. Kalashknikova, trans. S. Dinamov, foreword. Moscow: Gos. izd-vo khudozh. lit-ry, 1936.

Imperialisticheskaia voina 1914–1918gg. Ob'iasnitel'nyi tekst k serii diapositivov. M. Gaivoronskii, compiler. Moscow: Fabrika Diafoto no. 7, 1933.

Isserson, G. S. *Kanny mirovoi voiny: Gibel' armii Samsonova.* Moscow: Gos. voen. izd-vo, 1926.

Ivanov, V. V. *Bronepoezd no 14–69: Povest'.* Moscow: Krasnaia nov', 1923.

Jünger, Ernst. *Storm of Steel: From the Diary of a German Storm-Troop Officer on the Western Front.* New York: Howard Fertig, 1975.

Kandidov, Boris. *Religiia v tsarskoi armii.* Moscow: Bezbozhnik, 1928.

Katsov, Leonid. *Skvoz' plen.* Moscow: Federatsiia, 1930.

———. *Skvoz' plen.* Moscow: Mos. t-vo pisatelei, 1934.

Khmelevskii, G. *Mirovaia imperialisticheskaia voina, 1914–1918: sistematicheskii ukazatel' knizhnoi i stateinoi voenno-istoricheskoi literatury za 1914–1935 gg.* Moscow: Voennaia akademiia RKKA im. M. V. Frunze, 1936.

Klychkov, Sergei. *Sakharnyi nemets.* Paris: YMCA Press, 1982. Reprint of Moscow: Federatsiia, 1929.

Kollontai, A. *Otryvki iz dnevnika 1914 g.* Leningrad: Gosizdat, 1924.

Korol'kov, G. *Nesbyvshiesia Kanny: Neudavshiisia razgrom russkikh letom 1915 g.* Moscow: Voenizdat, 1926.

Korsun, N. G. *Erzerumskaia operatsii na Kavkazskom fronte mirovoi voiny v 1915–1916 gg.* Moscow: Gos. voen. izd-vo, 1938.

Latsis, Martin Ivanovich. *V poslednoi skhvatke s tsarizmom.* Moscow, 1935.

Lemke, Mikh. *250 dnei v tsarskoi stavke: 25 cent. 1915–2 iiulia 1916.* Petersburg: Gos. izd-vo, 1920.

Lenin, V. I. *Collected Works,* vol. 21. Moscow: Progress Publishers, 1964.

———. *Ob imperialisticheskoe voine.* F. Blumental', comp. Ia. Berman, ed. Moscow: Gos. izd-vo, Otdel voen. lit-ry, 1929.

Levin, Kirill. "The Wild Battalion: A Story." In *We Did Not Fight: 1914–18 Experiences of War Resisters,* Julian Bell, ed. London: Cobden-Sanderson, 1935.

———. *Za koliuchei provolokoi.* Moscow: OGIZ–Molodaia gvardiia, 1931.

———. *Zapiski iz plena.* Moscow: Federatsiia, 1931.

———. *Zapiski iz plena.* Moscow: Mos. t-vo pisateli, 1934.

Lidin, Vladimir. "Mogila neizvestnogo soldata." *Novyi mir* no. 3 (1931): 18–41.

———. *Mogila neizvestnogo soldata.* Moscow: Federatsiia, 1932.

Littauer, Vladimir. *Russian Hussar: A Story of the Imperial Cavalry, 1911–1920.* Shippensburg, Pa.: White Mane Publishing Co., 1993.

Maizel', D. "O *Tikhom Done* i odnom 'dobrom kritike.'" *Zvezda* no. 8 (1929): 189–198.

Maksimov, A., E. Medvedev, and Sh. Iusupov, eds. *Tsarskaia armiia v period mirovoi voiny i Fevral'skoi revoliutsii: Sbornik.* Kazan: Tatizdat, 1932.

Malakhova, Vera Ivanovna. "Four Years as a Front-line Physician." In *A Revolution of Their Own: Voices of Women in Soviet History,* Barbara Alpern Engel and Anastasia Posadskaya-Vanderbeck, eds. Boulder, Colo.: Westview Press, 1997.

Mashbits-Verov, I. *"Tikhii Don." Novyi mir* no. 10 (1928): 225–236.

Mavrodin, V. *Brusilov.* Moscow: Pravda, 1943.

McKay, Claude [Mak Kei]. "Vozvrashchenie soldata." In *Sudom lincha.* A. M. and P. Okhrimenko, trans. Moscow: Ogonek, 1925: 37–44.

Mirovaia voina: Ukazatel' literatury. A. S. Mazel', ed. Leningrad: Bibliotechnaia metodicheskaia baza Leningradskogo oblprofsoveta, Bibliotechnyi kollektor KOGIZ'a, 1934.

Mirovaia voina: Ukazatel' literatury, 1914–1934. Leningrad, Bibliotechnaia metodicheskaia baza Leningradskogo oblprofsoveta, Bibliotechnyi kollektor KOGIZ'a, 1934.

Molostvova, E. B. *Soldatskiia pis'ma.* Kazan: Umid', 1917.

Na chuzhbine: Sbornik proizvedenii russkikh voinov. "Russkii soldat-grazhdanin vo Frantsii," 1919.

Nashi chudo-bogatyri v voine 1914 goda. Petrograd: Gramotnost', 1915.

"Novye podvigi Koz'my Kriuchkova i ego tovarishchei." In *Pamiatka otdel'nykh podvigov russkikh voinov velikoi voiny 1914–1915 gg., II.* Vyborg: Vestnika Vyborgskoi Krepostnoi Artillerii, 1915.

Okunev, Ia. *Na peredovykh pozitsiiakh: Boevyia vpechatleniia*. Petrograd: M. V. Popov, 1915.

Os'kin, D. *Zapiski praporshchika*. Moscow: Federatsiia, 1931.

⸺. *Zapiski soldata*. Moscow: Federatsiia, 1929.

Owen, Wilfred. *The Collected Poems of Wilfred Owen*. New York: New Directions Books, 1963.

Paduchev, Vl. *Zapiski nizhnego china: 1916 god*. Moscow: Mos. t-vo pisatelei, 1931.

Pasternak, Boris. *Doctor Zhivago*. New York: Pantheon Books, 1958.

Pasternak, L. O. *Zapisi raznykh let*. Moscow: Sovetskii khudozhnik, 1975.

Pavlov, I. U. *Boevoi put': Zapiski krasnogo letchika*. Moscow: Izd-vo TSK VLKSM Molodaia gvardiia, 1937.

Pireiko, A. *Na fronte imperialisticheskoi voiny: Vospominaniia bol'shevika*. Moscow: Starii Bol'shevik, 1935.

⸺. *V tylu i na fronte imperialisticheskoi voiny: Vospominaniia riadovogo*. Leningrad: Priboi, 1926.

Pokrovskii, M. N. *Imperialisticheskaia voina: Sbornik statei*. Moscow: Gos. sots-ekon izd-vo, 1934.

Puchkov, S. V. *Moskovskoe gorodskoe bratskoe kladbishche*. Moscow: Gorodskaia tipografiia, 1915.

Puliakov, M. "V tsarskoi i v krasnoi." In *Za chto borolis'?* M. Kudrin, ed. Moscow: Gosizdat, 1928.

Remarque, Erich Maria. *All Quiet on the Western Front*. New York: Ballantine Books, 1982.

⸺ [Remark]. *Na zapadnom fronte bez peremen,* Dm. Umanskii, ed. Foreword by Karl Radek. Sergei Miatezhnyi and Petr Cherevin, trans. Moscow-Leningrad: Zemlia i fabrika, 1929.

⸺. *The Road Back*. Boston: Little, Brown, 1931.

Rolland, Romain. *Klerambo*. Petrograd: Gosizdat, 1923.

Romanov, Panteleimon. *Rus'*. Moscow: Gos. izd-vo khudozh. lit-ry, 1936.

Rossiia v mirovoi voine, 1914–1918 v tsifrakh. Moscow: TSU, 1925.

Rozenfel'd, Semen. *Gibel'*. Berlin: Petropolis, 1931.

⸺. *Gibel'*. Leningrad: Izdatel'stvo pisatelei, 1931.

Rozhdestvenskii, M. *Lutskii proryv*. Moscow: Voenizdat, 1938.

Sel'vinskii, Il'ia. *General Brusilov*. In *Lirika i drama*. Moscow: OGIZ, 1947.

Sergeev-Tsenskii, S. N. *Brusilovskii proryv*, I. Moscow: Sovetskii pisatel', 1943.

⸺. *Brusilovskii proryv*, II. Moscow: Sovetskii pisatel', 1944.

⸺. *Massy, mashiny, stikhii*. Moscow: Gos. izd-vo khudozh. lit-ry, 1936.

⸺. *Sobranie sochinenii v desiati tomakh*. Moscow: Gos. izd-vo khudozh. lit-ry, 1955–1956.

⸺. *Zauriad-polk*. Moscow: Gos. izd-vo khudozh. lit-ry, 1935.

Sergeyev-Tsensky, S. *Brusilov's Breakthrough: A Novel of the First World War*. Helen Altschuler, trans. London: Hutchinson, 1945.

Shadr, I. D. "Pamiatnik miromy stradaniiu," *Tvorchestvo* no. 5 (1918): 21–24.

Sheppard, Canon H.R.L. "Foreword." In *We Did Not Fight: 1914–18 Experiences of War Resisters,* Julian Bell, ed. London: Cobden-Sanderson, 1935.

Shklovskii, Viktor. *Sentimental'noe puteshestvie: Vospominaniia, 1917–1922*. Orange, Conn.: Antiquary, 1986. Reprint of Moscow-Berlin: Gelikon, 1923.

Shklovsky, Viktor. *A Sentimental Journey: Memoirs, 1917–1922*. Ithaca, N.Y.: Cornell University Press, 1970.

Sholokhov, Mikhail. *Quiet Flows the Don.* Robert Daglish, trans. Brian Murphy, ed. New York: Carroll and Graf, 1996.

——. *Tikhii Don.* Vstupitel'naia stat'ia Iu. Lukina. Illiustratsii S. G. Korol'kova. Moscow Gos. izd-vo khudozh. lit-ry, 1941.

——. *Tikhii Don, Kniga pervaia.* Graviury A. Kravchenko. Moscow: Gos. izd-vo khudozh. lit-ry, 1934.

——. *Tikhii Don, Kniga pervaia.* Illiustratsii S. G. Korol'kova. Moscow: Gos. izd-vo khudozh. lit-ry, 1935.

——. *Tikhii Don, Kniga vtoraia.* Moscow: Gos. izd-vo khudozh. lit-ry, 1933.

Shub, Esfir. *Padenie dinastii Romanovykh (The Fall of the Romanov Dynasty).* Sovkino, 1927; Kino International, 1991.

Shukhmin, Khristofor. *Diuzhina nemtsev na odnom kazatskom shtyke.* Moscow, 1915.

Slezkin, Iurii L'vovich. *Brusilov.* Leningrad: Sovetskii pisatel', 1947.

"Smert' sviashchenika geroia." In *Nashi chudo-bogatyri v voine 1914 goda.* Petrograd: Gramotnost', 1915.

Soboleff, Leonid. *Romanoff.* Alfred Fremantle, trans. New York: Longmans, Green and Co., 1935; repr. Westport, Conn.: Hyperion Press, 1975.

Sobolev, Leonid. *Kapital'nyi remont.* Leningrad: Gos. izd-vo khudozh. lit-ry, 1933.

Sokolovskii, Nikolai. *Na zapade bez peremen: Radio-p'esa po romanu Remarka.* Unpublished manuscript in RGALI, f, 613, op. 1, d. 7787.

Solzhenitsyn, Alexander. *August 1914.* Michael Glenny, trans. New York: Farrar, Straus and Giroux, 1972.

Stepnoi, N. [Pseudonym of Nikolai Aleksandrovich Afinogenov]. *Zapiski opolchentsa,* 3rd ed. Kineshma: Izd-vo. kollektiva raboche-krest'ianskikh pisatelei, 1924.

Stepun, Fedor. [N. Lugin] *Iz pisem praporshchika-artillerista.* Moscow: Zadruga, 1918; repr. Tomsk: Vodolei, 2000.

Svechin, A. A. *Iskusstvo vozhdeniia polka po opytu voiny 1914–1918 gg.* Moscow: Gosizdat, 1930; repr. Moscow: Assotsiatsiia voennaia kniga Kuchkovo Pole, 2005.

Tagirov, A. *Soldaty.* B. Kh. Cherniak and V. Ia. Tarsis, trans. (from Bashkir). Moscow: Gos. izd-vo khudozh. lit-ry, 1934.

Tikhii Don. Moscow: Soiuzkino, 1931.

Timofeev, Boris. *Chasha skorbnaia.* Tsentral. Ispon. Kom. Sovet, 1918.

Tolstoi, Aleksei. *Khozhdenie po mukam I-II.* Moscow: Sovetskaia literatura, 1934.

——. "Na Kavkaze." In *Polnoe sobranie sochinenii,* tom 3. A. S. Miasnikova, A. N. Tikhonova, L. I. Tolstaia, eds. Moscow: Gos. izd-vo khudozh. lit-ry, 1949.

——. "Otechestvo." In *Polnoe sobranie sochinenii,* tom 3. A. S. Miasnikova, A. N. Tikhonova, L. I. Tolstaia, eds. Moscow: Gos. izd-vo khudozh. lit-ry, 1949.

——. "Po Galitsii." In *Polnoe sobranie sochinenii,* tom 3. A. S. Miasnikova, A. N. Tikhonova, L. I. Tolstaia, eds. Moscow: Gos. izd-vo khudozh. lit-ry, 1949.

——. "Po Volyni." In *Polnoe sobranie sochinenii,* tom 3. A. S. Miasnikova, A. N. Tikhonova, and L. I. Tolstaia, eds. Moscow: Gos. izd-vo khudozh. lit-ry, 1949.

Tolstoy, Alexei. *Road to Calvary,* vol. 1. Edith Bone, trans. New York: Alfred A. Knopf, 1946.

Tsarskaia armiia v period mirovoi voiny i fevral'skoi revoliutsii: materialy k izucheniiu imperialisticheskoi i grazhdanskoi voiny. Vstup. stat'ia M. Vol'fovich; sostavili A. Maksimov, E. Medvedev, i Sh. Iusupov; pod red. A. Maksimova; Tsentral'nyi arkhiv Tatarskoi respubliki. Kazan': Tatizdat, 1932.

Tsekhnovitser, O. V. *Literatura i mirovaia voina: 1914–1918*. Gos. izd-vo khudozh. lit-ry, 1938.

Tsikhovich, Ia. K. *Strategicheskii ocherk voiny 1914–1918 g.g.* Russian S.F.S.R. Komissiia po issledovaniiu i ispol'zovaniiu opyta mirovoi i grazhdanskoi voiny. Russian S.F.S.R. Armiia, Voenno-istoricheskaia komissiia. Moscow: Vysshii voennyi redaktsionnyi sovet, 1920.

Usievich, E. "Roman o pervoi mirovoi voine." *Znamia* 11 (1945): 136–149.

Vavilov, Artem (Artur). *Zapiski soldata Vavilova.* Reworked by Boris Brodianskii. Moscow-Leningrad: Gosizdat, 1927.

Veber, Iu. "Proryv." In *Artilleristy: Sbornik statei i rasskazov,* E. A. Boltin, L. V. Zhigarev, and M. M. Kaplun, eds. Moscow: Molodaia gvardiia, 1939.

Veselyi, Artem. *Rossiia, krov'iu umytaia.* Moscow: Sovetskii pisatel', 1935.

Vinogradov, S. "Na pomoshch' zhertvam voiny" (1914). In N. I. Baburina, ed., *Russia 20th Century: History of the Country in Poster.* Moscow: Panorama Publishing House, 2000.

Voitolovskaia, A. L. *Po sledam sud'by moego pokoleniia.* Syktyvkar: Komi Knizhnoe Izdatel'stvo, 1991.

Voitolovskii, L. *Po sledam voiny: Pokhodnye zapiski, 1914–1917,* I. Leningrad: Gos. izd-vo, 1925.

———. *Po sledam voiny: Pokhodnye zapiski, 1914–1917,* II. Leningrad: Gos. izd-vo, 1927.

———. *Po sledam voiny.* Leningrad: Izdatel'stvo pisatelei, 1934.

———. *Vskhodil krovavyi mars: Po sledam voiny.* Moscow: Goslitizdat, 1931; repr. Moscow: Voennoe izdatel'stvo, 1998.

Voronitsyn, I. *U nemtsev: Ocherki politicheskoi tiurmy i ssylki.* Khar'kov, 1923.

"Vysochaishee nagrazhdenie Georgievskim krestom devitsy Tychininoi." In *Nashi chudo-bogatyri v voine 1914 goda.* Petrograd: Gramotnost', 1915.

Zagorskii, M. B. *Gogol' i teatr.* Moscow: Iskusstvo, 1952.

———. *Predatel'.* Unpublished manuscript in RGALI, f. 2452, op. 3, d. 1703.

———. *Pushkin i teatr.* Moscow: Iskusstvo, 1940.

Zaionchkovskii, A. M. *Mirovaia Voina 1914–1918.* Moscow: Voenizdat, 1924.

Zakharova, Lidiia. *Dnevnik sestry miloserdiia na peredovykh pozitsiiakh.* Petrograd: Izd-vo biblioteka Velikoi voiny, 1915.

Zhdanov, N., and A. Svechin. *Russkie voennoplennye v mirovoi voine 1914–1918 gg, I–III.* Moscow: Vseroglavshtaba, 1920.

Secondary Sources

Alabin, M. M., A. C. Dibrov, and V. D. Sudravskii, eds. *Moskovskoe gorodskoe bratskoe kladbishche: Opyt biograficheskogo slovaria.* Moscow: Gos. publichnaia istoricheskaia biblioteka, 1992.

Anderson, Benedict. *Imagined Communities: Reflections on the Origins and Spread of Nationalism,* rev. ed. London: Verso, 1991.

Audoin-Rouzeau, Stéphane, and Annette Becker. *14–18: Understanding the Great War.* New York: Hill and Wang, 2003.

Becker, Annette. *War and Faith: The Religious Imagination in France, 1914–1930.* Oxford: Berg, 1998.

Belov, G. "Russkii polkovodets A. A. Brusilov." *Voenno-istoricheskii zhurnal* no. 10 (October 1962): 41–55.

Bernstein, Frances Lee. *The Dictatorship of Sex: Lifestyle Advice for the Soviet Masses.* DeKalb, Ill.: Northern Illinois University Press, 2007.

Borenstein, Eliot. *Men Without Women: Masculinity and Revolution in Russian Fiction, 1917–1929.* Durham, N.C.: Duke University Press, 2000.

Brandenberger, David. *National Bolshevism: Stalinist Mass Culture and the Formation of Modern Russian National Identity, 1931–1956.* Cambridge, Mass.: Harvard University Press, 2002.

Brown, Kate. *A Biography of No Place: From Ethnic Borderland to Soviet Heartland.* Cambridge, Mass.: Harvard University Press, 2004.

Browning, Christopher. *Ordinary Men: Reserve Police Battalion 101 and the Final Solution in Poland.* New York: HarperCollins, 1998.

Carlson, Maria. "Fashionable Occultism: Spiritualism, Theosophy, Freemasonry, and Hermeticism in Fin-de-Siècle Russia." In *The Occult in Russian and Soviet Culture,* Bernice Glazer Rosenthal, ed. Ithaca, N.Y.: Cornell University Press, 1997, 135–152.

Chatterjee, Choi. *Celebrating Women: Gender, Festival Culture and Bolshevik Ideology, 1910–1939.* Pittsburgh: University of Pittsburgh Press, 2002.

Clark, Katerina. *Petersburg: Crucible of Cultural Revolution.* Cambridge, Mass.: Harvard University Press, 1995.

———. *The Soviet Novel: History as Ritual.* Chicago: University of Chicago Press, 1981.

Clements, Barbara Evans. *Bolshevik Feminist: The Life of Alexandra Kollontai.* Bloomington: Indiana University Press, 1979.

Clements, Barbara Evans, Rebecca Friedman, and Dan Healey, eds. *Russian Masculinities in History and Culture.* Houndmills, UK: Palgrave, 2002.

Cohen, Aaron J. "Oh, That! Myth, Memory, and the First World War in the Russian Emigration and the Soviet Union." *Slavic Review* 62, no. 1 (Spring 2003): 69–86.

Coleman, Heather J. *Russian Baptists and Spiritual Revolution, 1905–1929.* Bloomington: Indiana University Press, 2005.

Comerchero, Vincent Alan. "From Outcasts to Allies: Red Army Veterans and the Soviet State from the Introduction of the New Economic Policy through the First Five Year Plan." Ph.D. diss., Indiana University, 1997.

Confino, Alon. "Collective Memory and Cultural History: Problems of Method," *American Historical Review* 102, no. 5 (December 1997): 1386–1403.

Corney, Frederick C. *Telling October: Memory and the Making of the Bolshevik Revolution.* Ithaca, N.Y.: Cornell University Press, 2004.

Danchev, Dmitrii. "Sergei Nikolaevich Sergeev-Tsenskii." In *Dictionary of Literary Biography,* vol. 272: *Russian Prose Writers Between the Wars,* Christine Rydel, ed. Detroit: The Gale Group, 2003: 361–370.

Danilenko, I. S. "Borets protiv lzhi i bezmolviia." In A. A. Svechin, *Iskusstvo vozhdeniia polka.* Moscow: Assotsiatsiia voennaia kniga Kuchkovo Pole, 2005.

Davidian, Irina. "The Russian Soldier's Morale from the Evidence of Tsarist Military Censorship." In *Facing Armageddon: The First World War Experienced,* Hugh Cecil and Peter Liddle, eds. London: Cooper, 1996.

Dawson, Graham. *Soldier Heroes: British Adventure, Empire, and the Imagining of Masculinities.* London: Routledge, 1994.

Dowling, Timothy C. *The Brusilov Offensive.* Bloomington: Indiana University Press, 2008.

Dunham, Vera S. *In Stalin's Time: Middleclass Values in Soviet Fiction*. Durham, N.C.: Duke University Press, 1990.

Edele, Mark. "Paper Soldiers: The World of the Soldier Hero According to Soviet Wartime Posters." *Jahrbucher fur Geschichte Osteuropas* 47 (1999): 89–108.

Eksteins, Modris. "*All Quiet on the Western Front*." *History Today* 45, no. 11 (November 1995): 29–34.

———. *Rites of Spring: The Great War and the Birth of the Modern Age*. Boston: Houghton Mifflin, 1989.

Engel, Barbara, and Anastasia Posadskaya-Vanderbeck, eds. *A Revolution of Their Own: Voices of Women in Soviet History*. Boulder, Colo.: Westview Press, 1997.

Enteen, George M. *The Soviet Scholar-Bureaucrat: M. N. Pokrovskii and the Society of Marxist Historians*. University Park: Pennsylvania State University Press, 1978.

Ermolaev, Herman. *Censorship in Soviet Literature, 1917–1991*. Lanham, Md.: Rowman and Littlefield, 1997.

———. *Mikhail Sholokhov and His Art*. Princeton, N.J.: Princeton University Press, 1982.

Field, Deborah. *Private Life and Communist Morality in Khrushchev's Russia*. New York: Peter Lang, 2007.

Figes, Orlando. *A People's Tragedy: The Russian Revolution, 1891–1924*. New York: Penguin Books, 1996.

Figes, Orlando, and Boris Kolonitskii. *Interpreting the Russian Revolution: The Language and Symbols of 1917*. New Haven, Conn.: Yale University Press, 1999.

Fitzpatrick, Sheila. "The Civil War as a Formative Experience." In *Bolshevik Culture: Experiment and Order in the Russian Revolution*, Abbott Gleason, Peter Kenez, and Richard Stites, eds. Bloomington: Indiana University Press, 1989.

———. "Cultural Revolution as Class War." In *Cultural Revolution in Russia, 1928–1931*, Sheila Fitzpatrick, ed. Bloomington: Indiana University Press, 1978.

———. "The Foreign Threat During the First Five-Year Plan." *Soviet Union/Union Sovietique* 5, no. 1 (1978): 26–35.

Frantzen, Allen J. *Bloody Good: Chivalry, Sacrifice, and the Great War*. Chicago: University of Chicago Press, 2004.

Fuller, William C., Jr. *The Foe Within: Fantasies of Treason and the End of Imperial Russia*. Ithaca, N.Y.: Cornell University Press, 2006.

Fussell, Paul. *The Great War in Modern Memory*. New York: Oxford University Press, 1975.

Gatrell, Peter. *Russia's First World War: A Social and Economic History*. Harlow, UK: Pearson, 2005.

———. *A Whole Empire Walking: Refugees in Russia during World War I*. Bloomington: Indiana University Press, 2005.

Geertz, Clifford. "Deep Play: Notes on the Balinese Cockfight." In *Interpretation of Cultures: Selected Essays*. New York: Basic Books, 1973.

Goldberg, Anatol. *Ilya Ehrenburg: Revolutionary, Novelist, Poet, War Correspondent, Propagandist*. New York: Viking, 1984.

Guillory, Sean Christopher. "We Shall Refashion Life on Earth! The Political Culture of the Young Communist League, 1918–1928." Ph.D. diss., UCLA, 2009.

Halfin, Igal. *Terror in my Soul: Communist Autobiographies on Trial*. Cambridge, Mass.: Harvard University Press, 2003.

Hallett, Richard. "Soviet Criticism of *Tikhiy Don* 1928–1940." *Slavonic and East European Review* 46, no. 106 (January 1968): 60–74.

Harrison, Richard W. *The Russian Way of War: Operational Art, 1904–1940.* Lawrence: University Press of Kansas, 2001.

Hartzok, Justus Grant. "Children of Chapaev: The Russian Civil War Cult and the Creation of Soviet Identity, 1918–1941." Ph.D. diss., University of Iowa, 2009.

Haslam, Jonathan. "Soviet-German Relations and the Origins of the Second World War: The Jury Is Still Out." *Journal of Modern History* 69, no. 4 (December 1997): 785–797.

Hellberg, Elena. "The Hero in Popular Pictures: Russian Lubok and Soviet Poster." In *Populare Bildmedien,* R. Brednich and A. Hartmann, eds. Göttingen: Volker Schmerse, 1989.

Hellman, Ben. "Pervaia mirovaia voina v lubochnoi literature." In *Rossiia i Pervaia Mirovaia Voina: Materialy mezhdunarodnogo nauchnogo kollokviuma,* N. N. Smirnov, ed. St. Petersburg: D. Bulanin, 1999.

———. *Poets of Hope and Despair: The Russian Symbolists in War and Revolution (1914–1918).* Helsinki: Institute for Russian and East European Studies, 1995.

Heretz, Leonid. *Russia on the Eve of Modernity: Popular Religion and Traditional Culture Under the Last Tsars.* Cambridge: Cambridge University Press, 2008.

Higgonet, Margaret R., and Patrice L.-R. Higgonet. "The Double Helix." In *Behind the Lines: Gender and the Two World Wars,* Margaret R. Higgonet, Jane Jenson, Sonya Michel, Margaret C. Weitz, eds. New Haven, Conn.: Yale University Press, 1987.

Hoffmann, David L. "Was there a 'Great Retreat' from Soviet Socialism? Stalinist Culture Reconsidered." *Kritika: Explorations in Russian and Eurasian History* 5, no. 4 (Fall 2004): 651–674.

Holquist, Peter. "From Estate to Ethnos: The Changing Nature of Cossack Identity in the Twentieth Century." In *Russia at a Crossroads: History, Memory and Political Practice,* Nurit Schliefman, ed. London: Frank Cass, 1998.

———. *Making War, Forging Revolution: Russia's Continuum of Crisis, 1914–1921.* Cambridge, Mass.: Harvard University Press, 2002.

Horne, John, and Alan Kramer. *German Atrocities, 1914: A History of Denial.* New Haven, Conn.: Yale University Press, 2001.

Huss, Marie-Monique. "Pronatalism and the Popular Ideology of the Child in Wartime France: The Evidence of the Picture Postcard." In *The Upheaval of War: Family, Work, and Welfare in Europe, 1914–1918,* Richard Wall and Jay Winter, eds. Cambridge: Cambridge University Press, 1988.

Hynes, Samuel. *A War Imagined: The First World War and English Culture.* London: Bodley Head, 1990.

Iuniverg, Leonid. "Abram Vishniak i ego izdatel'stvo 'Gelikon.'" In *Russkoe evreistvo v zarubezh'e: Stat'i, publikatsii, memuary i esse* I (VI). Jerusalem: M. Parkhomovskii, 1998.

Ivanits, Linda J. *Russian Folk Belief.* Armonk, N.Y.: M. E. Sharpe, 1989.

Jahn, Hubertus. "Kaiser, Cossacks, and Kolbasniks: Caricatures of the German in Russian Popular Culture." *Journal of Popular Culture* 31 (Spring 1998): 109–122.

———. *Patriotic Culture in Russia during World War I.* Ithaca, N.Y.: Cornell University Press, 1995.

James, Pearl, ed. *Picture This: World War I Posters and Visual Culture.* Lincoln: University of Nebraska Press, 2009.

Jeffords, Susan. *The Remasculinization of America: Gender and the Vietnam War.* Bloomington: Indiana University Press, 1989.

Jones, David R. "The Imperial Army in World War I." In *The Military History of Tsarist Russia*, Frederick W. Kagan and Robin Higham, eds. New York: Palgrave, 2002.

Kaganovsky, Lilya. "How the Soviet Man was (Un) Made." *Slavic Review* 63, no. 3 (2004): 578–579.

Katagoshchina, Mariia. "Muzei velikoi voiny." *Moskovskii zhurnal*, no. 5 (1992): 39–44.

——. "Pamiatniki velikoi voiny." *Voennaia byl'*, no. 3 /132 (July–September, 1993): 14–17.

Kavanagh, Gaynor. "Museum as Memorial: The Origins of the Imperial War Museum." *Journal of Contemporary History* 23, no. 1 (January 1988): 77–97.

Kelly, Andrew. *Filming* All Quiet on the Western Front: *'Brutal Cutting, Stupid Censors, Bigoted Politicos.'* London: I. B. Tauris, 1998.

Kelly, Catriona. "The Education of the Will: Advice Literature, *Zakal,* and Manliness in Early Twentieth-Century Russia." In *Russian Masculinities in History and Culture,* Barbara Evans Clements, Rebecca Friedman, Dan Healey, eds. Houndmills, UK: Palgrave, 2002.

Kenworthy, Scott. "The Mobilization of Piety: Monasticism and the Great War in Russia, 1914–1916. *Jahrbücher für Geschichte Osteuropas* 52 (2004): 388–401.

King, David. *The Commissar Vanishes: The Falsification of Photographs and Art in Stalin's Russia.* New York: Metropolitan Books, 1997.

Kirschenbaum, Lisa A. *The Legacy of the Siege of Leningrad, 1941–1945: Myth, Memories, and Monuments.* New York: Cambridge University Press, 2006.

Kizenko, Nadieszda. "The Savior on the Waters Church War Memorial in St. Petersburg," in *Picturing Russia: Explorations in Visual Culture,* Joan Neuberger and Valerie Kivelson, eds. New Haven, Conn.: Yale University Press, 2008, 124–127.

Klimenko, Michael. *Ehrenburg: An Attempt at a Literary Portrait.* New York: Peter Lang, 1990.

Kolonitskii, Boris I. "Kerensky," in Edward Acton, Vladimir Iu. Cherniaev, and William G. Rosenberg, eds. *Critical Companion to the Russian Revolution.* Bloomington: Indiana University Press, 1997.

—— *Tragicheskaia erotika: Obrazy imperatorskoi sem'i v gody Pervoi Mirovoi Voiny.* Moscow: Novoe literaturnoe obozrenie, 2010.

Kornblatt, Judith. *The Cossack Hero in Russian Literature: A Study in Cultural Mythology.* Madison: University of Wisconsin Press, 1992.

Korotkov, I. A. *Istoriia Sovetskoi voennoi mysli.* Moscow: Nauka, 1980.

Kremleva, I. A. "Pokhoronno-pominal'nye obychai i obriady." In *Russkie,* V. A. Aleksandrov, I. V. Vlasova, and N. S. Polishchuk, eds. Moscow: Nauka, 2003, 517–532.

Krylova, Anna. "'Healers of Wounded Souls': The Crisis of Private Life in Soviet Literature, 1944–1946." *Journal of Modern History* 73, no. 2 (June 2001): 307–331.

——. "Stalinist Identity from the Viewpoint of Gender: Rearing a Generation of Professionally Violent Women-Fighters in 1930s Stalinist Russia." *Gender & History* 16, no. 3 (November 2004): 626–653.

Leed, Eric J. *No Man's Land: Combat and Identity in World War I.* Cambridge: Cambridge University Press, 1979.

Lehmann, Maike. "Bargaining Armenian-ness: National Politics of Identity in the Soviet Union after 1945," in *Representations on the Margins of Europe: Politics and Identities in the Baltic and South Caucasian States,* Tsypylma Darieva and Wolfgang Kaschuba, eds. Frankfurt: Campus Verlag, 2007.

Lincoln, W. Bruce. *Passage Through Armageddon: The Russians in War and Revolution, 1914–1918.* New York: Simon and Schuster, 1986.

Lohr, Eric. *Nationalizing the Russian Empire: The Campaign Against Enemy Aliens During World War I.* Cambridge, Mass.: Harvard University Press, 2003.

Mannherz, Julia. "Popular Occultism in Late Imperial Russia." Ph.D. diss., Cambridge University, 2005.

Marks, Steven G. *How Russia Shaped the Modern World: From Art to Anti-Semitism, Ballet to Bolshevism.* Princeton, N.J.: Princeton University Press, 2002.

Martin, Terry. *The Affirmative Action Empire: Nations and Nationalism in The Soviet Union, 1923–1939.* Ithaca, N.Y.: Cornell University Press, 2001.

Masing-Delic, Irene. *Abolishing Death: A Salvation Myth of Russian Twentieth-Century Literature.* Stanford, Calif.: Stanford University Press, 1992.

Mavrodin, V. V. "Predislovie," in A. A. Brusilov, *Moi vospominaniia.* Moscow: Voenizdat, 1963.

McReynolds, Louise. "Mobilizing Petrograd's Lower Classes to Fight the Great War" in Gazeta Kopeika," *Radical History Review* 57 (1993): 160–180.

Melman, Billie, ed. *Borderlines: Genders and Identities in War and Peace, 1880–1930.* New York: Routledge, 1998.

Merridale, Catherine. "The Collective Mind: Trauma and Shell-shock in Twentieth-century Russia." *Journal of Contemporary History* 35, no. 1 (2000): 39–55.

⸻. *Night of Stone: Death and Memory in Twentieth-Century Russia.* New York: Viking, 2000.

Mikhailova, Yulia. "Images of Enemy and Self: Russian 'Popular Prints' of the Russo-Japanese War." *Acta slavica iaponica* 16 (1998): 30–53.

Millichap, Joseph R. *Lewis Milestone.* Boston: Twayne, 1981.

Mosse, George L. *Fallen Soldiers: Reshaping the Memory of the World Wars.* New York: Oxford University Press, 1990.

⸻. *The Image of Man: The Creation of Modern Masculinity.* Oxford: Oxford University Press, 1996.

Murphy, A. B., V. P. Butt, H. Ermolaev, eds. *Sholokhov's* Tikhii Don: *A Commentary in 2 Volumes.* Birmingham Slavonic Monographs No. 27. Birmingham, UK: Department of Russian Language and Literature, the University of Birmingham, 1997.

Natter, Wolfgang G. *Literature at War, 1914–1940: Representing the "Time of Greatness" in Germany.* New Haven, Conn.: Yale University Press, 1999.

Nekrich, Aleksandr. *The Punished Peoples.* New York: Norton, 1978.

Niqueux, Michel. "Kratkaia khronika zhizni i tvorchestva Sergeia Klychkova." In Sergei Klychkov, *Sakharnyi nemets.* Paris: YMCA Press, 1982; repr. of Moscow: Federatsiia, 1929.

Norris, Stephen M. "Russian Images of War: The Lubok and Wartime Culture, 1812–1917." Ph.D. diss., University of Virginia, 2002.

⸻. *A War of Images: Russian Popular Prints, Wartime Culture, and National Identity, 1812–1945.* DeKalb, Ill.: Northern Illinois University Press, 2006.

Orlovsky, Daniel. "Velikaia voina i rossiiskaia pamiat'." In *Rossiia i Pervaia Mirovaia Voina: Materialy mezhdunarodnogo nauchnogo kollokviuma,* N. N. Smirnov, ed. St. Petersburg: D. Bulanin, 1999, 49–57.

Page, Stanley W. "The Russian Proletariat and World Revolution: Lenin's Views to 1914." *American Slavic and East European Review* 10, no. 1 (February 1951): 1–13.

Papernyi, Vladimir. *Kul'tura "Dva."* Ann Arbor, Mich.: Ardis, 1985.

Paret, Peter, Beth Irwin Lewis, and Paul Paret, eds. *Persuasive Images: Posters of War and Revolution.* Princeton, N.J.: Princeton University Press, 1992.

Peris, Daniel. *Storming the Heavens: The Soviet League of the Militant Godless.* Ithaca, N.Y.: Cornell University Press, 1998.

Pervaia mirovaia voina: Ukazatel' literatury, 1914–1993 gg. V. A. Vinogradov, ed. Moscow: INION, 1994.

Petrone, Karen. "Family, Masculinity, and Heroism in Russian Posters of the First World War." In *Borderlines: Genders and Identities in War and Peace, 1880–1930,* Billie Melman, ed. New York: Routledge, 1998.

———. *Life Has Become More Joyous, Comrades: Celebrations in the Time of Stalin.* Bloomington: Indiana University Press, 2000.

———. "Masculinity and Heroism in Imperial and Soviet Military-Patriotic Cultures." In *Russian Masculinities,* Barbara Clements, Rebecca Friedman, and Dan Healey, eds. Houndmills, UK, 2002.

———. "Motherland Calling: National Symbols and the Mobilization for War." In *Picturing Russia: Explorations in Visual Culture,* Valerie Kivelson and Joan Neuberger, eds. New Haven, Conn.: Yale University Press, 2008.

Phillips, Laura L. *Bolsheviks and the Bottle: Drink and Worker Culture in St. Petersburg, 1900–1929.* DeKalb, Ill.: Northern Illinois University Press, 2000.

———. "Gendered Dis/ability: Perspectives from the Treatment of Psychiatric Casualties in Russia's Early Twentieth-Century Wars." *Social History of Medicine* 20, no. 2 (2007): 333–350.

Plaggenborg, Stefan. "Gewalt und Militanz in Sowjetrußland 1917–1930." *Jahrbücher für Geschichte Osteuropas* 44, no. 3 (1996): 409–430.

Plamper, Jan. "Fear: Soldiers and Emotion in Early Twentieth-Century Russian Military Psychology." *Slavic Review* 68, no. 2 (Summer 2009): 259–283.

Platt, Kevin M. F., and David Brandenberger. "An Internationalist's Complaint to Stalin and the Ensuing Scandal," in *Epic Revisionism: Russian History and Literature as Stalinist Propaganda,* Kevin M. F. Platt and David Brandenberger, eds. Madison: University of Wisconsin Press, 2006, 315–323.

Pluksh, P. I. *Sergeev-Tsenskii—pisatel', chelovek.* Moscow: Sovremennik, 1975.

Porshneva, O. S. *Krest'iane, rabochie i soldaty Rossii nakanune i v gody Pervoi Mirovoi Voiny.* Moscow: Rosspen, 2004.

Prost, Antoine. "The French Contempt for Politics: The case of Veterans in the Inter-War Period." In *Republican Identities in War and Peace: Representations of France in the 19th and 20th Centuries.* Oxford: Berg, 2002, 277–310.

———. *In the Wake of War: 'Les Anciens Combattants' and French Society 1914–1939.* Oxford: Berg, 1992.

———. *Republican Identities in War and Peace: Representations of France in the Nineteenth and Twentieth Centuries.* Jay Winter and Helen McPhail, translators. Oxford: Berg, 2002.

Pyle, Emily E. "Village Social Relations and the Reception of Soldiers' Family Aid Policies in Russia, 1912–1921." Ph.D. diss., University of Chicago, 1997.

Rayfield, Donald. "The Soldiers' Lament: World War One Folk Poetry in the Russian Empire." *Slavonic and East European Review* 66 (1988): 66–90.

Reese, Roger R. *Red Commanders: A Social History of the Soviet Army Officer Corps, 1918–1991.* Lawrence: University of Kansas Press, 2005.

Renan, Ernest. "What is a Nation?" In *Becoming National: A Reader,* Geoff Eley and Ronald Grigor Suny, eds. New York: Oxford University Press, 1996, 42–55.

Rhoades, Michelle K. "Renegotiating French Masculinity: Medicine and Venereal Disease During the Great War." *French Historical Studies* 29, no. 2 (Spring 2006): 293–327.

Riasanovsky, Nicholas V., and Mark D. Steinberg. *A History of Russia*, 7th ed. New York: Oxford University Press, 2005.

Roberts, Mary Louise. *Civilization Without Sexes: Reconstructing Gender in Postwar France, 1917–1927*. Chicago, University of Chicago Press, 1994.

Robinson, Paul F. "'Always with Honour': The Code of the White Russian Officers." *Canadian Slavonic Papers/Revue canadienne des slavistes* 41, no. 2 (June 1999): 121–141.

Roper, Michael. "Between Manliness and Masculinity: The 'War Generation' and the Psychology of Fear in Britain, 1914–1950." *Journal of British Studies* 44, no. 2 (April 2005): 343–362.

———. "Slipping out of view: Subjectivity and Emotion in Gender History." *History Workshop Journal* 59 (2005): 57–72.

Rosenberg, William G. "Problems of Social Welfare and Everyday Life." In *Critical Companion to the Russian Revolution, 1914–1921*, Edward Acton, Vladimir Iu. Cherniaev, and William G. Rosenberg, eds. Bloomington: Indiana University Press, 1997.

Rothstein, Robert A. "The Quiet Rehabilitation of the Brick-Factory: Early Soviet Popular Music and its Critics." *Slavic Review* 39, no. 3 (September 1980): 373–388.

Rouhier-Willoughby, Jeanmarie. *Village Values: Negotiating Identity, Gender, and Resistance in Urban Russian Life-Cycle Rituals*. Bloomington, Ind.: Slavica, 2008.

Rowland, Daniel. "*Blessed is the Host of the Heavenly Tsar*: An Icon from the Dormition Cathedral of the Moscow Kremlin." In *Picturing Russia: Explorations in Visual Culture*, Valerie A. Kivelson and Joan Neuberger, eds. New Haven, Conn.: Yale University Press, 2008, 33–37.

Rubenstein, Joshua. *Tangled Loyalties: The Life and Times of Ilya Ehrenburg*. New York: Basic Books, 1996.

Ruud, Charles A. *Russian Entrepreneur: Publisher Ivan Sytin of Moscow, 1851–1934*. Montreal: McGill-Queen's University Press, 1990.

Sanborn, Joshua A. *Drafting the Russian Nation: Military Conscription, Total War, and Mass Politics, 1905–1925*. Dekalb, Ill.: Northern Illinois University Press, 2003.

———. "The Mobilization of 1914 and the Question of the Russian Nation," *Slavic Review* 59, no. 2 (Summer 2000): 267–289.

Scherr, Barry P., and Richard Sheldon. "Westward Flows the Don: The Translation and the Text." *Slavic and East European Journal* 42, no. 1 (Spring 1998): 119–125.

Sedakova, O. A. *Poetika obriada: Pogrebal'naia obriadnost' vostochnykh i iuzhnykh slavian*. Moscow: Indrik, 2004.

Segall, Helen. "Il'ia Gregor'evich Erenburg." In *Dictionary of Literary Biography*, vol. 272: *Russian Prose Writers Between the Wars*, Christine Rydel, ed., 56–77. Detroit: The Gale Group, 2003.

Sherman, Daniel. *The Construction of Memory in Interwar France*. Chicago: University of Chicago Press, 1999.

Sirotkina, Irina. *Diagnosing Literary Genius: A Cultural History of Psychiatry in Russia, 1880–1930*. Baltimore, Md.: The Johns Hopkins University Press, 2002.

Slepyan, Kenneth D. "The Limits of Mobilisation: Party, State and the 1927 Civil Defence Campaign." *Europe-Asia Studies* 45, no. 5 (1993): 851–868.

Slezkine, Yuri. *The Jewish Century*. Princeton, N.J.: Princeton University Press, 2004.

Smith, Alexandra. "Aleksei Nikolaevich Tolstoi." In *Dictionary of Literary Biography,* vol. 272: *Russian Prose Writers Between the Wars.* Christine Rydel, ed., 432–445. Detroit: The Gale Group, 2003.

Smith, John T. "Russian Military Censorship During the First World War." *Revolutionary Russia* 14, no. 1 (June 2001): 71–95.

Smith, S. A. "Citizenship and the Russian Nation During World War I." *Slavic Review* 59, no. 2 (Summer 2000).

Sokolov, Iu. V. *Krasnaia zvezda ili krest? Zhizn' i sud'ba generala Brusilova.* Moscow: Rossiia molodaia, 1994.

Solntseva, Natal'ia. *Poslednii lel': O zhizni i tvorchestve Sergeia Klychkova.* Moscow: Moskovskii rabochii, 1993.

Solzhenitsyn, Aleksandr. *August 1914.* Michael Glenny, trans. New York: Farrar, Straus and Giroux, 1972.

Steinberg, Mark D. *Proletarian Imagination: Self, Modernity, and the Sacred in Russia, 1910–1925.* Ithaca, N.Y.: Cornell University Press. 2002.

Stepanov, A. I. *Rossiia v pervoi mirovoi voine.* Moscow, 2000.

Stites, Richard. "Days and Nights in Wartime Russia: Cultural Life, 1914–1917." In *European Culture in the Great War: The Arts, Entertainment, and Propaganda, 1914–1918,* Aviel Roshwald and Richard Stites, eds. Cambridge: Cambridge University Press, 1999.

Stockdale, Melissa K. "'My Death for the Motherland is Happiness': Women, Patriotism, and Soldiering in Russia's Great War, 1914–1917." *American Historical Review* 109, no. 1 (February 2004): 78–116.

———. "United in Gratitude: Honoring Soldiers and Defining the Nation in Russia's Great War." *Kritika: Explorations in Russian and Eurasian History* 7, no. 3 (Summer 2006): 459–485.

Stoecker, Sally W. *Forging Stalin's Army: Marshal Tukhachevsky and the Politics of Military Innovation.* Boulder, Colo.: Westview Press, 1998.

Stoff, Laurie S. *They Fought for the Motherland: Russia's Women Soldiers in World War I and the Revolution.* Lawrence: University Press of Kansas, 2006.

Stone, David R. *Hammer and Rifle: The Militarization of the Soviet Union, 1926–1933.* Lawrence: University Press of Kansas, 2000.

Stone, Norman. *The Eastern Front, 1914–1917.* New York: Charles Scribner's Sons, 1975.

Theweleit, Klaus. *Male Fantasies,* vols. 1 and 2. Minneapolis: University of Minnesota Press, 1987, 1989.

Timasheff, Nicholas S. *The Great Retreat: The Growth and Decline of Communism in Russia.* New York: E. P. Dutton, 1946.

Tims, Hilton. *Erich Maria Remarque: The Last Romantic.* New York: Carroll and Graff, 2003.

Trice, Thomas Reed. "The 'Body Politic': Russian Funerals and the Politics of Representation, 1841–1921." Ph.D. diss., University of Illinois, 1998.

Trifonov, N. A. "Nespravedlivo zabytaia kniga," in Sof'ia Fedorchenko, *Narod na voine.* Moscow: Sovetskii pisatel', 1990.

Tumarkin, Nina. *Lenin Lives: The Lenin Cult in Soviet Russia.* Cambridge, Mass.: Harvard University Press, 1983.

———. *The Living and the Dead: The Rise and Fall of the Cult of World War II in Russia.* New York: Basic Books, 1994.

Verhey, Jeffrey. *The Spirit of 1914: Militarism, Myth and Mobilization in Germany.* Cambridge: Cambridge University Press, 2000.

von Hagen, Mark. *Soldiers in the Proletarian Dictatorship: The Red Army and the Soviet Socialist State, 1917–1930.* Ithaca, N.Y.: Cornell University Press, 1990.

———. *War in a European Borderland: Occupations and Occupation Plans in Galicia and Ukraine, 1914–1918.* Seattle: University of Washington Press, 2007.

von Geldern, James, and Louise McReynolds, eds. *Entertaining Tsarist Russia.* Bloomington: Indiana University Press, 1998.

von Geldern, James, and Richard Stites, eds. *Mass Culture in Soviet Russia.* Bloomington: Indiana University Press, 1995.

Voronova, O. *Shadr.* Moscow: Molodaia gvardiia (Zhizn' zamechatelnykh liudei), 1969.

Wanke, Paul. *Russian/Soviet Military Psychiatry, 1904–1945.* London: Frank Cass, 2005.

Weitz, Eric. *A Century of Genocide: Utopias of Race and Nation.* Princeton, N.J.: Princeton University Press, 2005.

Wells, William W. Memorandum for the Director of Central Intelligence on "*Military Thought* (USSR): The Brusilov Case—How an Historical Error was Corrected." July 9, 1976. Declassified December 2004.

Westwood, J. N. "Novikov-Priboi as Naval Historian," *Slavic Review* 69, no. 2 (June 1969): 297–303.

White, Stephen. *The Bolshevik Poster.* New Haven, Conn.: Yale University Press, 1988.

Wildman, Allan K. *The End of the Russian Imperial Army,* vols. 1 and 2. Princeton, N.J.: Princeton University Press, 1980, 1987.

Wingfield, Nancy M., and Maria Bucur, eds. *Gender and War in Twentieth-Century Eastern Europe.* Bloomington: Indiana University Press, 2006.

Winter, Jay. "Introduction: Henri Barbusse and the Birth of the Moral Witness." In Henri Barbusse, *Under Fire.* Robin Buss, trans. New York: Penguin, 2003.

———. *Remembering War: The Great War Between Memory and History in the Twentieth Century.* New Haven, Conn.: Yale University Press, 2006.

———. *Sites of Memory, Sites of Mourning: The Great War in European Cultural History.* Cambridge: Cambridge University Press, 1995.

Winter, Jay, and Antoine Prost. *The Great War in History: Debates and Controversies, 1914 to the Present.* Cambridge: Cambridge University Press, 2005.

Wood, Elizabeth A. *The Baba and the Comrade: Gender and Politics in Revolutionary Russia.* Bloomington: Indiana University Press, 1997.

Wortman, Richard. *Scenarios of Power: Myth and Ceremony in Russian Monarchy,* vol. 2. Princeton, N.J.: Princeton University Press, 2000.

Youngblood, Denise. *Russian War Films: On the Cinema Front 1914–2005.* Lawrence: University of Kansas Press, 2007.

———. "A War Forgotten: The Great War in Russian and Soviet Cinema." In *The First World War and Popular Cinema,* Michael Paris, ed. New Brunswick, N.J.: Rutgers University Press, 2000.

Zavgorodnii, A. F. *Deiatel'nost gosudarstvennykh organov i obshchestvenno-politicheskikh organizatsii po sotsial'noi zashchite voennosluzashchikh Krasnoi Armii i ikh semei v mezhvoennykh period (1921-iiun' 1941 gg.).* St. Petersburg: Nestor, 2001.

Zubova, N., and M. Katagoshchina. "Pamiatnik velikoi voiny." *Moskovskii zhurnal* 5 (1994): 52–55.

INDEX

Italicized page numbers indicate illustrations.

15th Siberian Rifle Regiment, 168
53rd Infantry Regiment, 191
105th Artillery Regiment, 52
410th Usmanskii Regiment, 113
1914 (Feinberg and Telingater), 169–170, 181, 235, 240–243, *242*

About Imperialist War (Lenin), 203
Academy of Sciences, 288
Afinogenov, Aleksandr Nikolaevich, 333n10
Afinogenov, Nikolai Aleksandrovich, 251, 333n10
afterlife, 56, 58, 60, 68
Albert (France), 31, 34
alcohol consumption, 84, 101, 109
Aleksandr Nevskii (film), 207
All Power to the Soviets (Bonch-Bruevich), 284
All Quiet on the Western Front (film), 186, 230–231
All Quiet on the Western Front (Remarque): adaptations of, 227–231; camaraderie in, 82; censorship of, 200, 202; critical response to, 186, 224–227, 233; editions of, 200, 224, 330n73; enhanced status during Great Break, 244; futility of heroism in, 100; interpretations of, 225, 226, 227, 233–234; popular response to, 147–148, 231–234; sequel to, 227; soldier-officer relationships in, 111–112; stormy reception of, 11; translations of, 224–225; violence in, 97, 147–148
All-Russian Central Executive Committee, 319n165
All-Russian War Cemetery. *See* Moscow City Fraternal Cemetery (All-Russian War Cemetery)
All Saints Monastery, 299–300
Almast, Mak, 331n78
amputees, 90, 115, 122, 123, 315n70
anti-German sentiment: class differences in, 190–191; ethnic cleansing, calls for, 194–195; in literature, 267; and Nazi military threat, 204; purge era, 203–204, 205, 268; and Slavic racial consciousness, 328n17; tsarist-Soviet continuity in, 290; during World War I, 29, 192, 204–205; World War I experiences as basis for, 204, 328n17
anti-Semitism, 29, 157, 191, 196, 290. *See also* Jews, violence against
Anulov, F. A., 217
apocalyptic movements, 55, 73, 309n69
"apolitical" pacifism, 226
"The Appearance of the Holy Mother from the Heavens to the Russian Troops before Battle" (*Iavlenie Bozhei Materi na nebe pered srazheniem russkomu voinstvu*) (poster), 35–36, *35*

Arakcheev, A. A., 210
Armenian Communist Party, 288, 337n19
Armenian genocide commemoration, 288–289
Armiakov (Russian scout), 118
Arras (France), 250
Arsenal (film), 312n125
The Art of Leading a Regiment (Svechin), 216
artillerists, 268–269, 271
Artillerists (*Artilleristy*), 222–223, 268
"Artillerists of the World War" (Barsukov), 268, 269, 271
Astakhov (Cossack), 97
At the Front of the Imperialist War (Pireiko), 260–261
atheism, 73–74
"atrocities," 320n10
Audoin-Rouzeau, Stéphane, 127
August 1914 (Solzhenitsyn), 286–288
Austria, Nazi annexation of, 268
Austria-Hungary: Jewish population, Russian violence against, 158–159; national character of, 85, 132, 167, 192–193, 269, 270; occupation of Russian Ukraine, 323n100; prisoners of war from, 160; prisoners of war in, 48–50, 49, 104–105, 117, 317n115; Russian offensive against, 25–26, 101, 271–272
Averbakh, L., 21–22, 101
Avgustovo, battle at, 42–43

Babel', Isaak: arrest of, 121; Civil War, writings about, 25, 317n121; diary of, 162; *Mariia*, 121–124; "Murderers Who Have Yet to Be Clubbed to Death," 161; *Red Cavalry* cycle, 162–163, 254; as Russian-Jewish author, 231
Baptist pacifist soldiers, 137
Baranovichi, 3, 4. *See also* Brusilov offensive (1916)
"barbed-wire psychosis," 116
Barbusse, Henri, 10, 21–22, 304n57, 331n78
Barnet, Boris: *Borderlands* (*Okraina*) (film), 70–71, 186–189, 289, 326n74; translation of works of, 11
The Barracks (*Kazarrma*) (Grigor'ev), 137, 262–263, 334n37

Barsukov, E. Z., 216–217, 218, 268, 269, 271
Basel. *See* International Socialist Congress (Basel)
Bashkir Autonomous Republic, 323n97, 326n81
Bazarevskii, A. Kh., 219, 330n56
Becker, Annette, 127
Bednyi, Dem'ian, 79, 237
Belaia gvardiia (Bulgakov), 265
Belgium, World War I in, 28, 330n56
Bell, Julian, 181
Belolipetskii, V. E., 330n58
Belorussia, 25, 232
Belov, I. A., 147–148
bereavement. *See* mourning, individual
"Big Bertha" (German gun), 269
The Big Refit (*Kapital'nyi remont*) (Sobolev), 50, 264, 265–266
A Biography of No Place (Brown), 73
Birzhevye vedomosti (Stock Exchange Gazette), 12, 84
Blavatskaia, E. P., 311n114
Bleiman, M., 326n74
Bochkareva, Mariia, 86, 87–88, 258, 334n23
bogatyr' (Russian medieval warrior), 75
"Boldly We Go into Battle" (revolutionary song), 310n76
Bol'shaia Sovetskaia Entsiklopediia. See The Great Soviet Encyclopedia
Bolsheviks: acceptable wartime behavior, 103; afterlife, beliefs about, 58; antiwar attitudes of, 14, 169; as best hope for preservation of Russian nation, 60; class solidarity paradox, 172–173; conscientious objectors, opportunities for, 134; on Cossack brutality, 153; defeatism of, 174, 261; desertion by, 262; ignorance about, 260; massacre of White officers, 146; "peace" (slogan), 134; in Podillian legend, 73; posters issued by, 91; refusal of military service by, 174–175; storming Winter Palace, 80; violence, ideology of, 129; war against religion, 73; war enthusiasm of, 134, 171–173; war mobilization by, 171–172; World War I, ambivalence toward, 173–174; World War I, reflection on, 5, 91; World War I,

withdrawal from, 91. *See also* Old Bol-
sheviks
Bonch-Bruevich, M. D., 205, 216, 219, 284
Borderlands (Okraina) (film), 70–71, 186–
189, 289, 326n74
"Borderlands" *(Okraina)* (Finn), 184–186,
190, 326n63
Borenstein, Eliot, 314n29
Borodin, F. M., 330n58
bourgeois pacifism: accusations of, 226,
227, 233; criticism of, 181, 186, 230, 248;
role of, 178
Brandenberger, David, 120, 247, 328n23
bravery. *See* heroism/heroic masculinity
"Breakthrough" (Veber), 222–223, 270,
271–272
Brest-Litovsk, treaty of, 205
Brezhnev-era monuments, 282
Britain: Parliament, 230; peace pledge
movement, 183; postwar influence of
wartime violence, 128; ration of rum for
soldiers, 315n48; Russia as military savior of, 270; and war scare (1927), 204;
wartime censorship, 305n65
British Imperial War Museum. *See* Imperial War Museum (British)
Brown, Kate, 73
Brusilov (Slezkin), 283
Brusilov, Aleksei Alekseevich: biography
of, 223, 275; class alien status of, 222; coffin, 62–63, *62;* criticism of, 27, 223–224;
death, 60, 220, 221; deserters, punishment for, 274, 336n68; fall from favor,
283–284; funeral, 60–65, *62, 67;* heroization of, 63, 64, 65, 278, 283; later life, 220;
in literature, 330n71; Lutsk offensive (*see*
Brusilov offensive [1916]); memoirs (*see*
Brusilov, Aleksei Alekseevich, memoirs of); military service, 60; obituary,
61; occult practices, 66; pension for,
120; plays about, 223; relationship with
son, 66–67; on soldiers' lack of fighting
spirit, 170; Soviet recognition of, 220–
224; works by, 11, 244
Brusilov, Aleksei Alekseevich, memoirs of:
criticism of tsar and military advisors,
91; death of first wife, 65–66; editions of,

65–66, 216, 223, 283, 284; introduction
to, 65; officers as role models in, 265;
popularity of, 221; published excerpts of,
221; spiritualism in, 66, 311n114; translations of, 221, 311n111; women in, 106–107
The Brusilov Breakthrough (Vetoshnikov), 223
Brusilov offensive (1916): and anti-German
sentiment, 207; description of, 25–26;
fictional accounts of, 264, 268; as fore-
ordaining German defeat, 279; Ninth
Army, 330n56; publications about, 222–
223, 238, 330nn56,58; role of patriotism
in, 279; significance of, 27; Soviet de-
valuation of, 222; Soviet revaluation of,
222; troop losses during, 3, 222
Brusilova, Nadezhda Vladimirovna:
Brusilov's burial, 65; Brusilov's career,
221; Brusilov's fascination with supernatural, 66; Brusilov's funeral, 62, 64;
Brusilov's grave marker, 65; Brusilov's
memoirs, 65; emigration, 221; medical
care, 221; unpublished memoirs, 62, 64;
works by, 283
*Brusilov's Breakthrough (Brusilovskii pro-
ryv)* (Sergeev-Tsenskii): ambiguities in,
264; criticism of, 279–280, 280–281; fraternization in, 273; surrender in, 274; as
war mobilization literature, 280–281;
women in, 275–278
Budennyi, Semen, 63, 64, 66
Bukharin, Nikolai, 45, 308n46
Bulgakov, Mikhail, 45, 265, 335n45
Bulletin of Foreign Literature (Vestnik
inostrannoi literatury), 224

Cadet Corps, 298
camaraderie: betrayal of, 97; cross-class,
78, 87–88, 99–102, 109, 110–111, 318n137;
Russian Imperial depiction of, 125; Soviet depiction of, 82, 125
Cannae of the First World War (Isserson),
203–204
capitalism: as cause of World War I, 14,
24, 26, 134, 190, 270; commercialization
of war commemoration, 12–13; future
war with, 127, 233, 247–248; replacement

with socialism, 178; war as norm under, 14, 181, 251
case studies. *See* memory case studies
Caucasian people, 183
Cement (Gladkov), 162
cemeteries. *See* Moscow City Fraternal Cemetery (All-Russian War Cemetery); Novodevichii Cemetery; Piskarevskoe Memorial Cemetery (Leningrad); war cemeteries
censorship: of anti-German sentiment, 206–208; of antiheroic rhetoric, 259–262; chronology of, 21; as ecosystem, 247, 305n62; of ethnic violence, 254, 285; of heroic officers, 265; of ideology, 203–204, 207–208, 239; of Jewish military service, 262–263; for literary reasons, 239; of militaristic themes, 20, 99, 324n26; of military desertion, 105; of military secrets, 201–202; of military service avoidance, 261; of nationalistic themes, 20; nature of, 200–208; of pacifism, 251–252; of political themes, 201, 324n26; post-Stalin period, 286–288; psychology of, 201–202; of rape, 254–255, 258; of rejection of war, 138; of religious themes, 249–251, 285, 286; of sexual themes, 108–109, 148, 201, 255–258, 278; of soldiers' letters, 324n13; Stalin-era, 246, 327n1; tsarist legacy in, 24; of violence, 161, 252–255, 257–258, 285; of warrior's fear, 246, 248, 333n2; during wartime, 23, 305n65; of works by enemies of the people, 203; of works by purge victims, 202; of works published abroad, 286–288; World War II era, 273. *See also* censorship mechanisms
censorship mechanisms: addition of new topics to works, 201; physical alteration of items, 201, 203, 327n1; prepublication, 201; removal of books from libraries, 20, 202, 203, 204; self-censorship, 258
Central Asia, Russian conquest of, 312n3
Central Committee, 120–121, 223–224, 288, 319n165
Central Executive Committee of the Soviet Union, 216, 225

Chaadaeva, Ol'ga, 170–171, 176, 222, 324n21
Chapaev (film), 334n27
Chapaev (Furmanov), 259, 316n78
Chapel of the Transfiguration. *See* Transfiguration of the Savior "Reconciliation of Nations" (chapel)
Charskaia, Lidiia, 259, 334n24
Cheka (secret police), 67, 137
children: displacement of, 156; orphaned by violence, 41, 158; violence against, 59–60, 118, 119, 149–150, 151, 152, 153, 159; witnessing violence, 118–119, 156
Christianity. *See* Orthodox Christianity
Church of All Saints, 299
Church of the Transfiguration: consecration of, 1; demolition of, 3; design of, 36–37, *37, 294*; as individual memorial, 36–37; later construction on site of, 4, *296*; location of, 293, 338n26
churches as war memorials, 293–294
cinematography, influence on literature of, 241, 243
citizenship: gendered depiction of, 165; and military service, 79–80, 81; pacifism as subversive to, 135; under Provisional Government, 18; in Soviet State, 18
Civil War: atrocities, 24; civilian struggle for survival, 6; conscientious objectors, 134, 135; cult of, 305n68; death, burial, and mourning, 1, 6, 70, 302n20; films about, 130; heroes of, 5, 33, 91; honor code in, 130–131; memorials to, 299; militarism of, 24–25; nurses in, 317n121; plays about, 122–124; Red Terror victims, 298; use in Soviet war mobilization, 25; veterans, benefits for, 120; veterans' memoirs, 89; violence in, 129, 161–164; women in combat, 81, 313n27, 314n29. *See also* Red Army; White Army
civilians. *See* "rear" (civilians and officials)
Clark, Katerina, 15, 304n47, 305n62
class distinctions: camaraderie transcending, 78, 87–89, 109, 110–111; class-aliens, war accounts by, 238; in enthusiasm for war, 166, 171; and gendered behaviors, 149; and heroism/heroic masculinity, 81, 109–113, 271; and national-

ism, 167; nationalism as more important than, 267; in patriotism, 279; tension with need for effective Soviet officers, 290; and wartime violence, 129, 149–154. *See also* soldier-officer relationships; upper classes

class solidarity, 82, 186, 187. *See also* internationalism

class warfare: celebration of, 187; training for, 172–173; violence against class-enemies, 129, 146

clergy: criticism of, 50–52; heroism of, 250; promotion of war effort by, 35, 50–51, 69; violence committed by, 51–52

close analysis, 16

Cohen, Aaron, 5, 10, 113

Cold War, 269, 271, 335n56

Collected Works (Erenburg), 21

Collegium of Jewish Social Activists, 153

Comerchero, Vincent Alan, 319n165

commemoration. *See* memorialization

commendations, military, 83–84. *See also* St. George cross

Commissariat of Defense, 223

Communism and women's equality, 80–81

Communist Academy, 215

Communist Party members as purge victims, 334n31

Confino, Alon, 303n24

conscientious objectors, 134, 135, 136–137. *See also* pacifism

"conscious" revolutionaries. *See* revolutionary consciousness

Cossacks: anti-German sentiment of, 151, 152; Civil War service, 151; de-Cossackization campaign, 96; as ethnic "others," 96, 150; ethnic violence perpetrated by, 150, 151, 152; German atrocities against, 152; heroes (*see* Kriuchkov, Koz'ma); heroic traditions of, 69; honor code, 130, 146, 151, 152; as marauders, 152, 153; mythology of, 95–96, 100; nature of, 98–100, 142, 151–152, 290; pogroms instigated by, 118–119, 153, 160, 196; prayers of, 47–48; sexual violence perpetrated by, 153–154, 255, 256; status in Soviet Union, 96; as symbols of military mas-

culinity, 76; violence perpetrated by, 95–96, 146, 149–154; World War I service, 95–97, 151

Council of People's Commissars, 213

cowardice, 274–275, 280. *See also* heroism/heroic masculinity

Creative Work (Tvorchestvo), 38

Crimean War, 210, 263

Czechoslovakia, Nazi annexation of, 268

d'Annunzio, Gabriele, 128, 320n22

Darkness and Dawn (Tolstoi), 309n69

Dawson, Graham, 321n30

The Days of the Turbins (Bulgakov), 265, 335n45

"Dead, Rise Up!" (Masereel), 72, *73*

dead/death: communication with, 308n35 (*see also* séances); as God's punishment, 41; haunting the living, 66, 249; immortality through memory, 168–169; meaning in, search for, 33, 55, 57, 70; monuments to, 38, *39*; nationalism providing meaning, 168; relationship to living, 55; as release from torments of war, 147; remains, 40–42, 116; and resurrection, 55–71, 310n91 (*see also* resurrection); revolutionary cause providing meaning, 57, 70–71; as sacrificial Christ-figures, 69. *See also* eternal memory concept; mourning, civic/national; mourning, individual; Revolution (1917), death and resurrection themes; World War I, deaths

defeatism, 261, 263, 264, 280, 281

"defense literature," 245

Defense Section of the Union of Soviet Writers. *See under* Union of Soviet Writers

defensism, 261, 280

De-Lazari, A. N., 214

Delbrück, Hans, 203

Department of Special Purpose. *See under* Union of Soviet Writers

deportation of Korean population, 195

Deschanel, Paul, 243

desertion, 101–104; Bolshevik view of, 103, 173, 262; as dishonorable, 101–102; as heroic, 104–105, 173; by Jewish soldiers, 262; justification for, 260, 261–262; punishment for, 274, 336n68; as revolutionary act, 103; by "unconscious" soldiers, 103–104; in World War II–era discourse, 273–274. See also military service, avoidance of

diaspora. See émigrés, World War I accounts by; Russian diaspora

Dinamov, S., 255–256

"Disabled" (Owen), 114

disabled veterans. See wounded veterans

disappearance, 249–263; of desertion/evasion of service, 259–262; of ethnicity, 262–263; of gender relations, 255–259; of pacifism, 251–252; of religious discourse, 249–251; of violence, 252–255

discursive remasculinization, 333n4

displacement of civilians. See under "rear" (civilians and officials)

Divil'kovskii, A. A., 141

Dmitriev, V.: application to join Communist Party, 324n37; internationalism, 184; on surrender as heroic, 274; Volunteer: Remembrances about War and Captivity, 104–105, 175, 177

Dni Turbinykh (Bulgakov), 265, 335n45

Dobrovolets: vospominaniia o voine i plene (Dmitriev). See Volunteer: Remembrances about War and Captivity (Dmitriev)

Doctor Zhivago (Pasternak), 286

documentary pamphlet-lampoon (genre), 240

Domanskii, M., 40–42

Don Revolutionary Committee, 148

Dovzhenko, Aleksandr, 312n125

A Dozen Germans on One Cossack Bayonet (Shukhmin), 133

draft riots and evasion, 169, 174–175

Dragunovskii, Iakov, 135–137

Dubinskaia, Tat'iana, 149–150, 259

Dubrovskii, A., 186

"Dulce et Decorum Est" (Owen), 94

East Prussia, Russian advance into, 25

Easter, as catalyst for fraternization, 193

Eastern Europe, World War I memory in, 9

"editor's preface," 21

Egorov, Aleksandr, 63, 217

Eideman, Robert Petrovich, 65, 221

Eisenstein, Sergei, 207, 231, 313n23, 334n23

Ekaterinoslav, 174

Eksteins, Modris, 9

émigrés, World War I accounts by, 27–28, 86, 283. See also Purgatory (Khozdenie po mukam) (A. Tolstoi)

enemies of the state: censorship of, 202, 203; ethnicity in, 28–29; extermination of, 18, 148; as perpetrators of sexual violence, 255; and Russianness, 194–198; violence against, 130; World War II–era views of, 272–275

enemy combatants: anti-German sentiment toward, 190–191; censorship for, 201–202; change in definition of, 193; compassion toward, 135–136; drunkenness in, 85; ethnic stereotypes concerning, 191–192, 192–193; portrayals of, based on nationality, 132–133; violence against, honor code concerning, 130–131; World War II–era views of, 272–275. See also fraternization with the enemy

Engagement at the Border of the Western Front (Kiev military district), 204

England. See Britain

Erenburg, Il'ia: anti-Nazi propaganda during World War II, 11; Collected Works, 21; on commercialization of World War I, 12–13; The Extraordinary Adventures of Khulio Khurenito and His Disciples. . . . (Neobychainye pokhozhdeniia Khulio Khurenito i ego uchenikov. . . .), 12, 45–46, 137–138, 191–192, 308n46; The Face of War (Lik voiny) (see The Face of War [Lik voiny] [Erenburg]); on gender tensions, 107; memoir (see The Face of War [Lik voiny] [Erenburg]); pacifism, 11, 22, 52; "rear" as place of immorality, 107; religion, ambivalence about, 22, 46–47, 250; as Russian-Jewish author, 231; "the Thaw" (coining of term), 284; as war reporter, 11–12, 303n36

Erevan genocide monument, 289

Erlikh, A., 186–187

Ermolaev, Herman, 21, 316n86
Erzerum (Turkish fortress), 211
Esenin writers' circle, 139–141
espionage, anxiety about, 194, 195–196, 205
"Eternal Memory" (hymn), 56, 58, 64
eternal memory concept: in Orthodox Christian context, 56; representations of, 71; in revolutionary context, 56,
  310n76; in Soviet context, 56, 61, 67, 74
ethical code. *See* honor code
ethnic distinctions: and abuse of civilians,
  154; among soldiers, 157; censorship
  of conflicts, 254, 285; as "classed" phenomenon, 195–196; and espionage anxieties, 195–196, 205; between heroes and
  villains, 267; and innate desire to fight,
  171; and nationalism, 20; and wartime violence, 20, 149–154, 165, 191–192.
  See also anti-German sentiment; anti-
  Semitism; Jews, violence against; *individual ethnic groups*
European World War I memory: brutality
  of war, 151; class distinctions in, 109;
  commercialization of, 12–13; connection
  to future political and social agendas, 5;
  dead, relationship to living, 55; fostering
  patriotism, 13; heroic masculinity in, 82;
  "ironic" war accounts, 177; monuments
  and memorials, 4–5, 31, 42; mourning,
  5, 42; penetration of ideas into Soviet
  Union, 21–22; similarities to Soviet
  memory, 74; tropes of, 77; veterans'
  rights organizations, 119; World War I
  as break with the past, 8–9
evangelical pacifism, 134, 135
Evening Moscow (Vecherniaia Moskva), 225
Evert, Aleksei, 26
"The Exploit of Sister E. P. Korkina" (*Podvig sestry E. P. Korkinoi*) (poster), 88
*The Extraordinary Adventures of Khu-
  lio Khurenito and His Disciples. . . .
  (Neobychainye pokhozhdeniia Khulio
  Khurenito i ego uchenikov. . . .*) (Erenburg), 12, 45–46, 137–138, 191–192, 308n46

The Face of War (*Lik voiny*) (Erenburg):
  censorship of, 22–23, 249–251, 253–254;

criticism of, 21; editions of, 21, 22–23,
  250, 253–254, 303n35; excerpts from, 12;
  interpretation of war, 12, 24, 305n67;
  pacifist themes in, 11, 22, 251; as part of
  Collected Works, 21; religious themes in,
  22, 46, 51–52, 249–251; translation of, 11;
  violence in, 51–52, 253–254
Fadeev, Aleksandr, 25, 70
fakul'tet osobogo naznacheniia (Department of Special Purpose). *See under*
  Union of Soviet Writers
Falkenhayn, Erich von, 203
The Fall of the Romanov Dynasty (*Padenie
  dinastii Romanovykh*) (film), 51, 56–57,
  106, 109–110, 190
A Farewell to Arms (Hemingway), 255–256,
  334n16
fascism, 128, 334n16
fatherland/motherland: defense of, 20,
  170–171, 176, 241, 281; woman as, 276–
  277. *See also* nationalism; patriotism
father-son relationships, 66–67, 69. *See
  also* soldier-officer relationships, paternalistic
fear: as aberration, 333n2; in heroic warriors, 246, 333n1; as normal, 333n2
February Revolution, 238, 313n25
Federation (publishing house), 224
Fedorchenko, Sof'ia: authenticity of,
  332n109; autobiography, 237; career, 237;
  censorship of, 161; children's books by,
  237; civilian displacement in works by,
  155–156; as class-alien, 238; *glasnost'*-era
  publication of, 285, 286; interpretation
  of, 332n109; *The People at War* (*Narod
  na voine*) (see *The People at War* [*Narod
  na voine*] [Fedorchenko]); post–World
  War II publication of, 285; repression of
  works of, 17, 244, 332n107; translation of
  works of, 11; violence in works by, 153,
  156–157, 158–159; during World War I,
  236, 237
Fedorov, N. F., 58
Fedorovna, Elisaveta, 1
Feinberg, Il'ia, 169–170, 181, 235, 240–243, 242
Feu (*Under Fire*) (Barbusse), 22
Field (Niva). *See Niva* (Field)

15th Siberian Rifle Regiment, 168
53rd Infantry Regiment, 191
Figes, Orlando, 311n108
"Fighting Empires" (Telingater), 241, *242*
Finn, Konstantin: "Borderlands"
("Okraina"), 184–186, 190, 326n63
First Cavalry Army, 317n121
First World War. *See* World War I
Five-Year Plans, 244
folk religion, 52–53, 69, 310n91
food, procurement of. *See* marauding
For St. George Crosses (*Za krestami*) (Gromov), 17, *18,* 101
foreign enemies. *See* enemy combatants
forests, in folk beliefs, 53
"forgetting." *See under* Soviet World War I
memory
The Forty-First (*Sorok pervyi*) (film),
130, 253
410th Usmanskii Regiment, 113
Fradkov, Mikhail, 293
France: blame for Russian entry in World
War I, 25, 26, 190, 270; Industrial Party
trial (1930), 204; miracle stories from,
46–47; 1916 campaign, 330n56; Russia as
military savior of, 270, 279; sexuality of
soldiers, 256; war monuments, 11; wartime censorship in, 305n65; wartime
violence's impact on postwar society,
128; women in, 107
Frantzen, Allen J., 307n23
Franz Ferdinand, Archduke of Austria, 241
fraternization with the enemy: as antinational trend, 193; and Brusilov offensive, 27; censorship of, 273; at Easter, 136,
193; punishment for, 189; revolutionary
demand for, 70, 173, 273; World War II–
era views of, 273
Freikorps (German right-wing paramilitary), 86, 128, 333n4
Friche, V., 38
Friend of the Invalid (voluntary society), 120
From the Letters of an Ensign-Artillerist
(Stepun), 153, 156
"From the Merchants of Moscow to the
Soldier-Invalids" (poster), 90
frontline combatants: in gendered terms,
85–86, 106–109, 125; tension with rear
support, 85–86, 125, 257–258; virtue of, 94
Frunze, M. V., 61, 220
Frunze Military Academy, 63, 65, 220,
328n26
funeral rituals: Orthodox Christian, 56, 61,
62; Soviet, 62–63
Furmanov, Dmitrii: as author, 17; *Chapaev,* 259, 316n78; Cossack myth transposed onto Bolshevik heroes, 312n6;
diary, 114–115, 151–153, 325n45; on ethical
conduct in wartime, 198; as medic, 114–
115; on Mennonites as orderlies, 137
Fussell, Paul, 9, 31, 306n3

Gai, G., 63
Galicia: Austrian recapture of, 25; civilian
displacement, 155; Cossack violence in,
118–119, 152, 153; Russian occupation of,
323n100; violence against Jews, 118–119, 157
Gance, Abel, 55, 249
gas attacks, 271–272
Gastev, Aleksei, 55
Gatrell, Peter, 5
Gelikon (publisher), 10, 303n35, 308n46
gender identity: and citizenship, 165; destabilization by war, 80; discursive regendering, 248; equality in Soviet State,
18; equality under Provisional Government, 18; in frontline combatants, 85–
86; front/rear tensions, 106–109, 257–
258; men, upright behavior of, 84; and
military culture, 79–82; in mourning,
69; and nationalism, 79; paradoxes of,
75–126; in rear support, 85–86; reestablishment of the ideal, 275–278; themes
and methods, 16–20; and war, 79–82.
See also heroism/heroic masculinity;
women
General Brusilov (Sel'vinskii), 223
Generalissimo Count Suvorov-Rymnikskii
(battleship), 50
genocide of Armenians, 288–289
Georgians, prejudice against, 195
Gerasimov, Sergei, 284–285
The [German] High Command (Falkenhayn), 203

Germany: atrocities committed by, 28, 152, 211; "barbed-wire psychosis," 116; as cause of war, 185; colonists in Galicia, 155; conflicts with Cossacks, 151, 152; detention of Russian nationals as enemy aliens, 178–179; drunken troops, 85; espionage by, 268; military strength of, 205–207, 269; national character of, 192, 270; National Socialists, takeover by, 230; normalization of violence in, 163; occult predictions concerning, 40; prisoners of war from, 131, 151, 184–186, 188–189; prisoners of war in, 48, 205–206; Rumanian declaration of war on, 270; Russian anxieties about, 25, 204, 247; Russian military success against, 269; Russian offensive against, 25; Social Democrats, 178–179, 181, 273; veterans, writings by, 86; wartime violence's impact on postwar society, 128; World War II, 272; wounded soldiers, 135–136. *See also* anti-German sentiment; pro-German sentiment, of Tatars; Russian-German elites

"Geroiskaia bor'ba kazaka Koz'my Kriuchkova s 11 nemtsami" (*Heroic Struggle of the Cossack Koz'ma Kriuchkov with Eleven Germans*) (poster), *76*

Gestapo, 205

Gil'chevskii, K., 214, 330n71

Gladkov, Fedor, 25, 162

glasnost', 286, 293, 298

Glavlit. See Main Administration for Literary and Publishing Affairs (*Glavlit*)

Gogol, Nikolai, 60

Gogol and the Theater (Zagorskii), 229

Goldberg (prisoner of war), 118–119, 154

"Golden Virgin" myth, 31, 34, 73

Gorbachev era. *See glasnost'*

Gorkii, A. M. (Maksim), 122, 237, 238–239, 332n113

Gorlitskaia operatsiia, 330n58

The Grave of the Unknown Soldier (*Mogila neizvestnogo soldata*) (Lidin), 11, 121

Great Break, 244

Great Britain. *See* Britain

"great retreat" (1915), 15, 26, 27, 167, 194

"great retreat" (1930s), 211

The Great Soviet Encyclopedia (*Bol'shaia Sovetskaia Entsiklopediia*), 71, *72, 73,* 282, 336n2

Great War. *See* World War I

The Great War and Modern Memory (Fussell), 31

grief. *See* mourning, individual

Grigor'ev, Sergei, 137, 262–263

Gromov, Moisei Georgievich, 17, *18,* 101

Guillory, Sean Christopher, 304n44

Gumilev, Nikolai: on drunkenness/sobriety of soldiers, 84, 85; glorification of violence, 131–132, 133, 320n22; *Notes of a Cavalryman* (*Zapiski kavalerista*), 84, 131–132; on Russian strength of spirit, 167

Gutor, A. E., 216

Harvard Project on the Soviet Social System, 99

Hašek, Jaroslav, 10

Haslam, Jonathan, 333n120

Hellman, Ben, 133, 306n77

"Help for War Victims" (Pasternak), 90, 91, *92, 93. See also* "The Price of Blood" (poster)

"Help for War Victims" (Vinogradov), 89

Hemingway, Ernest, 10, 255–256, 334n16

Heretz, Leonid, 328n17

"Heroic Struggle of the Cossack Koz'ma Kriuchkov with Eleven Germans" (*Geroiskaia bor'ba kazaka Koz'my Kriuchkova s 11 nemtsami*) (poster), 76

heroism/heroic masculinity: alcohol-fueled, 84, 101; ambiguous treatment of, 82; of artillerists, 271; in atheist orthodoxy, 17; censorship of, 248, 255–256, 257; challenges to, 18, 80, 82; class distinctions in, 271, 290; commendations for, 83–84 (*see also* St. George cross); and defensism, 280; desertion as, 173; disillusionment in, 177; epitome of, 83–84; fear in, 246; fraternization with enemy as, 173; ideal of, 9, 81–82, 314n32; justified violence in, 24–25; killing as, 141; literary attacks on, 101; loss of, from failure to protect the innocent, 154, 160–161; mechanized warfare as challenge to, 18, 76–78; morality of, 129, 253; national discourse on, 168; and national identity, 165, 270; nature of, 98–100, 167–168, 171, 255, 256–257; of nurses, 86–87, 107; of officers, 264–265, 266–267; and pacifism, 137; paradoxes of, 83–84; and patriotism, 278; price of, 94; proof of, as reason for volunteering, 177, 187; religious questioning of, 9; remasculinization of, 18, 248, 333n4; and resurrection, 67; revolutionary-era, 63, 81, 124–126, 290; Russian definition of, 193; sexuality in, 255–257; of soldiers, 83, 271; Soviet challenges to, 105, 124–125, 263–264, 290–291; Soviet ideal of, 60, 81, 91–105, 187–188, 193, 259–262; surrender as, 104–105; as theme, 17, 20; tsarist-era, 60, 105, 263–264, 271, 290; in violent death, 69; volunteers as quintessential heroes, 169; and war enthusiasm, 175; and war mobilization, 126; war's toll on, 79, 89–90, 129, 148; World War I, 82–106; World War II, 272–275. See also Brusilov, Aleksei Alekseevich; cowardice; Kriuchkov, Koz'ma; masculinity

Hindenburg, Paul von, 11

History of Military Art within the Framework of Political History (Delbrück), 203

The History of Soviet Military Thought (Korotkov), 215

homosexuality, 153–154

honor code: difficulty of upholding, 131, 160; as impossible goal, 152, 156; justified killing under, 130–131, 133, 143, 146; tsarist, 146; violation of, 131, 142, 149, 151, 152, 157

Hoover Institution poster collection, 315n70

Horne, John, 320n10

How the Steel was Tempered (Ostrovskii), 89

humanism, Soviet criticism of, 225–226

Hungary. *See* Austria-Hungary

"I Shall Manifest Myself to Him" (print), 36

Iakimichev (editor), 216

Iakovlev (Cossack captain), 161

Iakubovskii (editor), 216

Ianushkevich, N. N., 155, 205

"Iavlenie Bozhei Materi na nebe pered srazheniem russkomu voinstvu" (*The Appearance of the Holy Mother from the Heavens to the Russian Troops before Battle*) (poster), 35–36, 35

Ignat'ev, I., 43

immortality through memory, 168–169

Imperial Russia. *See* Russian Empire

Imperial War Museum (British), 208–209, 329n31

imperialism, as cause of war, 190, 251

In the Footsteps of War (Po sledam voiny) (Voitolovskii): censorship of, 138, 239–240, 251–252; challenge of newspapers' creation of heroes, 94–95; Cossack violence in, 153; critical acclaim for, 238–239; desertion in, 101–102; editions of, 235, 239–240, 251–252, 332n114; enhanced status during Great Break, 244; ethnic distinctions in, 192–193; as ethnographic work, 238, 332n109; interpretation of war, 305n67; nationalism in, 192–193; pacifism in, 138, 240, 251–252; soldier-officer relationships in, 91, 101–102; twentieth anniversary discourse, 238–240; warrior's fear in, 333n2

In the Rear and at the Front of the Imperialist War (Pireiko), 260

In the Trenches (V okopakh) (Dubinskaia), 149–150, 254, 259

"In the Tsarist Barracks" (Grigor'ev), 262

Industrial Party trial (1930), 204

infidelity, censorship of, 257–258

insanity. *See* mental illness

International Socialist Congress (Basel), 178, 179, 181

internationalism: censorship of, 273; in combat, 188; enemies of, 190–193; in Great Break, 244; Leninist definitions of, 184, 189–190; and nationalism, 178–190; and pacifism, 178–179; and patriotism, 193, 279; rejection of war, 179; and Russianness, 184–190. *See also* class solidarity

inventions, Russian, 269, 335n56

"ironic" war accounts, 177
Iskusstvo vozhdeniia polka (Svechin), 216, 318n137
Islam, 52, 338n24. *See also* Muslim soldiers
Isserson, G. S., 203–204
Istoriia voennogo iskusstva v ramkakh politicheskoi istorii (Delbrück), 203
Istpartotdel. See Tatar Oblast' Party Committee's Department of the History of the Party (*Istpartotdel*)
Italy: fascism in, 334n16; normalization of violence in, 163; Russia as military savior of, 270; wartime violence's impact on postwar society, 128
Iusupov, G. D., 209
Ivankov, Mikhail, 96, 97, 98
Ivanov, Sergei, 293
Ivanovich, Semen, 155
Iz pisem praporshchika-artillerista (Stepun), 153, 156
Izvestiia (News), 186, 225, 237

J'accuse (film), 55, 249
James, Pearl, 319n168
Japan: Russo-Japanese War (*see* Russo-Japanese War); Soviet conflict with (1930s), 195
Jaurès, Jean, 181
Jeffords, Susan, 333n4
Jews: censorship of, 262–263; criticisms of, 86; desertion of, 260, 262; displacement of, 155; espionage accusations against, 196; as hostages, 155; military service of, 157, 260, 262–263; nature of, 290; pogroms against, 66, 102–103, 118–119, 160, 161, 196; rape of, 118–119, 154, 157; on Russian-Austro-Hungarian border, 196; as Soviet citizens, 260; violence against, 157, 158–159, 254, 260. *See also* anti-Semitism; Russian-Jewish authors; synagogues, in memorials
Jünger, Ernst, 82, 86, 109, 130–131

Kadishev, A., 262
Kak zakalialas' stal' (Ostrovskii), 89
Kandidov, Boris, 42–43, *44*
Kanny mirovoi voiny (Isserson), 203–204

Kapital'nyi remont (Sobolev). See *The Big Refit* (*Kapital'nyi remont*) (Sobolev)
Katkov, A. M., 36–37
Katkov, M. V., 36–37
Katsov, Leonid, 231, 259–260, 262, 274, 334n31
Kautsky, Karl, 241
Kazan District Military Censorship Committee, 43, 176
Kazarma (Grigor'ev). See *The Barracks* (*Kazarma*) (Grigor'ev)
Kelly, Catriona, 78
Kerenskii, Aleksandr, 80
Khozdenie po mukam (A. Tolstoi). See *Purgatory* (*Khozdenie po mukam*) (A. Tolstoi)
Khrushchev era, 282, 283
Kiev, fear of German occupation of, 25
Kiev military district, works by, 204
Kievskaia mysl' (Kievan Thought), 91
killing, act of, 139–149; as casual act, 139; dehumanization by, 146; as God's work, 146; impact on perpetrator, 148–149; justified vs. unjustified, 146, 147, 148; as masculine feat, 141; motivation for, 139, 140; psychic cost of, 139–143, 146, 148; rejection of, 146–147; repentance for, 142–143, 146, 147; as senseless and illogical, 139
Kir'ianov (critic), 228, 229–230
Kirov assassination, 240
Kirschenbaum, Lisa, 303n23
Kishinev, 231
"The Kitchen of War" (*Kukhnia voiny*) (poster), *182*
Klein, P. I., 1
Klychkov, Sergei, 17, 139–141, 202, 286
Kollontai, Aleksandra, 17, 178–179, 184, 198
Kol'tsov, Mikhail, 260, 334n31
Komarow, 161
Komsomol, 222–223, 232, 268, 304n44
Komsomol'skaia Pravda (Komsomol Truth), 213
Konovalov (Voitolovskii's servant), 101–102
Korchagin, Pavel, 89
Koreans in Soviet Union, deportation of, 195
Korkina, E. P., 87, *88*
Kornblatt, Judith, 312n6

Korol'kov, G. (historian), 218, 329n54
Korol'kov, S. G. (artist), 142, *145*
Korotkov, I. A., 215
Kovel, 86
Kramer, Alan, 320n10
Krasnaia nov' (Red Virgin Soil), 141
Krasnaia zvezda (Red Star), 212, 213, 225
Krasnoe koleso, uzel I (Solzhenitsyn), 286–288
Krasnyi arkhiv (Red Archive), 45, 113
Krasnyi kavalerist (Red Cavalryman), 161, 317n121
Kravchenko, A., 142, *145*
Kremlin Wall, burials in, 58
Kriuchkov, Koz'ma: bravery of, 98, 316n86; comparisons to, 133; and Cossack mythology, 95–98; criticism of, 94, 96–97, 100; heroism as God's will, 34; in popular culture, 75–77, *76*, 312n1; prisoners of war, treatment of, 131
Krupskaia, Nadezhda, 178
Kuhl, H., 203
"Kukhnia voiny" (*The Kitchen of War*) (poster), *182*
Kuropatkin, A. N., 26
Kursk railway station (Moscow), 114–115

Laboring Peasant Party, 202
Laemmle, Carl, 231
Land and Factory (publishing house), 224, 334n37
Lapchinskii, A. N., 216
Latvians, prejudice against, 195
Lavrenev, Boris, 130
Lawrence, T. E., 10
Lazarevich, V., 219
League of Nations, 230
Lemke, M., 23
Lenin, Vladimir: *About Imperialist War* (*Ob imperialisticheskoi voine*), 203; and alternative military service decree, 135; censorship of, 203; as Christ figure, 58; on citizen-soldier connection, 79; as critic, 240, 333n115; death and tomb of, 40, 58, 66; defeatism, 178; on effects of battle on the Russian soldier, 128; frat-

ernization at the front, call for, 70; resurrection of, 58–59, 67; on socialists' defense of fatherland, 241; transforming the imperialist war into civil war, call for, 14, 173, 178, 179; on war and religion, 32; on war mobilization, 171–172; World War I as imperialist war, 241
Lenin cult, 302n19
Lenin Library, 200, 202. *See also* Russian State Library (Moscow)
Leningrad, blockade of, 282
Leningrad, siege of, 240, 303n23
Leningrad Movie Theater (Moscow), 4, 300, 338n26
Leningrad Park (Moscow), 4, 293
Leninism: contradiction with patriotism, 279–280; defeatism of, 263, 264, 280, 281; internationalism of, 184, 189–190; and nationalism, 178–190; war motivation of, 172–173
Levichev, V. N., 217–218
Levin, Kirill: in international antiwar movement, 181, 183; *Notes from Captivity* (*Zapiski iz plena*), 48–50, 115–119; as prisoner of war, 48–50, *49*, 116–119, 206; as Russian-Jewish author, 231; translation of works of, 11; "The Wild Battalion," 183
Levshov, Erofei Mikhailovich, 298
libraries, censorship in, 20, 202, 203, 204
Lidin, Vladimir, 11, 121
Liebknecht, Karl, 179
Lik voiny. See The Face of War (*Lik voiny*) (Erenburg)
Lippai, Z., 226
Literary Critic. See Literaturnyi kritik
Literaturnaia gazeta (Literary Gazette), 225
Literaturnyi kritik (Literary Critic), 263–264, 266–267
Liutaia zima (Sergeev-Tsenskii), 335n44
Lloyd George, David, 10
Lodz Operation, 219
looting. *See* marauding
Lourdes Madonna, 46–47
lubki (popular prints): heroism of nurses as theme in, 87; holy war as theme in, 34–36, *35*. *See also individual posters*

The Lutsk Breakthrough (Rozhdestven-skii), 222

Lutsk offensive, 25–26, 222–223, 238. *See also* Brusilov offensive (1916)

Luzhkov, Iurii, 293

L'vov, battle for, 25, 84–85, 91, 132

Madonna imagery. *See under* religion

Madonna of Albert (legend). *See* "Golden Virgin" myth

Magnitogorsk model construction project, 232

Main Administration for Literary and Publishing Affairs (*Glavlit*), 10, 20, 201, 285

Makarov, S. O., 75, 312n3

male warrior hero. *See* heroism/heroic masculinity

Mamadyshkii uezd (Tatar Republic), 206

Manusevich, A., 207

marauding, 152, 153, 155, 156, 157

Marian apparitions, 73

Mariia (Babel'), 121–124

Mars Field (Petrograd), 40, 56–57, 58, 59, 311n107

Marxism, atheistic nature of, 294

masculinity: and class, 109–113; ideal, 79; maimed by war trauma, 113–119, 123; nationalization of, 81. *See also* heroism/ heroic masculinity

Masereel, Frans, 71, 72, 73

Mashbits-Verov, I., 98

mass burials, 56–57, 58

Masses, Machines, Elements (*Massy, mashiny, stikhii*) (Sergeev-Tsenskii), 264, 335n44

The Master and Margarita (Bulgakov), 45

Mavrodin, V. V., 223, 275

Mazereel, F. *See* Masereel, Frans

McKay, Claude, 319n168

mechanized warfare, heroic masculinity and, 76–78

medals and honors. *See* commendations, military

Memoirs of Peacetime and the Experience of War (Kuhl), 203

memorial cemeteries. *See* Memorial Park Complex of the Heroes of the First World War (Moscow); Moscow City Fraternal Cemetery (All-Russian War Cemetery); war cemeteries

Memorial Park Complex of the Heroes of the First World War (Moscow), 292–300; ceremonial opening of, 293; construction costs, 293; controversy concerning, 298–300; location of, 293; nationalist themes in, 294–295; obelisk, 295, *296, 297*, 298, 299; religious themes in, 293–294; Transfiguration of the Savior "Reconciliation of Nations" (chapel), 293–294, *296*, 299, 300; vandalism of, 299; World War I monuments, 295; World War II memorial, 295

memorialization: eternal memory concept in, 56, 67; in France, 11; immortality through, 168–169; national goals, realization through, 1; post-Soviet era, syncretic nature of, 295, 298; religious themes in, 1, 36–38, 40, 293–294, 338n24; Soviet rejection of, 6, 11, 51; spurring revolution, 56; of World War II, 282. *See also* Memorial Park Complex of the Heroes of the First World War (Moscow); Moscow City Fraternal Cemetery (All-Russian War Cemetery)

memory, definition of, 7, 303n24

memory, World War I. *See* European World War I memory; Soviet World War I memory

memory case studies, 208–243; *All Quiet on the Western Front*, 224–234; Brusilov's zigzags, 220–224; compiling a documentary history of World War I, 214–220; Moscow Military History Museum, rise and fall of, 208–214; World War I twentieth anniversary discourse, 235–243

Menning, Bruce, 329n49

Mennonites, 137

Mensheviks, 174, 195, 261

mental illness, 116–119, 122–123, 319n165

Menzelinsk, 43

Merkurov, S. D., 3

Merridale, Catherine, 5, 79, 113, 292, 319n165
"Mertvye, vosstan'te" (Masereel), *73*
methodology of author, 16–23
Miasoedov, S. N., 194
Milestone, Lewis, 186, 230–231
military heroism. *See* heroism/heroic masculinity
Military History Museum (Moscow): closure of, 213; exhibits, 209–210, 210–211; location of, 209, 212; number of visitors, 209, 329n31; opening of, 209; pressures on, 212–213; purpose of, 209; rise and fall of, 208–214; security for, 212–213
military mobilization. *See* mobilization for war
military museums. *See* Military History Museum (Moscow); war museums
Military Publishing House. *See* State Military Publishing House
military service: avoidance of, 251, 261 (*see also* desertion); connection to citizenship, 79–80, 81; Soviet, 79–80; tsarist, 79–80
Military-Historical Department of the Soviet general staff, 202, 206–207
Military-Legislative Council of the Revolutionary Military Council (Revvoensovet), 61, 62, 63, 220
Milstein, Lev. *See* Milestone, Lewis
Ministry of Defense, 220; Publishing House, 223
miracle stories, 31, 46–47, 73, 308n49
mobilization for war: causing personal grief, 169; definition of, 13–14; heroic masculinity notions in, 79, 126, 291; national enthusiasm for war, 166; 1930s, 248; and normalization of war, 127; opposition to, 169–170; religious imagery in, 34; by revolutionaries, 171–172, 174; role of boyhood adventure literature, 321n30; by Soviets, 13–15; in tsarist Russia, 125; war literature in, 280–281; for World War II, 272, 292. *See also* war enthusiasm
Mogila neizvestnogo soldata (Lidin). See

The Grave of the Unknown Soldier (*Mogila neizvestnogo soldata*) (Lidin)
Molodaia gvardiia (Young Guard), 224, 225
Molodechno pogrom, 239
Molotov-Ribbentrop pact, 207
montage (technique), 241, 243
monuments. *See* memorialization
Morskoi sbornik (Naval Collection), 268
Moscow: metro construction, 3; street fighting after October Revolution, 58
Moscow Art Theater, 265, 335n45
Moscow City Duma, 38
Moscow City Fraternal Cemetery (All-Russian War Cemetery): anti-Soviet resistance at, 298; architect of, 1; burials in, 1; closure as cemetery, 1–2; commemoration of World War I, 36–38; dedication of, 1; desecration of, 3; disrepair, 2; memorialization (1980s), 298; monuments, *4*; religious imagery in, 36–38, 40; restoration of (*see* Memorial Park Complex of the Heroes of the First World War [Moscow]); Soviet neglect of, 2, 3–4, 58; Soviet use of, 4
Moscow Military History Museum. *See* Military History Museum (Moscow)
Moscow University publications, 324n21
Moskovskoe gorodskoe bratskoe kladbishche (Puchkov), *2*
mosques, in World War II memorials, 338n24
Mosse, George, 7, 9, 128, 320n3
motherland/fatherland: defense of, 20, 170–171, 176, 241, 281; woman as, 276–277. *See also* nationalism; patriotism
mourning, civic/national, 31–32, 36. *See also* Memorial Park Complex of the Heroes of the First World War (Moscow); memorialization; Moscow City Fraternal Cemetery (All-Russian War Cemetery)
mourning, individual: dead, retrieval of, 40–42; elements of process, 68; and eternal memory, 56; gendered nature of, 69; and guilt, 67; monuments, 36–37; nature and labor as comfort for, 70; religion as comfort for, 68–69, 168; revolu-

tionary cause as comfort for, 57; service to nation as comfort for, 67, 69, 168; service to others as comfort for, 42, 50; in Soviet culture, 67–68

Mukhametov (soldier), 43, 45

"Murderers Who Have Yet to Be Clubbed to Death" (Babel'), 161

Museum of the Revolution, 221

Muslim clergy, 171

Muslim soldiers, 43, 45, 52, 197. *See also* Tatars

muzhik (male peasant), 88–89

"My First Goose" (Babel'), 162

mysticism, 52–53, 54–55

mythmaking, 7, 31–74. *See also* religion

"Na bor'by s imperialisticheskimi voinami" (poster). *See* "To the Struggle against Imperialist Wars" (*Na bor'by s imperialisticheskimi voinami*) (poster)

Na fronte imperialisticheskoi voiny (Pireiko), 260–261

Na literaturnom postu (On Literary Guard), 226

Narkompros. See People's Commissar of Enlightenment (*Narkompros*)

Narod na voine (Fedorchenko). *See The People at War* (*Narod na voine*) (Fedorchenko)

Nastuplenie Iugo-Zapadnogo fronta v mai-iiune, 330n58

national identity: defined through comparisons to enemies, 192–193; heroic masculinity in, 165, 270; providing meaning to wartime death, 168; religious aspects of, 165; as theme, 16–20. *See also* Russianness; Sovietness

National Socialists, 230

nationalism: bolstered by memory of war, 9; emphasized over class, 267; and internationalism, 178–190, 272; and Leninism, 178–190; in Memorial Park Complex of the Heroes of the First World War (Moscow), 294–295; and pacifism, 178–190; and prejudice, 188–189; in Russian Empire, 20, 167–169; Soviet chal-

lenges to, 290–291; World War II era, 273. *See also* patriotism

Naval Collection (*Morskoi sbornik*), 268

navy. *See* Russian Imperial Navy, tradition of prayer in

Nazis, 222, 230, 231, 243, 268

Nefterev, I. F., 219

Neobychainye pokhozhdeniia Khulio Khurenito i ego uchenikov. . . . (Erenburg). *See The Extraordinary Adventures of Khulio Khurenito and His Disciples. . . .* (*Neobychainye pokhozhdeniia Khulio Khurenito i ego uchenikov. . . .*) (Erenburg)

Nesbyvshiesia Kanny (G. Korol'kov), 329n54

Nevskii, Aleksandr, 207

New Economic Policy (NEP) era, 15, 212–213

New Soviet Man, 9, 20, 105, 123

New World (*Novyi mir*), 141

News (*Izvestiia*). *See Izvestiia* (*News*)

newspapers, accounts of war in, 85, 91, 94–95, 125

Nicholas II, Tsar, 25, 80, 206, 241. *See also* Romanov dynasty

Nikolai Nikolaevich, Grand Duke of Russia, 287

1914 (Feinberg and Telingater), 169–170, 181, 235, 240–243, 242

Ninth Army, 330n56

Niva (Field), 34, 40–42, 308n36

NKVD. *See* People's Commissariat of Internal Affairs (NKVD)

Nobel Prize, 232, 286, 338n13

Norris, Stephen, 326n76

Notes from Captivity (*Zapiski iz plena*) (Levin), 48–50, 115–119, 244, 309n53

Notes of a Cavalryman (*Zapiski kavalerista*) (Gumilev), 84, 131–132

Notes of a Militiaman (*Zapiski opolchentsa*) (Stepnoi), 251

Notes of a Soldier (*Zapiski soldata*) (Os'kin), 101, 324n27

Novel-Newspaper (*Roman-Gazeta*), 224

Novikov-Priboi, Aleksei, 263–264, 268, 280

Novodevichii Cemetery, 62, 63, 65

Novodevichii Monastery, 61, 63, 220

Novyi mir (New World), 141
nurses: absence of, in interwar period discourse, 275; Civil War service, 317n121; heroism of, 86–87, *88*, 107, 317n121; immorality of, 86, 107, 317n122; memorial to, 294–295; in World War II discourse, 277–278

Ob imperialisticheskoi voine (Lenin), 203
occult practices, 32, 66
occult publications, 40
October (film), 313n23
October Revolution: in film, 187, 189, 313n23; masculine gender of, 313n25; Moscow street fighting, 58; storming of Winter Palace, 80; Women's Battalion of Death in, 80, 258, 313n23
Odessa, fear of German occupation of, 25
officers: as Bolsheviks in the making, 266; as class enemy, 265; decadent lifestyle of, 211, 212; ethical dilemmas of, 102; ethnic hatred by, 150, 191, 326n81; inadaptability of, 265; masculinity of, questioned, 109–110; moral traits in, 266–267; as role models, 264–265, 267; sexual violence of, 149–150, 255, 256; as "superfluous man," 266; training materials for, 208; as ultimately doomed, 265–266; valorization of, 288. *See also* soldier-officer relationships
Ogon' (Barbusse), 21–22
Ogorodnikov, F. E., 216
"Okraina" (Finn). *See* "Borderlands" (*Okraina*) (Finn)
Okunev, Ia., 85, 88–89, 132
Old Believers, 54, 309n68
Old Bolsheviks, 261
Old Moscow Society, 2, 8, 301n5
On Literary Guard (Na literaturnom postu), 226
105th Artillery Regiment, 52
The Operation of the Breakthrough on the Southwestern Front in 1916 (Vetoshnikov), 223
Ordeal (A. Tolstoi), 309n69
Ordeal of Sevastopol' (*Sevastopol'skaia strada*) (Sergeev-Tsenskii), 263, 281

Order of St. George, 63, 64, 295
Orlovsky, Daniel, 5
orphans, 158
Orthodox Christianity: as component of Russianness, 273; funeral ritual, 56, 61, 62; influence on Soviet commemorative practices, 40; "just" killing, belief in, 146; memorialization projects, 1, 36, 293, 338n24; mourning rituals, 68–69; restoration of, 33, 298; resurrection and salvation beliefs, 55, 58; soldiers' abuse of non-Orthodox peers, 171; World War I, support for, 35, 51; World War I as holy war, 17, 34
Os'kin, Dmitrii, 101, 108, 110, 324n27
Ostrovskii, Niikolai, 25. *See also How the Steel was Tempered* (Ostrovskii)
overcoats, theft of, in literature, 59–60
Owen, Wilfred, 77–78, 94, 114

pacifism: "apolitical," 226; censorship of, 251–252; criticism of, 141; evangelical, 134, 135; gender associations of, 141, 179; as improbable ideology, 287–288; international antiwar movement, 181, 183; and nationalism, 178–190; posters advocating, 179, *180*, 181; prevention of war through fighting, 183; secular, 138; Soviet promotion of, 134–138, 181; Soviet rejection of, 130, 135, 137–138; World War II–era views of, 273. *See also* bourgeois pacifism; conscientious objectors; Tolstoian pacifism
Padenie dinastii Romanovykh (film). *See The Fall of the Romanov Dynasty* (*Padenie dinastii Romanovykh*) (film)
Palitsyn, F. F., 287
Panchuk, Filipp, 119–120
Pankratova, A. M., 223–224, 278
Pasternak, Boris, 286, 288, 338n13
Pasternak, Leonid, 90, 91, *92*, *93*
patriarchal relationship. *See* father-son relationships; soldier-officer relationships, paternalistic
patriotism: allowing forgetting of horrors of war, 13; bolstered by memory of war, 9; censorship of, 20; class distinc-

tions in, 279; conflict with class solidarity, 20, 167; conflict with Leninist
doctrine, 279–280; heroic masculinity
in, 278; ideal female role model in, 277;
and internationalism, 193, 279; in memorialization, 1; resurgence (late 1930s),
268; in Russian Empire, 20, 166–167,
170, 171; as theme, 17, 20; war enthusiasm, 169; World War I–era, 27–28, 176;
World War II–era, 223, 279. *See also* nationalism
Paul I, Emperor, 210
peace pledge movement, 181, 183
Peace Pledge Union, 181
Pearse, A., 312n1
Pelepeiko, Sotnik (Lieutenant), 83
The People at War (*Narod na voine*) (Fedorchenko): authenticity of, 52–53, 309n61,
332n109; author's introduction to, 235;
brutal nature of war in, 235; censorship
of, 109, 201, 235, 249, 254–255, 257–258,
285–286; criticism of, 237; editions of, 53,
235, 249, 254, 257–258, 309n61, 332n104;
ethnic violence in, 254, 285; folk religion
in, 52–53; infidelity in, 257–258; as inspiration, 310n93; interpretation of, 332n109;
killing in, 139; mourning in, 67–68; officers' violence against women, 149;
praise for, 237; rape in, 254–255; religious
themes in, 249, 285; sexuality of soldiers
in, 256–257, 258; supernatural in, 237–
238; twentieth anniversary discourse,
235–238; war enthusiasm in, 175, 324n35
People's Commissar for Military and Naval Affairs, 61
People's Commissar of Enlightenment
(*Narkompros*): ideological struggle with
Red Army, 244; and military museums,
209, 212, 213; orientation against tsar-
ist military history, 215; study of World
War I, 200
People's Commissar of Provisioning, 3
People's Commissariat of Defense, 222
People's Commissariat of Internal Affairs
(NKVD), 3
People's Commissariat of Military and
Naval Affairs, 63

People's Court, 217
Peschanaia Street (Moscow), 3
Pesn' o rodine (*Song of the Motherland*), 277
Peter the Great, 263, 294
Peterburgskii listok (Petersburg Leaflet), 57
Petliura, S. V., 265
Petrograd, 25, 205
pilgrimages, 73
Pimen, Patriarch, 298
Pireiko, Aleksandr: censorship of, 259,
260–261; draft evasion by, 102, 174–175;
evasion of military service by, 102–103;
memoirs, 105, 174–175, 260–261, 317n112;
shielding Jewish civilians from Cos-
sacks, 102–103, 160
Piskarevskoe Memorial Cemetery (Lenin-
grad), 282
Plamper, Jan, 333n2
Plekhanov, Georgii Valentinovich, 241
Po sledam voiny (Voitolovskii). See *In
the Footsteps of War* (*Po sledam voiny*)
(Voitolovskii)
Podillian legends, 73
podvig (exploit), 307n20
"Podvig sestry E. P. Korkinoi" (*The Exploit
of Sister E. P. Korkina*) (poster), 88
pogroms: Cossack instigation of, 118–119,
153, 196; in Galicia, 118–119; impact on
witnesses, 118–119; in Komarow, 161;
in Molodechno (1915), 239; predictions
about, 66; protection from, 102–103;
White Army instigation of, 161
Poincaré, Raymond, 10, 241, 243
poison gas attacks, 271–272
Poklonnaia Gora (Homage Hill) (Mos-
cow), 338n24
Pokrovskii, M. N., 207
Poland: Soviet-Polish War, 60, 94, 161;
World War I, 25, *77*
popular unrest, 71–74
Porshnev, S. V., 332n109
Porshneva, O. S., 332n109
Portugal (Red Cross hospital ship), 38, *39*, 40
Poslednyi lel' (Klychkov). See *The Sugary
German* (*Sakharnyi nemets*) (Klychkov)
posters and popular prints. See *lubki*
(popular prints); *individual posters*

Prague émigré archive, 283
Pravda (Truth), 56, 61, 186–187
Pravdukhin, V. P., 141
prayer, 41, 47–48, 49, 50, 52
Preobrazhenie Rossii (Sergeev-Tsenskii), 264
Presidium of the Central Executive Committee of the USSR, 216
"The Price of Blood" (poster), 91, 93. See also "Help for War Victims" (Pasternak)
prisoners of war: from Austria-Hungary, 160; in Austria-Hungary, 48–50, 49, 104–105, 117, 317n115; cemetery, 117; development of revolutionary consciousness in, 175; from Germany, 131, 151, 184–186, 188–189; in Germany, 48, 205–206; mental illness in, 116–119; praise for All Quiet on the Western Front by, 147–148; violence against, 131, 160, 188–189
pro-German sentiment, of Tatars, 206, 328n19
Proletarian Cinema (Proletarskoe kino), 230
proletarian solidarity. See class solidarity; internationalism
Proletarskoe kino (Proletarian Cinema), 230
Prost, Antoine, 9
prostitution, 108, 149
Protazanov, Iakov: The Forty-First (Sorok pervyii) (see The Forty-First [Sorok pervyii] [film])
Protestants, 134
Provisional Government: equality of sacrifice and entitlements, 28; gender equality under, 18, 80, 313n22; masculinity of, 80; revolutionary burial grounds, 40; women in combat, 80, 81, 258
Przemysl (Austro-Hungarian fortress), 25, 211
psychological trauma. See mental illness
Puchkov, S. V., 2, 37, 40
Pulemetchitsa (Dubinskaia), 259
Pulko-Dmitriev, A. D., 206–207
Purgatory (Khozdenie po mukam) (A. Tolstoi), 53–55, 59–60, 249
purge era: anti-German sentiment during, 203–204, 205, 268; authors as victims, 200, 201, 202, 240, 244–245, 334n31;

burial of victims, 3; censorship of victims of, 202; local party organizations as victims, 282; military historians as victims, 219; military specialists as victims, 215
Pushkin, Aleksandr Sergeevich, 329n54
Pushkin and the Theater (Zagorskii), 229

Quiet Flows the Don (film), 284–285, 316n94
Quiet Flows the Don (Tikhii Don) (Sholokhov): author's analysis of, 16–17; censorship of, 99, 148, 246, 248, 273, 324n26; Civil War in, 148; conscious revolutionaries in, 253; contradictions in, 98, 100; Cossacks in, 95–97, 98–100, 154, 246; criticism of, 146; desertion in, 103, 262; editions of, 142; film version, 284–285, 316n94; honor code in, 142, 160; illustrations from, 142, 144, 145; internationalism in, 189–190, 273; killing, impact on perpetrator, 141–143, 146, 148–149; Lenin quotations in, 173, 324n26; "Marxist-Leninist-Stalinist" views of characters in, 240; mourning, discussion of, 68–70; officers in, 265; pacifism in, 98, 146–147; popular success of, 316n94; prayer in, 47–48; publication history, 235; religion in, 47–48; serial publication of, 98; soldier-officer relationships in, 111–112; war motivation in, 172–173; warrior's fear in, 246, 248; women in, 259; as work to emulate, 240

Rabochaia gazeta (Workers' Gazette), 56
Rabochaia Moskva (Worker's Moscow), 212
Radek, Karl, 200, 202, 224, 260, 334n31
rape and sexual violence: as amusement, 255; censorship of, 254–255, 258; child victims of, 159; by Cossacks, 153–154, 255, 256; female soldier as victim of, 149–150; as inevitable in war, 163, 254; Jews as victims of, 118–119, 154, 157; justification for, 157, 162–163; by officers, 149–150, 255, 256; same-sex violence, 153–154; by White Army, 161, 162; witnesses as victims, 154
Rasputin, Grigorii, 194

rationalism, 34

Rava-Russkaia, 160

reanimation, 53

"rear" (civilians and officials): chauvinistic attitudes toward Germans, 184–186, 188–189; debt owed to soldiers, 114; displacement of, 155–156, 159 (*see also* refugees); in gendered terms, 106–109, 125; immorality of, 94, 107, 108; military abuse of, 154–161, 254, 323n100 (*see also* marauding; pogroms; rape and sexual violence); and military honor code, 130–131; tension with frontline combatants, 85–86, 125, 257–258

Reconciling the Nations (chapel). *See* Transfiguration of the Savior "Reconciliation of Nations" (chapel)

Red Archive. *See Krasnyi arkhiv* (Red Archive)

Red Army: Academy of the General Staff, 223; burials, 1; Central Directorate, 217; challenge of German invincibility myth, 207; Chief Directorate, 217–218; Chief of Staff, 219; Commissar for Military and Naval Affairs, 215; Commission for the Study of War Experience, 8, 217; Commission on the Research and Use of the Experience of World War I, 214; Fifth Department, 203, 218; founding of, 214; General Staff and Political Administration, 213, 217, 219, 270; glorification of, 25; heroes, 63; ideological tensions in, 215–216, 244; ideological tensions with Narkompros, 244; "Marxist" historiography, ascendance of, 216; military history, importance of, 212; Military History Department, 217, 218, 219; morale, 120–121; museum, 209; personal tensions in, 217, 244; prowess of, 268; publications by, 215; Scientific Military-Historical Department of the general staff, 202–203; Soviet-Polish war, 60; twenty-fifth anniversary of, 235, 243; volunteers, 177; war invalids, 319n165; women in, 81, 313n27; World War I documentary project, 200, 214–220, 221, 244, 268

Red Army Day (1925), 209

Red Cavalry (Babel'), 162–163, 254

Red Cavalryman (Krasnyi kavalerist), 161, 317n121

Red Guards, 148

Red Proletarian (publishing house), 224

Red Square (Moscow), 40, 58

Red Star (Krasnaia zvezda). *See Krasnaia zvezda* (Red Star)

Red Virgin Soil (Krasnaia nov'), 141

The Red Wheel, Knot 1 (Solzhenitsyn), 286–288

Reese, Roger, 329n49

refugees, 26–27, 155–156, 159, 239

refusal of service. *See* conscientious objectors

Religiia v tsarskoi armii (Kandidov). *See Religion in the Tsarist Army* (*Religiia v tsarskoi armii*) (Kandidov)

religion, 31–74; censorship of, 22–23, 249–251, 285, 286; healing the spirit, 69; and heroism/heroic masculinity, 9, 48–50, 55; impotence of, 49, 52; individual faith, 289–290; as justification for war, 32, 34–35, *35;* Madonna imagery, 31, 34, 42–43, 46–47, 73; miracle stories, 31, 46–47, 73, 308n49; in monument and memorials, 36–38, 40, 293–294; and national identity, 165; orthodox socialist views, 54; and pacifism, 54–55, 134–135, 137; pilgrimages, 73; popular, 73–74, 289; and popular unrest, 71–74; prayer, 41, 47–48, 49, 50, 52; providing meaning, 17–18; revival after the revolution, 33; of sailors at sea, 50; of soldiers, 31, 36, 43, 45; Soviet denial of, 32, 33, 289; in Soviet discourse, 17–18, 42–55; spiritual-revolutionary worldview, 54; as theme of study, 9, 16–20; tsarist religious imagery, 34–42, *35;* vanishing discourse about, 249–251; World War I as holy war, 17, 34–35, 43, 45, 168–169. *See also* afterlife; clergy; folk religion; Jews; Muslim clergy; Muslim soldiers; mysticism; mythmaking; Orthodox Christianity; Protestants

Religion in the Tsarist Army (*Religiia v tsarskoi armii*) (Kandidov), 42–43, *44*

Remarque, Erich Maria: *All Quiet on the Western Front* (see *All Quiet on the Western Front* [Remarque]); biographical play about, 228–230; depiction of war, 331n78; military service, 100; Nobel Prize, suggestions concerning, 232; *The Road Back,* 227; Russian translations of, 10; on warrior's fear, 333n1

Renan, Ernest, 302n18

Rennenkampf, P. K., 25, 205, 287

Reserve Regiment (Zauriad-polk) (Sergeev-Tsenskii), 264, 266–267, 335n44

resettlement. *See* "rear" (civilians and officials), displacement of; refugees

resurrection, 55–71; Christian imagery of, 69; connection to military heroism, 67; to fight in revolution, 228; imagery, 69; of Lenin, 58; making human suffering bearable, 40; messianic rhetoric, 55; metaphorical, 71; metaphysical, 68; millenarian and revolutionary rhetoric, 55–56; of revolutionary dead, 57–58, 71; of Russia, through dead martyrs, 57; of soldiers, 67–71; in Soviet discourse, 60; by technology, 58; of war victims, 310n91

retreat of 1915. *See* "great retreat" (1915)

"The Return of the Soldier" (McKay), 319n168

revolution: metaphorical resurrection through, 71; as purifying force, 108; war as necessary for, 134

Revolution (1905), 210

Revolution (1917): burials, 1, 40; death and resurrection themes, 33, 56–58, 70–71; executions, 148; fueled by rebellious soldiers, 264; Mars Field funeral, 56–57, 311n107; militaristic interwar myths about, 24–25; restoring masculine honor, 81; violence in, 128–129. *See also* February Revolution; October Revolution

revolutionary consciousness: contrasted with "unconscious" soldiers, 79; and desertion, 261, 262; development of, 43, 149, 187, 193; at expense of heroism, 124–126; paradoxes of, 261; in post–World War II discourse, 285; and violence, 253. *See also* Bolsheviks

Revvoensovet. *See* Military-Legislative Council of the Revolutionary Military Council (Revvoensovet)

Riga, 174

Right Bank Ukraine, 73

The Road Back (Remarque), 227

Road to Calvary (A. Tolstoi), 309n69

Rolland, Romain, 10

Roman-Gazeta (Novel-Newspaper), 224

Romanov dynasty, 28, 194. *See also* Nicholas II, Tsar

Roper, Michael, 314n32

Rosenfel'd, Mikhail, 213

Rostov on the Don, 232

The Rout (Razgrom) (Fadeev), 70

Rowland, Daniel, 338n25

Rozhdestvenskii, M., 222, 330n68

Rumania, declaration of war on Germany by, 270

Russell, Bertrand, 181

Russian Association of Proletarian Writers (RAPP), 21

Russian diaspora, 10. *See also* émigrés, World War I accounts by

Russian Empire: censorship in, 23, 305n65; civilian hardship in, 23–24; downfall, 27; fall of, 28; France, influence of, 25, 26; glorification of war, 82–83; impact of war's violence on postwar society, 128; militaristic culture, 32, 87; as military savior of Britain and France, 270; mobilization for war, 17, 32; national consciousness, 27–28; nationalism, 167–169; patriotism, 20, 27–28; relationship to the West, 271; war mobilization, 27; wartime killing in, 130–133. *See also* Russian Imperial Army; Russian Imperial Navy, tradition of prayer in

Russian Federation: coat of arms, 294–295; World War I memory in, 293

Russian Gazette (Russkie vedomosti), 83

Russian Imperial Army: alternative service, 137; Austria-Hungary, offensives against, 25; East Prussia, invasion of, 25, 26; Germany, offensives against, 25, 26; Southwestern Front, mood of, 168; "The Wild Division" (Caucasian unit), 183

Russian Imperial Navy, tradition of prayer in, 50
Russian Liberation Army, 299, 300
Russian Orthodoxy. *See* Orthodox Christianity
"Russian Soldier" (poster), 87
Russian State Library (Moscow), 200. *See also* Lenin Library
Russian Word (Russkoe slovo), 23–24
Russian-German elites, 194–195, 267, 328n13
Russian-Jewish authors, 231
Russianness: backwardness, 166; bravery, 269; creating civil disorder, 167; definition of, 165–198; development of, 29, 166, 167; identification with, by multiethnic populations, 166; inventiveness, 268, 269, 335n56; military prowess, 268–272, 269, 271; and religion, 273; spirit (*dukh*), strength of, 167–168; technological prowess, 271; traits of, 166–168, 268–272, 269, 271, 335n56; in tsarist era, 167–169, 176; tsarist-Soviet continuities in, 167, 268–272; in World War I, 165–198
Russkie vedomosti (Russian Gazette), 83
Russkoe slovo (Russian Word), 23–24
Russo-Japanese War, 94, 147, 210, 263–264, 312n3
Russo-Turkish war, 210, 312n3
Ruzskii, N. V., 91

Sakharnyi nemets (Klychkov). See *The Sugary German* (*Sakharnyi nemets*) (Klychkov)
"Salt" (Babel'), 162–163
Samsonov, A. V., 25, 204, 286, 287
Sanborn, Joshua, 314n46
Sassoon, Siegfried, 181
séances, 32, 66
Second International Socialist Congress, 181
Second World War. *See* World War II
self-censorship, 258
self-defense, as fatal for the soul, 140
self-mutilation, 136
Sel'vinskii, I. L., 223, 283
Sergeev-Tsenskii, Sergei: *Brusilov's Breakthrough* (*Brusilovskii proryv*), 223, 264, 273–278, 279–281, 330n71; *Liutaia zima,*

335n44; *Masses, Machines, Elements* (*Massy, mashiny, stikhii*), 264, 335n44; military service, 335n47; misogynistic undercurrent in, 276, 278; *Ordeal of Sevastopol'* (*Sevastopol'skaia strada*), 263, 281; Orthodox Christianity, attitude toward, 273; *Reserve Regiment* (*Zauriadpolk*), 264, 266–267, 335n44; *The Transfiguration of Russia* (*Preobrazhenie Rossii*), 264; translation of works of, 11
Sevastopol, 335n47; siege of, 210
Sevastopol'skaia strada (Sergeev-Tsenskii). See *Ordeal of Sevastopol'* (*Sevastopol'skaia strada*) (Sergeev-Tsenskii)
Seventeenth Party Congress, 181
sexual violence. *See* rape and sexual violence
sexuality: censorship of, 108–109, 148, 201, 255–258, 278; in heroism/heroic masculinity, 255–257; prostitution, 108, 149; of soldiers, 256–257, 258; Soviet views of, 256. *See also* infidelity, censorship of
Shadr (Voronova), 39
Shadr, I. D., 38, 39, 40
Shakhty trial (1928), 204
Shantsev, V., 293
Shaposhnikov, B. M., 215, 217, 219, 221
Shchusev, A. V.: design of Church of the Transfiguration, 1, 36–37, 37, 294; design of Lenin's Mausoleum, 40; location of Church of the Transfiguration, 296, 338n26
shell-shock victims, 117–119. *See also* mental illness
Sheppard, Canon H. R. L., 181, 183
Shklovskii, Viktor, 241, 326n74
Shlikhter, Aleksandr Grigorievich, 3, 8
Shlikhter, Sergei Aleksandrovich, 3, 4, 293, 300
Sholokhov, Mikhail: Civil War service, 96; mockery of prayer, 50; *Quiet Flows the Don* (see *Quiet Flows the Don* [*Tikhii Don*] [Sholokhov]); rejection of nationalism, 198; translation of works of, 11; transposing Cossack myth onto Bolshevik heroes, 312n6

Shub, Esfir: *The Fall of the Romanov Dynasty* (film) (*see The Fall of the Romanov Dynasty [Padenie dinastii Romanovykh]* [film]); pacifist approach of, 52
Shukhmin, Khristofor, 133
Shvandin (violin-maker), 48–50, 309n53
Skobelev, M. D., 75, 210, 312n3
Skuratov, M. M., 285
Slezkin, Iurii, 283
Slezkin, Lev, 283
Slezkine, Yuri, 328n13
smallpox, 116
"Smelo my v boi poidem" (revolutionary song), 310
Smith, John T., 305n65
Smolensk infantry reserve battalion, 113
Sobolev, Leonid, 50, 110, 264, 265–266
Social Democrats: censorship of, 273; criticism of, 178–179, 181; internationalism among, 189–190; refusal of military service by, 174. *See also under* Germany
Socialist Realism, 188, 326n77
Socialist Revolutionaries, 174
Society of Old Bolsheviks, 261
Sokol region (Moscow), 2, 298–299
Sokolovskii, Nikolai, 227–228
Soldaty (Tagirov), 154
soldier-officer relationships: Bolshevik view of, 136; brutality in, 63–64, 96, 109, 113, 149, 188, 260; camaraderie in, 99, 100, 101–102, 109, 110–111, 318n137; contest for masculinity, 109–110; museum exhibit about, 211; paternalistic, 63, 87, 111–113, 125, 275; rebellion of soldiers, 264; strained nature of, 113, 143; in World War II–era discourse, 274, 275
soldiers: alienation from "rear," 78, 82, 107; conflicts with civilians, 154–155; and ethnic distinctions, 194–197; fatalism of, 83; fear in, 70, 83, 314n37; and heroism, 82, 271; internationalism in, 184; letters from, 43, 168–169, 176, 194–197; loyalty to tsar, 183; mistreatment of, 171; morale of, 333n1; motivation through vodka, 84; as noble laborers, 132; patriotism in, 176; powerlessness of, 48; and religion, 43; resurrection of, 67–71; sexuality of, 256–257, 258; "unconscious" military service, 43, 103–104, 106, 175, 187; as victims, 82. *See also* artillerists; camaraderie; desertion; volunteers for war
Soldiers (Tagirov), 154
A Soldier's Notebook (Brusilov), 311n111
Solov'ev, Staff-Captain, 83
Solzhenitsyn, Aleksandr, 286–288
Song of the Motherland (*Pesn' o rodine*), 277
Sorok pervyi (film). See *The Forty-First* (*Sorok pervyi*) (film)
Soviet ideology: continuity with Russian discourse, 29; continuity with tsarist *mentalité*, 9; inherent contradictions in, 14–15; reintroduction of traditional Russian culture into, 211
Soviet State Publishing House, 308n46
Soviet Union: commemorative practices, Orthodox roots of, 40; fall of, 288; founding myths, Orthodox roots of, 40; gender equality under, 18; League of Nations, entrance into, 230; mobilization for war, 13–15; pacifism in, 181; recognition by United States, 230; relationship to the West, 271; violence against citizenry, 129; World War II, 272
Soviet Worker (publishing house), 224
Soviet World War I memory: ambiguous themes in, 14; antiheroism in, 15; bolstering patriotism and nationalism, 9; continuity in discourse, 9; creators of, 7–8; disappearance of, 244, 282–289; documentary history, 214–220; forgetting, 5, 13, 302n18; heroism in, 15; individual mourning, lack of, 6; marginalization of, 8, 14, 213, 291–292; memorials, 299; museums as, 208–209, 300 (*see also* Military History Museum [Moscow]); in Russian Federation, 293; Soviet struggles over (*see* memory case studies); themes in, 17; transformation in, 8, 268; transnational contexts, 8–13; tropes of, 24; twentieth anniversary commemoration, 181; twentieth anniversary discourse, 235–243; during World War II war mobilization, 292. *See also* European World War I memory

Sovietness: construction of, through conscious forgetting, 5, 302n18; development of, 167; lack of legitimating myth,
7; national and patriotic myth, 20; New
Soviet Man, 9, 20, 105, 123; and revolution mythology, 5; tsarist-era links
to, 269. *See also* national identity; Russianness
Soviet-Polish War (1920), 60, 94, 161
spies. *See* espionage, anxiety about
spirit (*dukh*), in Russian people, 167–168
spirituality. *See* religion
St. George, emblem of, 293
St. George, Order of, 63, 64, 295
St. George cross: fictional recipients of,
97, 99, 100, 122, 259, 284–285; in monuments, 295, *296, 297,* 299; recipients of,
75, 87, 114–115
St. Petersburg: Poincaré's visit to, 241; war
protests in, 170
Stalin, Josif: critique of Second International Socialist Congress, 181; "cult
of personality," 288; death of, 284; enjoyment of *The Days of the Turbins*
(play), 335n45; foreign policy, 333n120;
and Moscow City Fraternal Cemetery,
3; Order 227 ("not one step back"), 274,
336n68; overthrow, attempts at, 205; and
pacifism, 230; paranoia in, 283; post–
World War II rebuilding efforts, 282;
and professionals, 269, 335n55; purges,
3, 240 (*see also* purge era); revolutionary
policies, abandonment of, 15; Seventeenth Party Congress, speech to, 181
Stalin-era censorship, 99, 246, 327n1
Stalinist prison camps, 135
The Standard (Znamia). See *Znamia* (The
Standard)
State Historical Museum, 209, 213. *See also*
Military History Museum (Moscow)
State Literature Publishing House: *All
Quiet on the Western Front* (Remarque),
227–230; letters to, 98, 147–148; *Mariia*
(Babel'), 121; *The People at War* (Fedor-
chenko), 237, 285–286
State Military Publishing House, 243, 262
State Publishing House, 216, 221

Steinberg, Mark, 321n33
Stepnoi, N., 251, 333n10
Stepun, Fedor, 153, 156, 323n93
Stites, Richard, 5
Stock Exchange Gazette. See *Birzhevye ve-
domosti* (Stock Exchange Gazette)
Stockdale, Melissa K., 313n22
Stone, Dave, 328n27, 329n49, 337n7
Storm of Steel (Jünger), 86, 109
Strategic Outline of War, 1914–1918, 214
The Sugary German (*Sakharnyi nemets*)
(Klychkov): censorship of, 202; criti-
cism of, 141; editions of, 139, 140, 321n51;
honor code in, 143; psychic costs of kill-
ing in, 139–141
Sukhomlinov, V. A., 194
supernatural. *See* religion
surrender, 104–105, 177, 273–274
Suvorov, A. V., 210, 275
Svechin, A. A., 8, 214, 216, 318n137, 323n100
synagogues, in memorials, 338n24
Sytin, P., 216

Tagirov, Afzal, 154, 323n97, 326n81
Tambov infantry detachment, 168
"tamizdat" (works published abroad),
286–288
Tannenberg, Battle of, 25, 194, 204, 205, 287
Tarle, E. V., 207
Tatar Oblast' Party Committee's Department of the History of the Party (*Istpar-
totdel*), 43, 45
Tatars: deportation of, 328n19; nature of,
290; pro-German sentiment of, 206,
328n19; as soldiers, 52, 171, 176, 196–197
(*see also* Muslim soldiers)
Teatr i dramaturgiia (Theater and Drama-
turgy), 121
Telingater, Solomon, 169–170, *240–243*
"the Thaw," 284, 285–286, 288
Theater and Dramaturgy (Teatr i drama-
turgiia), 121
Theweleit, Klaus, 333n4
thick description, 16, 304n48
Through Captivity (Katsov), 259–260, 274
Tikhii Don. See *Quiet Flows the Don*
(Sholokhov)

Tikhon, reestablishment of patriarchate under, 33
Timasheff, Nicholas, 15
"To the Struggle against Imperialist Wars" (*Na bor'by s imperialisticheskimi voinami*) (poster), 179, *180*, 181
Tolstoi, Aleksei: emigration, 53; glorification of wartime violence, 133; Peter the Great in works by, 263; *Purgatory* (*Khozdenie po mukam*), 53–55, 249; "rear" as place of immorality, 107; on strength of spirit of Russians, 167; translations of works of, 309n69; violence in works by, 132–133; war as purgatory, 314n35; war as purification, 84, 89, 167; as war correspondent, 83, 84–85, 86; wartime violence as everyday work, 132
Tolstoi, Lev, 98, 132, 138, 316n90
Tolstoian pacifism, 135–138, 141, 251, 273, 287
Tomb of the Unknown Soldier (Moscow), 282
tombs of unknown soldiers, 31, 282
"Toward a History of the Versailles Treaty" (Manusevich), 207
The Traitor (play), 228–230
traitors, anxiety about, 194, 195–196, 204
The Transfiguration of Russia (Sergeev-Tsenskii), 264
Transfiguration of the Savior "Reconciliation of Nations" (chapel), 293–294, *296*, 299, 300
treason. *See* traitors, anxiety about
Trice, Thomas, 57
Trotskii, Lev, 205, 214, 217
Truth (Pravda). See *Pravda* (Truth)
tsarist army. *See* Russian Imperial Army
The Tsarist Army in the Period of World War and the February Revolution (*Tsarskaia armiia v period mirovoi voiny i Fevral'skoi revoliutsii*), 200–201
tsarist era. *See* Russian Empire
Tsarskaia armiia v period mirovoi voiny i Fevral'skoi revoliutsii (*The Tsarist Army in the Period of World War and the February Revolution*), 200–201
Tsekhnovitser, Orest, 320n22

Tsement (Gladkov), 162
Tsereteli, I., 195
Tsisernakaberd monument to genocide victims, 288
Tsushima straits, 263–264
Tsusima (Novikov-Priboi), 263–264, 268, 280
Tukhachevskii, Marshall Mikhail, 203, 215
Tumarkin, Nina, 302n19
Turks, 132–133, 195, 288–289
Tver' Bolsheviks, 173–174
Tvorchestvo (Creative Work), 38
"Two Medals" (Telingater), 241, *242*
Tychinin (woman volunteer in World War I), 87

Ukraine: Austro-Hungarian occupation of, 323n100; national forces, 265
Ukrainian Academy of Sciences, 3
Umanskii, Dm., 200
Under Fire (Barbusse), 21–22
Union of Soviet Writers: Defense Committee, 235, 240, 241, 243, 259, 328n22; Drama Section, 207; *1914* exhibition, 241
Union of Zemstva medical services, 114, 137
United Kingdom. *See* Britain
United States, recognition of Soviet Union by, 230
United States Signal Corps, Photographic Division, 231
Universal Pictures, 230
unrest, popular, 71–74
upper classes: ethnic hatred by, 190–191, 195; future war against, 189–190; Russian-German elites, 194–195, 267, 328n13
Ural Cossacks, 309n69
Usievich, E., 266–267, 279–280
Utro Rossii, 303n36

V okopakh (Dubinskaia). See *In the Trenches* (*V okopakh*) (Dubinskaia)
V tylu i na fronte imperialisticheskoi voiny (Pireiko), 260
Vakhtangov Theater, 122
Vaniuk (soldier), 154
Varshavsko-Ivangorodskaia operatsiia, 330n58

Vavilov, Artur (Artem), 175, 177, 324n35
Veber, Iu., 222–223, 270, 271–272, 279
Vecherniaia Moskva (Evening Moscow), 225
venereal diseases, 108, 149, 154
Verdun, 25–26, 51–52
Veresaev, V. V., 237
Vestnik inostrannoi literatury (Bulletin of
  Foreign Literature), 224
veterans: European rights organizations,
  119; importance in Soviet interwar remembrance, 119–124; pensions, 119–121;
  popularity of *All Quiet on the Western
  Front* (Remarque) with, 232–233. *See
  also* wounded veterans
Vetoshnikov, L. V., 223
Viatka province, 58–59
Victory Day, 282
Vietnam War, 333n4
Vinogradov, S., 89
violence: aestheticization of, 128; and
  afterlife, 68; alternatives to, 55; in art,
  71; "atrocities," 320n10; begetting more
  violence, 59; bystanders and protectors,
  158–161; caused by necessity, 152; censorship of, 252–255, 257–258, 285; Civil
  War, 161–164; and class identity, 149–
  154; as compensation for suffering, 156;
  in defense of civilians, 161–162; dehumanizing nature of, 77, 89, 97, 124, 131,
  136, 147, 150–151, 225, 257–258; encouraging pacifism, 135–137; eroticization of,
  131, 147; and ethnic differences, 151, 152–
  153; and ethnic identity, 149–154, 165; as
  everyday work, 132; glorification of, 132,
  133; and heroic masculinity, 69, 271–272;
  and honor code, 130–131, 133; horrors of,
  132; hunting metaphor for, 131–132; ideal
  revolutionary use of, 252–253; ideal Soviet use of, 130; justification for, 24–25,
  129, 130, 151, 152–153, 156, 161–162; killing,
  act of (*see* killing, act of); leading to violence of revolution, 128–129; male desire to commit, 162; morality of, 18, 20,
  22; normalization of, 128, 132; paradoxes
  of, 129–130; patriotic, 130; perpetrated
  by clergy, 51–52; perpetrators of, 127, 129,

133, 138, 147, 156, 162, 164, 251–254, 257–
  258; in popular prints, 132; postwar Europe, impact on, 128, 320n3; psychic
  costs of, 129; religious justification for,
  34–35; sanitization of, by historians, 127;
  Soviet depiction of, 163–164; of Soviet
  regime, toward citizens, 127; as sport,
  131–132; as theme, 16–20; tragedy of early
  death, 67; tsarist-era, 130–133; victims of,
  129, 132–133, 149–150
Vishnevskii, Vs., 264, 280
vodka. *See* alcohol consumption
voenizatsiia. See mobilization for war
Voina i revoliutsiia (War and Revolution),
  65, 208, 221
Voitolovskaia, Adda, 238
Voitolovskii, Lev Naumovich: anguish and
  complexity in works by, 105; censorship
  of works of, 17, 138; daughter's memoirs,
  238; death, 240; *In the Footsteps of War
  (Po sledam voiny)* (see *In the Footsteps of
  War* [*Po sledam voiny*] [Voitolovskii]);
  ill health, 240; on immorality of the
  "rear," 108; letter from Gorkii, 238–239,
  332n113; on marauding, 153; memoir,
  110–111, 265; on obsession with traitors
  on the frontlines, 195–196; photograph
  of, *95*; publication of works by, 286; as
  Russian-Jewish author, 231; on war causing destruction of masculinity and selfhood, 114; on wounded soldiers, 114
Volgograd memorial complex, 282
Vologda province, soldiers from, 168–169
voluntary societies, disbanding of, 2
*Volunteer: Remembrances about War and
  Captivity* (Dmitriev), 104–105, 175, 177
Volunteer Corps, 298, 299, 300
volunteers for war: disillusionment and
  regret of, 177; as quintessential heroes,
  169; reasons for volunteering, 171, 175,
  187; Soviet paradox of, 169–178; tsarist-
  era, 170–171; World War I, 169–178, 173,
  324n27
Voronova, O., 39
Voroshilov, Kliment, 61, 63, 215, 221
Vostochno-Prusskaia operatsiia, 330n58

Vsekhsviatskoe (village). *See* Moscow City Fraternal Cemetery (All-Russian War Cemetery)

war: as battle of "Good" and "Evil," 45; dehumanizing influence of, 97; as destroyer of culture, 252; as emasculating experience, 185; as epic struggle, 263–264; glorification of, fostering patriotism, 13; as inevitable, 134, 251; as manifestation of evil, 45–46; meaninglessness of, 42; nature of, in Soviet discourse, 290–291; as norm for international relations, 14; as pointless sacrifice, 188; propaganda, 272; as punishment from God, 45, 134; religious questioning of, 9; Soviet justification for, 32–33; transforming men into animals, 97; tsarist glorification of, 82–83; tsarist justification for, 32; victims of (*see* dead/death)
War and Peace (L. Tolstoi), 132
War and Revolution (Voina i revoliutsiia). See *Voina i revoliutsiia* (War and Revolution)
war cemeteries, 58, *117*, 243, 282. *See also* Moscow City Fraternal Cemetery (All-Russian War Cemetery); Tomb of the Unknown Soldier (Moscow)
war enthusiasm: of Bolsheviks, 171–172; and disillusionment, 169, 177; in Europe, 241; family grief over, 175; and heroic masculinity, 175; Leninist framework of, 172–173; tsarist-era, 170, 171; of "unconscious" soldiers, 175
War Industries Committees, 27
war mobilization. *See* mobilization for war
war museums, 208–209, 328n29. *See also* Military History Museum (Moscow)
"war on war," 178, 179, 181
warrior hero. *See* heroism/heroic masculinity
Warsaw, fortification of (1914), 202
wartime violence. *See* violence
We Did Not Fight: 1914–1918 Experiences of War Resisters, 181, 183
weaponry, effective use of, 271
Weimar Republic, 333n4

Die Weltbühne (journal), 82
White Army: atrocities, 24; burials, 1; censorship of, 265; Civil War combatants, 334n23; honor code, 130–131; officers, 265; rape, 161, 162
White Guard, 298
The White Guard (Bulgakov), 265
"White Horseman," 53
widows, retrieving husband's remains, 40–42, 116, 308n37
"The Wild Batallion" (Levin), 183
"The Wild Division" (Caucasian unit of Russian Imperial Army), 183
Wilhelm II, Kaiser: on medal, 241; memoirs, 10; occult predictions concerning, 40; in popular prints, 75; reputed thirst for war, 241; Russian accounts of, 28; as Russian enemy, 57
Winter, Jay, 9, 128, 303nn25,26, 306n3
Winter Palace, 80, 313n23
Witte, Sergei, 311n114
Wolf, Erika, 309n58
Woman Machine Gunner (Dubinskaia), 259
women: abandoning wounded soldiers, 114, 115; association with "rear," 106, 258; in combat, as challenge to masculinity, 80; in combat, denigration of, 275–276, 278; in combat, in exchange for rights, 80; in combat, under Provisional Government, 81; in combat during Civil War, 81, 313n27, 314n29; in combat during World War I, 86, 87; economic opportunities for, 107; as frivolous, 84; ideal role for, 276–278; immorality of, 163; as inferior, 277, 290; in literature, 259; as Motherland, 276–277; under Provisional Government, 313n22; rights for, 80–81, 313n22; Soviet depiction of, 106; under Soviets, 80–81; treatment of, by officers, 149; tsarist representations of, 106; tsarist-Soviet continuity in views of, 290; as victims of war, 106, 258; in war effort, 275; wartime roles, 106, 276. *See also* nurses; rape and sexual violence
Women's Battalion of Death: defense of Provisional Government during October Revolution, 258; defense of Winter

Palace, 80, 313n23; film depiction of, 334n23; founder of, 86; inspiration for, 57
Workers' Gazette (Rabochaia gazeta), 56
Worker's Moscow (Rabochaia Moskva), 212
World War I: apocalyptic views of, 55; as beginning of new age, 167; as break with the past, 8–9; as catalyst for revolution, 178; causes of, 190, 207, 241; deaths, 1, 6, 56, 57, 71, 179, 302n20; as ethnic conflict, 191–192; events leading to, 241; fictional accounts of, 332n108; as German war, 205–206; as holy war, 17, 34–35, 43, 45, 168–169; as imperialist war, 205; as national liberation for Slavs, 63; patriotic demonstrations, 169; popular enthusiasm for, 166; as prelude to revolutionary events, 288; as preordained scourge on Russian land, 54; as purification/cleansing for nation, 167; Russian hardships during, 23–24; as Second Patriotic War, 205; strategic analysis of, 214–215. *See also* European World War I memory; Soviet World War I memory; *specific topics, people, and works*
World War II, 272–278; commemoration of, 282, 295, 299, 302n19, 338n24; deaths, 282; deportations during, 183; discourse about, themes in, 269; gender norms during, 275–278; German attack on Soviet Union, 272; heroism and enemies, 272–275; mobilization for, 13–15, 272, 292; patriotism during, 223; preparation for, 220
"The Wounded Soldier" (poster). *See* "Help for War Victims" (Pasternak)
wounded soldiers: abandonment of, 114–115; aid for, 89, 90; destroyed masculinity of, 114; posters of, 89–90; as tsarist sacrifices, 89
wounded veterans, 119–124; lack of government support for, 120–121; number of, 319n165; plays about, 121–124; treatment of, 121, 123, 319n168

Yiddish language, 196, 205
Young Guard. See Molodaia gvardiia (Young Guard)
Youngblood, Denise, 188, 312n125, 326n77

Za krestami. See For St. George Crosses (Za krestami) (Gromov)
Zagorskii, Mikhail Borisovich, 229–230, 331n83
Zaionchkovskii, A. M., 214, 221
Zapiski iz plena (Levin). *See Notes from Captivity* (Levin)
Zapiski kavalerista (Gumilev). *See Notes of a Cavalryman* (Gumilev)
Zapiski opolchentsa (Stepnoi), 251
Zapiski soldata (Os'kin). *See Notes of a Soldier* (Os'kin)
Zarobian (First Secretary of Armenian Communist Party), 337n19
Zauriad-polk (Sergeev-Tsenskii). *See Reserve Regiment* (Sergeev-Tsenskii)
Zherve, B. B., 216
Znamia (The Standard), 266, 279, 280, 335n44
Zweig, Arnold, 10

Karen Petrone

is Professor of History at the University of Kentucky. She is author of *Life Has Become More Joyous, Comrades: Celebrations in the Time of Stalin* (Indiana University Press, 2000); editor (with Valerie Kivelson, Michael S. Flier, and Nancy Shields Kollmann) of *The New Muscovite Cultural History: A Collection in Honor of Daniel B. Rowland*; and editor (with Jie-Hyun Lim) of *Gender Politics and Mass Dictatorship: Global Perspectives*.

www.ingramcontent.com/pod-product-compliance
Lightning Source LLC
Chambersburg PA
CBHW060324100426
42812CB00003B/872